五十嵐威暢

This book showcases selected works that I produced over fifty years.

In most cases the projects required the creative input, influence,

advice and criticism from clients, friends and staff members.

I also ackowledge generous support and encouragement from my family.

The various people have helped me make right decisions.

I would like to express my deepest gratitude to Shigeru Takeo, B. Martin Pedersen,

Shoji Usuda and Yasuhito Nagahara.

Takenobu Igarashi

Chapter 1 The Unique World of Three-Dimensional Design 8

Chapter 2 The Epitome of Impromptu 130

Chapter 3 Building the Future of Hokkaido 252

Appendix 285

Striving for Freedom, Beauty, and Purity

When I started working as a designer, I hoped to create at least one work every year that satisfied me, regardless of its importance. One day, I discovered an ingenious drafting device that allowed me to draw lines freely in a precise and controlled manner, and ventured into the world of three-dimensional alphabets. When my work was recognized internationally, I felt that I found my place in the world of design. As a designer, I hoped that the importance of design as a profession would be recognized and I did my best to prove its significance. But the market was overflowing with goods, draining scarce resources, and the earth was screaming. The approach to design and what was expected of it deteriorated rapidly, and its crucial role in society was no longer a concern.

Torn between my doubts and the desire to create, at the age of forty I was prepared to quit, and ten years later at the age of fifty I left Tokyo and moved to Los Angeles. In order to change myself, I had to change my way of thinking, viewpoint, position, lifestyle, location, and work. I started my new life carving marble and became completely absorbed in the world of creating objects of art. For three years, I pondered over the possibility of working with my own hands and experiencing the joy of carving.

Whether in design or in art, what is important is being different. I would like to make sculptures that no one has made—and if the result is not what I had expected, that is even better. I am happy to make mistakes; failure is a gift from God. The three fundamental rules in achieving a goal are not to force yourself, not to give up, and to keep making an effort.

We are surrounded by design. I started making sculptures because I also wanted to be surrounded by art, and suddenly I began receiving orders for public art. I feel that I found my special place at the crossroads of design and sculpture by realizing their different viewpoints. Without overthinking, I am only doing what my hands and the material teach me—just going my way.

Takenobu Igarashi

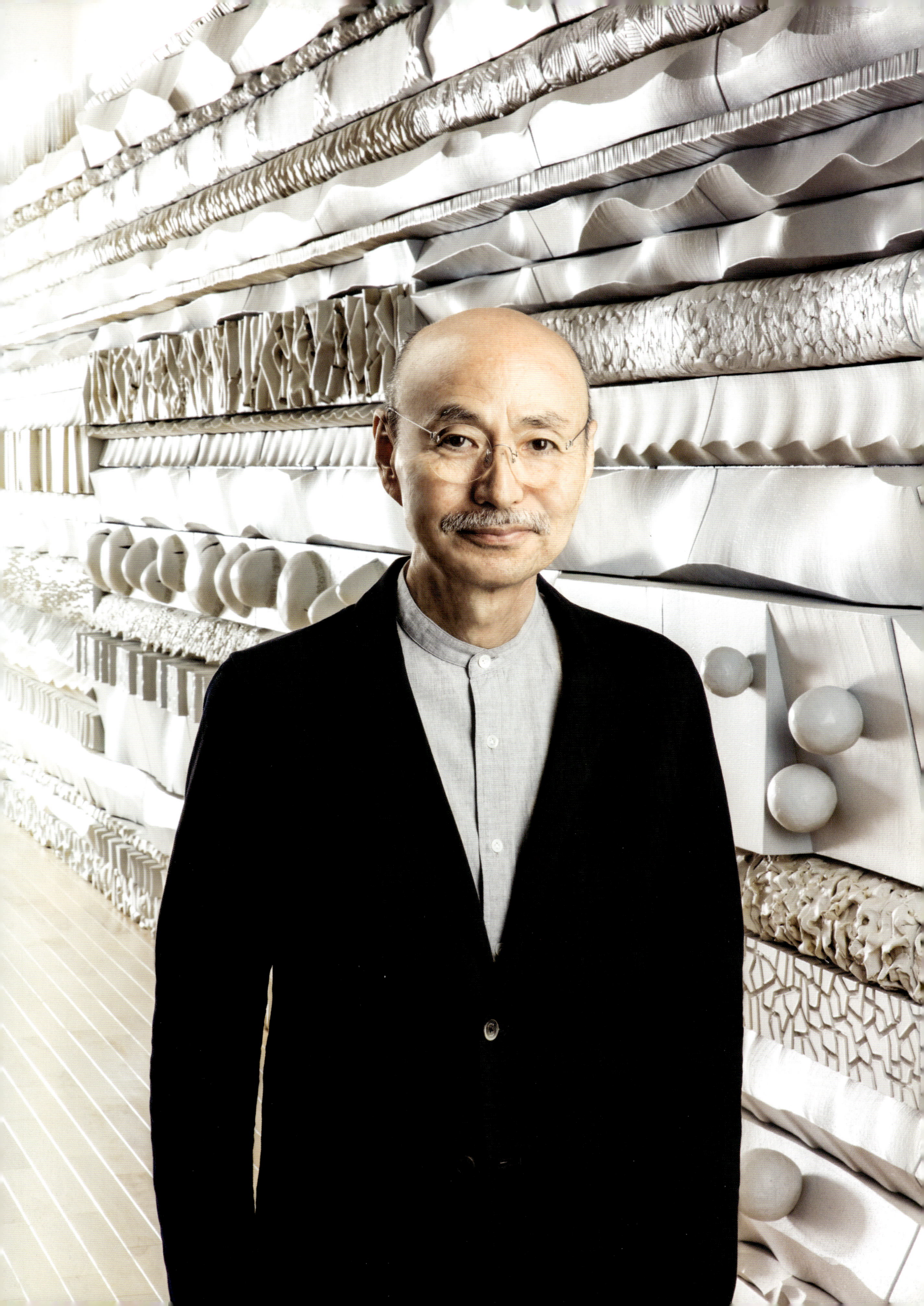

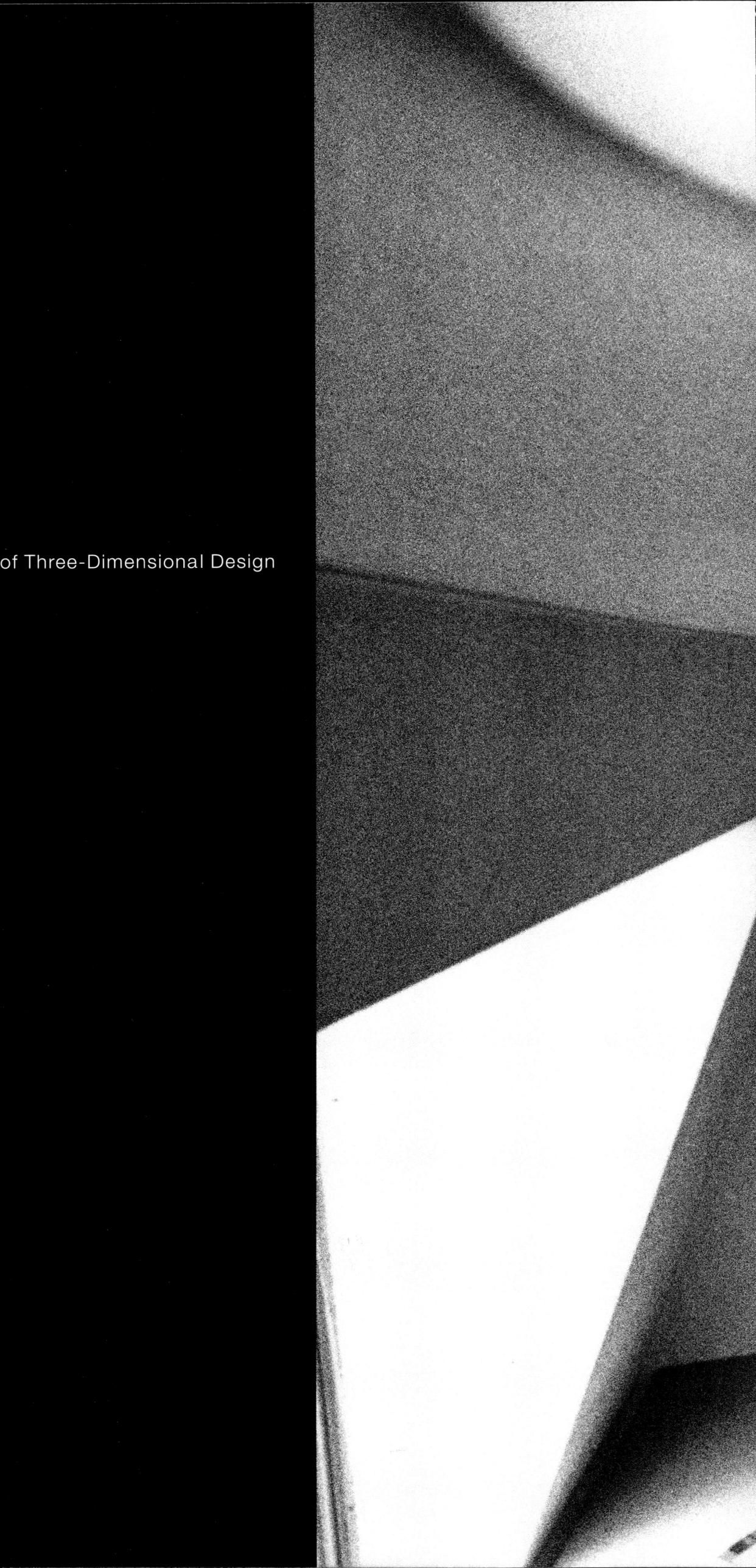

of Three-Dimensional Design

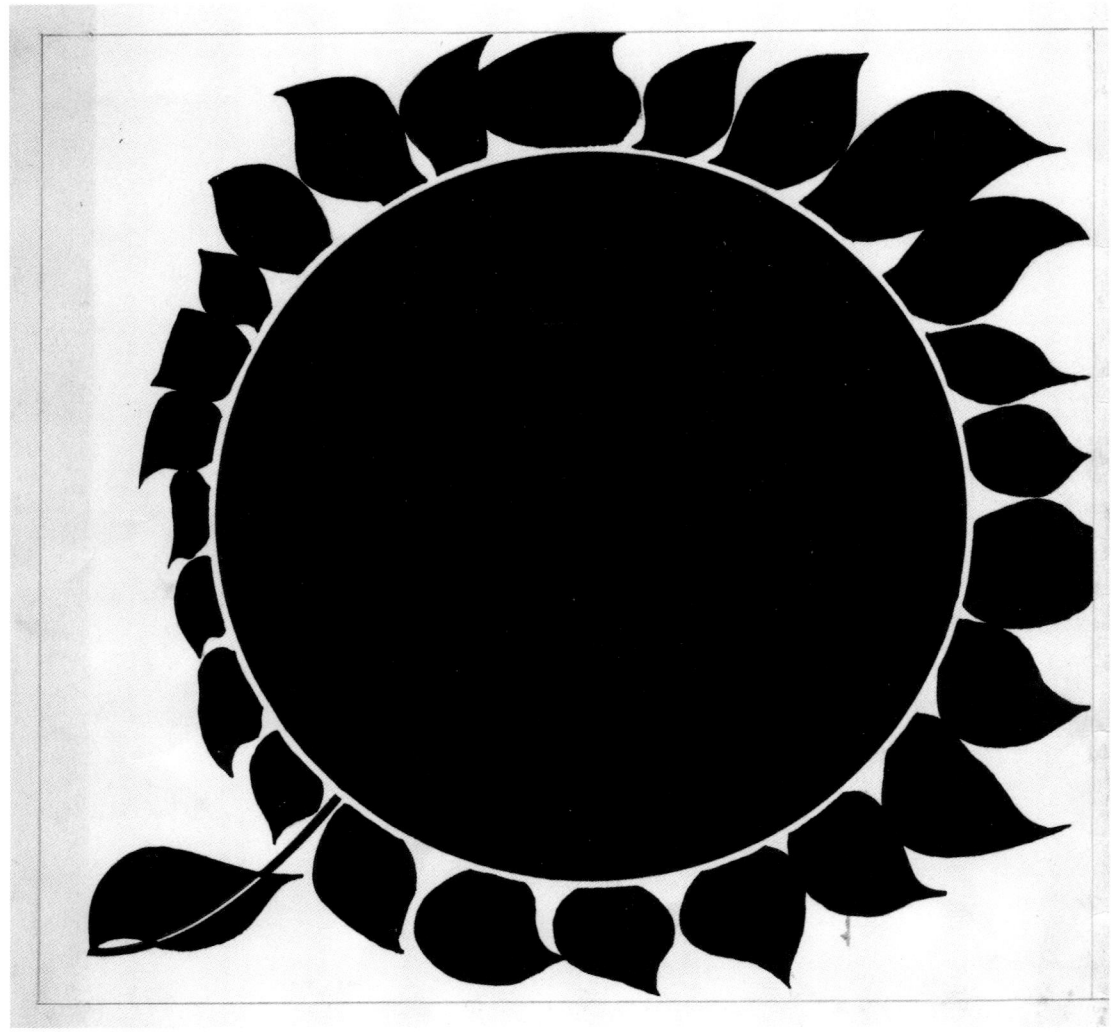

Cover Design Illustration
Seijo Gakuen Senior High School graduation texts collection, Japan, 1964

Discovering Design—From Boyhood to Youth

Takenobu Igarashi was born in 1944 in Takikawa, Hokkaido—a year before Japan surrendered—ending the Second World War. His father ran a food and liquor wholesale business and he grew up in a progressive family with parents who spoke foreign languages.

"I first heard the word *design* through my uncle, an architect, who said, 'There is a field called design. In architecture your choice of color is limited to the color of material you choose, but in design you are free to use any color. If you want to use color freely, then you should go into the field of design.' That was when I was in junior high school. After that, I became aware of design and started looking at design books and magazines at the bookstore." His uncle Tadashi Igarashi was the first authorized Class-I architect in Hokkaido, who built around 500 buildings in thirty years in Obihiro, the main city in the Tokachi area, and he always seemed to enjoy his work. His uncle's influence must have been crucial since the young Igarashi chose to pursue graphic design over all his other interests in the three-dimensional worlds of architecture, industrial design, and environmental design.

Igarashi lost his father when he was in fifth grade. His mother wisely arranged for her children to move to Tokyo, where Igarashi lived with his older brother and sister in Setagaya. First, he entered Toyama Metropolitan High School, one of the best preparatory schools in Tokyo. However, he could not adjust to the rigid atmosphere of the school whose sheer goal was to prepare students for entering the renowned Tokyo University. After a year, he transferred to Seijo Gakuen High School, a private school with an unrestrictive atmosphere. In the evenings, Igarashi studied basic design and design theory at the Visual Design Institute led by Professor Masato Takahashi at the Tokyo University of Education, and in 1964, he entered Tama Art University. "I had a lot of free time in my first year at Tama Art University because Professor Jutaro Ito was also teaching at the Visual Design Institute, so the assignments were mostly identical and I had done them all already…(laughs). Since there was no need to attend class every day, I spent my time at the sculpture department learning from famous professors like Kakuzo Tatehata and Katsuzo Entsuba. Professor Tatehata even commented on the works I made."

Tama Art University offered solid foundation courses and had traditionally produced graduates who moved into the field of advertising or illustration. However, Igarashi was in search of another direction. In his third year at Tama, a new course titled *Pure Graphics* was set up and he was one of seventeen students who were enrolled in the class. Originally Shigeo Fukuda, a young and energetic designer, was assigned to teach the course; however, due to disagreements with the administration, Jutaro Ito and Akio Kanda taught the course instead. In Kanda's lecture, the corporate identity program for Chase Manhattan Bank, designed by Chermayeff & Geismar and introduced in the newest issue of *IDEA* design magazine, was selected for discussion. Since the mid 1950s, starting with IBM—leading the way in corporate identity design—interest in CI was growing and it was slowly playing a role in visual communication design in Japan. "Professor Kanda's lecture filled me with enthusiasm right away. He taught us so many things, and in time he got to know and understand me and allowed me to work for him. I would go to his apartment and work on small jobs like a poster, program, or flyer for the Yomiuri Nippon Symphony Orchestra. Not satisfied with the phototypesetting ordered for a poster, Professor Kanda would enlarge the original metal typeface and draw Mincho and Gothic typefaces, adding his own changes. His concern about every detail really impressed me."

Kanda also worked for *Graphic Design Magazine* edited by Masaru Katsumie, a design critic who successfully led the pictogram design project for the Tokyo Olympics, which received international recognition. Through this connection, Igarashi was exposed to classic graphic and visual communication design represented by Herbert Bayer, which made him aware that "there are people doing such serious professional work." The Swiss magazine, *Neue Grafik*, and Bayer's famous World *Geo-Graphic Atlas* inspired him the most. Early issues of the Neue Grafik with a colored band around them are treasured in Igarashi's collection.

Igarashi's early work
Tama Art University, Japan, 1964

Studying Abroad

After graduating from Tama Art University, Igarashi worked there as an assistant, yet he hoped to study abroad. He consulted Professor Masaaki Tanaka at the Joshibi University of Art and Design, who was well-informed about design universities around the world. In those days, neither European nor American universities were prepared to take in foreign students, except for a few places such as the Art Center College of Design and the University of California, Los Angeles (UCLA). The former was a famous school with two graduates teaching at Tama Art University at that time.

"Shortly before, I was very impressed by the exhibition *From Space to Environment* held at Matsuya department store in Ginza. It was the first time I heard the word environment, and since UCLA graduate school offered Environmental Design, I enrolled at UCLA. To my disappointment it turned out to be landscape design, so that was a big mistake (laughs)." In order to get out of this situation, Igarashi decided to look into other universities by visiting Harvard University, Massachusetts Institute of Technology (MIT), Pratt Institute, and Yale University, just to name a few. Next he flew to Denmark to attend a design seminar and stayed in Copenhagen for three weeks. He liked the city but he found out that the education offered was not forefront. He also looked for a job but had no success. Following an extensive search, he came to the conclusion that, "after all, all universities are alike. So I decided to get my Master's degree as soon as possible and return to Japan and do as I like." After one quarter at UCLA majoring in Environmental Design, he changed his major to Graphic Design.

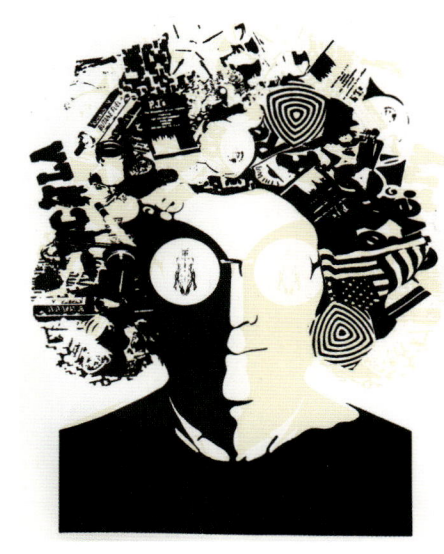

Illustration
UCLA, Los Angeles, CA, USA, 1969

"The educational policy of the Design Department was to give students a broad background, and not as I had imagined, to teach specialized courses in visual design or sign design. So I had to learn to do pottery and many other things for the first time. I hardly had any experience in photography, but taking a class by Professor Robert Heinecken, who made photo-sculptures, encouraged me. I was also influenced by Professor John Neuhart's camera work for Charles Eames' short films. It inspired me to create a visual presentation of the traffic problems of Los Angeles using three slide projectors and three screens.

"Professor Mitsuru (Mits) Kataoka, a second-generation Japanese-American, was a wonderful educator. He was in charge of communication and video in visual design. He was an idealist who said 'always talk to the top person, because you have nothing to lose. Just try,' or, 'the broader your base, the higher the pyramid built on top.' He encouraged and influenced me enormously. My graduation thesis was *Visual Communication and the Designer's Social*

Responsibility. I truly believed in the power of design so I was not interested in doing advertising at all." (Igarashi's diverse design activities do not include advertising.)

UCLA has a quarter system, which means there are four academic terms in a year. Most students take the summer quarter off to work and earn money. Igarashi started his studies in the summer and completed his courses in five quarters, and in spite of changing majors, he earned his master's degree in one and a half years instead of the usual two years. "I set a record that is still unsurpassed (laughs). I was told that once I return with my master's degree, Tama Art University would hire me, first as a teaching assistant and eventually as a lecturer. However, because of the student riots at that time, I could not return to the university (laughs)."

Since he finished his studies early, before returning to Japan Igarashi used his remaining time to travel around America with a friend in a second-hand car. "In Boston I visited Gyorgy Kepes, who collaborated in setting up the *New Bauhaus* and explored the concept of *visual language*. He was a professor at the Center of Advanced Visual Design at MIT. Without an appointment, I knocked on his office door and told the secretary that I came from Japan to see Mr. Kepes. Of course I did not say that I came from Los Angeles (laughs). We met for about an hour and he even took time to look at slides of my work. He then asked me if I thought I was a good designer. I said, 'I am,' and he laughed and said if I wanted to come to study, I should follow formal procedures. Since I had just finished my studies, I did not want to return to school again. Perhaps that was a mistake…(laughs)."

New Challenge in Geometric Thinking

After returning to Japan in December 1969, Igarashi set up *Environmental Design International* (EDI) in March of the following year with his best friend Takeshi Sashiyama. Although it reflected his intention to do graphic design in harmony with the environment, the name EDI was a bit exaggerated. For an unknown designer it was a tough beginning, and in April 1971, he changed the name to *Takenobu Igarashi Design Office*. After searching in the dark for about three years he came to know leading interior designer Shiro Kuramata, whose philosophy of "returning to the origin" inspired him. Kuramata gave him advice and also recommended him for jobs. Shigeru Uchida, an interior designer of the same generation, as well as his former professors Akio Kanda and Jutaro Ito, also helped him. Slowly his circle of acquaintances was expanding and with it his business grew.

Igarashi started experimenting with the axonometric drawing technique using the drafting board that led to his famous three-dimensional alphabets. One of his earliest attempts to create a three-dimensional structure from alphabets was the *ZEN Environmental Design logo* (1974) for Zenichi Nakamura, professor of environmental design at Kyushu Sangyo University.

In 1973, Igarashi had his first exhibition, *Animal Illustrations,* at the Fujie Gallery, showing simple yet witty drawings made by using a compass and a ruler. Fujie Gallery was a new gallery specializing in design owned by Fujie Textile and run by leading graphic designer Ikko Tanaka. Kuramata's exhibition was the first show opening the gallery, and it was he who recommended Igarashi to them. Around this time, Igarashi received an offer to teach at UCLA: "Actually, when I graduated from UCLA, they said I could come back to teach after about five years, and really after five years I received a letter with an offer to teach for them. I think it was 1974 when I went to Los Angeles collecting materials for *IDEA* magazine's special issue and I showed some slides of my work to my former professors. Just at that time I was working on a big environmental project for the Seibu department store, so I was not sure whether to accept or not—but since it was such a rare opportunity teaching abroad, I accepted the offer. The contract was for two years, but I came back after a year because I started working on the CI program of the Summit store, which was a lot of work and also very exciting."

There were no other professors teaching graphic design at UCLA besides Igarashi. He taught senior and graduate students, but it was difficult teaching some students who did not have basic design knowledge. During this time, he became acquainted with Charles and Ray Eames, who had been receiving international attention for their molded plywood furniture,

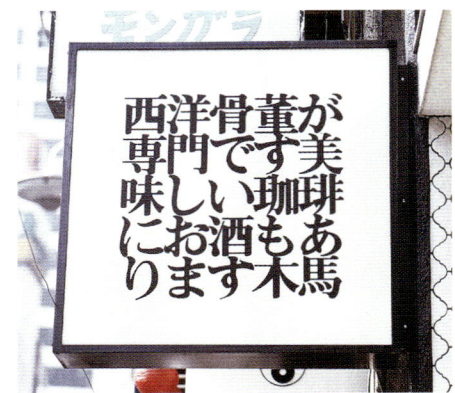

1-1 Logo, Sign
Mokuba, Jazz Café, Tokyo, Japan, 1973

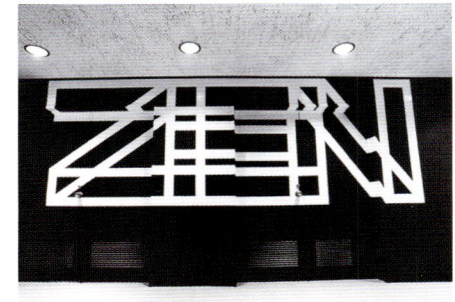

1-2 Wall Graphics with Logotype
Zen Environmental Design
Fukuoka, Japan, 1974

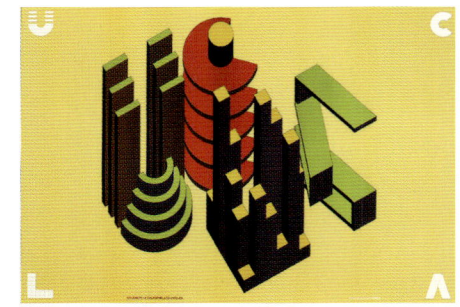

1-3 Poster Design
UCLA, Los Angeles, CA, USA, 1976

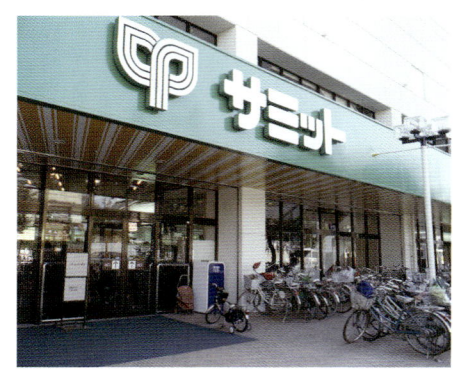

CI, Summit Store, Tokyo, Japan, 1976

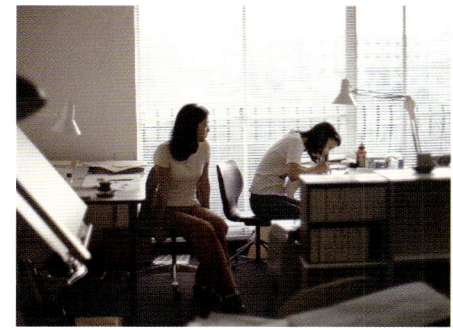

Igarashi Studio
Akasaka, Tokyo, Japan, c.1976

their exhibition designs such as *Mathematica*, and their experimental films like *Toccata for Toy Trains*. The encounter with the Eameses was an intellectual stimulus for Igarashi.

In the 1970s corporate identity design prevailed in full-scale in Japan. The Summit store, a food supermarket chain of the Sumitomo Group, was an example. "People at Summit did not know much about design but were aware of its importance. Shinya Arai from the Sumitomo Corporation, who later became the chairman of Summit, was the executive director at that time and he understood the key points in design to use it effectively. Aside from designing I worked as a consultant at the same time, preaching about the importance of following the rules that were set up for the CI, educating employees, and advising every time a new store opened. I told Mr. Arai that we should review and reconsider the design after twenty years, but he said there is no need for it and the design has not changed to this date (laughs)."

Igarashi's corporate identity design for Summit has lasted for over forty years to this date. Although corporate identity is meant to be long lasting, international competition not only in the distribution industry but also in all sectors of the economy has forced companies to merge, resulting in a continuous rise and fall of corporate identity programs. In this respect, it is significant that the Summit corporate identity still continues to exist.

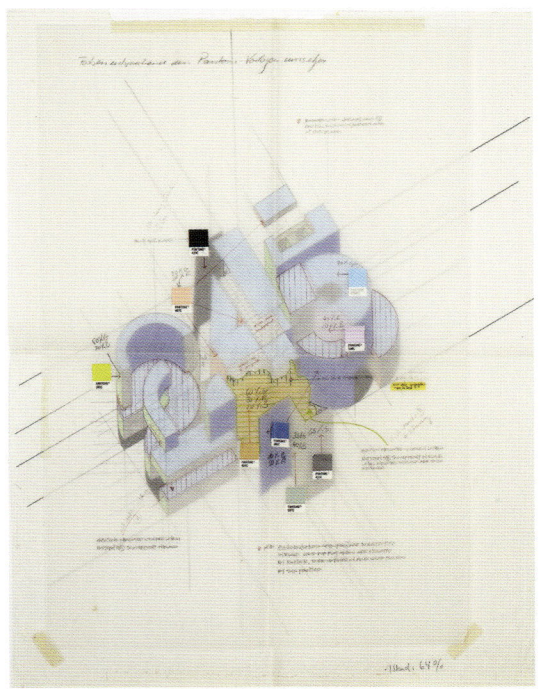 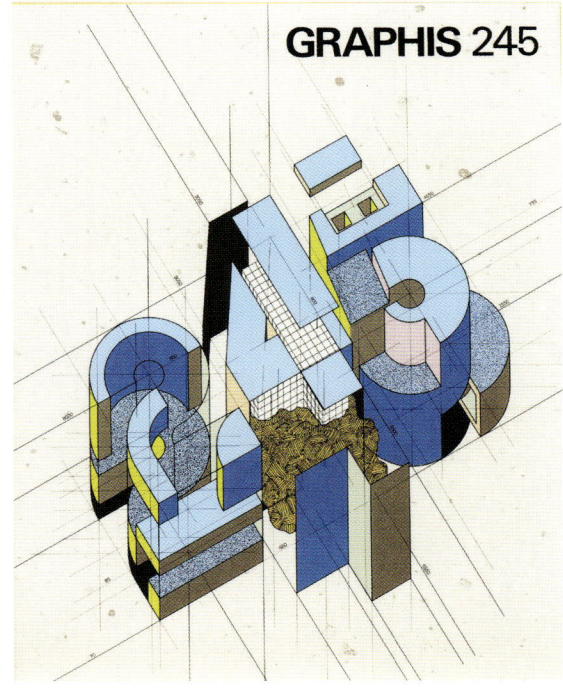

Layout master for the cover of Graphis Magazine   1-4 **Cover**, Graphis Magazine, Issue 245, 1986

Igarashi's absence during his teaching at UCLA proved to be a loss in terms of his business in Japan. However, his work for Summit was featured in two Japanese design magazines, *IDEA* and *Design*, and soon after, Walter Herdeg of *Graphis Magazine* in Switzerland contacted him. "I was asked to send slides of my work for Summit. It was a dream for every designer to be featured in *Graphis Magazine*, so I wanted to personally deliver the material to Mr. Herdeg. After showing him my other works, he decided to show them as well, and on top of that he said 'do you know AGI (Alliance Graphique Internationale), a group of top international designers? There is only Shigeo Fukuda from Japan, so you should become a member,' and he recommended that I join." Igarashi received the support he needed and became an AGI member in 1980, joining the international league of designers.

Also in the early 1980s, an American cosmetic magnate purchased some Japanese posters, including Igarashi's works while visiting Japan, and later donated them to New York's Museum of Modern Art (MoMA). When Stewart Johnson, curator at MoMA at the time, contacted Igarashi and asked him to send more works, Igarashi personally delivered them, which led to the MoMA Poster Calendar project. "It all starts with meeting people. Words are precious, and I learned a lot from what people say. I am the type of person who acts immediately. Instead of contemplating and studying, I work intuitively and act in anticipation of what could happen. For this reason, I know exactly what should be talked about when meeting people."

Three-Dimensional Alphabets—From Drawings to Sculptures

Igarashi started drawing alphabets and numerals using the drafting board in the 1970s. His geometric approach based on his own methodology attracted international attention. "Normally, letters and numerals are expressed two-dimensionally on the x and y axes. By adding the z-axis, they become three-dimensional. I was interested in the geometry of form, and at the origin of my approach was Max Bill, whom I admired since my high school days." Max Bill (1908–1994) was a Swiss painter, sculptor, designer, and architect. He studied at Bauhaus and was one of the founders of the Ulm School of Design (HfG Ulm), serving as its first rector. Igarashi was most influenced by Bill's *15 Variations on a Single Theme*, a correlation of changing geometric form, known for its clear form and functional beauty. "I was extremely impressed by the beauty of mathematical order consisting of dots, lines, and planes, the aesthetics inherent in integers, the balance of division and partition, clarity of minimal color, and the clear concept behind the variations. It is an intellectual and poetic world." Max Bill's influence is at the root of many of Igarashi's works, such as in his animal illustrations and later in his three-dimensional alphabets and logo designs. "Like Max Bill, more and more I came to think that working in ratios of whole numbers—not, for example 5.6 x 6.3 but 5.0 or at most 5.5—was best. I was drawing and exploring the world in which everything was ordered by whole numbers. So that was my attempt in axonometric drawings."

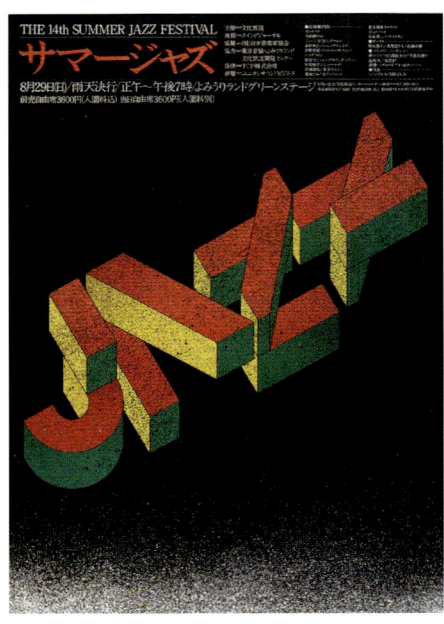

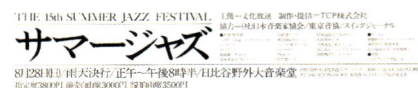

The axonometric method is a drawing technique that turns a plane diagonally, usually 30 or 60 degrees, to show a bird's-eye view which gives it a three-dimensional touch. The first axonometric works were a series of concert posters. When he showed them to his former professor Akio Kanda, he said, "You finally found it," encouraging his departure into a new phase of artistic creativity. In 1975, his second exhibition at the Fujie Gallery, *Takenobu Igarashi Exhibition 2*, was held, and in 1976, Igarashi showed his *Jazz 15 Variations* at the newly set up Tokyo Designers Space (TDS). Pieter Brattinga, a graphic designer, publisher, and gallery owner from Amsterdam, saw the exhibition, which was recommended to him by Ikko Tanaka, one of the initiators of Tokyo Designers Space. As a result, in 1978, *Jazz 15 Variations* was shown in Amsterdam. Between 1976 and 1984, Igarashi created a series of posters for the Summer Jazz Festival with variations of the word *jazz*. These early ingenious works successfully visualize pauses and changes of pace that are typical in jazz.

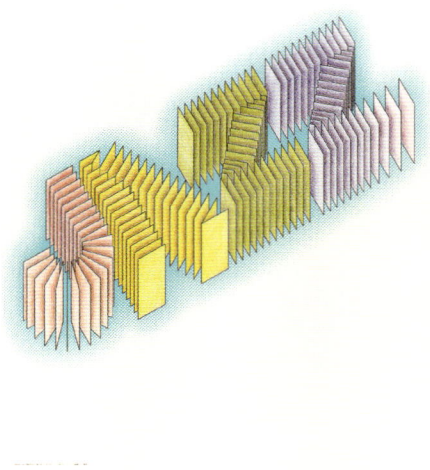

1-5 Poster Series
Summer Jazz, Nippon Cultural Broadcasting Inc.
1976–1984

Thirty-five years later in 2013, the exhibition, *Jazz 1976 + 2013 Takenobu Igarashi*, was held at Sapporo's Gallery Retara, showing the lithograph version of *Jazz 15 Variations* together with his newest terracotta works that were improvised like in jazz. The exhibition was held for the same period of time as the one in Amsterdam.

Other highlights of Igarashi's three-dimensional alphabet posters include *Graphic Designers of the West Coast* (1975), *ZEN* (1976) for ZEN Environmental Design, *Noh* (1981) for the UCLA Asian Performing Arts Institute, and *Expo '85*, the official poster for the International Exposition, Tsukuba, Japan, 1985. His other non-alphabet posters also attracted attention such as those for *Polaroid Impulse* (1988) and for *Kanagawa Art Festival* (1984), which show his finest handiwork. As discussed through these examples, Igarashi stands out in the field of poster design as a brilliant mastermind. His other three-dimensional works include a series of 26 letters for IBM and variations of the word *Design* for the cover of *Design News*, a magazine published by the Japan Institute of Design Promotion.

The next challenge was to create solid objects out of alphabets, which started in the 1980s. "I started making solid alphabets out of my own personal interest, and not for someone else. In making three-dimensional objects, you have to think about what material to use. Designers must work with many different materials. On the other hand, sculptors and artists usually limit their material to just one or two. Since I was a designer, I felt free to use any material, and wanted to try all the materials that I had learned to work with before. But I was not actually making them with my own hands, but in collaboration with different craftsmen depending on the material."

"Working on the three-dimensional plan basically means working in the world of geometry, and I started to realize that the most beautiful proportion is found in the multiple of 5." What were the difficulties in the actual production? "Drawing on a plane using the axonometric technique is actually drawing an architectural ground plan and elevating that to the three-dimensional. That is basically the thought behind it, but in reality, making a solid object in a physical world does not necessary function as it does in the drawings. The freedom of thought on paper cannot be realized so easily in the solid world. With material and technique as fixed points, you build upon them."

Igarashi's alphabet sculptures are fascinating objects that stimulate the senses through their brilliance. Letters and numerals are the most important communication signs employed by mankind and by using them Igarashi aesthetically revolutionized the way of expression through them. His first sculpture exhibition, *Alphabet Art of Takenobu Igarashi* (1981), was held at the Design Gallery 1953 in the Matsuya Department Store in Ginza. Kazumasa Nagai, an internationally known graphic designer who helped organize the show, praised it, "fascinating art—clean, pleasant, and refreshing—typical of his work...their sheer existence adding modernity and grace to space." Shiro Kuramata immediately commissioned him to work on the sign design for *Part 3*, the third store of Parco, a shopping center in Shibuya that sets the trends in fashion and culture.

His works were also exhibited at the street gallery outside. In 1983, a large-scale exhibition of the alphabet sculptures was held at a gallery within the Mikimoto store, the leading jewelry store for pearls in Ginza. International attention grew instantly as well, with an exhibition at New York's Reinhold Brown Gallery in the same year.

In 1987, ABC Verlag in Zurich, Switzerland published a collection of his works, *Igarashi Alphabets*, a compilation of axonometric drawings and sculptures in monochrome. Itsuo Sakane—who covered the new developments in the fusion of art and science—soon featured the book in the *Asahi Shimbun* newspaper. Further articles presenting his work followed, expanding beyond the borders. "James Miho, a famous American graphic designer, visited me in my office. At that time the first alphabet sculpture had just been delivered, and he asked to take a picture of it. Shortly after, the International Typeface Corporation (ITC) did a feature on it in their typographic magazine *U&lc* (Upper and Lower Case Magazine) after seeing James Miho's photos with his recommendation. *U&lc* issues about 20,000 copies, so a lot of professionals around the world saw my work and soon Graphis Magazine did a feature."

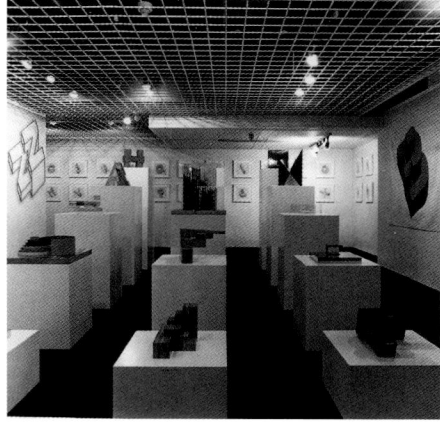

Takenobu Igarashi Alphabet Art Exhibition
Matsuya Design Gallery, Tokyo, Japan, 1981

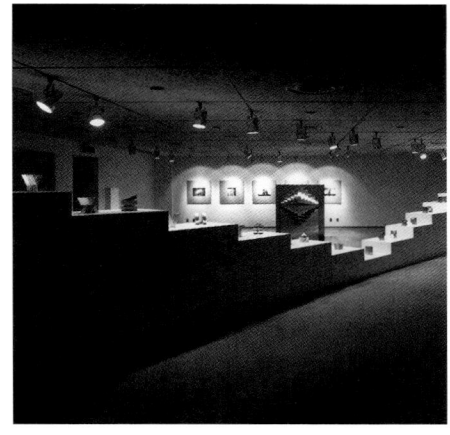

Alphabet Sculptures Exhibition
Ginza Mikimoto Hall, Tokyo, 1983

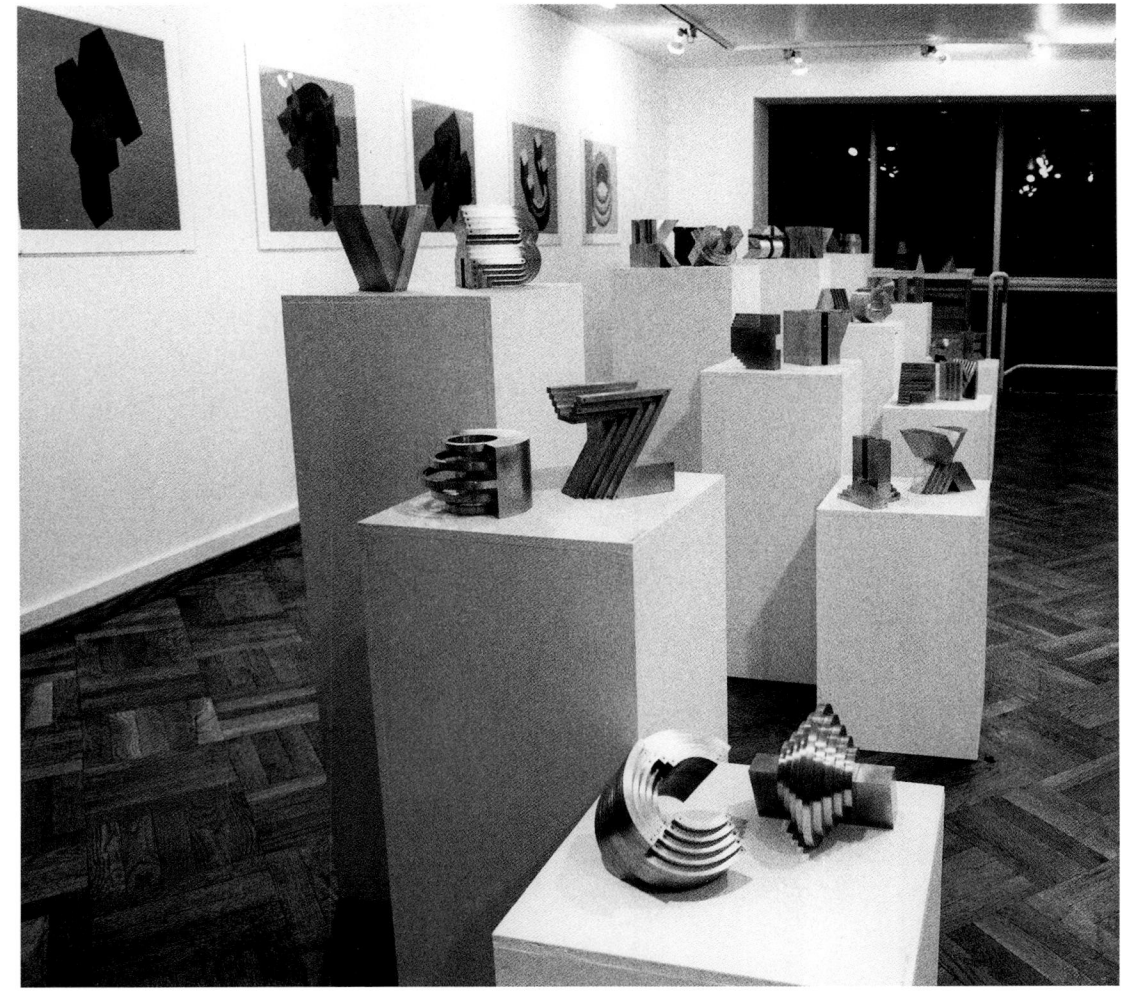

Exhibition at the Reinhold Brown Gallery, New York, NY, USA, 1983

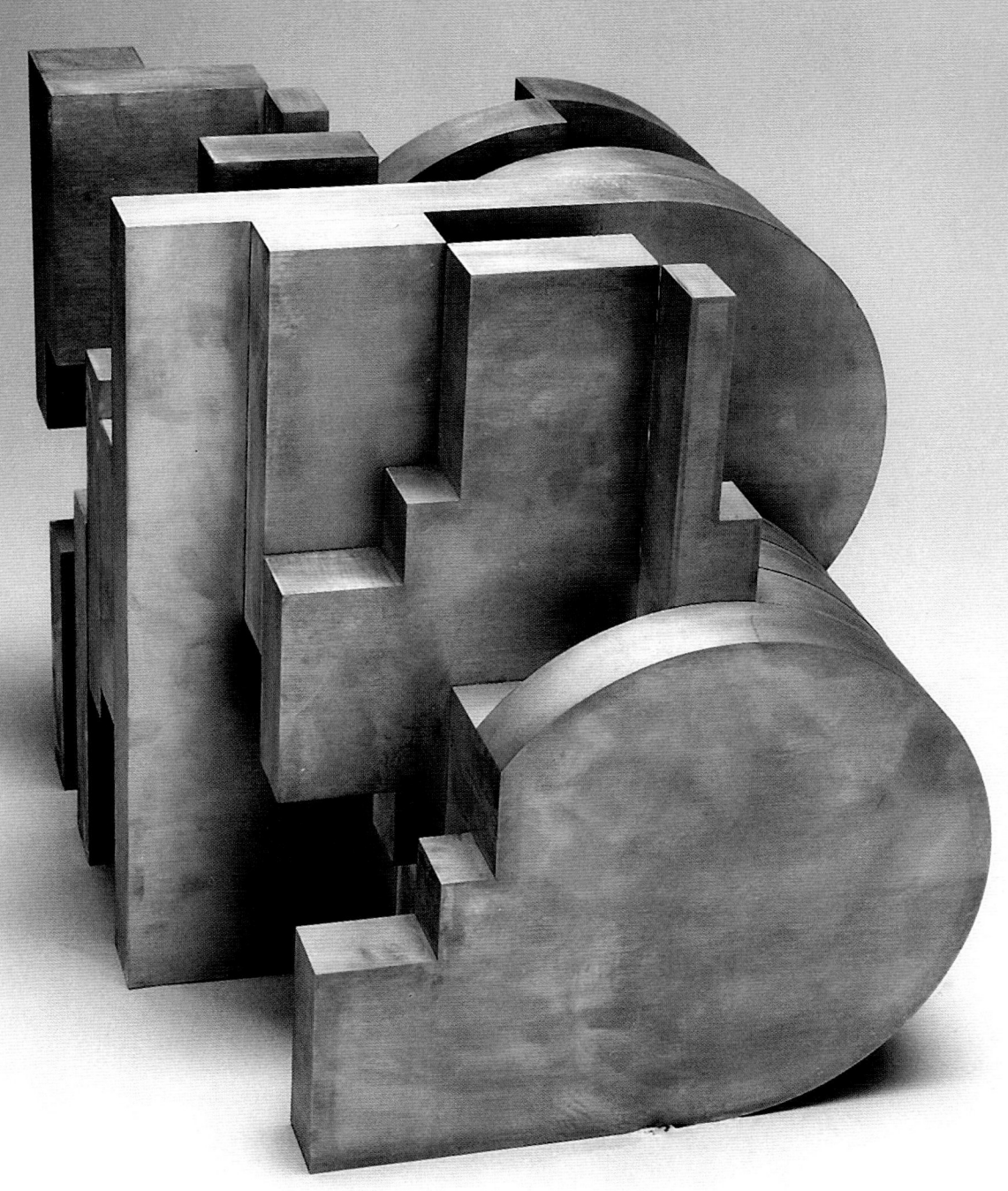

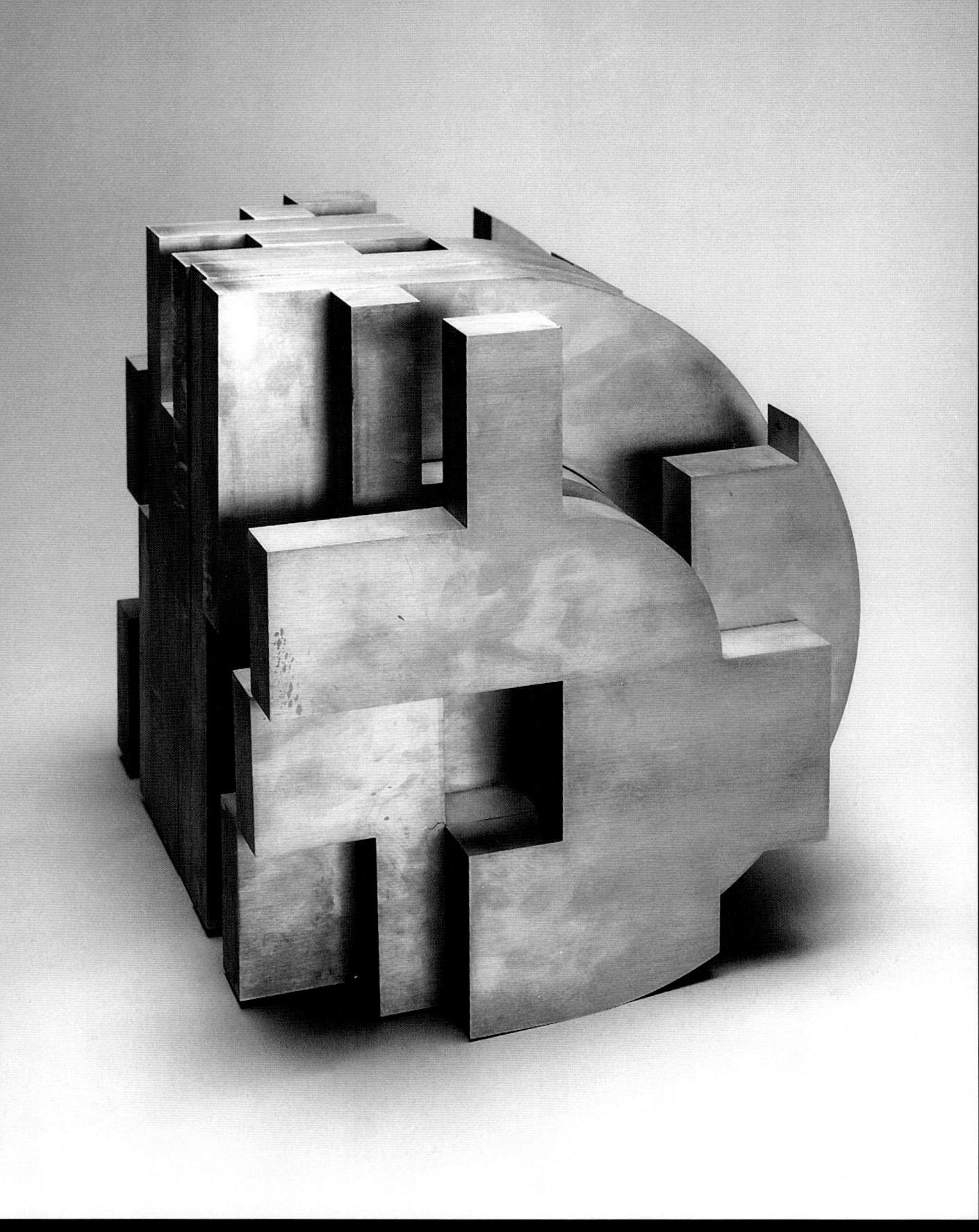

1-7 Stainless Steel Alphabet D, 1984

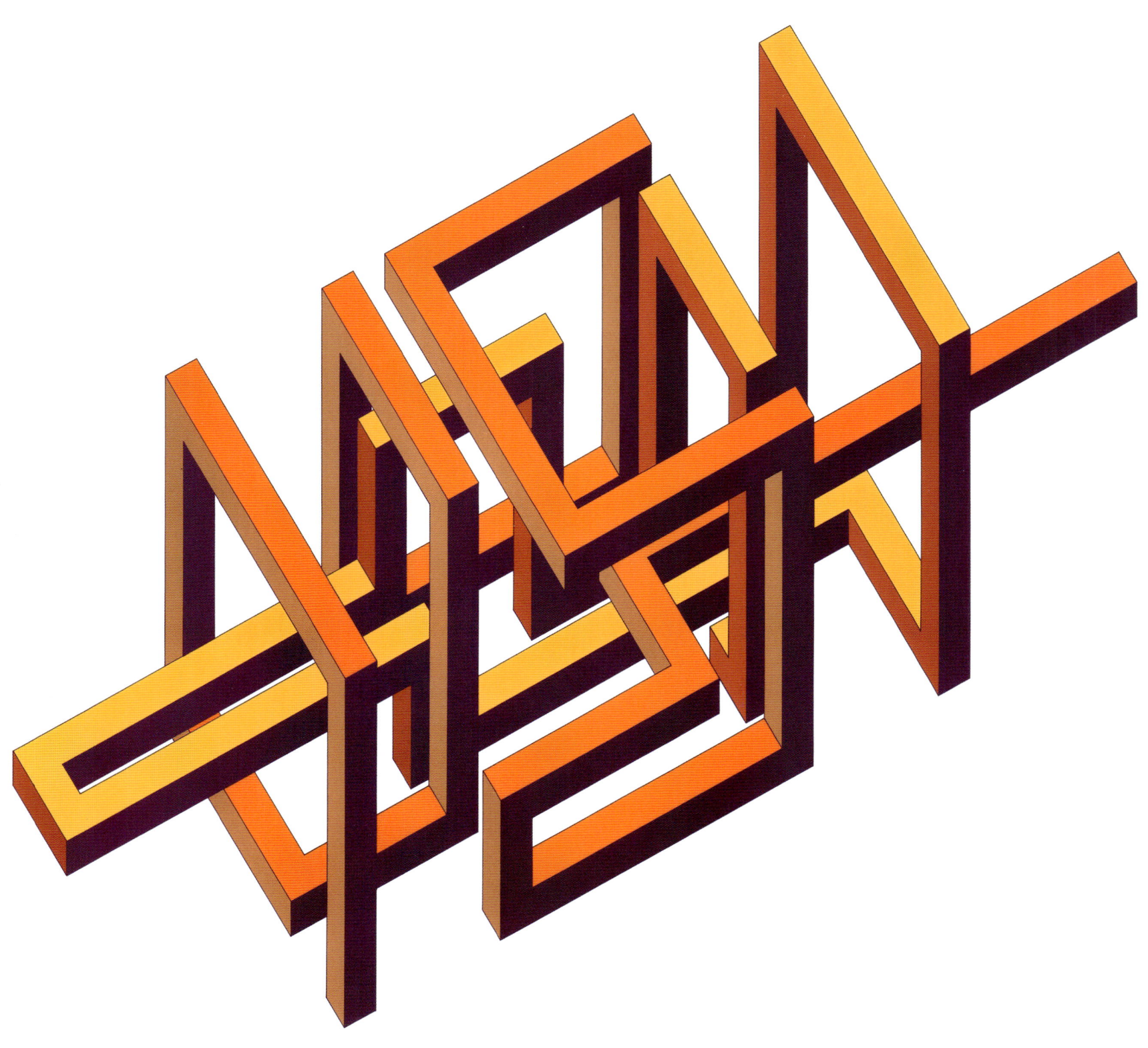

1-8 Art Print, 1985

The Fruits of Hard Work—MoMA Poster Calendars

The MoMA poster calendars are some of Igarashi's most significant works recorded in the history of international graphic design. The calendars that were created each year from 1984 to 1991 are celebrations of space in a magnificent polyphony of axonometric numbers. It originally started as a project for Parco *Part 3*, but unfortunately remained unfinished. "It was so much work to draw all the numbers. It was just impossible to have all twelve months finished in time and in the market on sale for the next calendar season. So we tried selling month for month, but it did not sell and we were behind schedule. After half a year the president of Parco said 'I don't think this will work,' and the project was cancelled."

Igarashi flew to New York after receiving a letter from MoMA's curator. Among other works, he also presented the six poster calendars for Parco, which lead to MoMA's calendar project. However, this was an enormous task—365 days a year meant 622 different numbers, each to be drawn by hand with a renewed design year after year. "I was drawing numbers for the calendar using a drafter and a ruling pen. Soon I realized that I had to come up with a better way because it was taking too much time to work that way. Basically, the form of the two-dimensional numbers was the same. I made a three-dimensional grid using a 5 mm unit. In drawing a circle varying in size by 5 mm, the center is fixed and does not change. You start by drawing a sketch using a compass with a pencil, and then you draw over it in ink using a compass with a ruling pen. I prepared a sheet with all the necessary basic forms printed in blue to use as a mount…Since it is so time-consuming to adjust the compass, I had compasses prepared for drawing different diameters like 10 mm, 15 mm, 20 mm and so on, having all the tools ready at hand to reduce work…Moreover, since it was difficult to work on a large B1 size paper, each number was drawn in ink separately and was then pasted onto the big paper. Of course, it is not impossible to work on a large paper, but it is very demanding."

Although he had the help of his staff, much of Igarashi's energy was spent on working on the MoMA calendar. Originally he had planned to continue for at least ten years, but then the Mac was introduced. "Our office started using the Mac in 1987. I realized how tedious it was to draw everything by hand. After about six years, photographer Mitsumasa Fujitsuka said, 'Isn't it enough?' Imagine working with a ruling pen side by side with someone on a computer (laughs). I continued for seven years. The eighth year was a re-make of the best 12, and then I was finished."

In Philip B. Meggs' comprehensive book *A History of Graphic Design*, he called Igarashi "A paradigm of the blending of Eastern and Western ideas."[1] It is unclear what Meggs means by Eastern ideas, but in the East Asian cultural sphere Chinese characters, or *Kanji*, were traditionally recognized as constructions with architectural qualities. *Kanji* as a hieroglyph contains its own universe in itself. It may be said that Igarashi's three-dimensional alphabets and the MoMA calendars are products of the thrilling and blessed union of his inherent Asian understanding of the script with the Western logical analysis of space. Aside from the calendars, Igarashi created shopping bags, greeting cards, and playing cards for MoMA. The shopping bag employing dots is especially striking through its lucidity that is typical of Igarashi's design.

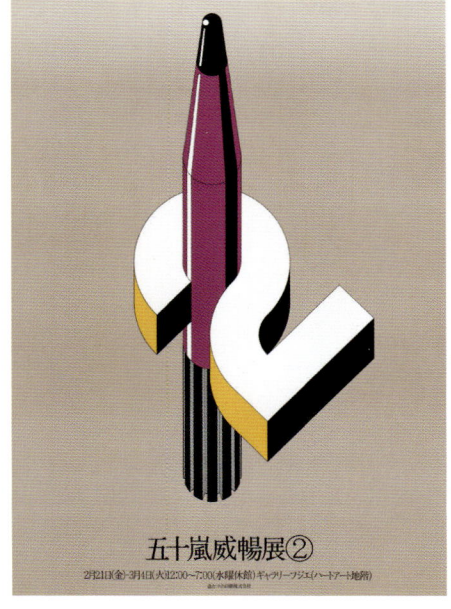

1-9 Postcard Design
Takenobu Igarashi Exhibition 2
Gallery Fujie, Tokyo, Japan, 1975

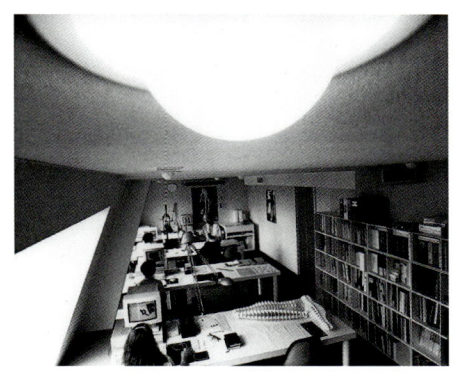

Igarashi Studio, Aoyama, Tokyo, c. 1992
Macintosh computers were introduced to staff members.

[1] Meggs, Philip B. (1998) *A History of Graphic Design*. New York: John Wiley & Sons, Inc.

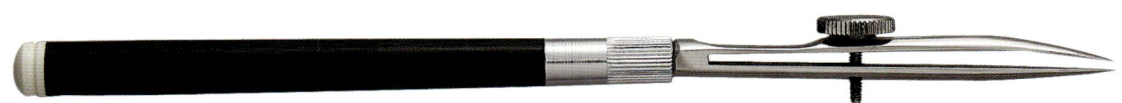

Igarashi's ruling pen used for various projects between the 70s and the 80s

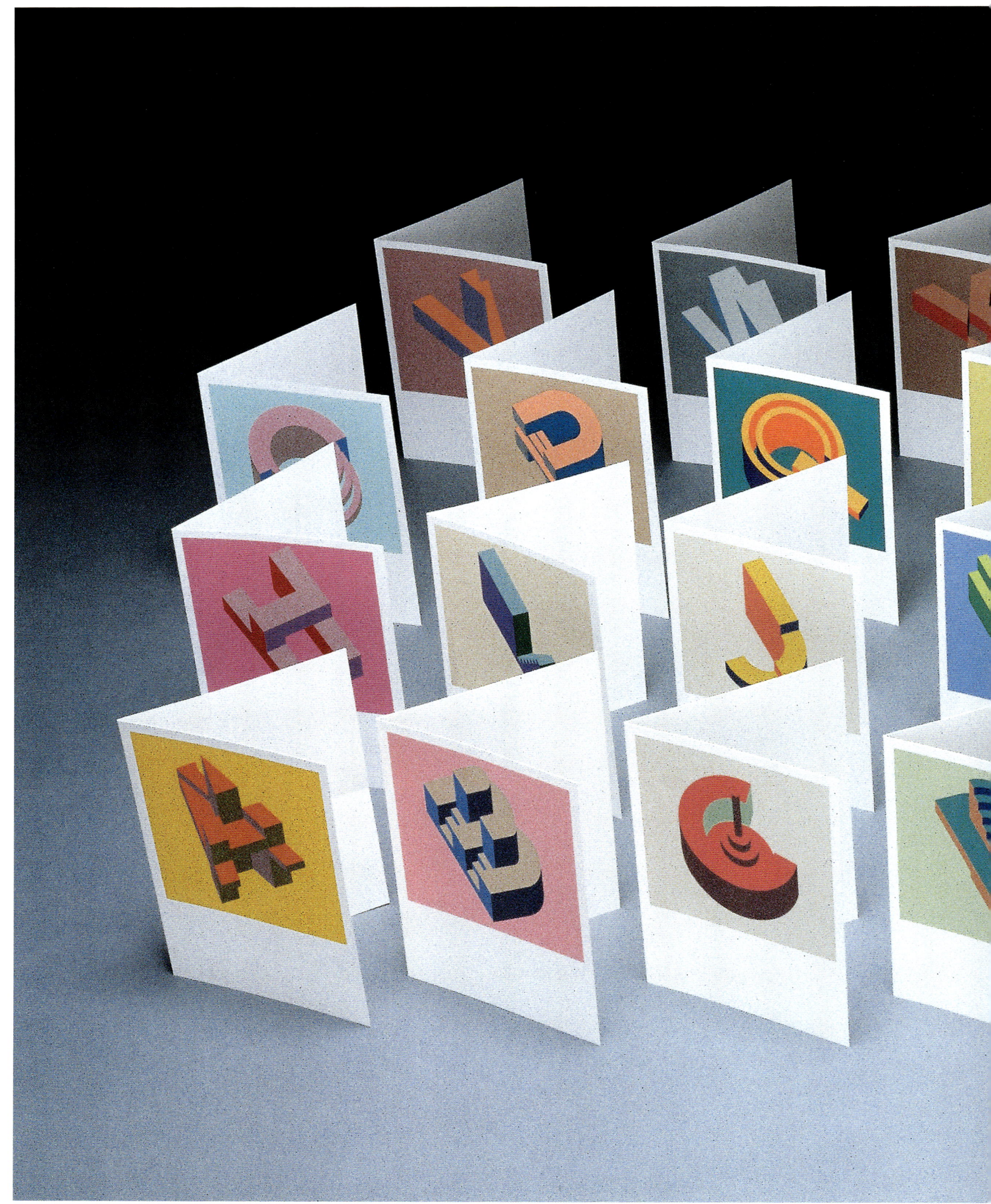

1-10 Alphabet Card
Alphabet Gallery, Tokyo, Japan, 1983

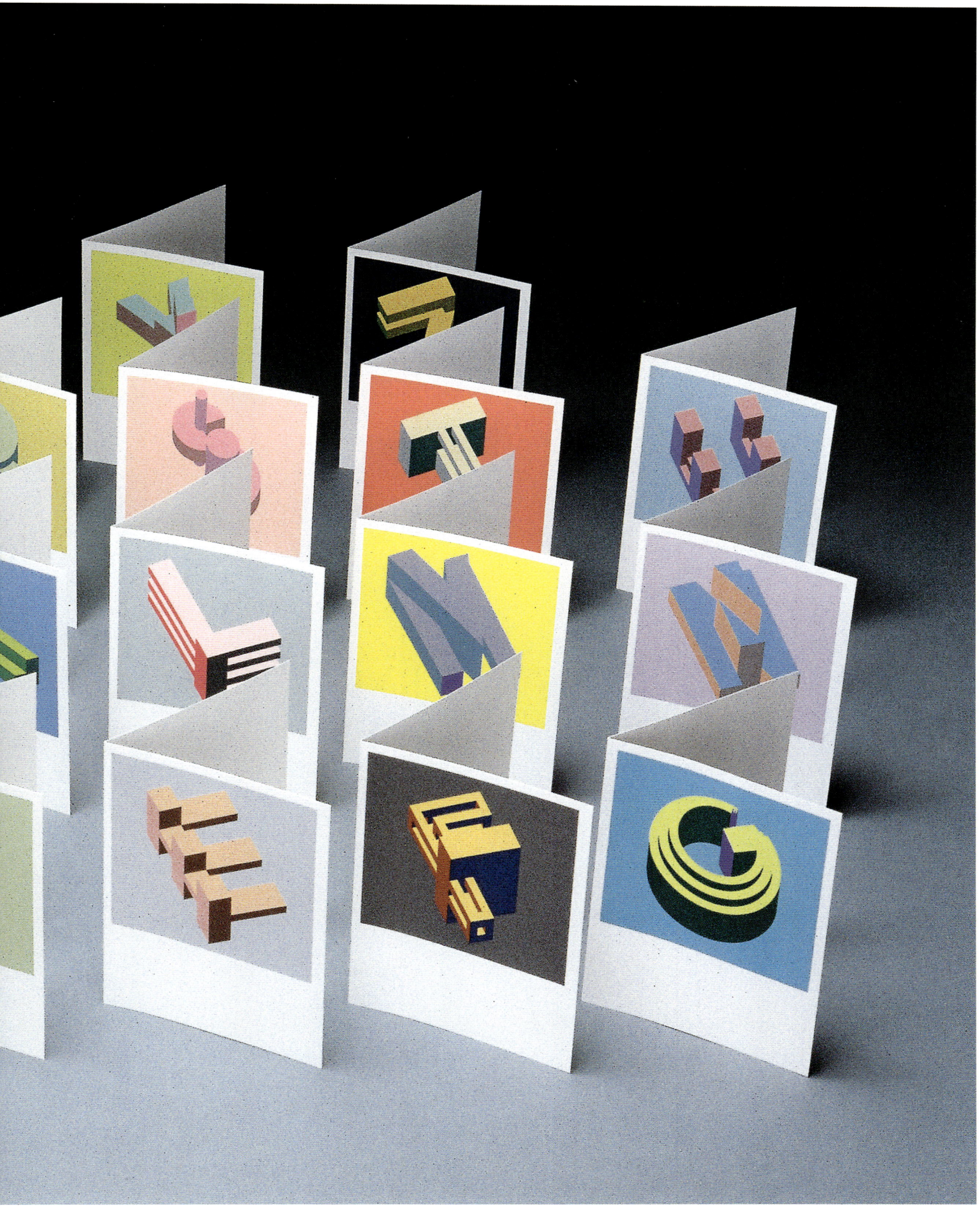

Hibiki—Another Successful Concept for Suntory

Hibiki logo for the Suntory Hall that was opened in 1986 is another stunning work of Igarashi. Suntory, an internationally operating beverage company, was planning to build a concert hall in Akasaka, Tokyo, with superb acoustics for experiencing ultimate live performances. Suntory's president at the time asked Igarashi to design a logo with a Japanese impression. The exquisite logo not only breaks from the traditional concept of symbol marks but also expresses the premonition of the coming digital age. "I presented about ten ideas; one of them was the visualization of the *Kanji Hibiki*, which means sound, resonance, and echo. He immediately liked it and the decision was made."

At the entrance of the concert hall, there is a monumental sculpture of fourteen golden arches of varying sizes. It is the three-dimensional variation of the logo, which forms the base. "After the logo was chosen, it occurred to me to try the three-dimensional version using the arch. The logo was symmetrical on the sides, so by connecting the respective sides with an arch, a three-dimensional form appears automatically, sort of an arch-alphabet. From working on the alphabet sculptures, I already had the idea of an arch, which I then used for a *Kanji*."

"I then had to make signs for the concert hall, with its many entrances: one for the backstage, one for the VIP, one for the back door, and so on. I designed five different three-dimensional symbols of the arch and placed them on the walls of the respective entrances. There is a small arch at the main entrance above the door, and one can catch a glimpse of it when entering. And on the other side, there is another bronze arch by the exit. The largest sculpture is the gold monument placed at the entrance square." The monument, like a creature inhabiting the square, serves its role beautifully as a landmark for music lovers visiting the hall and is renowned internationally for its outstanding acoustics.

There are also other three-dimensional alphabets and numbers aside from the Suntory sculpture, like *180* for Nike, *D* for the Italian design magazine Domus, *K* for Kokuyo, *150* commemorating the 150th anniversary of Kajima construction company used for the title page of their publication, and *T*, an intricate three-dimensional logo for the Japan Typography Association's bulletin. There is also a wooden sculpture of the *T*. In spite of its complex structure, the letter T is clearly discernible at certain angles. The large-scale object *3* was commissioned by Michael Peters of London, of which a variation of it was later placed at the Third Elementary School in Takikawa, where Igarashi attended as a child.

Sign Design and Corporate Identity

In the early 1970s, when Igarashi had difficulty finding work, he depended on Shigeru Uchida and Shiro Kuramata's recommendations to design logos and signs for shops and restaurants. In 1977, Architect Minoru Takeyama asked him to design the sign for Misawa Homes Institute of Research and Development Co., Ltd., and in 1979, he designed the sign system for the Kanazawa Tamagawa Library that was built by architect Yoshio Taniguchi. Taniguchi also commissioned Igarashi to design the sign system for the Akita Chuo City Library in 1983. He also designed the sign for Fumihiko Maki's Nissei Toranomon NN Building (1981) and for the libraries of both Mita and Hiyoshi campuses of Keio University (1985). All three architects were cosmopolitans and had studied at Harvard University.

"Sign design is not really understood, I felt like I had been working in vain. In spite of all the hours spent on meetings deciding on a sign system, after a while people just improvise and use a temporary sign or paste paper over it...it's really horrible. Additional signs are made without the designer, and everything gets so messy. That is why I don't like to do it anymore (laughs)...On the contrary, I started putting my efforts into designing CI programs in the '80s, the first one being the one for Summit. Thanks to Motoo Nakanishi, pioneer of CI design in Japan, companies were becoming aware of the importance of CI and started to utilize them. It was a time when orders totally expanded." As Igarashi mentions, CI design for Calpis Food Industry Co., Ltd. (1983), Mitsui Bank Ltd. (1984), Suntory Holdings Ltd. (1986), and Meiji Milk Products Ltd. (1986) followed during this period.

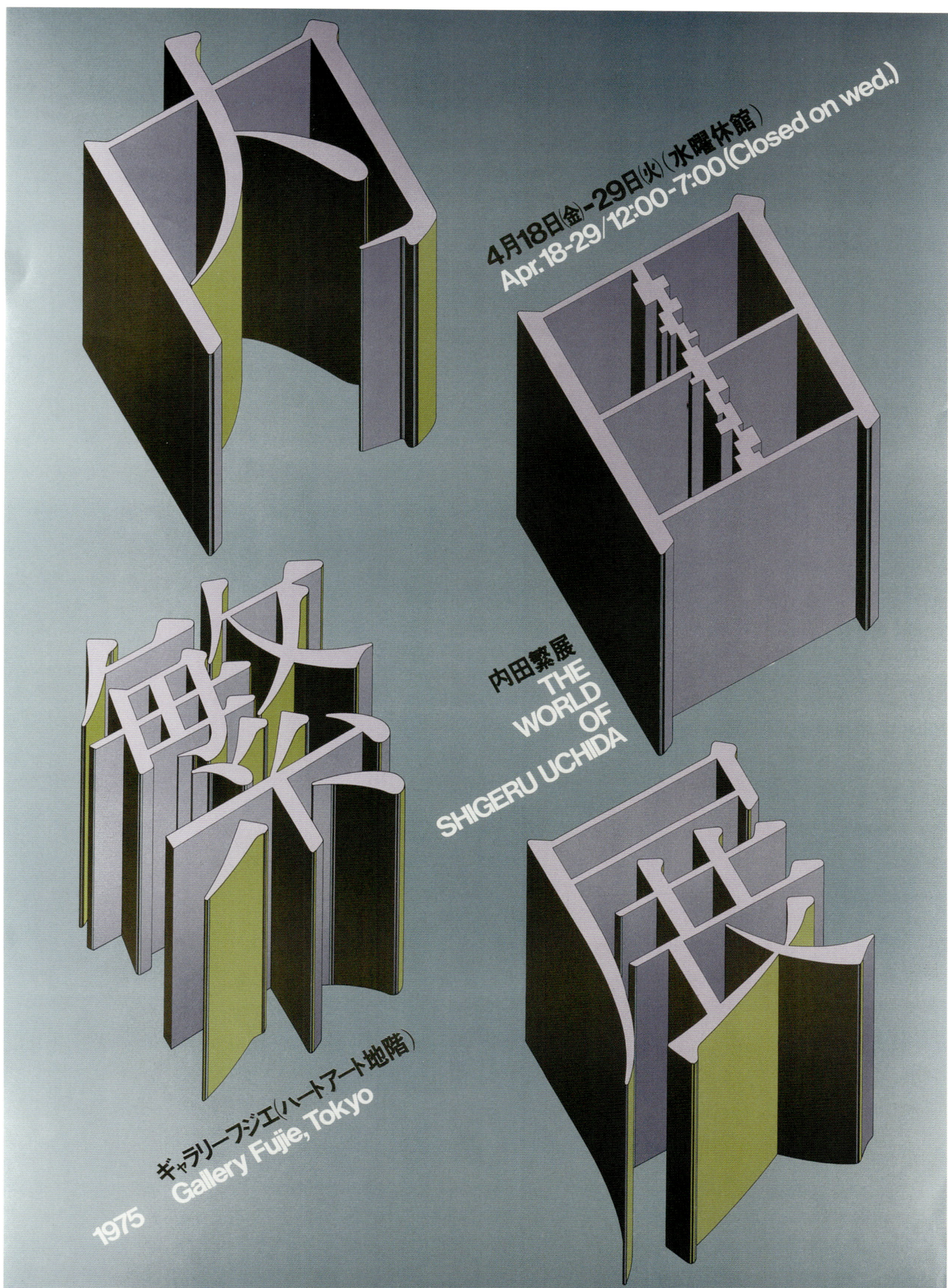

1-11 Poster
Shigeru Uchida Exhibition, Gallery Fujie, Tokyo, Japan, 1975

"I had only two weeks to work on the logo for Calpis. It was a competition among advertising agencies, and I think I was working for Dentsu. You need manpower to work on sign systems with all the work rushing in at the end, but doing a complete CI is even more work, and it is absolutely necessary to have people working for you. I would draw the idea on a graph paper, and then all the staff would do a clean drawing in ink. Luckily, at that time I had stocked my office with employees, so I was able to cope without a problem. I will never forget that we worked on 100 ideas for Calpis in just two weeks! For Suntory we presented 250 ideas, but we had a whole year for that. For Meiji we had more than half a year to a year's time to work on the CI. So I also got used to working on projects with a long duration."

Igarashi's remarkable achievements were only possible through his practical knowledge acquired and cultivated by working on variations influenced by Max Bill and on the MoMA poster calendars. "By devising methods and tools enabling a speedy drawing technique, I was able to increase the output of variations on a theme. Max Bill's influence is also undeniable. In the creative process, through analogy and estimation, it was possible to simulate a greater diversity of variations. So I was able to cope with more complex work in limited time, making design even more enjoyable." Rationalizing the work process and probing deeply into the possibilities of variation and simulation have resulted in the deepening of design's appeal to the senses. Igarashi's CI design is not only limited to corporations; it is also used for educational institutions like Kanazawa Institute of Technology (1981–1985), Tama Art University (1995), and Okazaki Women's University (2015).

While working on CI design, he published a collection of his works entitled *Igarashi Space Graphics*, from Shoten Kenchiku-Sha in 1983. The theme of the book was the effect of design on the environment, with an awareness of the role graphic design plays in the environment. "Take a logo, for example. A logo can be seen everywhere in the city, such as a billboard, as a sign, or as an advertisement. It becomes a part of the environment. For this reason, it needs to be inspected from an environmental viewpoint…I think I was sensitive to the effects of design on the environment more than most designers. In CI design, in choosing a certain corporate color, I always think about the medium through which it will be exposed. In an urban environment, there are signs everywhere, like signboards for a bank, for instance. I am especially sensitive to the color used and its influence on the environment. I think about this even when designing a poster." There are countless projects reflecting Igarashi's awareness of the environment. One example is his work for the German paper company Zanders, starting from design for their poster, booth for a trade fair in Dusseldorf (1986), and expanding to an entire showroom design. Other representative works include the floor design for Tokyo International Passenger Terminal at Tokyo Harbor (architect Minoru Takeyama) in 1990, sign and alphabet sculpture for The Square (1983), a shopping center situated in the Western outskirts of Tokyo, and CI and environmental design for APITA supermarket.

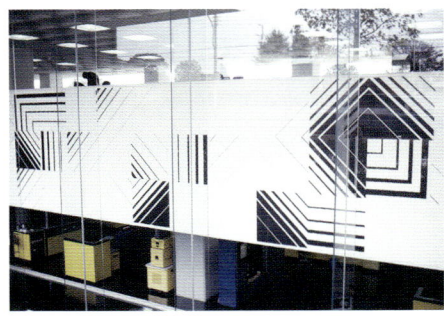

1-12 Wall Graphics
Misawa Homes CO., LTD., Tokyo, Japan, 1977
I produced this work on site with silkscreen printing. (TI)

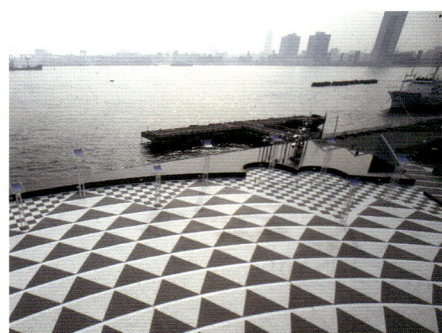

1-13 Floor Design for Harumi Passenger Ship Terminal
Tokyo Port Bureau of Port and Harbor
Tokyo Metropolitan Government
Tokyo, Japan, 1991

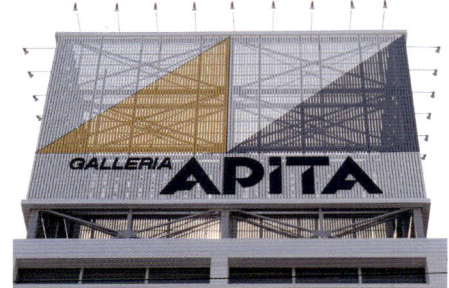

1-14 Logotype and Sign Design
Apita Commercial Complex, UNY Co., Ltd.
Nagoya, Aichi, Japan, 1983

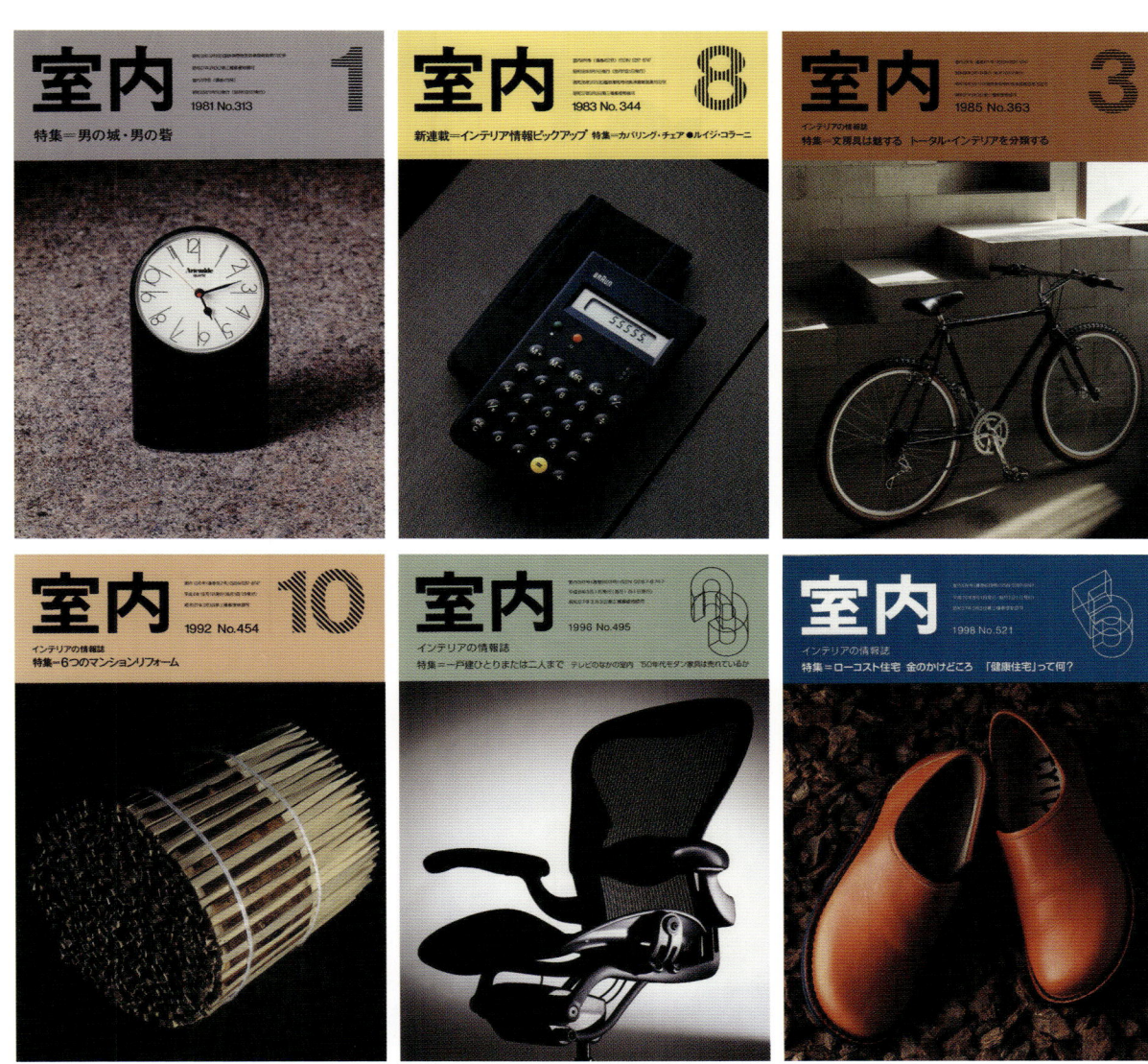

1-15 Cover Design
Shitsunai Interior, Design Magazine, Kosakusha, Tokyo, Japan, c. 1980–1997

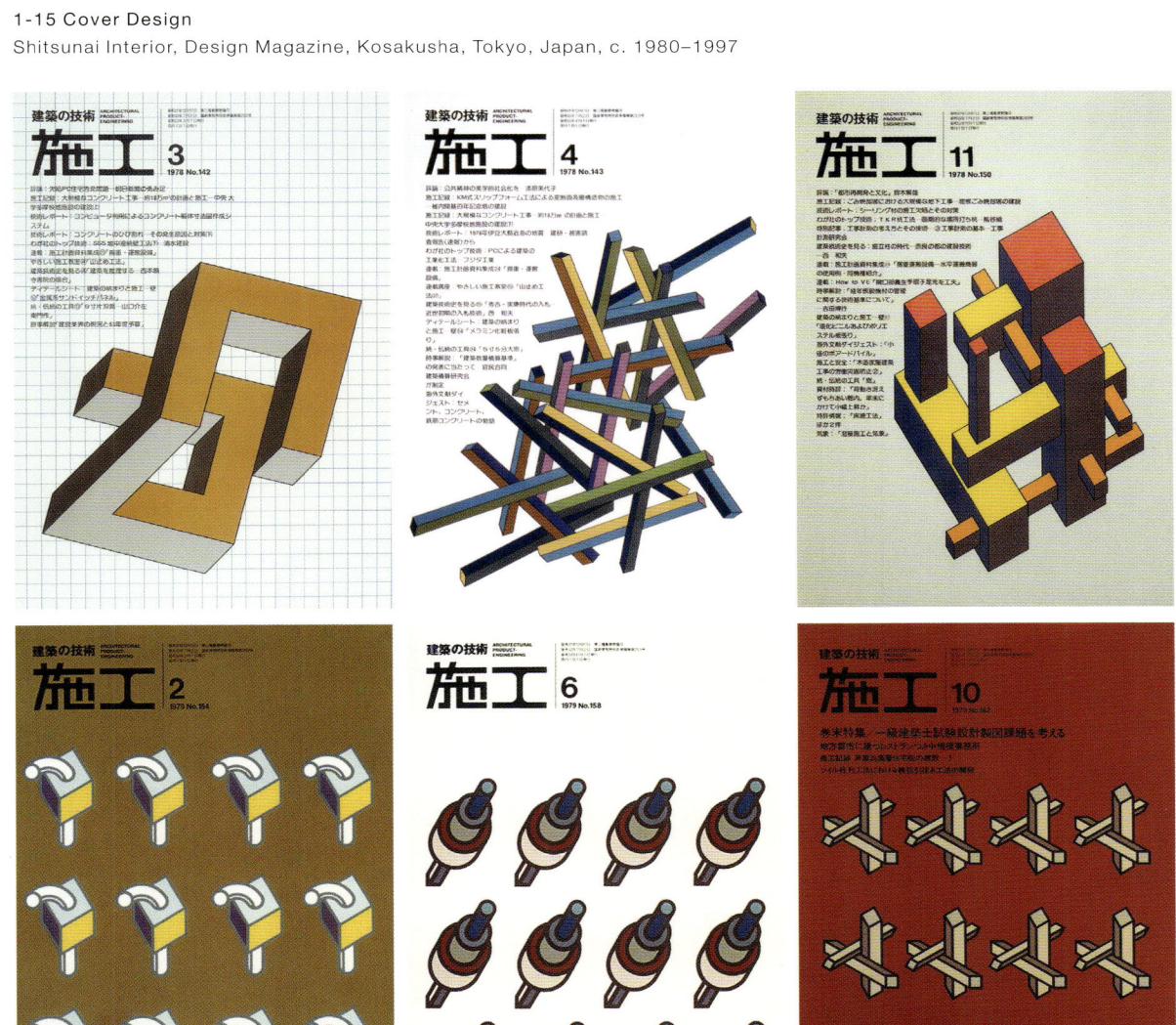

1-16 Cover Design
Seko, Architecture Magazine, Shokokusha, Tokyo, Japan, c. 1976–1982

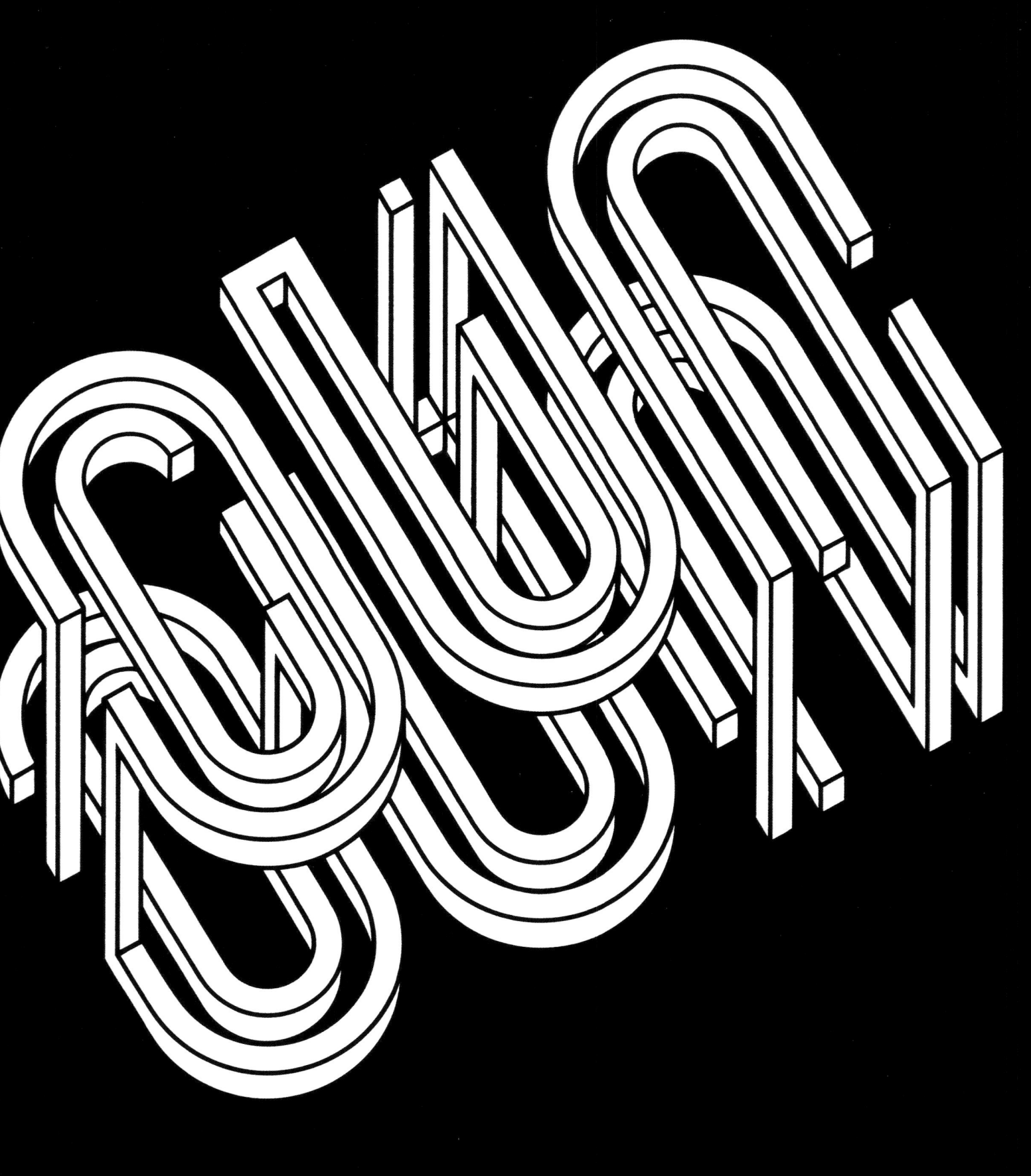

Getting Involved in Product Design—The OUN Project

Igarashi's involvement with product design can be traced back to his interest in architecture and industrial design and through designing covers from 1980 to 1997 for *Shitsunai*, an interior design magazine. Igarashi was supposed to design the cover using Mitsumasa Fujitsuka's photos of an interior or a piece of furniture. Together, they came up with a better idea. "The request to use a photo of an interior or a piece of furniture was too ordinary. We thought that products play an important role in forming the interior. So we suggested that we choose a new and exciting product each month, photograph it, and make a cover out of it. Moreover, there was a request from an agent to make a cover using bright colors. I didn't like that idea either, and used intermediate and subdued colors. For the January issue, we chose a clock designed in cooperation with Richard Sapper. Just when the proof print was finished, a young deliveryman from a noodle shop saw it and said, 'Wow, cool!' So eventually the magazine became a big hit and within a year the sales visibly increased. It was my first work with numerical results (laughs)."

Igarashi and Fujitsuka agreed that both had to concur on the products they choose. "If one of us disagreed, it was not chosen. We both choose intuitively, so when asked 'why is this good?' we would start thinking and discussing. These countless discussions were very valuable in that I questioned my decisions and also learned a lot from Fujitsuka's way of looking at products from the viewpoint of a photographer. It influenced me in the way I looked at products, what to look for, and so on." Originally as a one-year contract, the successful project continued for eighteen years. Some of them show Igarashi's own products as well. In the exhibition *50 Months of Shitsunai Cover Design* held in 1985 at Ginza Matsuya's Design Gallery 1953, the real products were also exhibited with the corresponding covers.

After a while Igarashi was asked to design products. "I think it was just by chance, or maybe it was the time. When I said, 'I am a graphic designer and I have no experience in industrial design so I have no idea,' the answer was, 'I want you because you are a graphic designer.' There was a certain expectation that something interesting might come out from the viewpoint of a graphic designer." One of his representative works is the *F Cordless Telephone* (1989) with its edgy form based on a grid that is fresh and modern. Fisso stationery products are also designed in this style.

In 1987, after working on the Suntory Hall project, Igarashi was asked by the same project planners to work on another project. Aside from its cultural contribution in the field of music, Suntory awards the Suntory Prize for Social Sciences and Humanities to honor individuals who have contributed to the society and culture through publications in research and criticism. The president of Suntory wanted to contribute to the field of design as well and Dentsu, one of Japan's leading advertising agencies, was entrusted with the task and contacted Igarashi.

"Together with Dentsu, we came up with the OUN project. There were three pillars of activity: design education, publication, and developing new products. All of this was supposed to take place on a global scale, so we started where we could. I thought that it would be no problem to do publishing. We were even planning to buy Graphis Magazine of Switzerland, but Martin Pedersen was a step ahead of us and bought the magazine and brought it to the US. It was Pedersen who did the layout of my feature in *ITC*'s *U&lc* in his younger days. For developing new products, we wanted to distribute them worldwide by bringing together international designers with international manufacturers. Since I was not an expert in the field, I suggested engaging experts as consultants. I chose Massimo Vignelli of New York and Alan Fletcher of London. Massimo Vignelli was an all-round designer versed in graphic, product, furniture, and interior design, as well as architecture. Alan Fletcher was one of the founders of Pentagram. I chose him for his connections in Europe. He was very popular and knew a lot of people."

Pentagram is a legendary design studio with a wide range of activities. Among the founders of Pentagram were industrial designer Kenneth Grange and architect Theo Crosby. With two specialists on board, they met every three months for a week during the preparation period of two years. They would travel around the world and meet with designers and manufacturers, consulting and discussing how to proceed. Finally, they developed over a hundred products, mainly paper products, and started selling them in American and European museums. "If the OUN project had worked 100% to its fullest, it would have been epoch-making. Unfortunately, we were not successful in making the distribution network to sell the products. After ten years there were still not enough stores and dealers. Maybe we were too ahead of time…but we did have some hit products, like the system album that I designed. I also designed two clocks, of which the first lots are sold out, although it took a long time."

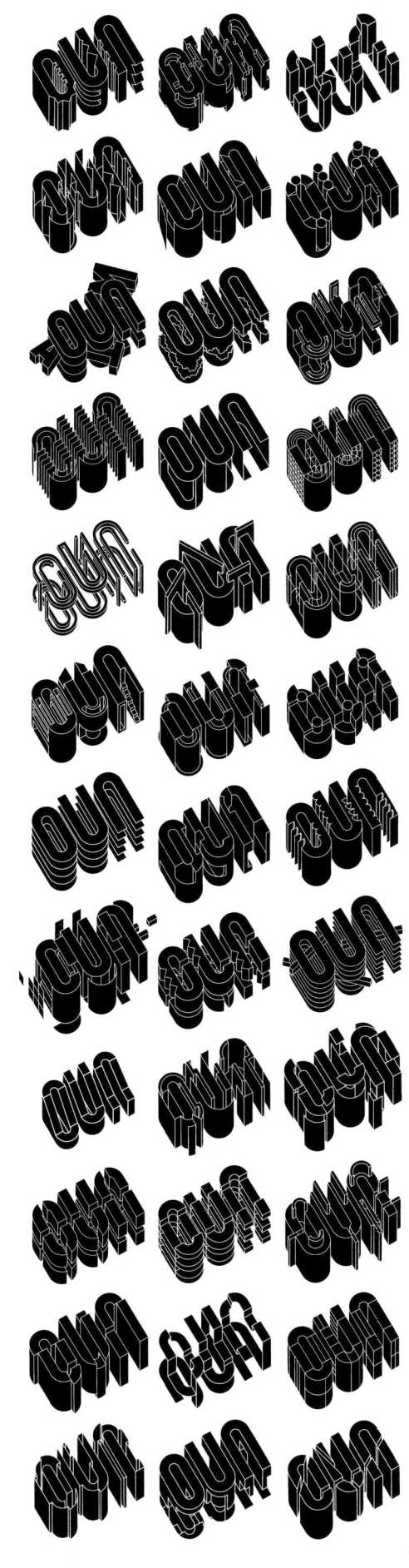

1-17 Logotype
OUN, Tokyo, Japan, 1987
This logo design varies in accordance with the type of the applied object.

The *Dual-Face Clock*, displaying two time-zones, and the *Ball Clock* (1987) both stand out for their functional beauty, devoid of unnecessary decoration, vividly showing Igarashi's sharp sensibility for form. The pioneering attempts on the OUN project unfortunately ended without being fully developed to its potentials. Learning from this failure, Igarashi proceeded to tackle another project working with Japanese local industries.

Y.M.D.—Product Development in Cooperation with Local Industries

Y.M.D. is a project initiated in 1989, bringing together Yamada Shomei Lighting Co., Ltd. with leading local craft industries from Hokkaido to Okinawa. Igarashi visited six different craft regions, from the woodworks of Hokkaido, the Aizu Lacquerware Cooperative Union, the ceramic producer in Seto, to flatware manufacturer of Tsubame-Sanjo, cast-metal of Yamagata and Toyama Prefectures, and assigned them to the staff. "I knew it would be difficult selling the products through my experiences with the OUN project. Local craft industries were having difficulties finding successors and were not in the position to develop new products. Having this situation in mind, our plan was to propose a design to the manufacturer. When they accepted it, they would work on a prototype at their own expense, and when the product was good, we would look for a network to sell the product. Once the distributor is found, the manufacturer gets the order to produce the product, and we would receive a percentage of the sales as royalty."

Igarashi was aware that selling these products in Japan would be difficult; therefore, he found distributors in the United States and in Germany. While he was searching for a way to sell the products, he was asked by the president of Yamada Shomei Lighting Co., Ltd. to design lamps. Igarashi accepted the offer and consulted the president about the methods of product distribution for support. This coincided with the generation change in administration at Yamada.

The products that were made for the Y.M.D. project in cooperation with six manufacturers throughout Japan were distributed throughout Yamada Shomei in Japan. Through the distributors in the United States and Germany, products were sold in museum stores and were presented at a trade show for gifts in New York, leading to several exhibitions in the U.S. and in European cities. Some products sold well, but soon the exchange rate of the dollar to the yen dropped drastically from 250 to 200 all the way down into the 100's (In September 1992, the yen reached its highest rate with $1=¥118.60 at the Tokyo foreign exchange market), making the products too expensive to sell abroad. The Y.M.D. project suffered a setback.

Although Igarashi's design, such as the cast-iron platters incorporating his three-dimensional and geometric design—stools, lamps, and stainless flatware were highly appraised— unfortunately the projects were stranded due to uncontrollable factors. "Basically, I was interested in systems and structures such as geometry of form and three-dimensional grids. It was a period in which I was pursuing that idea and materializing it in different forms, working within the physical limits of time and space, and trying to create my own form, my thoughts expanding in a Bauhaus-like universe. It was a lot of fun…Since I was a child, I was interested in architecture and sculpture, and wanted to do them myself. To me drawing a plan and then elevating it to obtain a three-dimensional result was a natural process. This interest is at the root of everything I do, whether it be graphic or product design."

Educating the Next Generation as Head of the Design Department

Igarashi's activity as a designer culminated with his appointment as Head of the Design Department, Faculty of Fine Art and Design Evening Division (today Faculty of Art and Communication Evening Division) at his Alma Mater, Tama Art University from 1989 to 1993. This period coincides with the turning point in design with the digital revolution. The building of new factories and establishment of new universities within the 23 wards of the city of Tokyo was forbidden by law—with the exception of the evening division. Tama Art University established a design department at the Kaminoge campus and asked Igarashi to create a new curriculum.

"In this age, I thought it was important to be able to speak English and to be able to design using the computer. So I immediately contacted Apple Computer and asked for support. We were the first in Japan to introduce 40 computers." Tama Art University led the way in training the talents of tomorrow who were able to work on an international scale with a thorough knowledge of digital technology. "Phototypesetting machines existed but did not conform

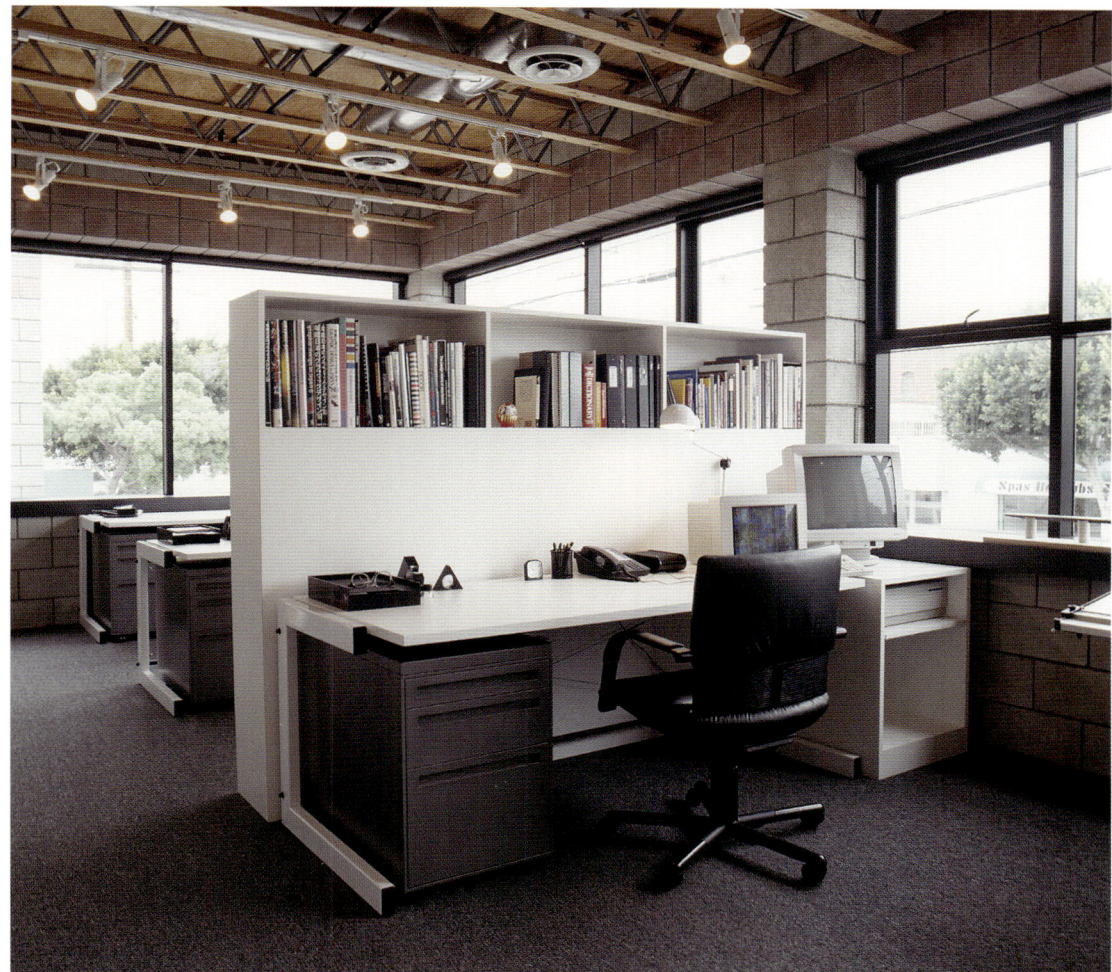

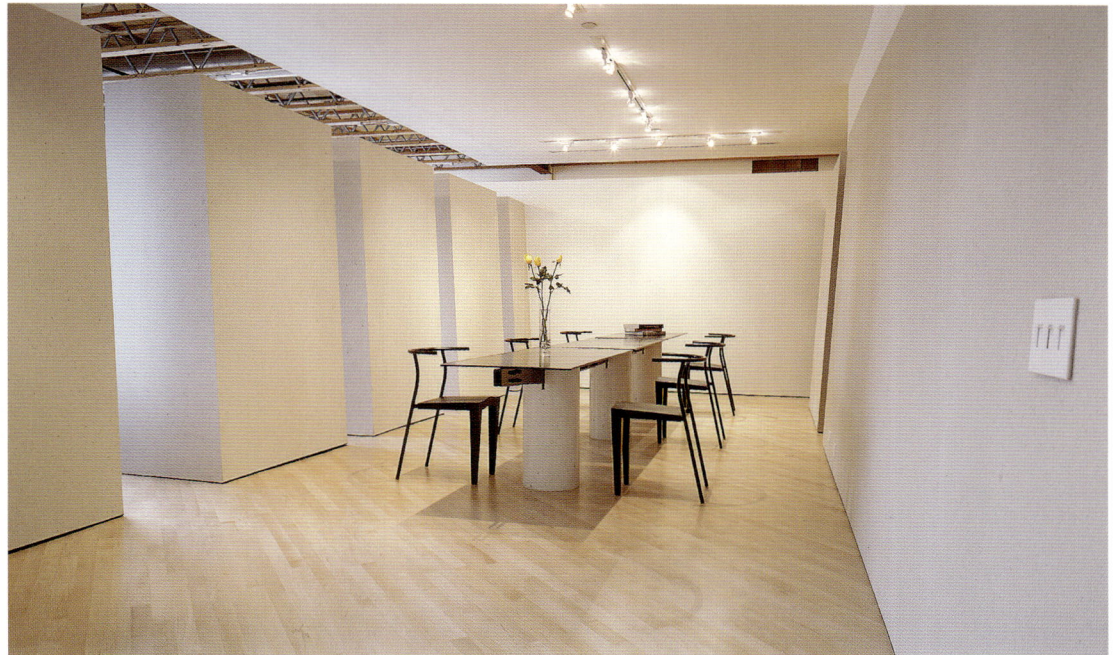

Igarashi International, Santa Monica, CA, USA
Interior design by Ken Tanaka, c. 1989

with the educational goals. However, there was also a lab of a printing company within the university, introducing the Israeli typesetting system to be used on a Sony computer. Morisawa and Type Bank allowed the use of their fonts for the typesetting machine 'as an exception only for educational purposes.' The fonts of both companies were available side by side for the computer. Moreover, since a printing company was involved, we could print student work in offset by sending data to the factory in Yokohama. Toppan Printing Co., Ltd., Dai Nippon Printing, and about 50 other major printing companies came to visit and were all amazed." Igarashi resigned after serving four years as the head of the faculty—sending off his first graduates and laying the foundation for raising the next generation of designers ready for the new age. In addition, Igarashi designed the present logo of the university in 1995 commemorating its 60th anniversary, and served as the ninth president of his Alma Mater from 2011 to 2014. Presently he is professor emeritus of Tama Art University.

Following the path of Igarashi, one is astounded by his devotion and his surging vigor in attaining his countless achievements. Igarashi, convinced that he had explored every possibility as a designer, moved on to become a sculptor in 1994.

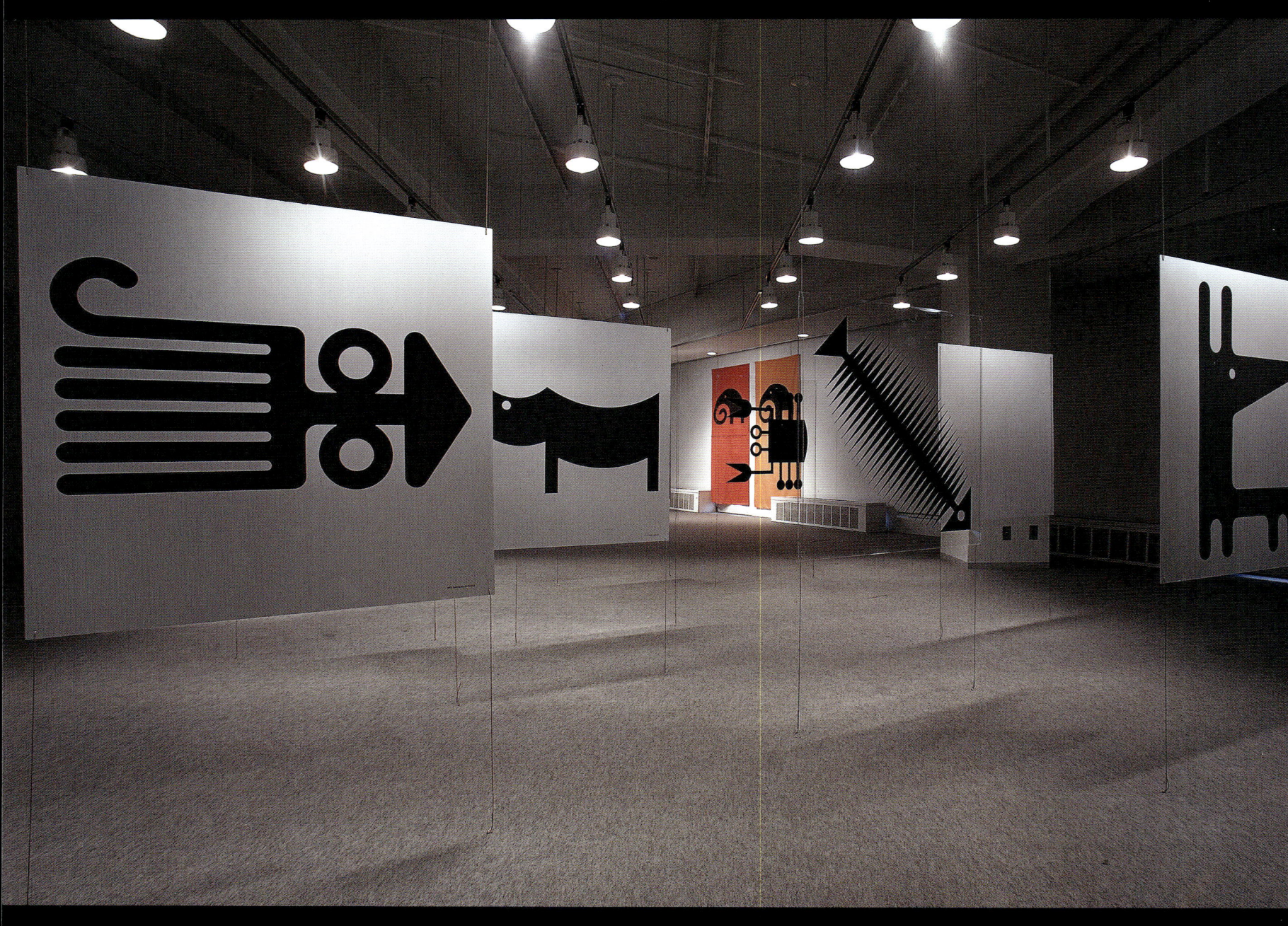

Solo Exhibition, Animal Illustrations, Gallery Fujie, Tokyo, Japan
Display Design: Shigeru Uchida, 1973

1-18 Animal Illustration
Other illustrations from the same series, 1973

Crab Fish
Fur Seal Peacock
Lion Bone of Fish

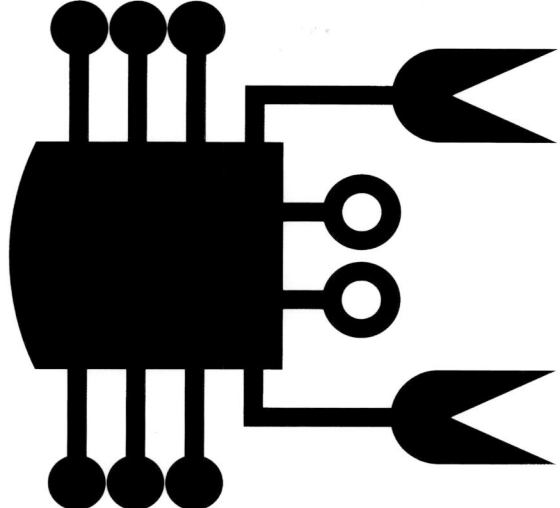
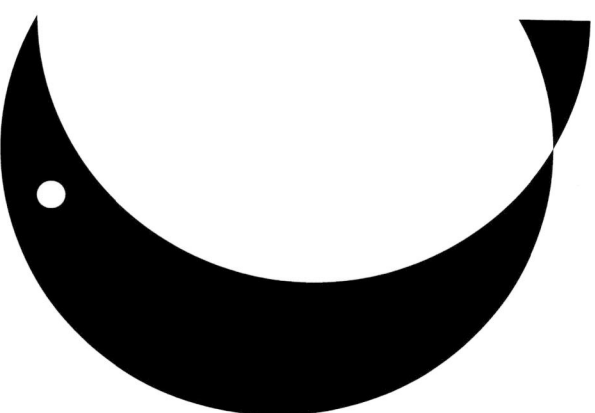
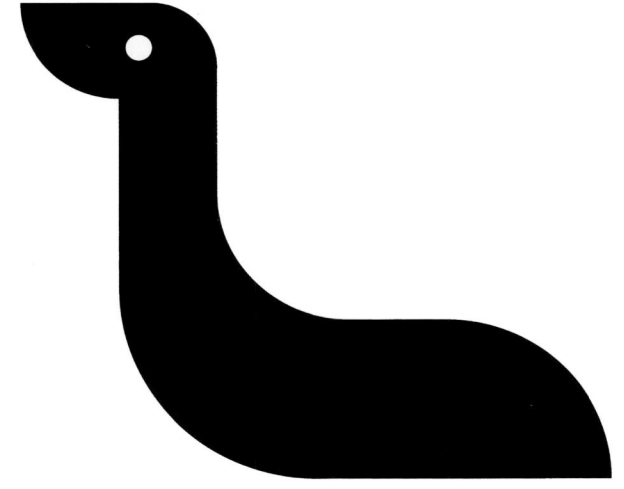
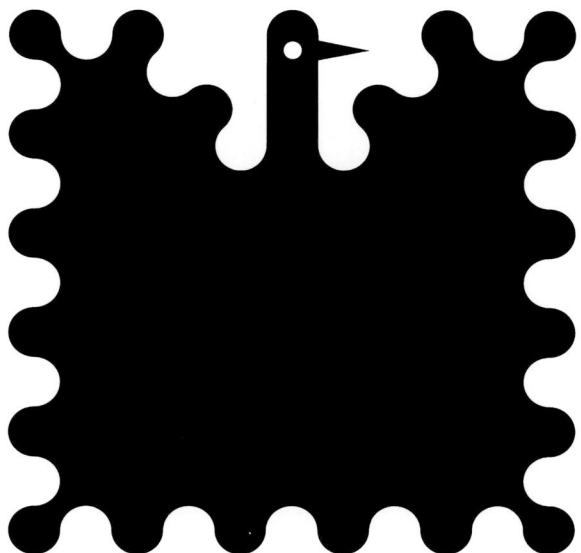
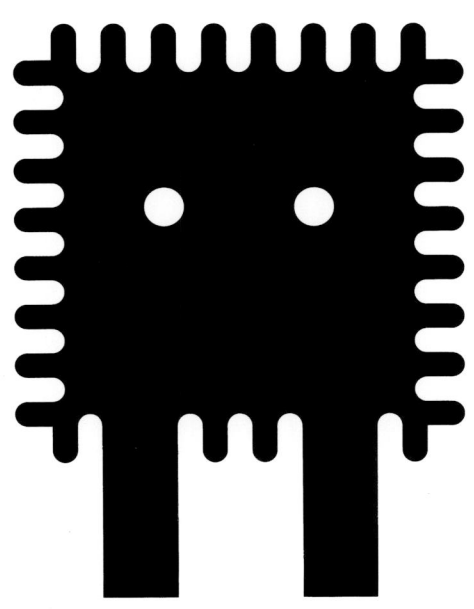
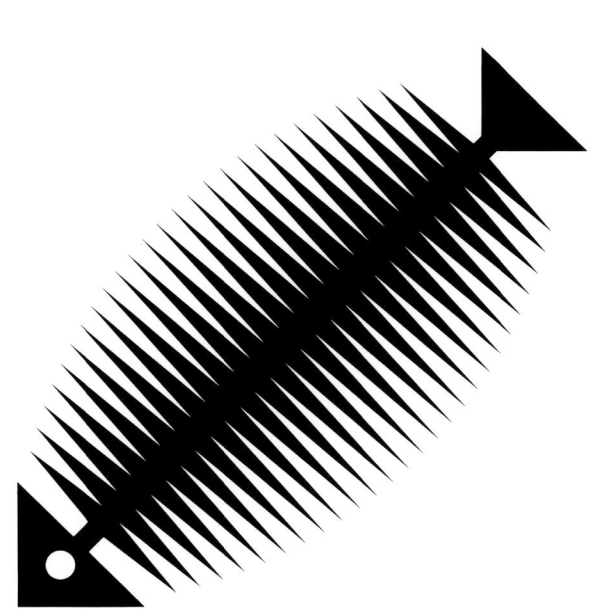

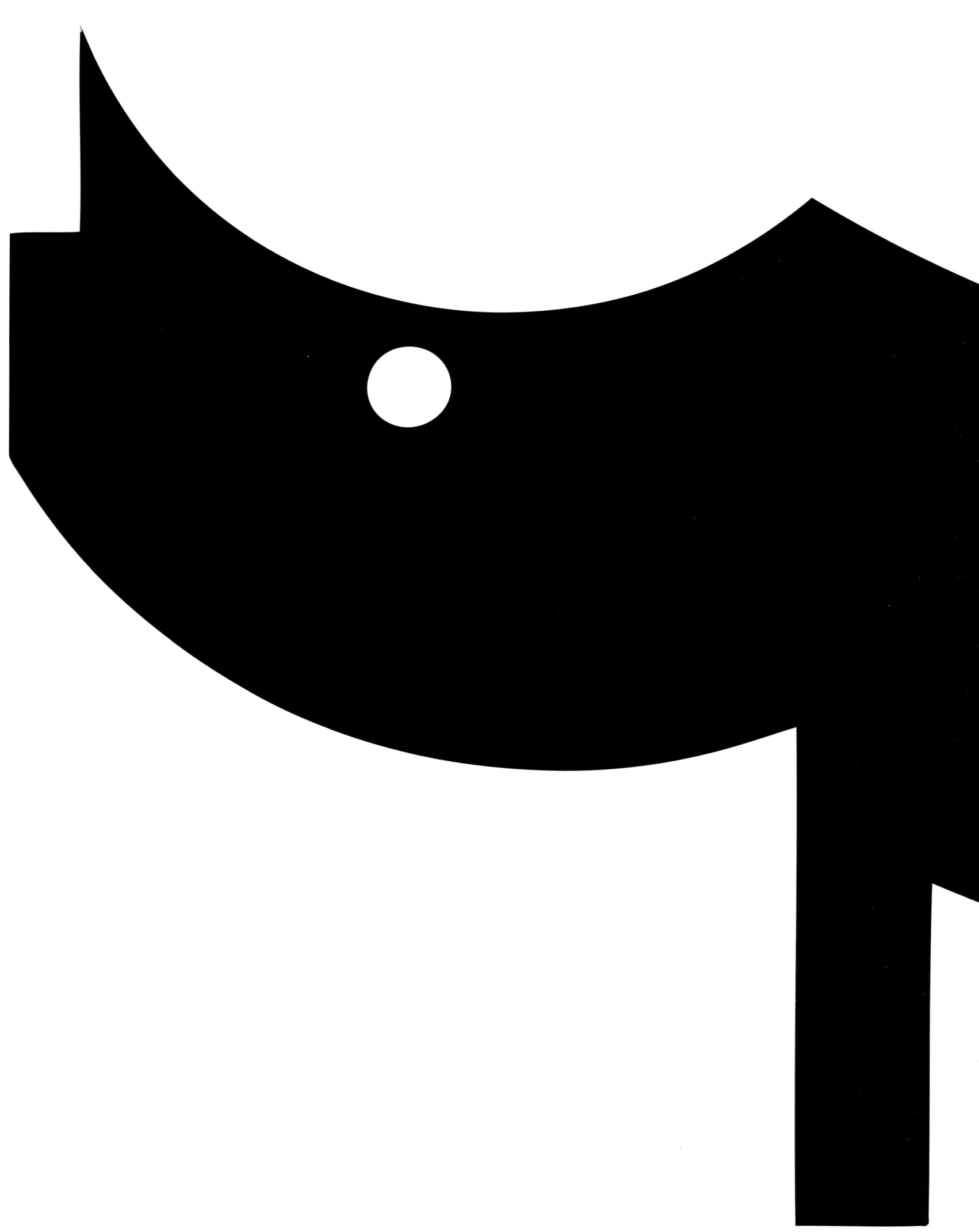

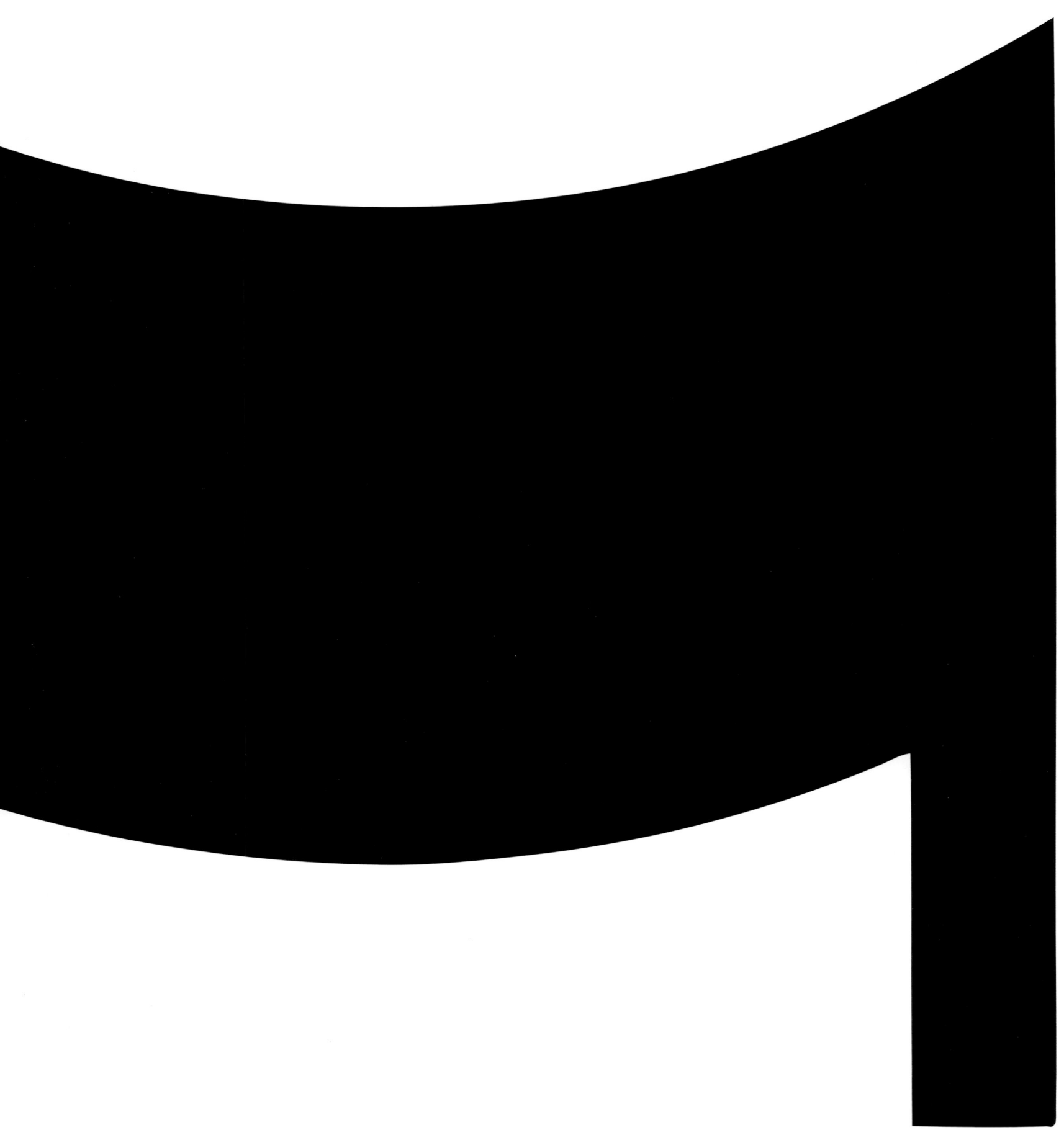

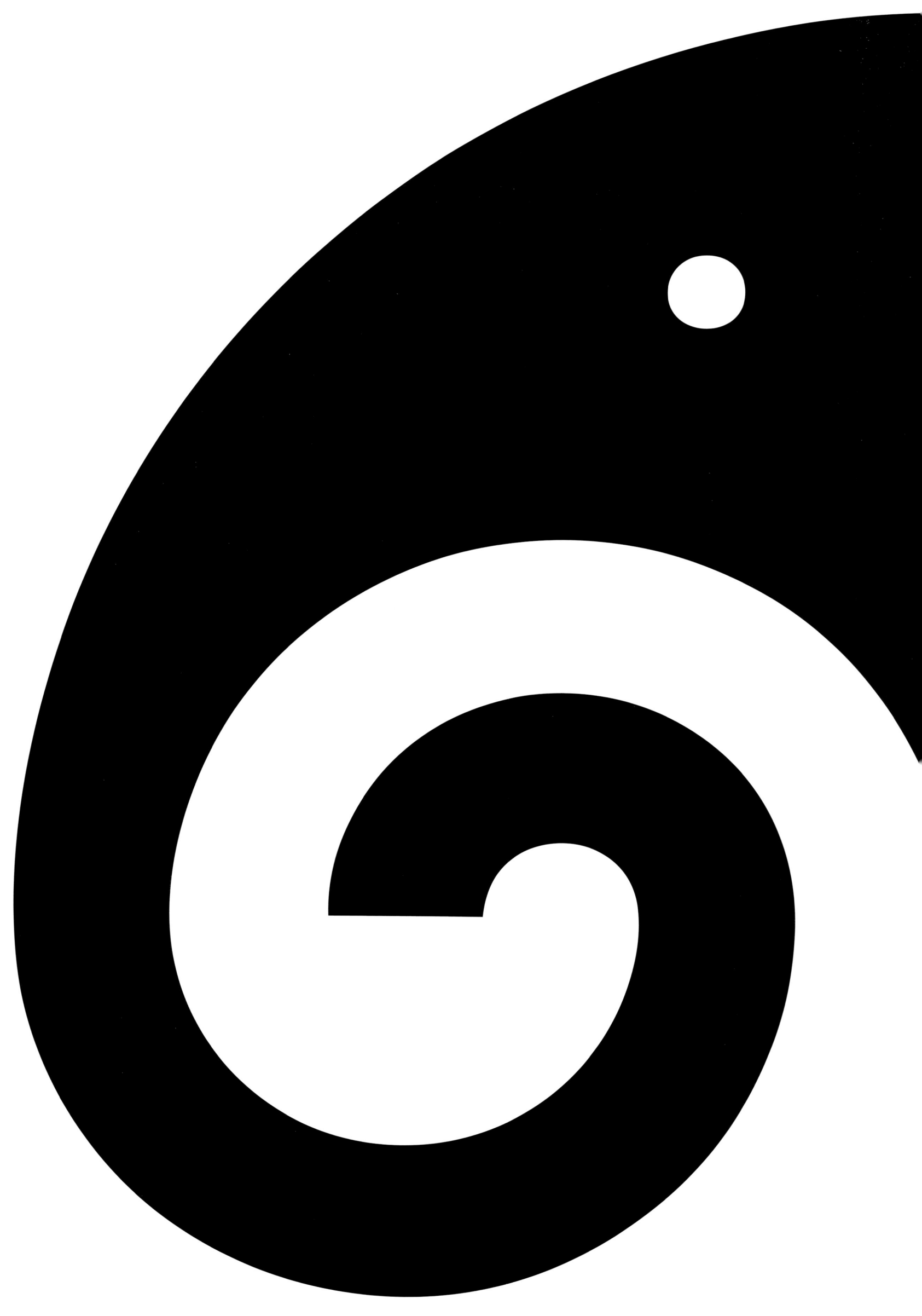

Elephant

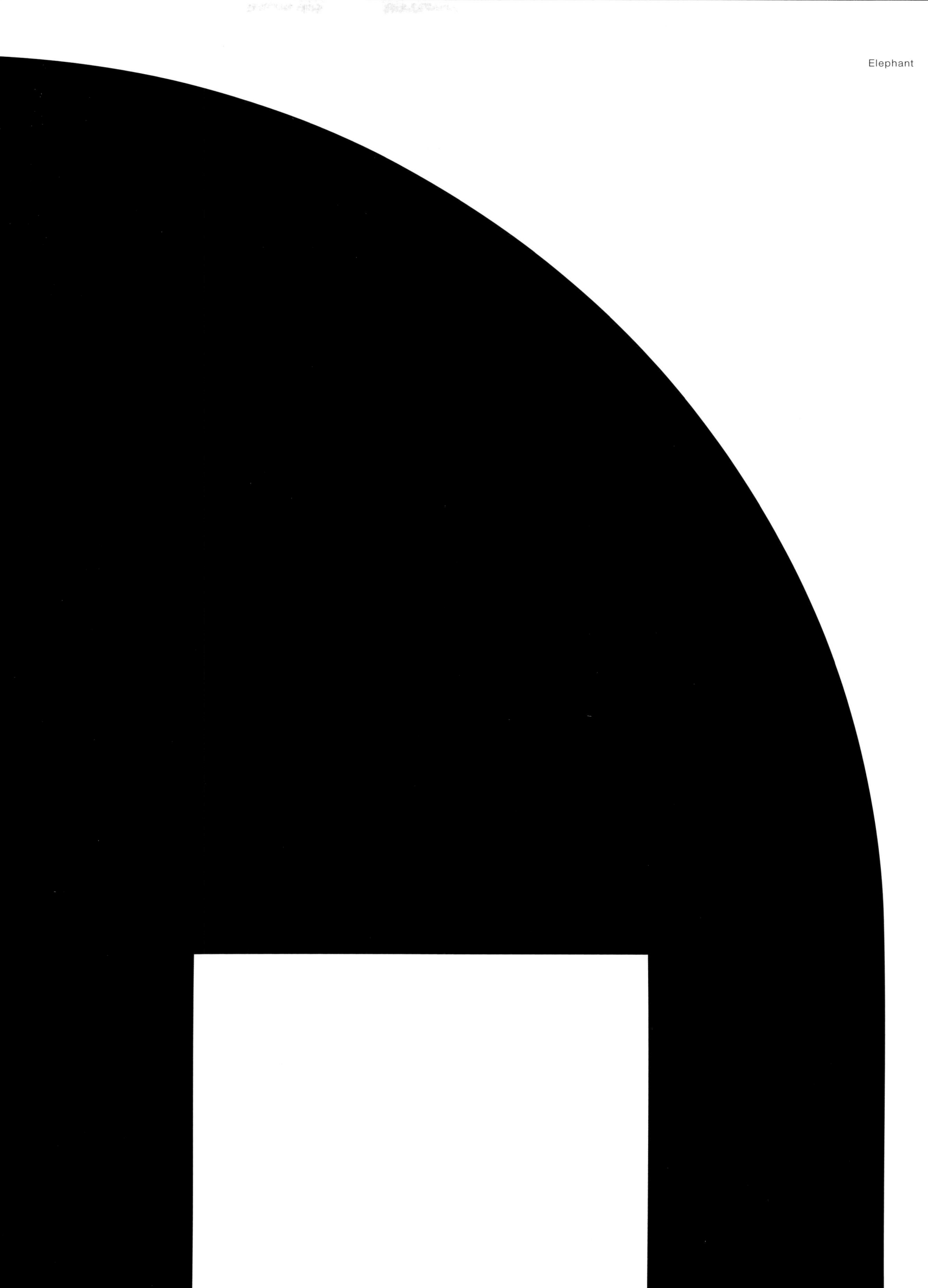

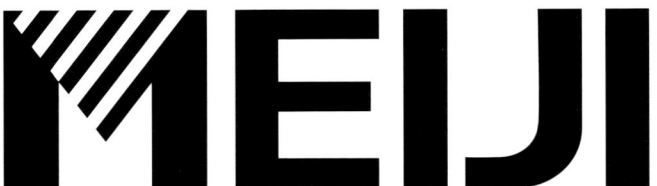

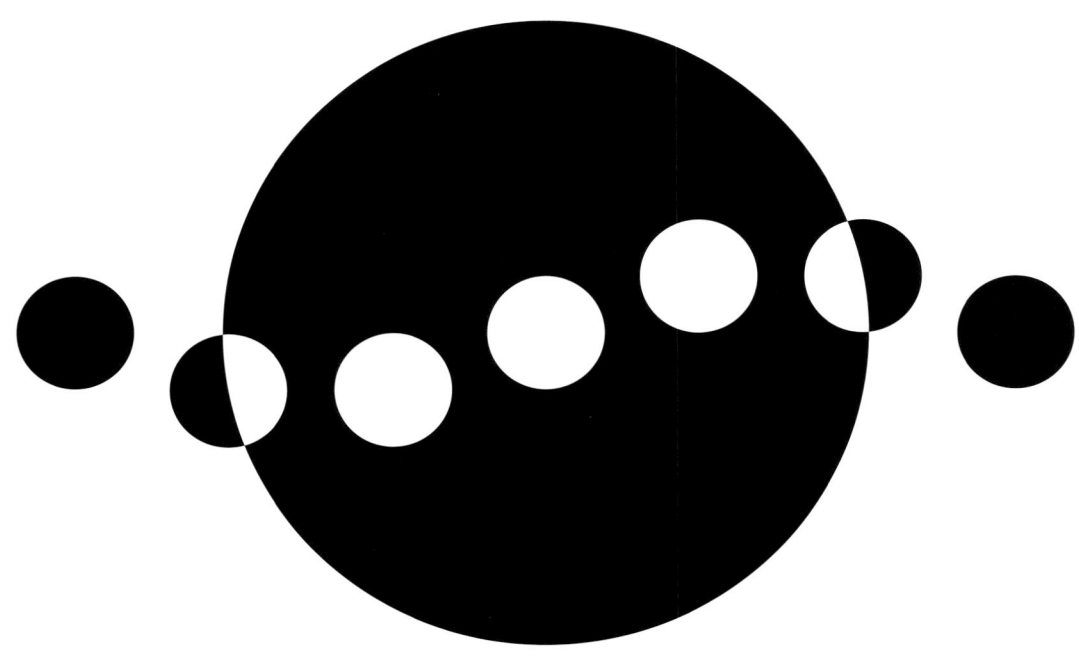

1-19 Logotype
Meiji Dairies Corporation
Tokyo, Japan, 1986

1-20 Symbol Mark
Calpis Co., Ltd.
Tokyo, Japan, 1983

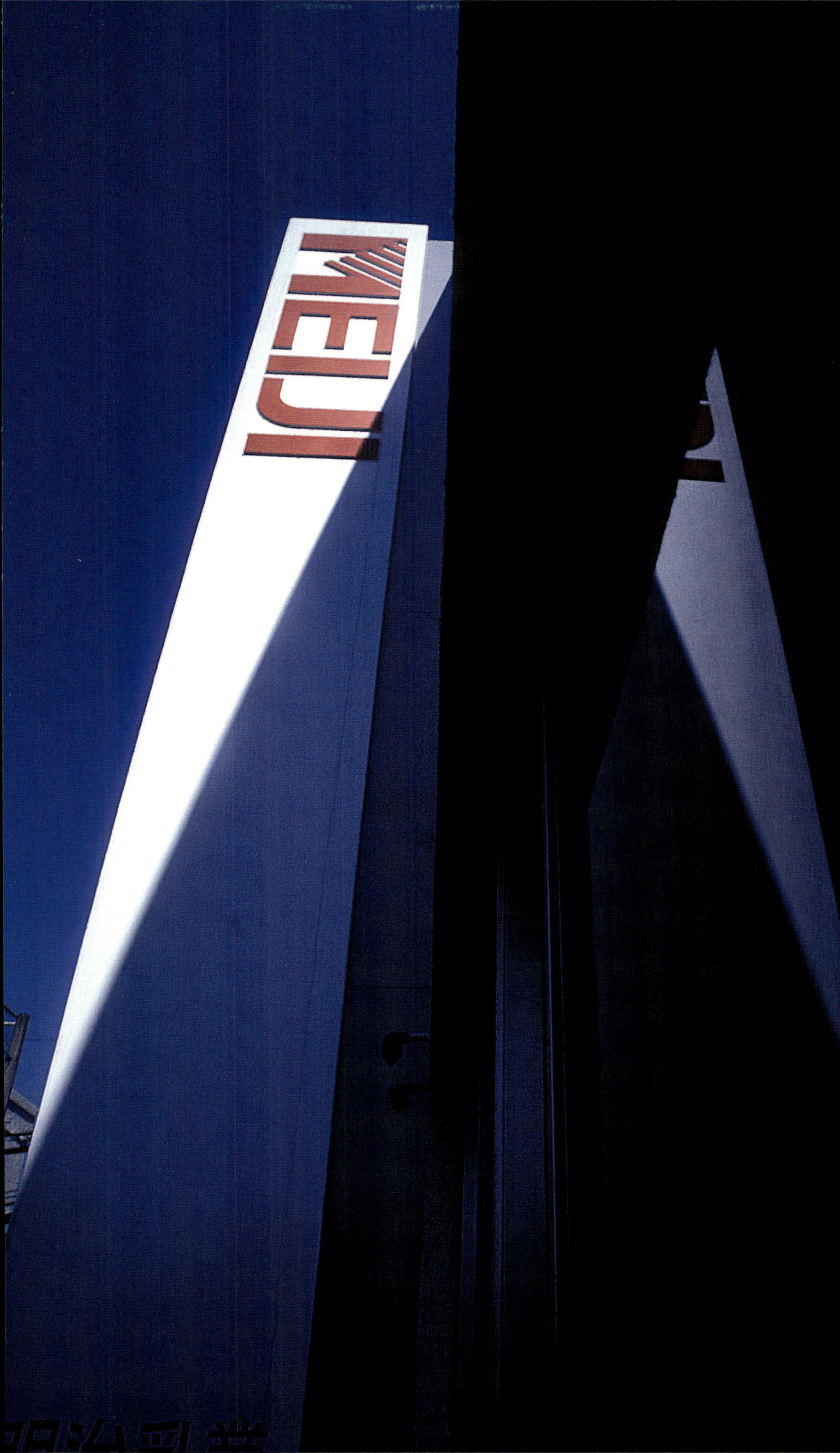

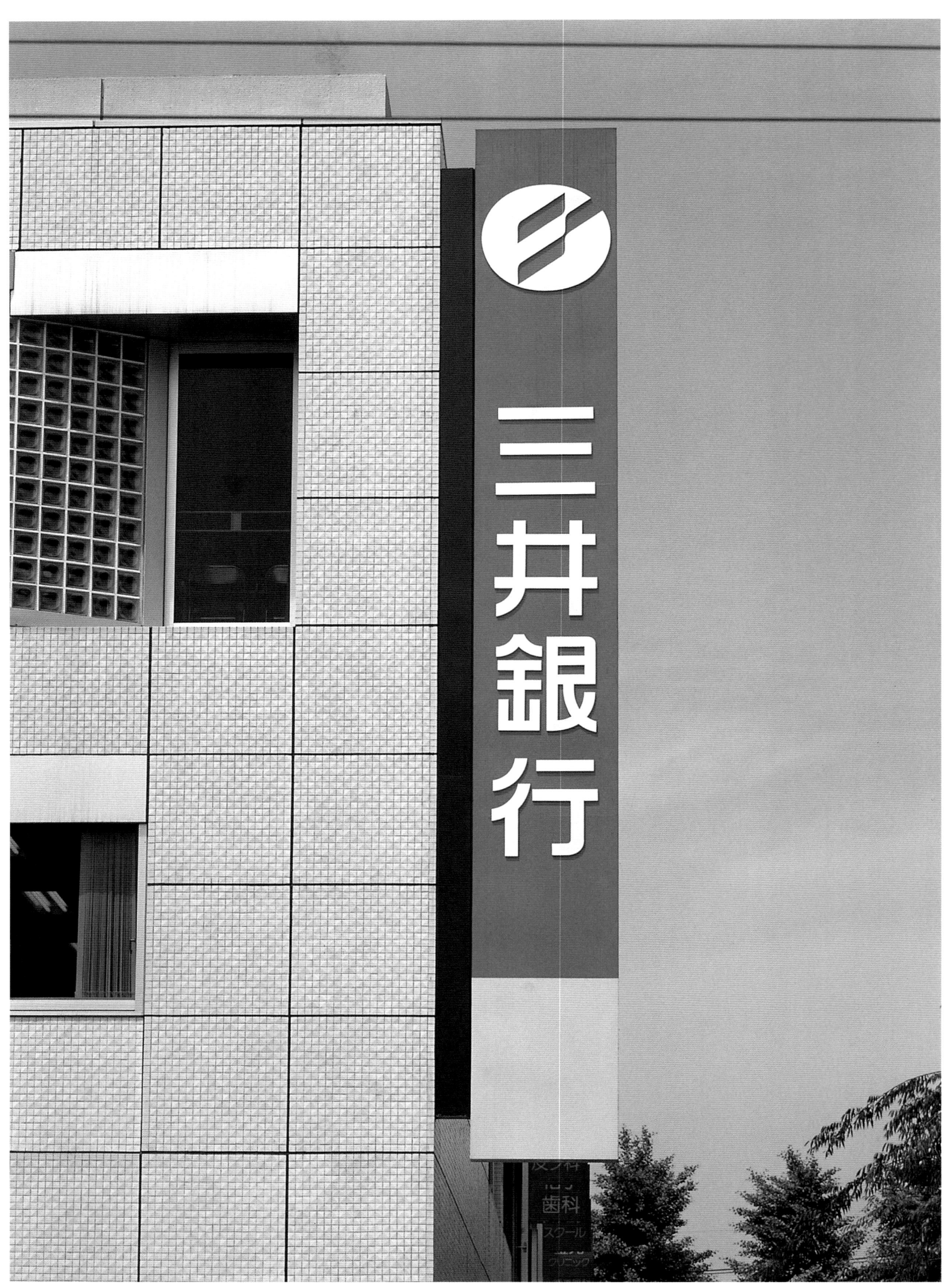

1-21 VI Design
Mitsui Bank
Tokyo, Japan, 1984

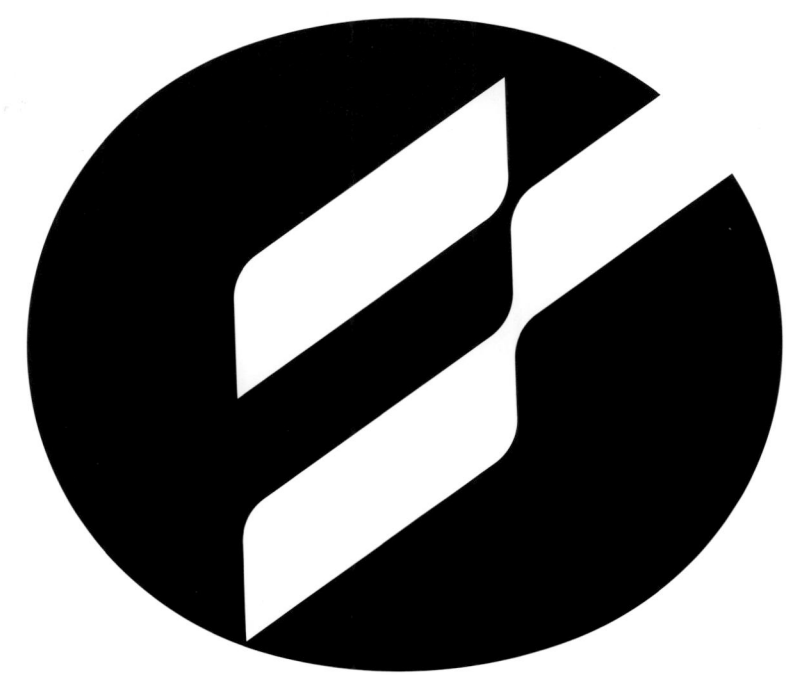

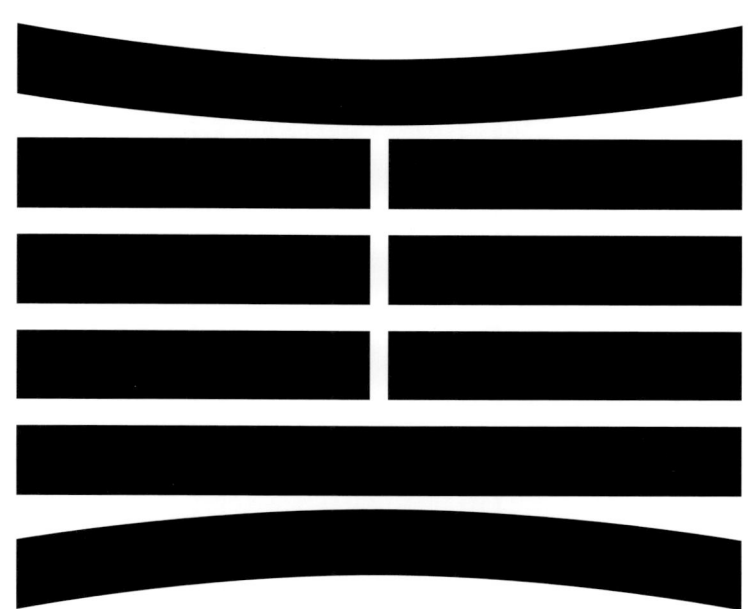

1-22 Symbol Mark
Tama Art University
Tokyo, Japan, 1995

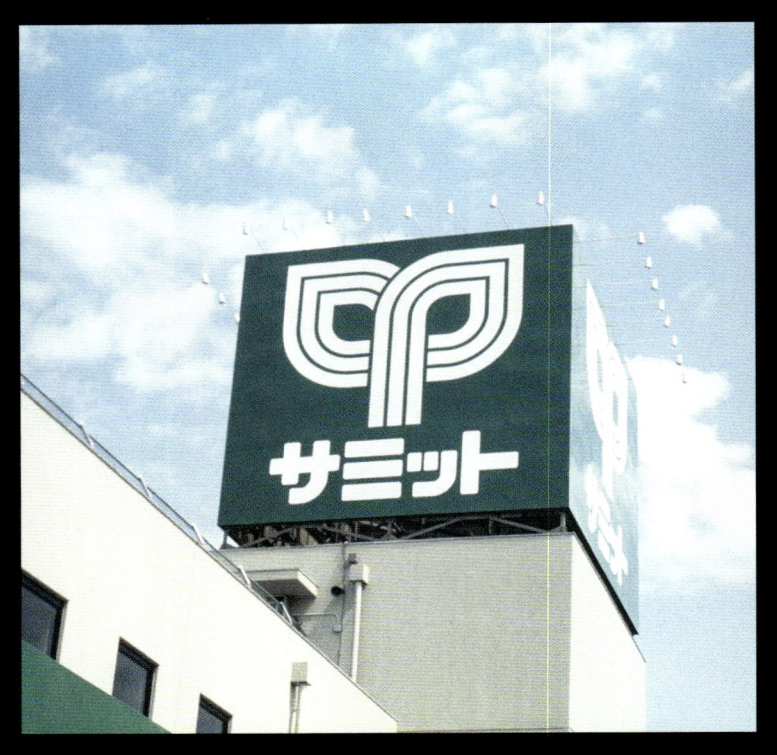
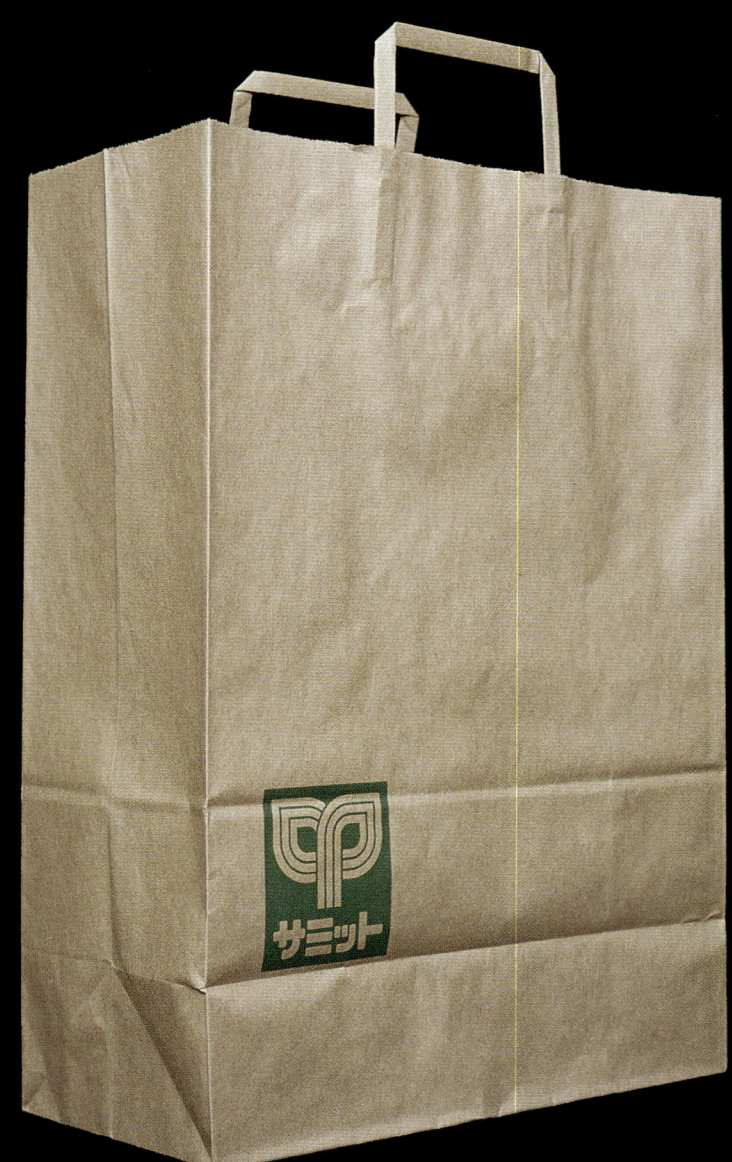

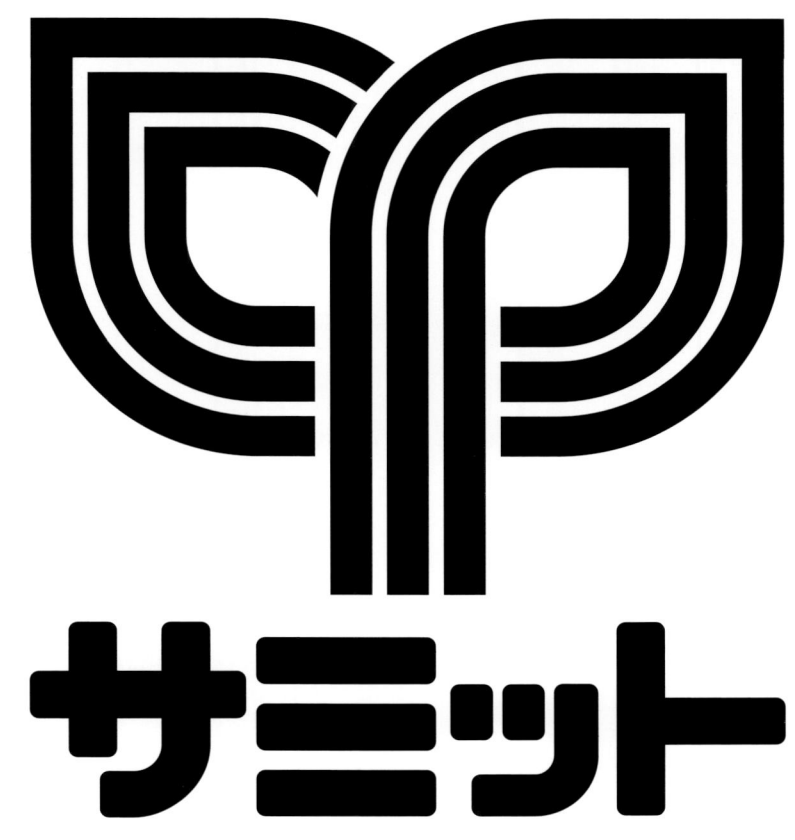

1-23 CI Design
Summit Store Supermarket
Tokyo, Japan, 1976–1985

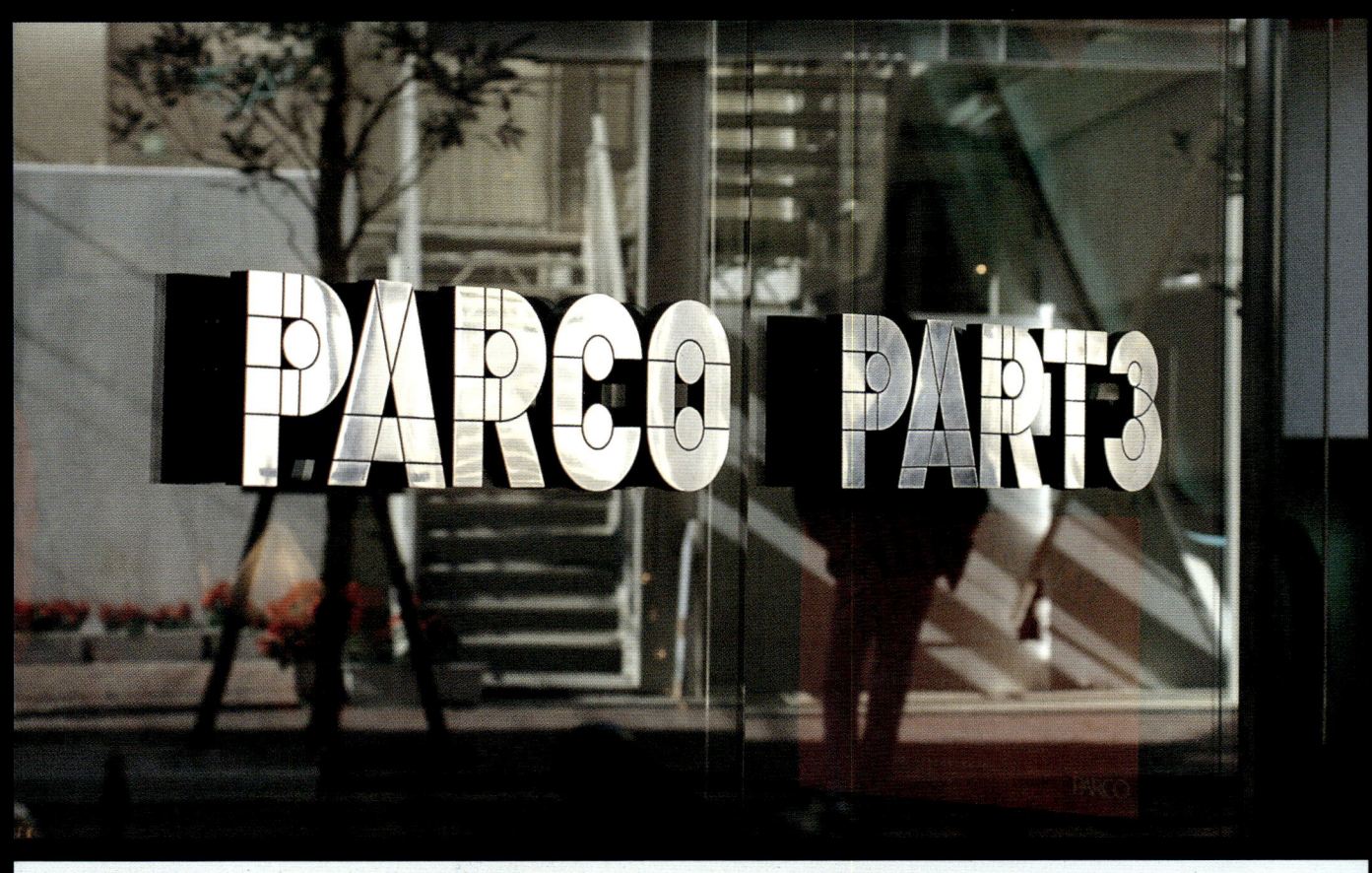
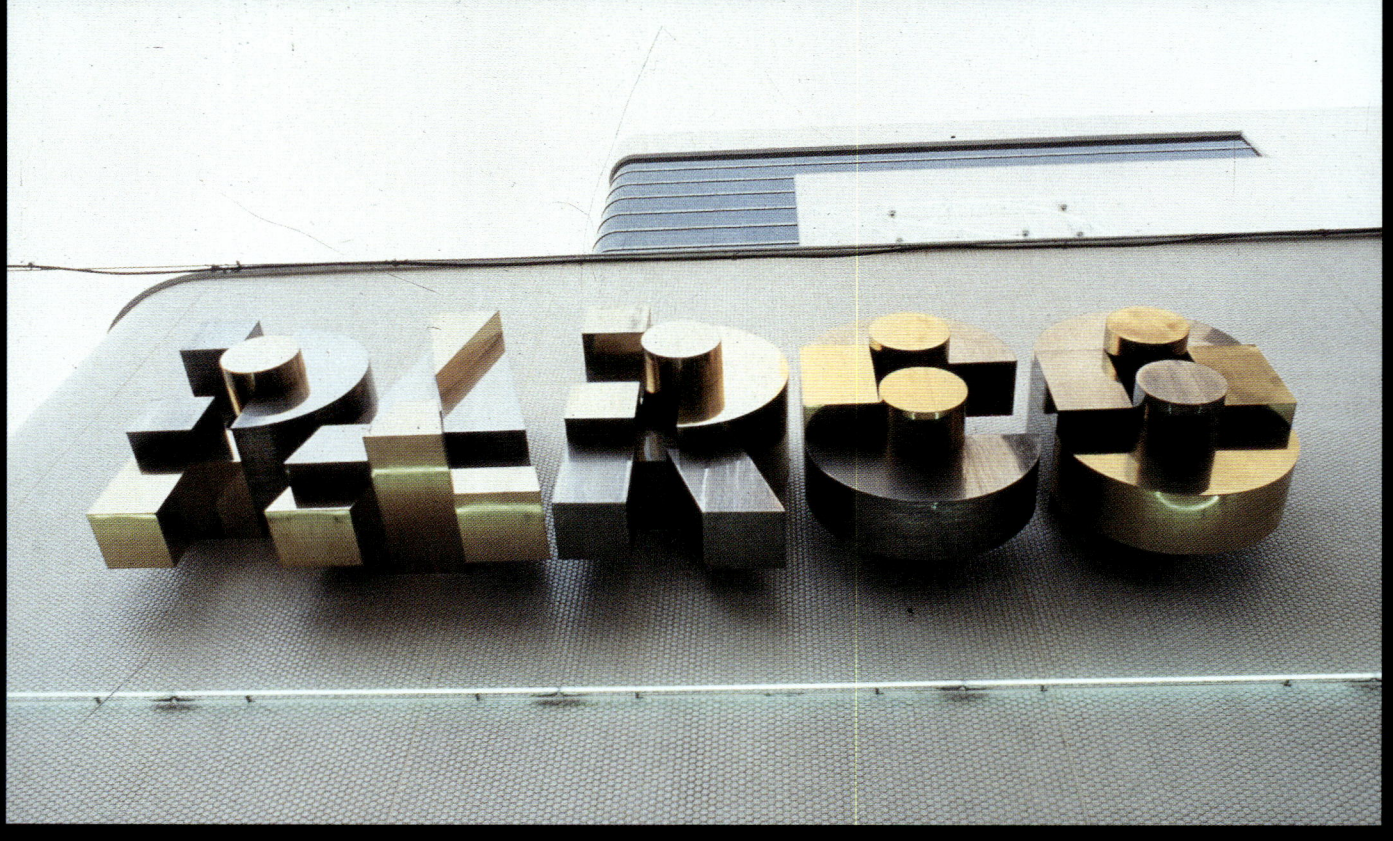

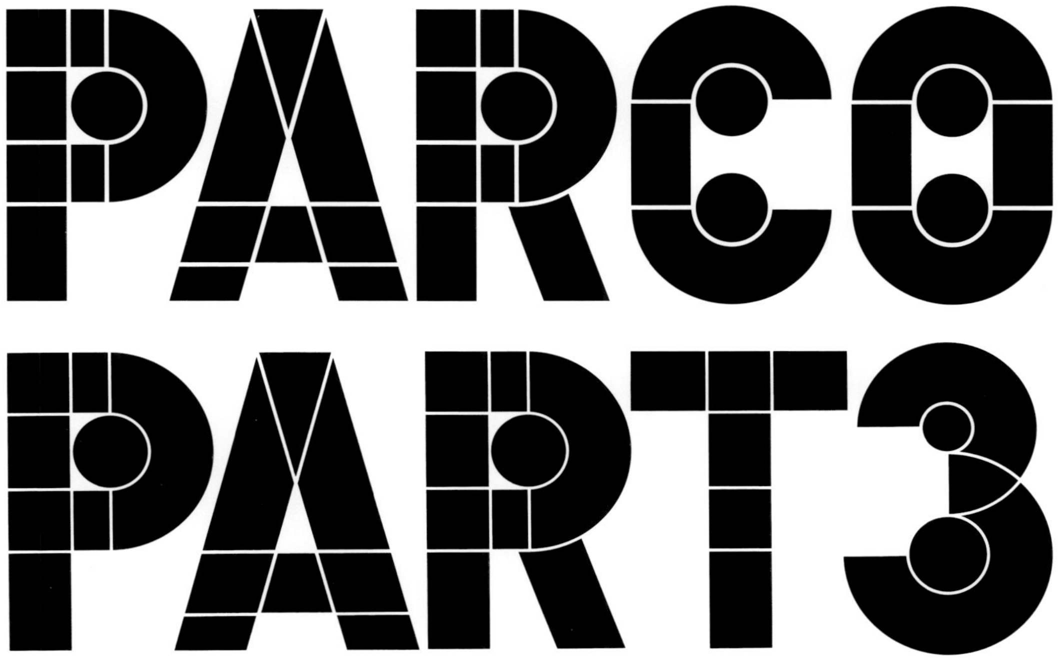

1-24 Logotype and Architectural Graphic
PARCO PART 3, Tokyo, 1981

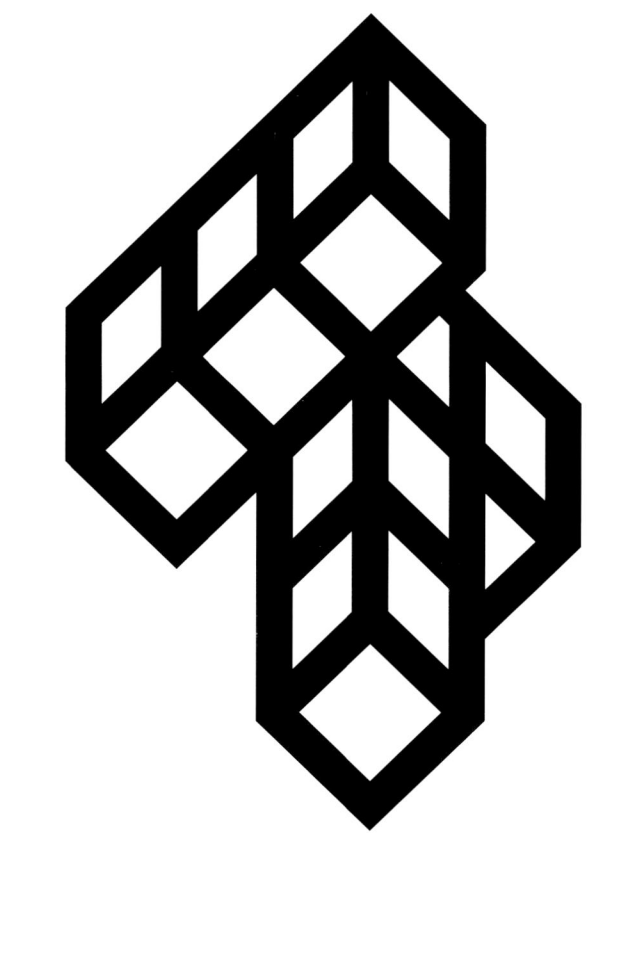

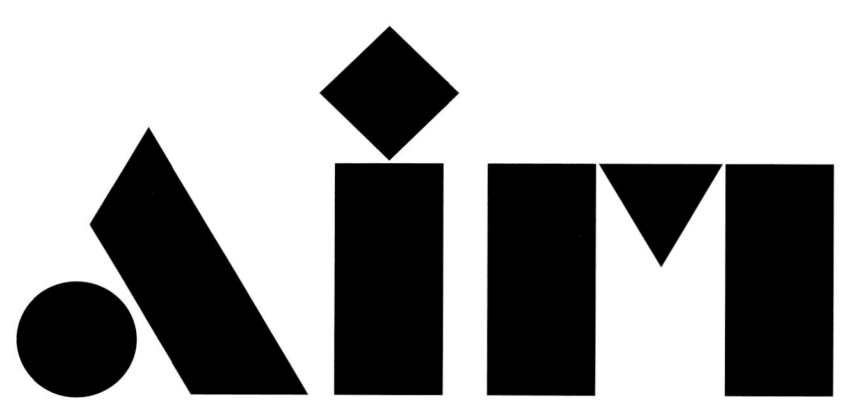

1-25 Symbol Mark and its three-dimensional model
Japan Typography Association, Tokyo, 1978

1-26 Logotype and Sign
AIM, Sapporo, Hokkaido, Japan, 1991

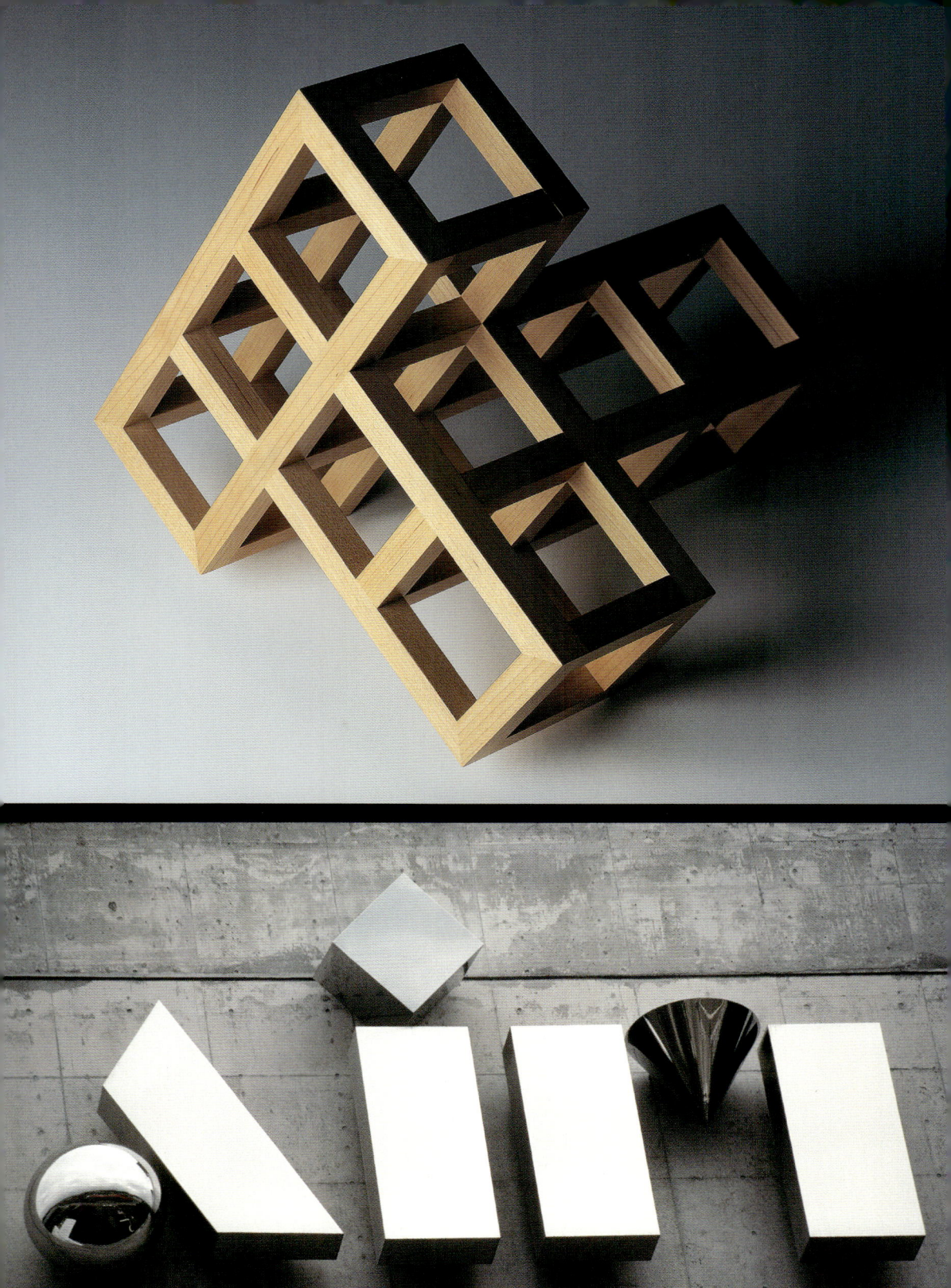

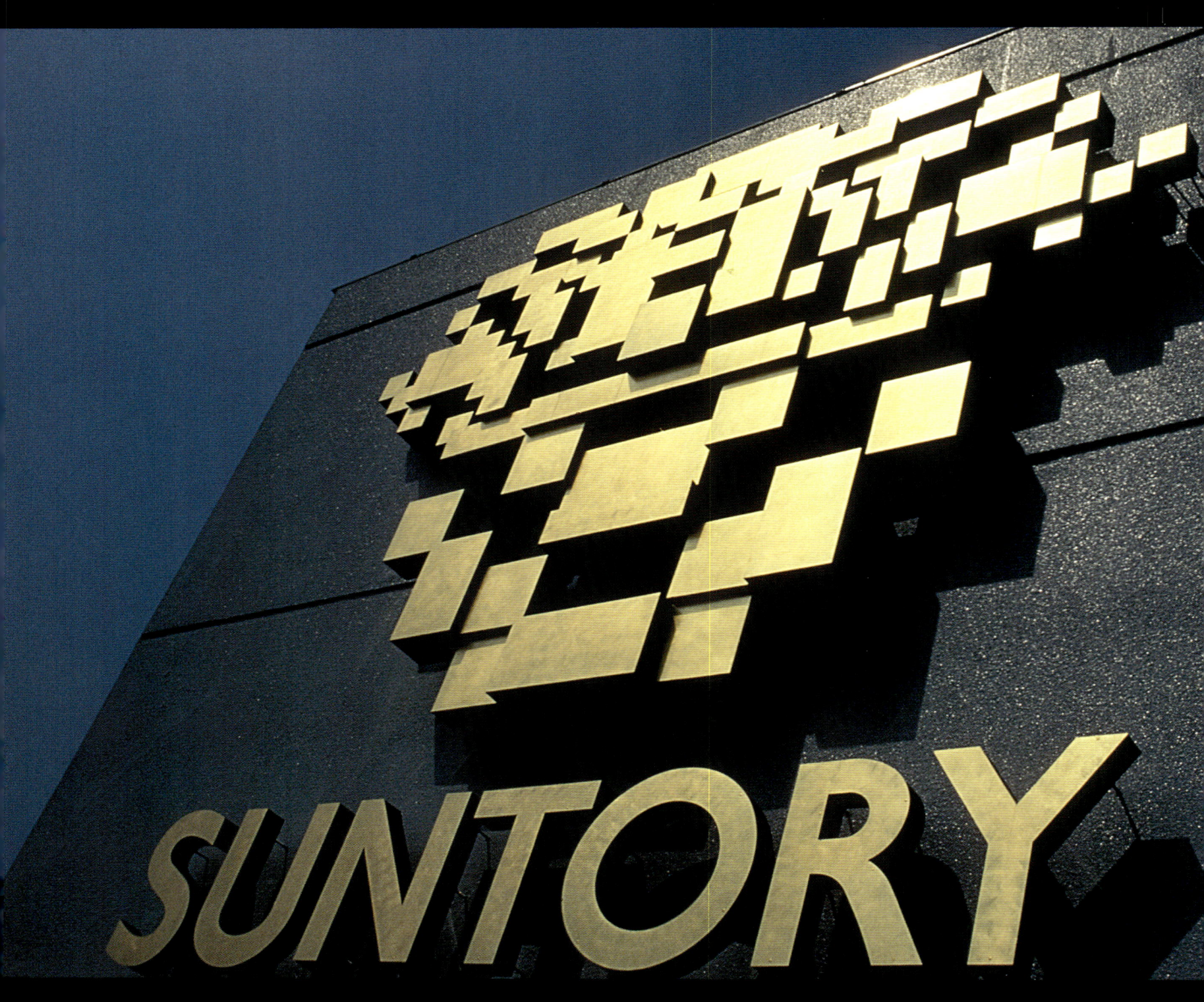

1-27 VI Design
Suntory, Tokyo, Japan, 1990

1-28 Metamorphosises
of Hibiki Logo
From new symbol mark to the
symbol of Suntory-Lion
Suntory, Tokyo, Japan, 1990

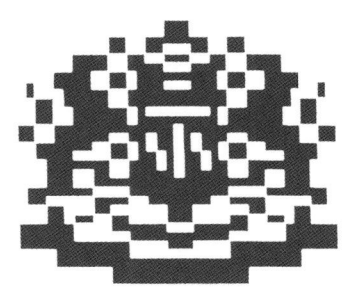
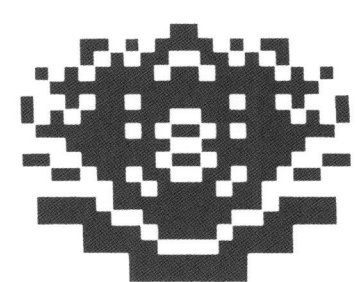
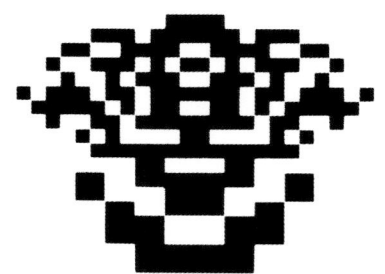

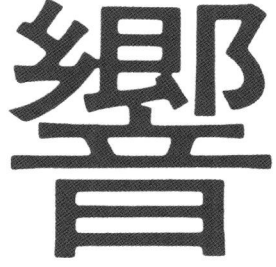

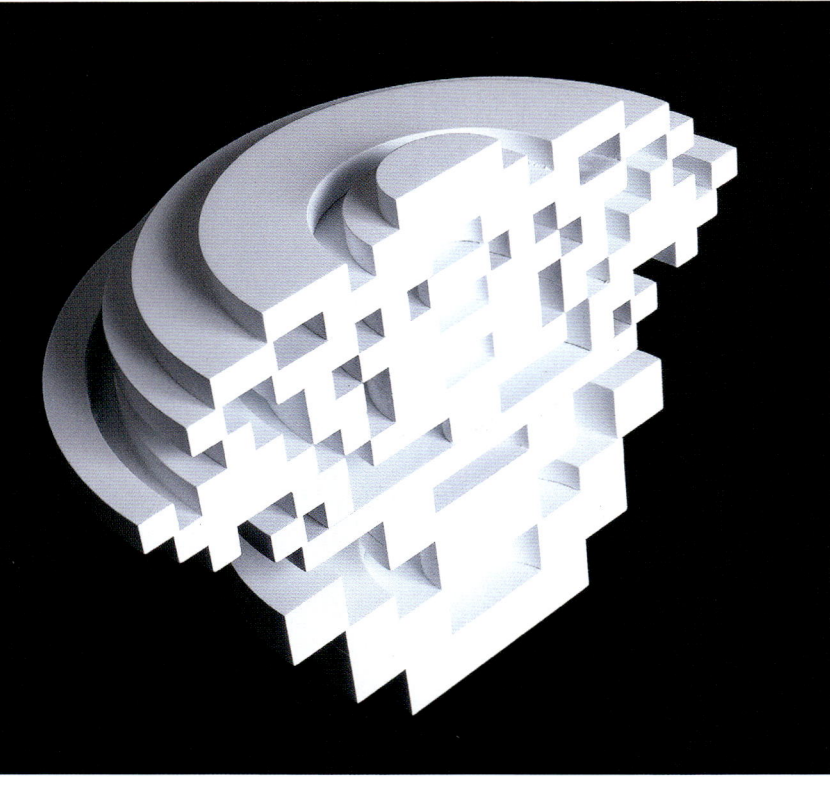

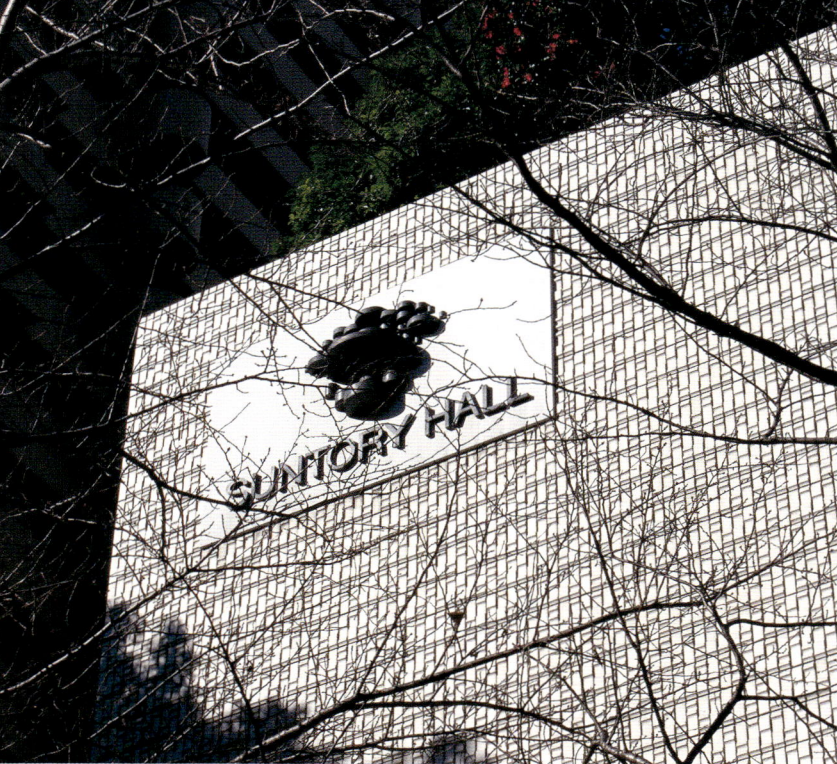

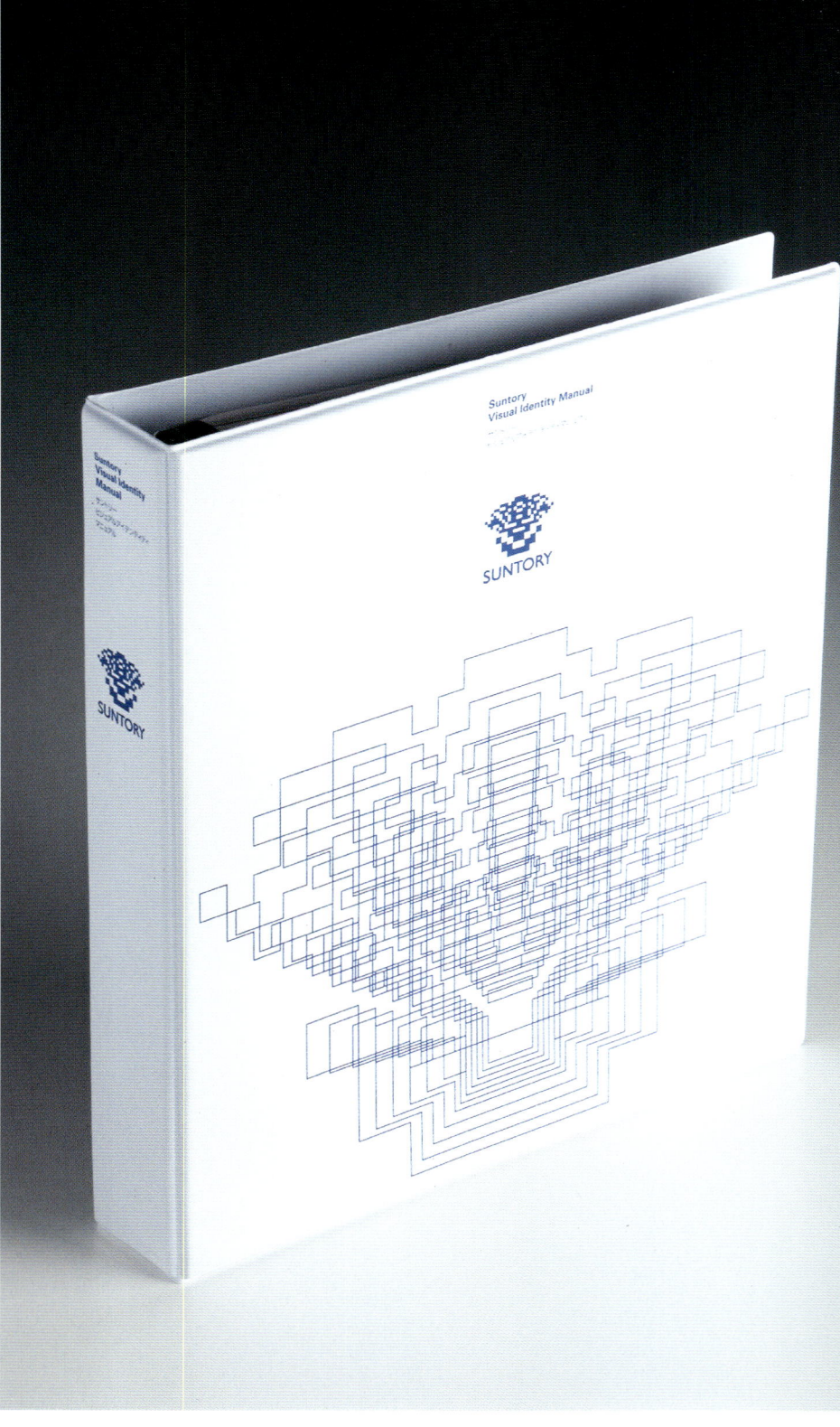

1-29 Hibiki, Model
1986

1-30 Architecture Sign
Suntory Hall, Tokyo, Japan, 1986

*There are varieties of large and small logo sculptures
installed in different parts of the concert hall building. (TI)*

1-31 VI Manual
Suntory, Tokyo, Japan, 1990
Between 1990 and 2004, this logo of Hibiki was used as a corporate logo.

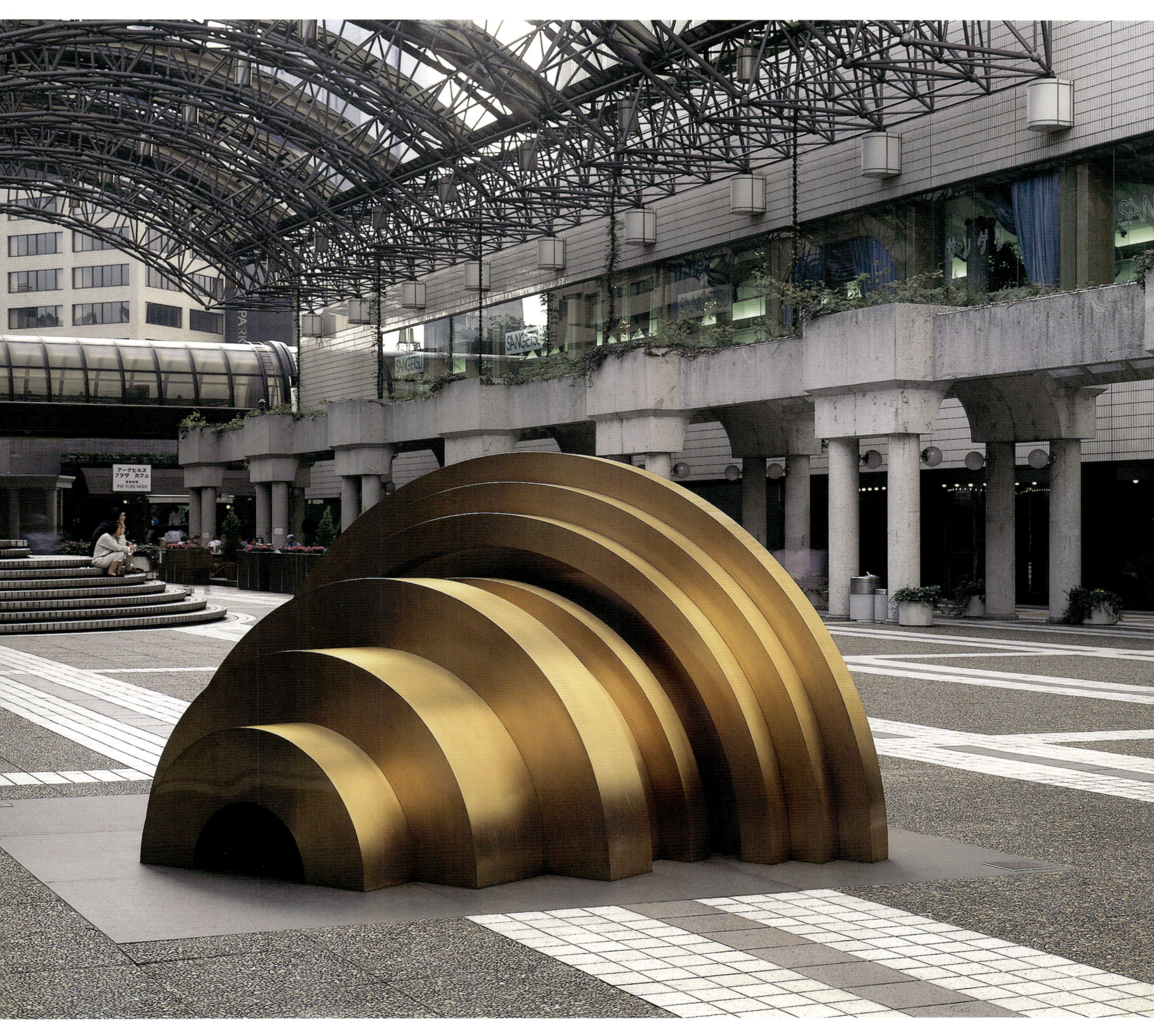

1-32 Hibiki
Suntory Hall, Tokyo, Japan, 1986

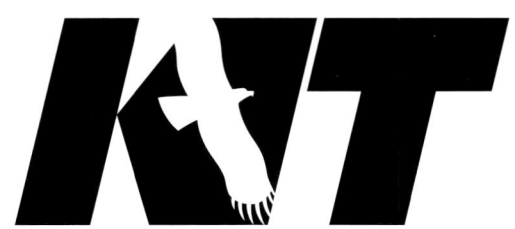

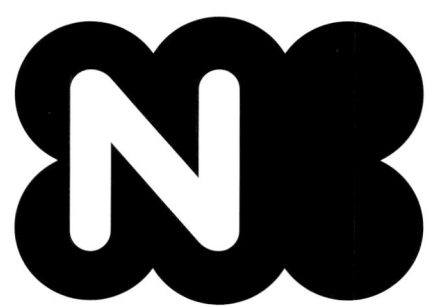

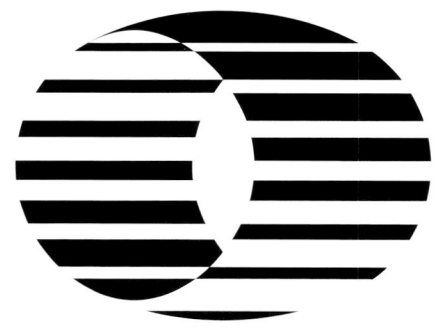

1-33 VI Design
Kanazawa Institute of Technology
Ishikawa, Kanazawa, Japan, 1983

1-34 Symbol Mark Design
NORITZ Corporation
Tokyo, Japan, 1984

1-35 VI Design
UHAG, COSA, Libermann Group
Zurich, Switzerland, 1985

1-36 VI Design
Kubota Computer
Osaka, Japan, 1987

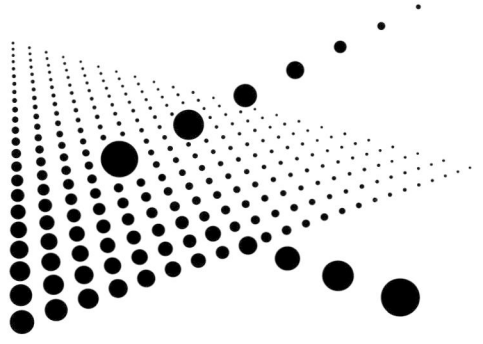

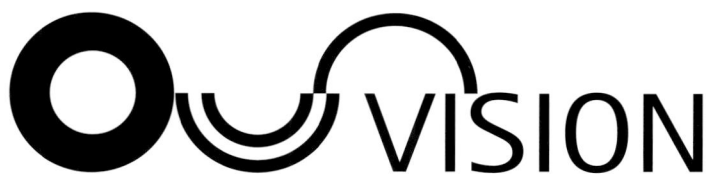

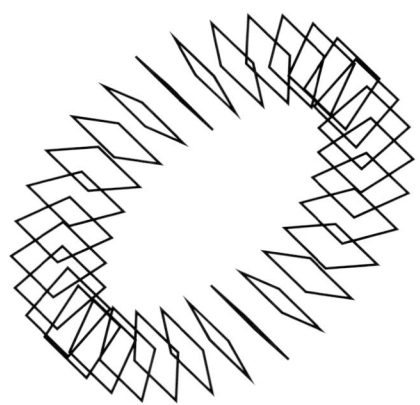

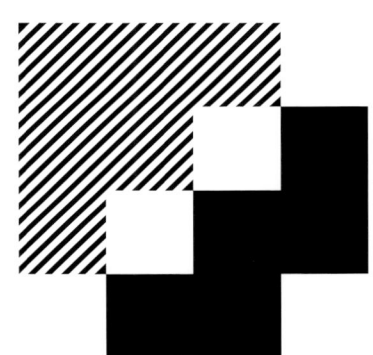

1-37 Logotype Design
Oun Vision
Sapporo, Hokkaido, Japan, 2004

1-38 VI Design
Polygon Pictures
Tokyo, Japan, 1987

1-39 VI Design
Field Stone Why Group
Tokyo, Japan, 1987

1-40 VI Design
Talvas Golf & Resort
Nasu, Tochigi, Japan, 1989

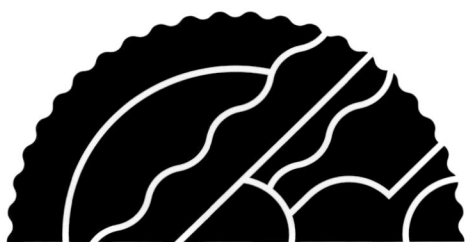

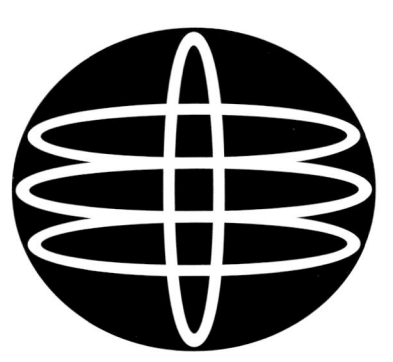

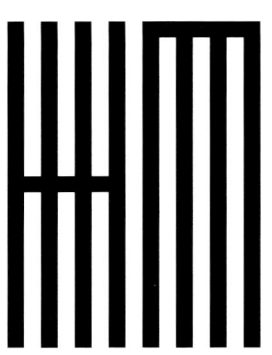

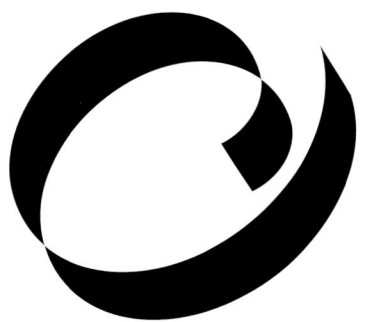

1-41 Symbol Mark Design
Oji Hall, Oji Paper Co., Ltd.
Tokyo, Japan, 1992

1-42 CI Design
Hida Takayama Museum of Art
Hida Takayama, Gifu, Japan, 1997

1-43 VI Design
Oji Paper Co., Ltd.
Tokyo, Japan, 1996

1-44 VI Design
Borou Noguchi Noboribetsu
Hokkaido, Japan, 2006

To beautifully create, it is necessary to have a trained eye to initially judge the horizontal or vertical, the millimeter, and the degree without tools. (TI)

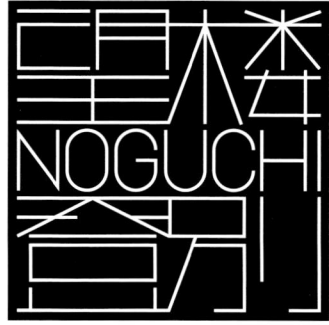

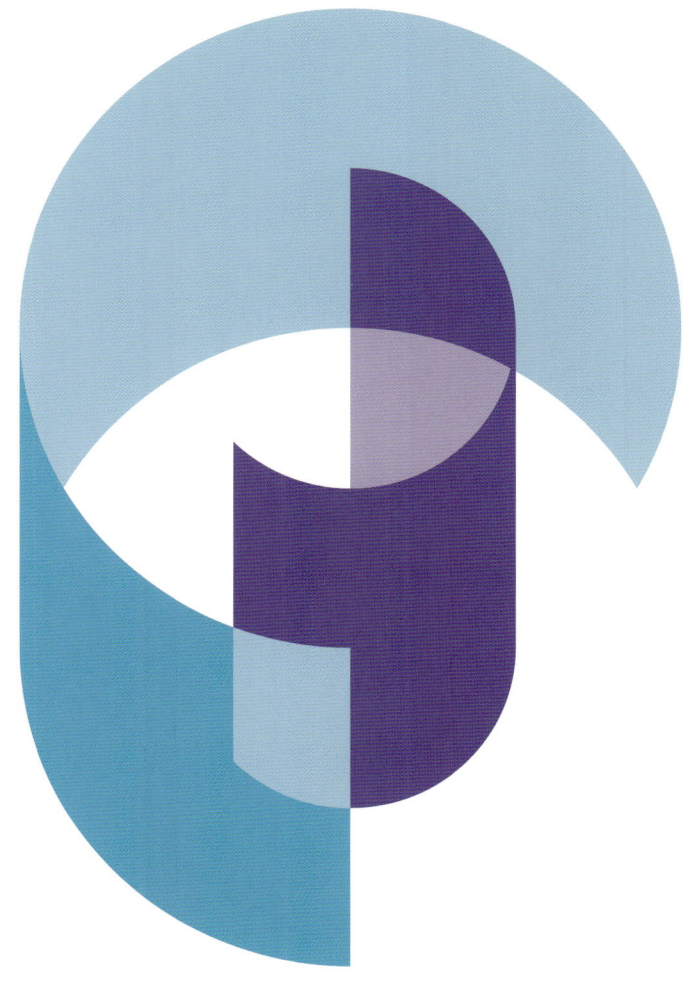

1-45 VI Design
Okazaki Women's Junior College
Seiko Gakuen Educational Corporation
Aichi, Japan, 2015

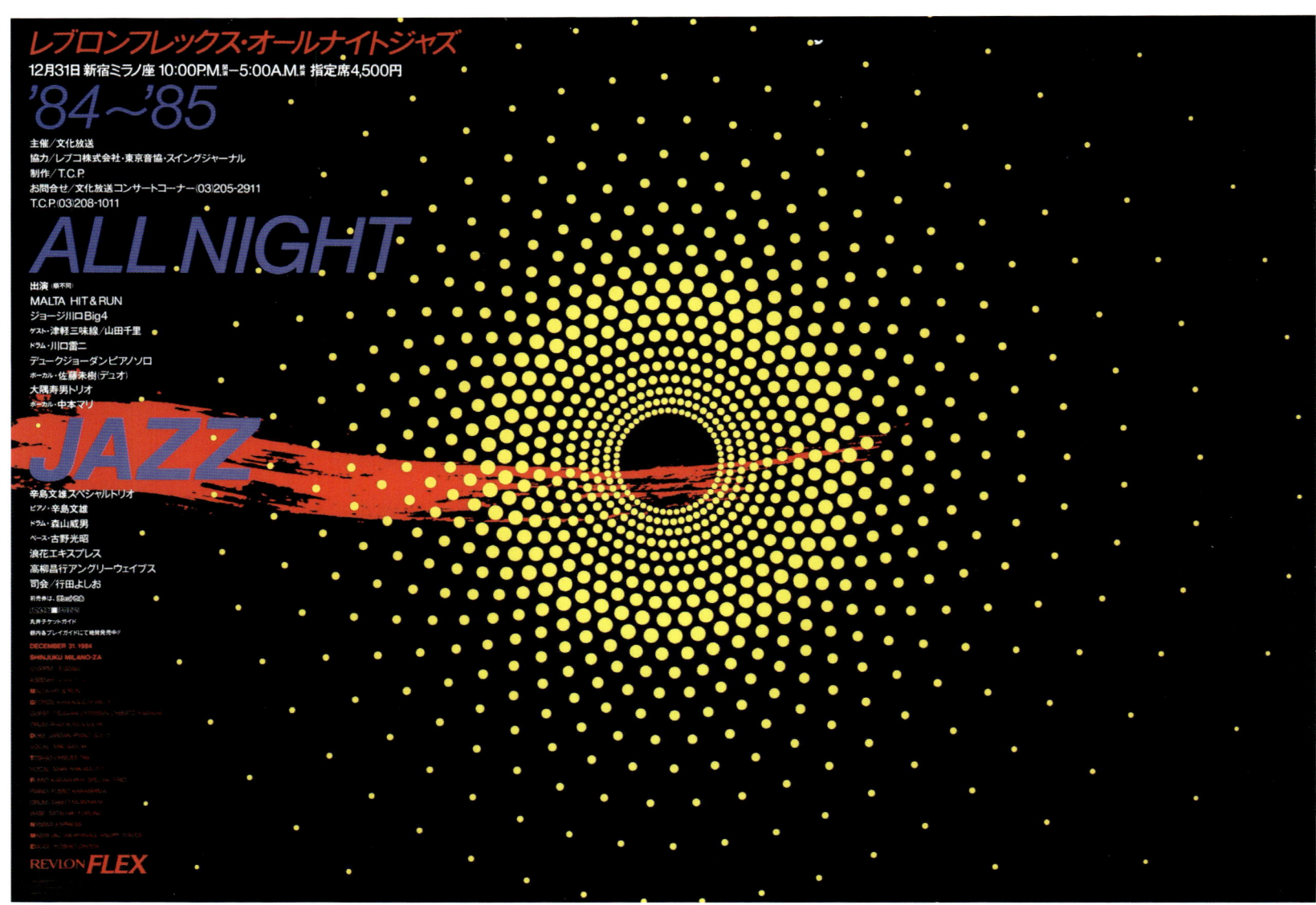

1-46 Poster
REVLON Flex All Night Jazz '84~'85, REVLON, Tokyo, Japan, 1984

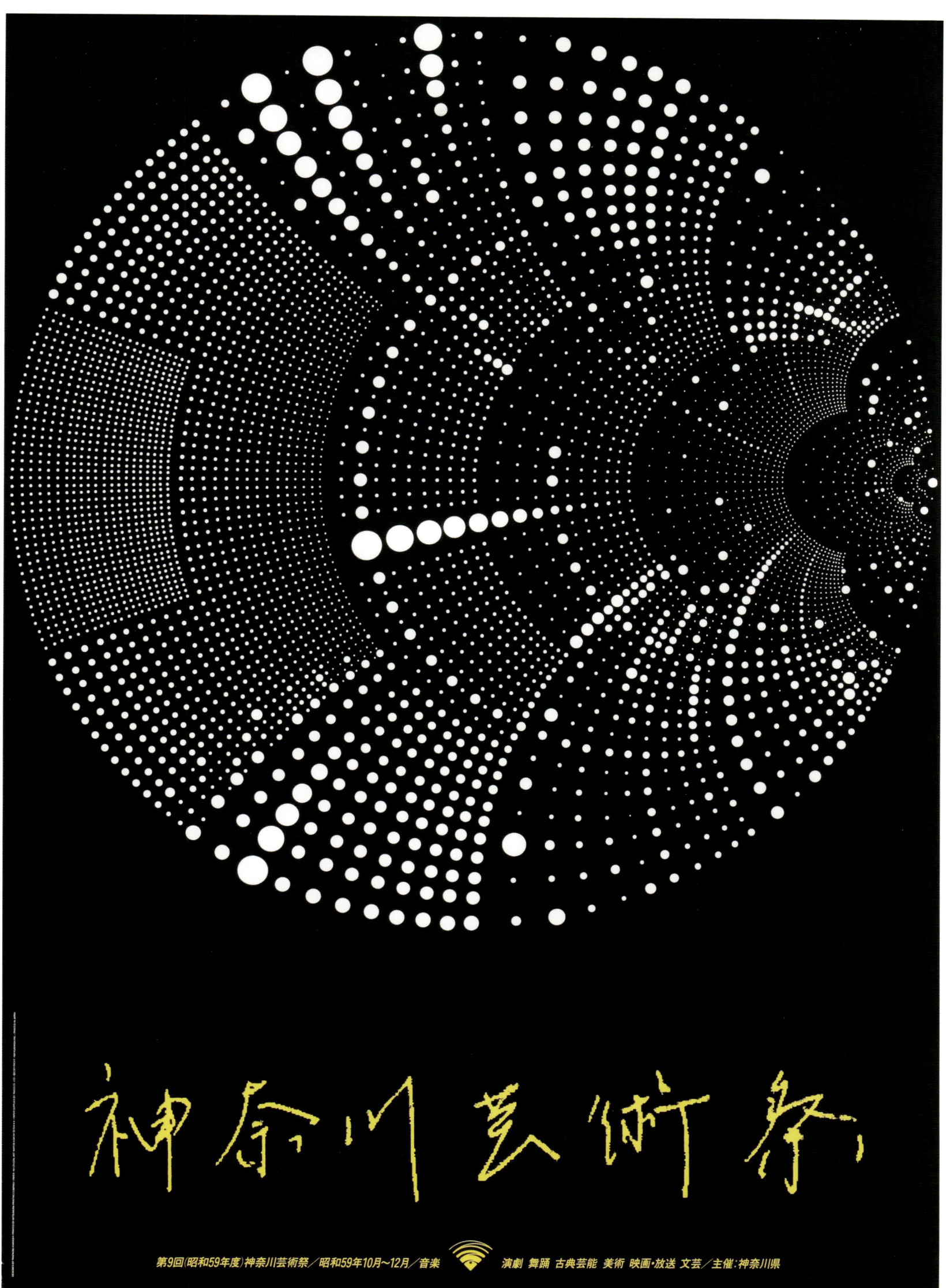

1-47 Poster
The 9th Kanagawa Art Festival, Kanagawa, 1984

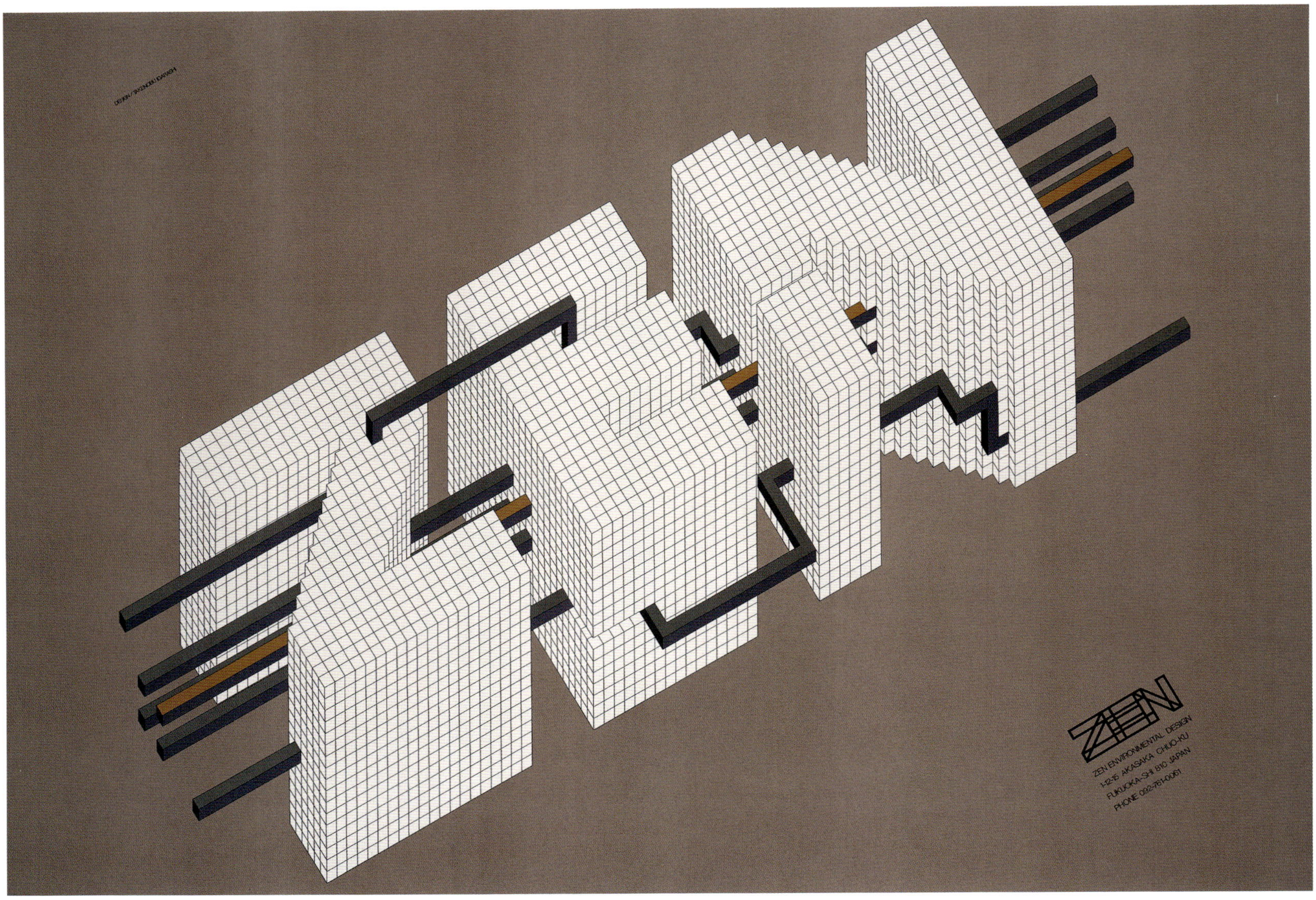

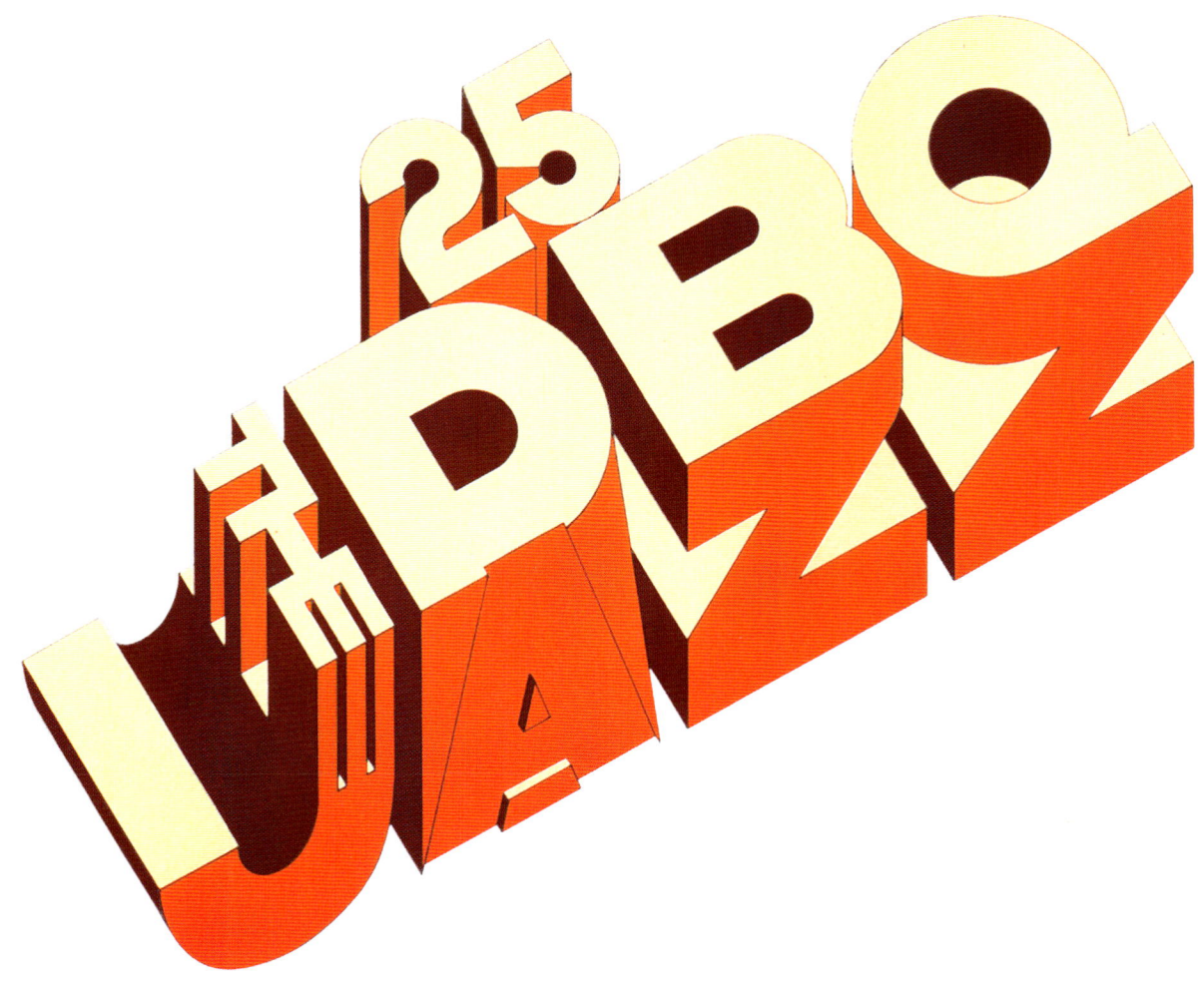

1-48 Poster
ZEN Environmental Design
Fukuoka, Japan, 1976

1-49 Illustration
Dave Brubeck Quartet 25th Anniversary Reunion Album
A&M Record, Los Angeles, CA, USA, 1976

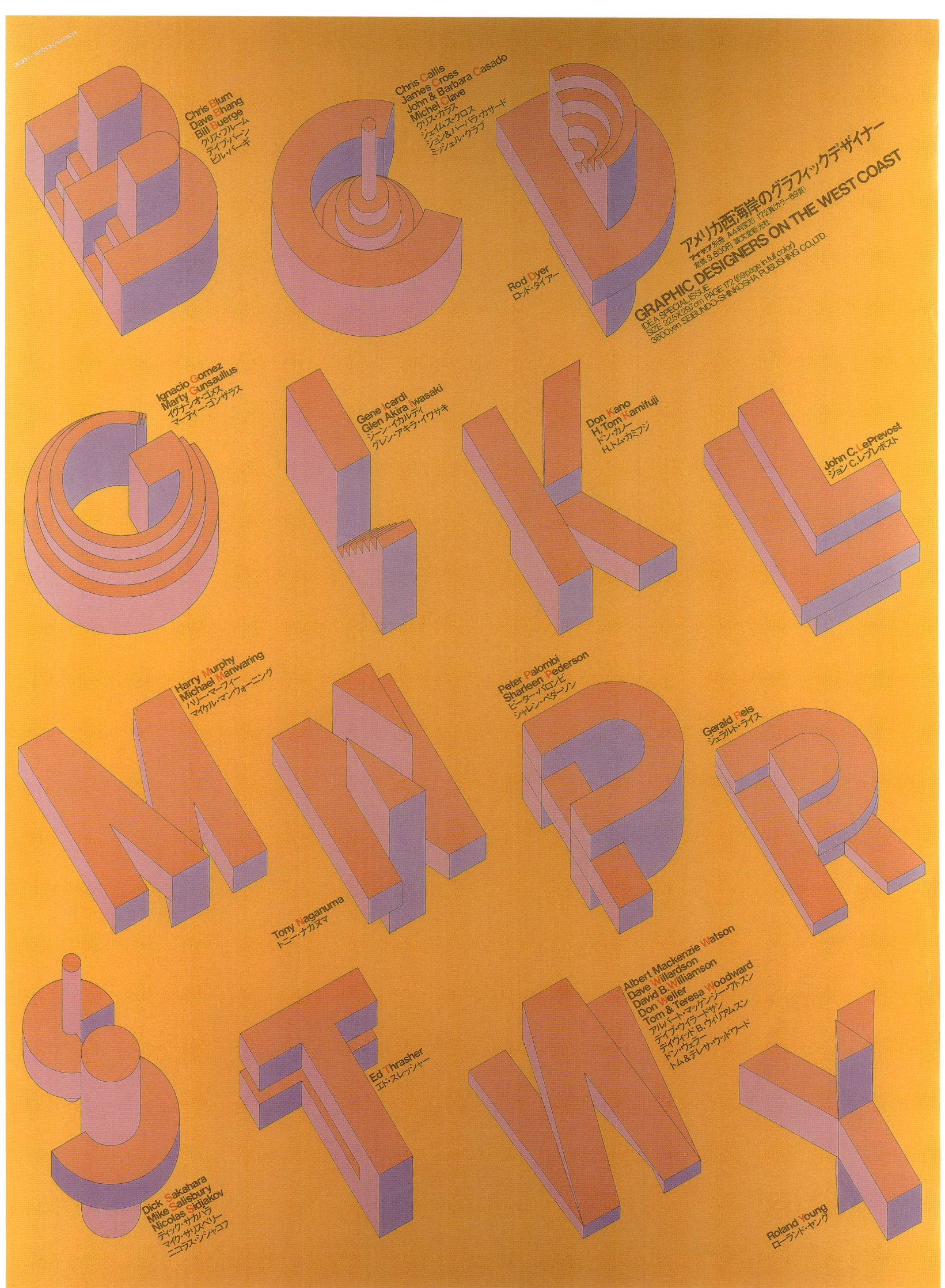

1-50 Poster
Graphic Designers on the West Coast
IDEA Special Issue, Seibundo Shinkosha
Tokyo, Japan, 1975

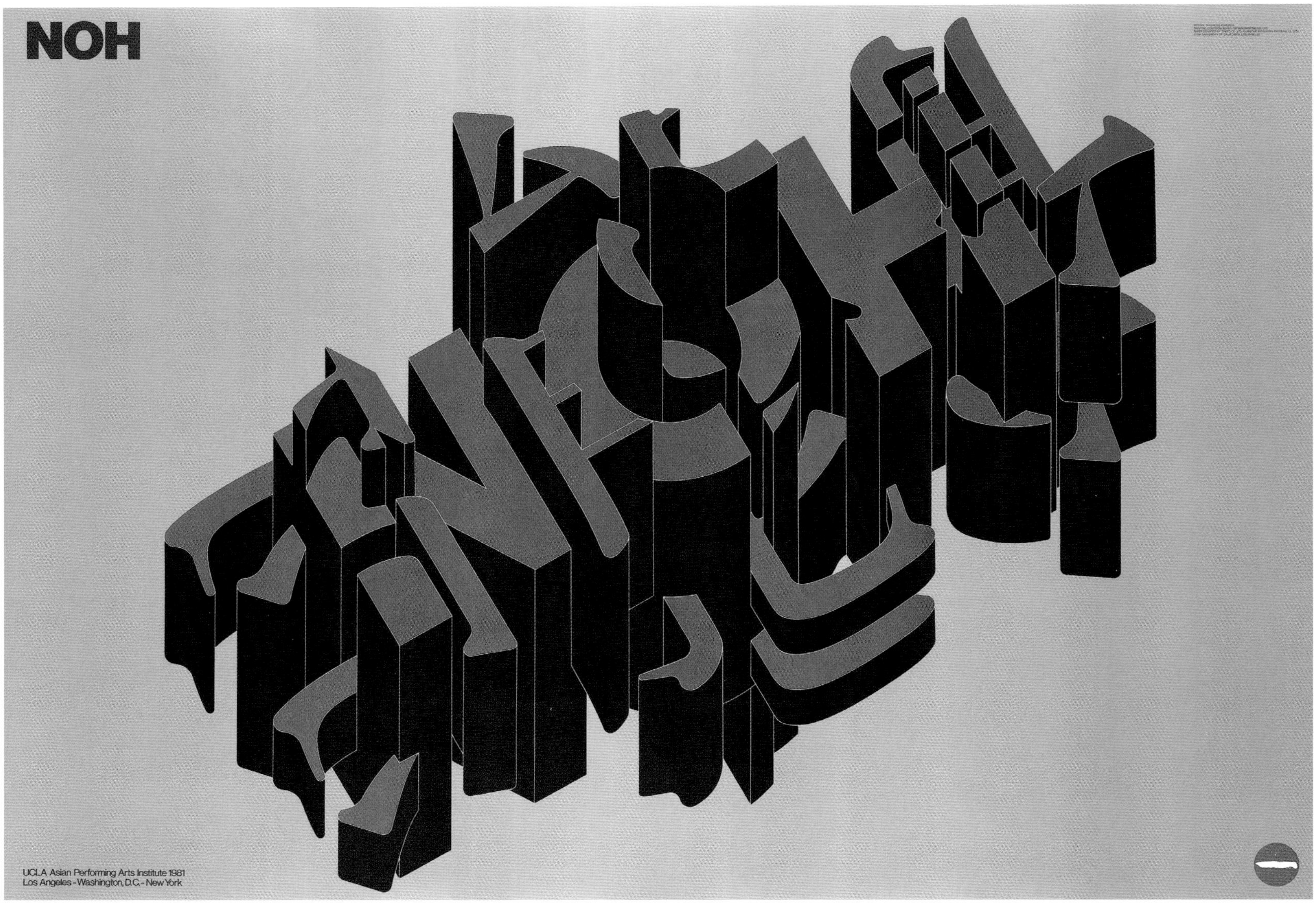

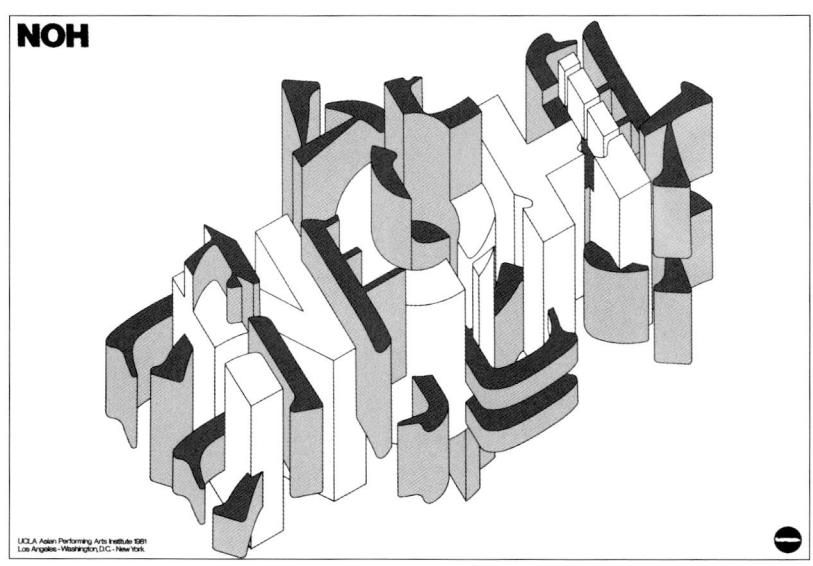
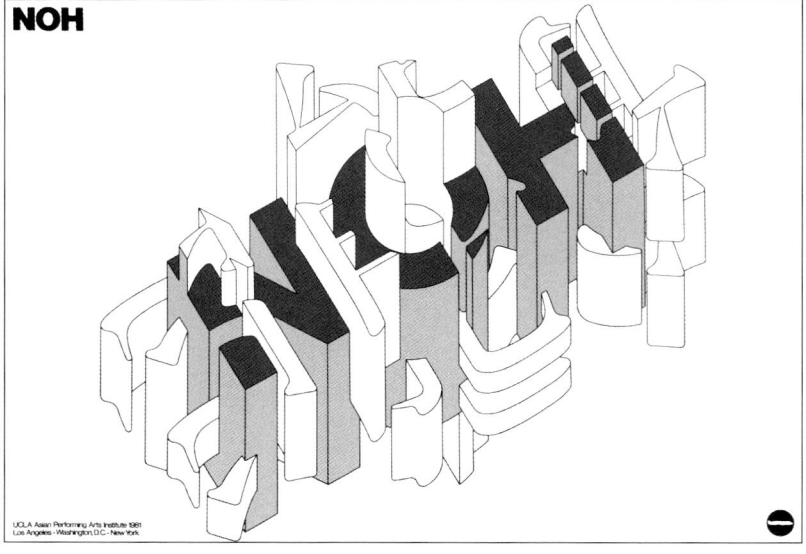

1-51 Poster
Noh, UCLA Asian Performing Arts Institute
Los Angeles, CA, USA, 1981

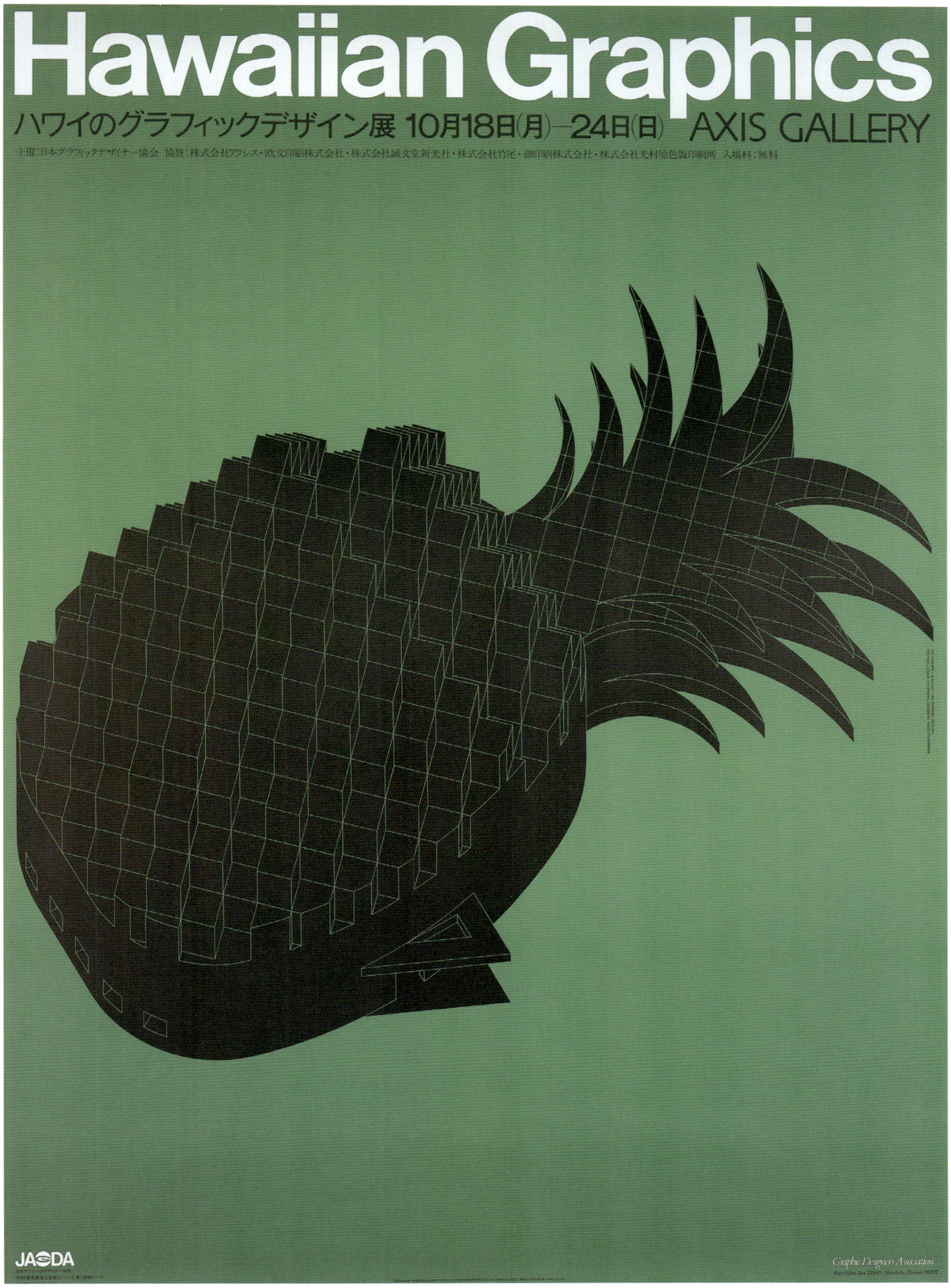

1-52 Poster
Hawaiian Graphics
Japan Graphic Designers Association Inc.
Tokyo, Japan, 1982

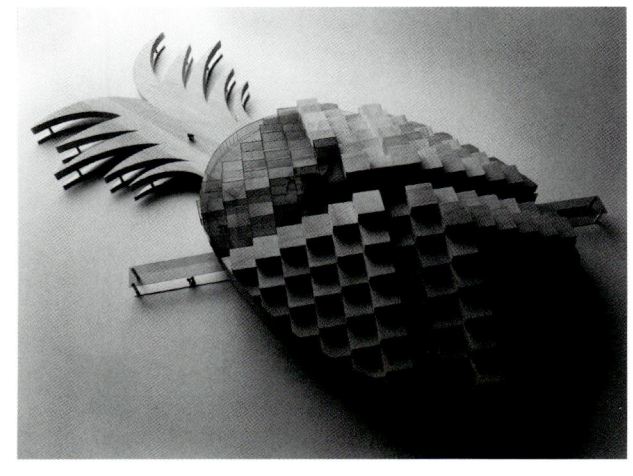

1-53 Pineapple Building, Model, 1982

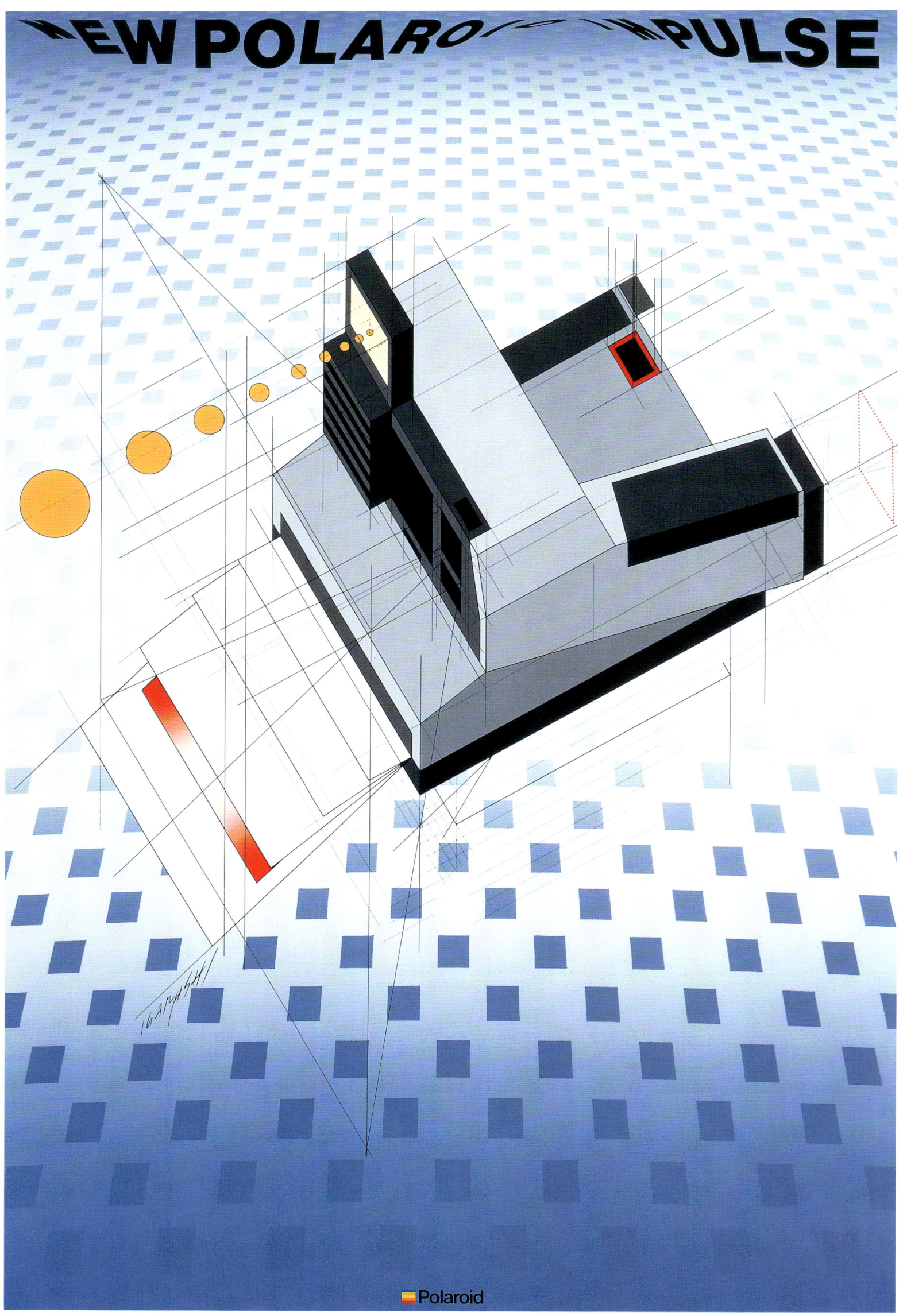

1-54 Poster
New Polaroid Impulse, Polaroid Corp, USA, 1988

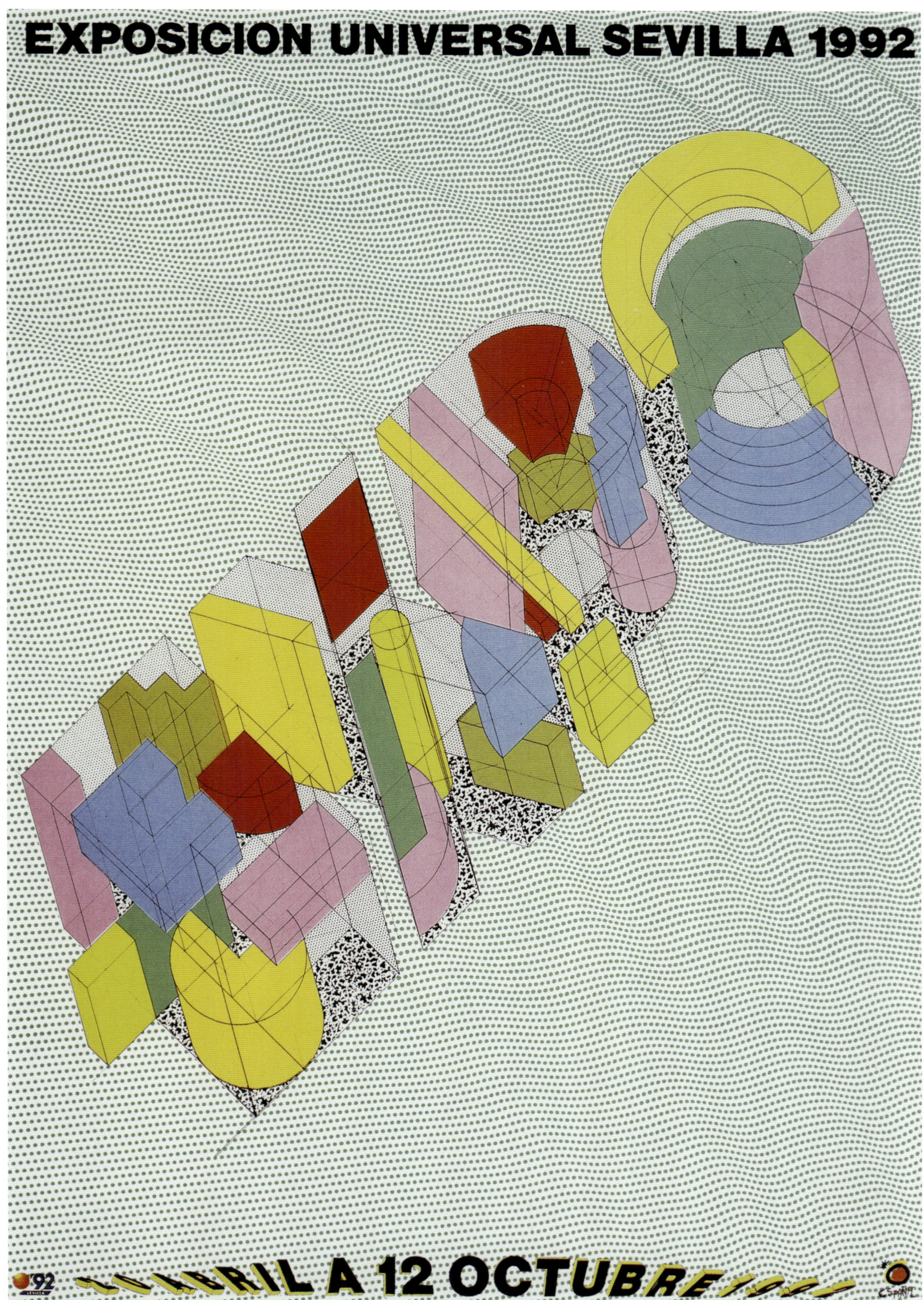

1-55 Poster
Exposición Universal de Sevilla 1992, EXPO'92 Executive Committee, Spain, 1988

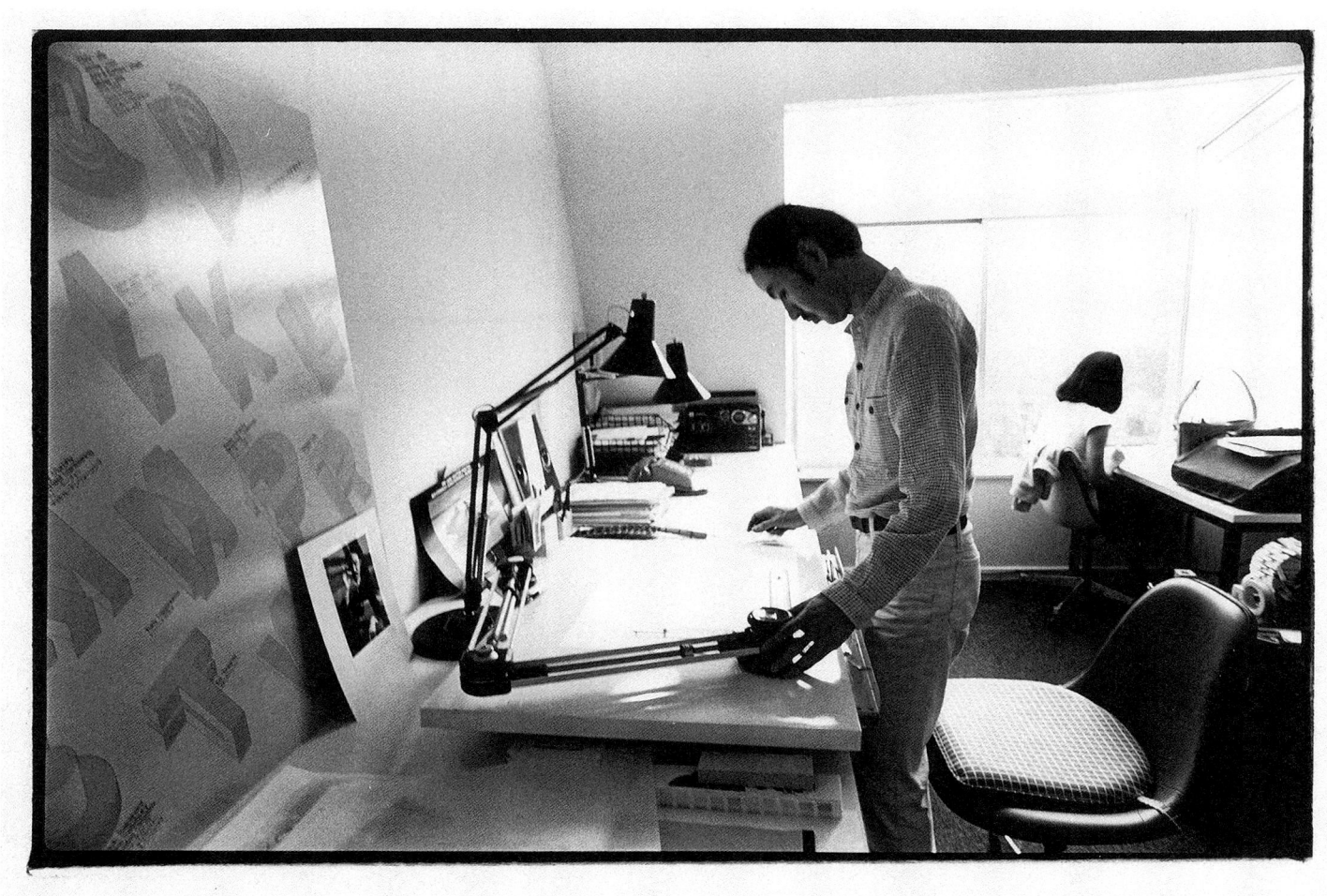

Igarashi is making a plan with a drafter at the studio in Aoyama, Tokyo, 1980.

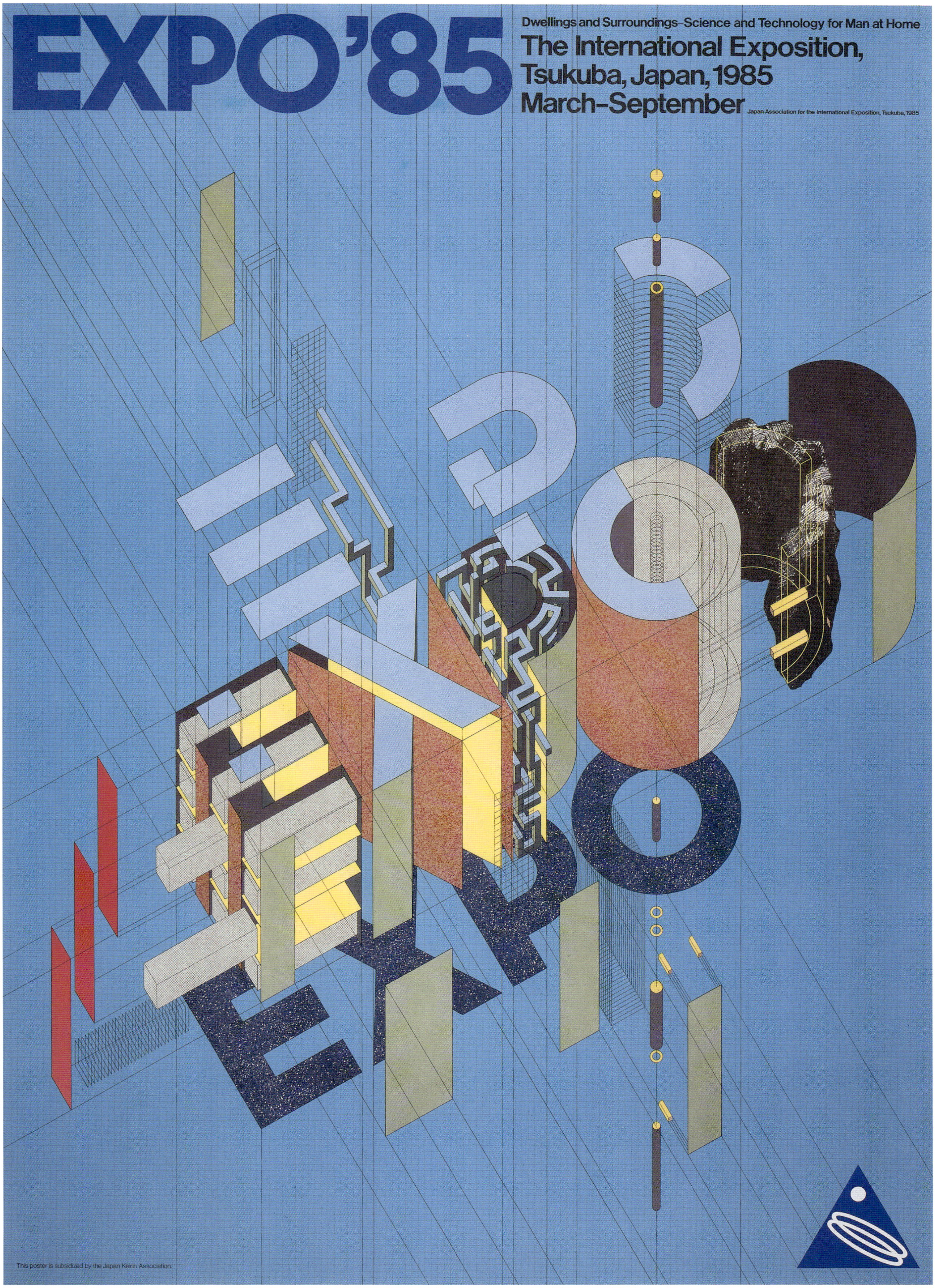

1-56 Poster
EXPO'85, Executive committee for The International Exposition, 1985
Tokyo, Japan, 1982

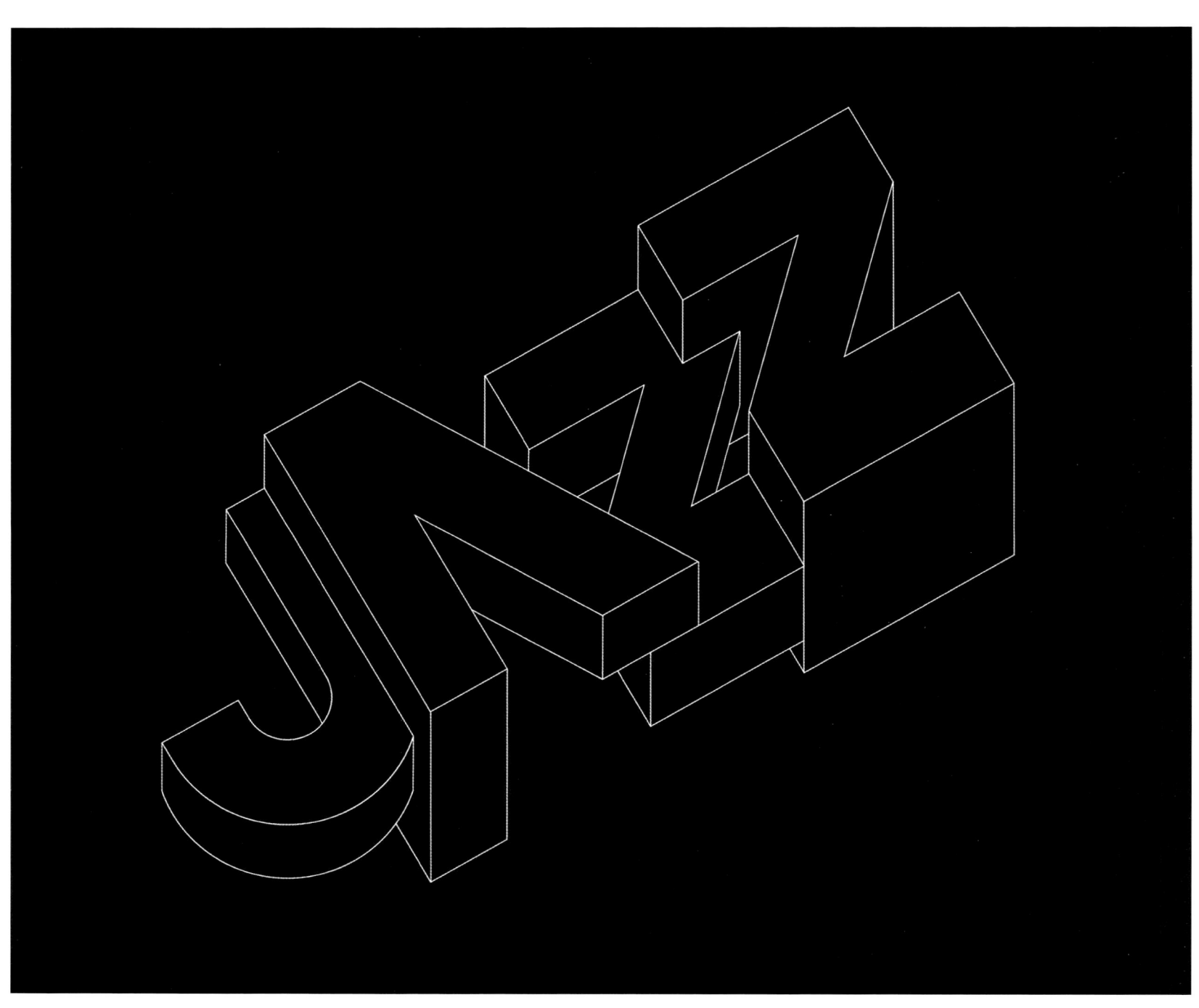

1-57 Photo Print
JAZZ15, Tokyo Designers Space, Tokyo, Japan, 1976
Print Gallery, Amsterdam, Netherland, 1978
Works from the same series

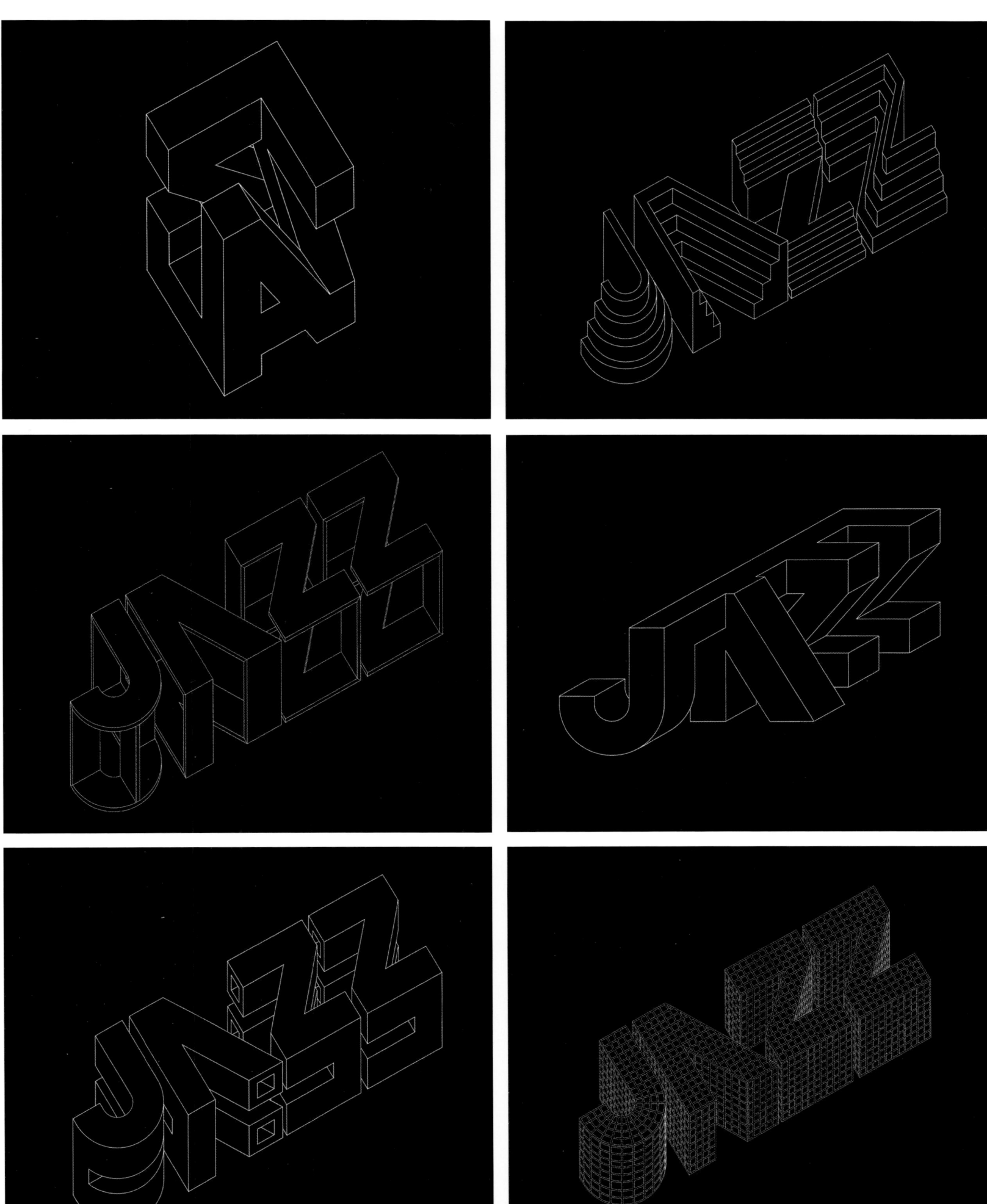

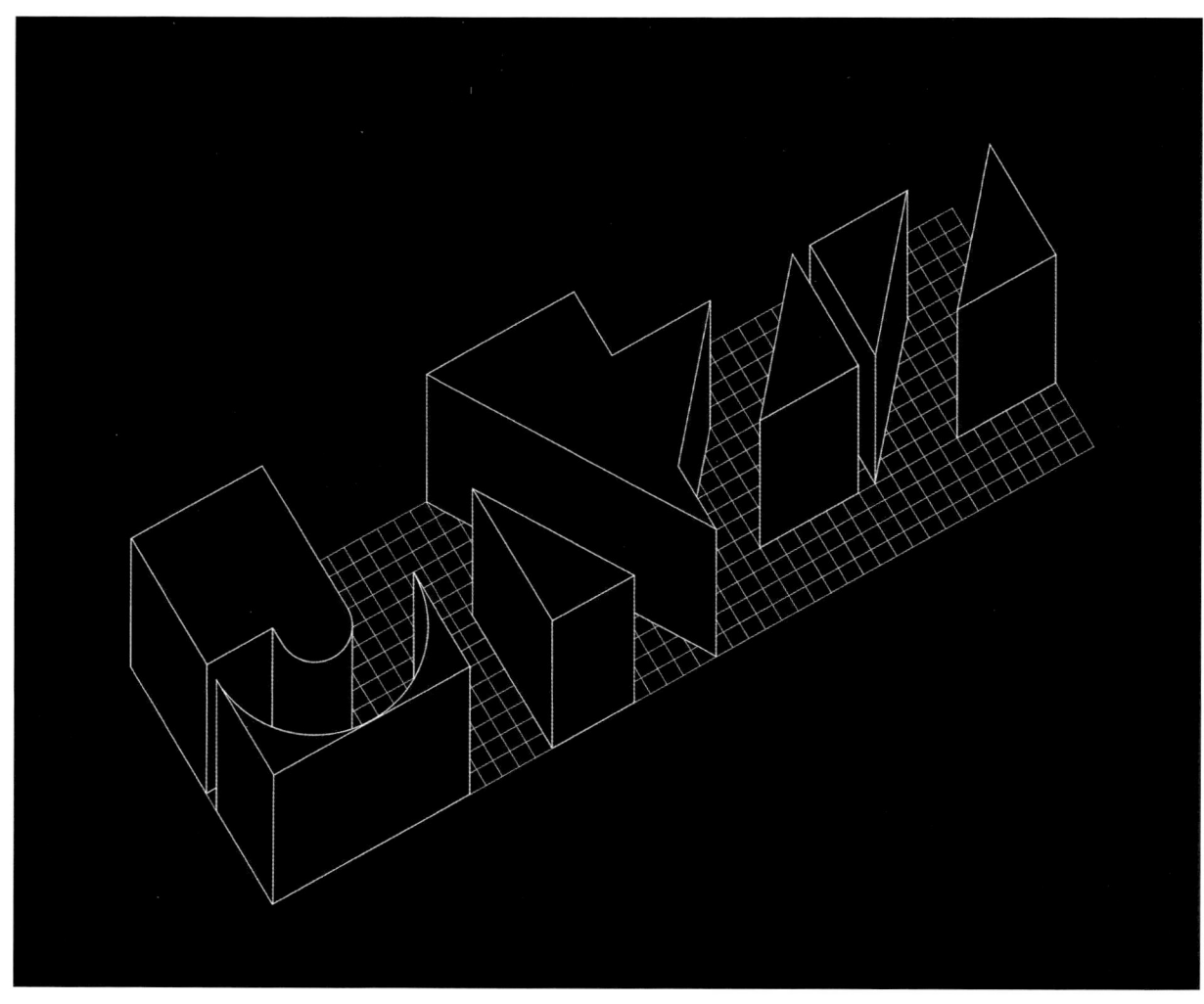
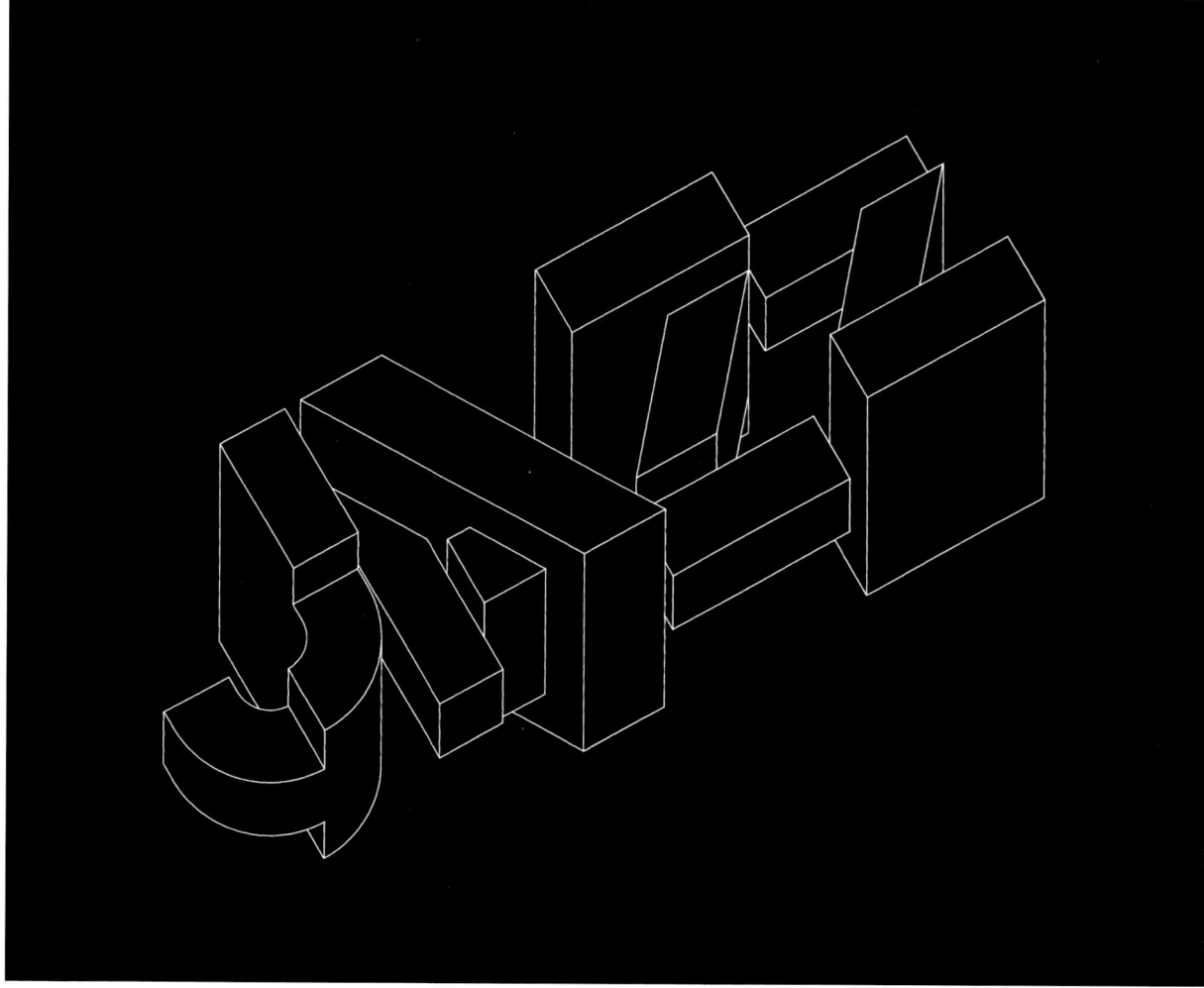

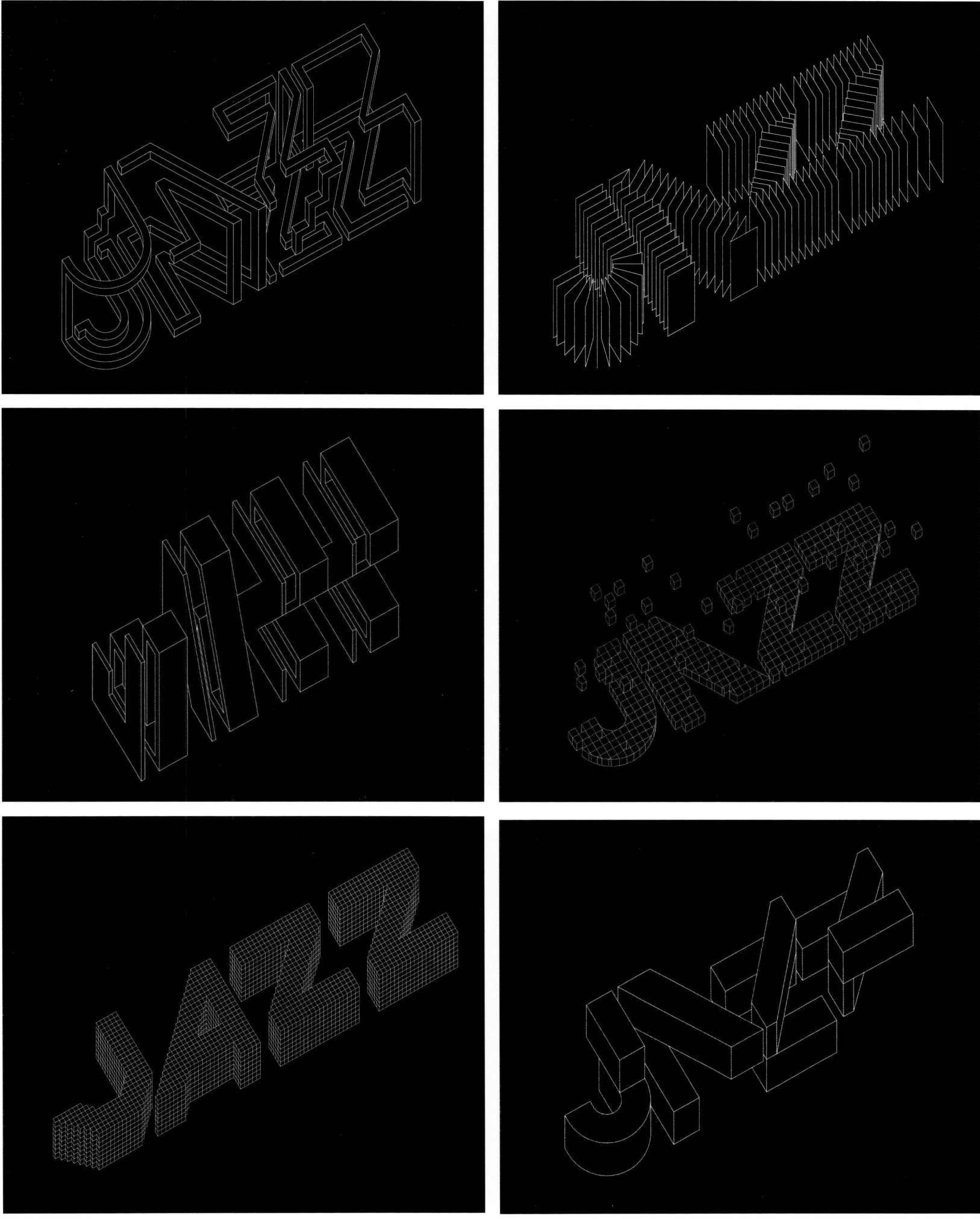

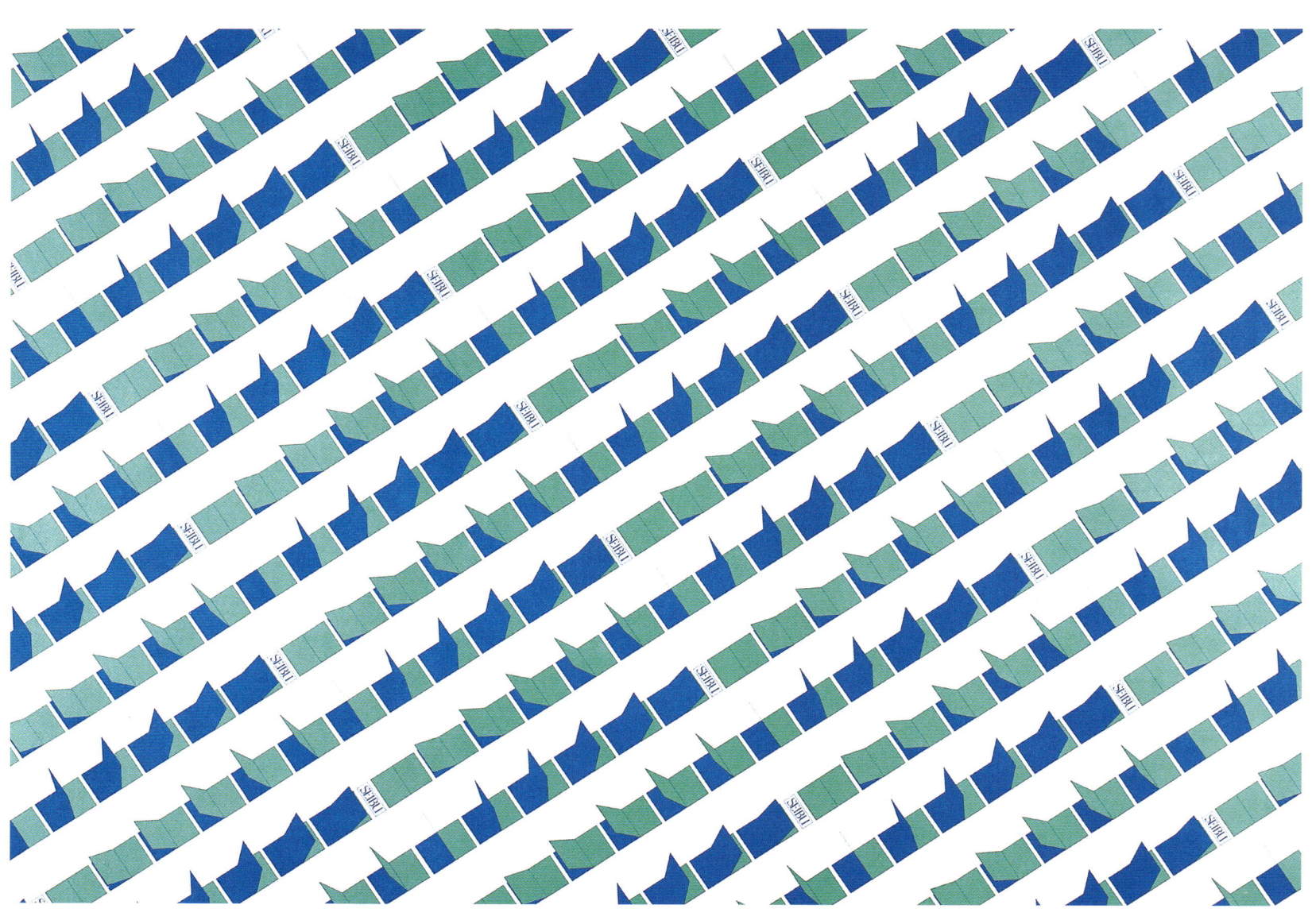

1-58 Wrapping Paper
Seibu Department Store Book Center
Tokyo, Japan, 1975

1-59 Shopping Bag
The Museum of Modern Art
New York, NY, USA, 1984

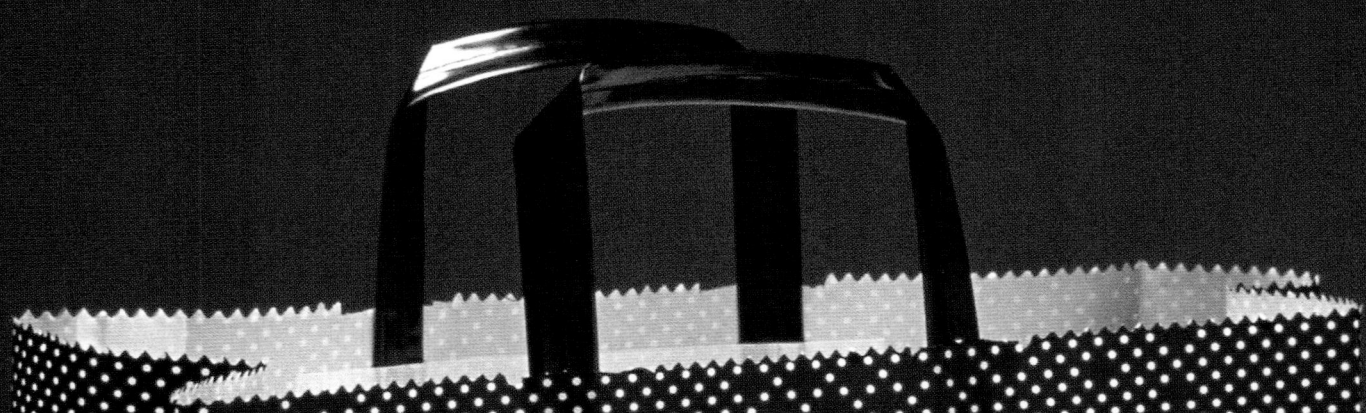

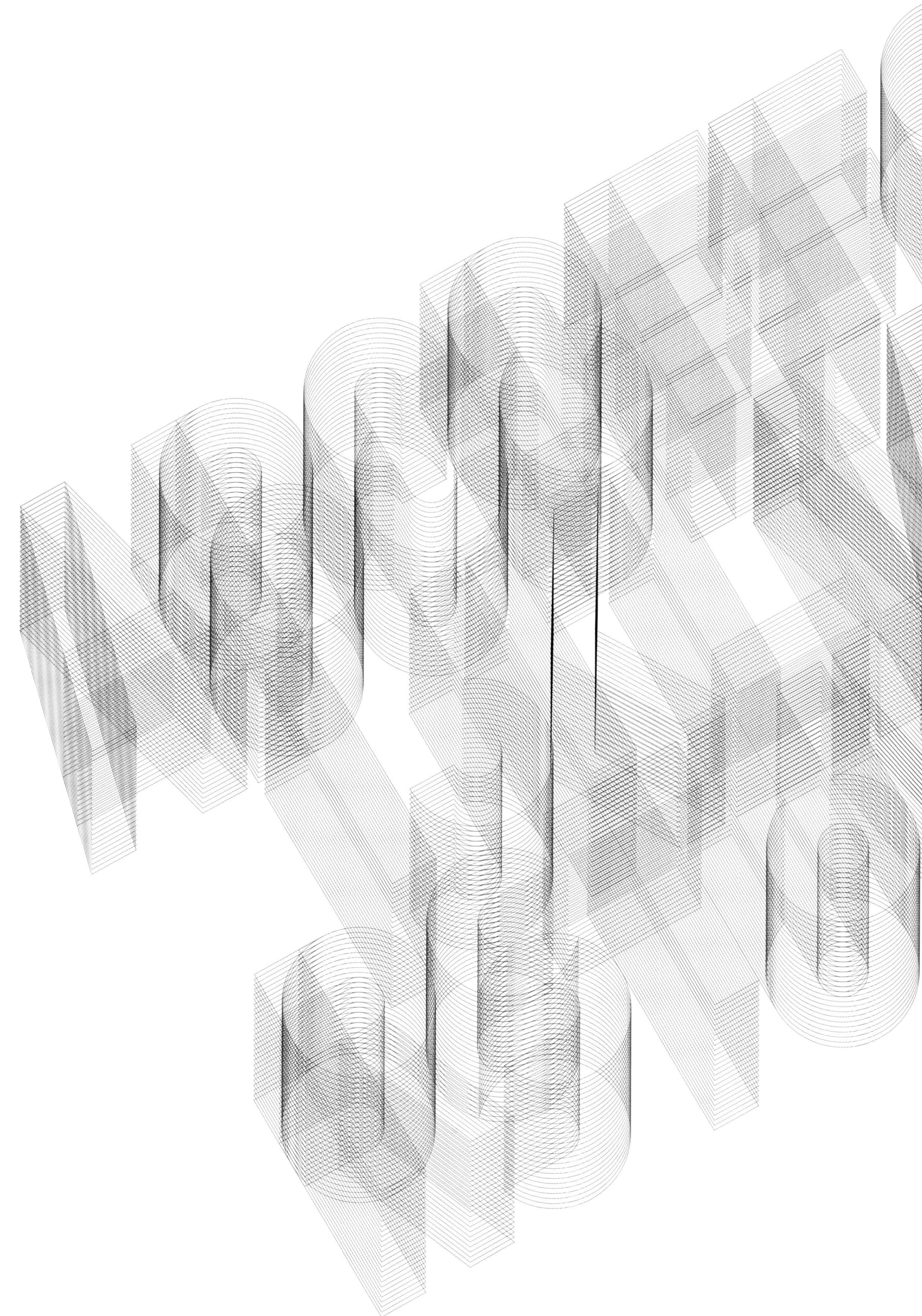

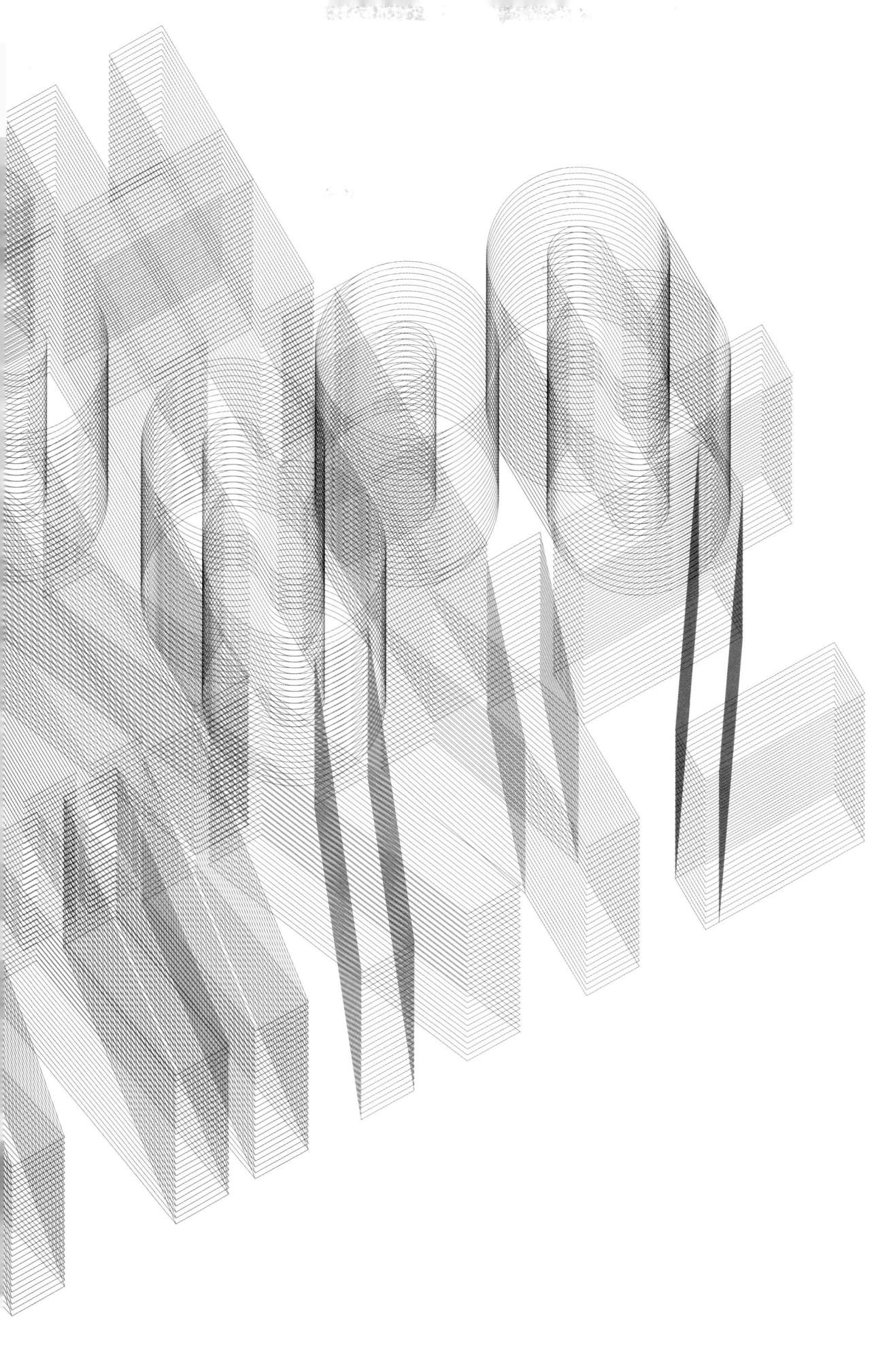

1-60 Original Illustration
Enigmatic Alphabet, HQ Magazine
Germany, 1986

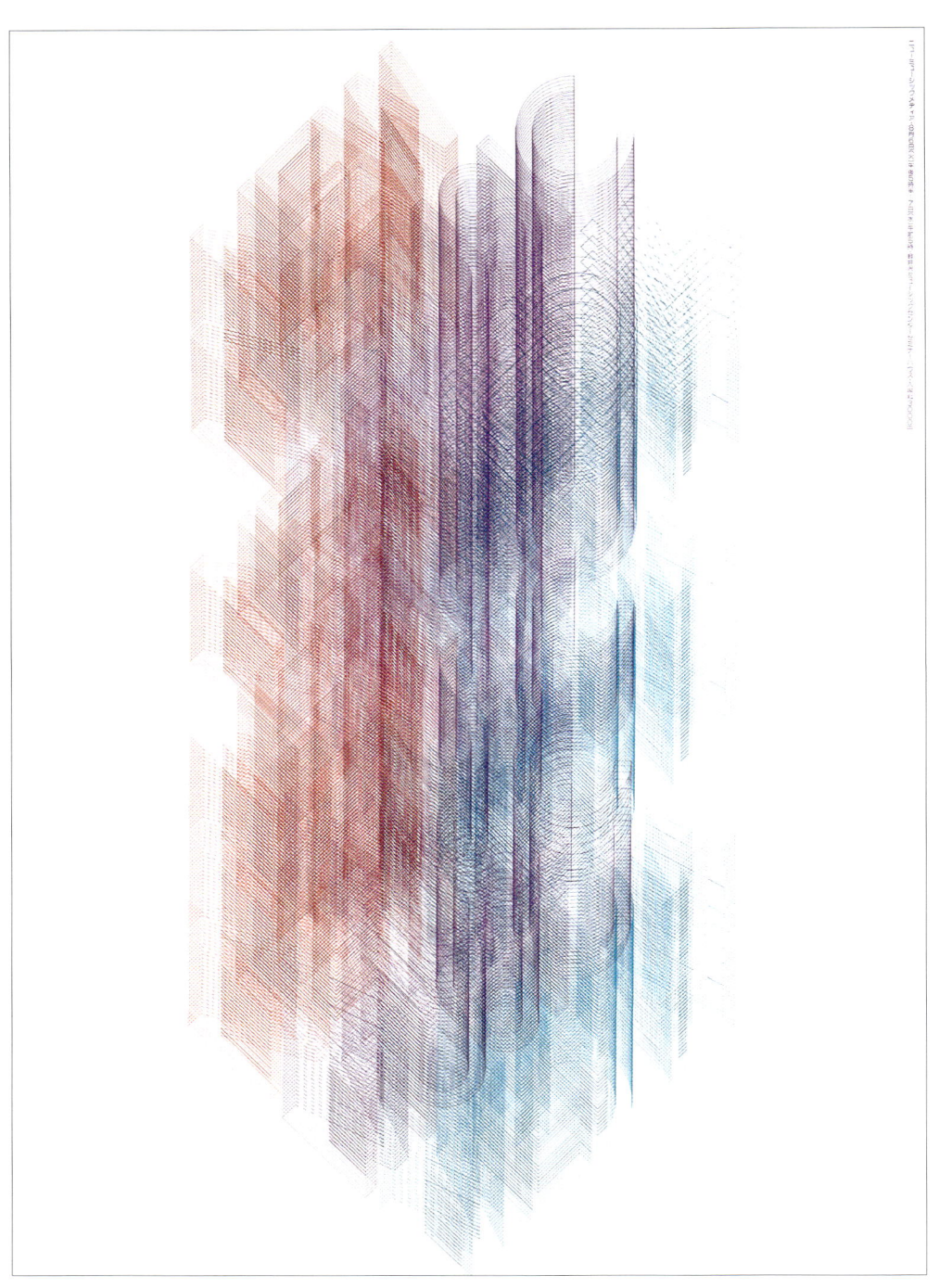

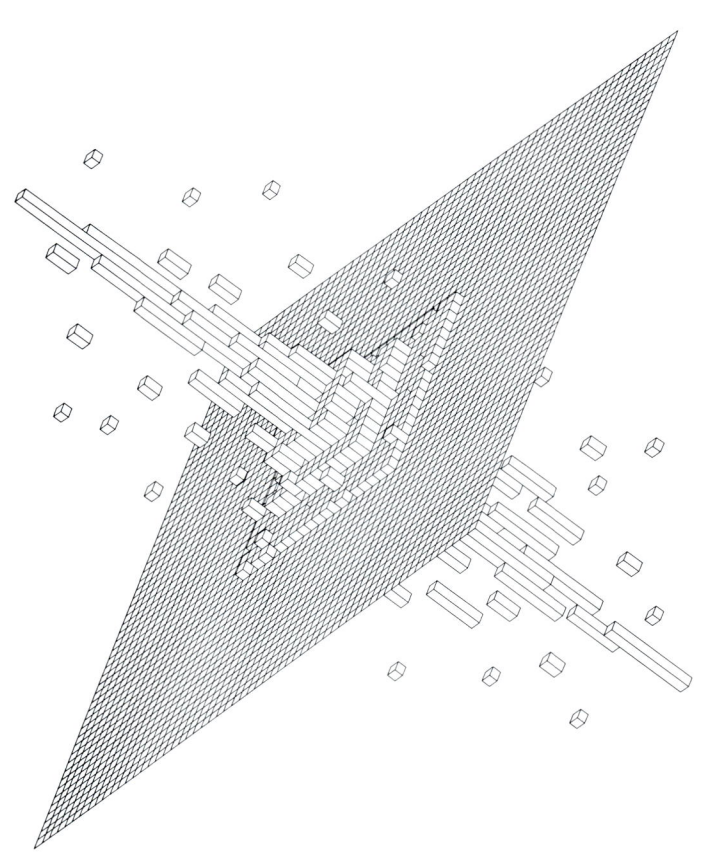

1-61 Poster
New Music Media
New Music Media Committee
Tokyo, Japan, 1974

1-62 Illustration for Poster Sylph
Sylph, Tokyo, Japan, 1981

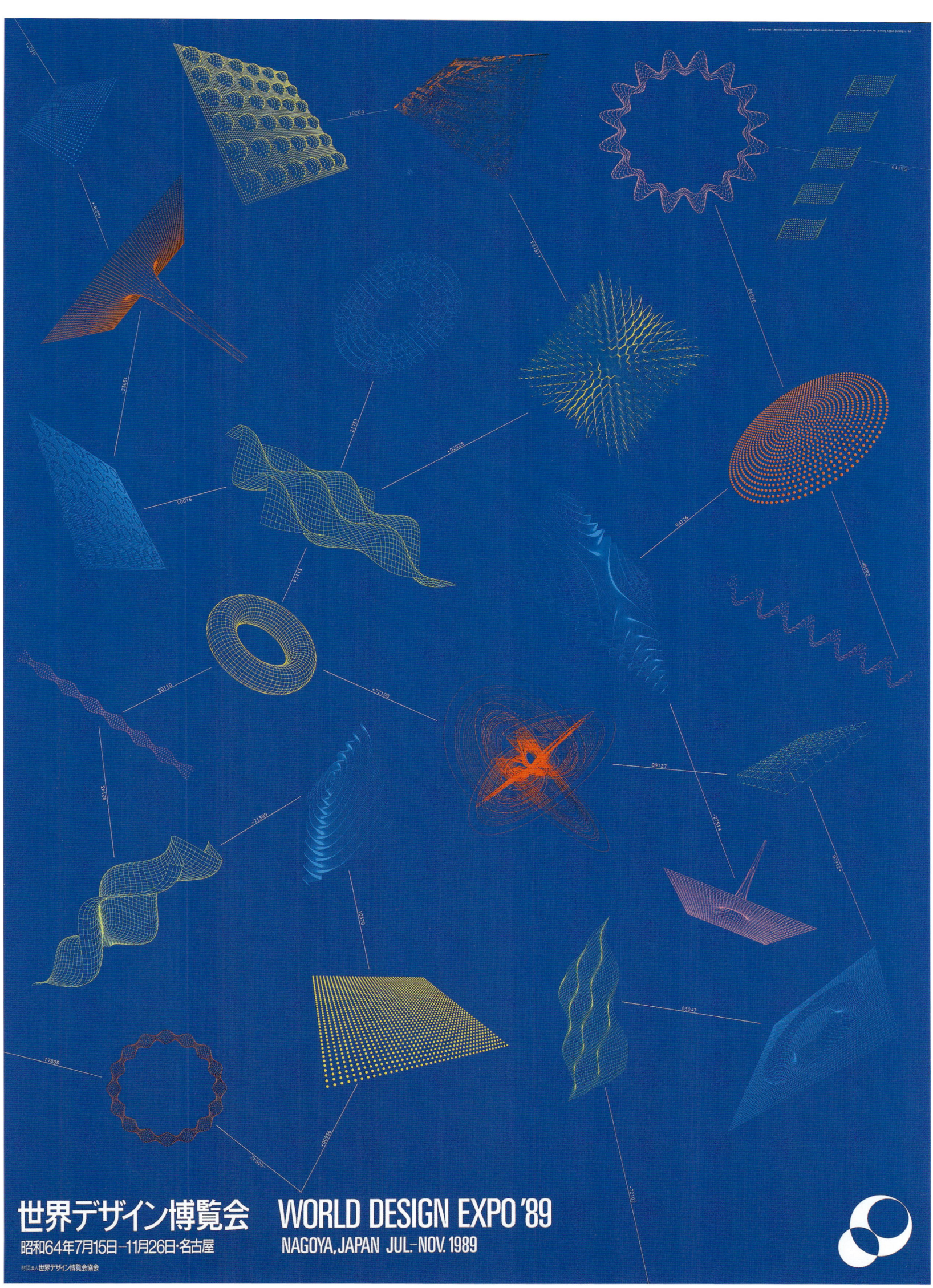

1-63 Poster
World Design Expo, World Design Expo Committee, Aichi, Japan, 1987

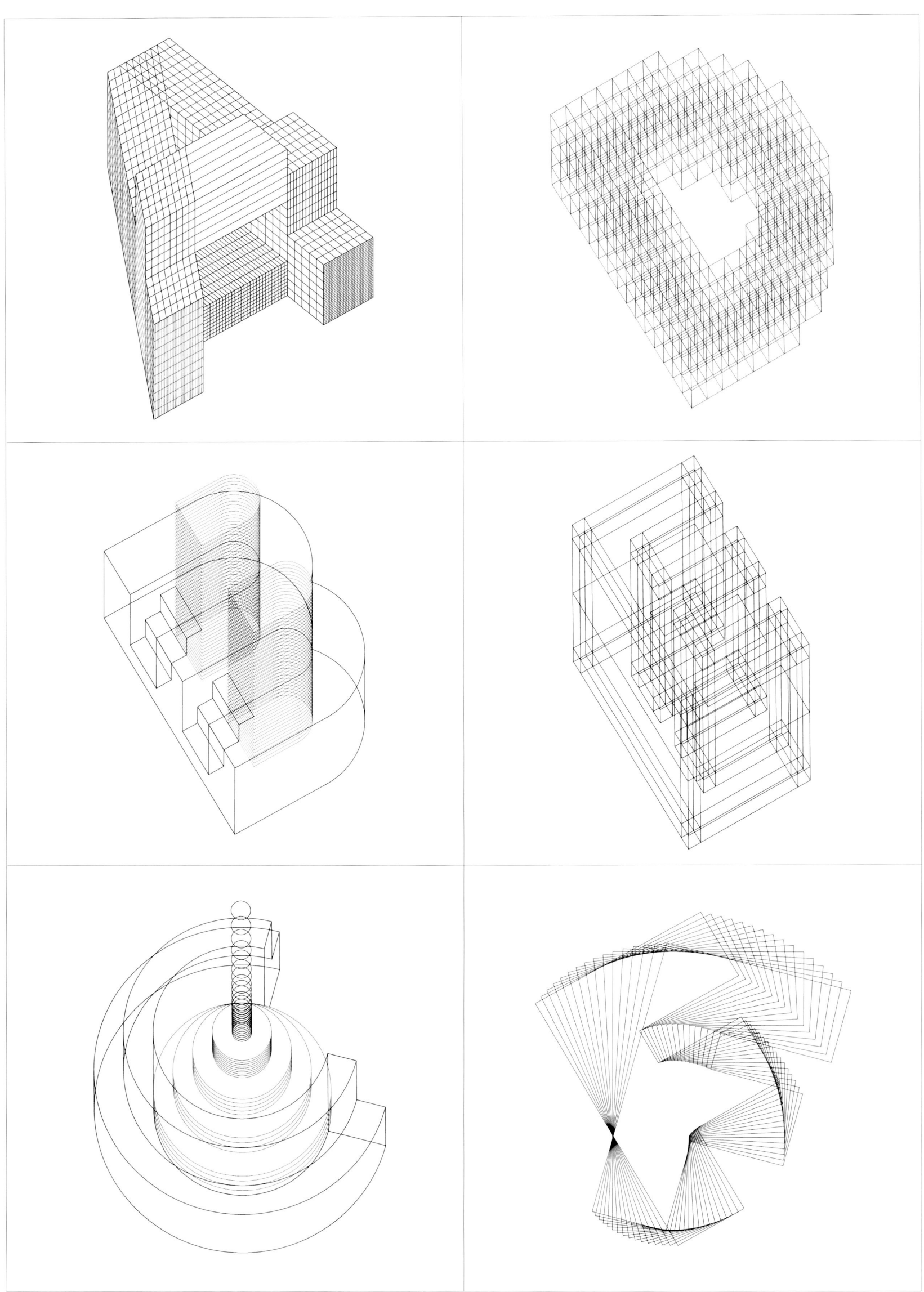

1-64 IBM Alphabet
IBM Japan, c. 1984-90

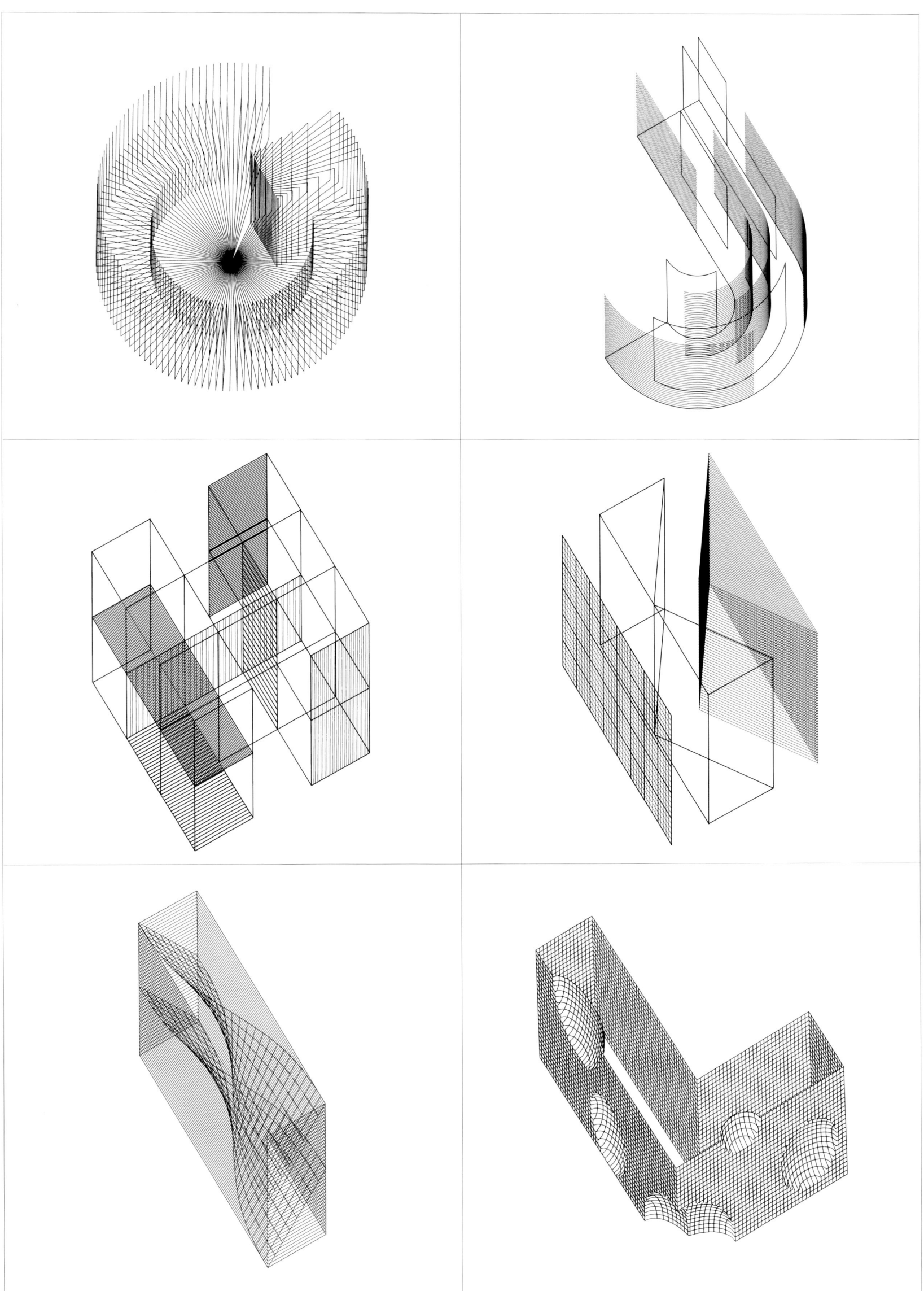

These works were created with a computer drafting system.

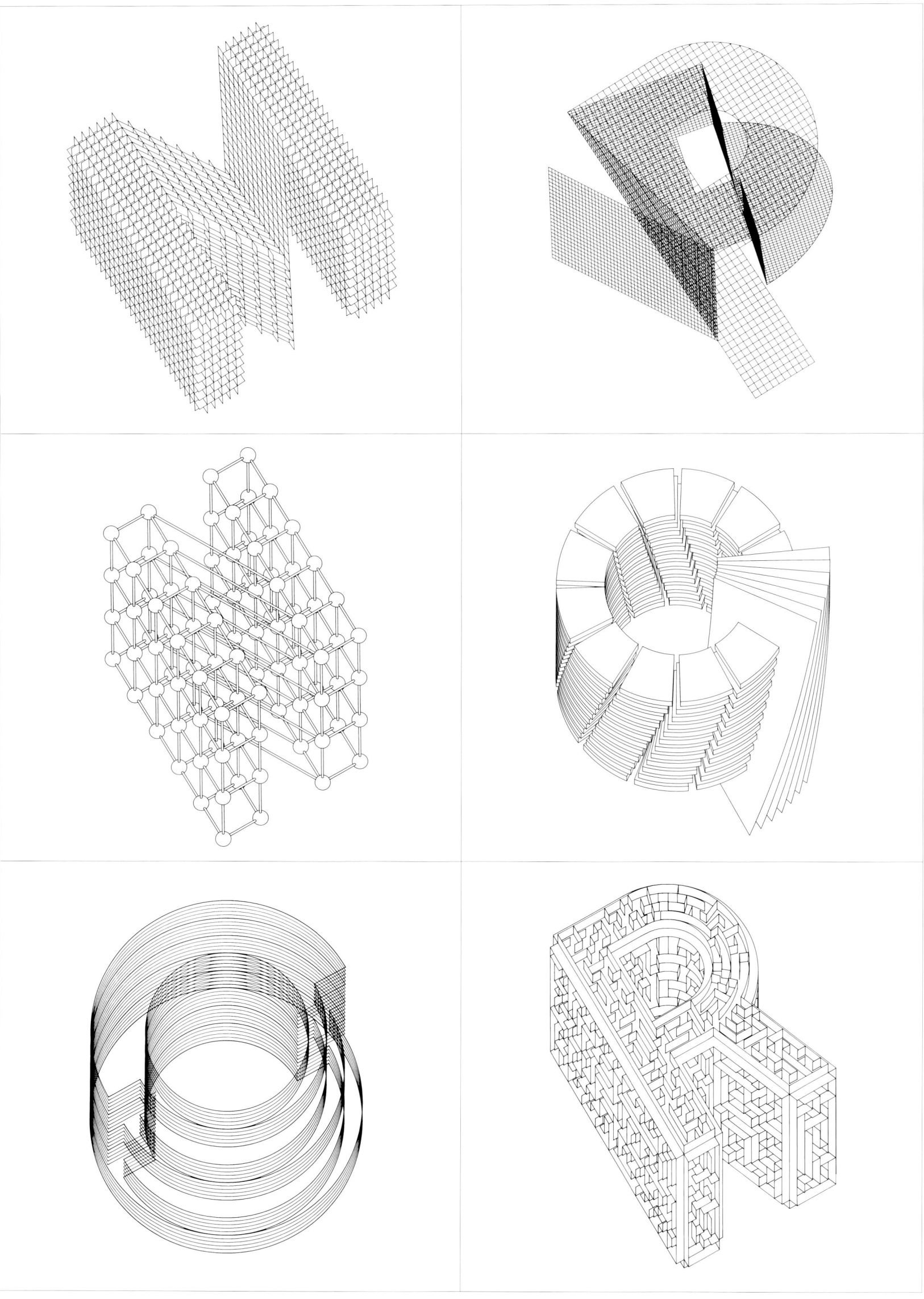

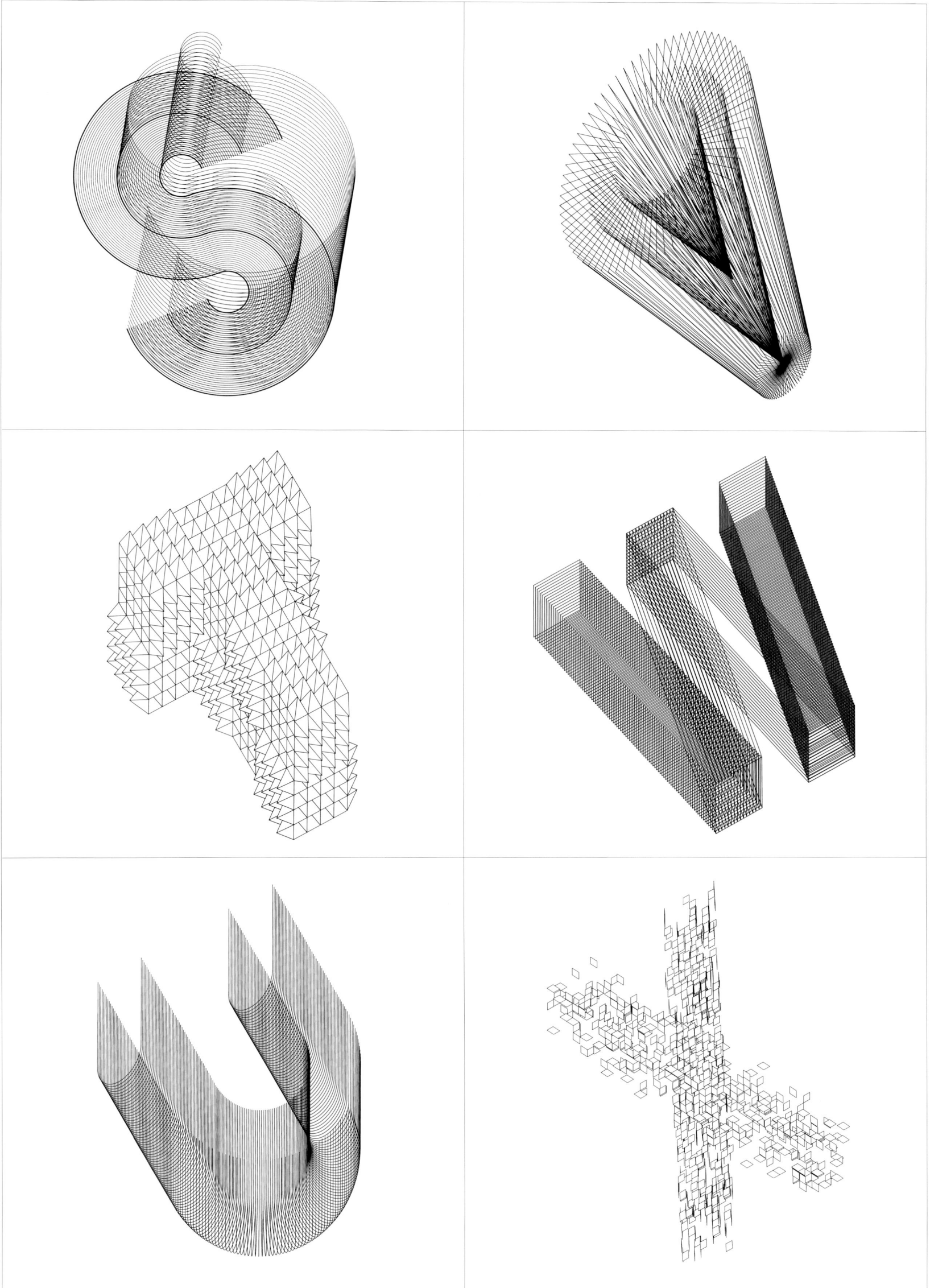

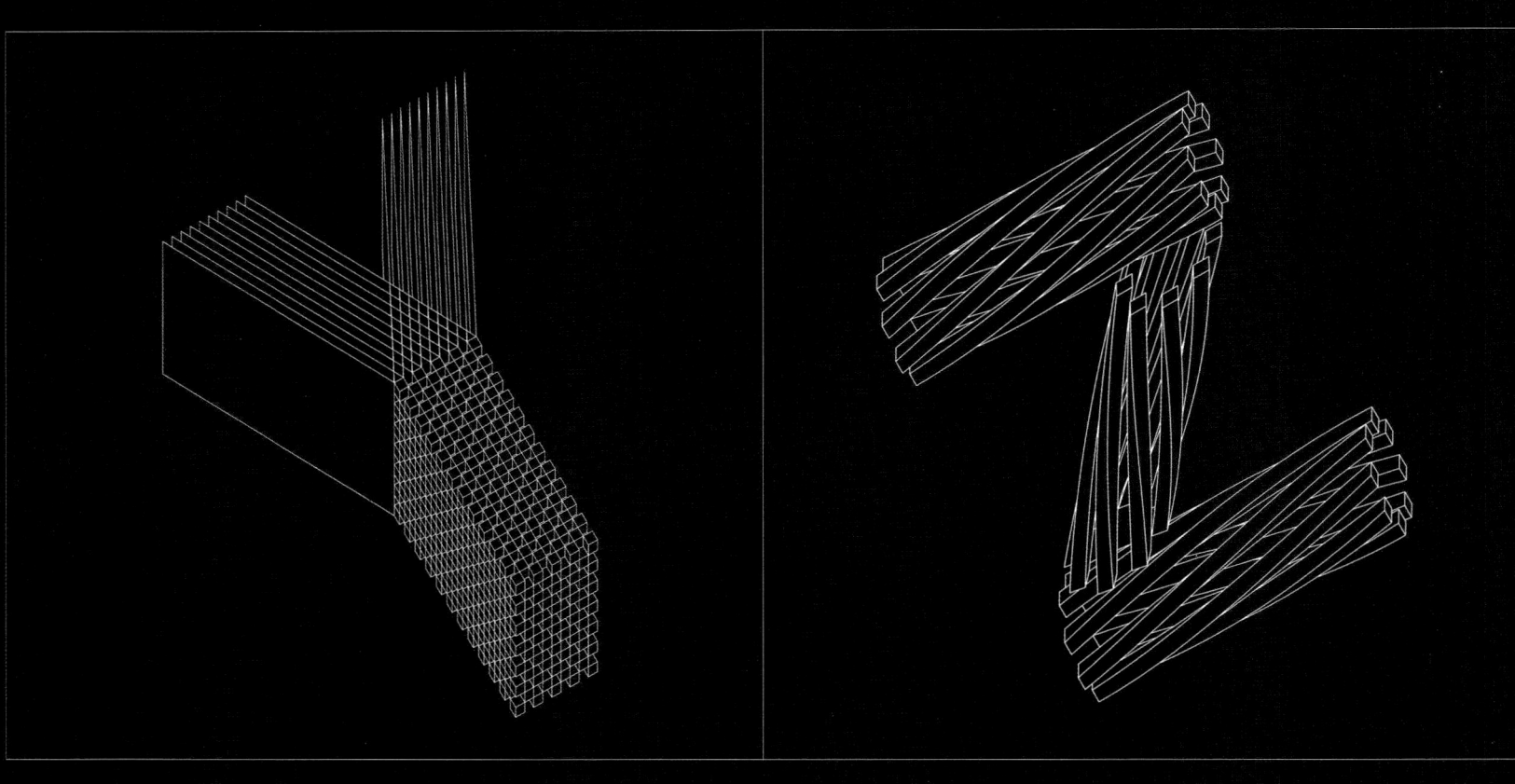

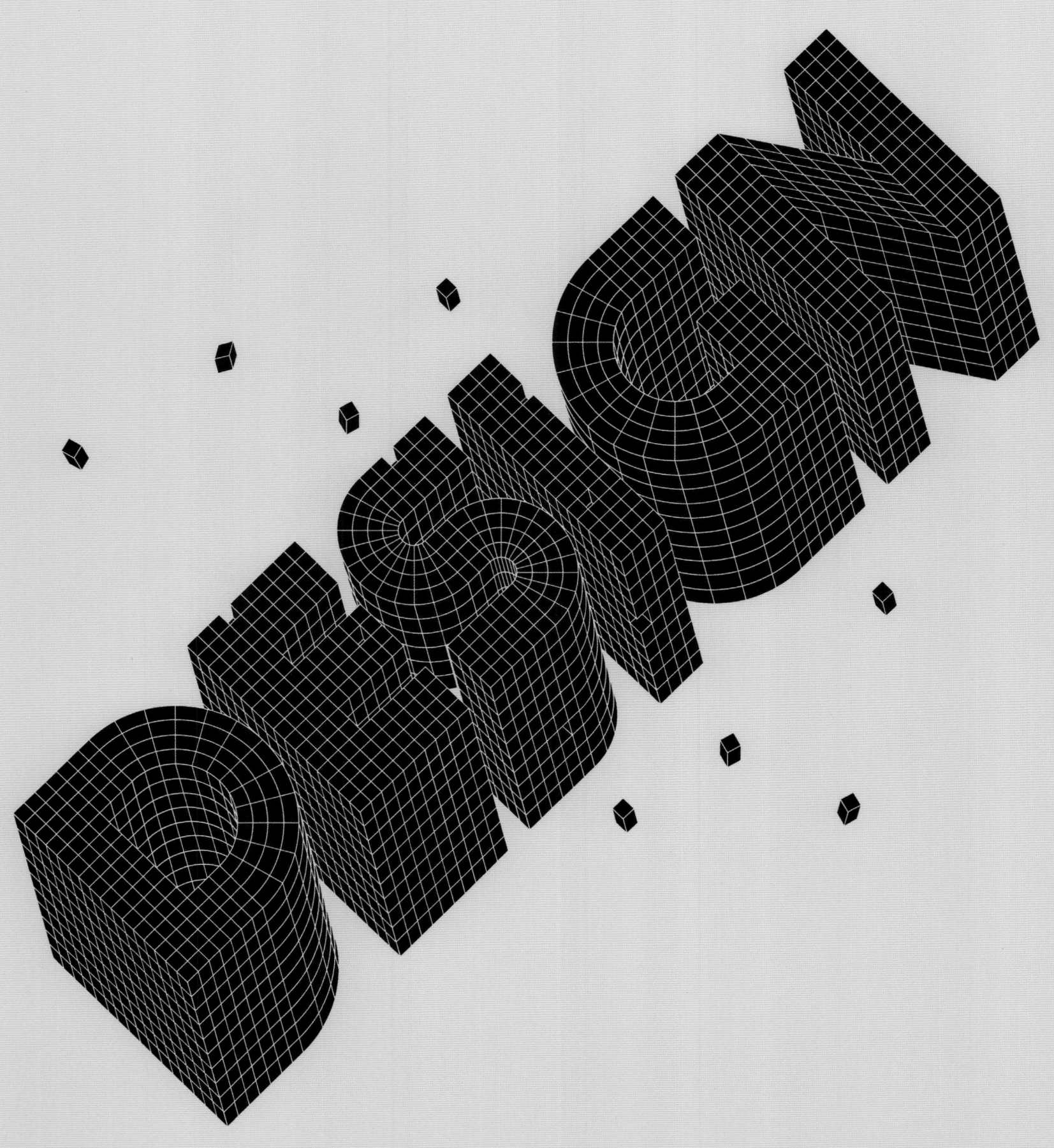

1-65 Cover Illustration
Design News Magazine
Japan Institute of Design Promotion
1980–1981
Works from the same series

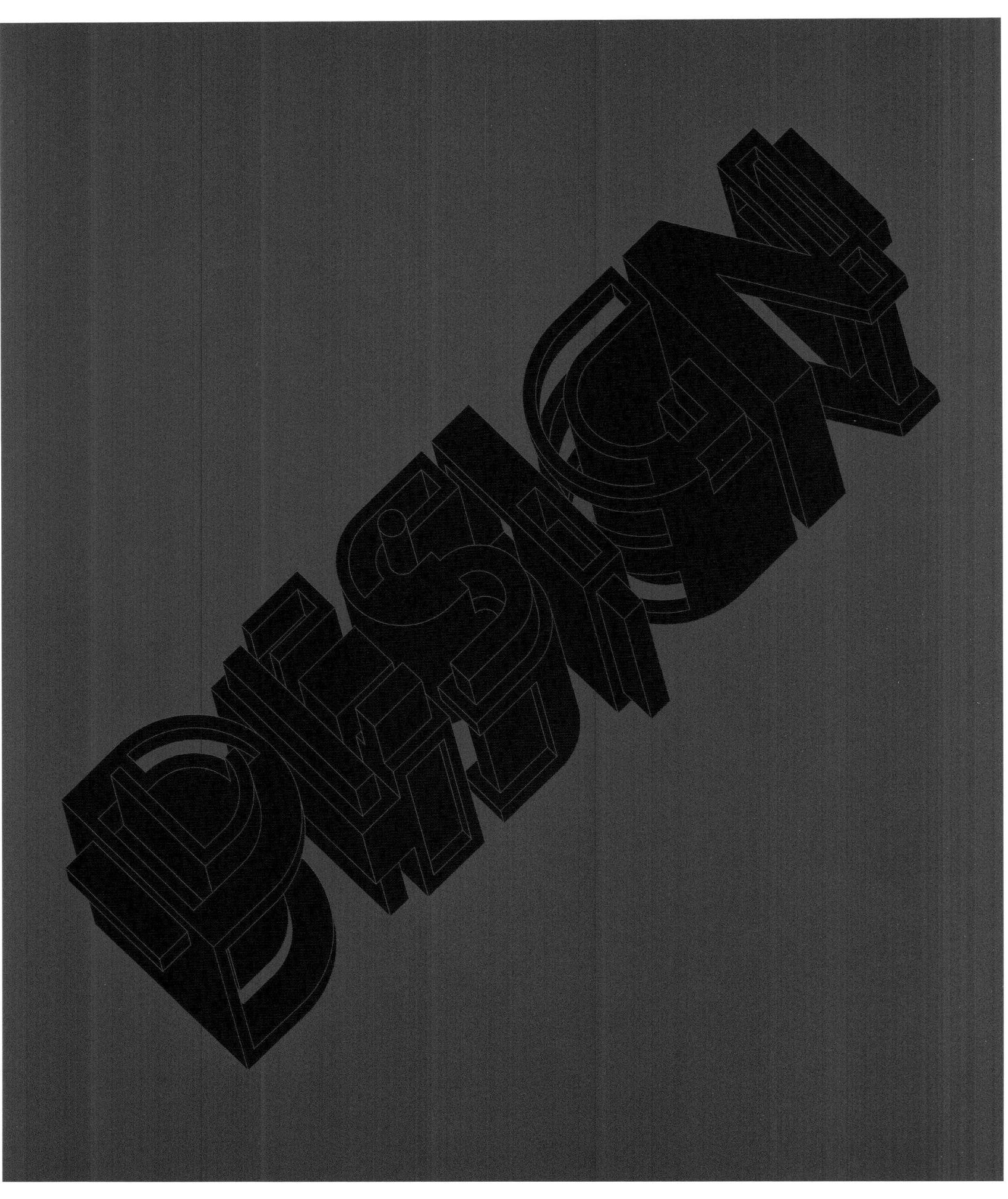

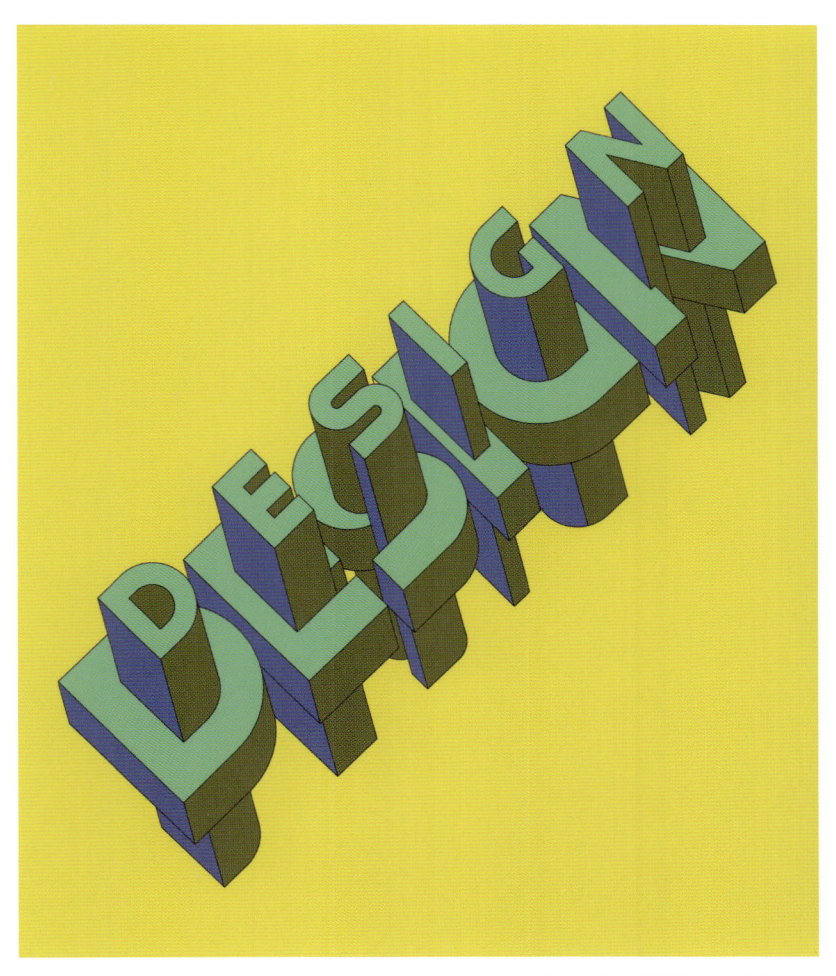
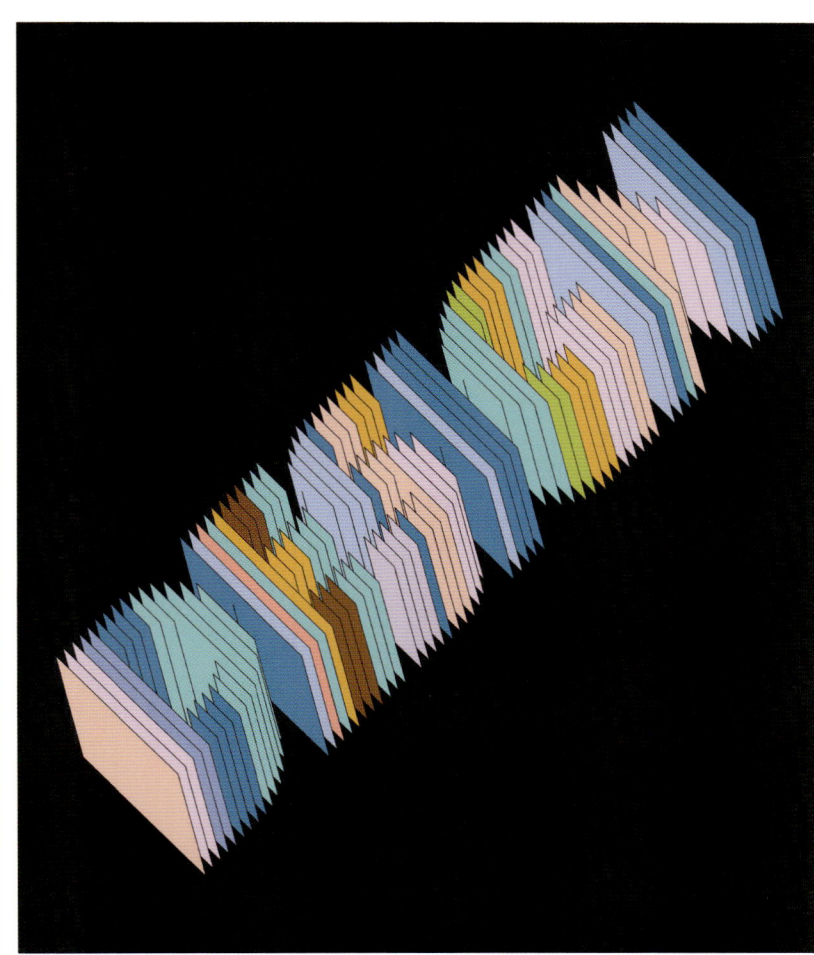
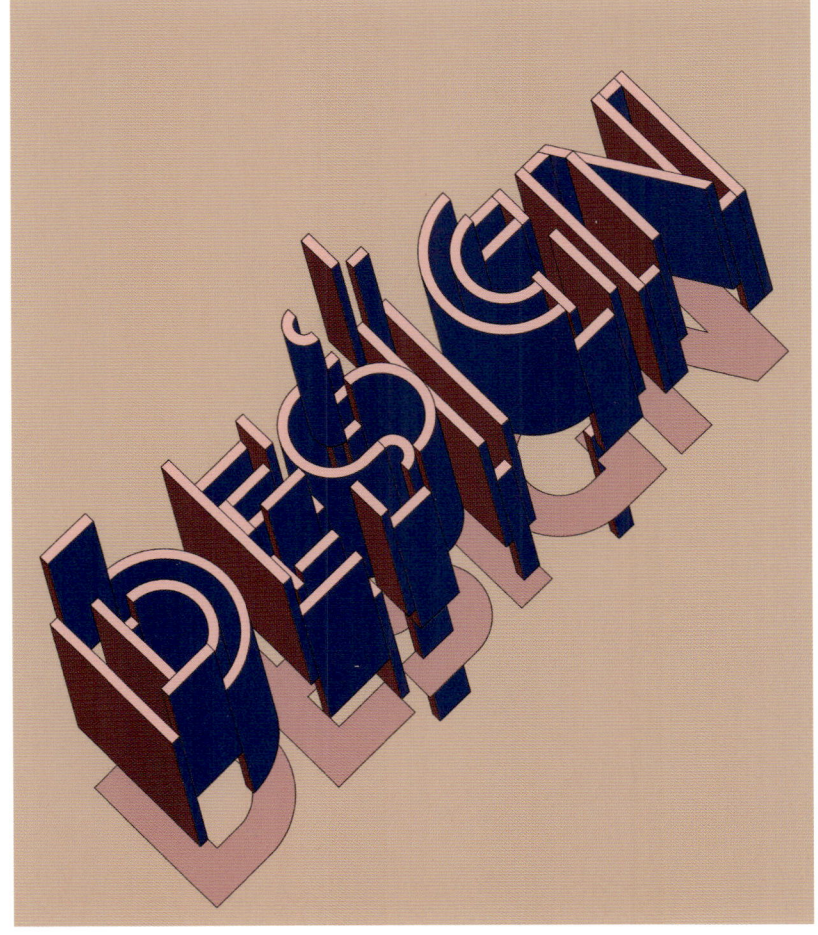
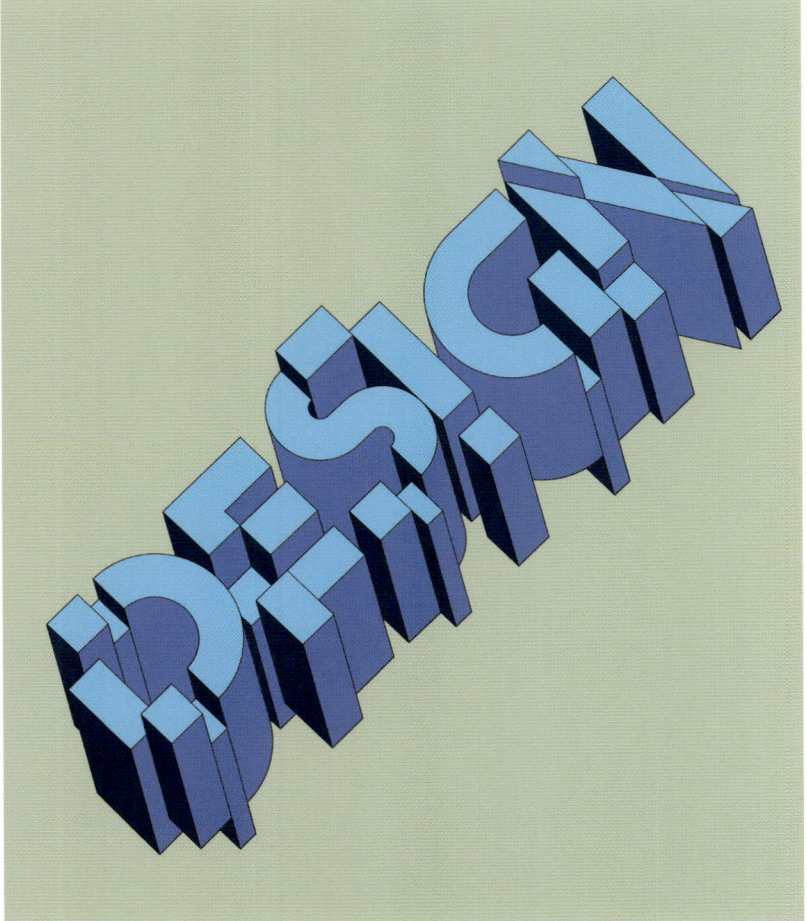

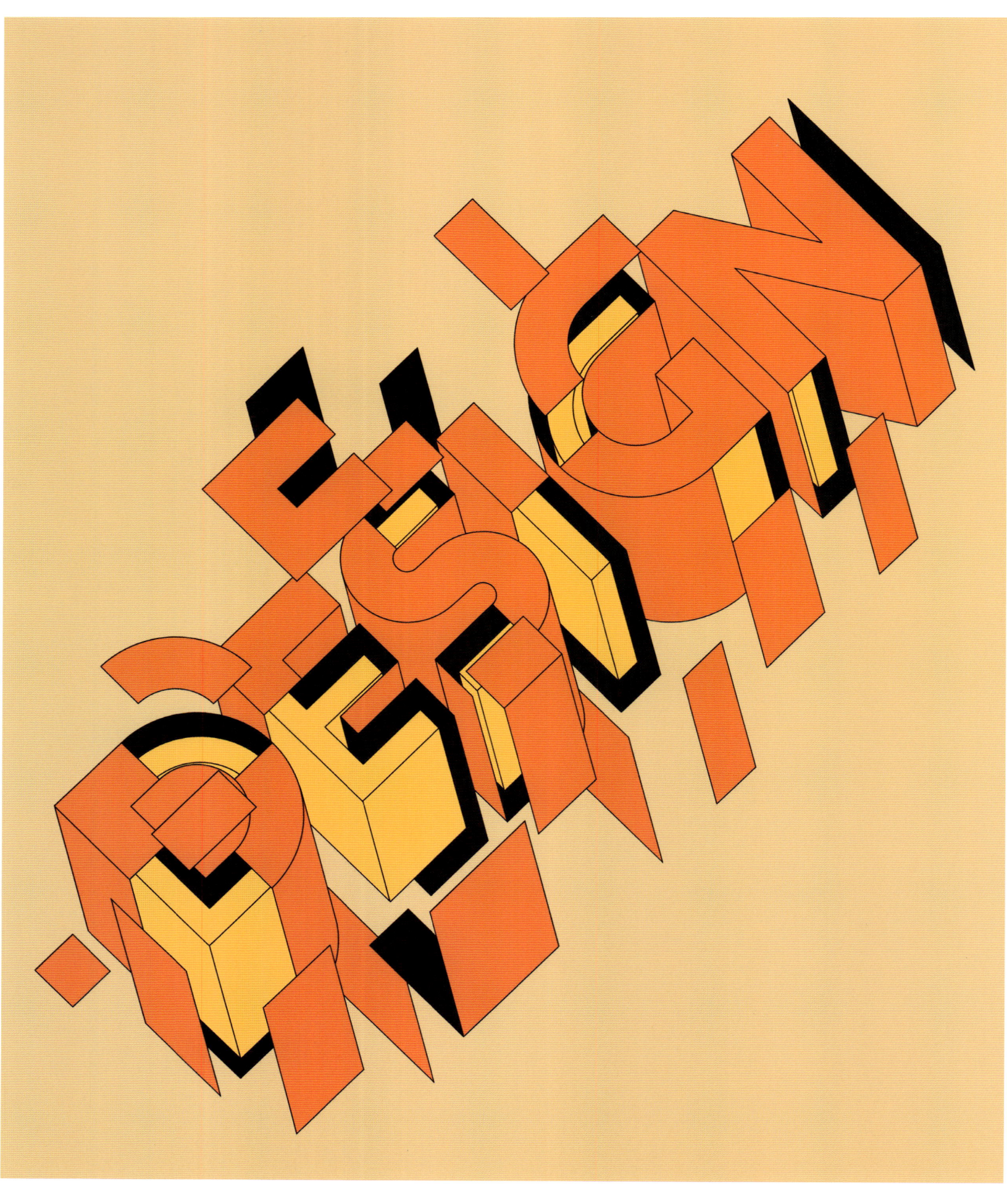

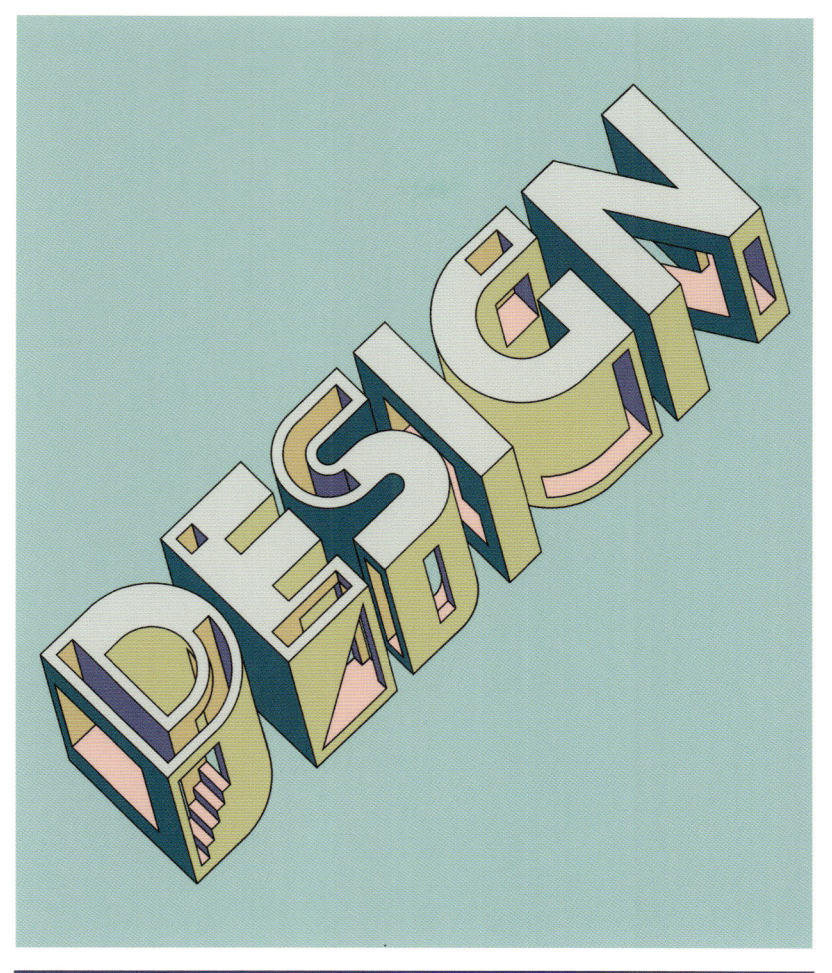
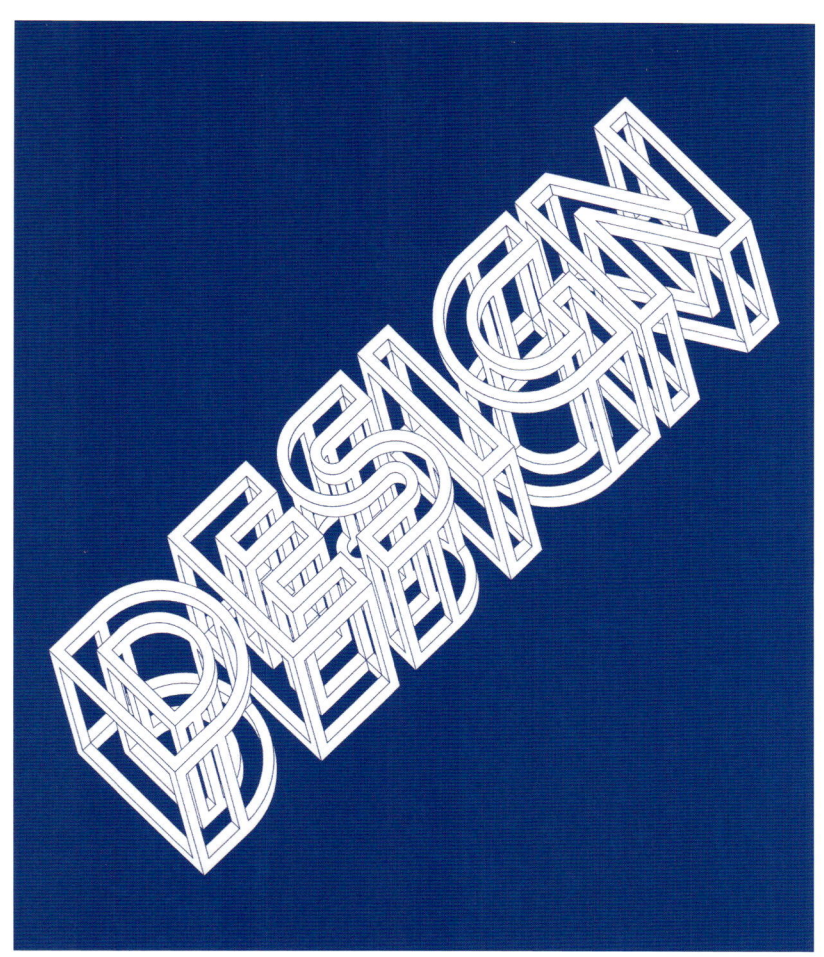
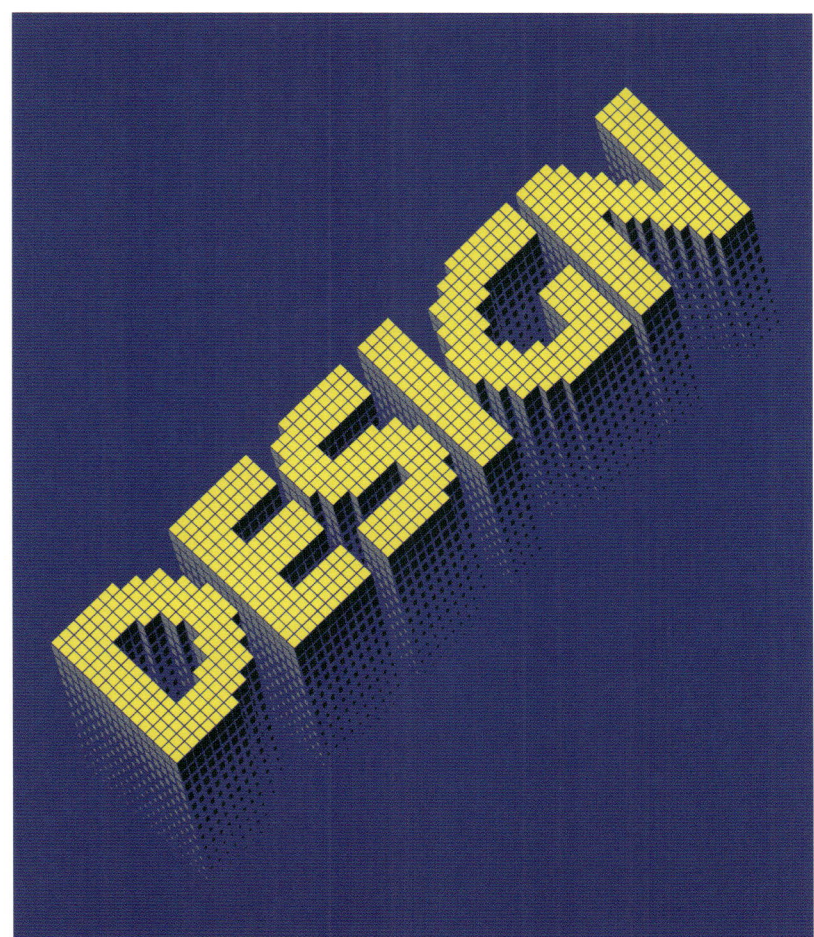
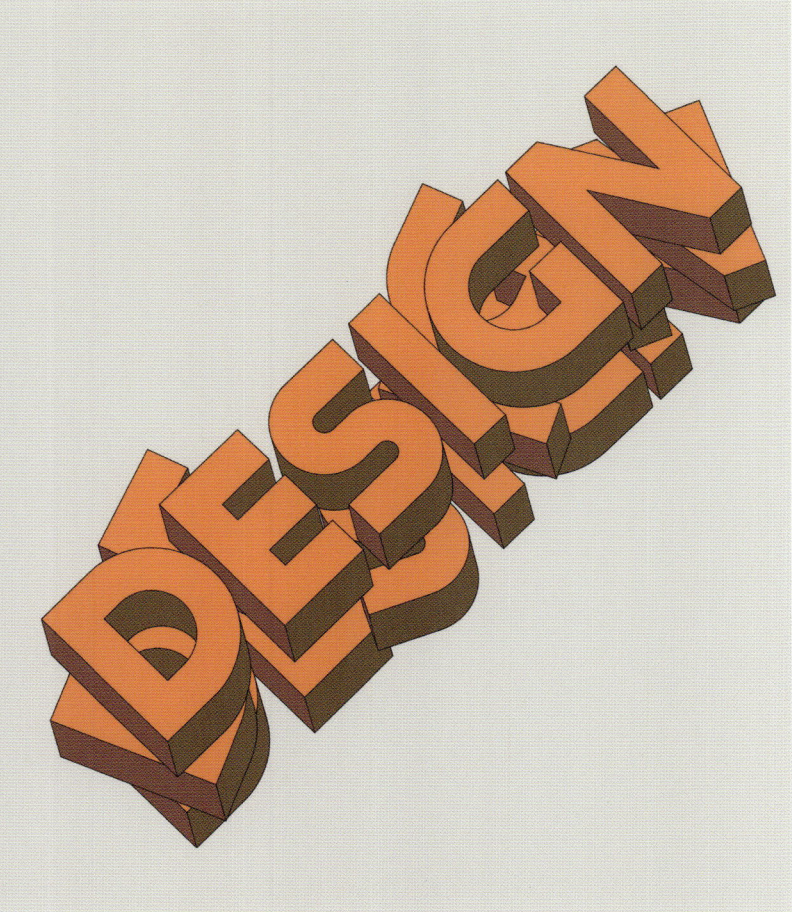

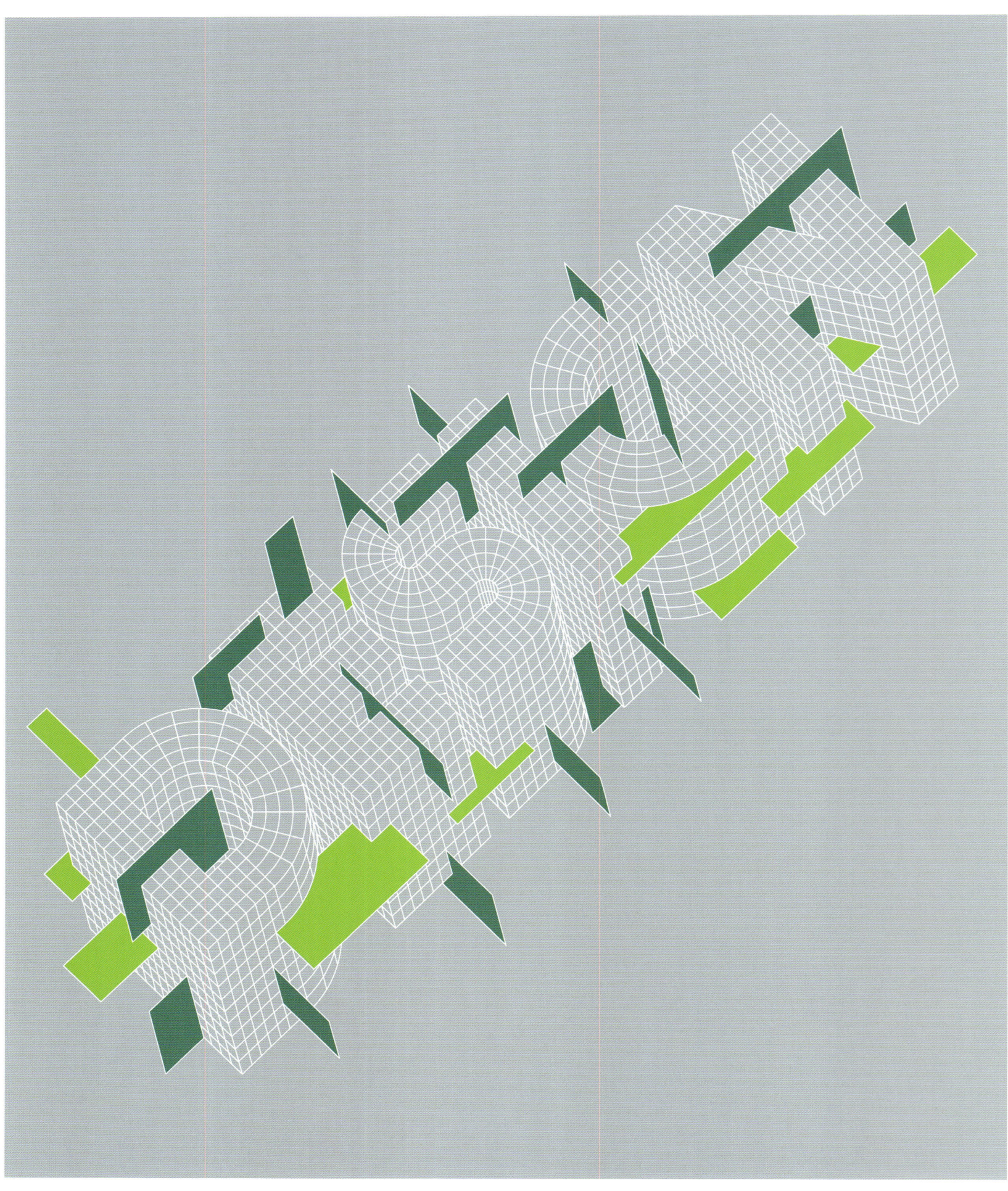

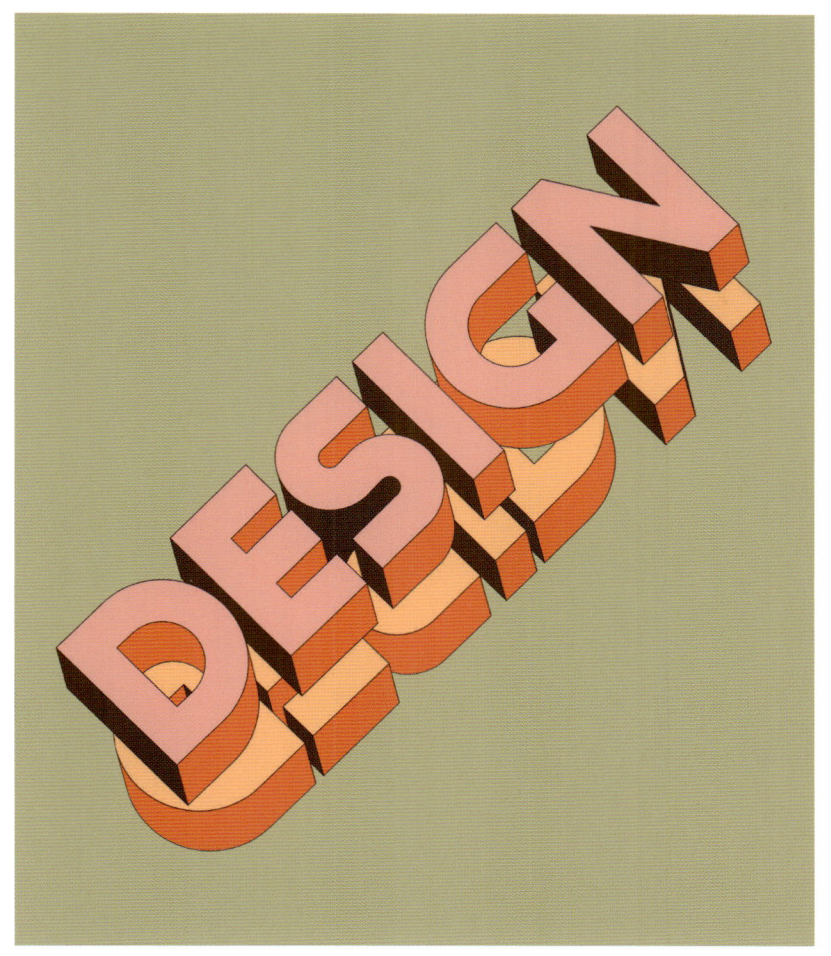
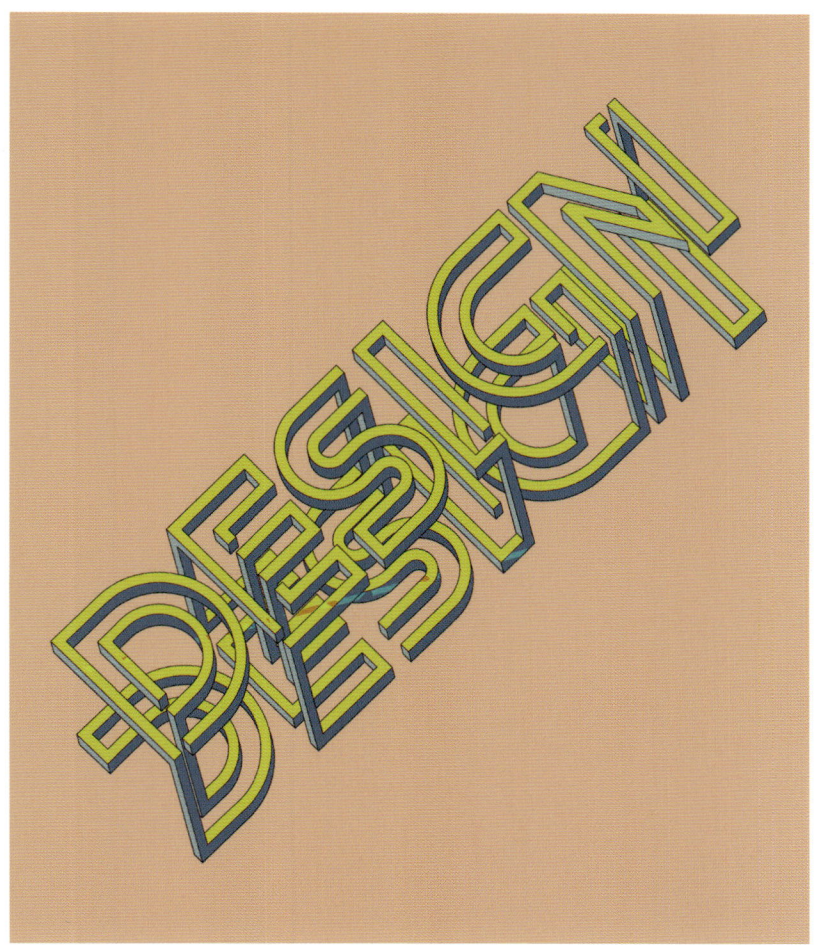
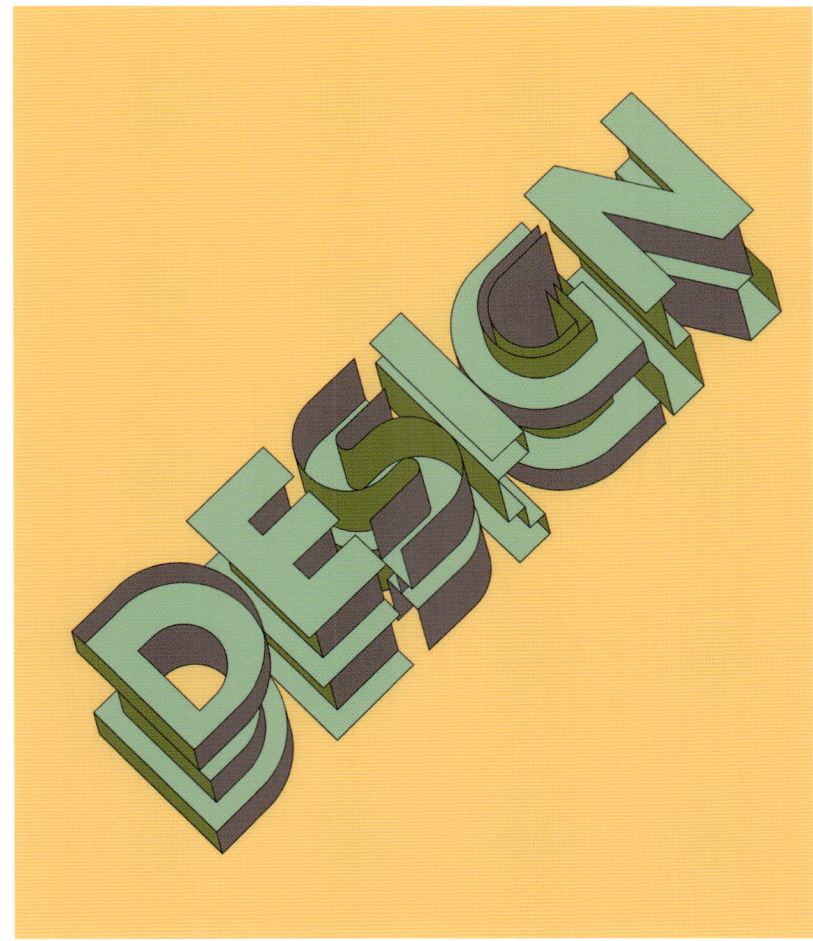
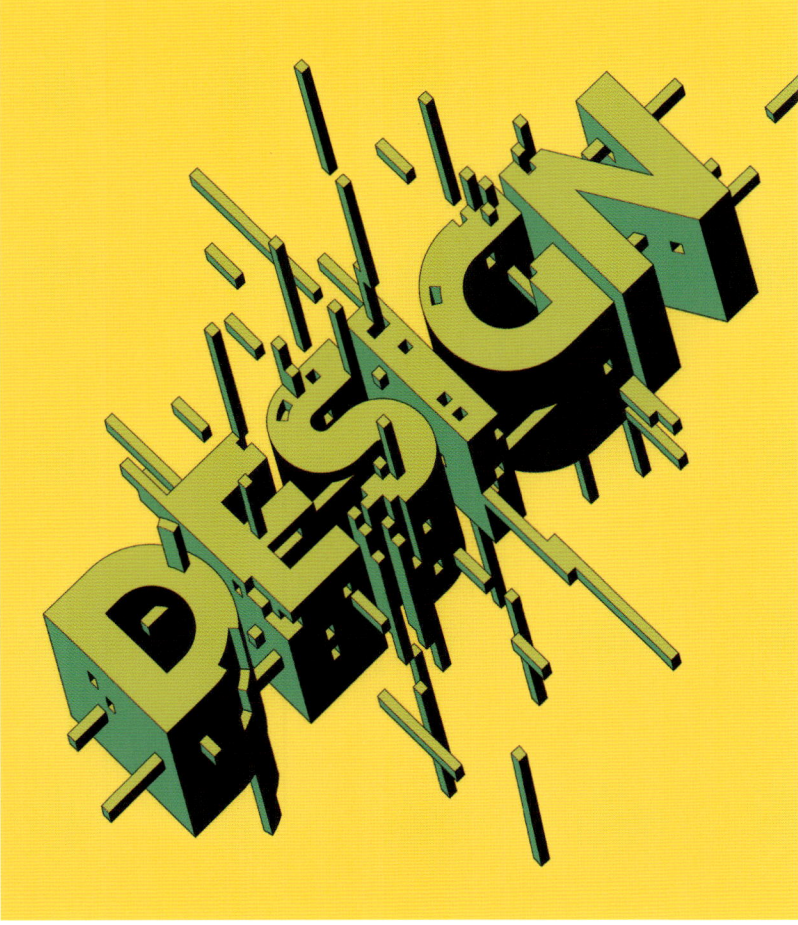

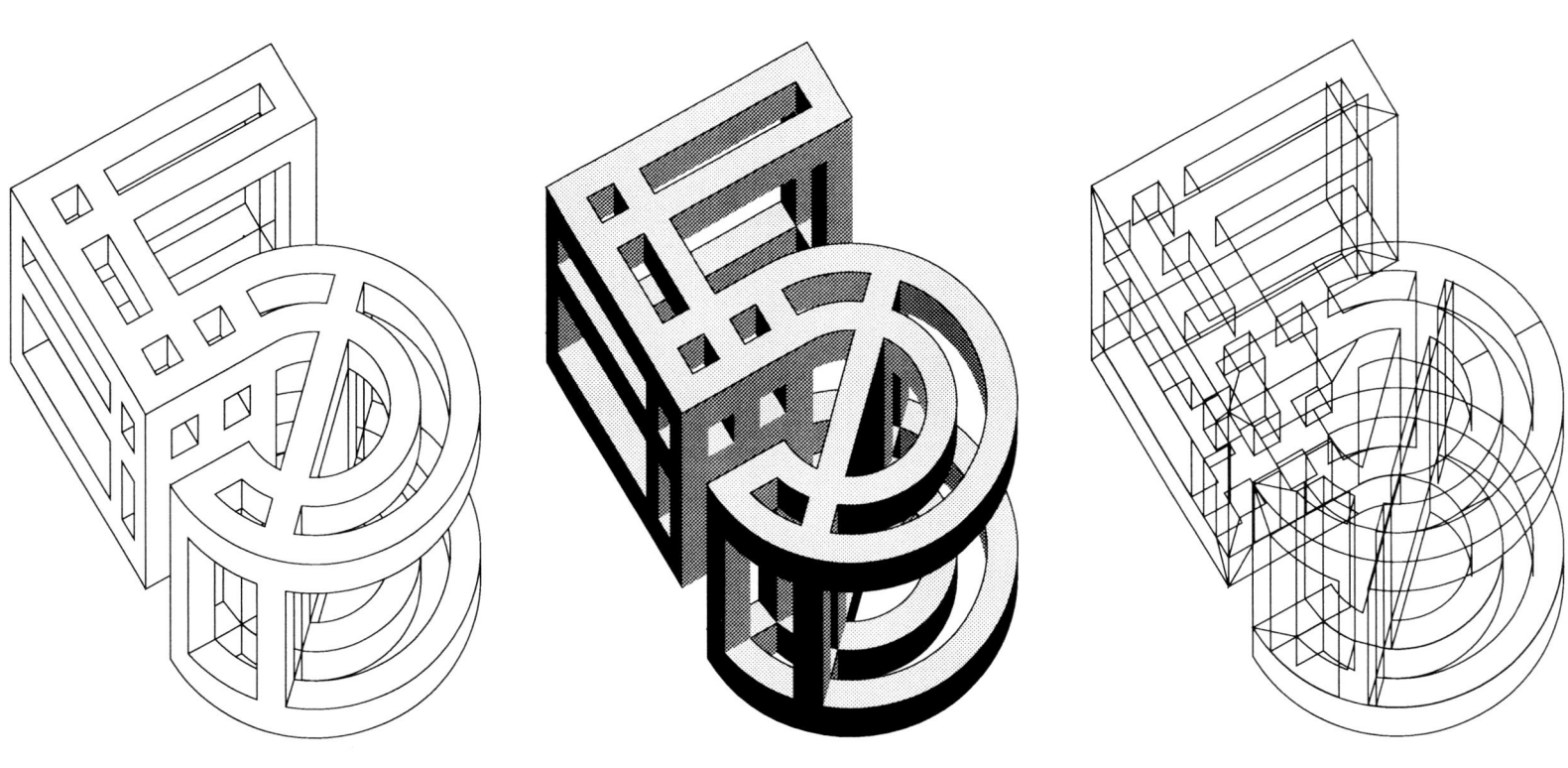

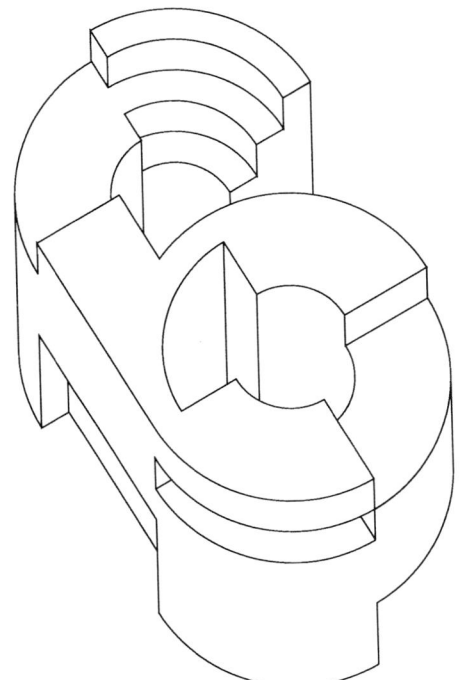 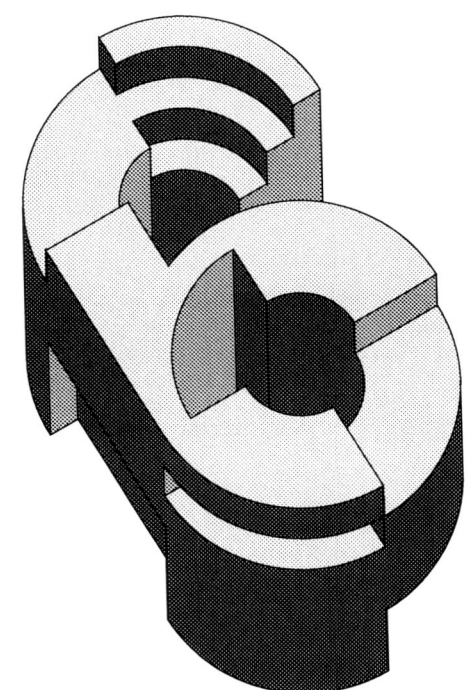 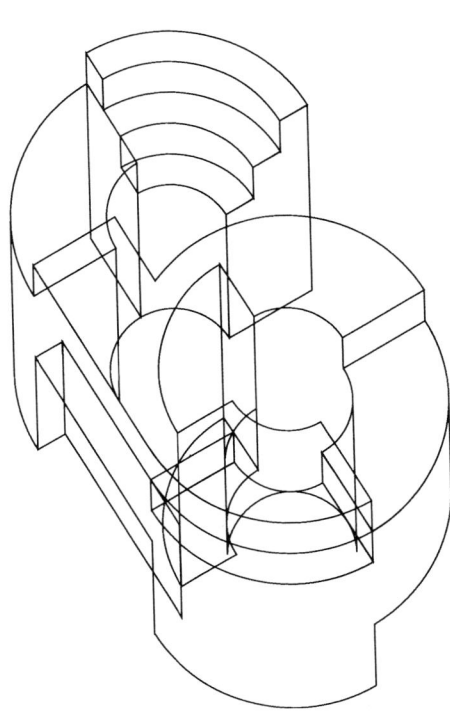

1-66 Graphic Chart
The Museum of Modern Art
New York, NY, USA, 1984–1991

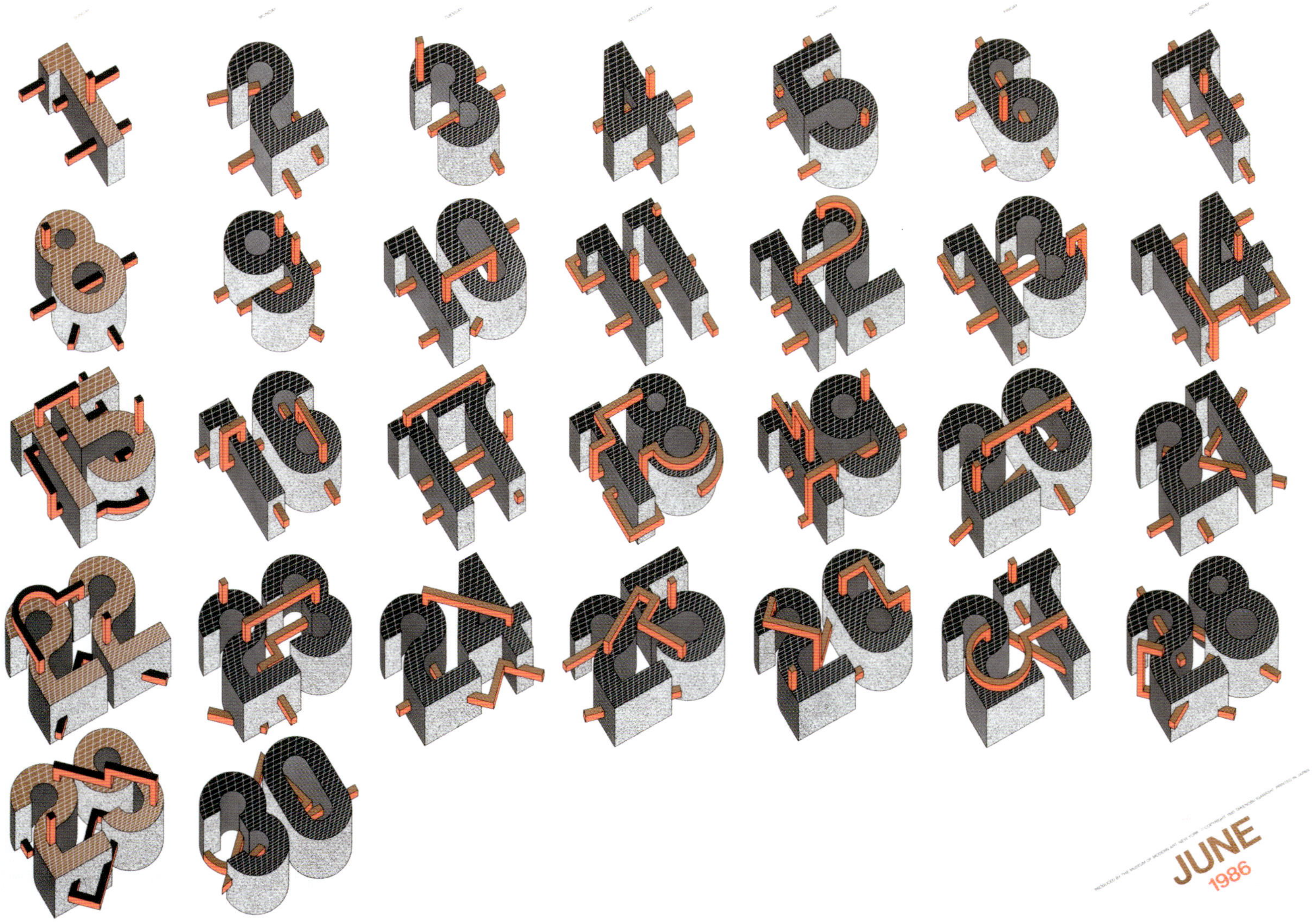

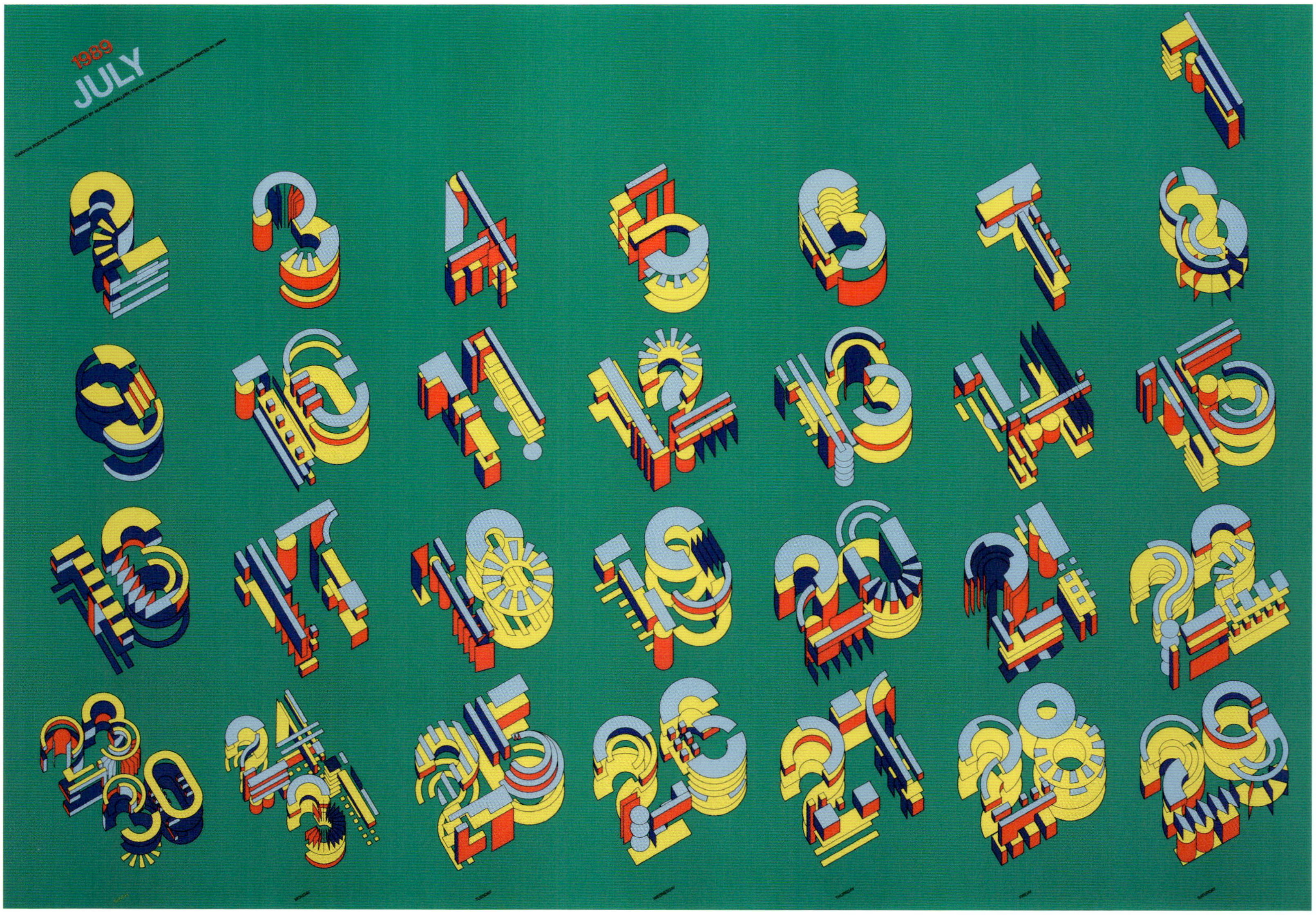

Calendar Poster
The Museum of Modern Art, New York, NY, USA, 1984–1991
Works from the same series

1-67 June, 1986
1-68 July, 1989

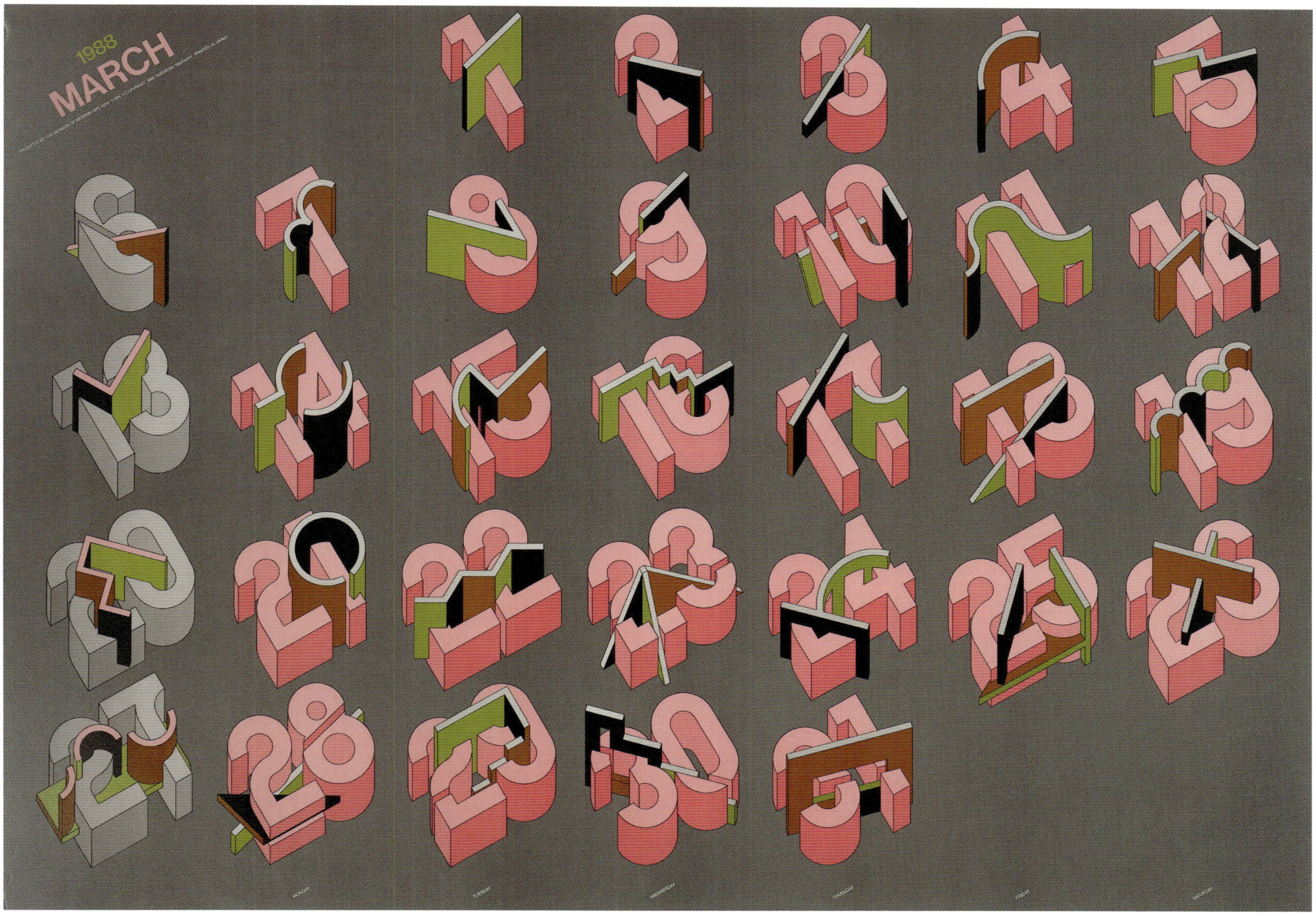

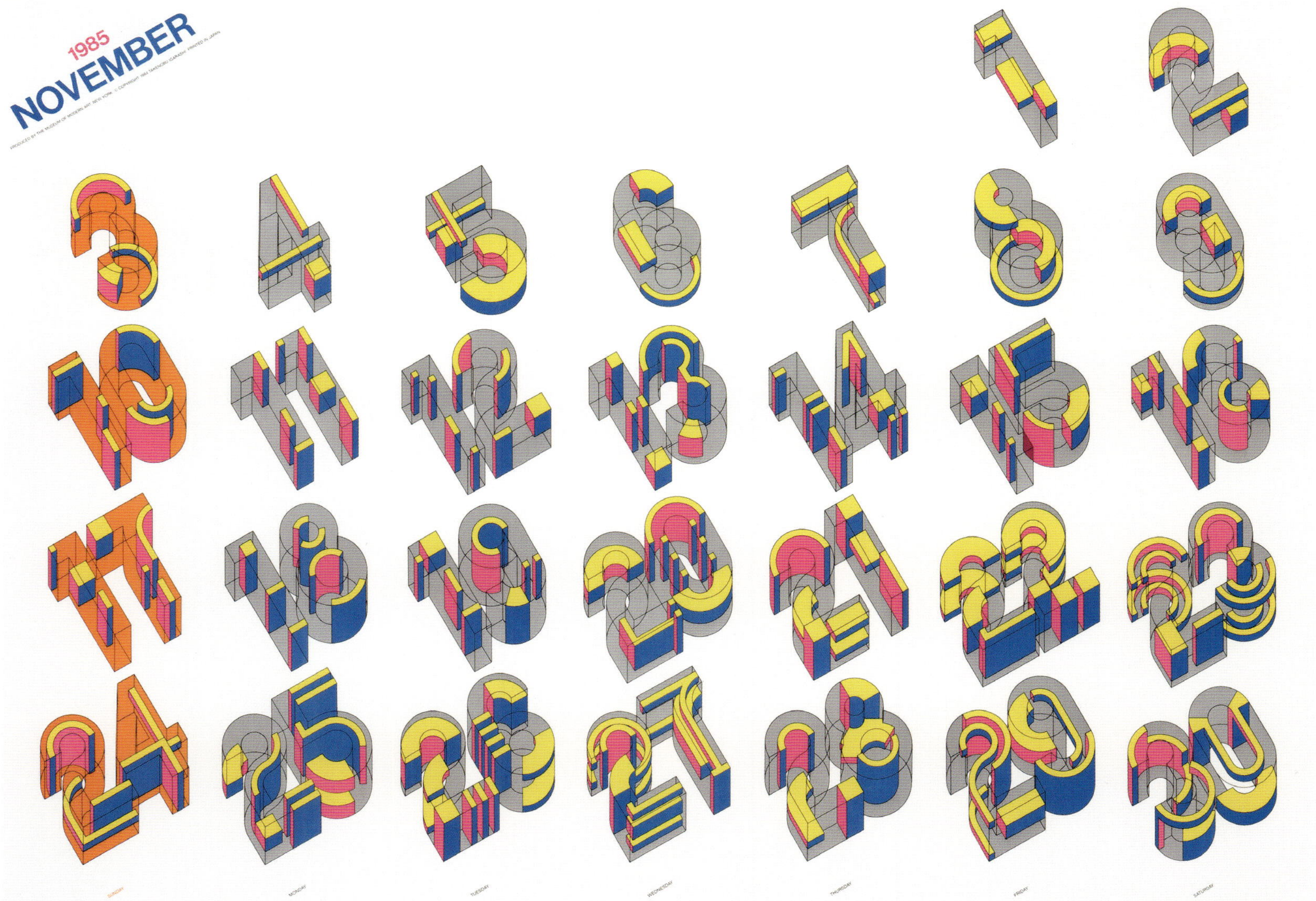

1-69 March, 1988
1-70 November, 1985

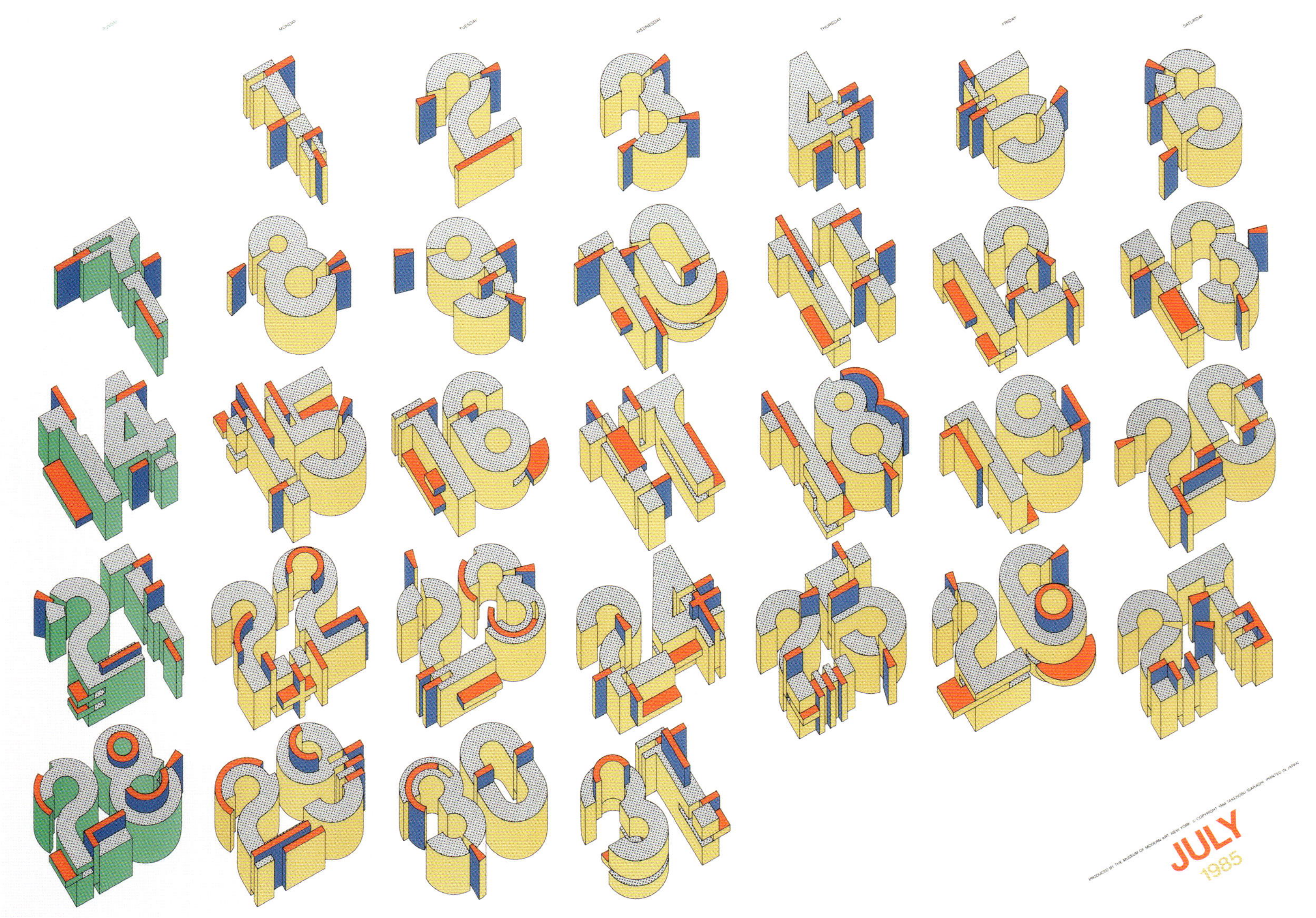

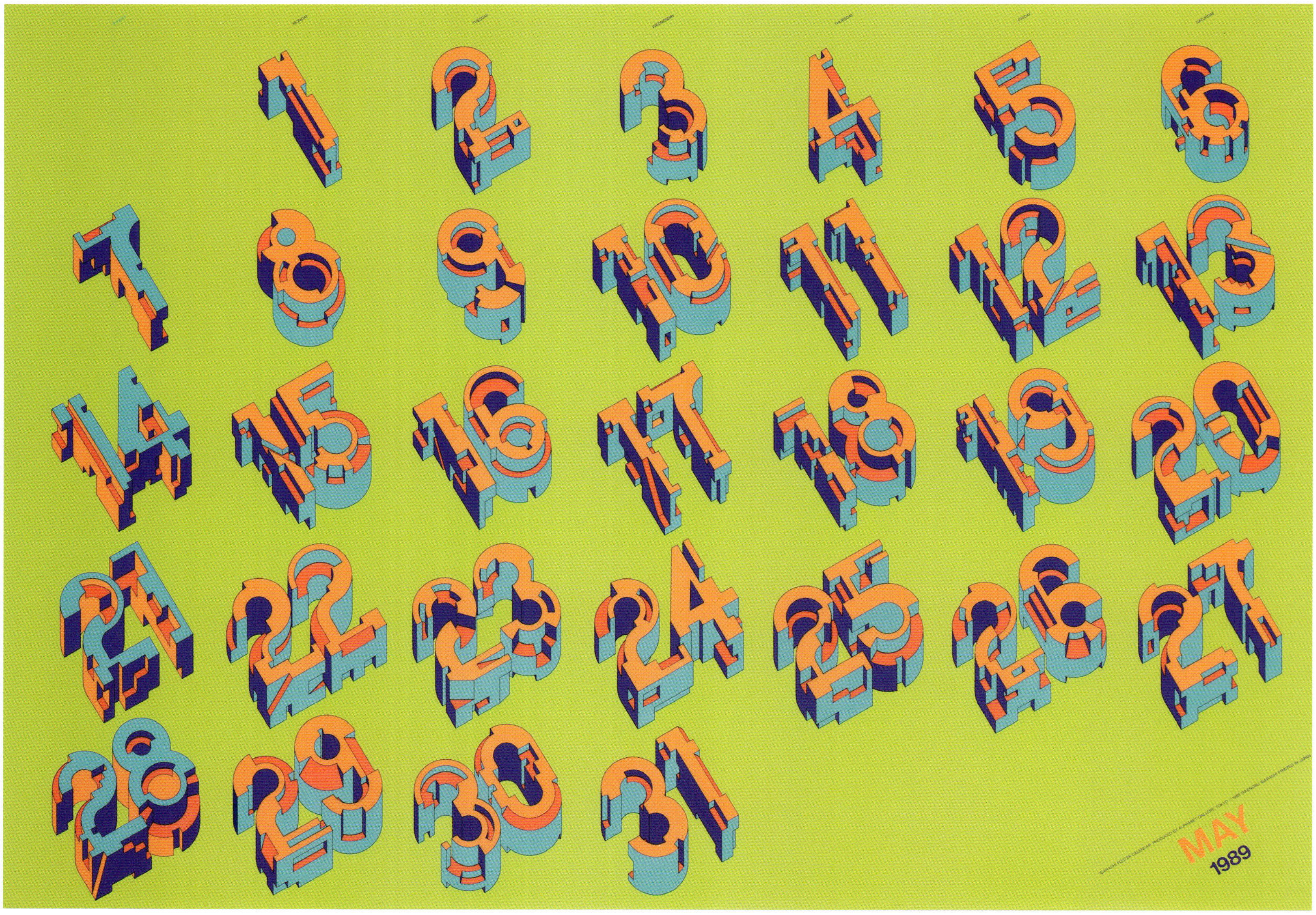

1-71 July, 1985
1-72 May, 1989

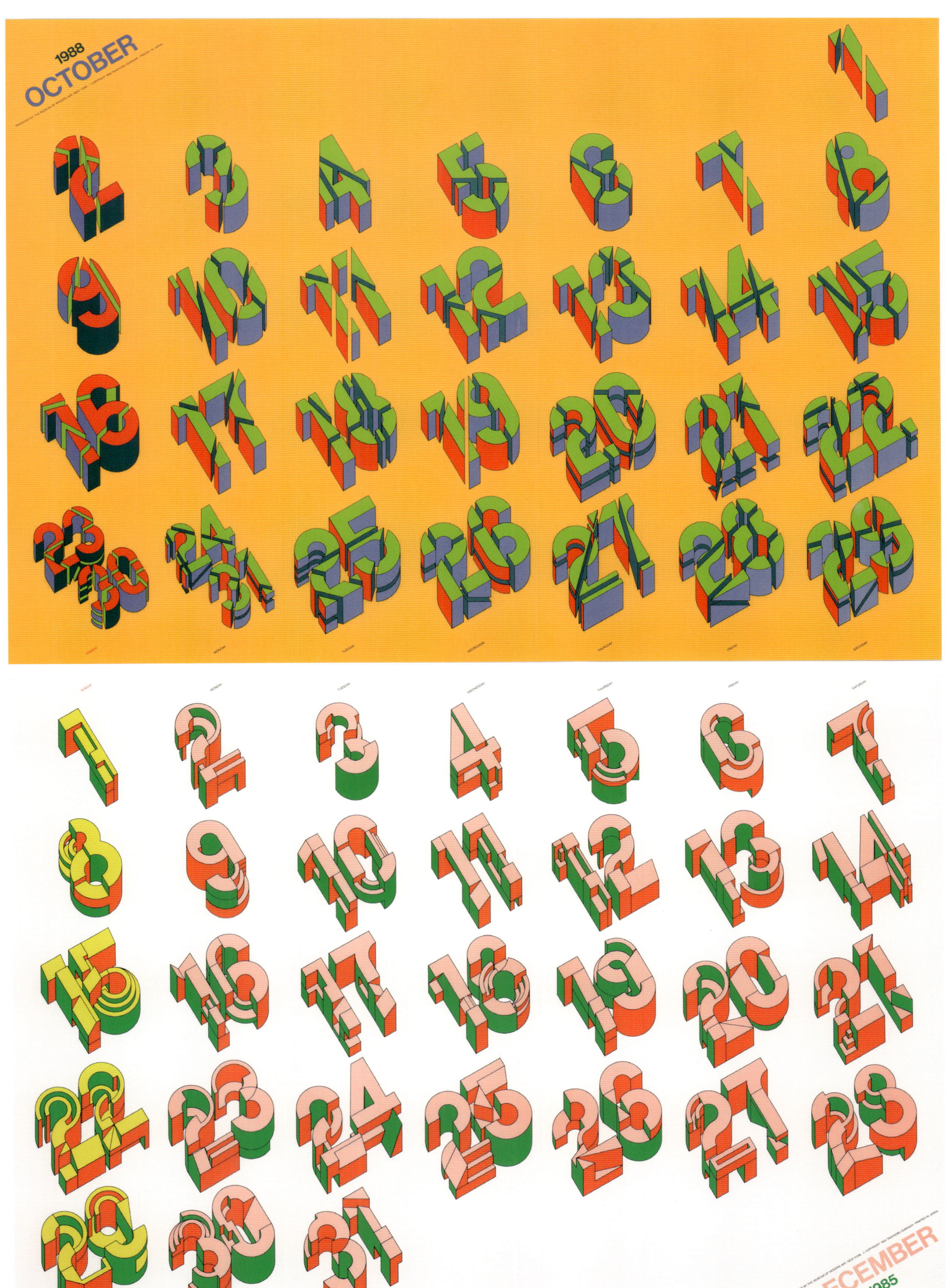

1-73 October, 1988
1-74 December, 1985

Full Scale (p92-97) 1-75 September, 1989
1-76 April, 1988
1-77 June, 1984

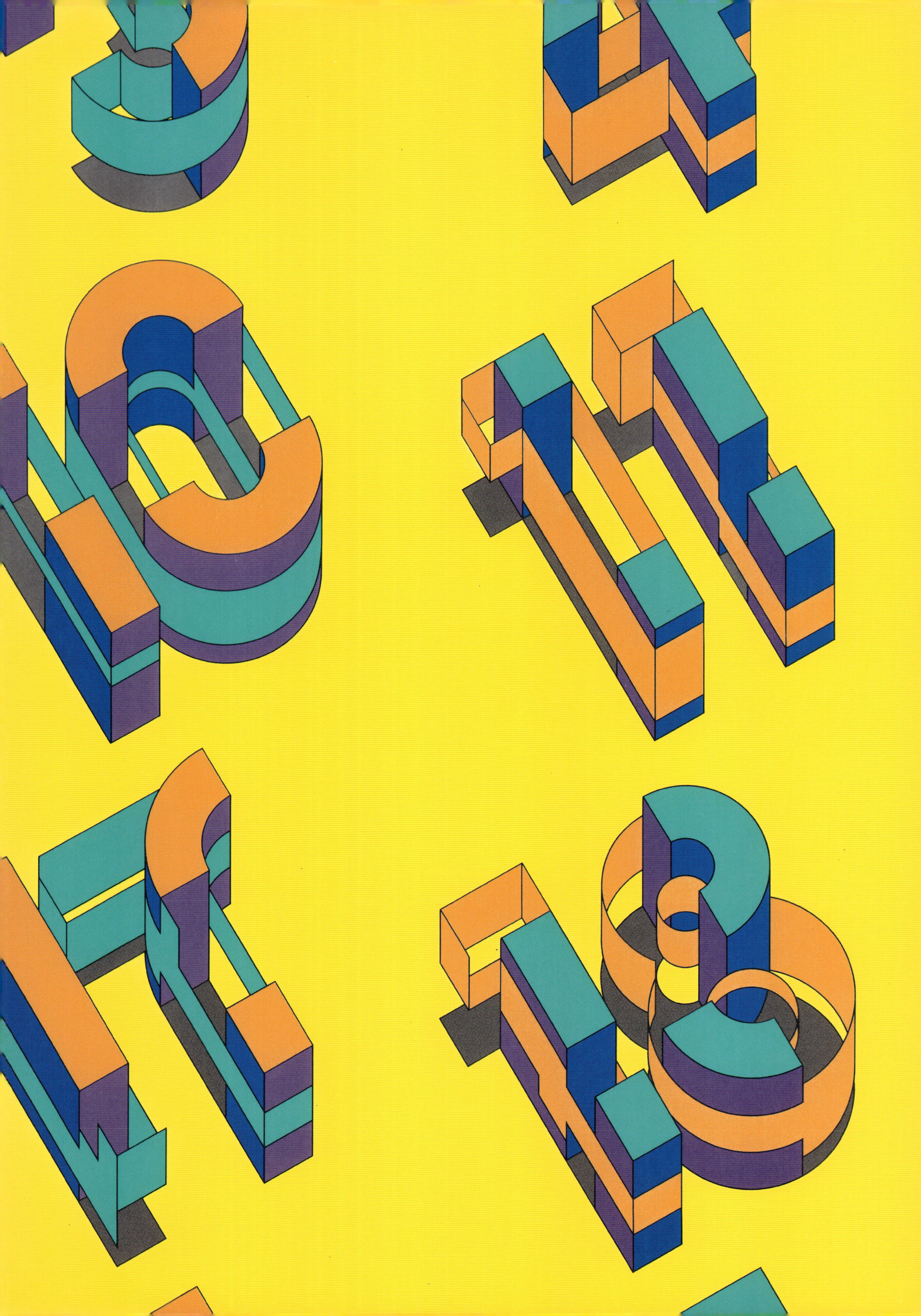

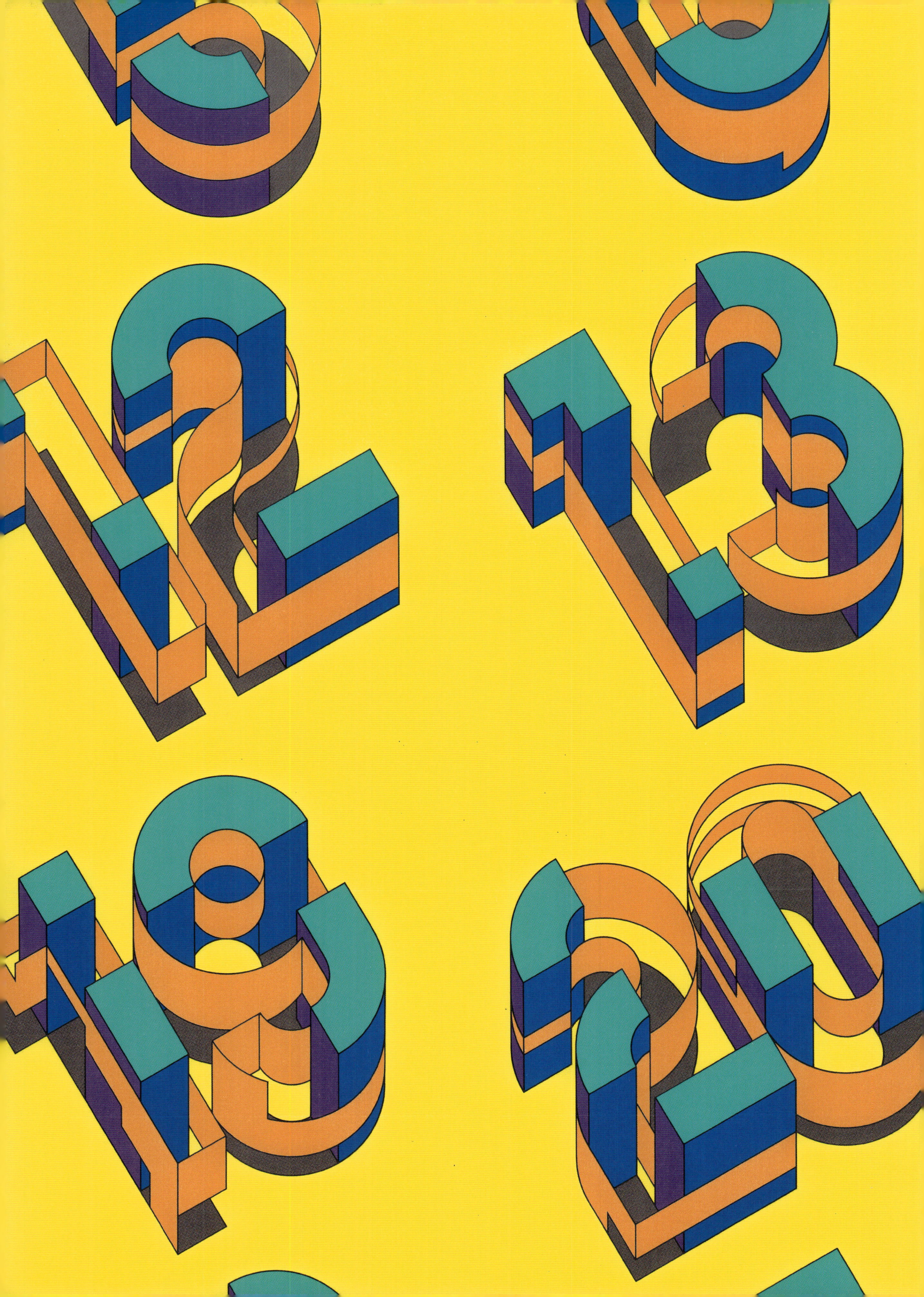

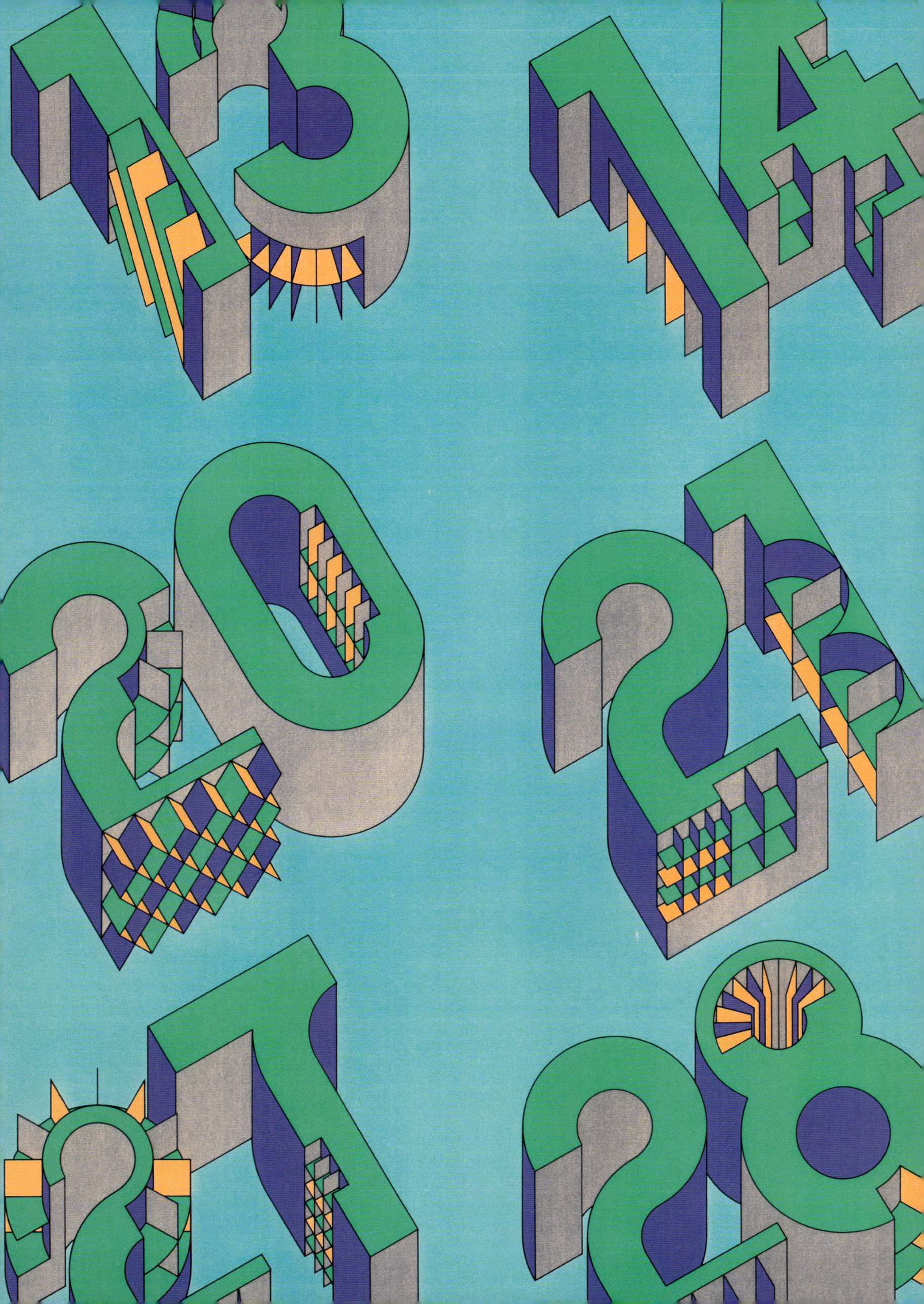

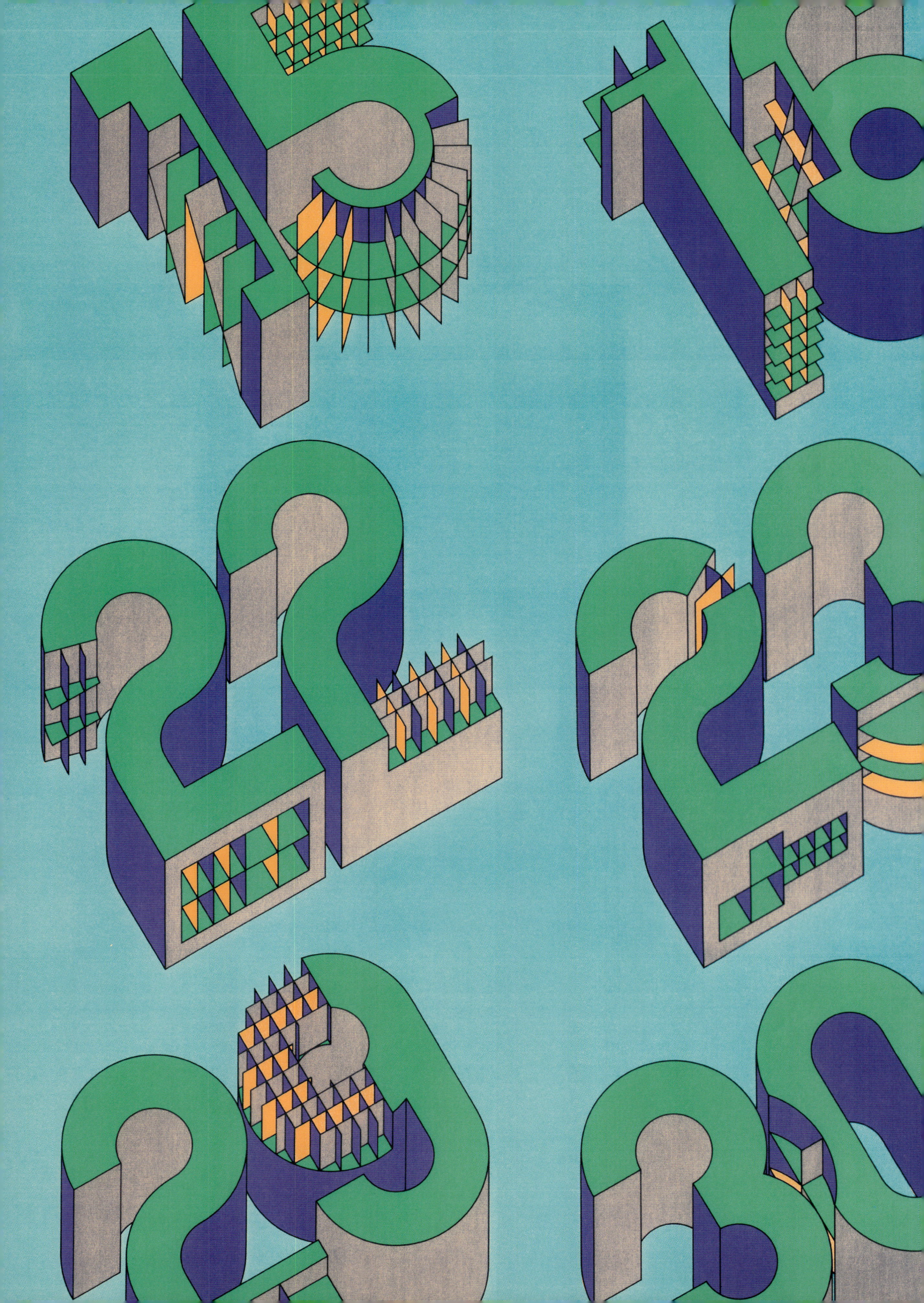

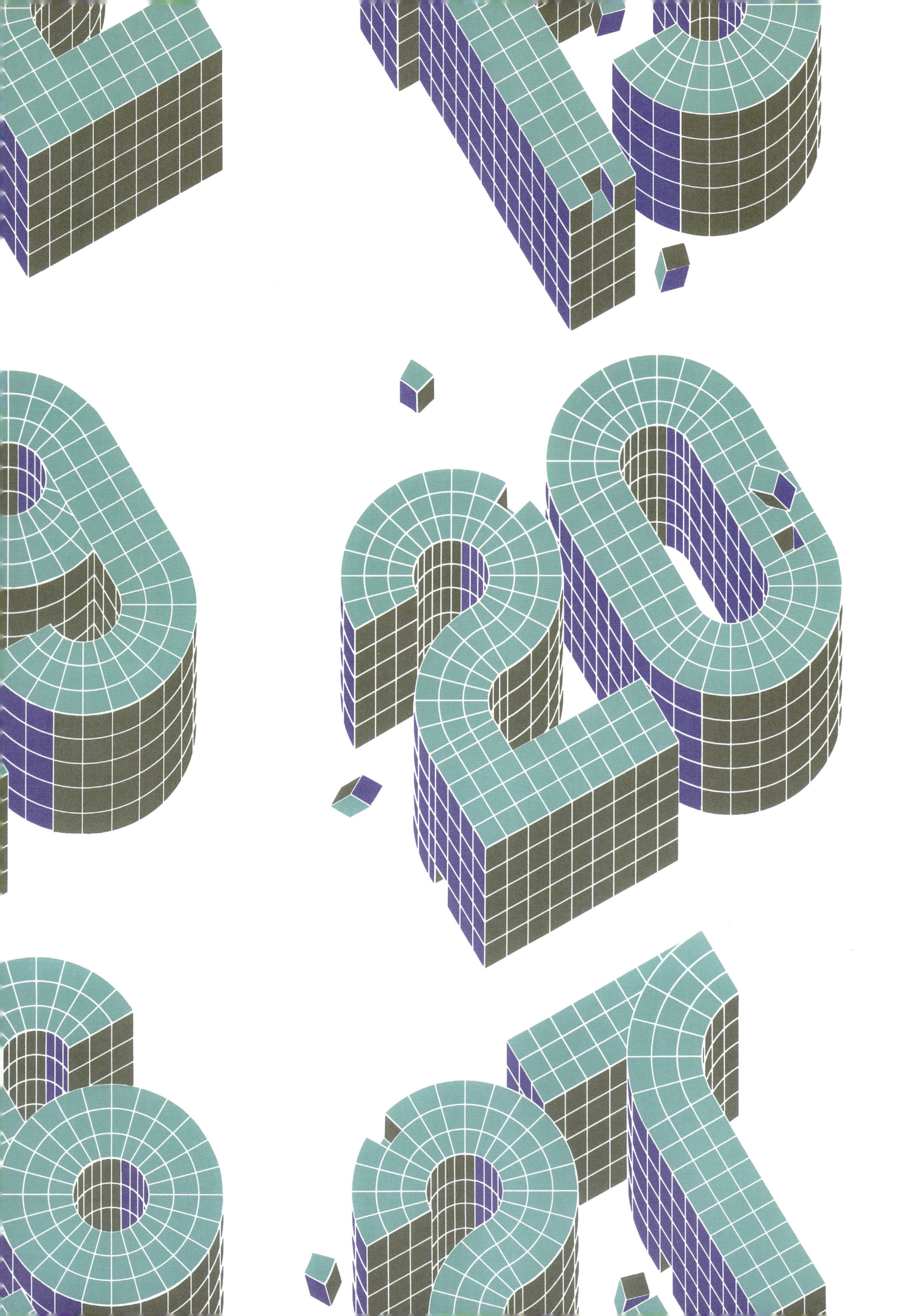

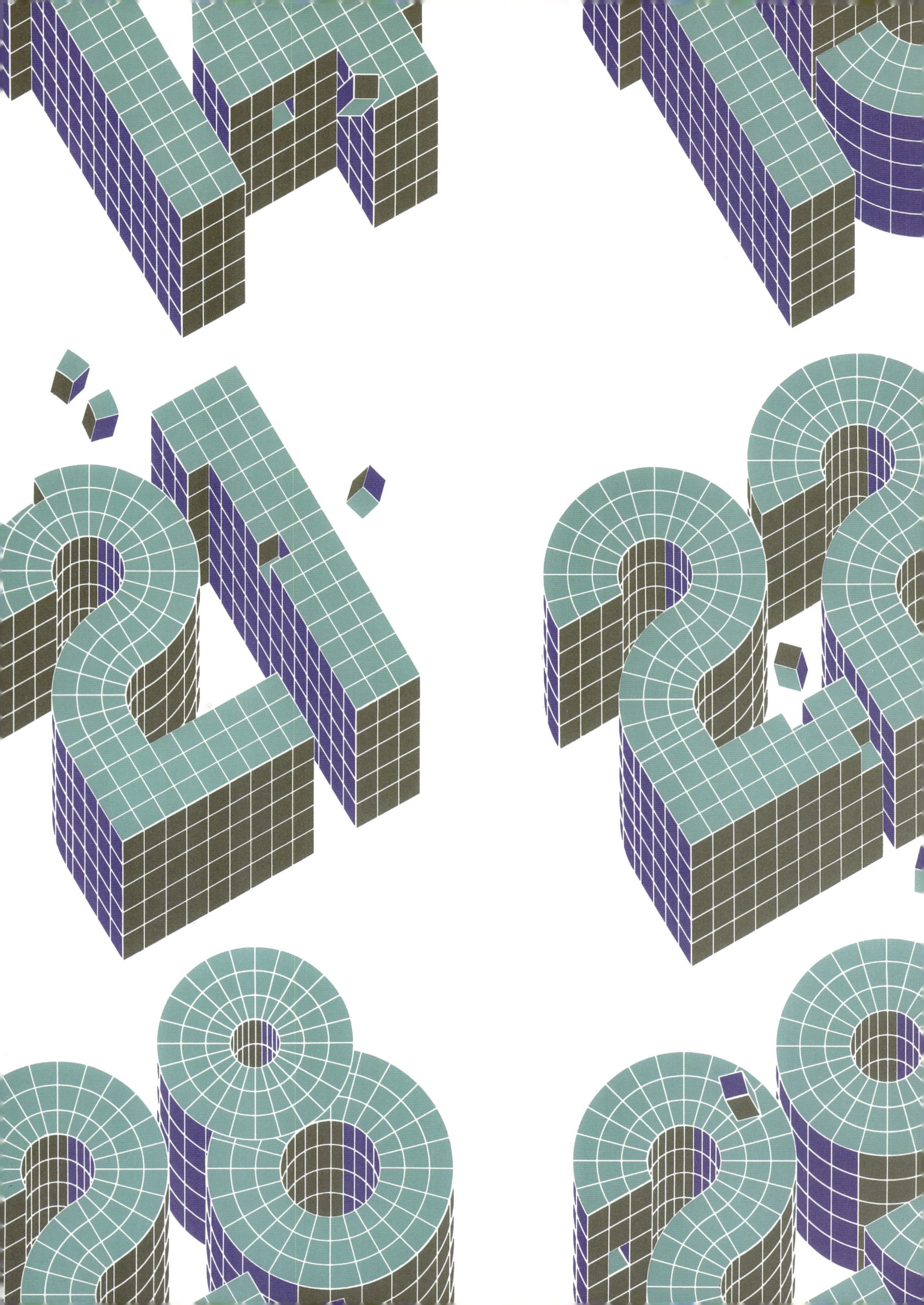

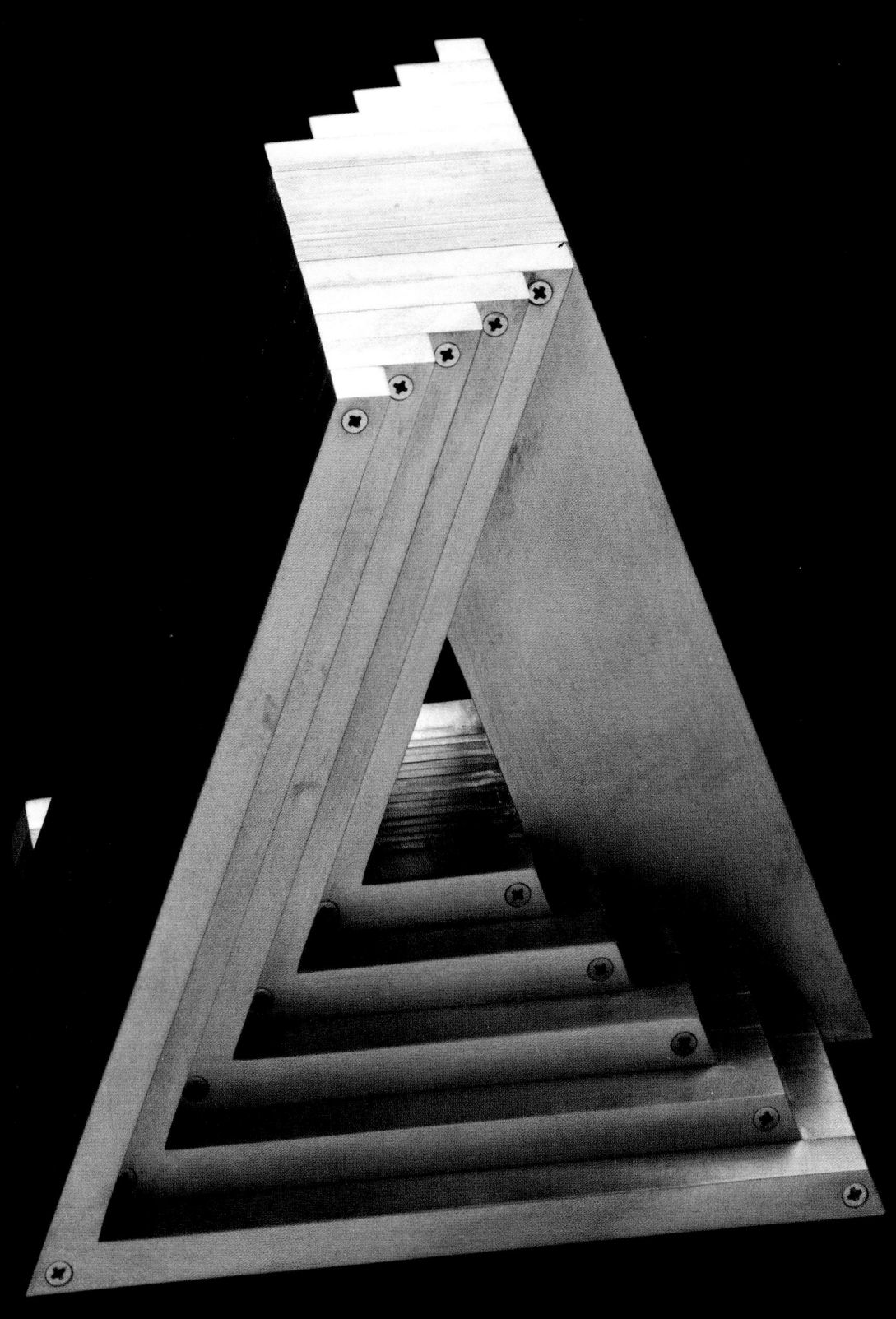

1-78 Aluminium Alphabet A, 1983

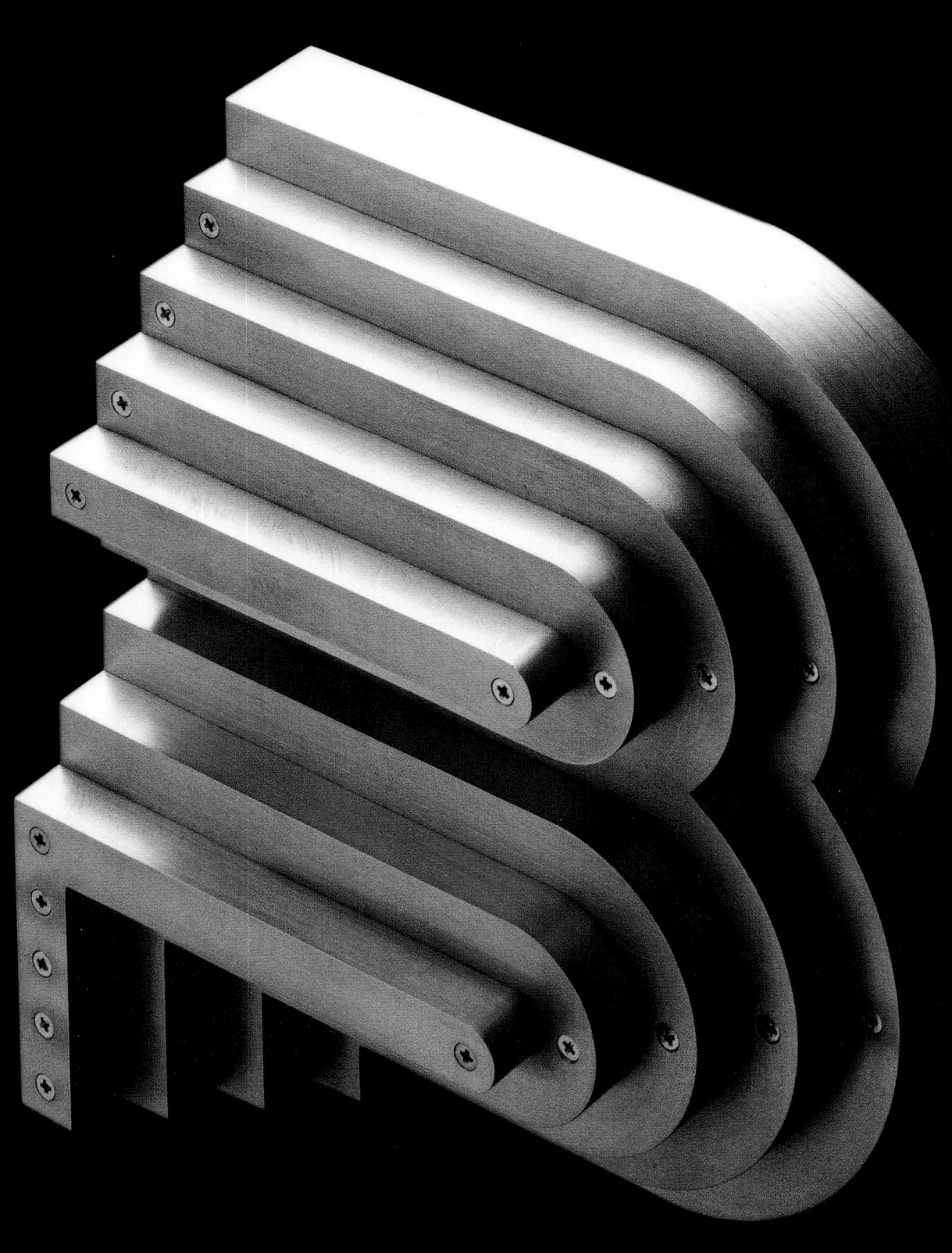

1-79 **Aluminium** Alphabet B, 1983

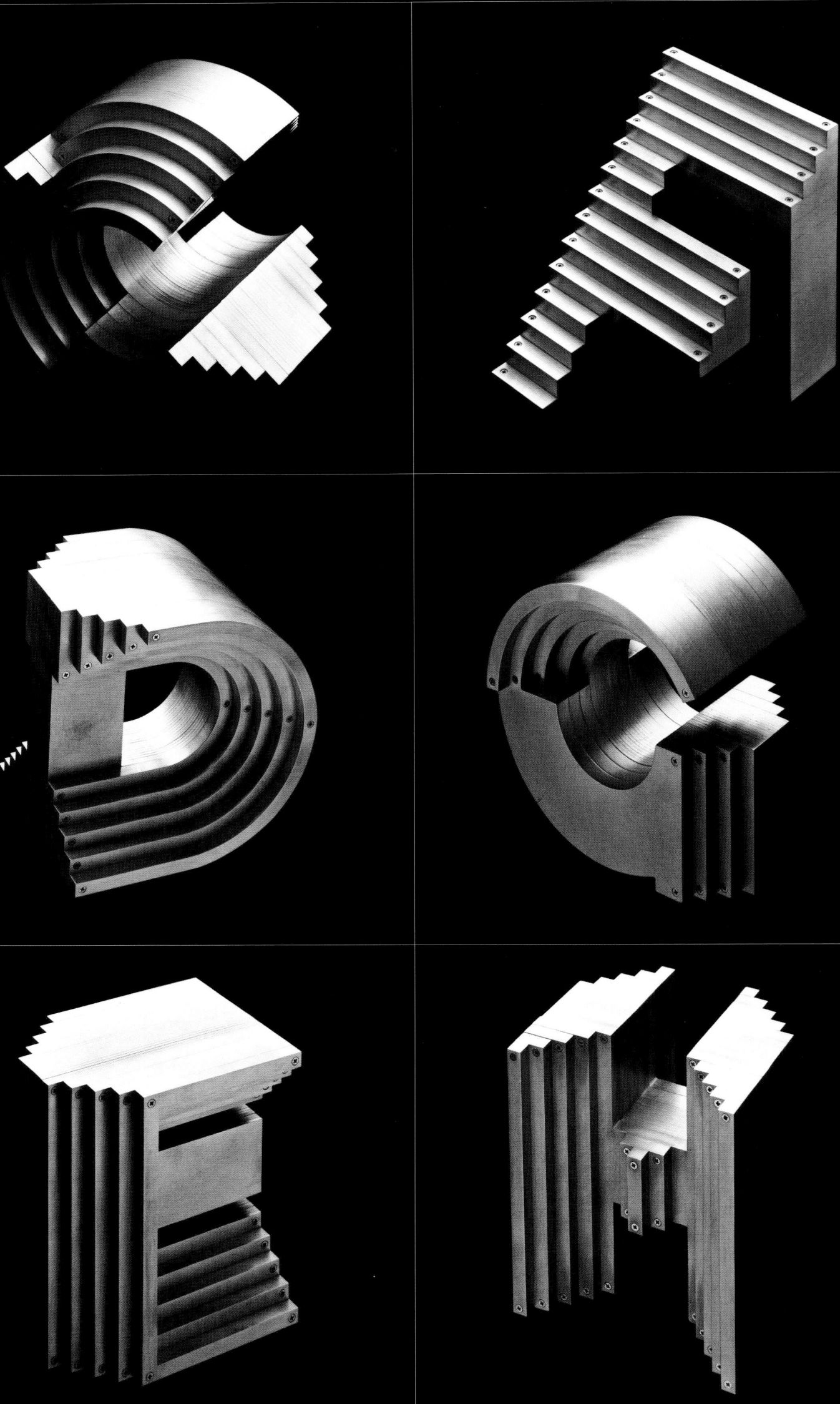

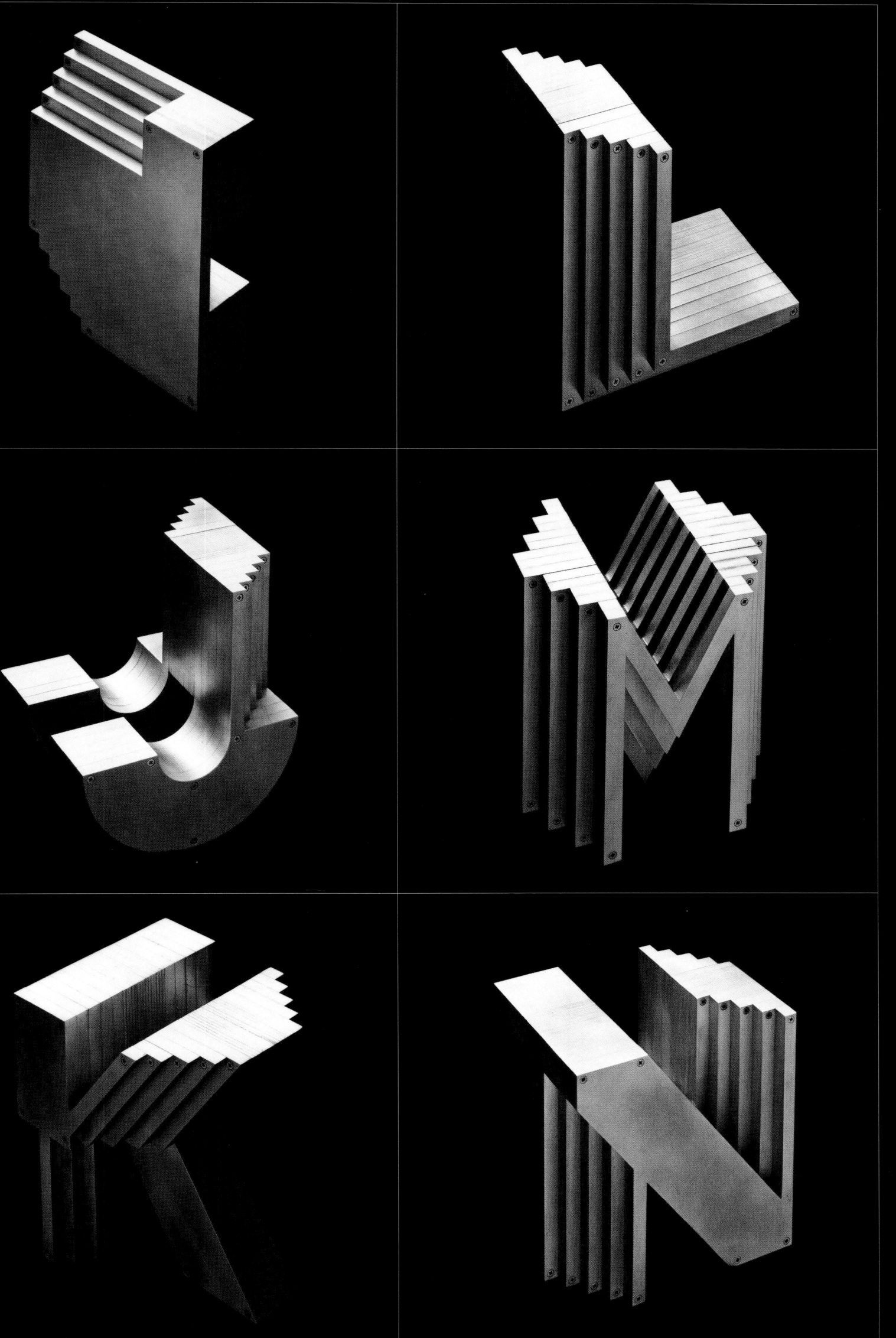

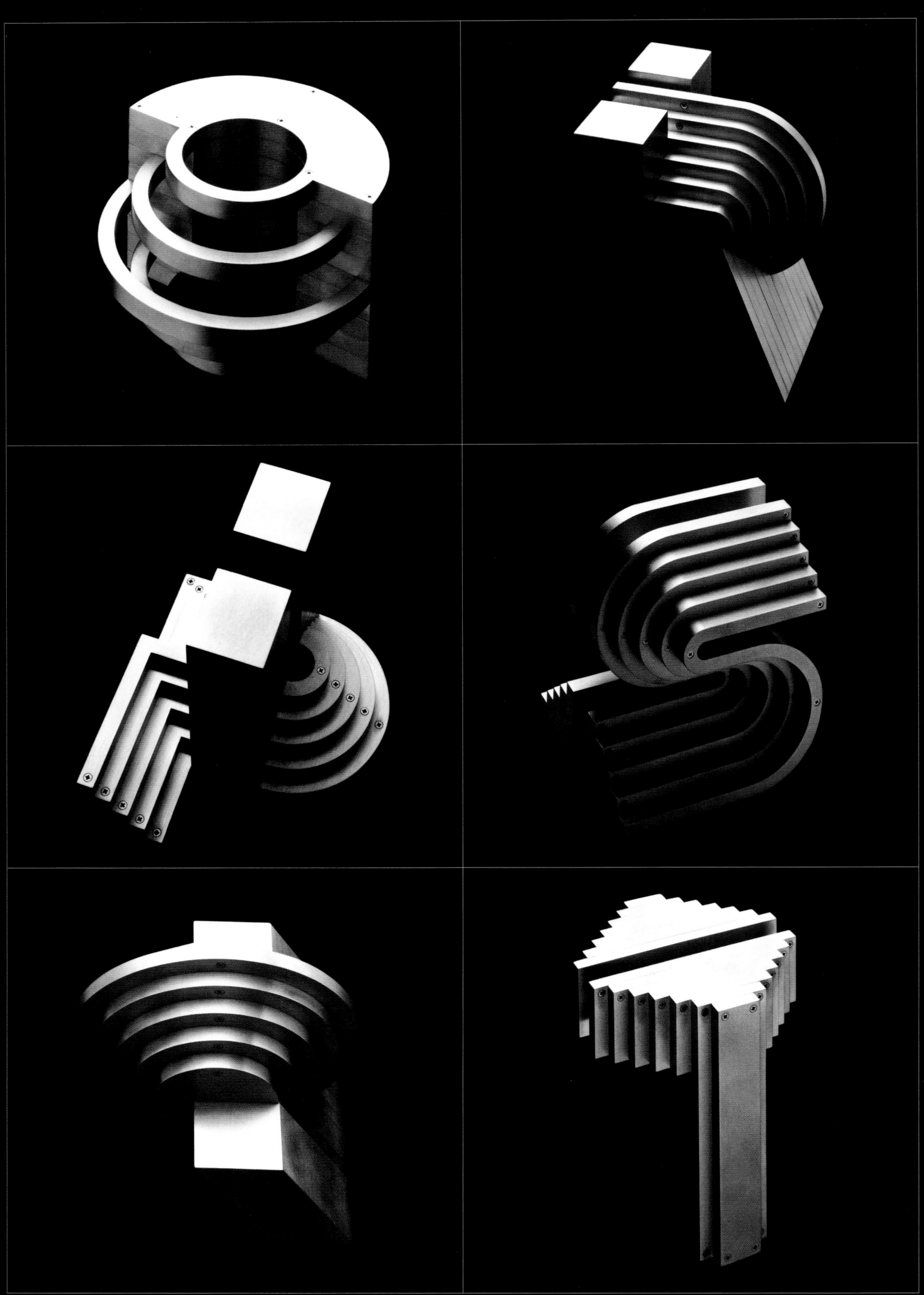

1-81 Aluminium Alphabets, O, P, Q, R, S, T, U, V, W, X, Y, Z, 1983

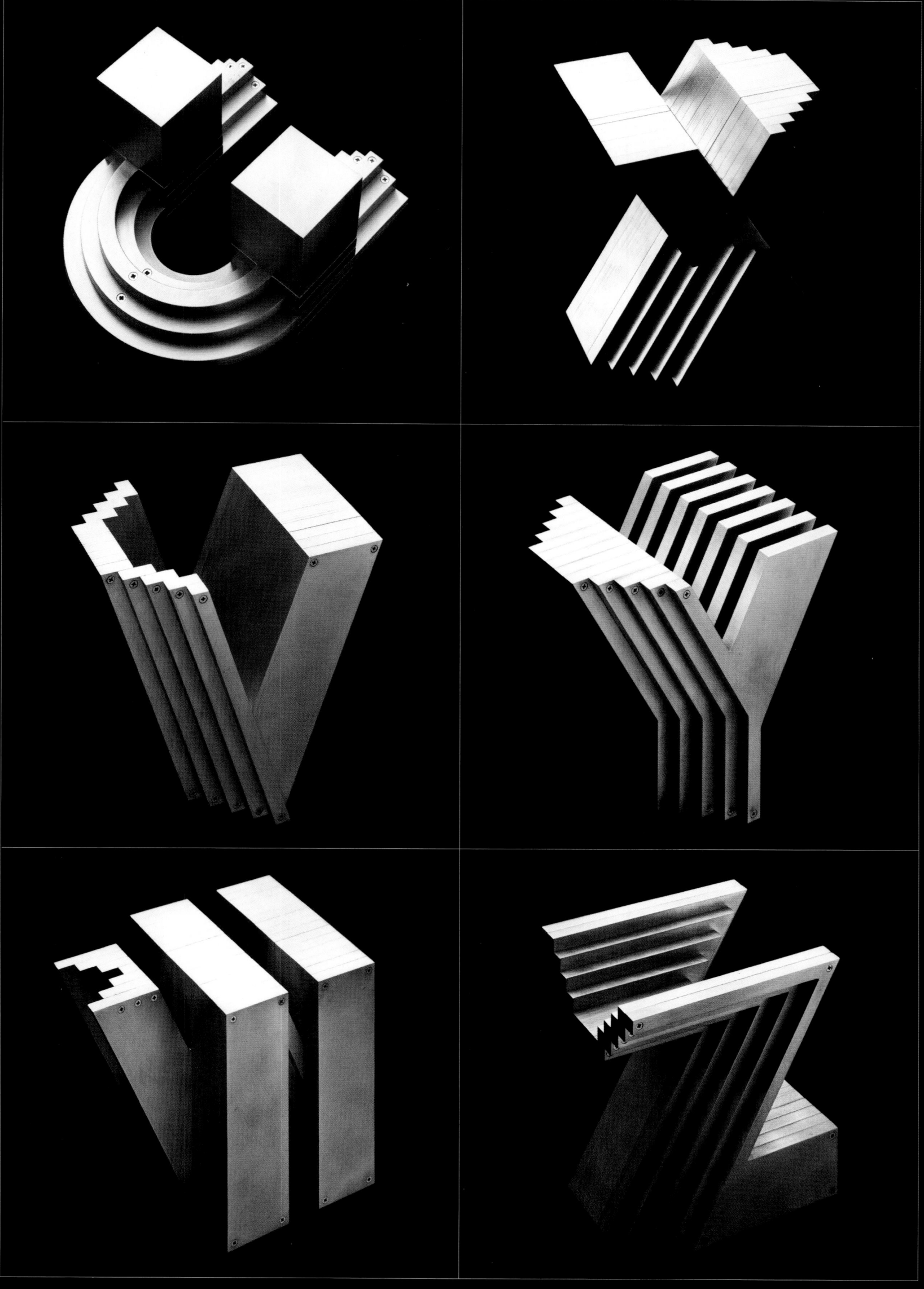

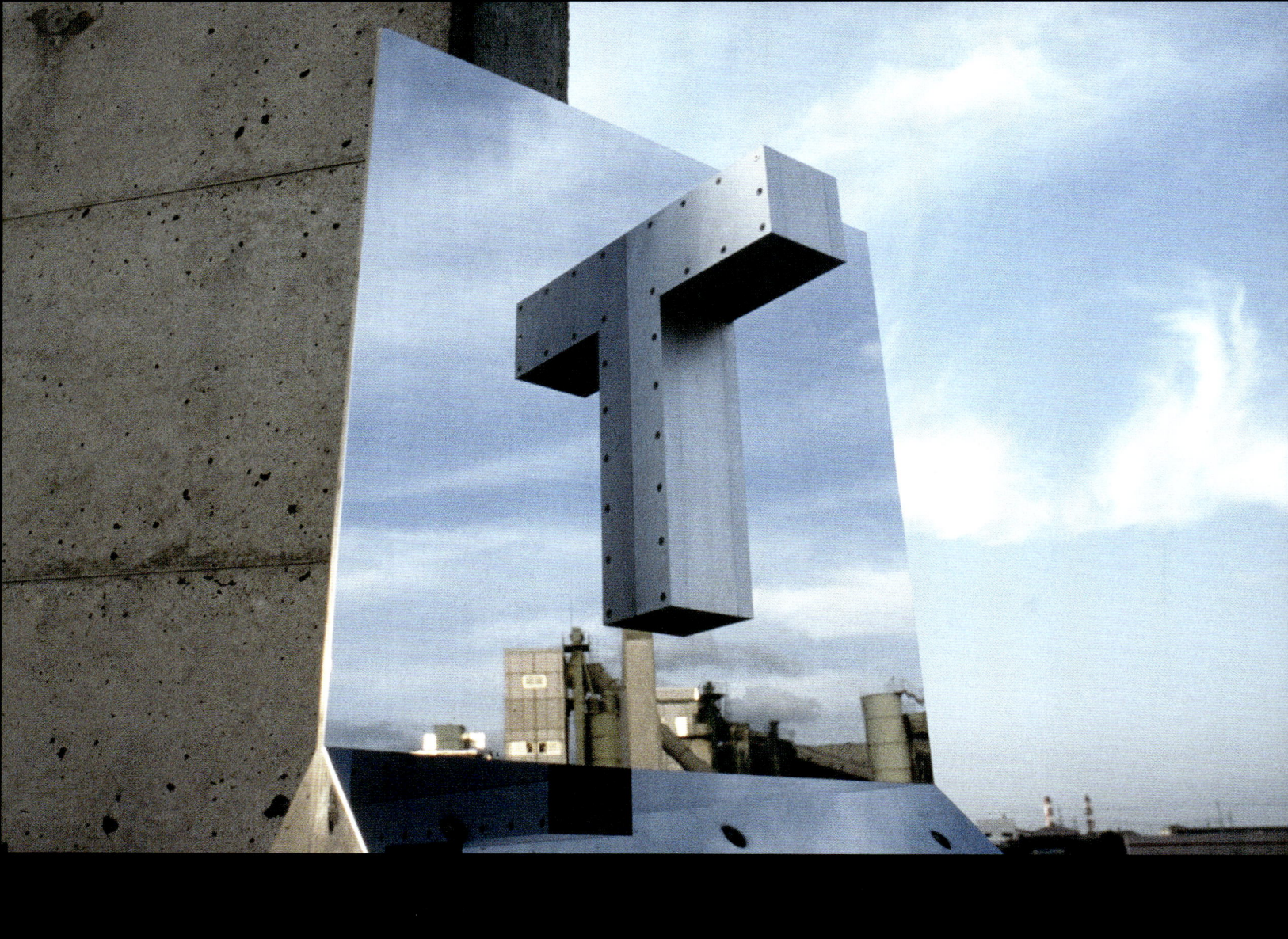

1-82 Mirror Alphabet T/Y, 1987
Same work, from different angles

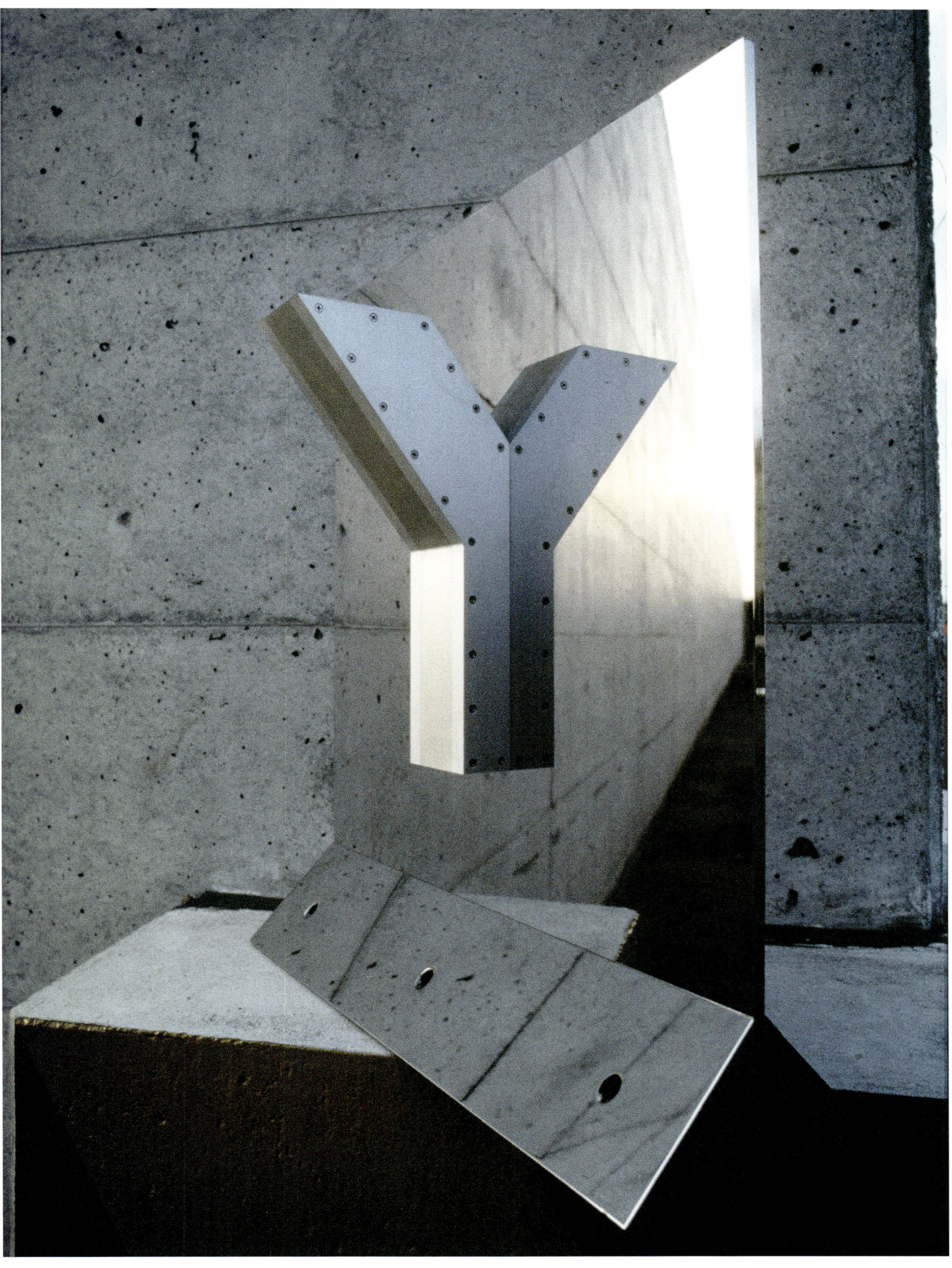

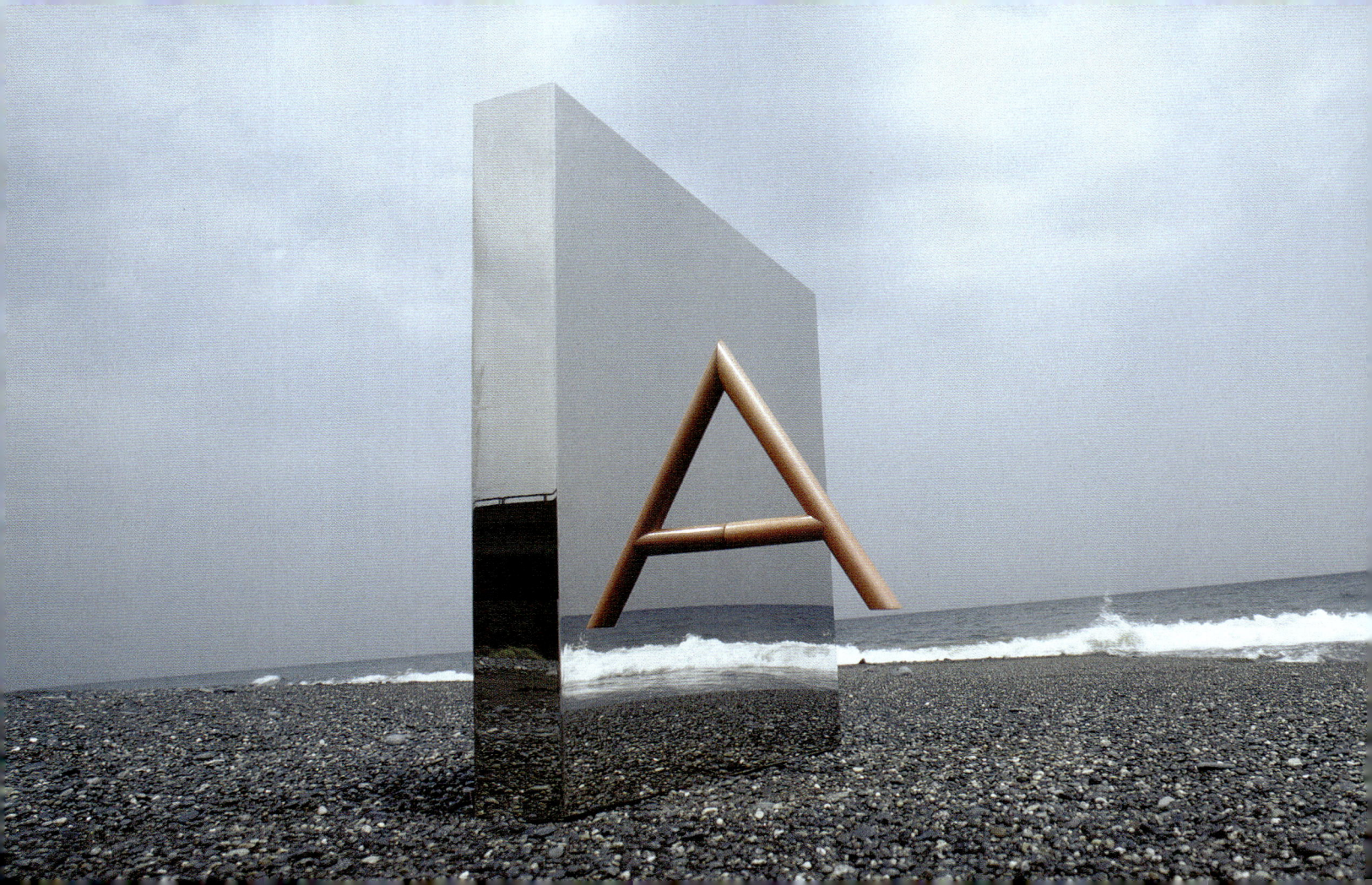

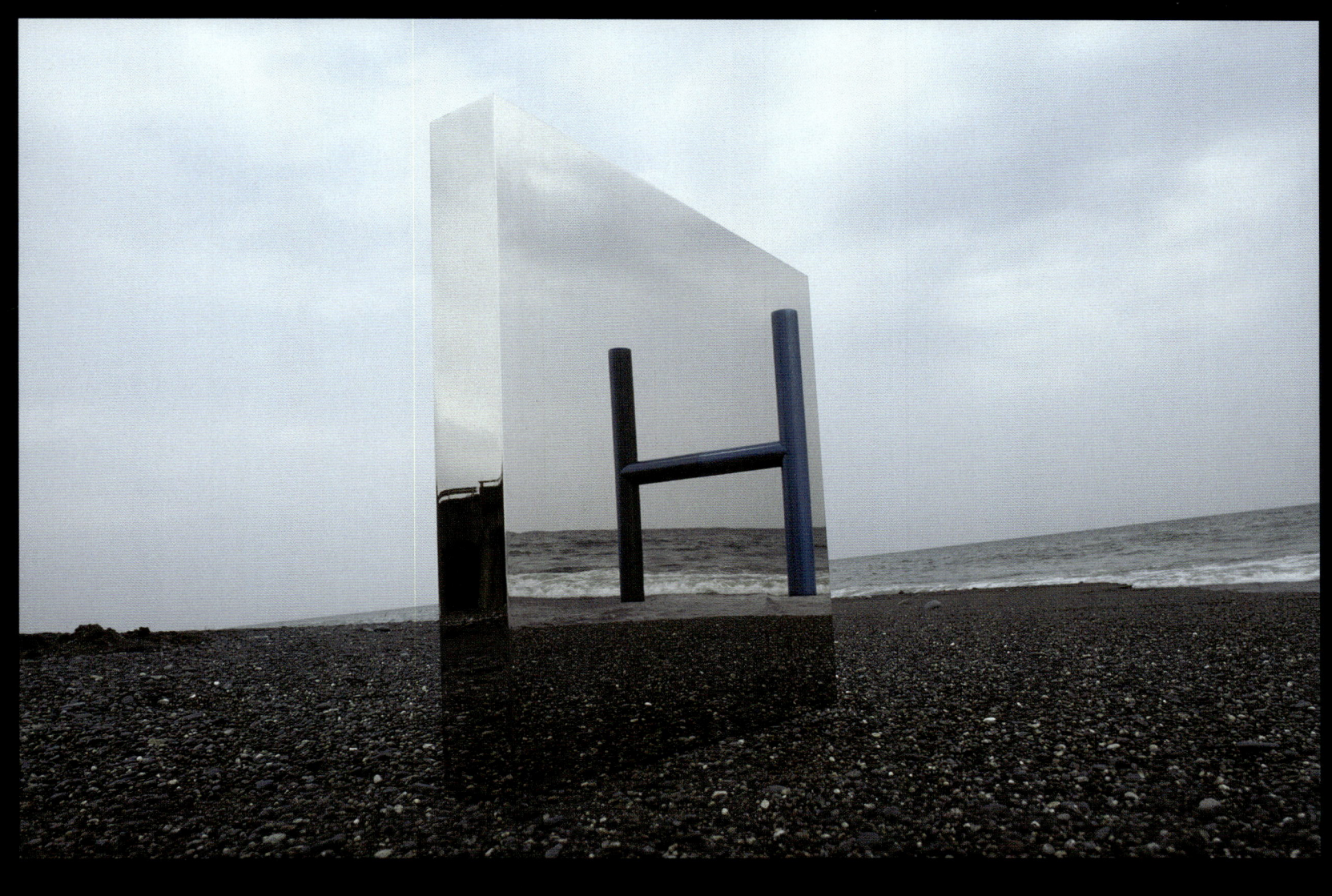

1-84 Mirror Alphabet H, 1981

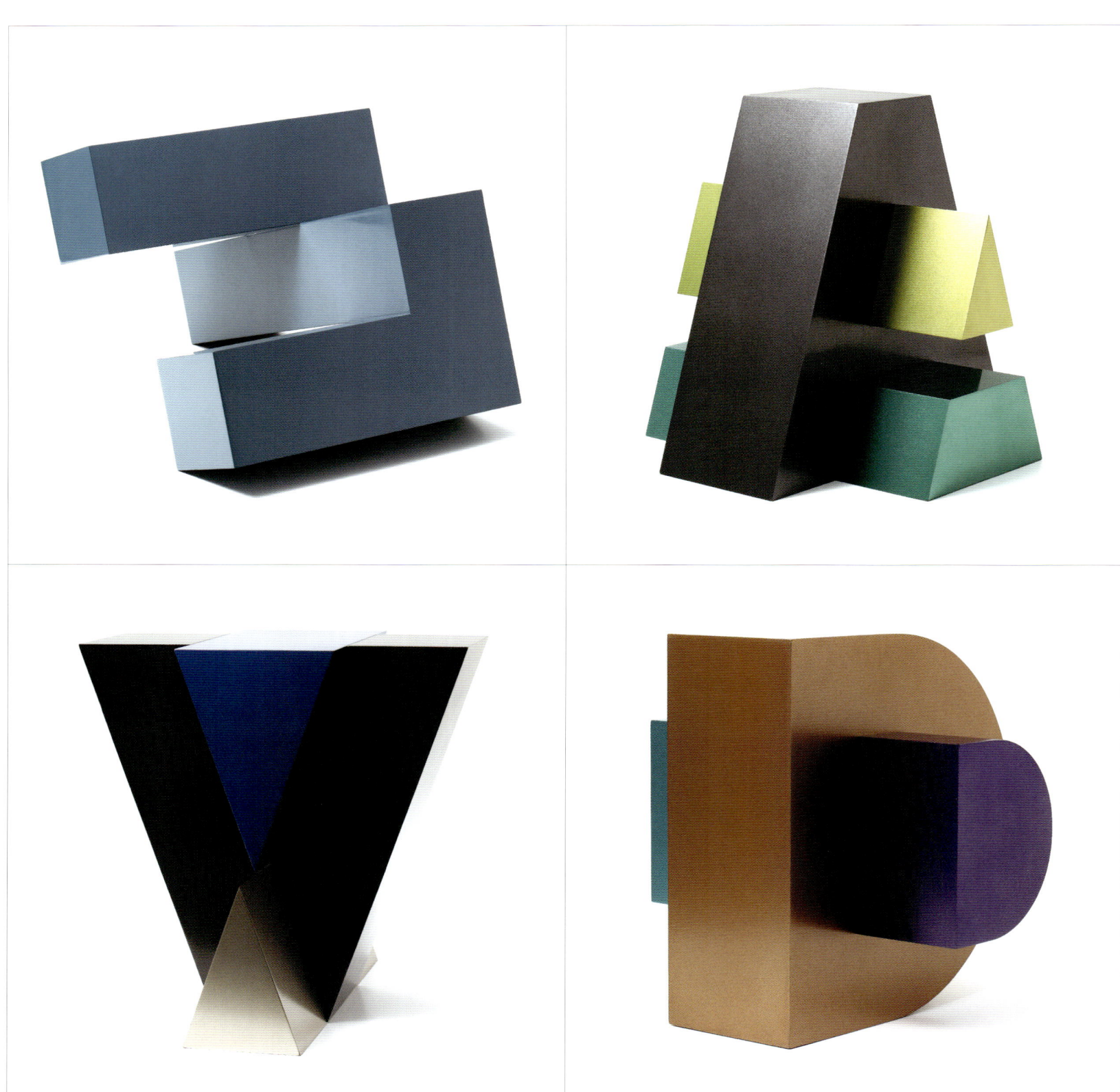

1-85 ABS Resin Alphabet F, 1981

1-86 ABS Resin Alphabet V, 1981

1-87 ABS Resin Alphabet A, 1981

1-88 ABS Resin Alphabet D, 1981

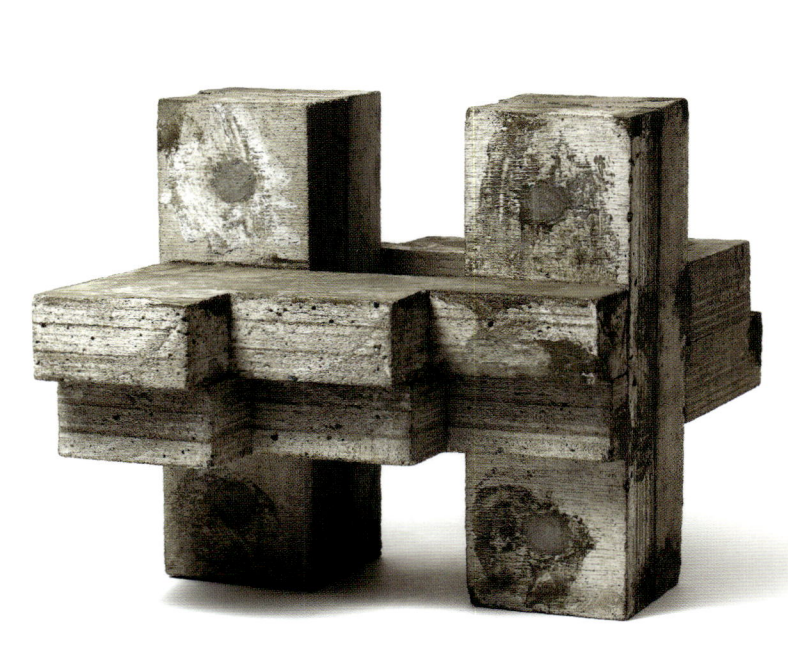
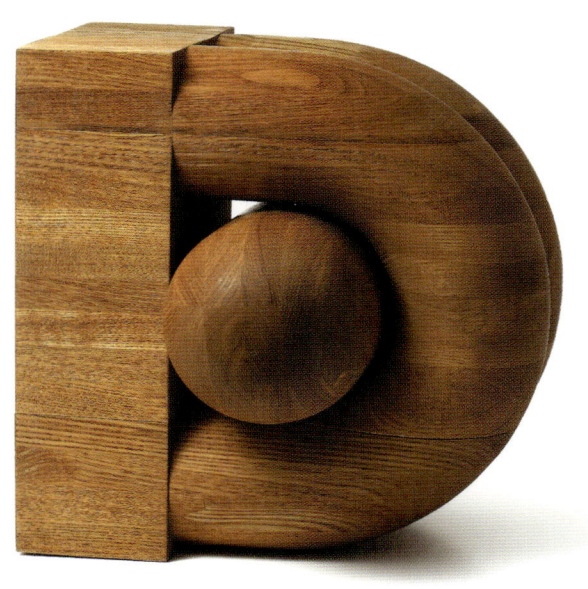
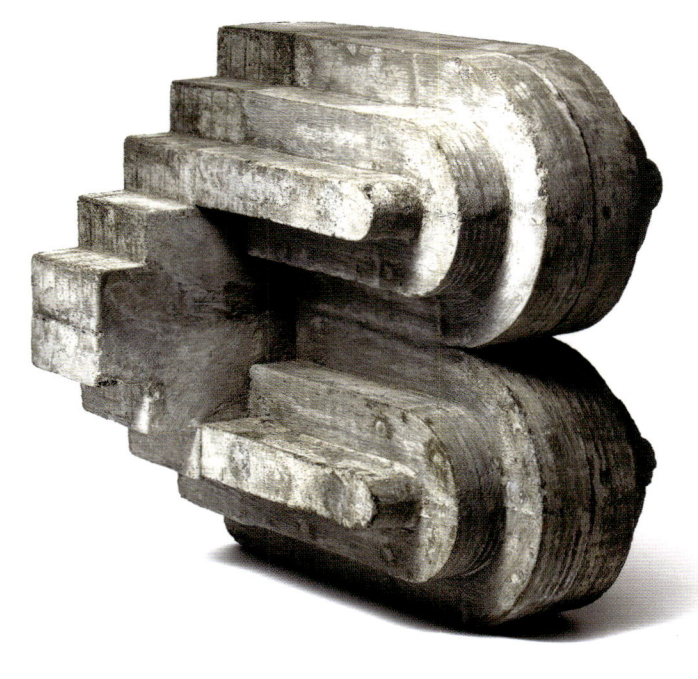
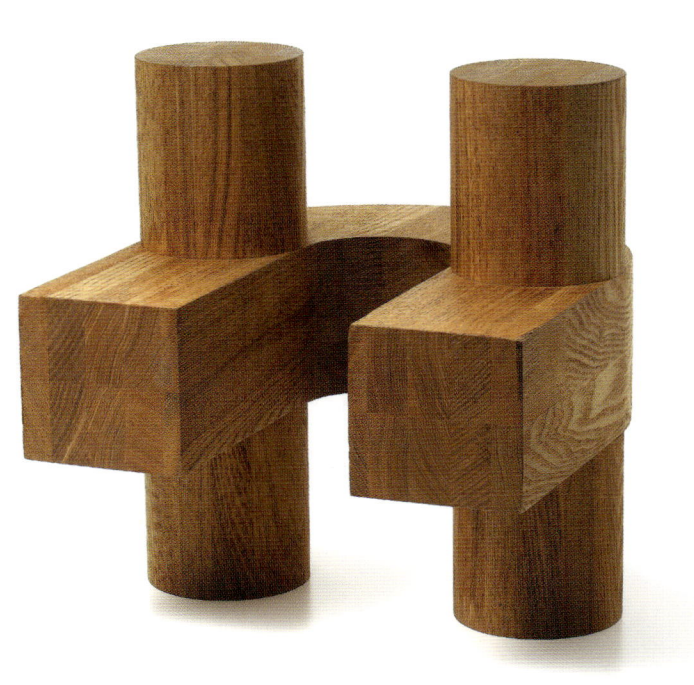

1-89 Concrete Alphabet H, 1981

1-90 Concrete Alphabet B, 1981

1-91 Wooden Alphabet D, 1981

1-92 Wooden Alphabet H, 1981

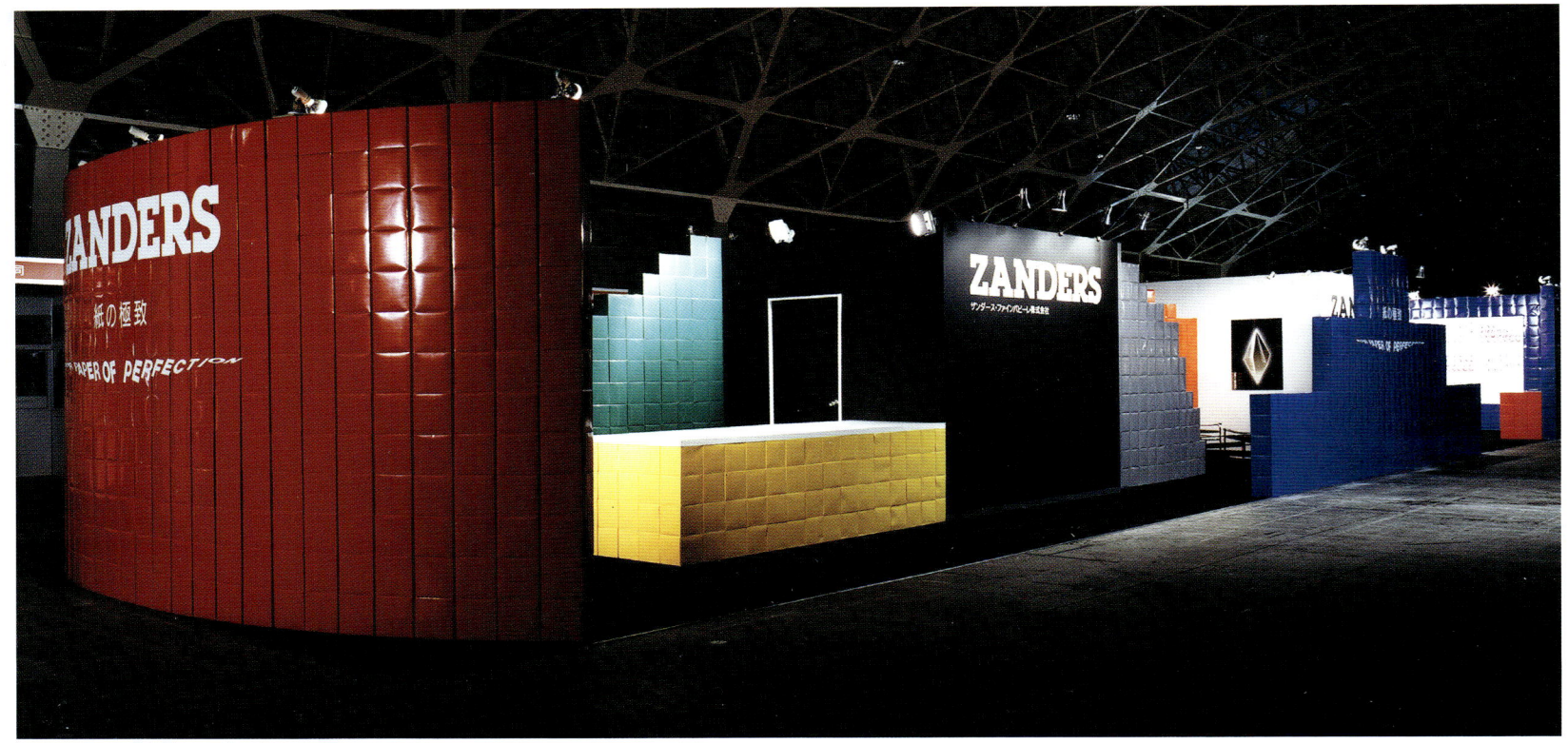

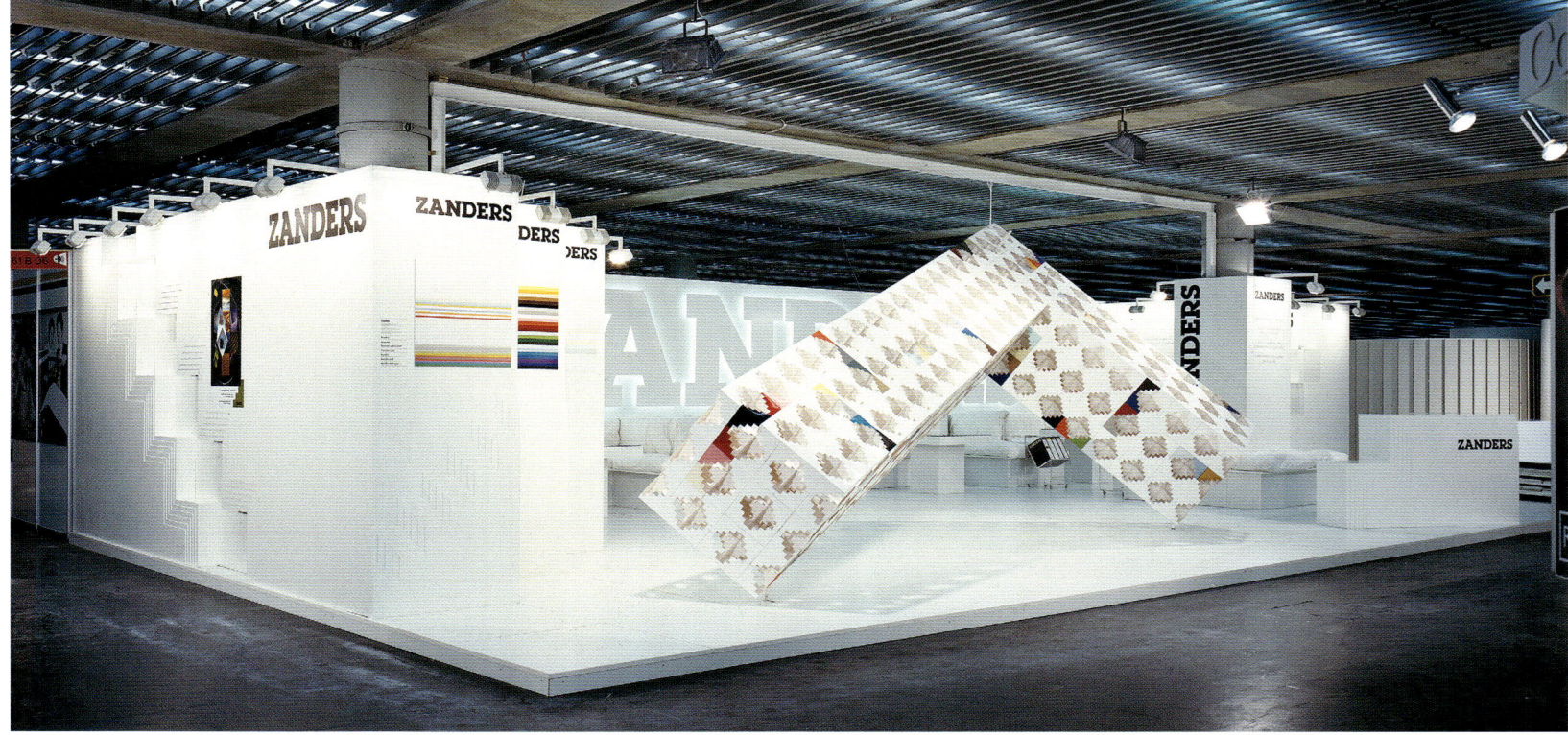

1-93 Exhibition Stand
Expo Paper Asia in Tokyo
Zanders the Papermakers
Germany, 1989

1-94 Exhibition Stand
Düsseldorf DRUPA
International Trade Fair
Zanders the Papermakers
Germany, 1989

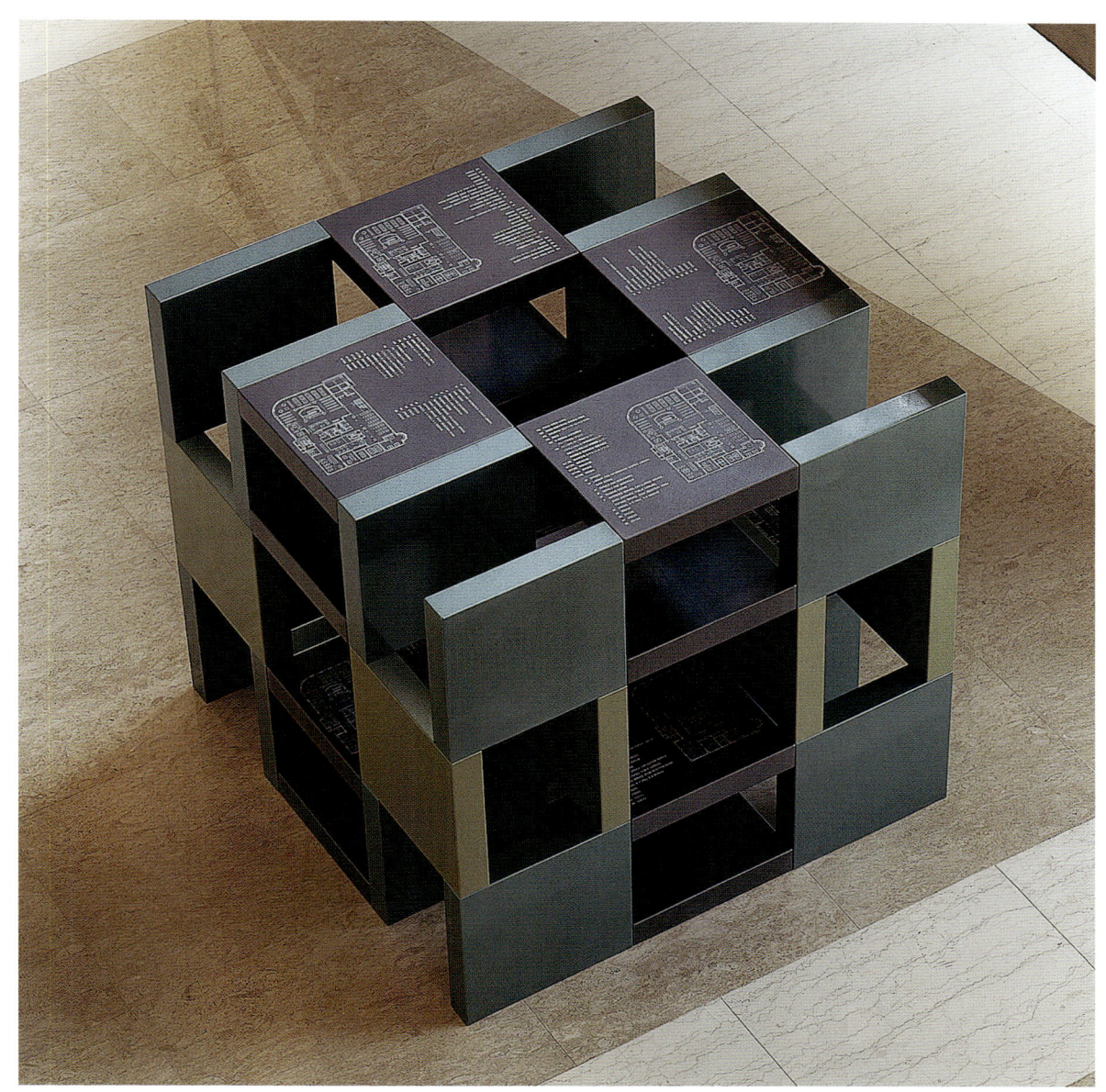

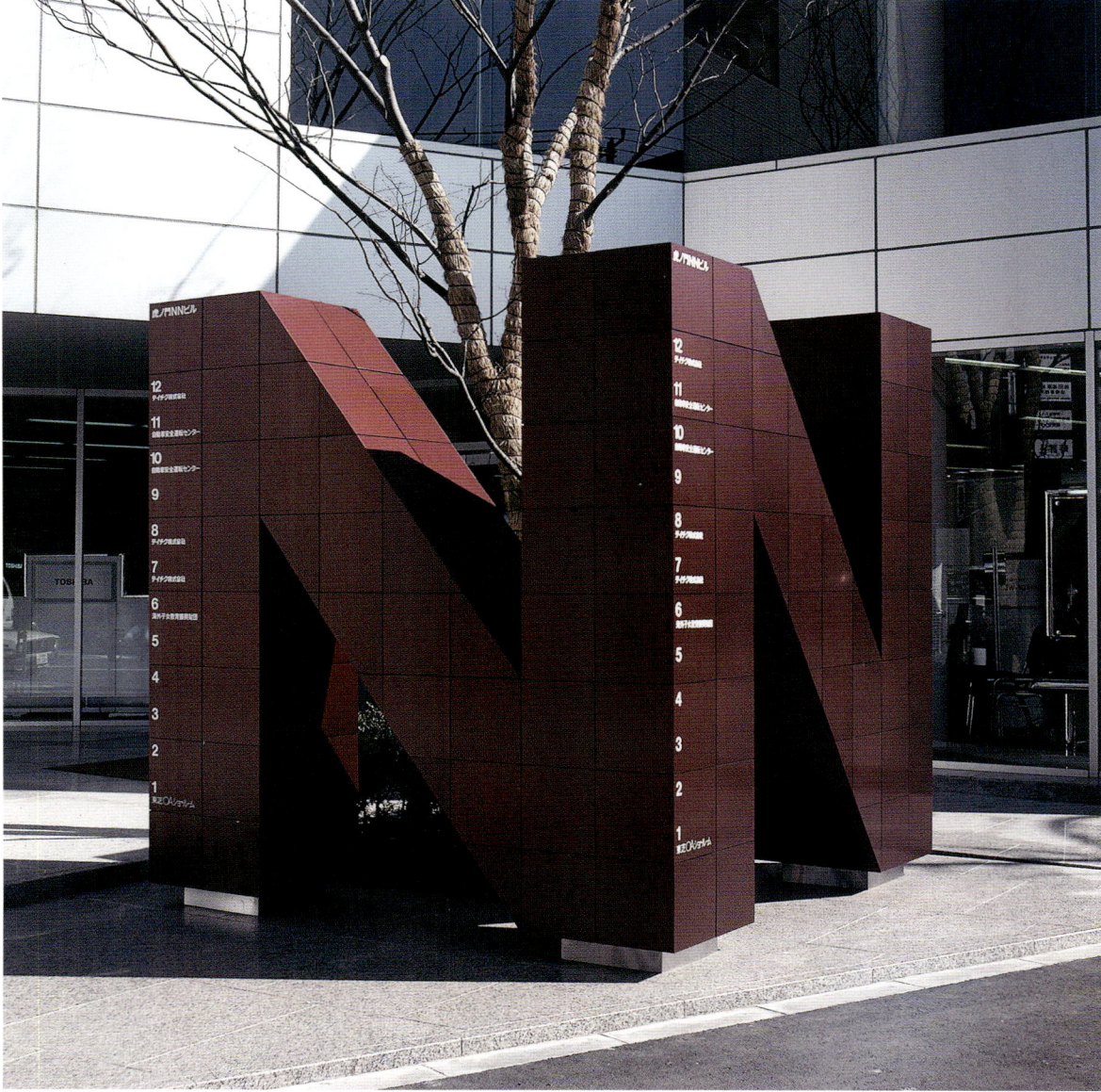

1-95 Library Sign
Keio University Mita Media Center
Tokyo, Japan, 1985

1-96 Directory Sign
Nippon Life Insurance Company
Toranomon NN Building
Tokyo, Japan, 1981

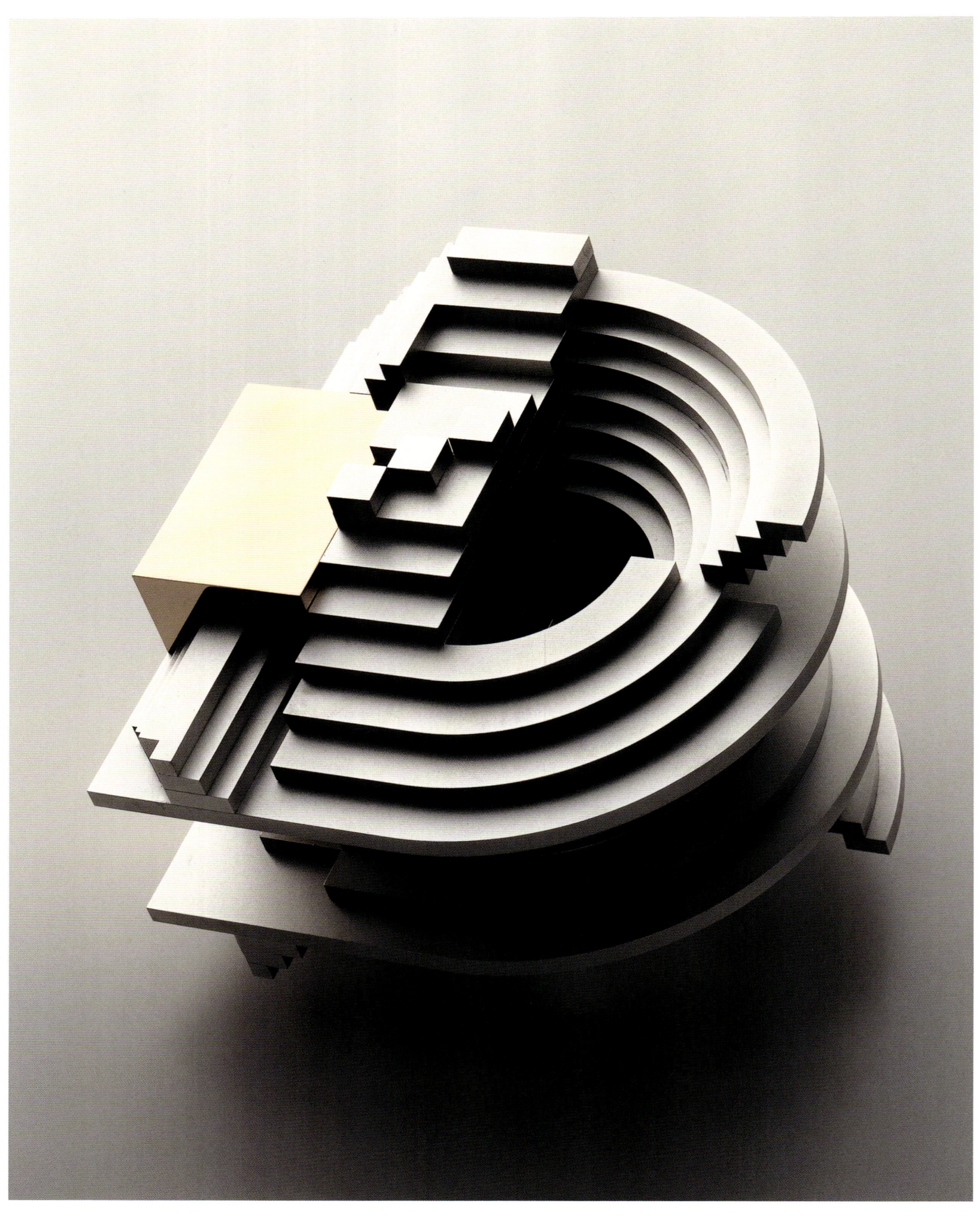

1-97 Sculpture D for a Magazine Cover
Domus, Italy, 1992

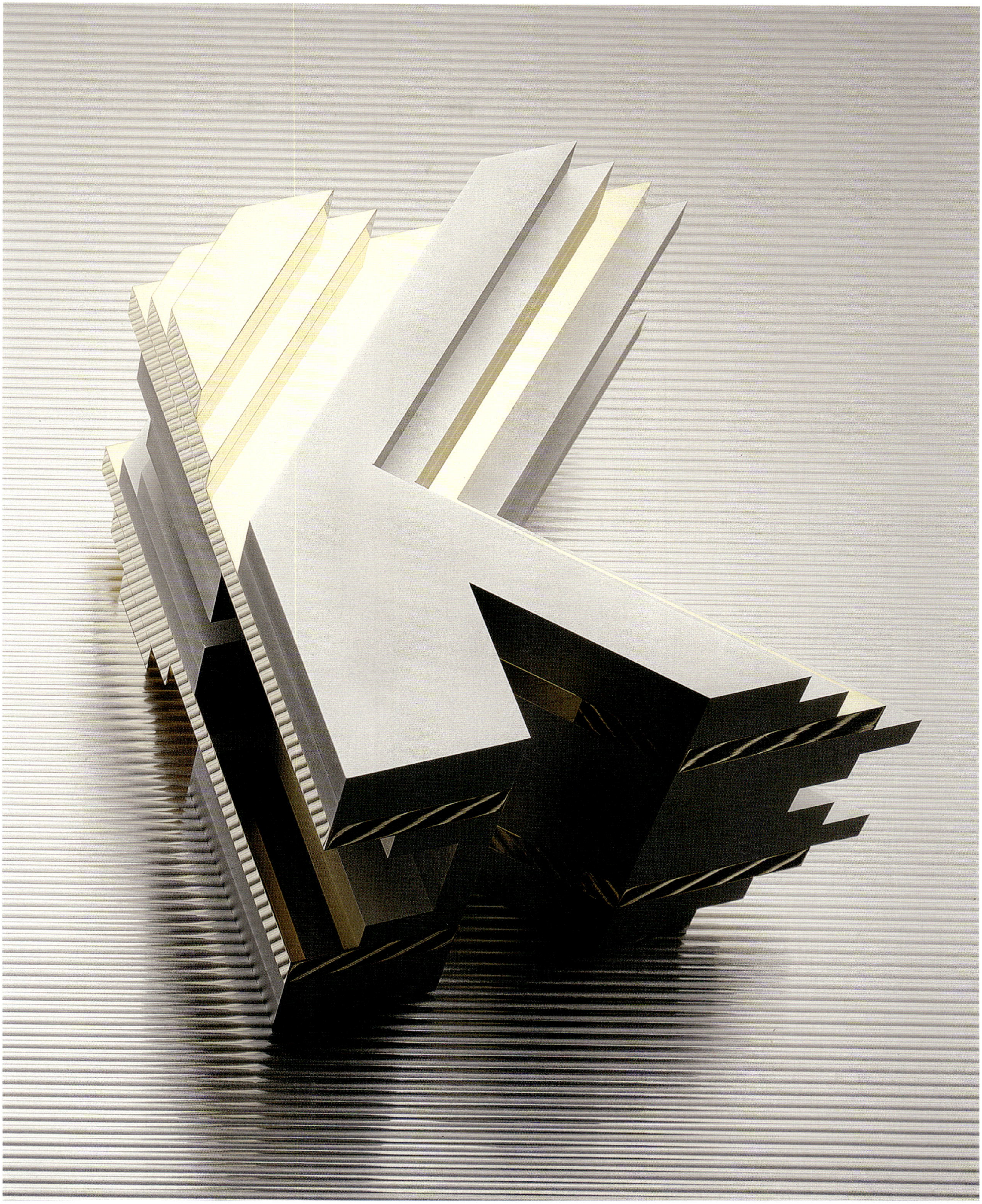

1-98 Sculpture K for a Catalog Cover
KOKUYO Co. Ltd. Tokyo, Japan, 1988

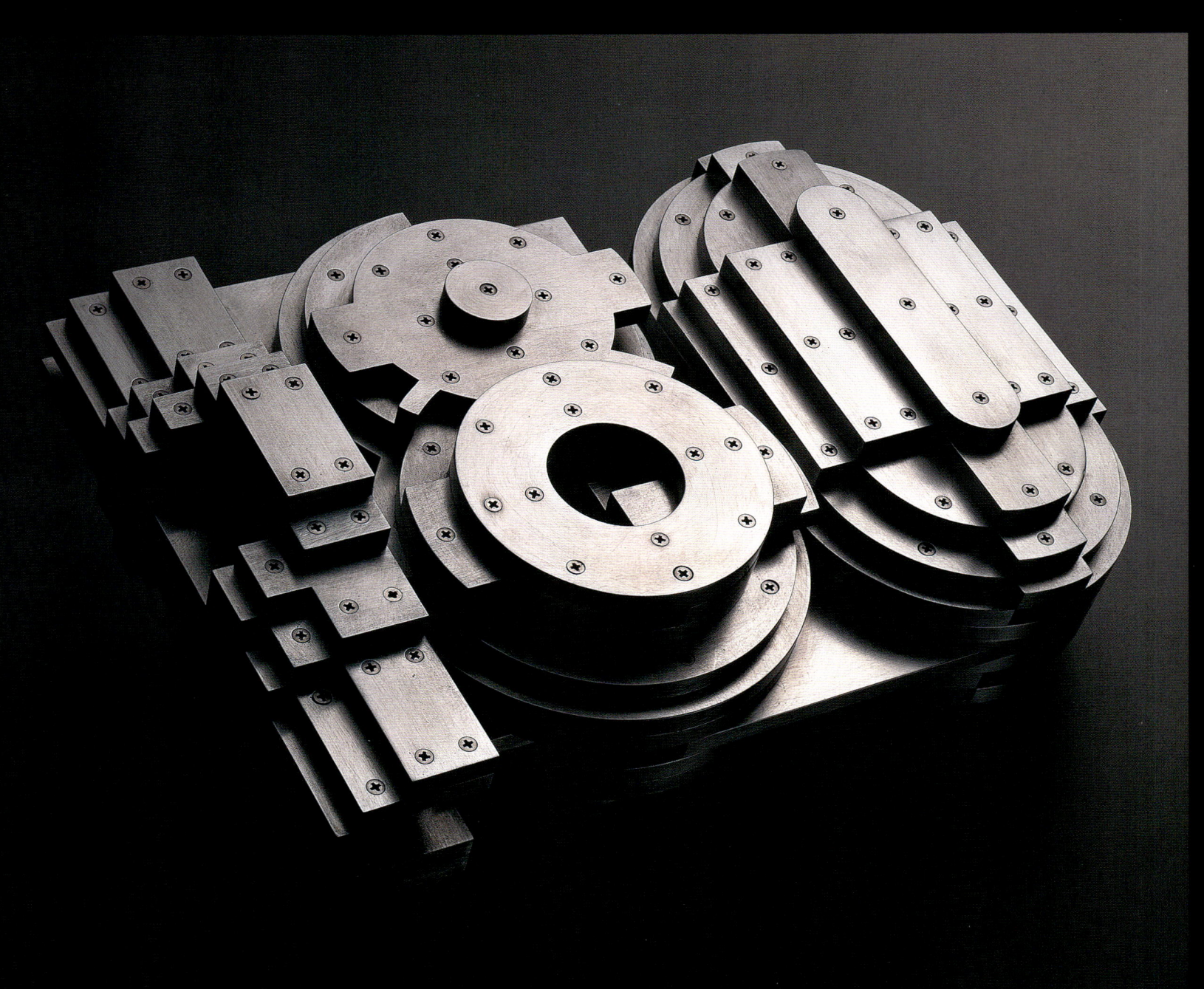

1-99 Sculpture for Nike180
Nike Air Shoes Campaign, Nike, Portland, OR, USA, 1990

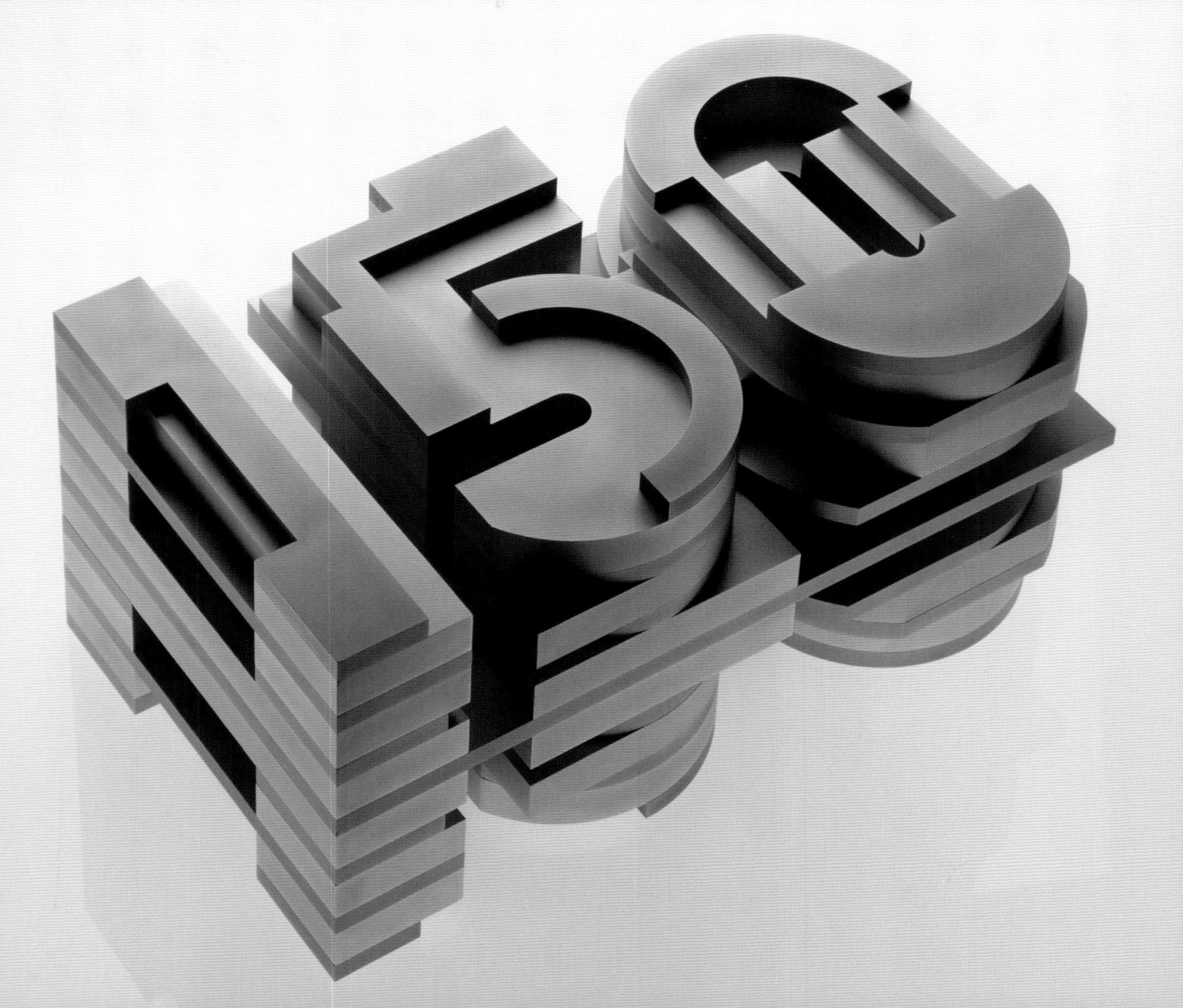

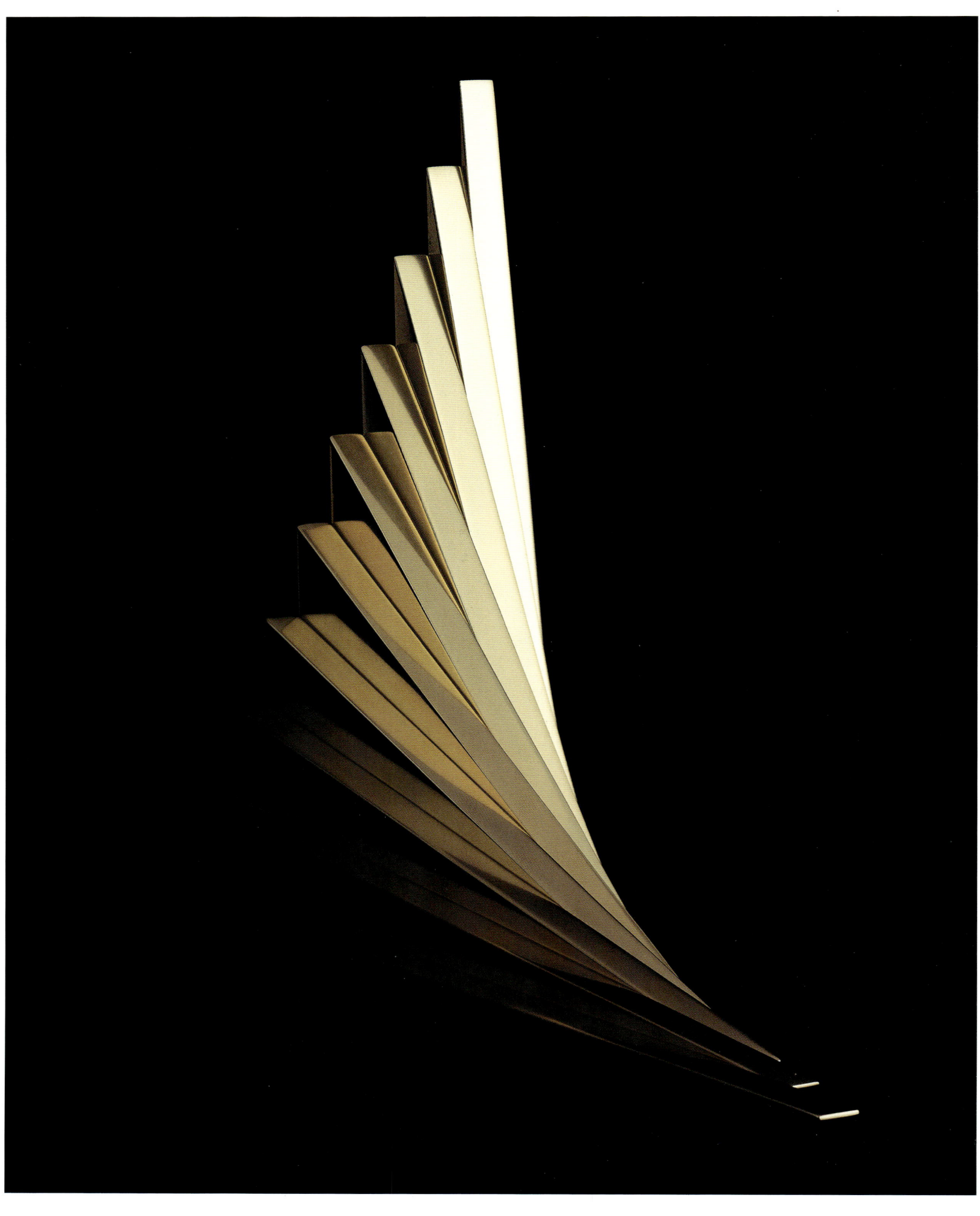

1-101 Trophy for Africa Prize
The Hunger Project
New York, NY, USA, 1987

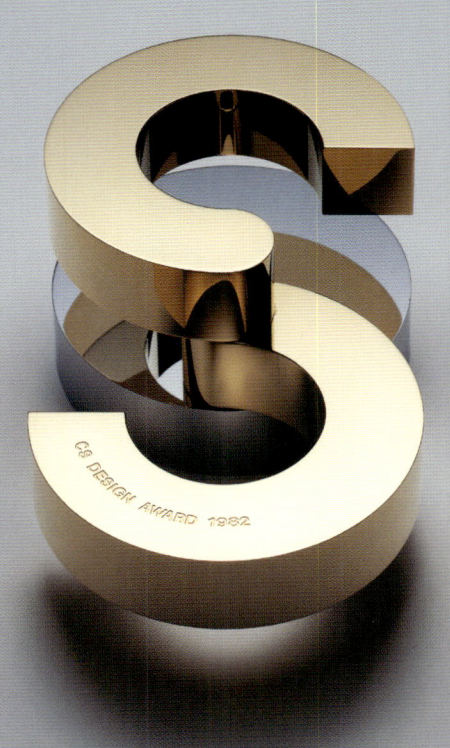
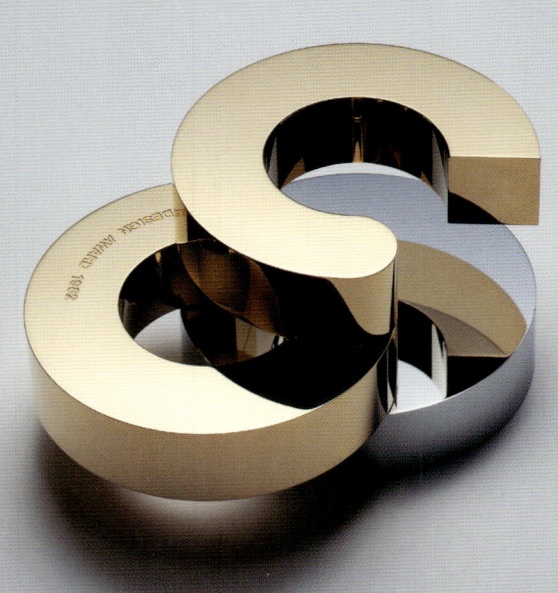

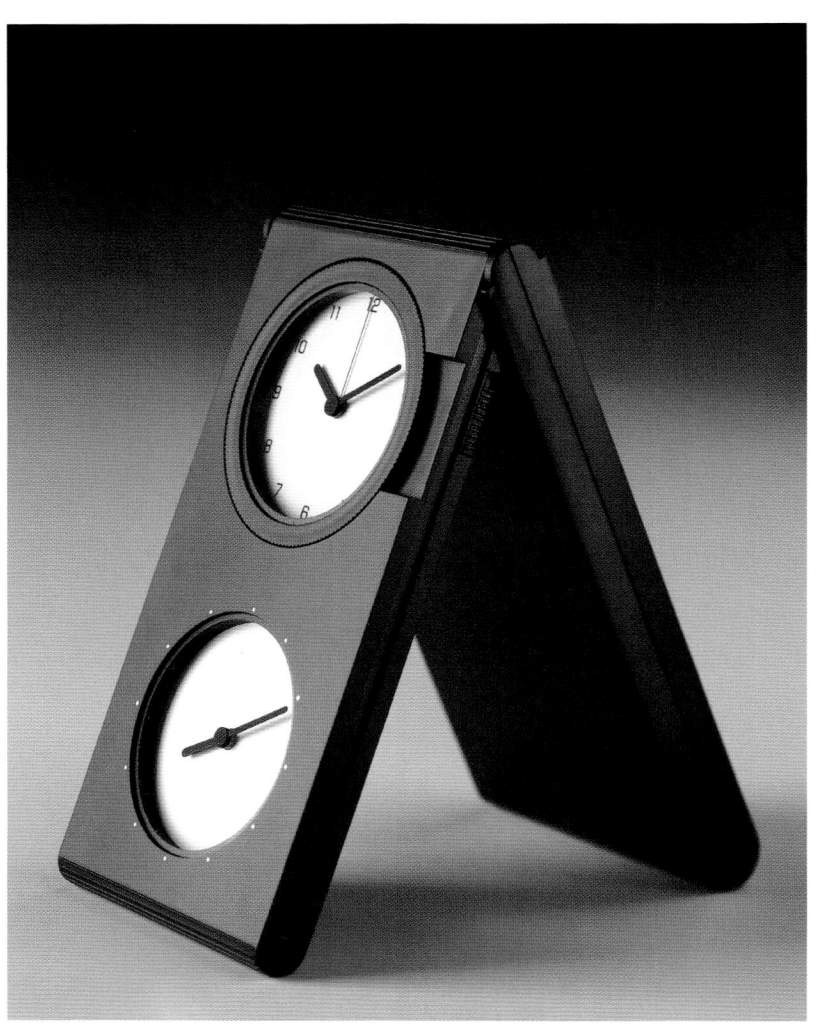
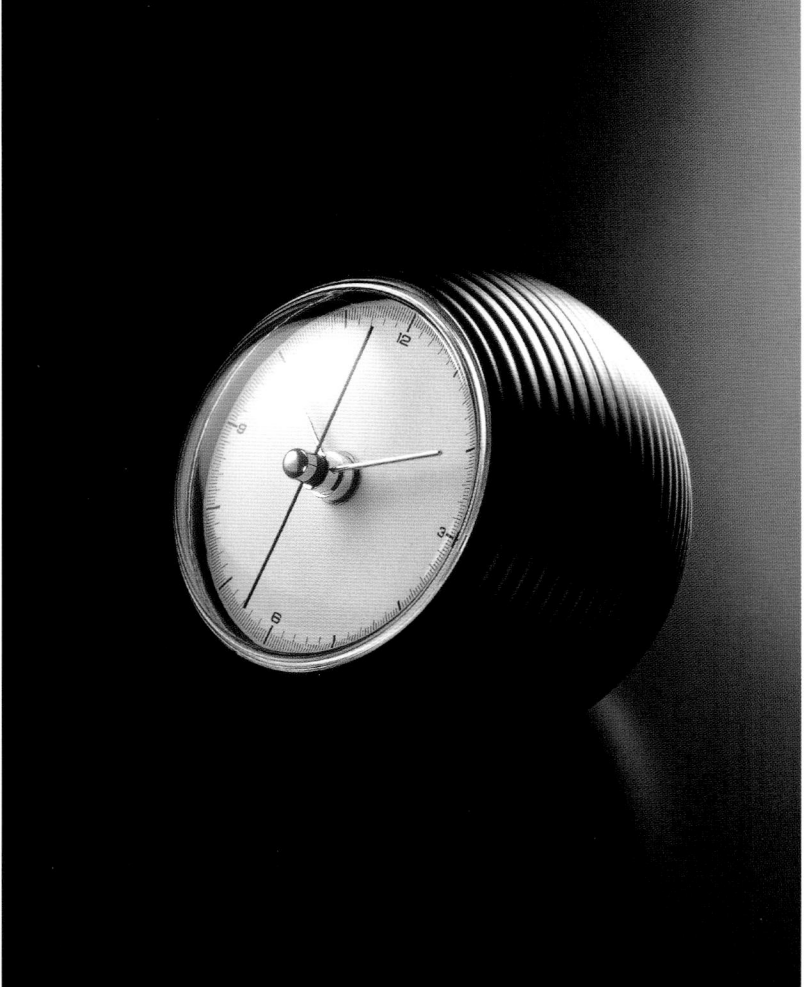

1-103 Clock
OUN, Tokyo, Japan, 1987

1-104 Clock
OUN, Tokyo, Japan, 1987

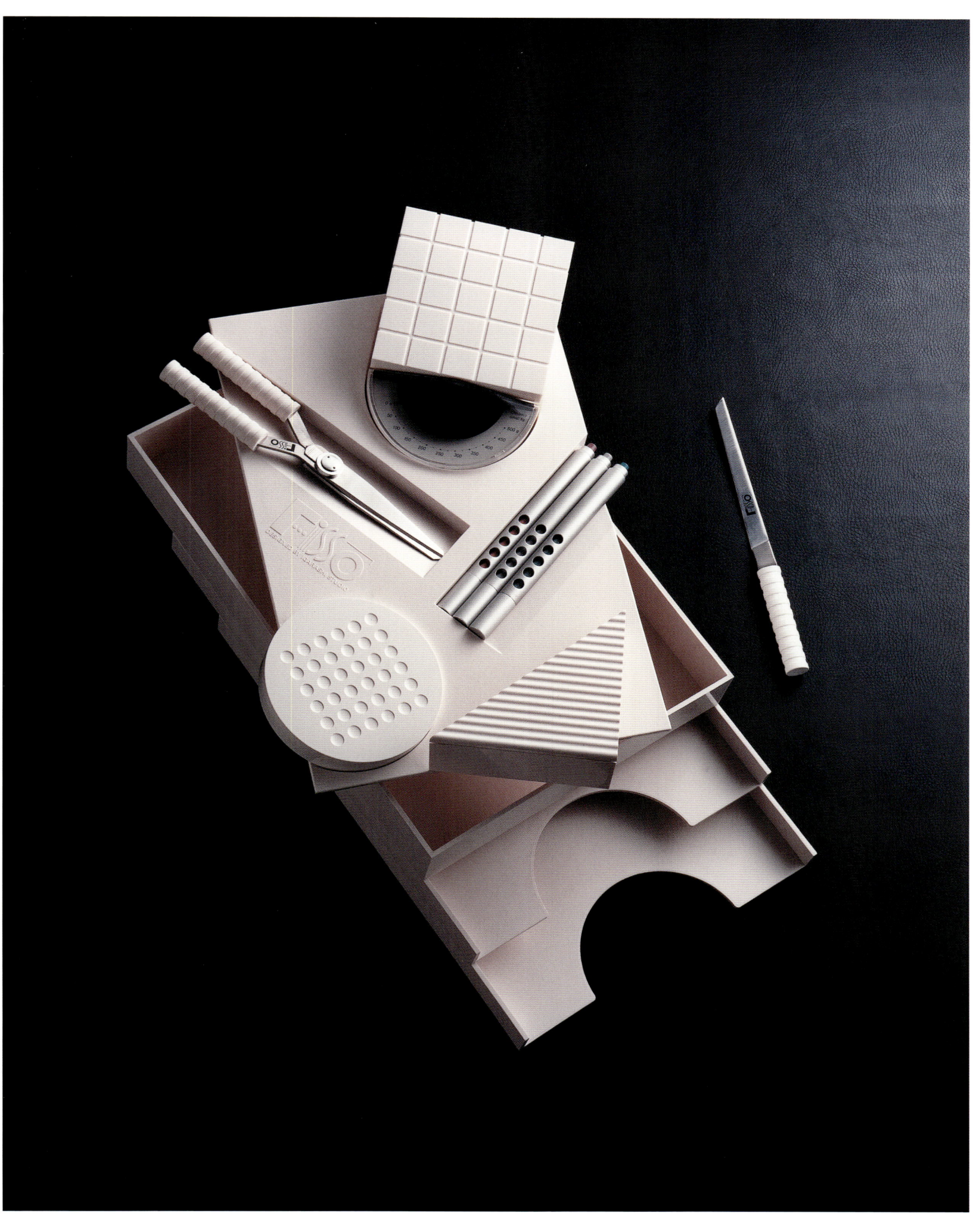

1-105 Desktop Accessory
Raymay Fujii, Tokyo, Japan, 1988

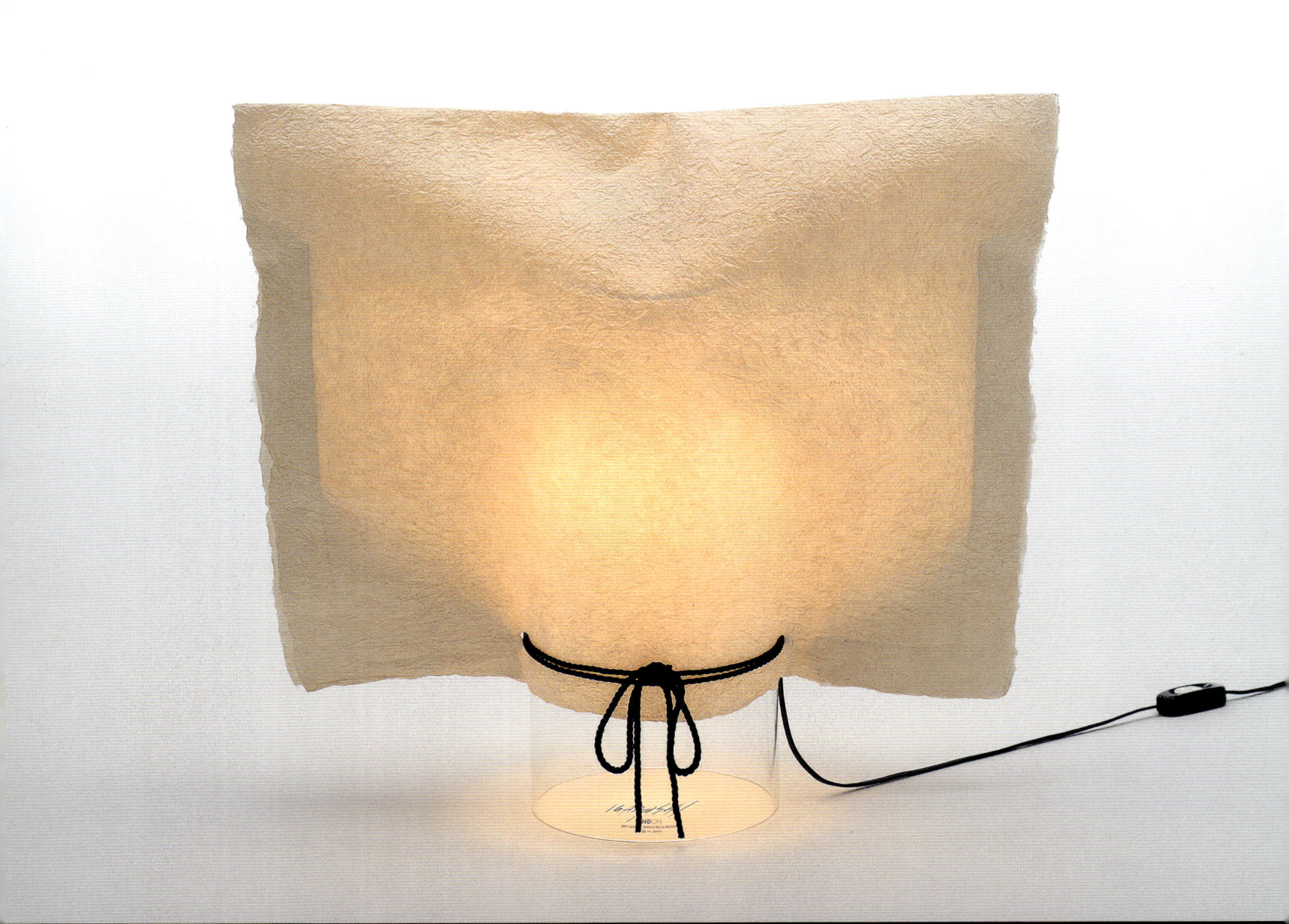

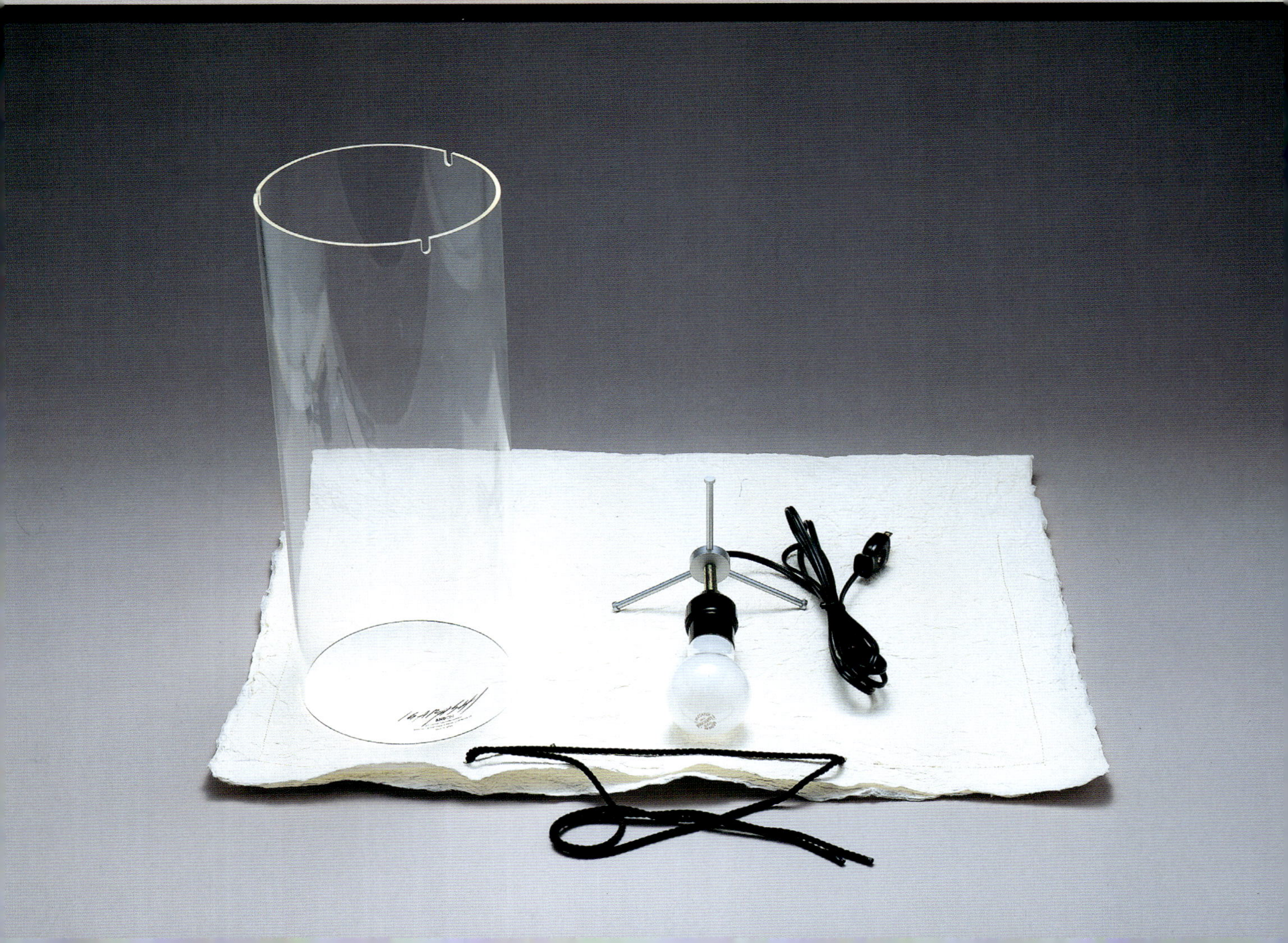

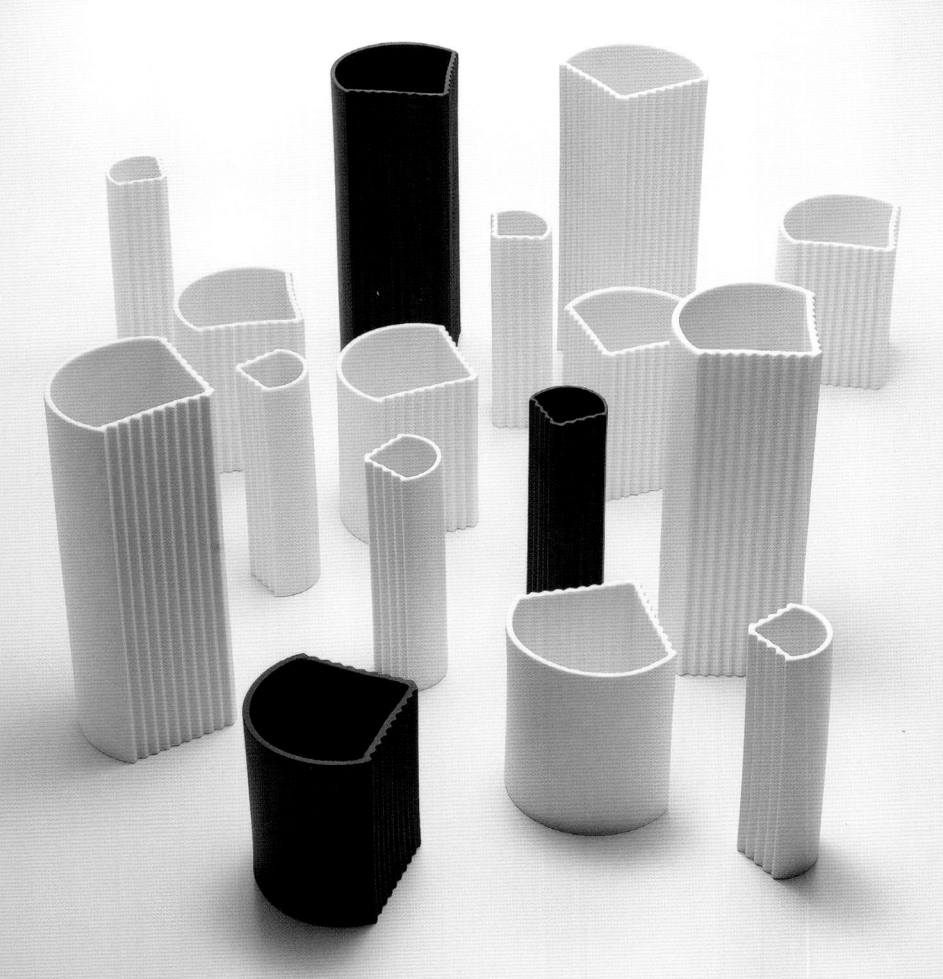

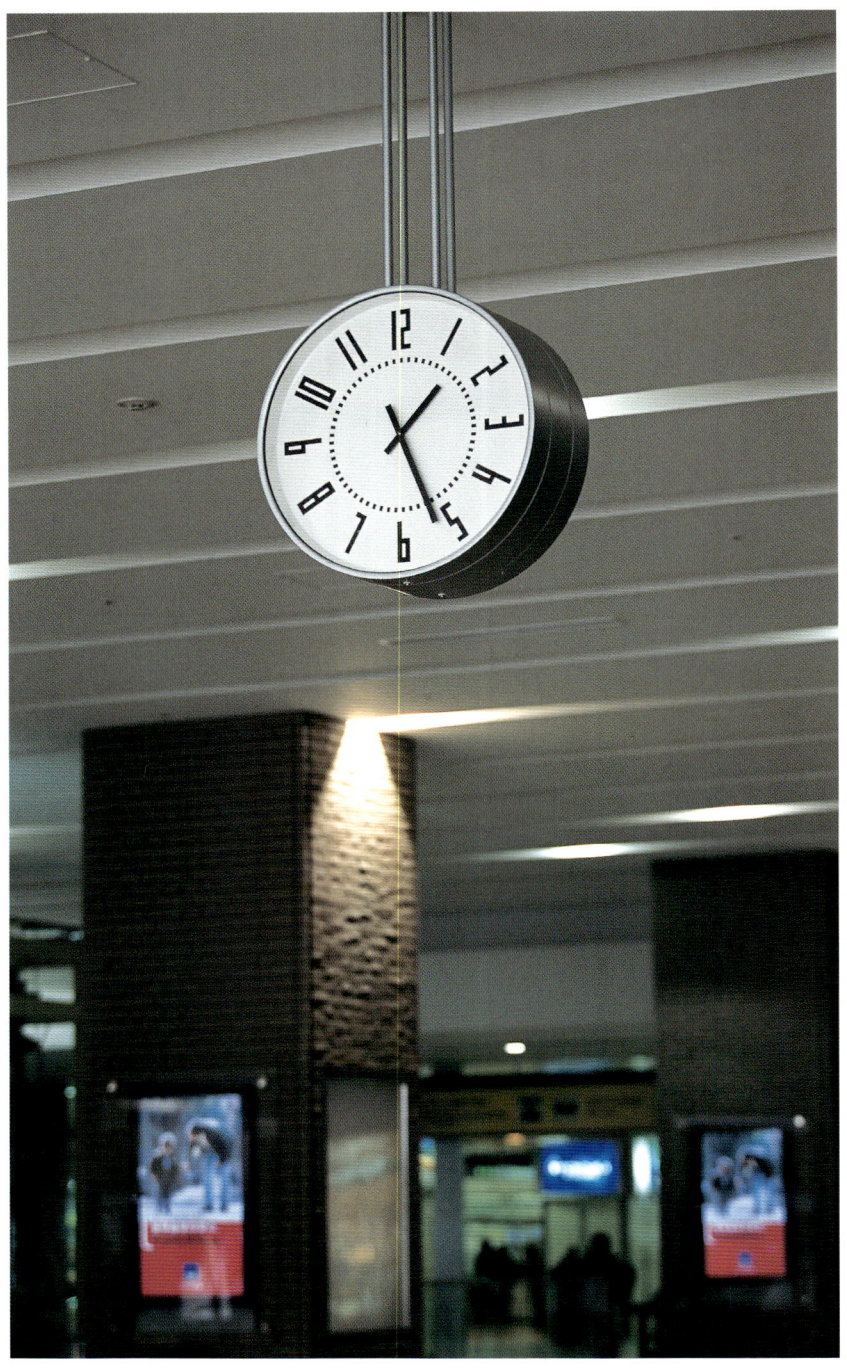
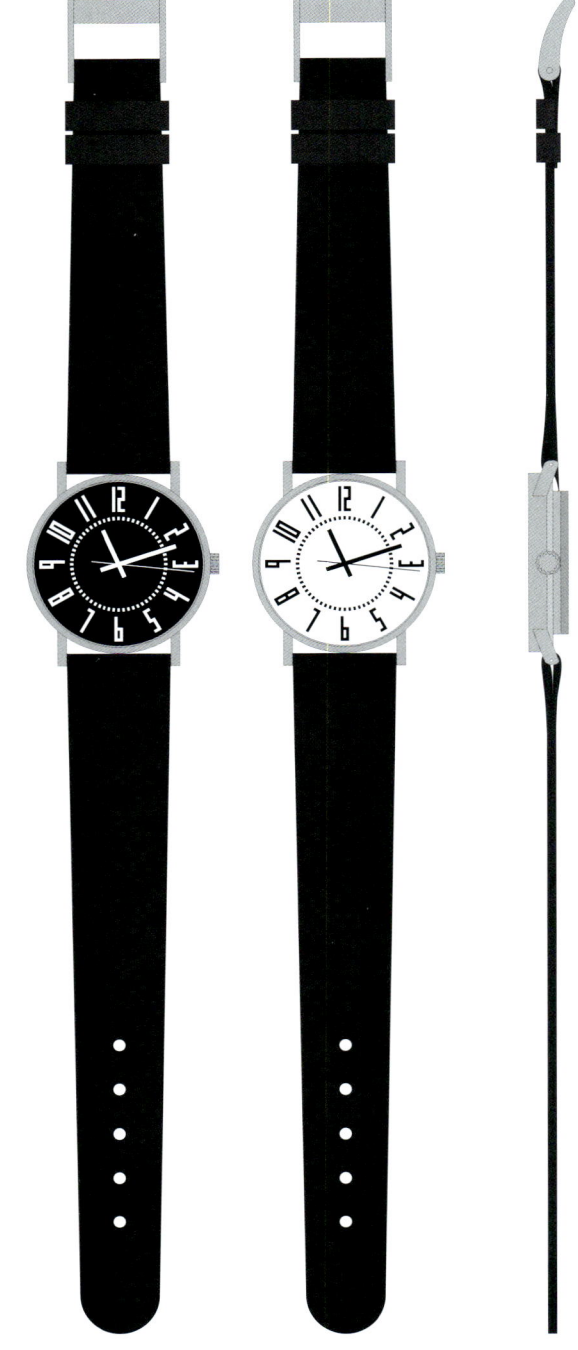

1-108 Clock for Sapporo Station South Gate Concourse
Sapporo Station General Development Co., Ltd., Hokkaido, Japan, 2006

1-109 Illustration for watch
m+h unit Inc., Tokyo, Japan, 2005

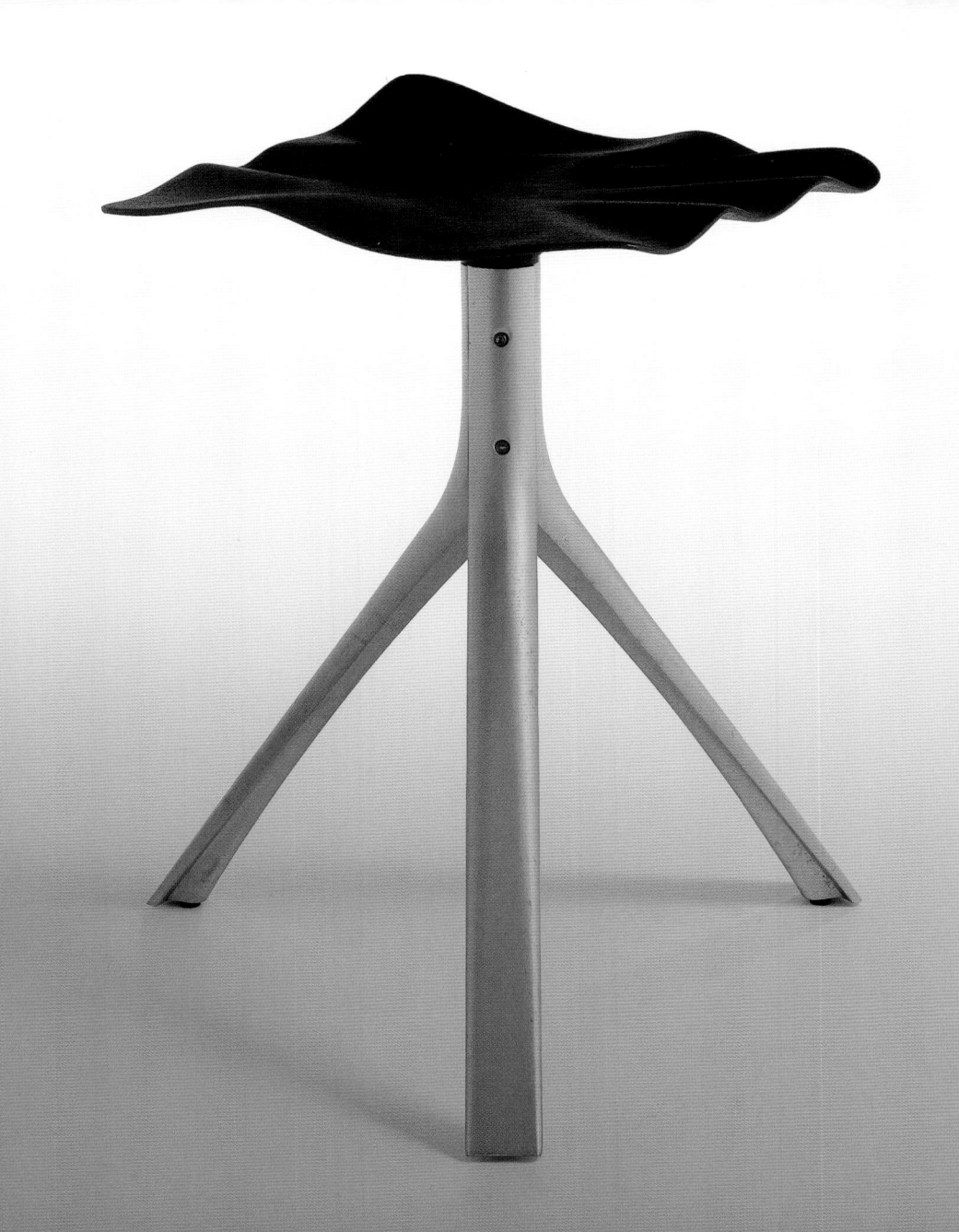

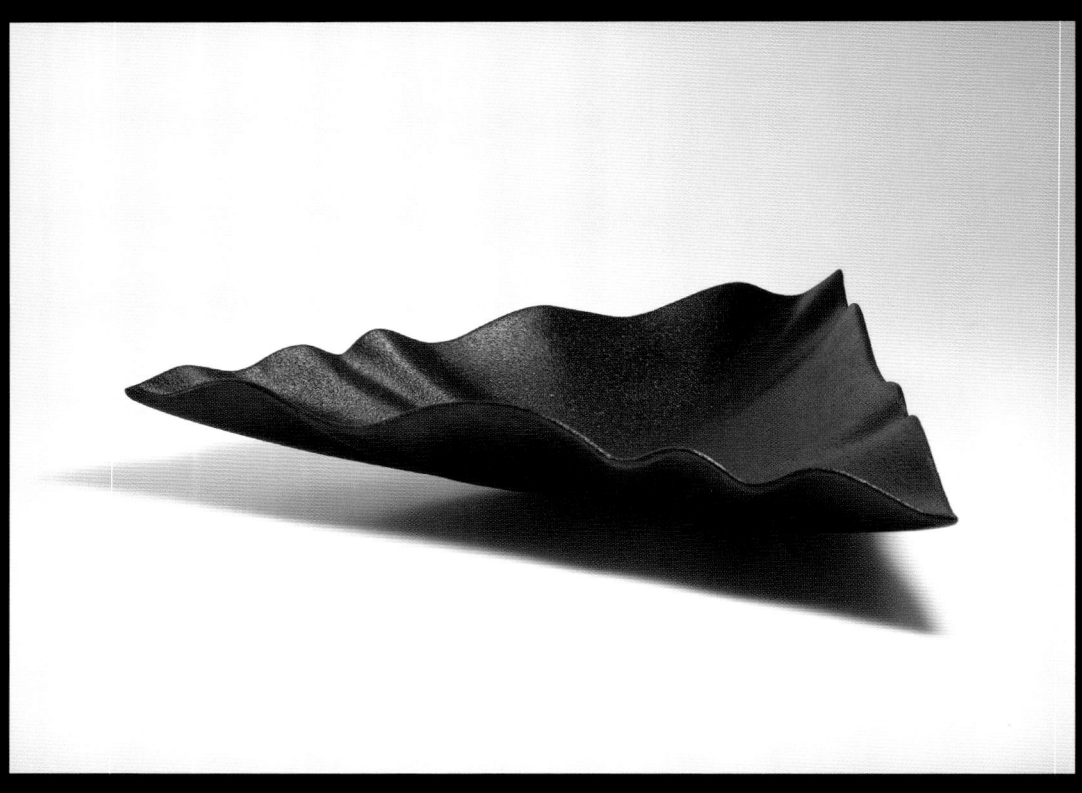

1-111 Platter/Triangle
Yamada Shomei Lighting Co., Ltd.
Y.M.D Department, Tokyo, Japan, 1989

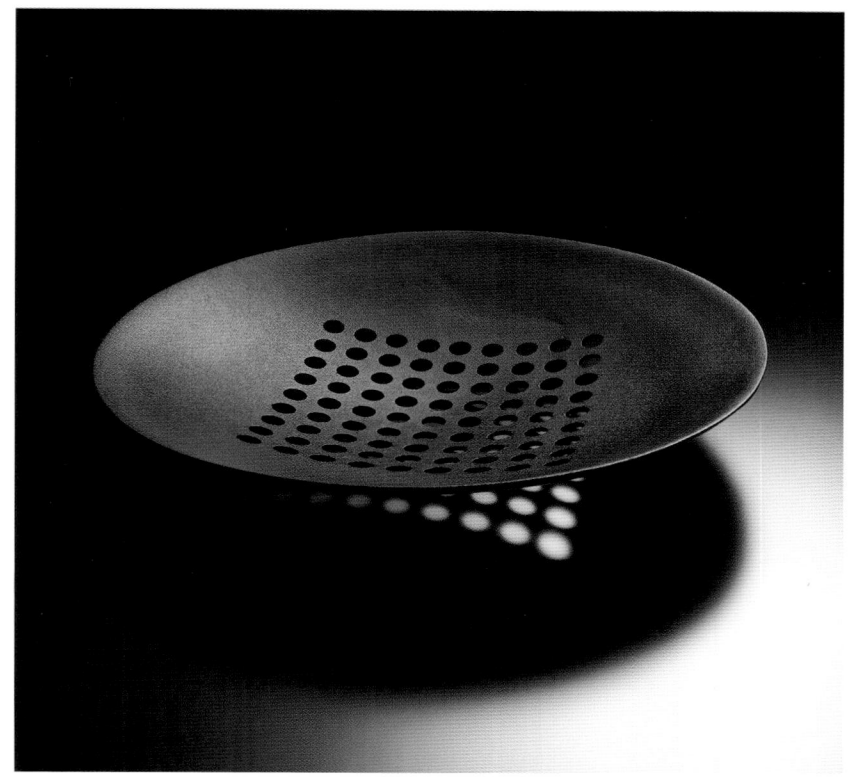

1-112 Platter/Dot
Yamada Shomei Lighting Co.
Ltd. Y.M.D Department
Tokyo, Japan, 1989

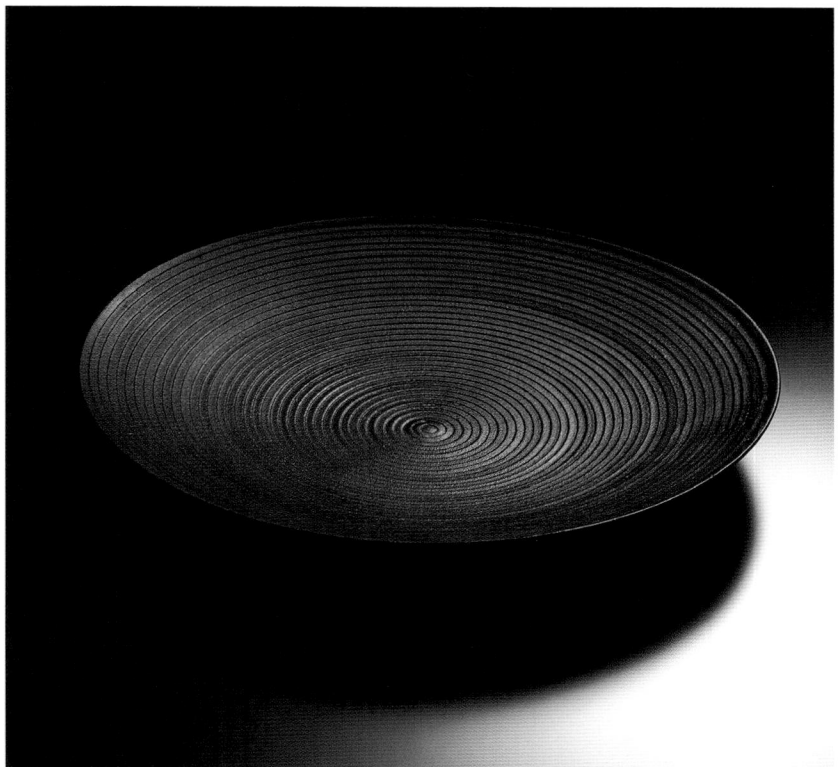

1-113 Platter/Line
Yamada Shomei Lighting Co.
Ltd. Y.M.D Department
Tokyo, Japan, 1989

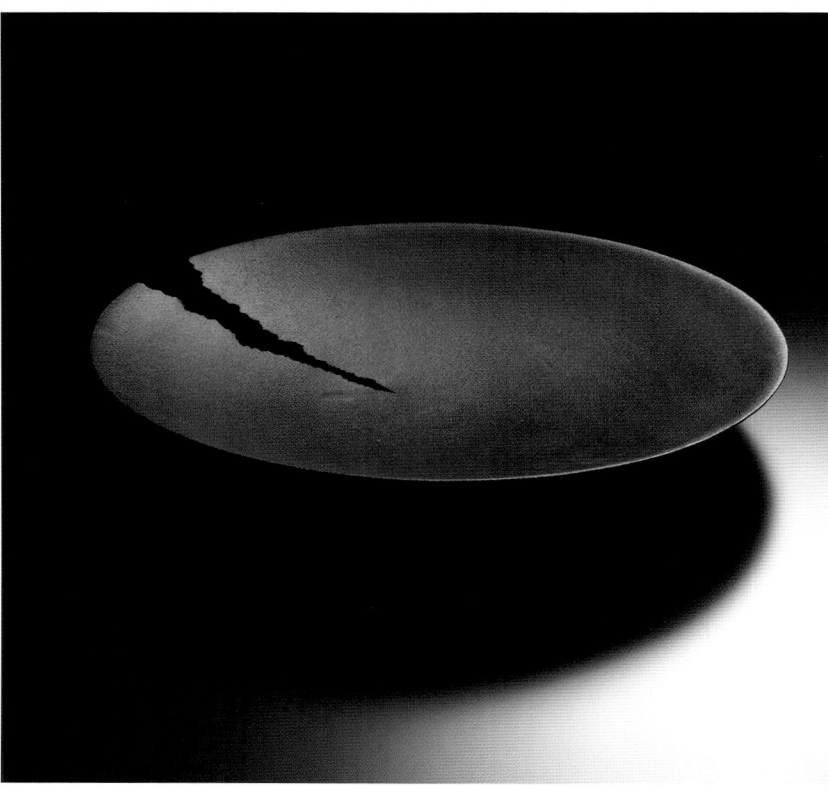

1-114 Platter/Crack
Yamada Shomei Lighting Co.
Ltd. Y.M.D. Department
Tokyo, Japan, 1989

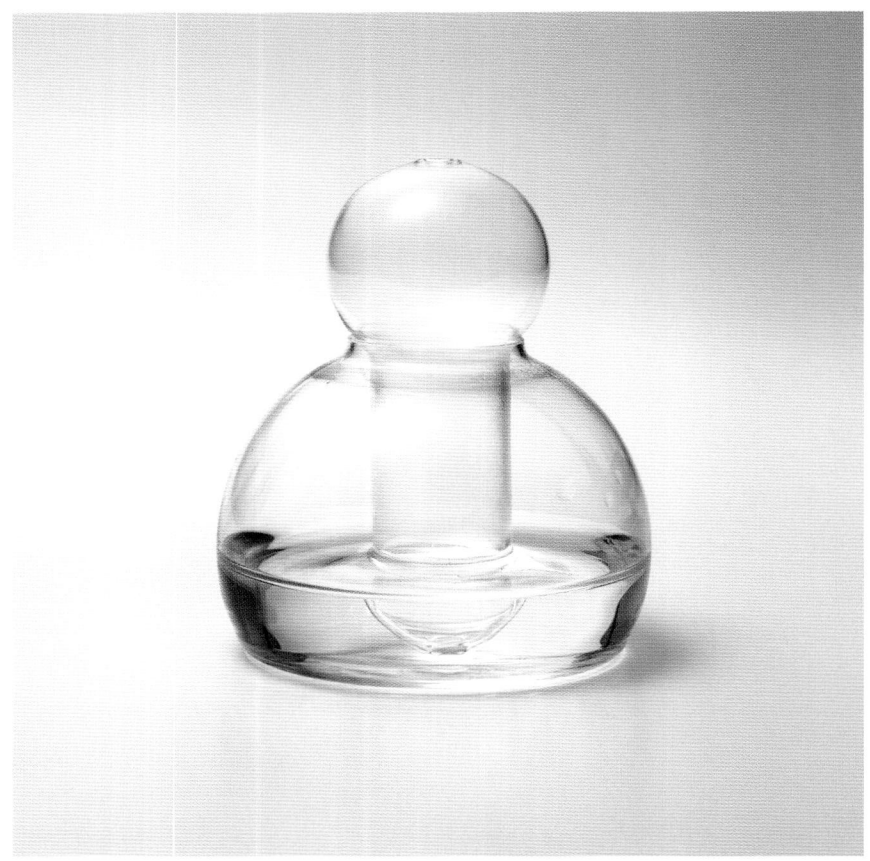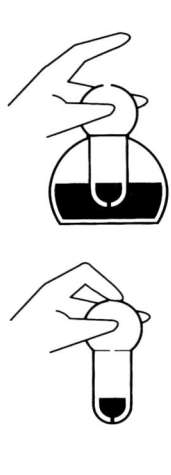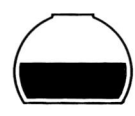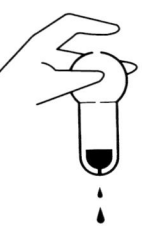

1-115 Soy Sauce Dispenser
Kimura Glass Co., Ltd.
Tokyo, Japan, 1995

1-116 Dinnerware
Yamada Shomei Lighting Co., Ltd.
Y.M.D. Department,
Tokyo, Japan, 1989-94

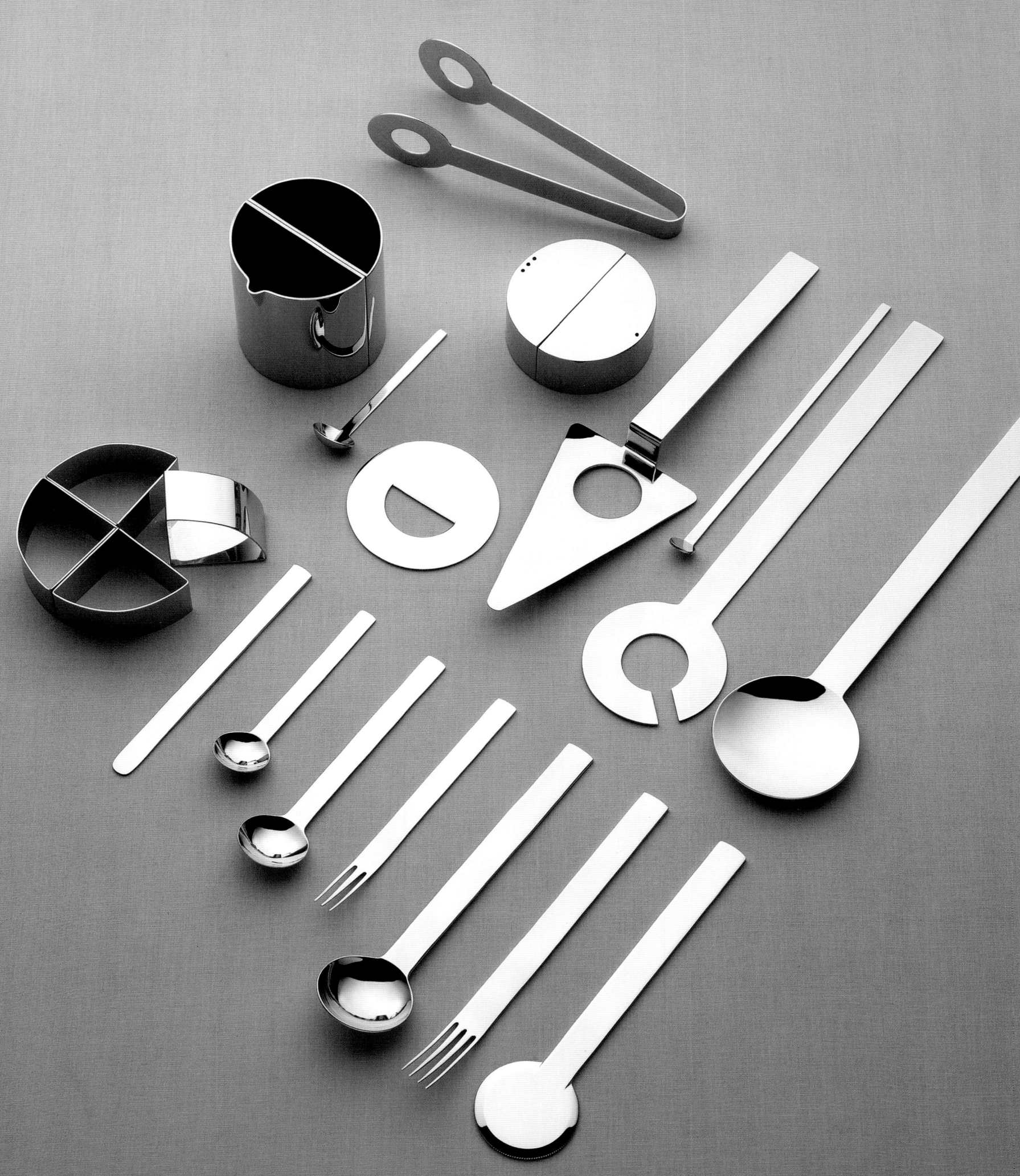

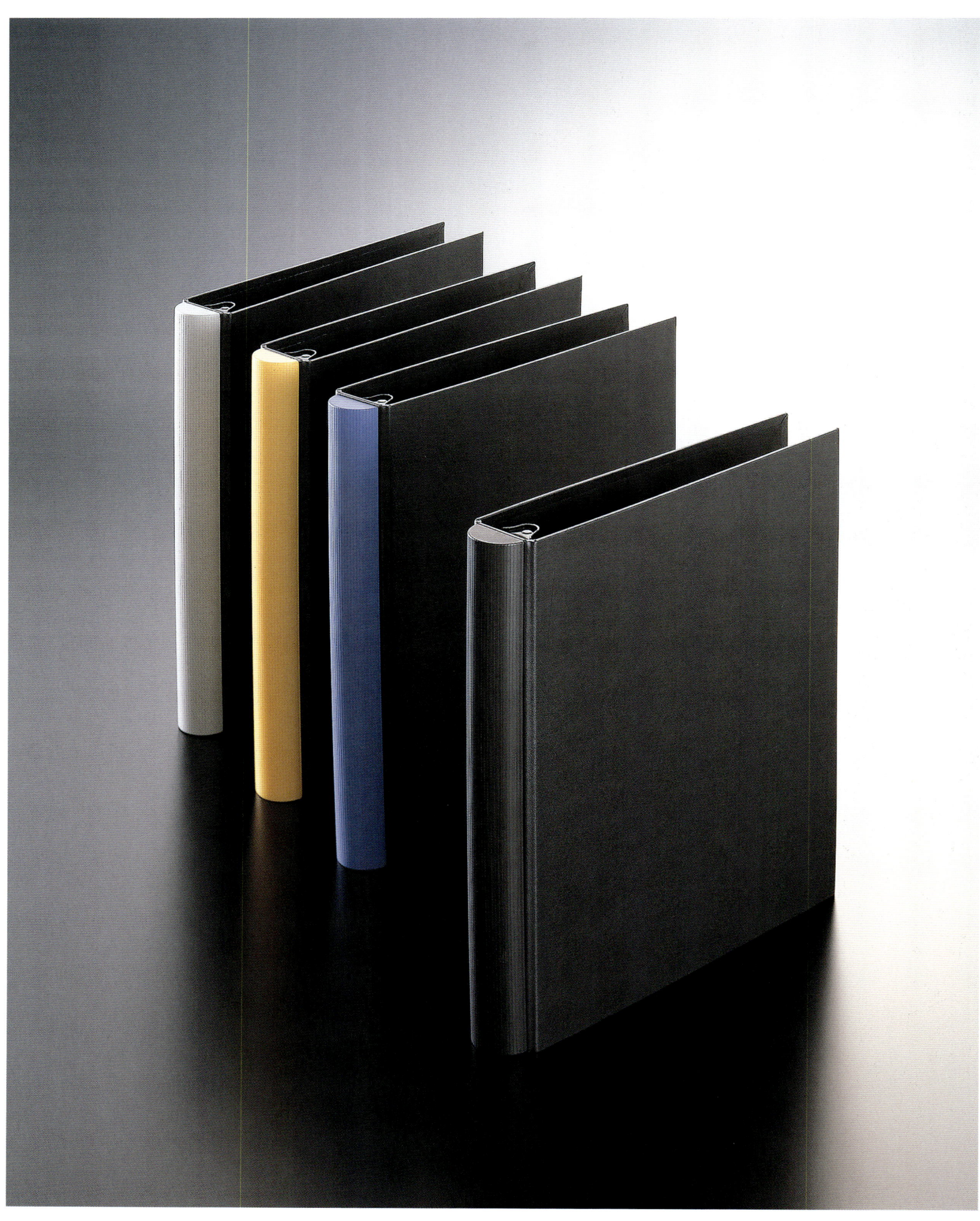

1-117 Photo Album
OUN, Tokyo, Japan, 1988

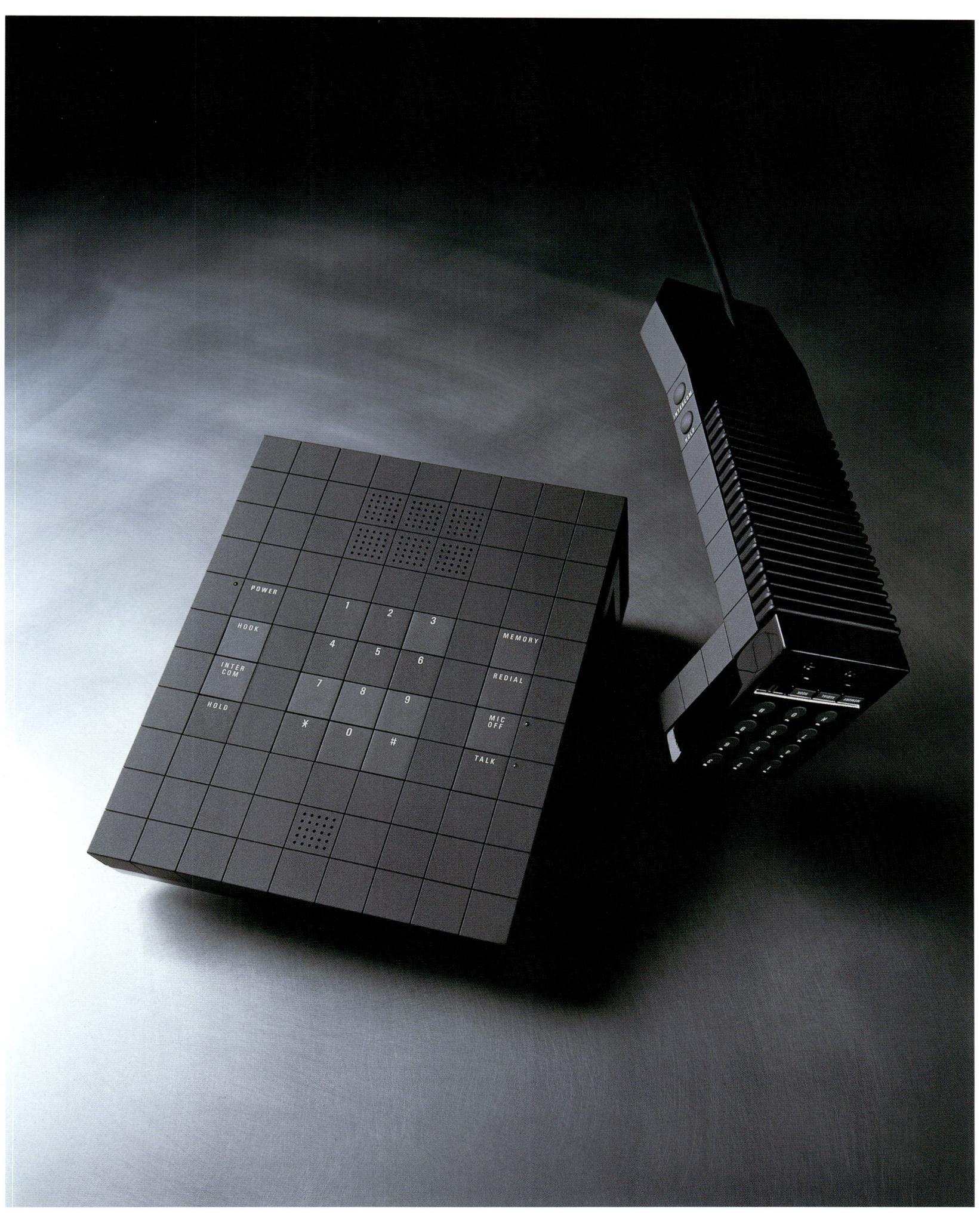

1-118 Cordless Telephone
Entex Corp., Tokyo, Japan, 1989

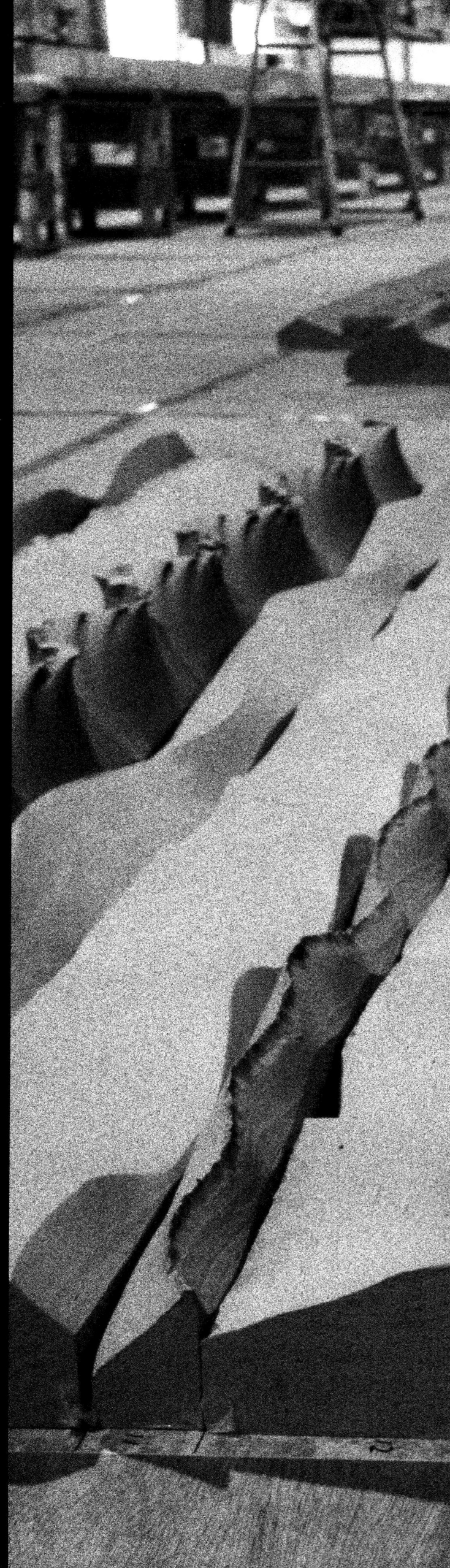

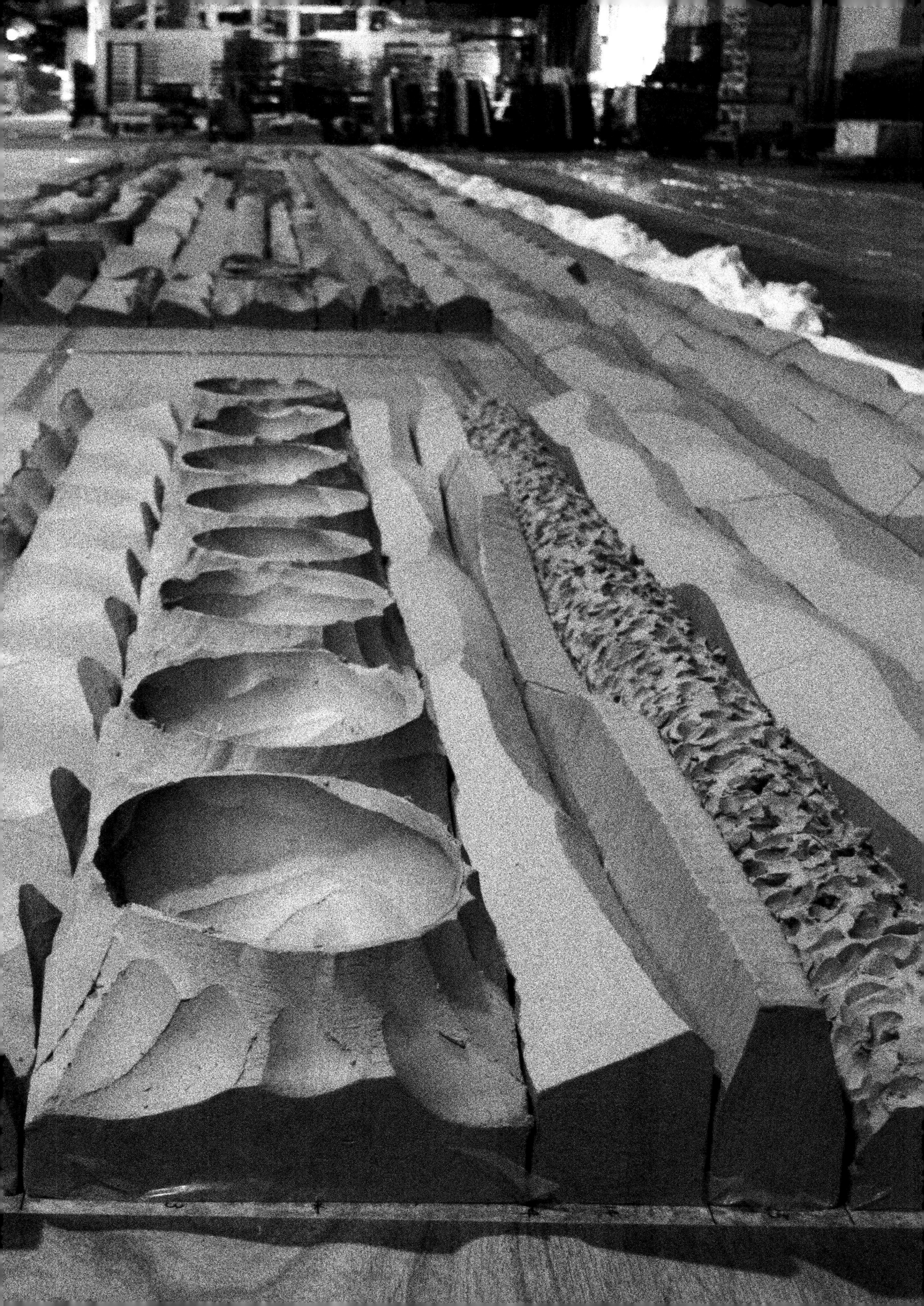

Becoming a Sculptor

As a sculptor, Takenobu Igarashi is internationally known for his abstract work, which is full of affection for the ever-changing rhythm of nature and human sensibility. For a quarter of a century, from his youth to the end of his forties, he was a graphic designer. He was always seeking to be true to his inner self without compromise; however, of all the choices he had made in life, nothing marks the turning point so distinctively as his decision to become a sculptor in 1994 at the age of fifty.

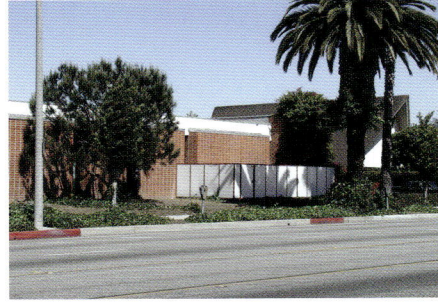

There are examples of famous European designers who have successfully extended their creative activities as painters, sculptors, or architects. In the case of Igarashi, who had been highly appraised internationally for his achievements in graphic design, this decision was like throwing away all that he had built up to that moment. In addition, from 1986 to 1991 Japan was booming with the Bubble Economy and the field of graphic design was basking in the benefits of prosperity. Although risk is inherent to creative life, what is even more surprising is that Igarashi left Japan to seek a new place to work in the United States. However, this seemingly abrupt move had been meticulously planned for about ten years. "When I turned forty in 1984, I thought another ten years of hectic work as a designer was enough. I wanted to do something different after that. In 1984, I obtained my U.S. permanent residency and established a base in Los Angeles, moving back and forth between Tokyo and Los Angeles. I could not just quit because I had employees and relationships with clients. I thought in the following ten years, I would reduce my workers by not replacing those who quit. Most workers quit after several years, so it was a natural process reducing the team. The remaining four employees were informed about my plan early enough. Finally, I closed my office in Tokyo and moved to Los Angeles, starting a new life as a sculptor in 1994."

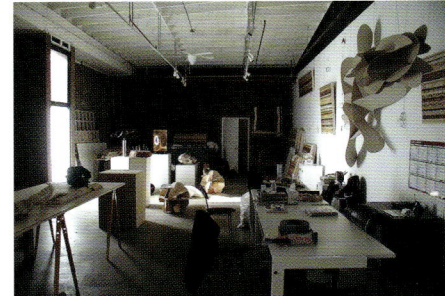

Igarashi's interest in sculpture started while he designed his *Alphabet sculptures*, which were all custom-made. He also made abstract sculptures in the 80s, one of which was to promote Nissan Motor Company's *Infiniti* (1988), a luxury limousine that was at first only to be sold in the United States. The sculpture was placed as a centerpiece in the showroom. "I received a phone call from an advertising agency in Boston, and I accepted the request with pleasure. It turned out to be a big project. The simple rectangular bar symbolizing the initial 'I' was softly inflated in the middle. The cast bronze sculpture was placed in over 150 showrooms scattered all over America. With such results, I thought it would be nice to do more work like that…(laughs)."

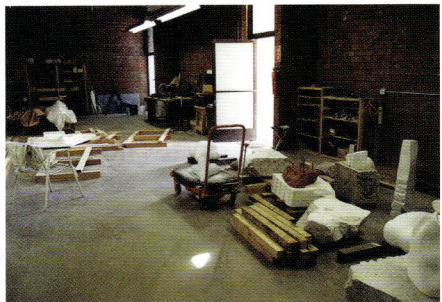

Igarashi's Atelier in Los Angeles, CA, USA

"Living in Los Angeles, getting to know fine artists like sculptors and painters, and having a close look at their lives made me aware of how naive I was. I realized that I had to totally change my way of life and my lifestyle, starting from the bottom. I started by doing what I could, step by step, moving toward my goal…This meant experiencing all the steps a sculpture student takes in learning to work with different materials like molding clay, chipping wood, carving stone, and so on. I went to see many exhibitions and made my own portfolio to show to the gallery owners as I looked for a place to exhibit my work. I led a modest life avoiding extravagance and saving wherever I could."

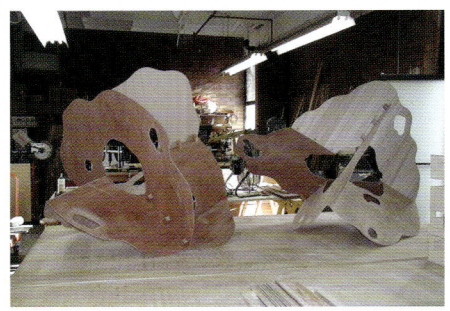

Work model for a hospital in San Francisco, CA, USA

Backed by the development of new tools, Igarashi ventured into a new start. Thirty years ago, working with stone required physical strength, but times had changed and Igarashi realized that age is no obstacle in working with stone with all the new tools that were available. However, after three years he was disappointed: "Stone is simply too heavy. It is hard labor just to move it around a bit." During this learning process he discovered wood by chance. Soon after he started working with wood, he won the art competition held by the Tokyo Metropolitan Subway. The project was to create an art piece improving what was usually a dull underground environment for then newly built Daimon Station of the Oedo Line. Since fire prevention measures forbade the use of wood in the underground premises, *Rhythm of Wave* (2000) was made out of terracotta. This was Igarashi's initial encounter with terracotta produced in Shiga Prefecture, famous for its ceramics.

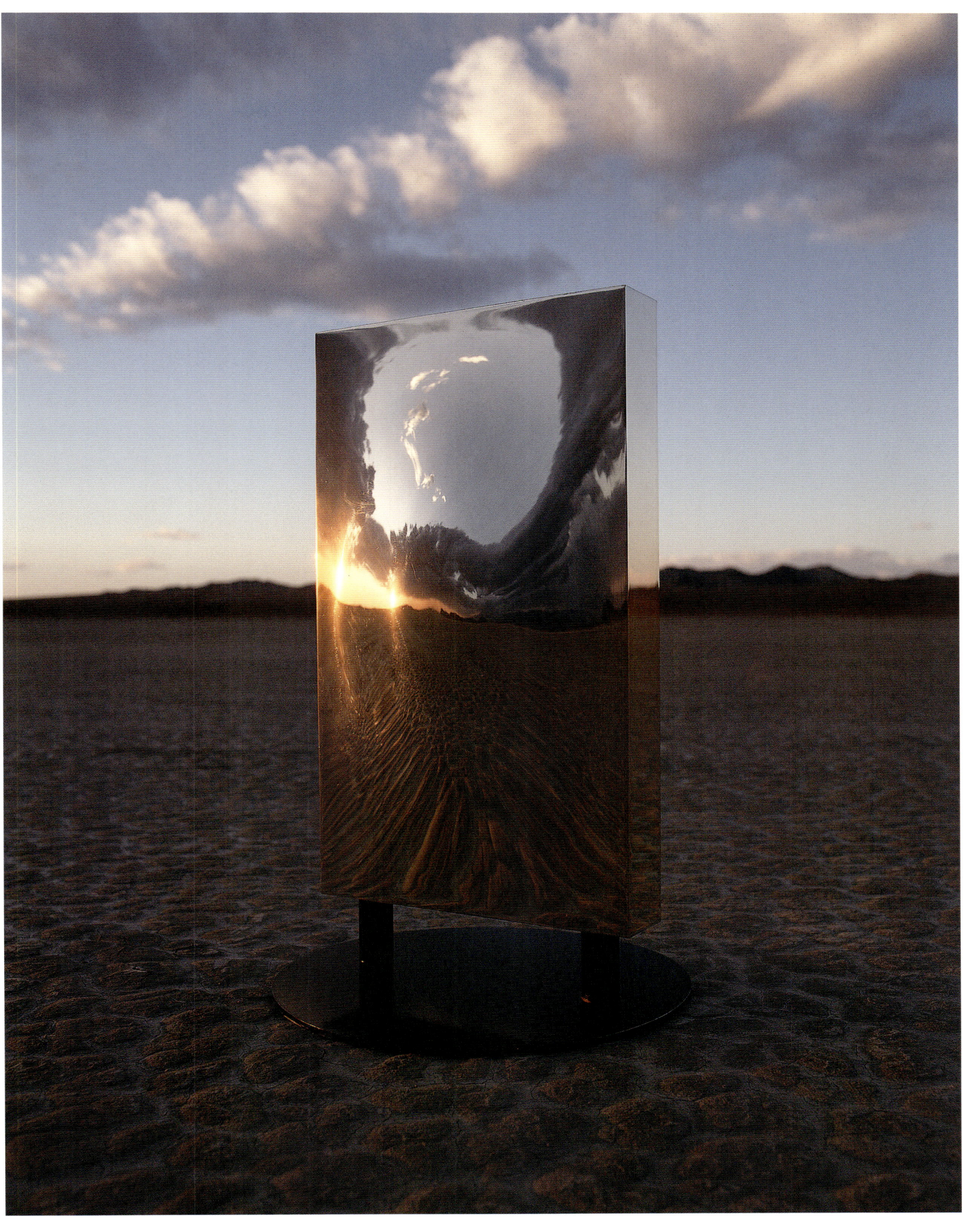

2-1 Infiniti
Nissan Infinity
USA, 1989

The original idea was titled *Sea of Words* (2000), and was installed at the entrance hall of the Tokyo University of Foreign Studies in Fuchu, in the western outskirts of Tokyo. His exhibition *Wood with String Works* (2000) at Gallery Natsuka in Ginza, Tokyo, can be considered as an extension of the same idea. "The studio I had rented in Los Angeles was within a factory. Parts sent to the factory from overseas were packed in a wooden box, which would be taken apart and discarded. I picked up a bundle of this wooden trash and started working with them. The wooden boards making up the boxes were about 3 to 10mm thick and 25 to 30mm in depth. I started carving these ordinary boards using different tools, and *Sea of Words* and a whole series entitled *Horizontal Feeling* (HF series) were born. 200 to 500 wooden pieces of five to ten different types of wood were used, depending on the size…There are no limits in the method of working with normal tools, changing the angle, roughing up the surface, carving with a band saw, and so on; it's all up to the imagination."

Without any sketch or pre-plan, he carved thin wood pieces and placed one upon the other as they were completed. To avoid deliberate expression, he chose colors without intention, using what is available or even mixing colors he disliked. *Horizontal Feeling #103101* (2003) for the Midland Square across from Nagoya station, *Horizontal Feeling* (2007) for the annex of Kajima Corporation's Akasaka complex, and *Horizontal Feeling* LHH (2008) installed at San Francisco's Laguna Honda Hospital, are some of the representative examples of the *HF* series. The series, which started in Los Angeles, had decreased in number upon his return to Japan and were not made until the spring of 2016, when Igarashi started making them again in his atelier set up within Kazenobi.

"I did not want to beg for orders from acquaintances of the past. Every time I returned to Japan, I made new acquaintances, and in ten years I got to know about 500 people, most of whom were young architects. In fact, about 95% of my sculptures were commissioned by people I met after quitting my career as a designer." There are enthusiastic individual collectors in Los Angeles who would make large investments and buy their favorite sculptures for their homes. On the contrary, in Japan the clients are big companies and public institutions like educational or medical institutions that purchase sculptures mostly for a new building. Modern sculpture in Japan exists in an urban context, shaping the space inside and outside of a building complex in a large open scale. Igarashi is no exception and his new acquaintances helped him and paved his way.

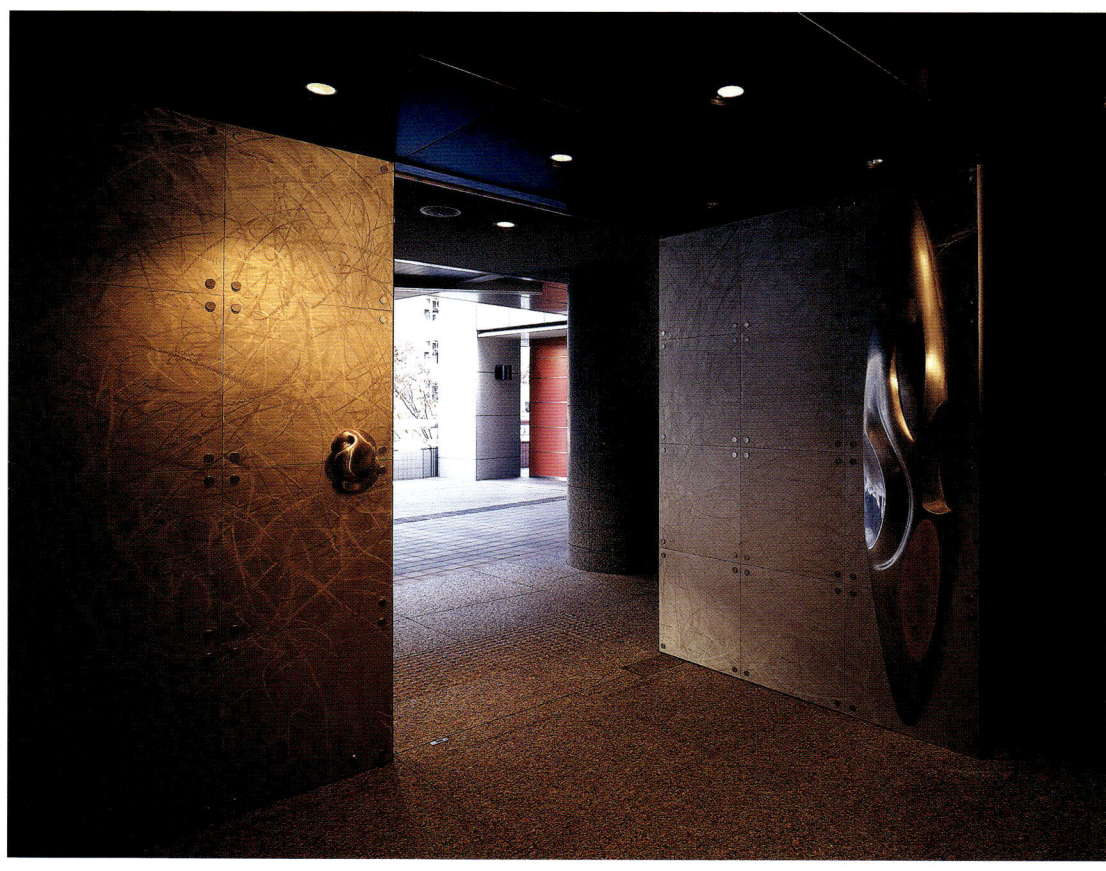

2-2 Listen to Music
Sumida Triphony Hall
Tokyo, Japan, 1997

2-3 Fuchujin
Fuchu Intelligent Park
Tokyo, Japan, 1991

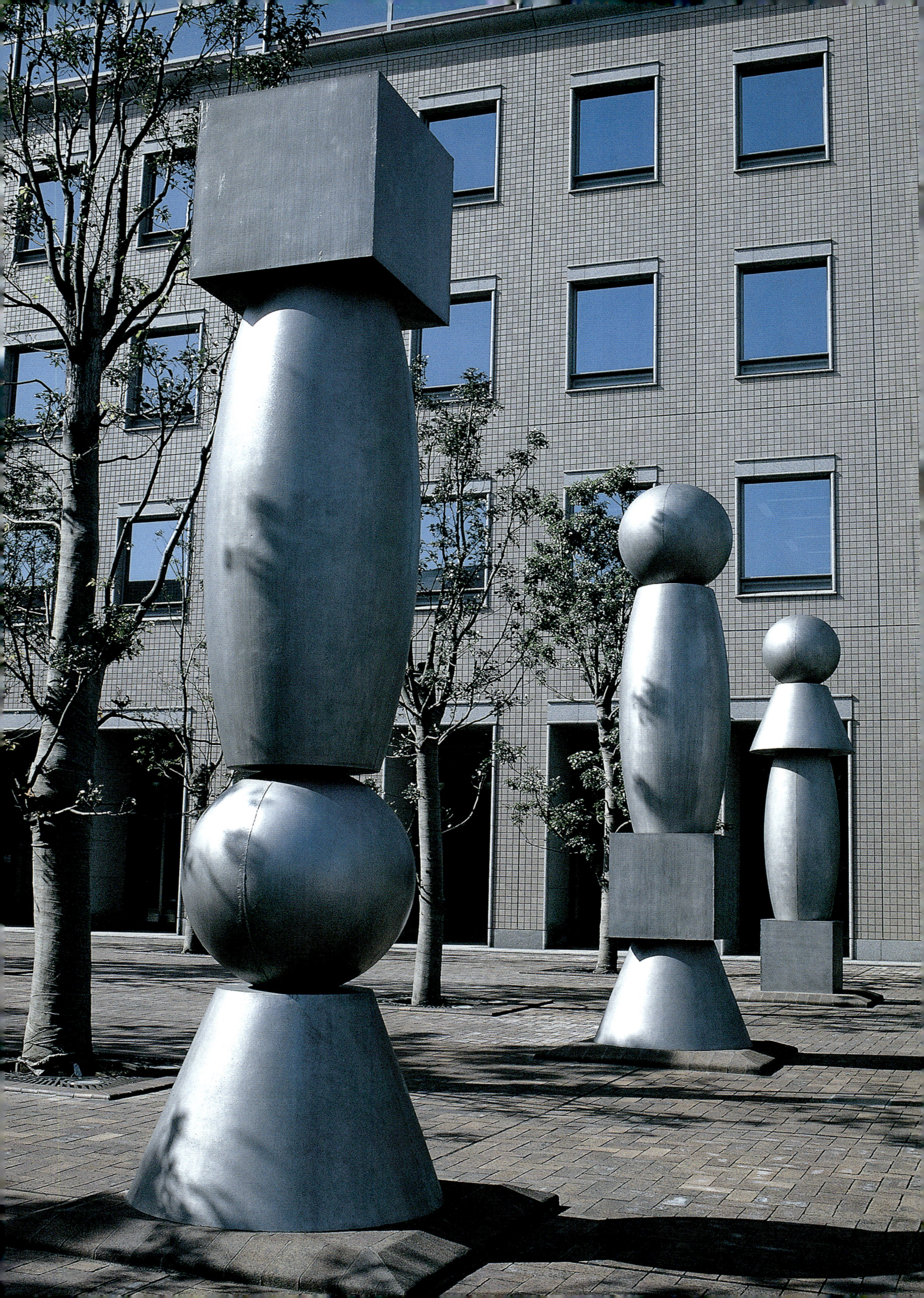

The Resonating Sound—Discovering the Joy of Working with Stone

For twenty years, Igarashi has been working with wood, clay, and stone, using his own hands as far as his physical strength allows him to work. Due to his farsightedness, the metal sculptures are made for him, since they are difficult for him to weld. "I discovered the joy of working with my own hands when I was working with stone in Los Angeles. I was carving marble with a hammer and chisel every day for three years. There are electrical tools, but my friend Minoru Ohira, a Japanese sculptor working in Los Angeles, advised me not to use them—and instead work with the same tools as Michelangelo did—It must be said that today, the chisel is equipped with an ultra-hard tungsten carbide edge, so it is amazingly easy to work with. The chisel carves the stone with the weight of the hammer hitting its core. On the other hand, it is very difficult to polish. It is hard labor just to move the stone around. But in terms of the joy of carving, the material is just fantastic. So I was learning all these things little by little. Now I also like working with wood, and terracotta is especially fun because it reacts and forms instantly."

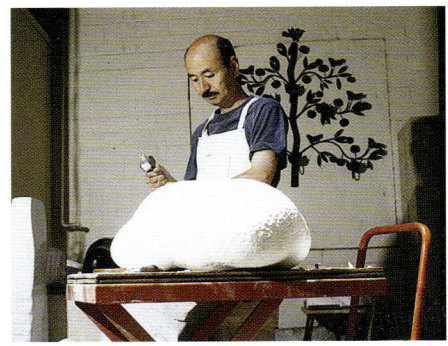

Making Sculptures in Pasadena
CA, USA, 1998

There are mainly two methods in sculpture: carving a hard material like stone and modeling a material with plasticity like clay and using the form to make a mold for casting bronze or plaster, or to make a figure in clay. Michelangelo is a master of the former method.

Igarashi describes the difference between design and sculpture as: "Design is at the base of my work. Design requires a plan to be worked out step by step, from studying to simulation. Basically it is about achieving the assumed result. Design is practically finished by making a concept and an image, and the rest of the work is just planning and preparation…in sculpture, working with my own hands, I do not have any image in mind when I start. There is no sketch, planning, or drawing. I started to realize that it is like a child's world. Children do not make sketches; they work straight with the material before them. In my case, it is the same when I work with terracotta." For Igarashi, design is a world of predictable results, while sculpture is a world full of indefinite factors.

"I look at the stone in front of me and wait until I have the desire to work with it. It might sound a bit affected, but when I start carving, the stone shows me what to do. What I mean is that there are parts of the stone that are easier to carve than others. So I keep carving in the direction that my chisel leads, eventually giving form to the stone. And the sound of hitting the stone is like music to my ears."

"In order to aim the chisel accurately, as you know the chisel is heavy, so automatically you hold it tightly. But if you forcefully hit a chisel, which is tightly held in position, it doesn't work. The forces counterbalance each other. It's like playing golf. You need to loosen your arms and shoulders for the ball to fly. So by easing your hands holding the chisel and the hammer, letting the sheer weight of the hammer hit the head of the chisel with a big arc, the power flows…So there is a lot of power in the hammer, but if you accidentally hit your hand with it, it hurts like hell as if the bones are all smashed. Of course you are wearing leather gloves, but it's still very painful, so if you do it many times, you learn not to do it again. After about six months you learn how to do it without any effort, working at your own pace for as long as you want and even chat while doing it, because you are not unnecessarily exerting yourself."

"In order to create a naturally curved three-dimensional surface at the final stage, you can use electrical tools like the grinder, but the final touch in creating a beautiful surface can be only achieved by hand-polishing. This is a lot of work that requires patience, sanding at first with a metal file and then with sandpaper. Finally, nitric acid and magnesium powder are used to treat the surface chemically for a smooth finish. I didn't like the last polishing part… On the other hand; the sensation of carving is indescribable. It is only possible to understand this feeling by actually doing it yourself. It is the most fulfilling experience. What a pleasant sensation it is to carve such a hard material with the control of my chisel and hammer!"

"This is accomplished by maintaining an equal relationship, with none of them taking the lead. At the end there is always an element of surprise, including failure. This curiosity, together with invention and discovery of tools and methodology nurtured during my designer period, apply to the process of making sculptures. I am convinced that a new aesthetic world can be found by working with the material, using tools in unusual or even abnormal but safe ways. It is not a process of drawing, but of making. It is about being face to face with the material and working with it. My way of thinking has not changed since my time as a designer."

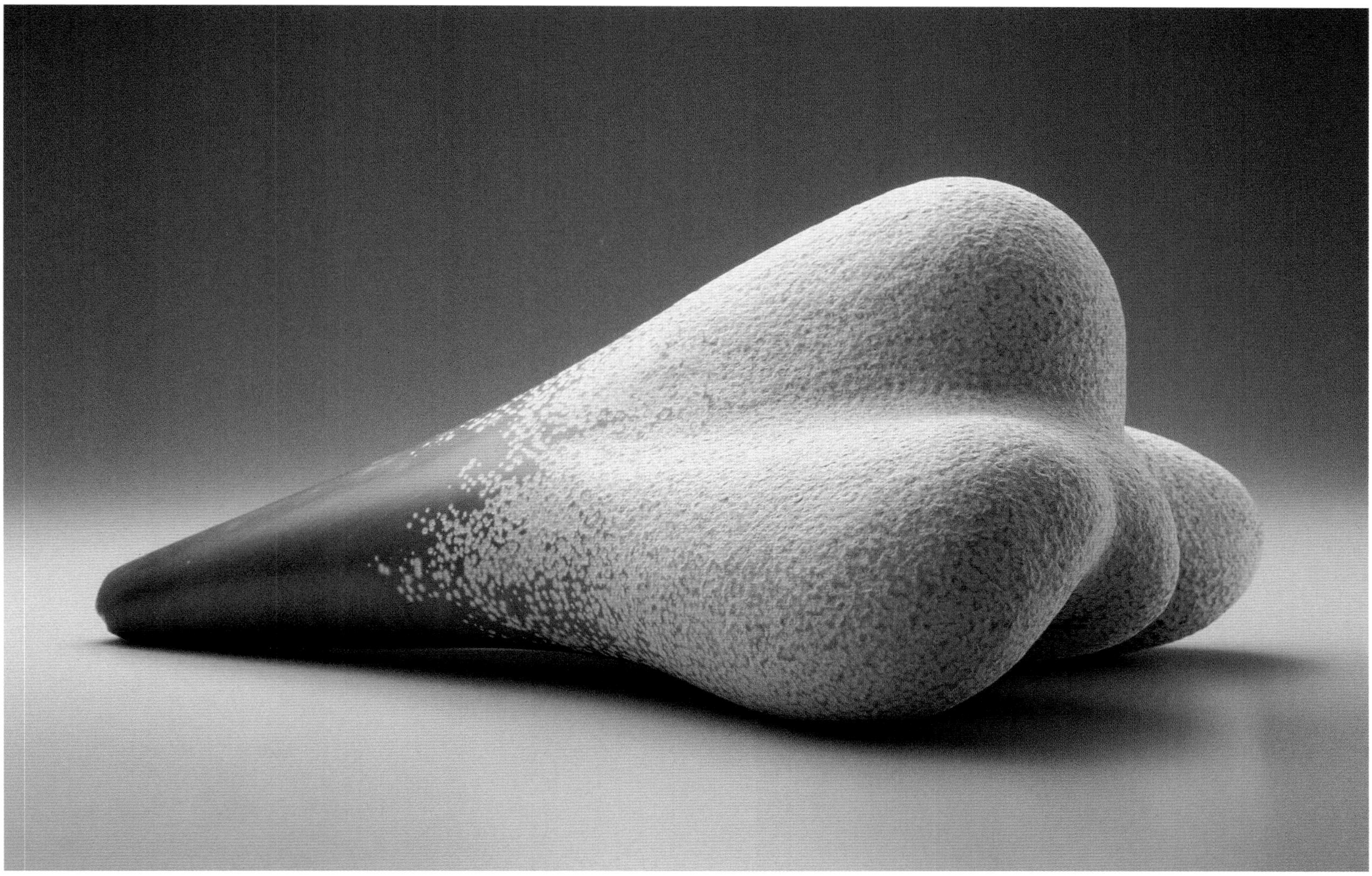

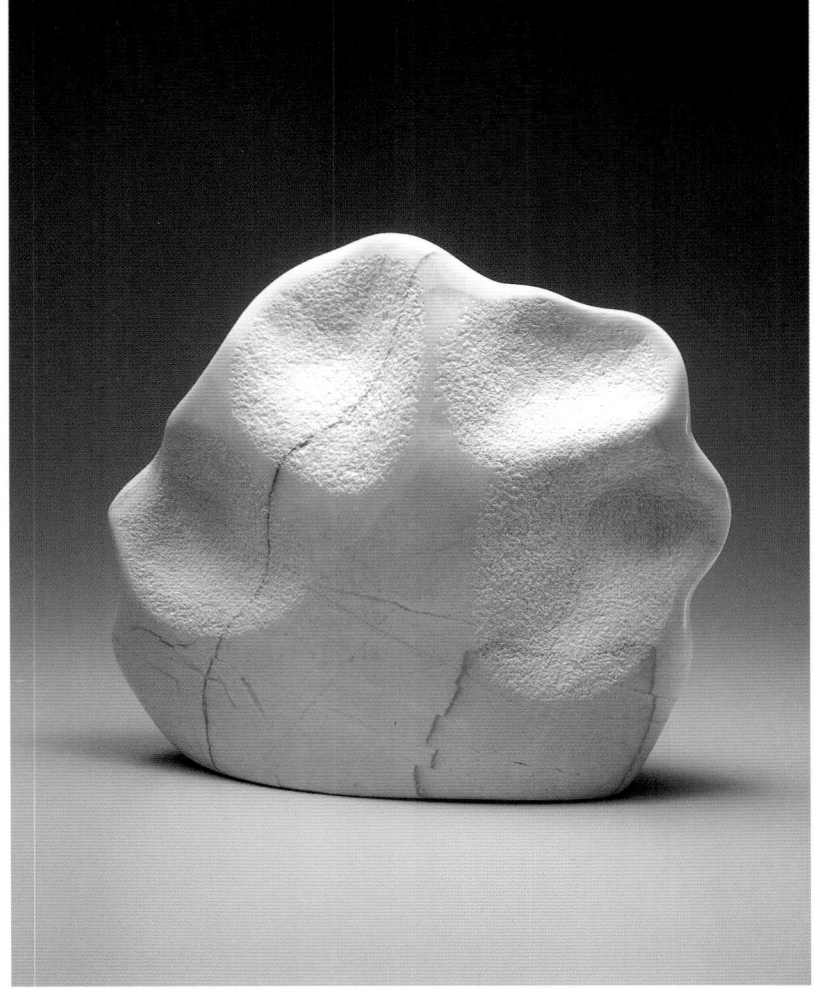
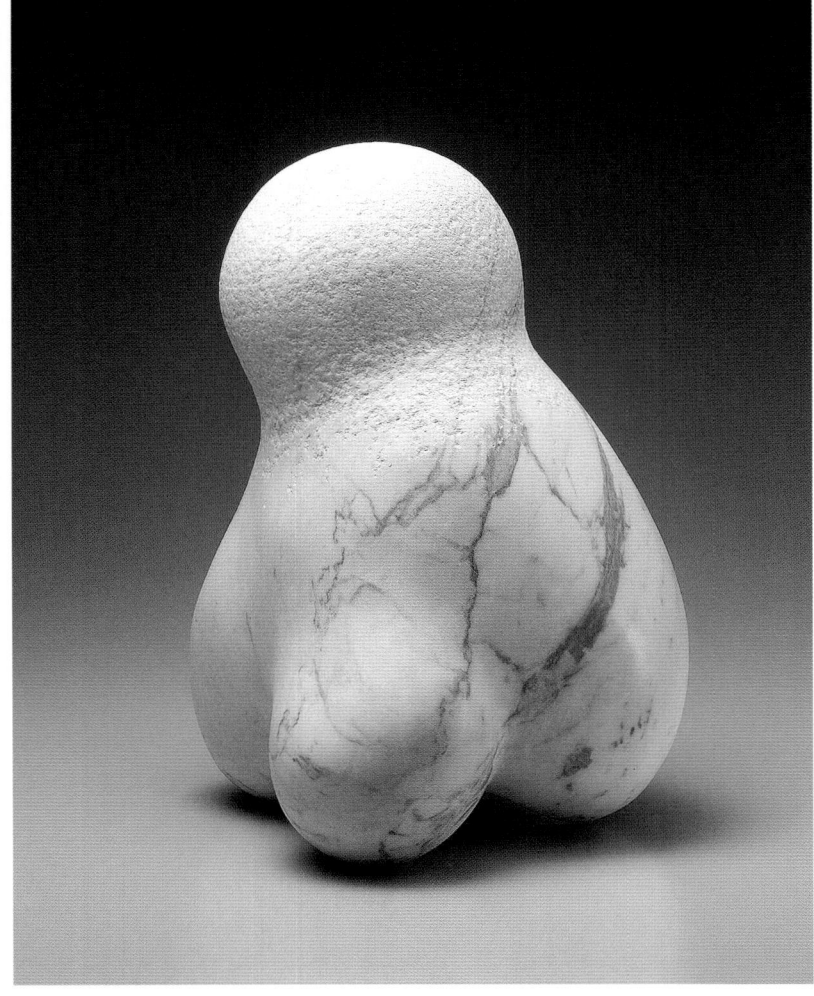

2-4 Snow Mountain, 2000

2-5 White Sun, 2000

2-6 Puppy, 2000

The Sensation of Terracotta—An Encounter with Deep Impact

Igarashi's way of making sculpture is similar to that of a child, purely facing the material without planning or making sketches in advance. A start from tabula rasa—a position based on "submitting to improvisation and ad lib," in Igarashi's own words. Similar to what the American improvisational violinist, Stephen Nachmanovitch, author of *Free Play: Improvisation in Life and Art* writes about improvisation, Igarashi's creative drive is about setting the spirit free or free play in motion. However, improvisation does not mean randomness or whim. As Nachmanovitch states, there are "rules": "Improvisation always has its rules, even if they are not prior rules. When we are totally true to our own individuality, we are actually following a very intricate design. This kind of freedom is the opposite of 'just anything.' We carry around the rules inherent in our organism… As our playing, writing, speaking, drawing, or dancing unfolds, the inner, unconscious logic of our being begins to show through and mold the material. This rich, deep patterning is the original nature that impresses itself like a seal upon everything we do or are." In fact, Igarashi's sculptures are vividly marked with a clear contour of his "original nature."[2] His affection for all living things is inherent in all his works, the fruits of which are even richer carried out without a strictly arranged plan. Igarashi entrusts himself to chance, allowing his "original nature" to unfold itself.

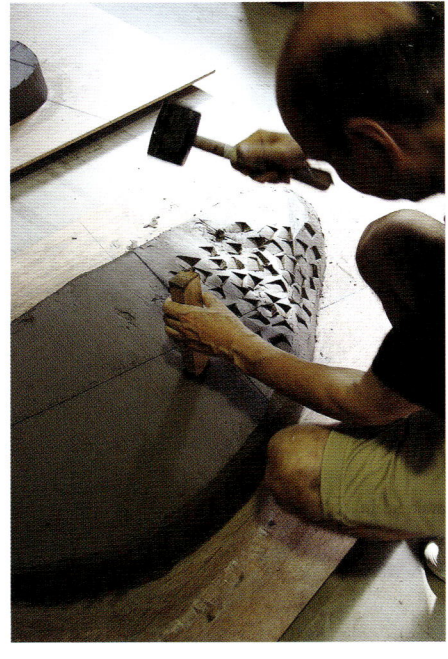

Working with clay at Creare Workshop.

Igarashi's career as a sculptor started by working with stone and metal and moving to wood and terracotta, but the epitome of the art of improvisation is found in terracotta. Aside from conventional tools and equipment, Igarashi uses found objects like sticks, ropes, small metal pieces, wires, pebbles, even bamboo or leaves and twigs to carve, pound, press, and scrape. *Rhythm of Wave*, installed at the premises of Tokyo Metropolitan Subway's Daimon Station of the Oedo Line, is his very first piece. The delicate foamy surface of the intricate layers that are piled up on top of each other are pleasing to the eye and are similar to the traditional mud walls in ancient Japanese temples and shrines—and as if guided by the earth, the bold gouge in the middle accentuates the piece.

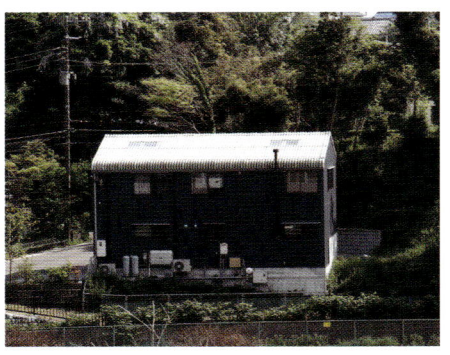

Igarashi's atelier in Akiya Yokosuka, Kanagawa, Japan

Moving back to Japan from Los Angeles in June 2004, Igarashi's creative activities accelerated around and after this time, producing key works that attracted attention such as *Landscape* (2003), installed at the observation deck of the Sapporo JR Tower in Hokkaido and *Forest of "Terminus"* (2011), a piece carved in vertical rhythm, for the underground plaza PASEO in the same Sapporo station area. Igarashi also designed the surrounding area, including graphics for the walls, *Land of Intelligence* (2012), a sculpture in three pieces for the Fukuoka University Library in Kyushu, and *The Mother Earth* (2012), a sculpture with a fountain and bench for the public area of Akasaka K-Tower, the main office building of the construction giant Kajima Corporation.

All works were made at the Shigaraki factory, including *White Legend* (2011), a monumental piece measuring 21 meters in length placed at the Kazenobi Museum, and *Diversity and Harmony* (2014), 108 colorful ceramic cubes of various glaze decorating the main entrance of Xinzhuang Joint Office Tower, a governmental building in Taiwan. By using the earth on which life grows (local earth was also partially used), the cubes symbolize the intermingling of different history and culture of Taiwan, existing in harmony.

Igarashi describes working with terracotta as "submitting myself to the pleasant sensation of the clay reacting to the tools employed, which are extensions of the movement of my hands, fingers, and body."[3] "My terracotta works are an extension of the idea explored in the wooden HF series. I work ad lib; using the hammer to hit tools and other objects into the clay…I guess the clay that I use is about five times as hard as that which is used for pottery. I have the factory prepare clods in a specified size. On average, the clods are in units measuring 50 to 200mm in thickness, about 250mm in depth, and 600mm in length. These units are then scraped and carved, sometimes using all of my weight. Of course, it is easy to cut using wire, but heavy tools help supplement the lack of muscle power. For example, I often use an old column to hit and transform the shape of the clay. For the same reason, everything that's made out of iron can possibly become a useful tool…without thinking, I try to see how the material reacts, submitting myself to the movement caused incidentally by the tools used. Even failure is considered God-given and no attempt is made to undo it. Cracks that occur during drying or baking are repaired but not re-made. I don't want the spontaneity to be lost."

[2] Nachmanovitch, Stephen. (1990) *Free Play: Improvisation in Life and Art*. New York: Jeremy P. Tarcher/Penguin.

[3] Igarashi, Takenobu. (2012) *Terra-cotta*. Igarashi Atelier.

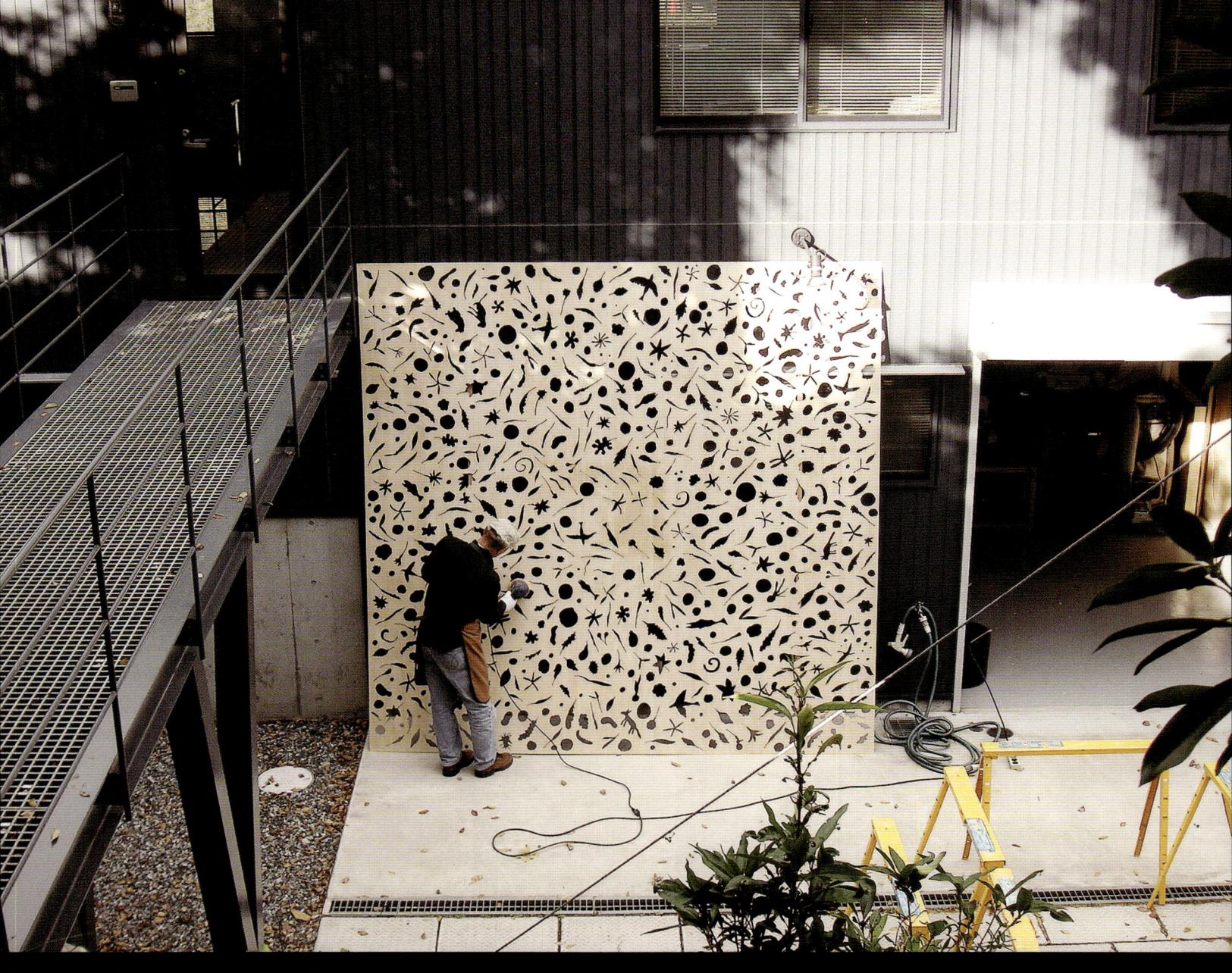
Making Komorebi series at the Atelier in Akiya.

Another series in wood is the *Calligraphy* series, in which Igarashi freely intersects and joins plywood as if creating brush strokes in space. Often the plywood pieces are bound together with silk strings, used in Japanese traditional musical instruments. Visiting the Ise Shrine, the origin of the Japanese soul, was the catalyst for the series. "I discovered a beautiful box in the treasure hall of the Ise Shrine. As if recollecting the form, pieces of wood were bound together with strings to form a box. The box was held together not by timberwork but by tying. I was so impressed by the gentle dignity emanating from the box. The *Calligraphy* series are made up of freely cut out plywood pieces bound together by silk strings. The holes for the strings are made by intuition. First, a stable triangular shape is built, upon which other pieces can be added. It is just like calligraphy, done instantaneously, and cannot be undone."

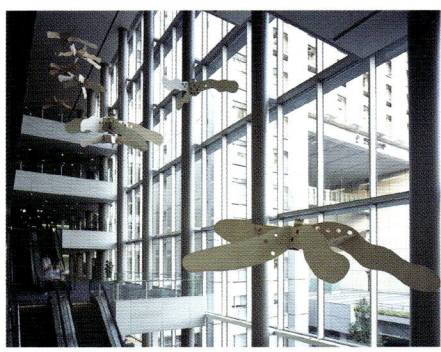

2-7 Sky Dancing
Shibaura Institute of Technology
Toyosu, Tokyo, Japan, 2005

Representative works of this series include *To the Sky* (2003), installed at the Tokyo University of Science; *Goka-kyoso* (2003) at the INA Central Hospital in Nagano Prefecture; and *Kaze Hana Tori* (2006) at the Kagetsu Children's Center in Hokkaido. *To the Sea of Premonition* (2006) is installed at the entrance lobby of the main tower of Tokyo Midtown, a multifunctional building complex built at the former site of the Ministry of Defense. For this piece, Igarashi produced an impromptu maquette. Using the CAD technique, an exact three-dimensional plan was drawn from the maquette, and the pieces were assembled together with glue and screws. Furthermore, there is another piece also titled *To the Sky* (2007) installed at the Midland Square owned by Toyota Motors and situated at Nagoya station, followed by two sculptures both titled *Sky Dancing*, one at the Toyosu campus of the Shibaura Institute of Technology (2005) and the other at the Sapporo's Odori Bisse (2010). Also *Zawa Zawa/Hyun Hyun/Gigii* (2015), onomatopoeia for rustle/whirl/creak, is installed at Osaki Bright Core, a high-rise building near Osaki station in Tokyo. In his book, *Lines: A Brief History*, Tim Ingold, an English cultural anthropologist, refers to East Asian brush calligraphy of *Kanji* (Chinese characters) as "dance." Igarashi's *Calligraphy* series are in fact a dynamic celebration of the "dancing wood."

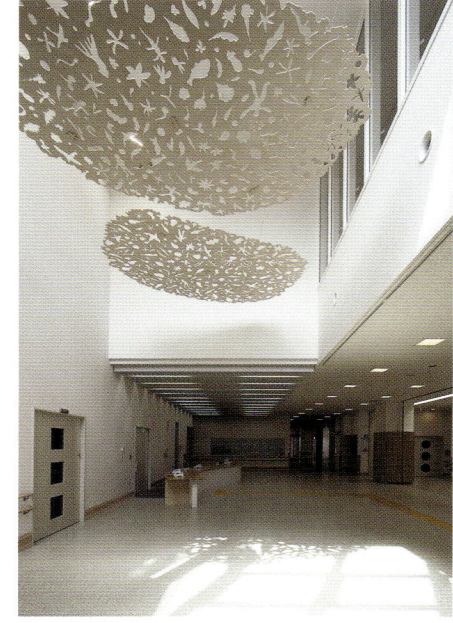

2-8 Komorebi
Hokkaido Medical Center for
Child Health and Rehabilitation
Sapporo, Hokkaido, Japan, 2007

Initially Igarashi used Finnish plywood, but recently he uses plywood produced domestically out of Japanese lime tree (Tilia japonica) from the Hidaka area of Hokkaido. These large sheets are cut out extemporaneously in the Komorebi (sunlight shining through leaves) series that is an ode to nature resembling lace work. Many of them are set up throughout Japan. The piece hanging in the air at the entrance hall of the Hokkaido Medical Center for Child Health and Rehabilitation (2007) is especially gentle and impressive. The *Komorebi* series exist also in metal, like the outdoor hollow steel column functioning as a landmark at Lucent Tower (2007), a high-rise office building near Nagoya station. The cutout model in plywood was traced and digitized, and the metal was cut using a laser. As it is apparent from the given examples, Igarashi's activity as a sculptor has been, from the very beginning, mainly that of a public artist livening up the urban environment and public space.

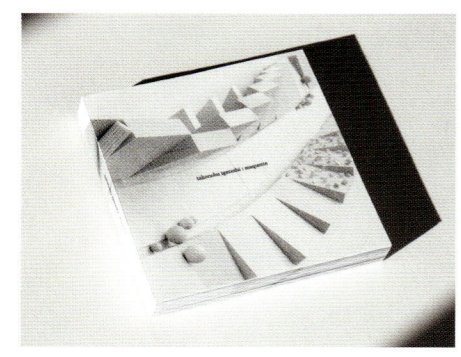

Exhibition Catalog for
Takenobu Igarashi Maquettes.

From the beginning of his career as a sculptor, Igarashi was strongly influenced by Richard Buckminster Fuller (1895–1983), architect, designer, system theorist, mathematician, philosopher, and poet. Born in Massachusetts, Fuller was a superstar visionary, most well known for his geodesic dome, consisting of equilateral triangles and polyhedrons. "The first thing I had in mind when I started doing sculpture was Fuller's unique inventions, attaining maximum power using minimum energy. The functional beauty of the geodesic dome, his pre-fabricated housing, and his mobile homes stimulated me...I thought of making a sculpture with minimum energy, and came up with the Revolving series. I made about 20 different pieces until I reached a limit in terms of form."

Fuchujin (1991) is a revolving sculpture installed as public art at the Intelligent Park in Fuchu. *Lotus* (1997) placed over water at a pharmaceutical company is another one of his early works. Fuller's spirit is resonant in Igarashi's sculptures connecting people and the environment, livening up the urban environment and public space. There are many sculptures like *Lotus* such as *Kumo* (1996) in Tokyo's stylish Azabu Juban shopping district and *Wave Light* (1999) installed in front of a high-rise building in Nakano-Sakaue re-development district, Tokyo, which represent Igarashi's early works.

Most metal sculptures are based on Fuller's concept of the geodesic dome. Employing the stable structure of a triangle as a base and interpreting its rules roughly, Igarashi experimented freely, developing new forms while maintaining strength. Igarashi's experience and intuition allowed him to create a free and dynamic sculpture such as *Dragon Spine* (2004).

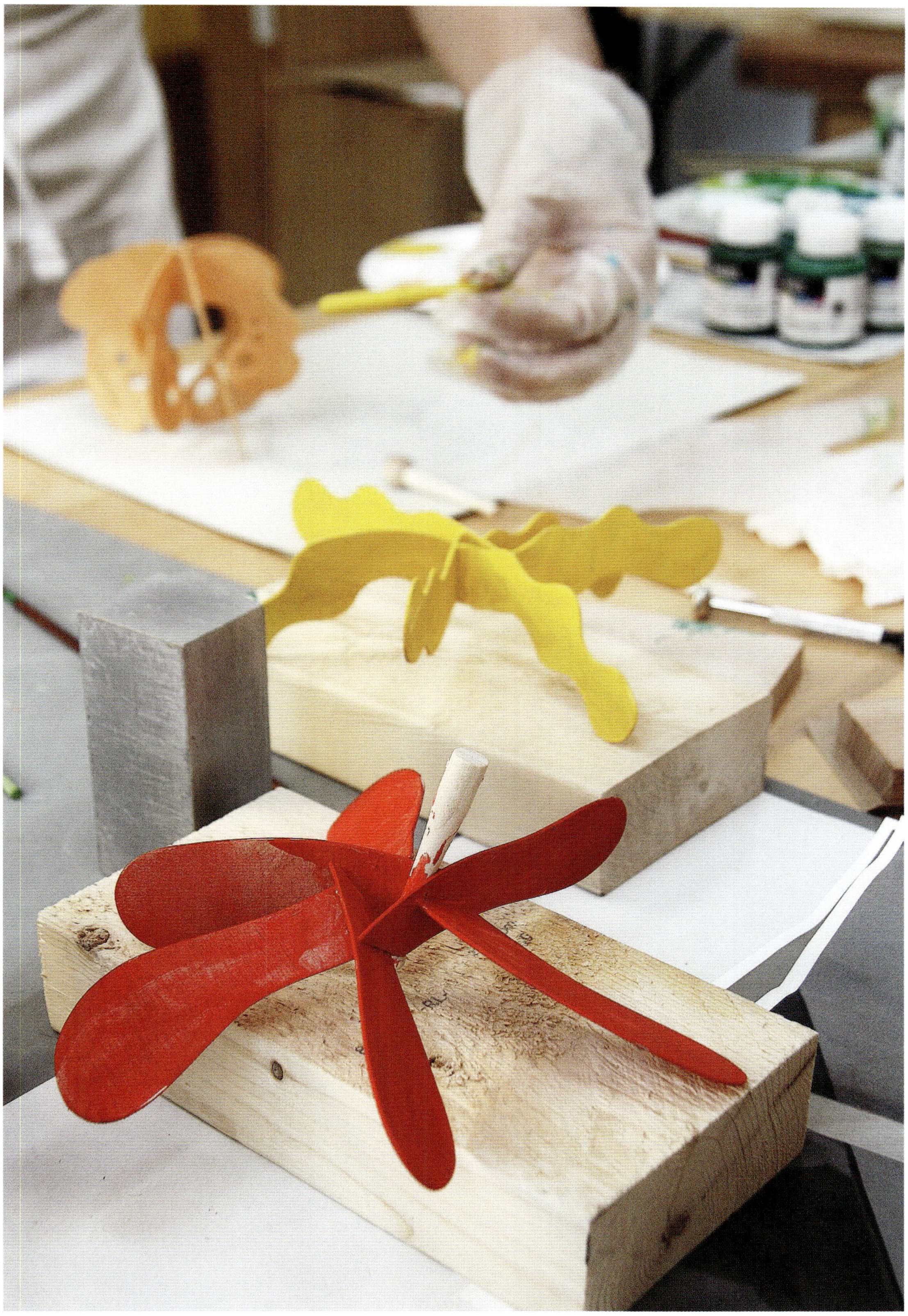

Making Maquettes

Igarashi's surging energetic accomplishments are indisputable. In 2009, he exhibited the prototypes of many of his works in the *Maquette Exhibition* at the designshop+gallery in a quiet residential area of Nishi-Azabu, Tokyo. *Maquette*, a French word for miniature model, is an essential collector's item in the West, but is hardly known in Japan. Igarashi's exhibition, in which he let people casually pick up and touch the items in the gallery, was probably the first exhibition of this kind in Japan. It was a rare occasion to be able to actually feel and touch the original forms created by a contemporary artist.

Freeing oneself and becoming one with life itself, Igarashi's world of expression has an overwhelming presence, unmistakably blooming in its own sensitivity and sparkling with joy.

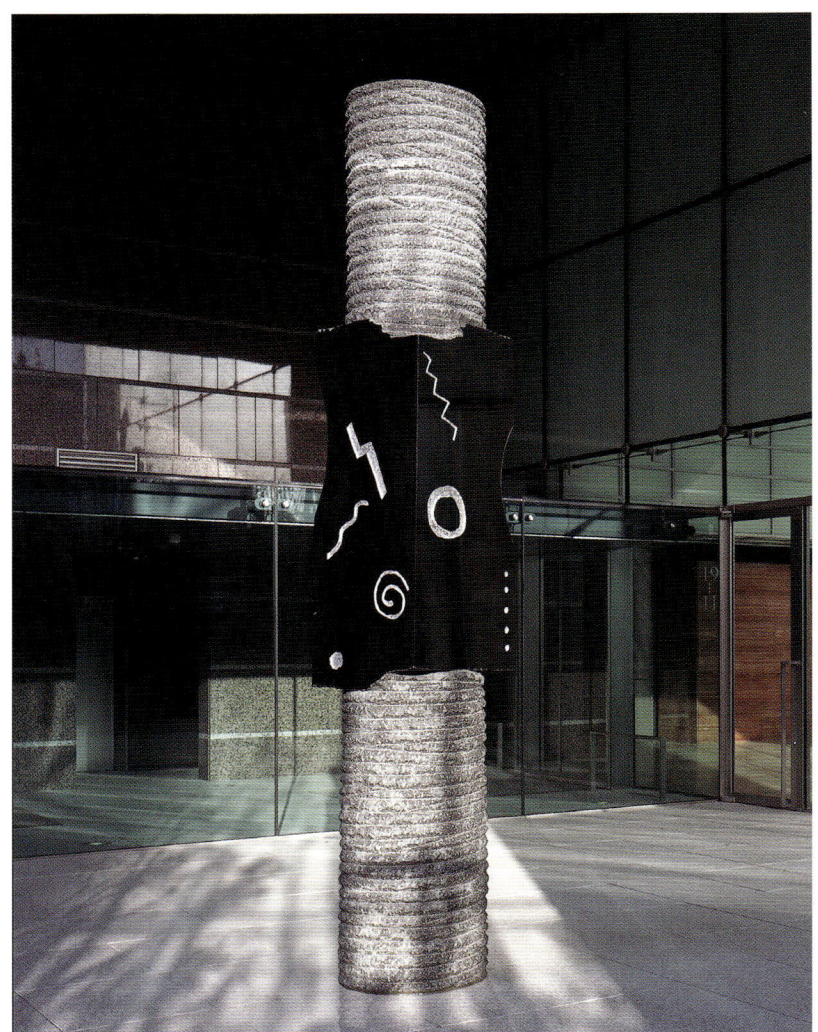 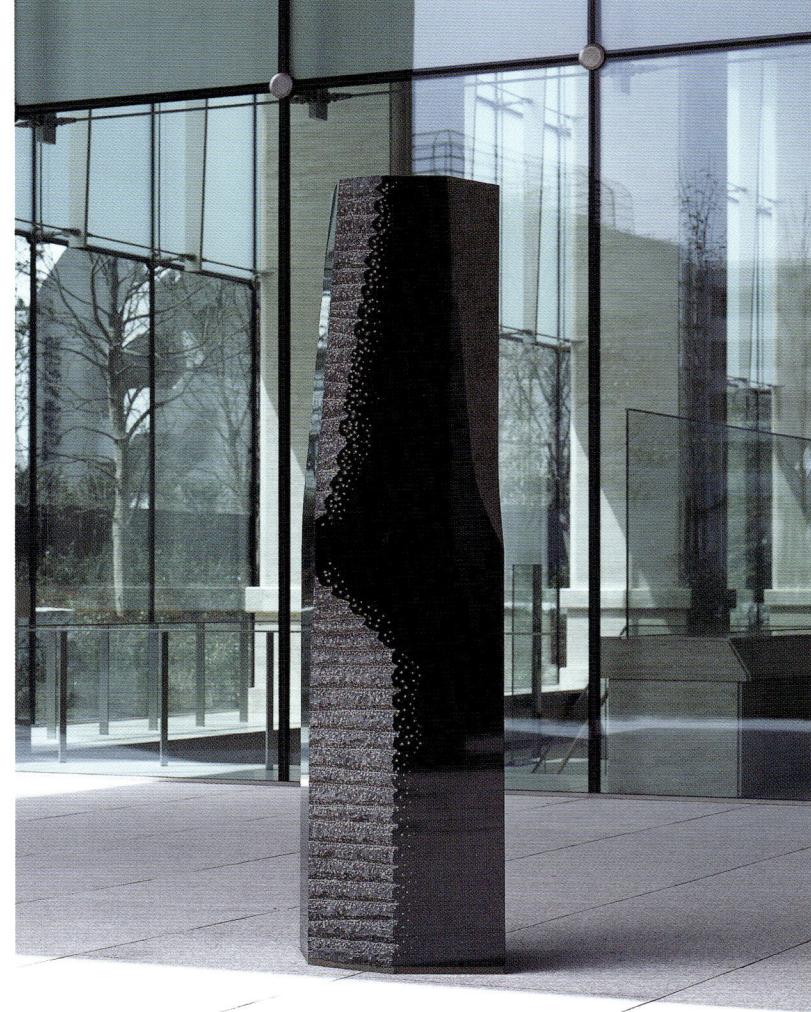

2-9 Sky Tree
Akasaka Garden City
Tokyo, Japan, 2005

2-10 Earth Mother
Akasaka Garden City
Tokyo, Japan, 2005

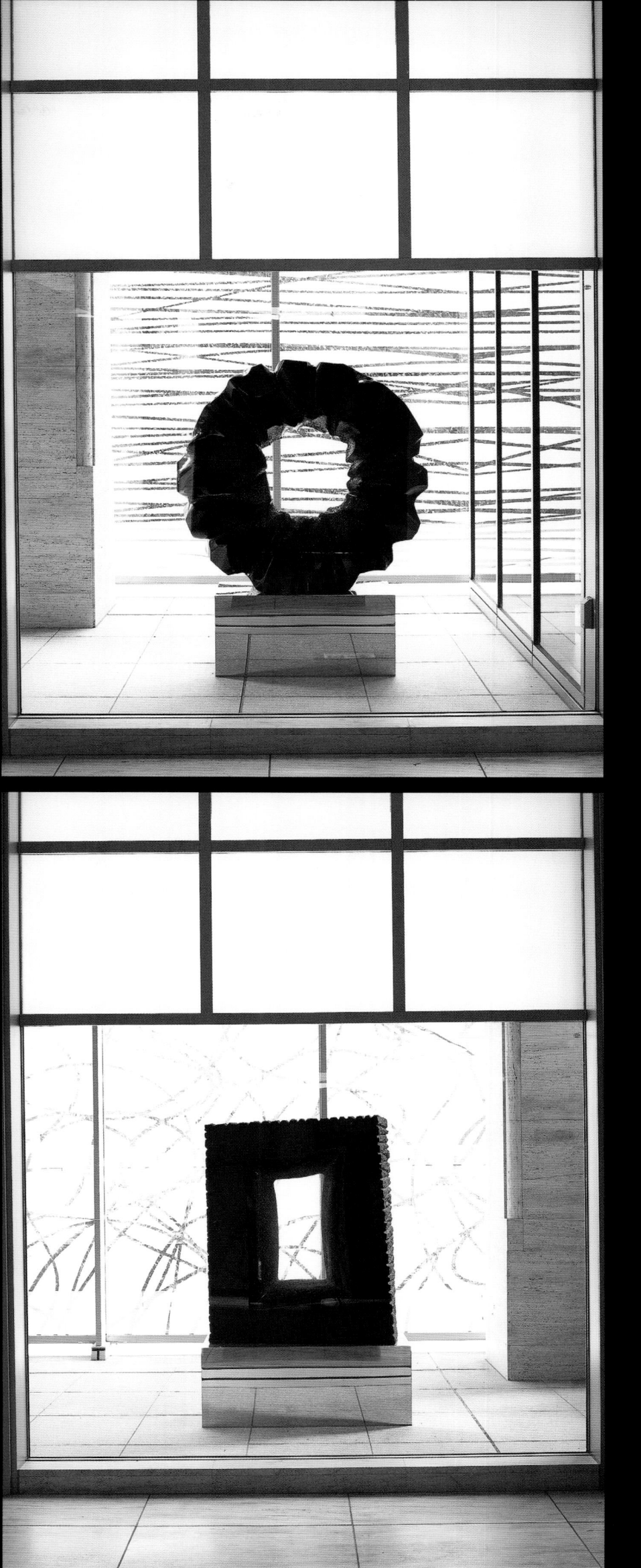

2-11 Fire Ball
Akasaka Garden City
Tokyo, Japan, 2005

2-12 Water Glass
Akasaka Garden City
Tokyo, Japan, 2005

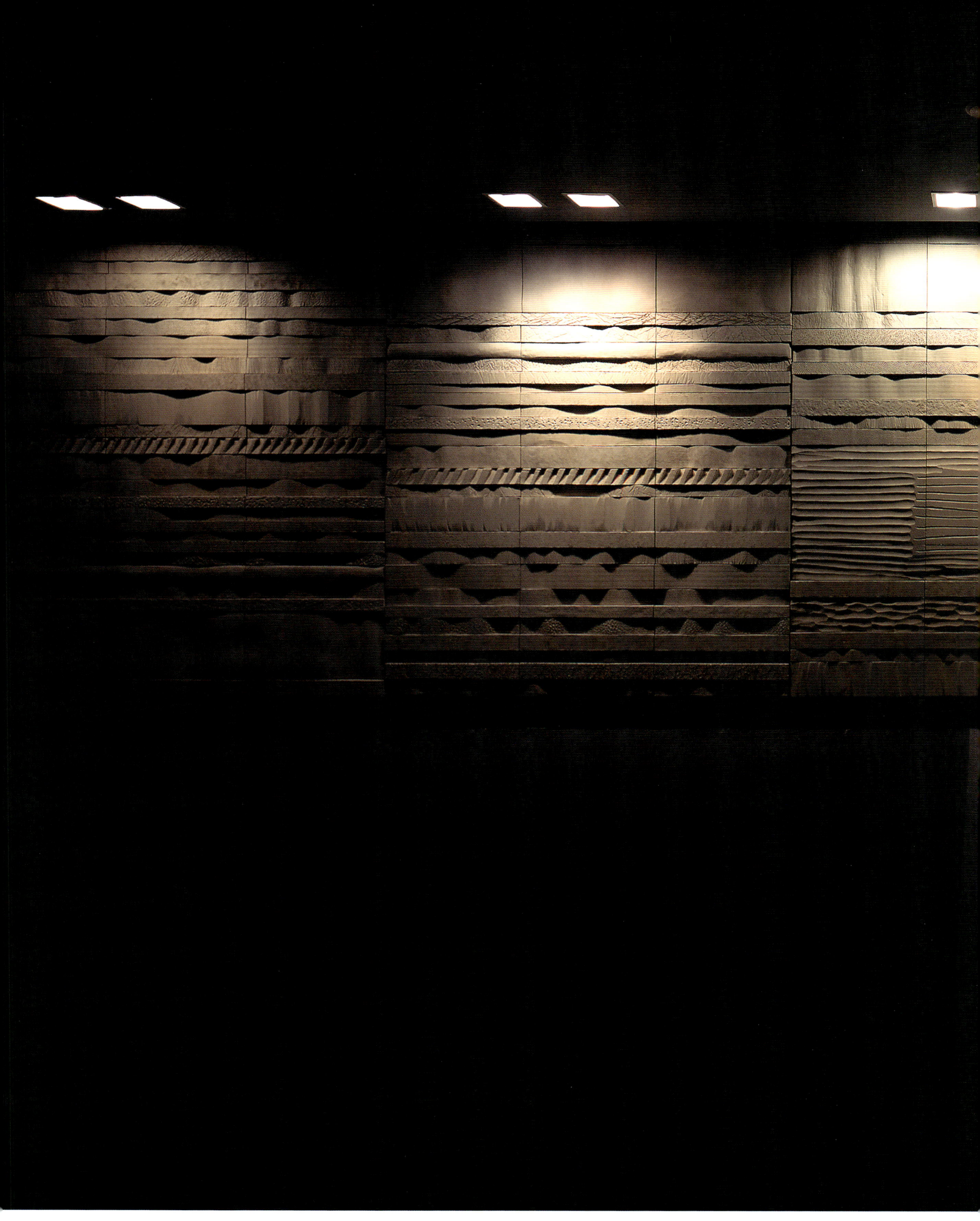

2-13 Rhythm of Wave
Metropolitan Subway, Oedo Line, Daimon Station
Tokyo, Japan, 2000

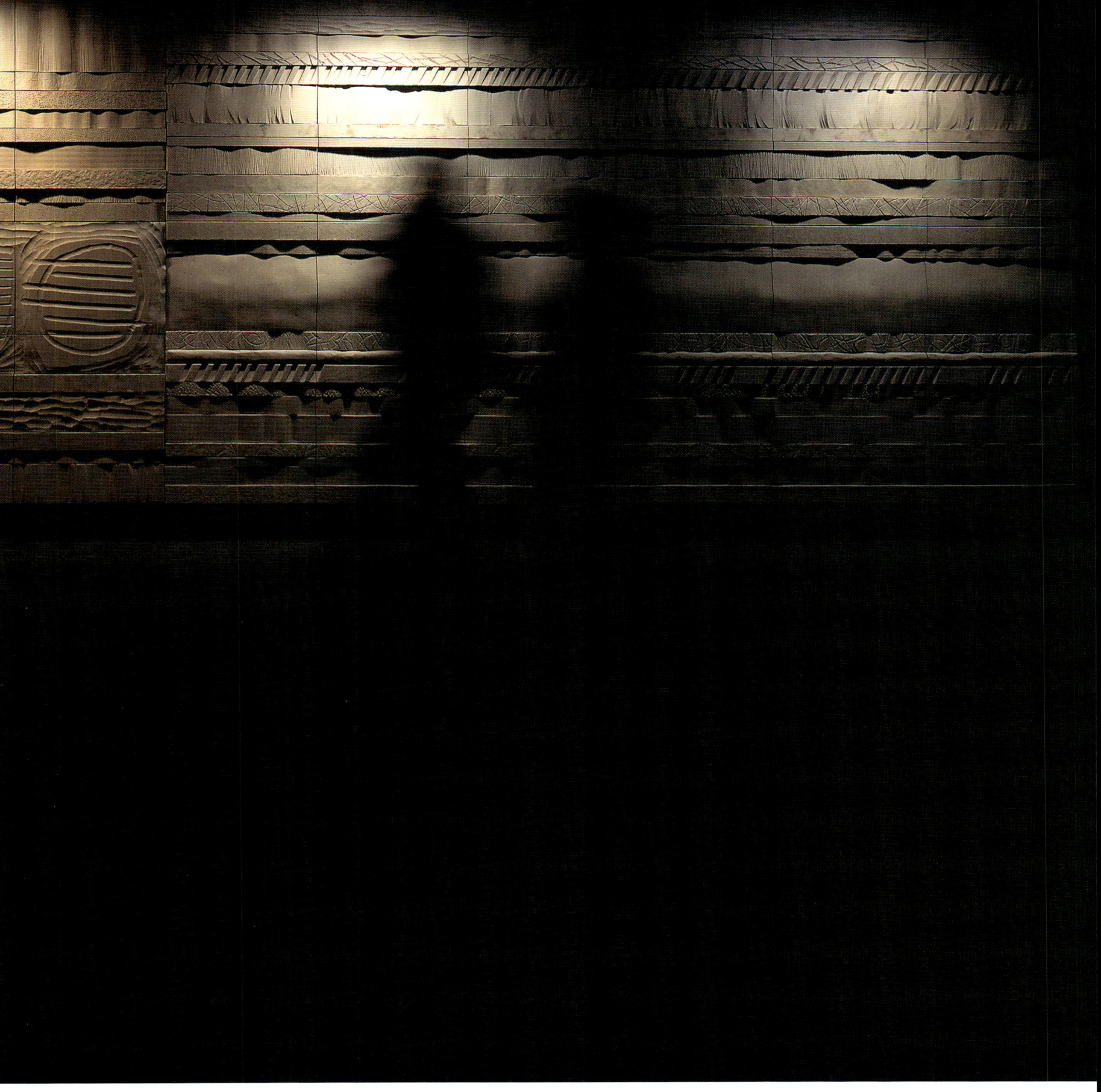

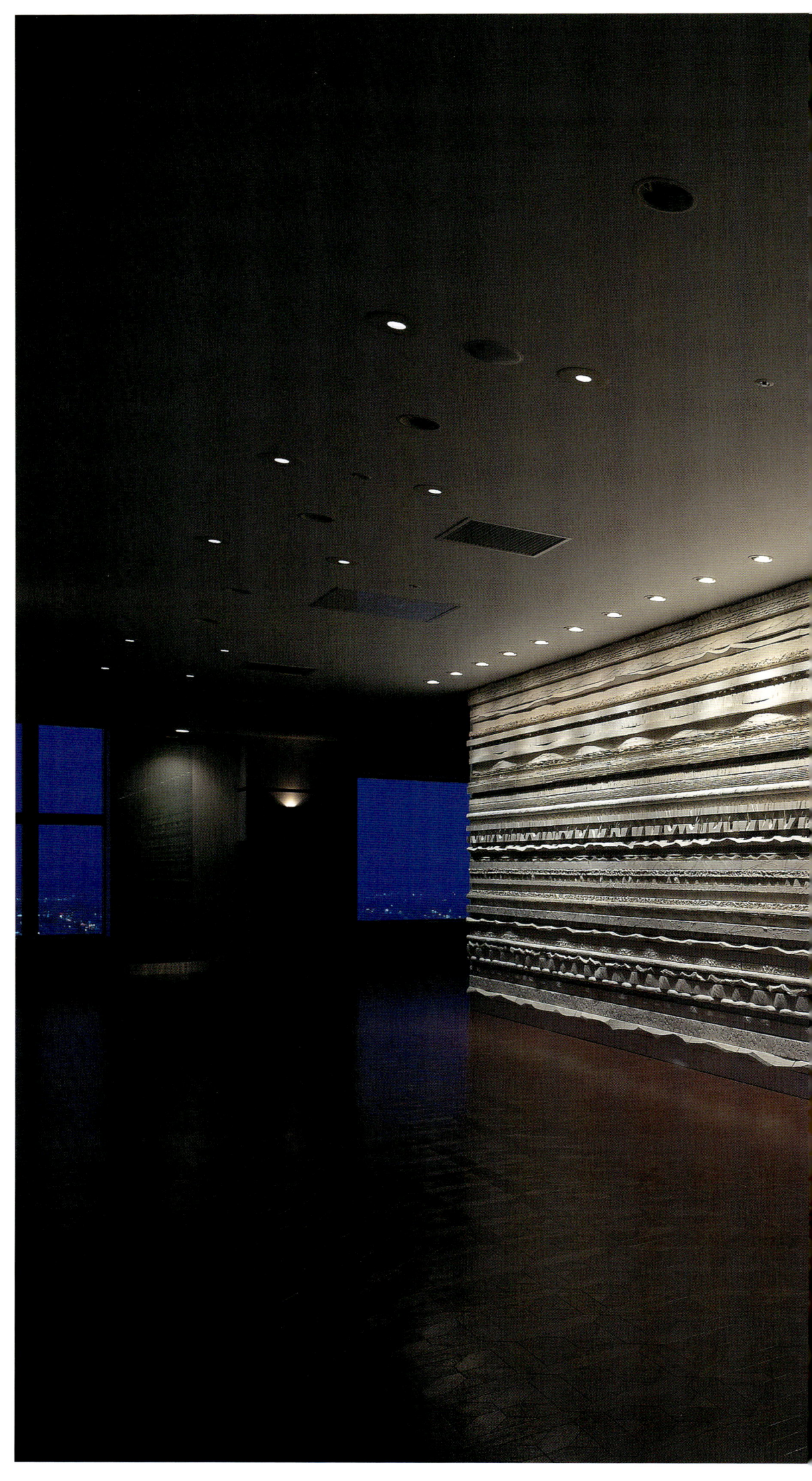

2-14 Landscape
JR Tower Observation Deck T38, Sapporo Station
Sapporo, Hokkaido, Japan, 2003

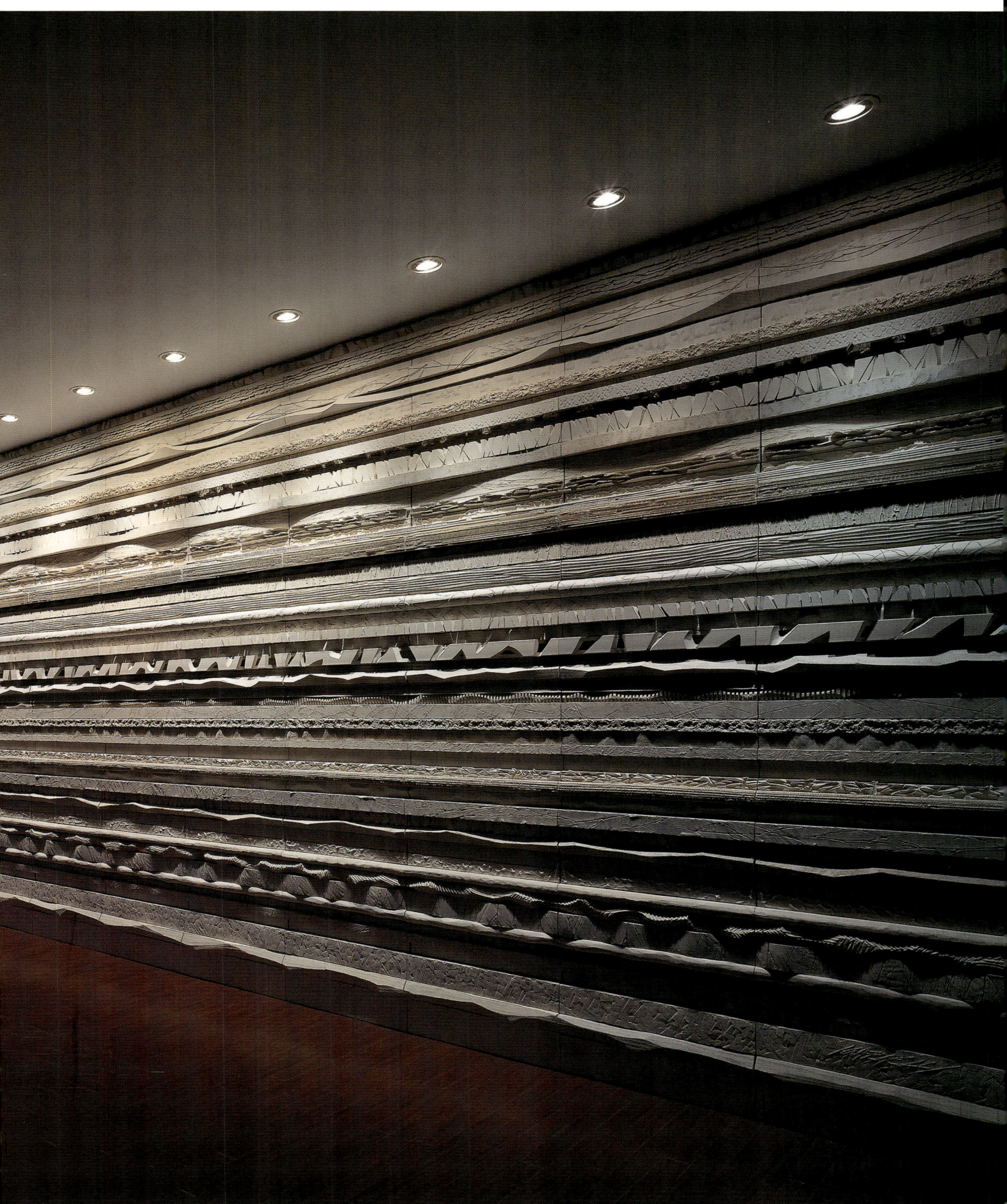

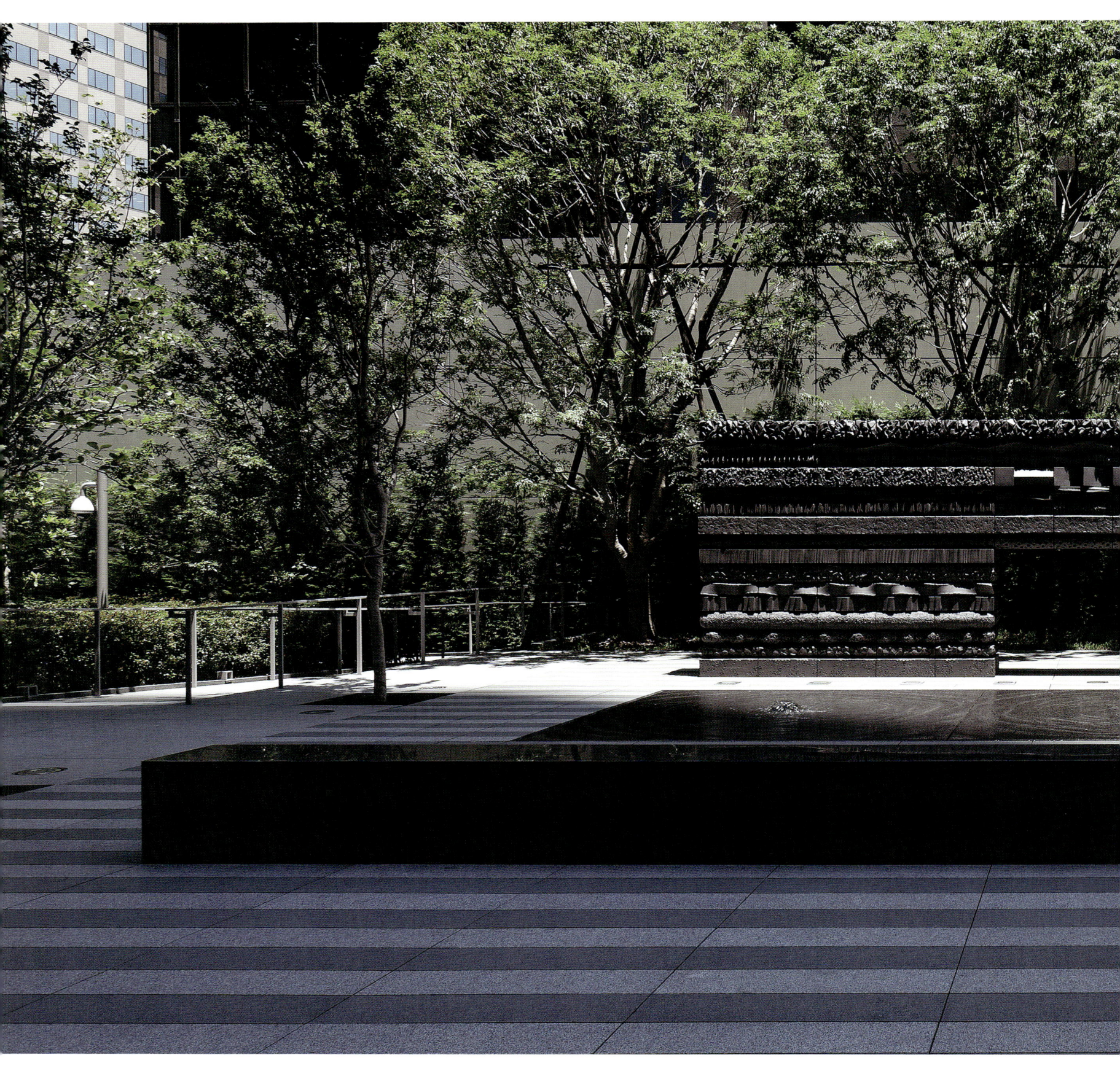

2-15 The Mother Earth (Sculpture)
Fountain Head (Fountain)
Akasaka K-Tower, Tokyo, Japan, 2012

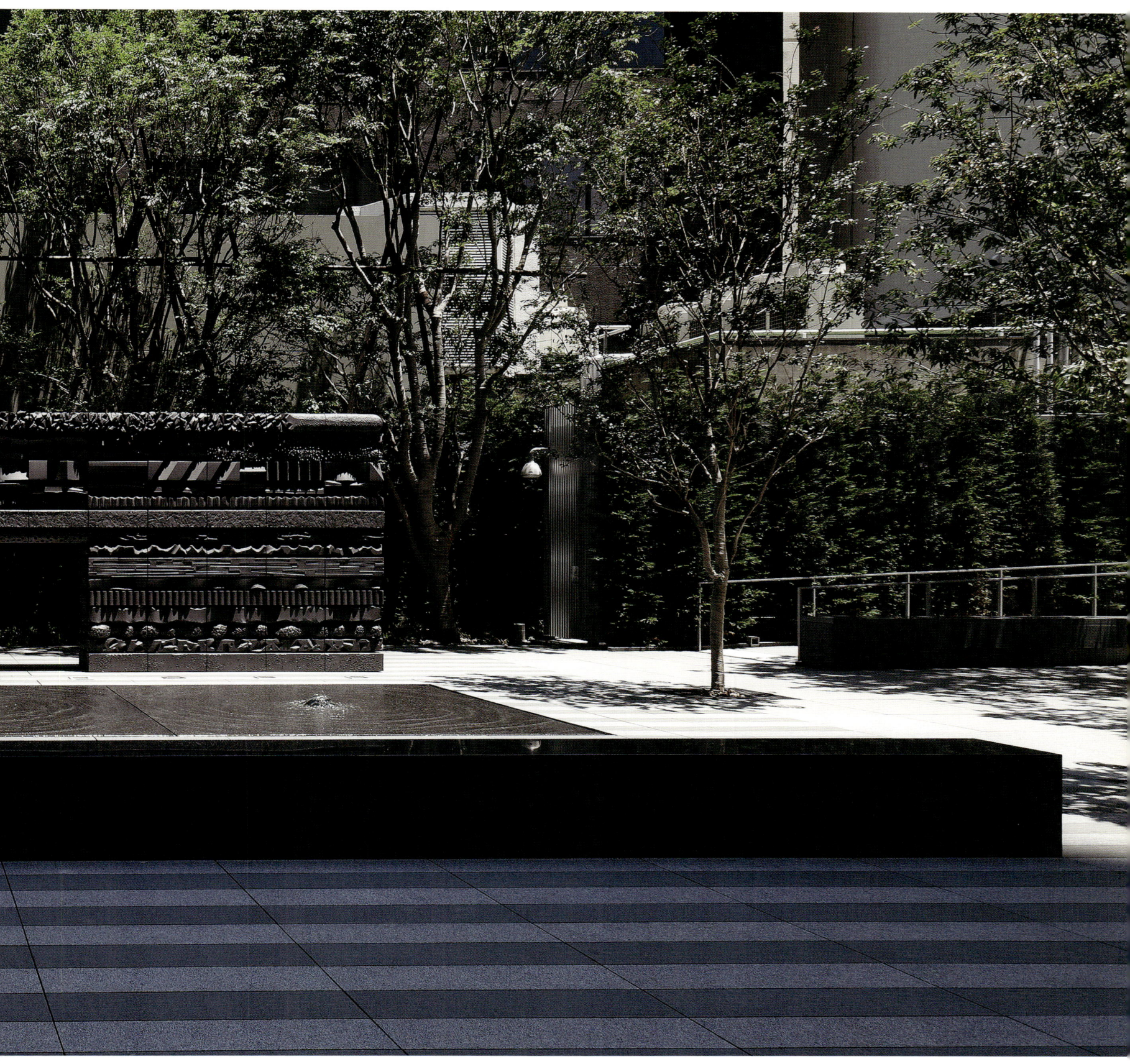

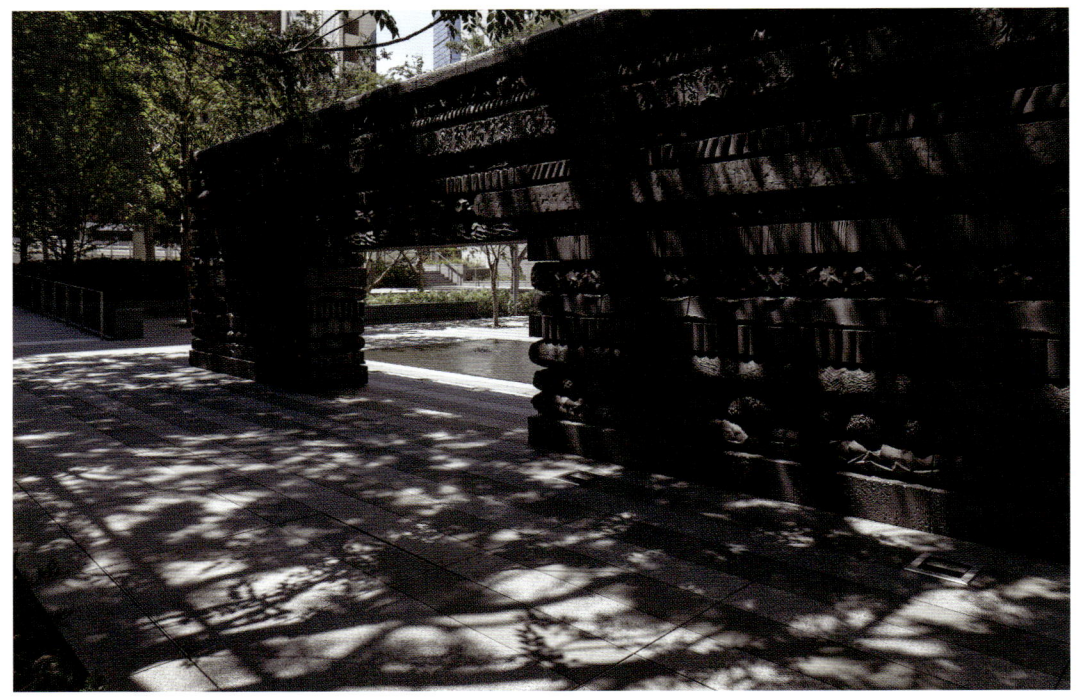

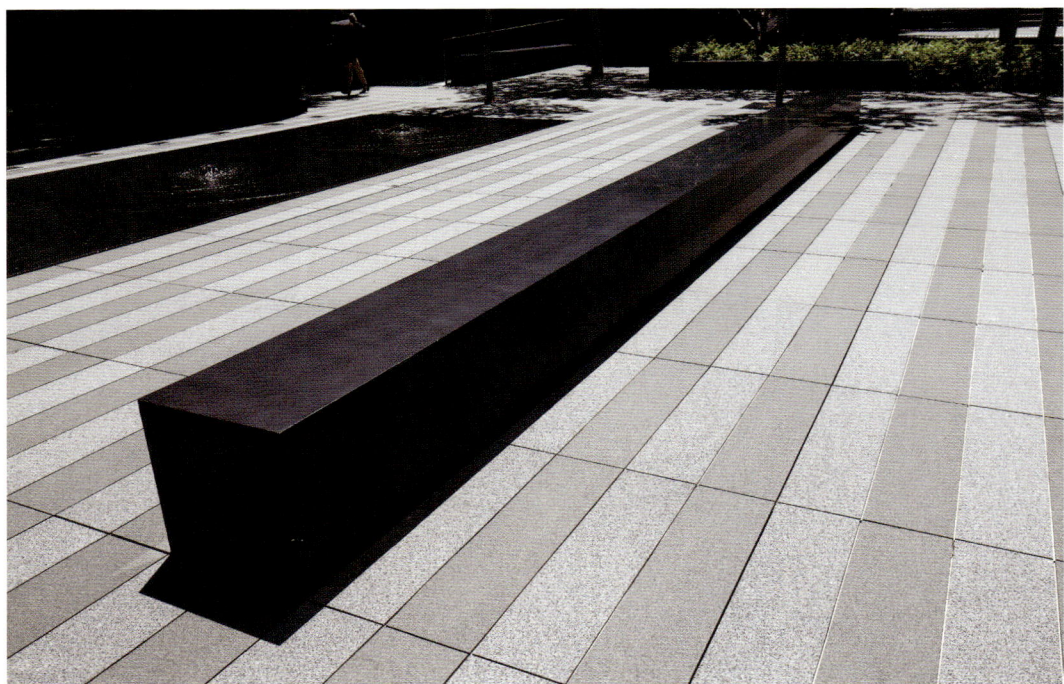

Akasaka K Tower The Mother Earth, Fountain Head and Bench, Land Detail
I came up with the idea of a place with a fountain, bench, sculpture, and floor. (TI)

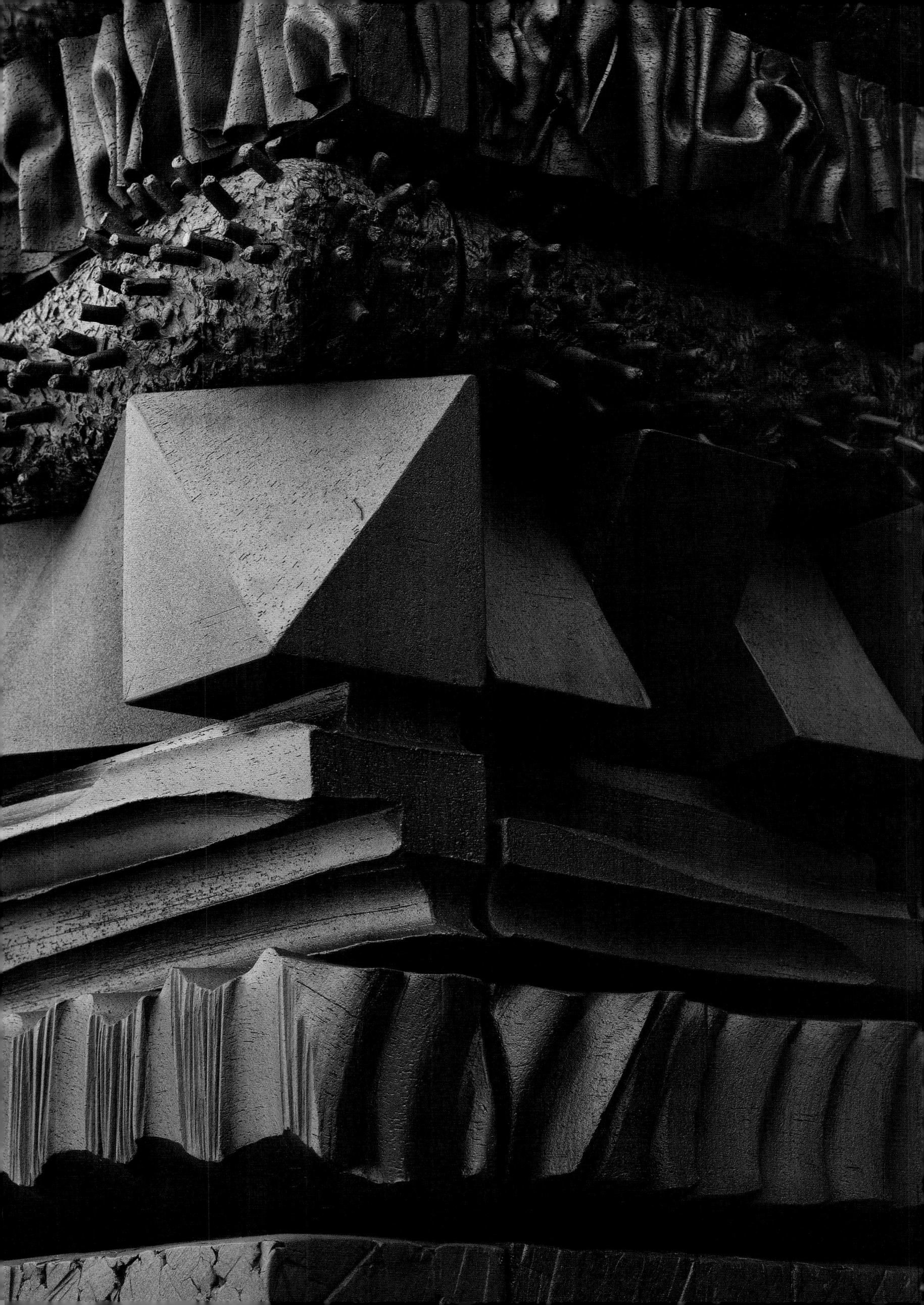

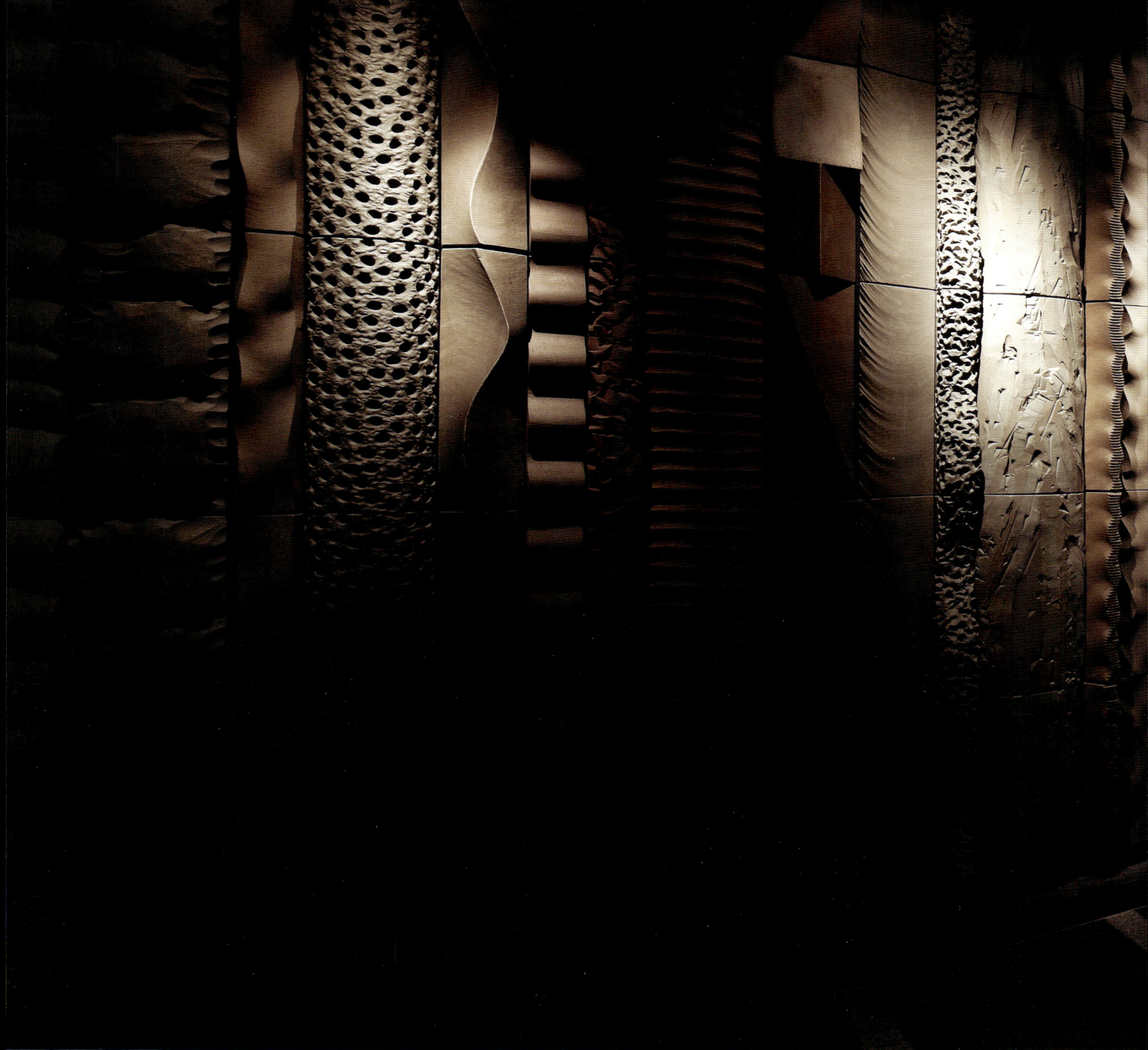

2-16 Forest of Terminus
Basement Plaza of Paseo, JR Sapporo Station
Sapporo, Hokkaido, Japan, 2011

*For Forest of Terminus, I added pigments to the clay to give it color.
With a wall sculpture, stone floor, a bench, and a stainless column,
the basement plaza is a place where people can relax and refresh. (TI)*

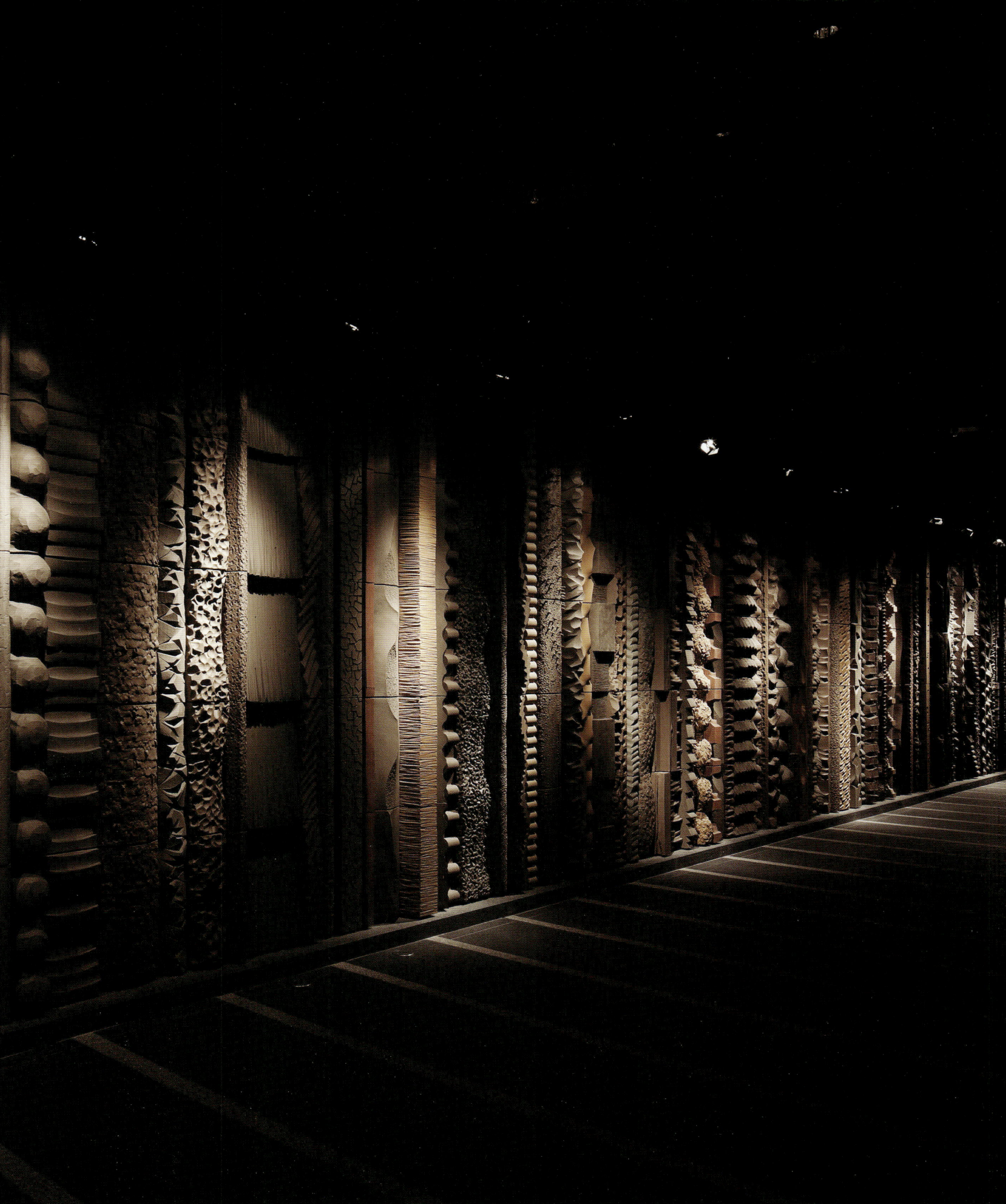

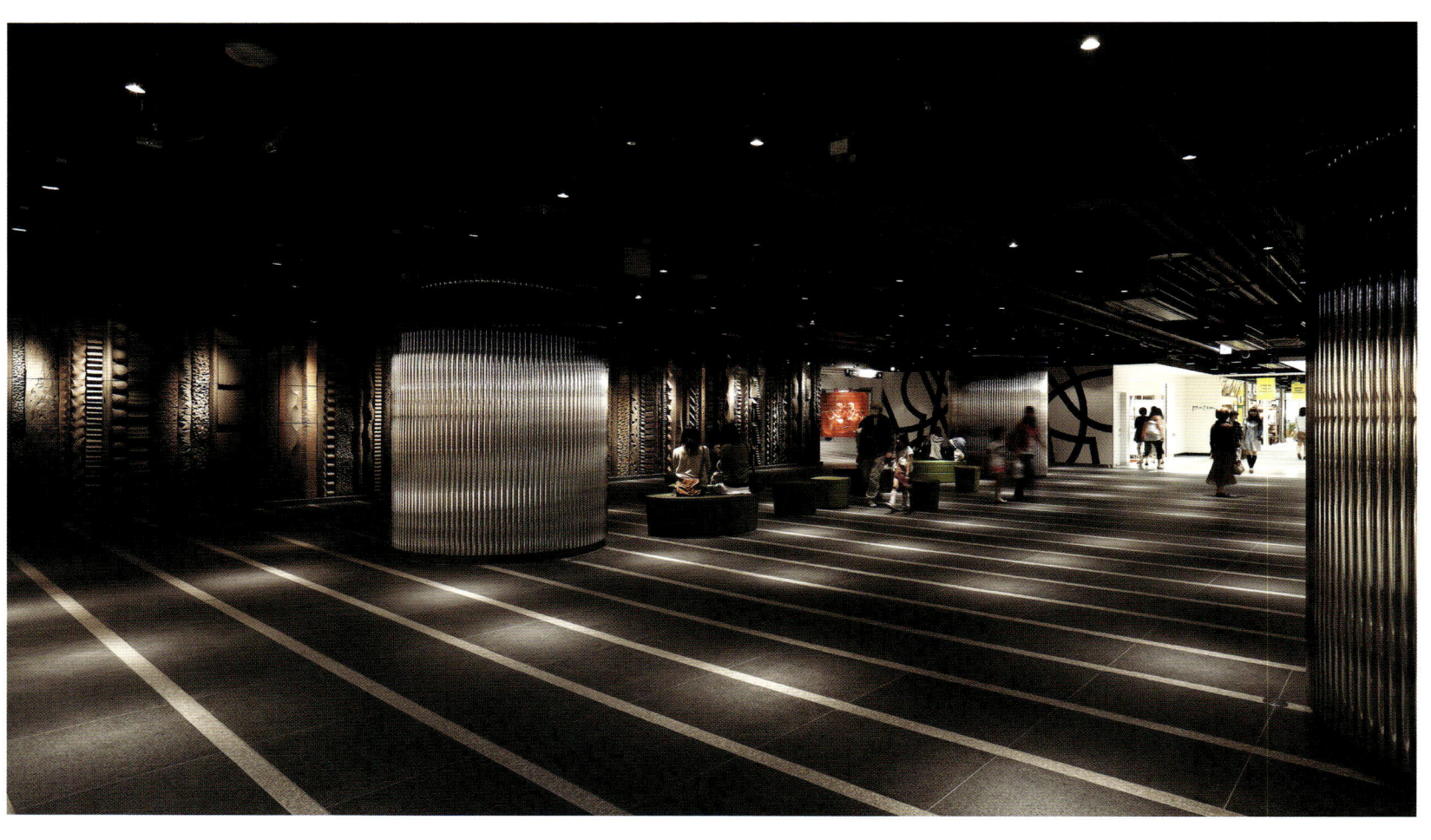

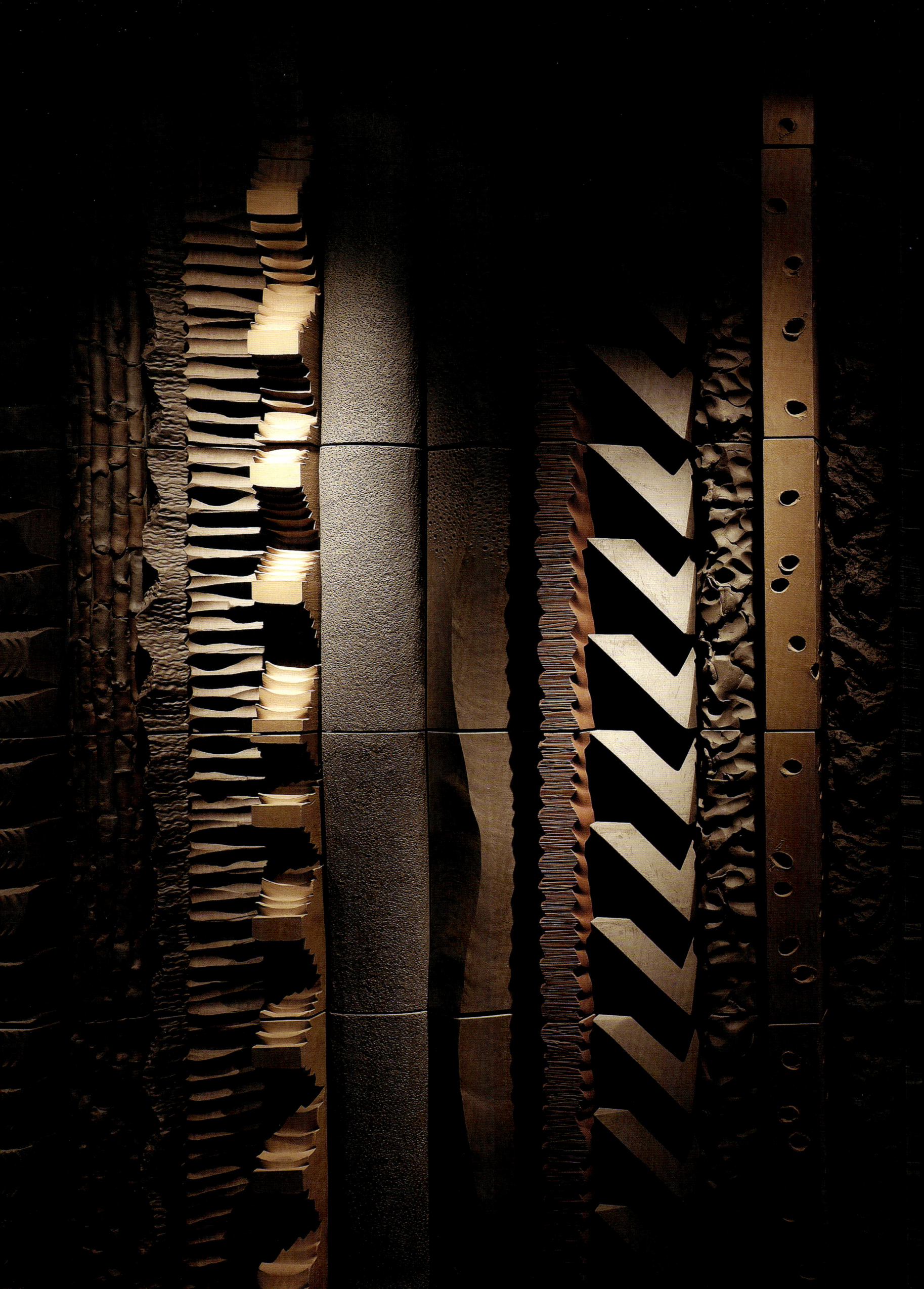

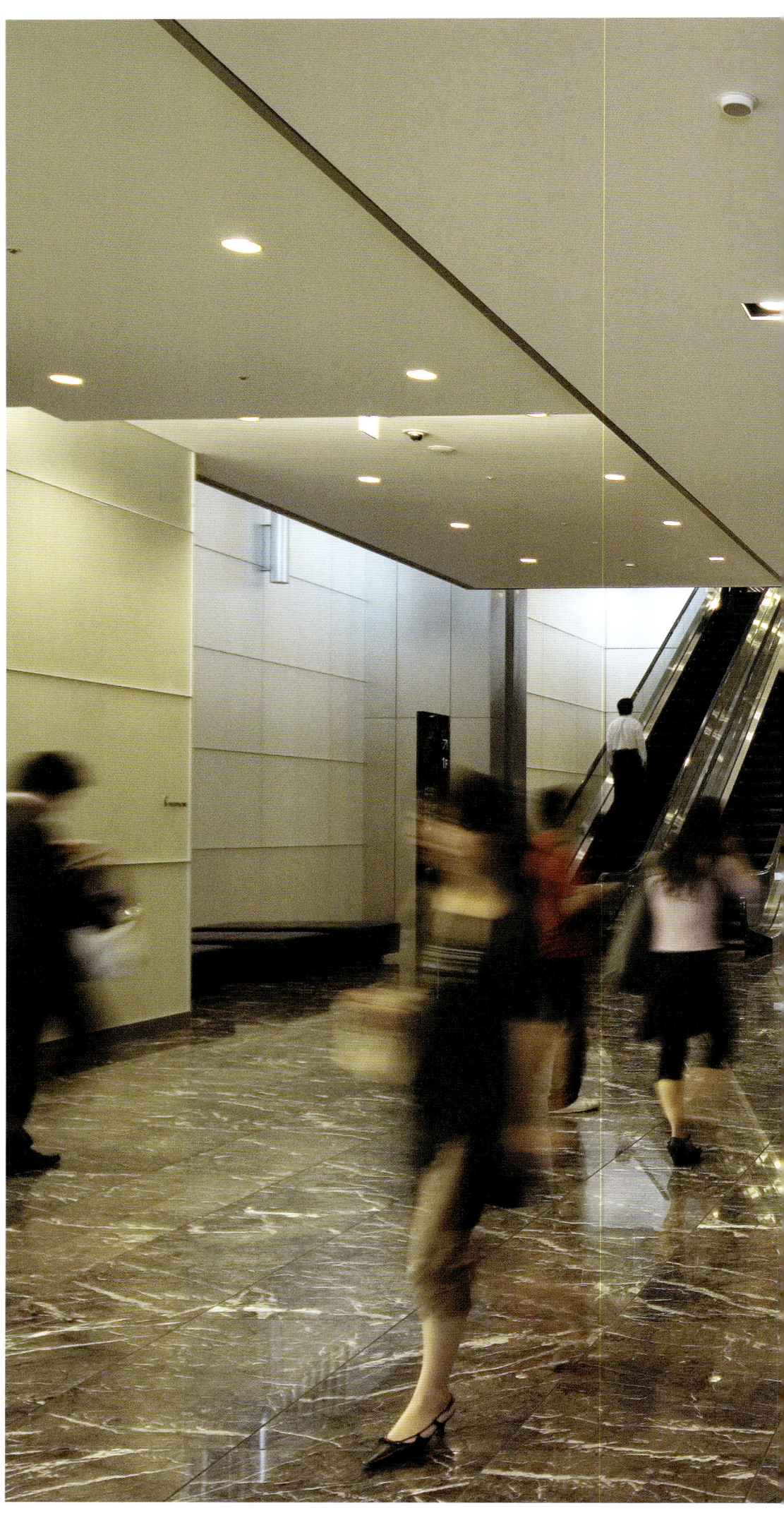

2-17 From the Land of Memory
Tokyo Midtown, Tokyo, Japan, 2006

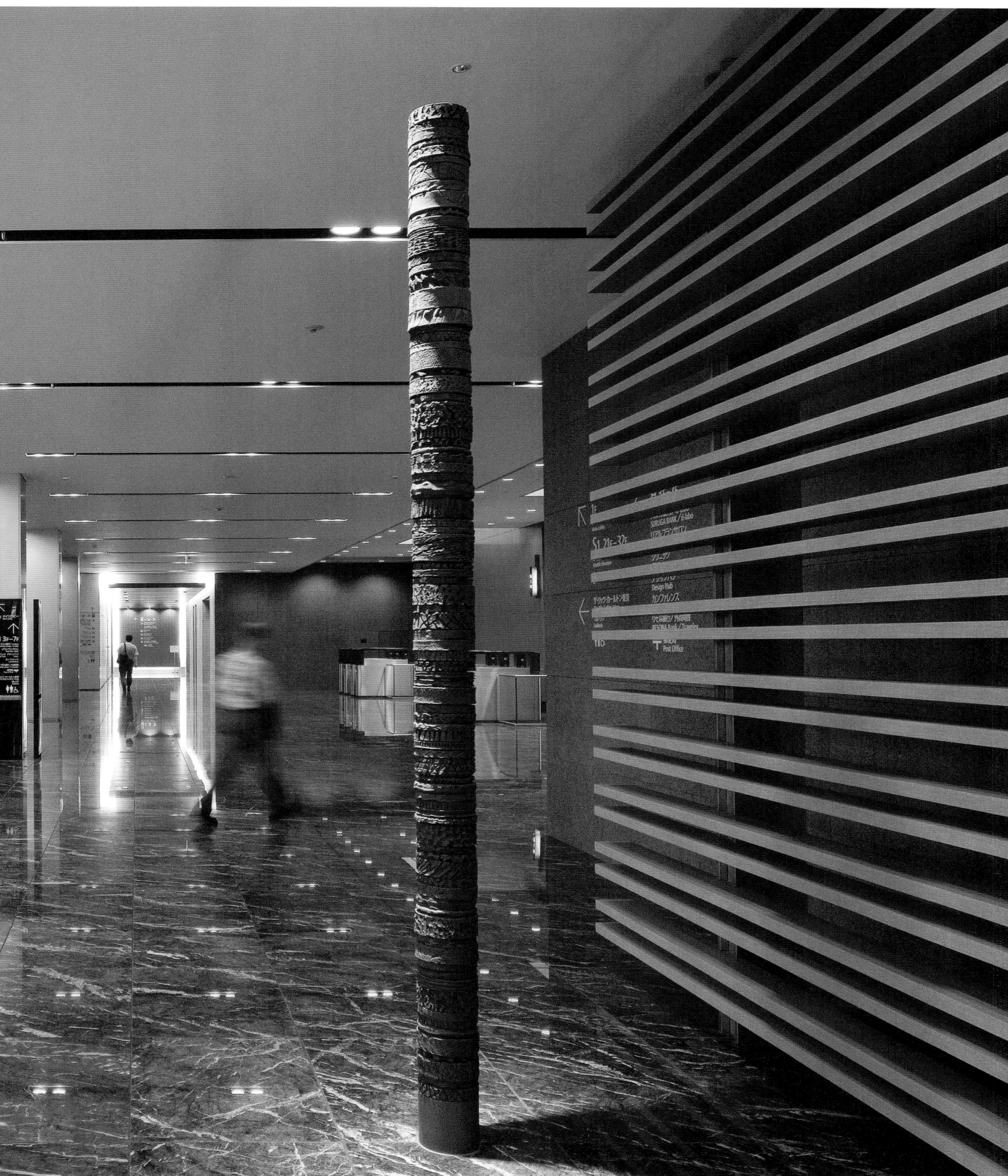

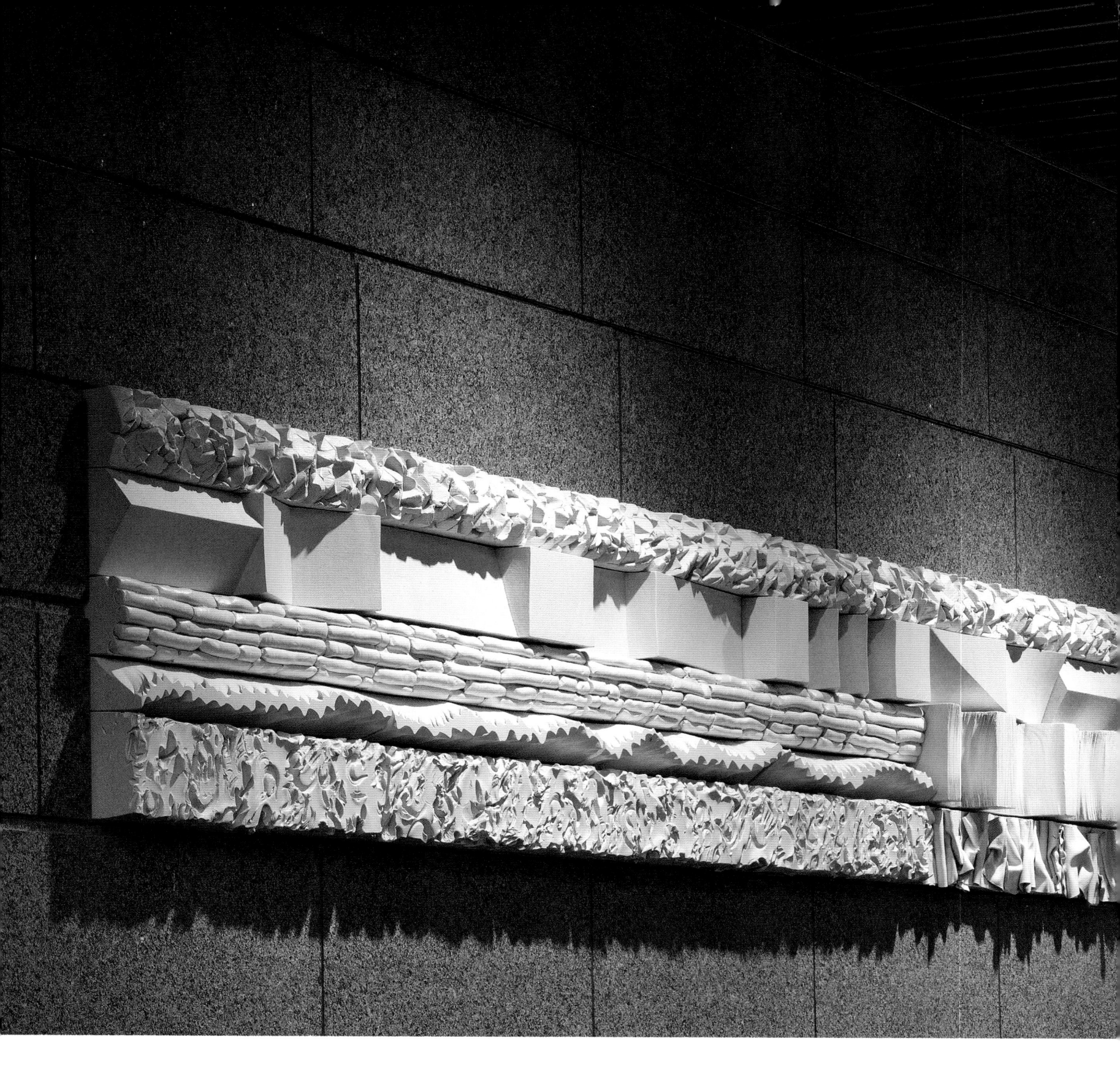

2-18 Land of Intelligence
Fukuoka University Library
Fukuoka, Japan, 2012

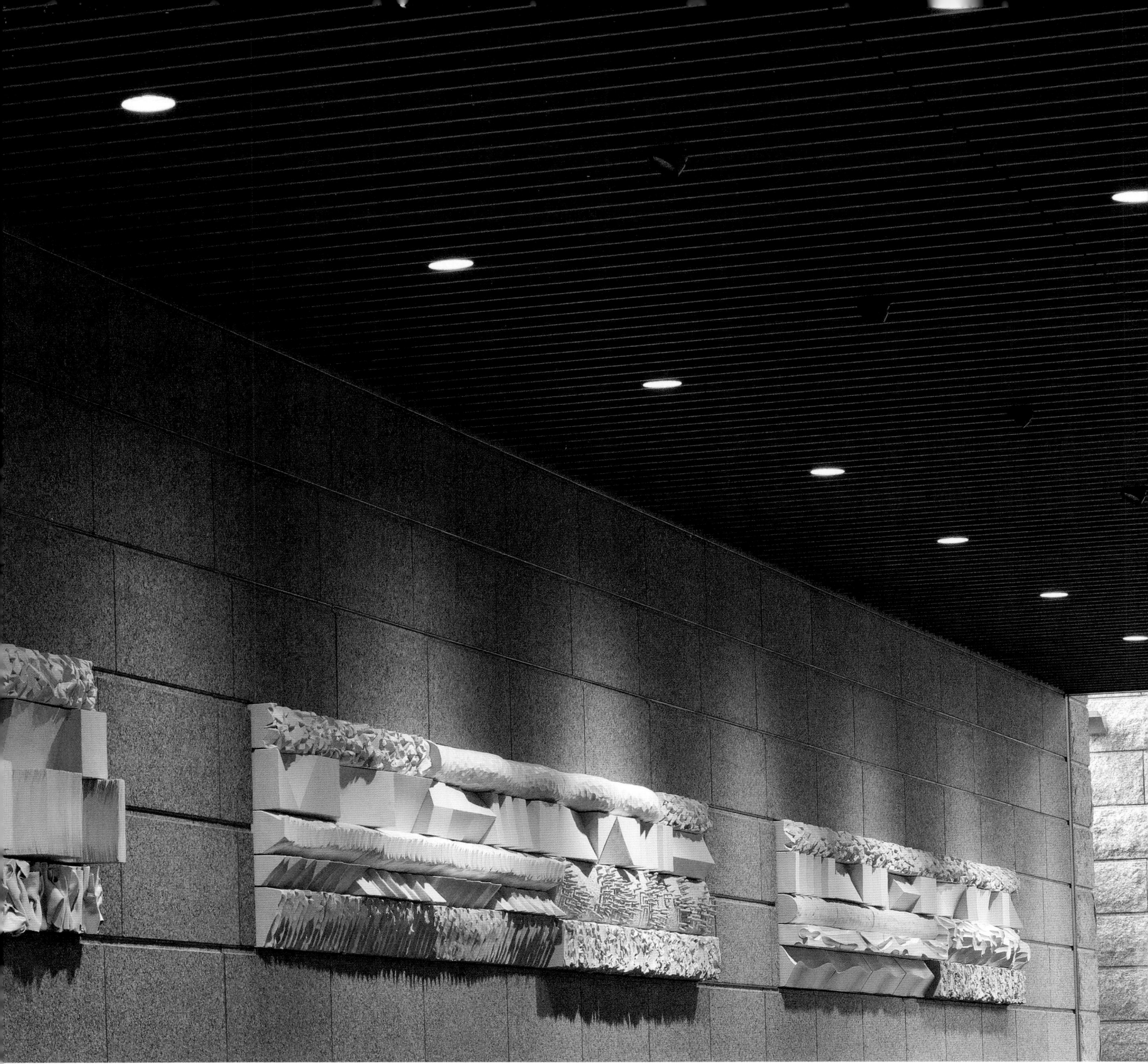

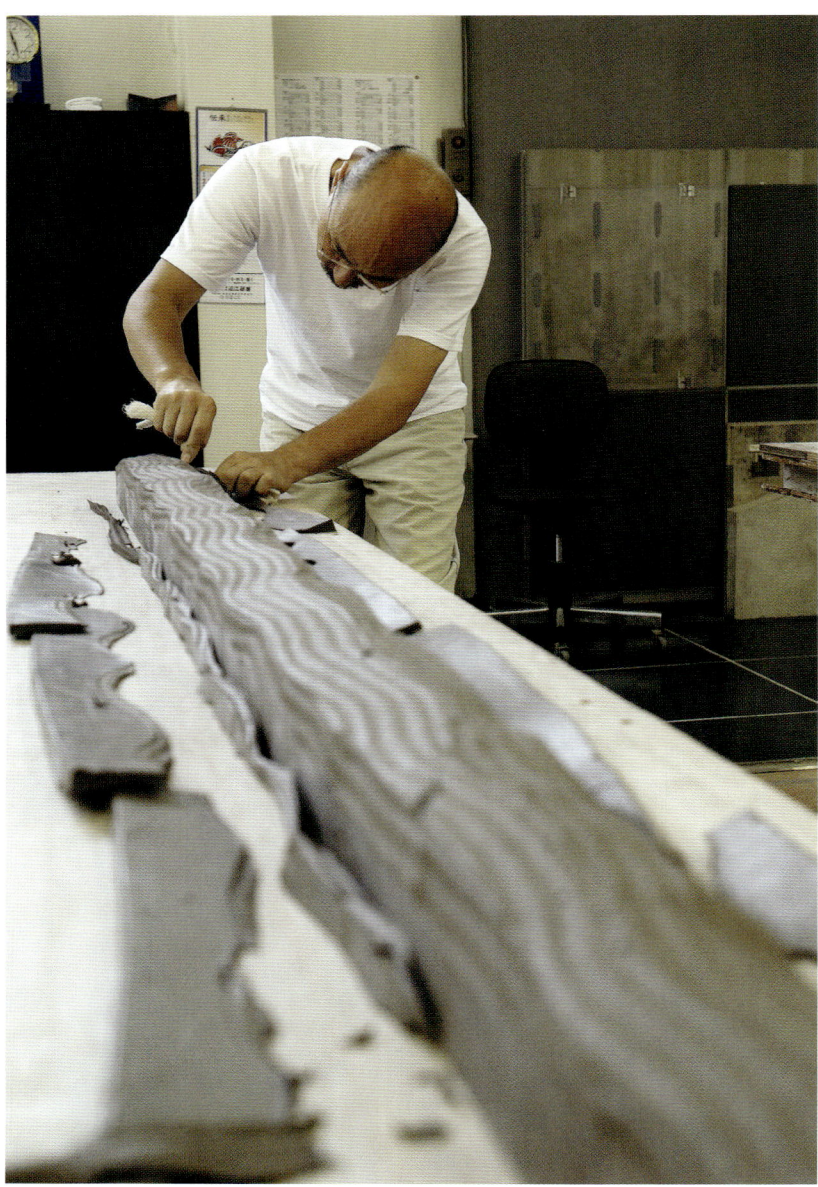

Igarashi used self-made tools to shave, carve and hit the clay at the factory of Shigaraki.

Making of Land of Intelligence.
*Photographer Shigeo Anzai
came to capture this moment. (TI)*

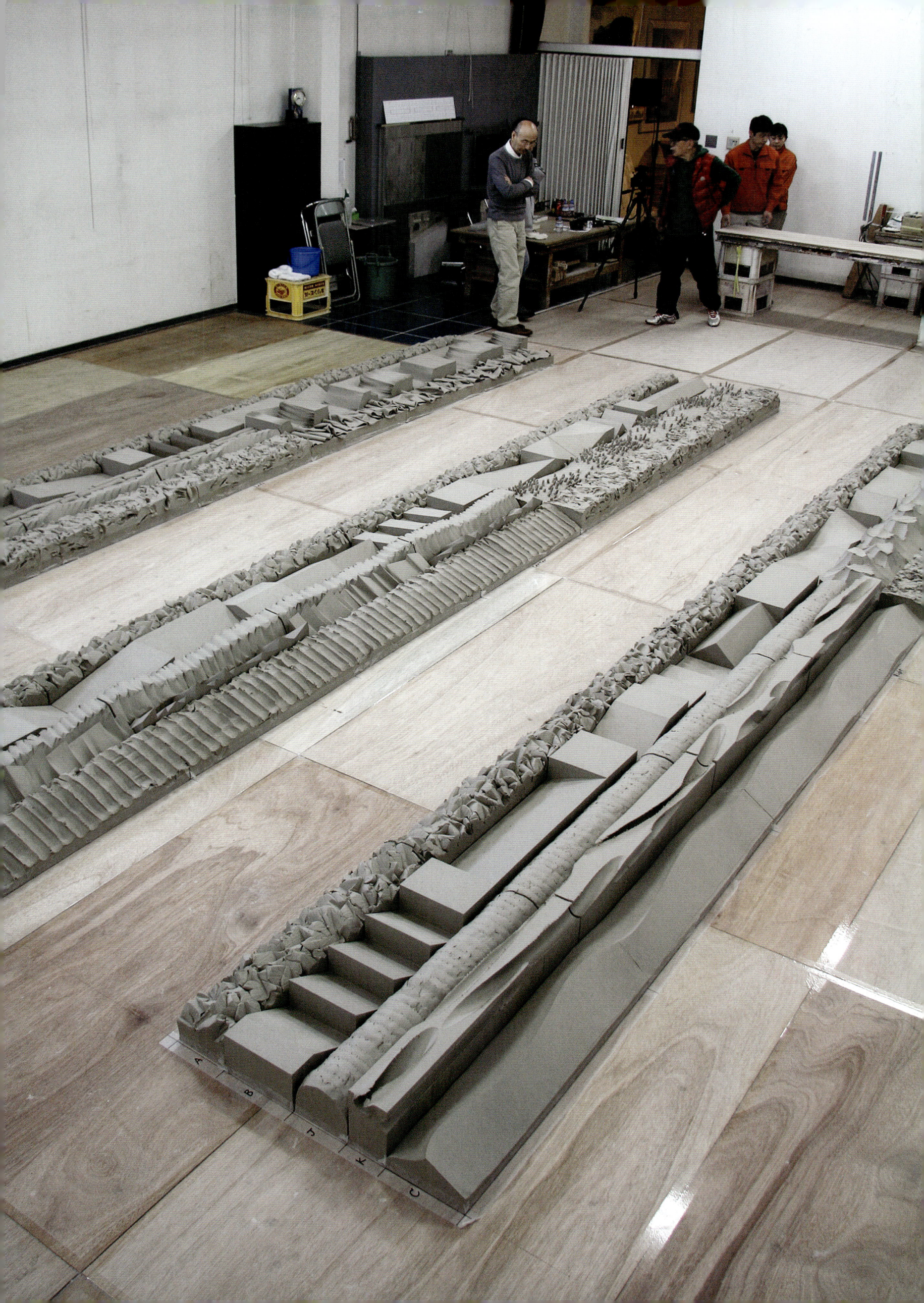

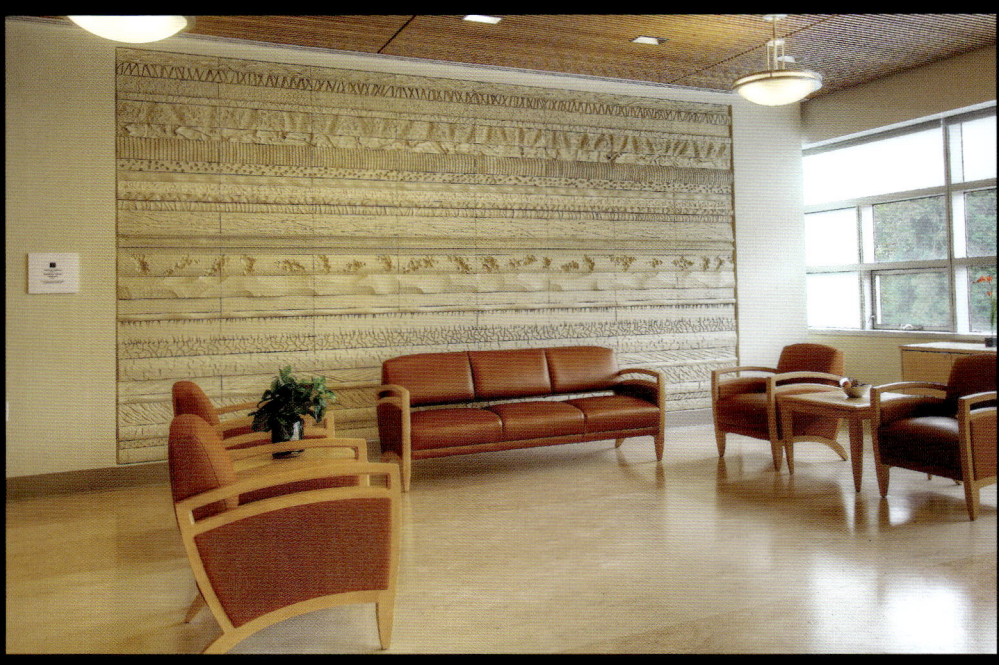

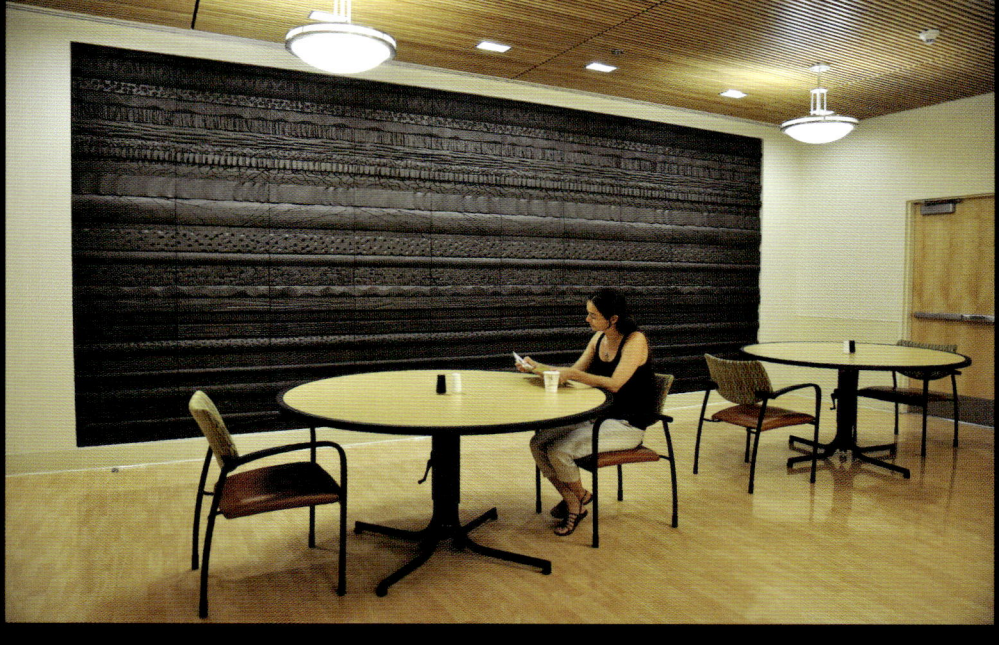

2-19 Horizontal Feeling Landscape
Laguna Honda Hospital
San Francisco, CA, USA, 2008

2-20 Horizontal Feeling Landscape
Laguna Honda Hospital
San Francisco, CA, USA, 2008

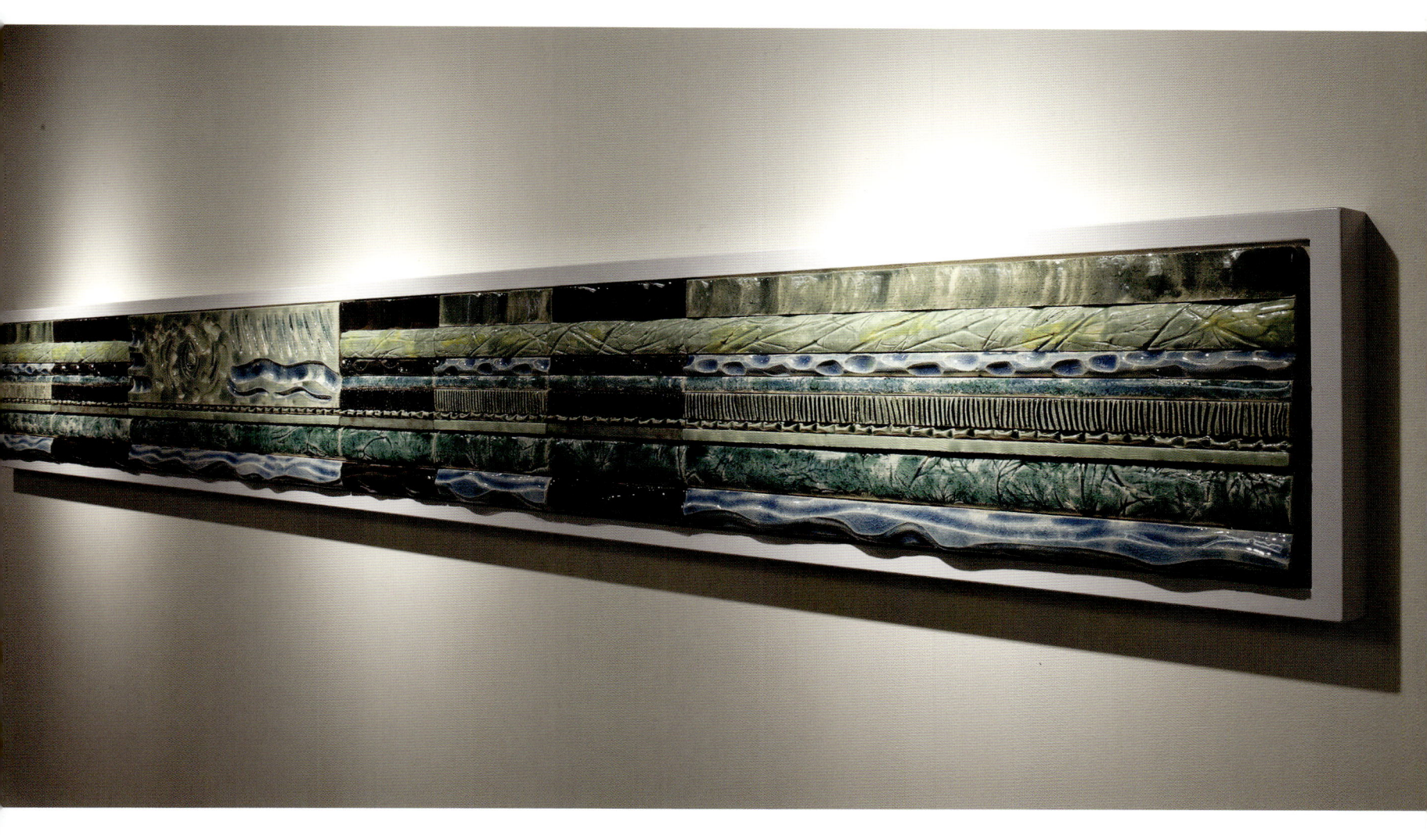

2-21 Horizontal Feeling LHH
Laguna Honda Hospital
San Francisco, CA, USA, 2008

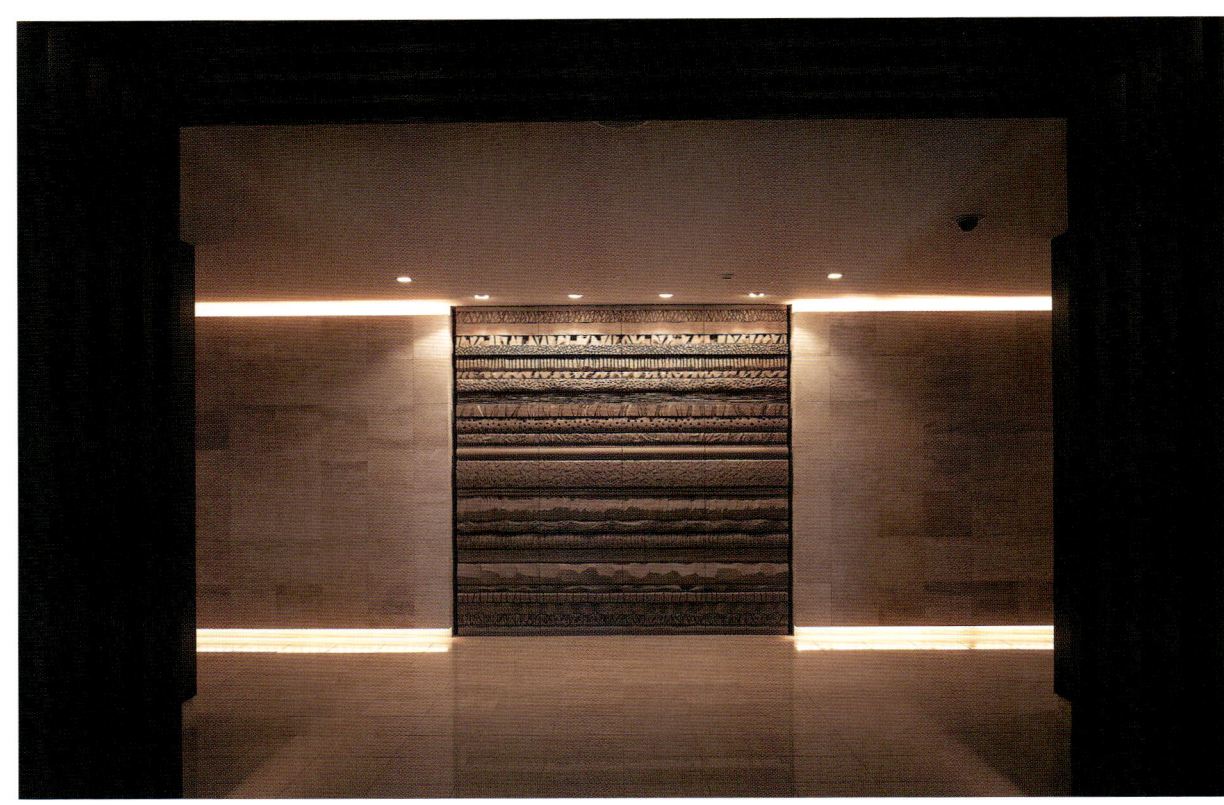
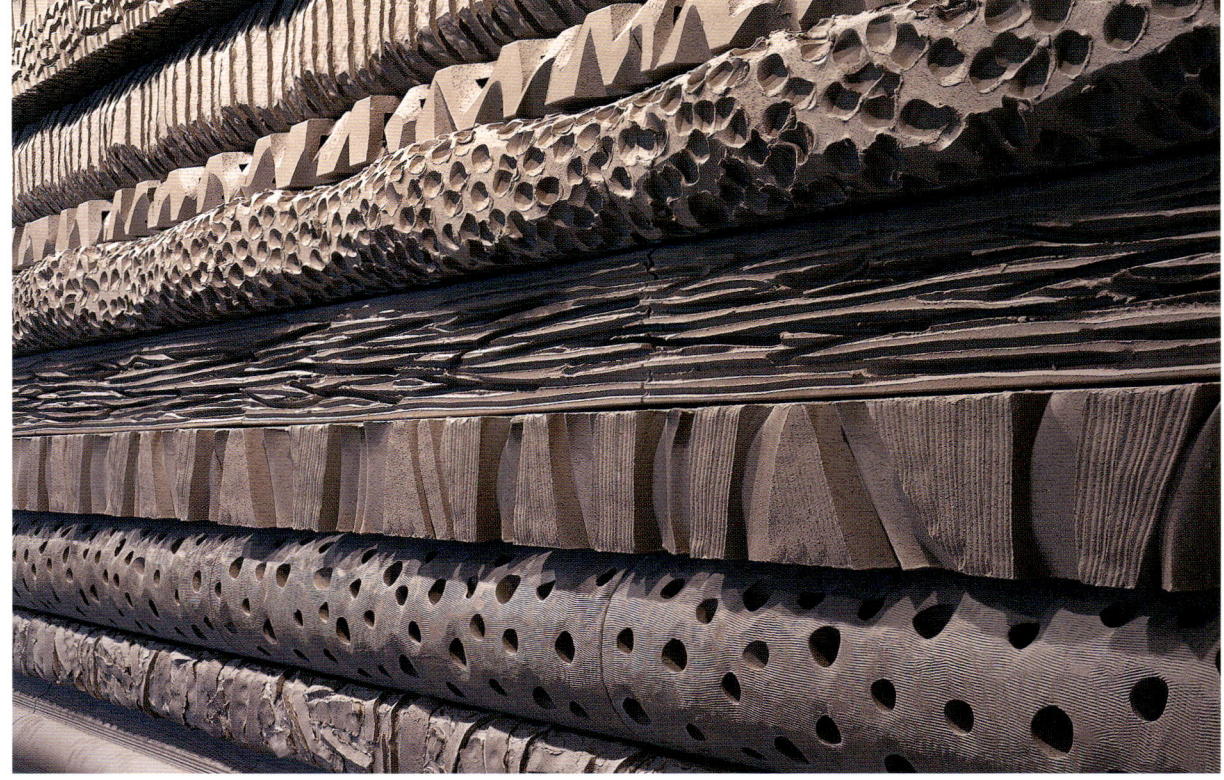

2-22 Untitled
Galleria Grande
Tokyo, Japan, 2006

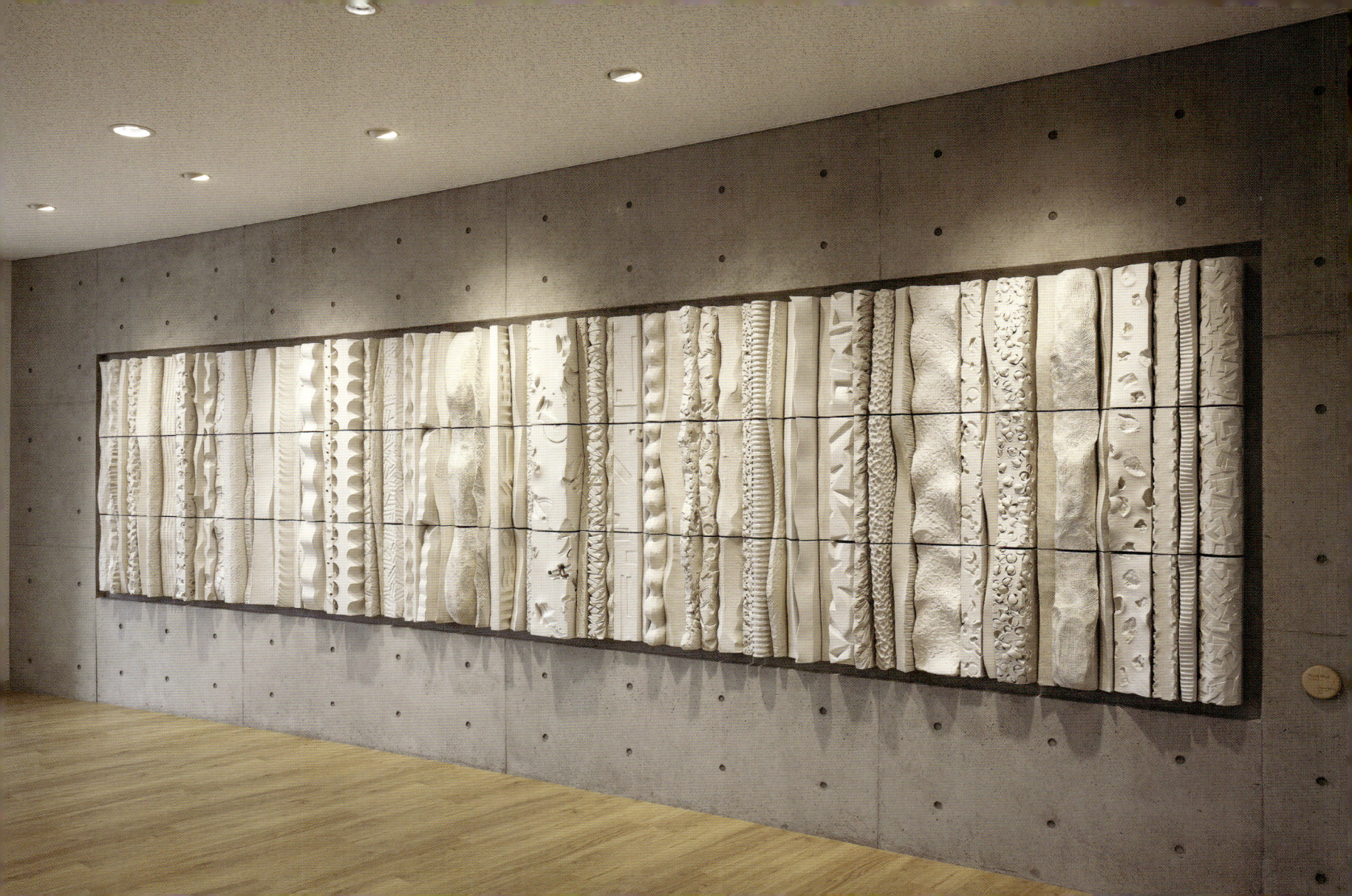

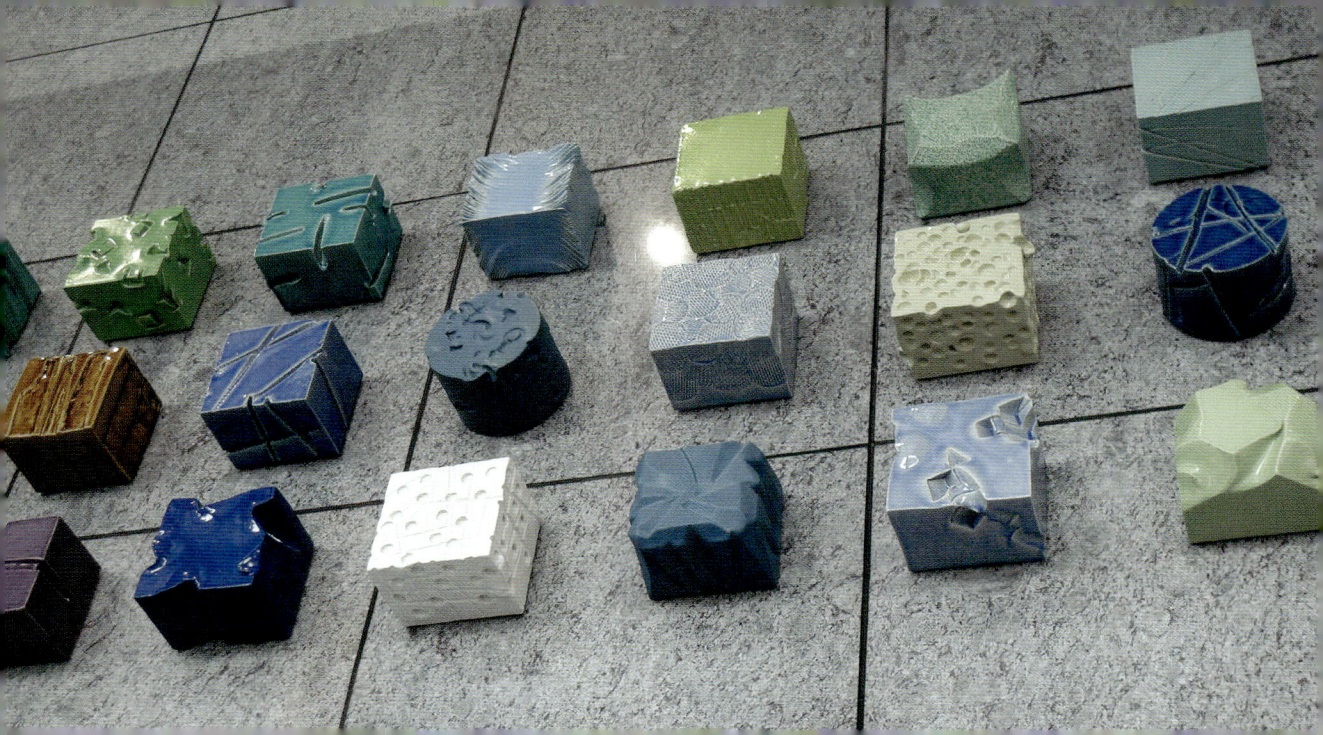

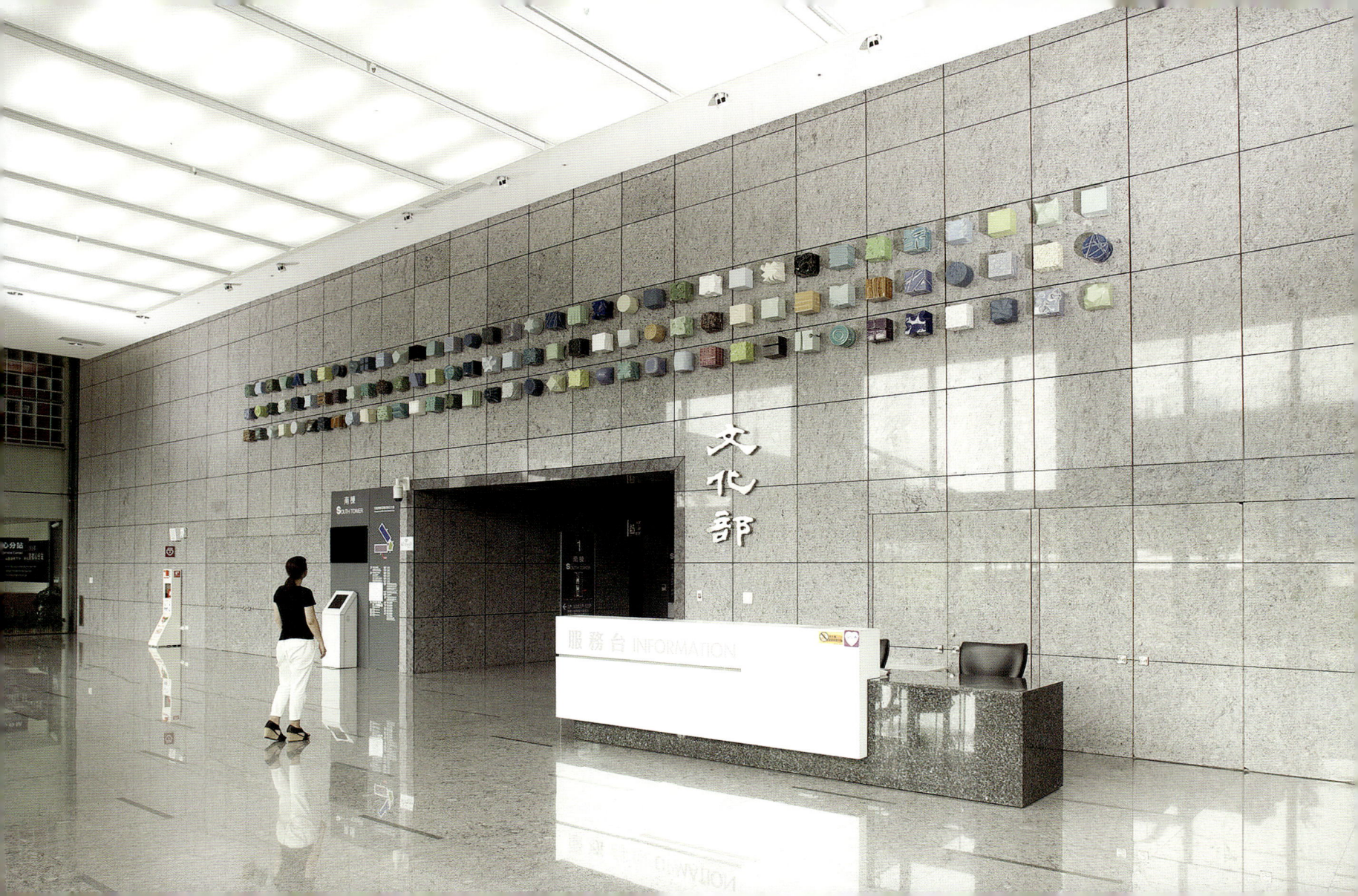

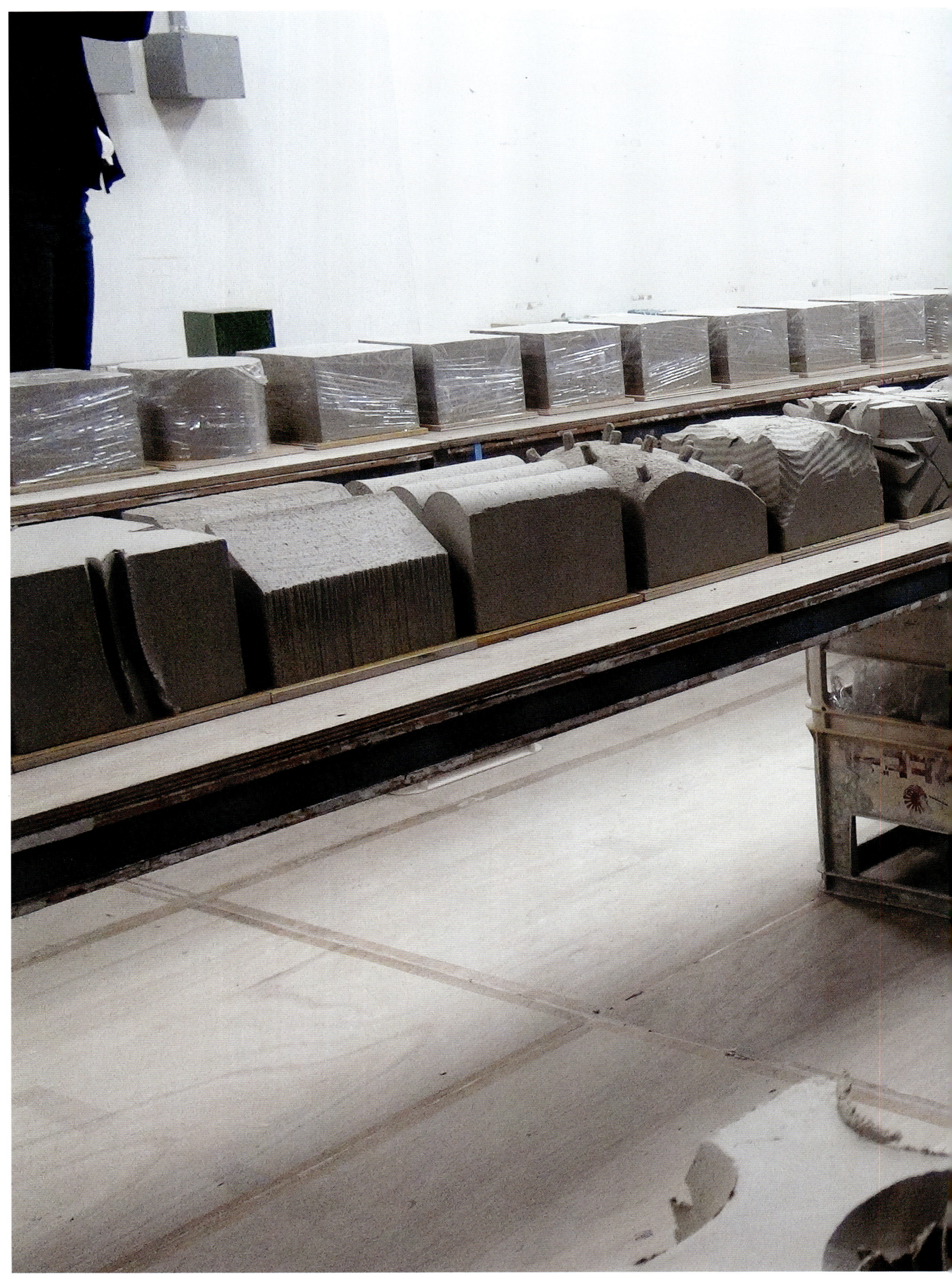

Making of Diversity and Harmony

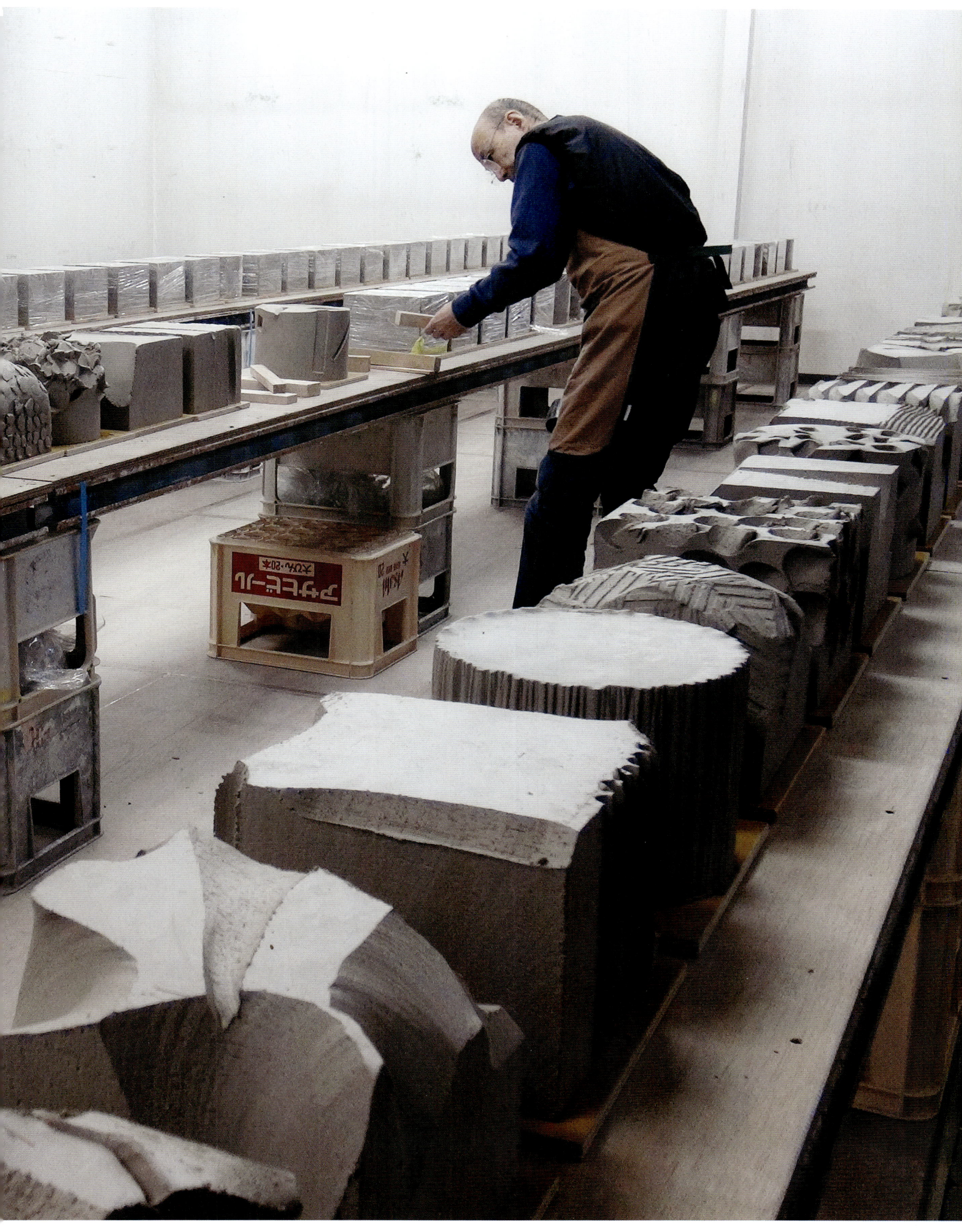

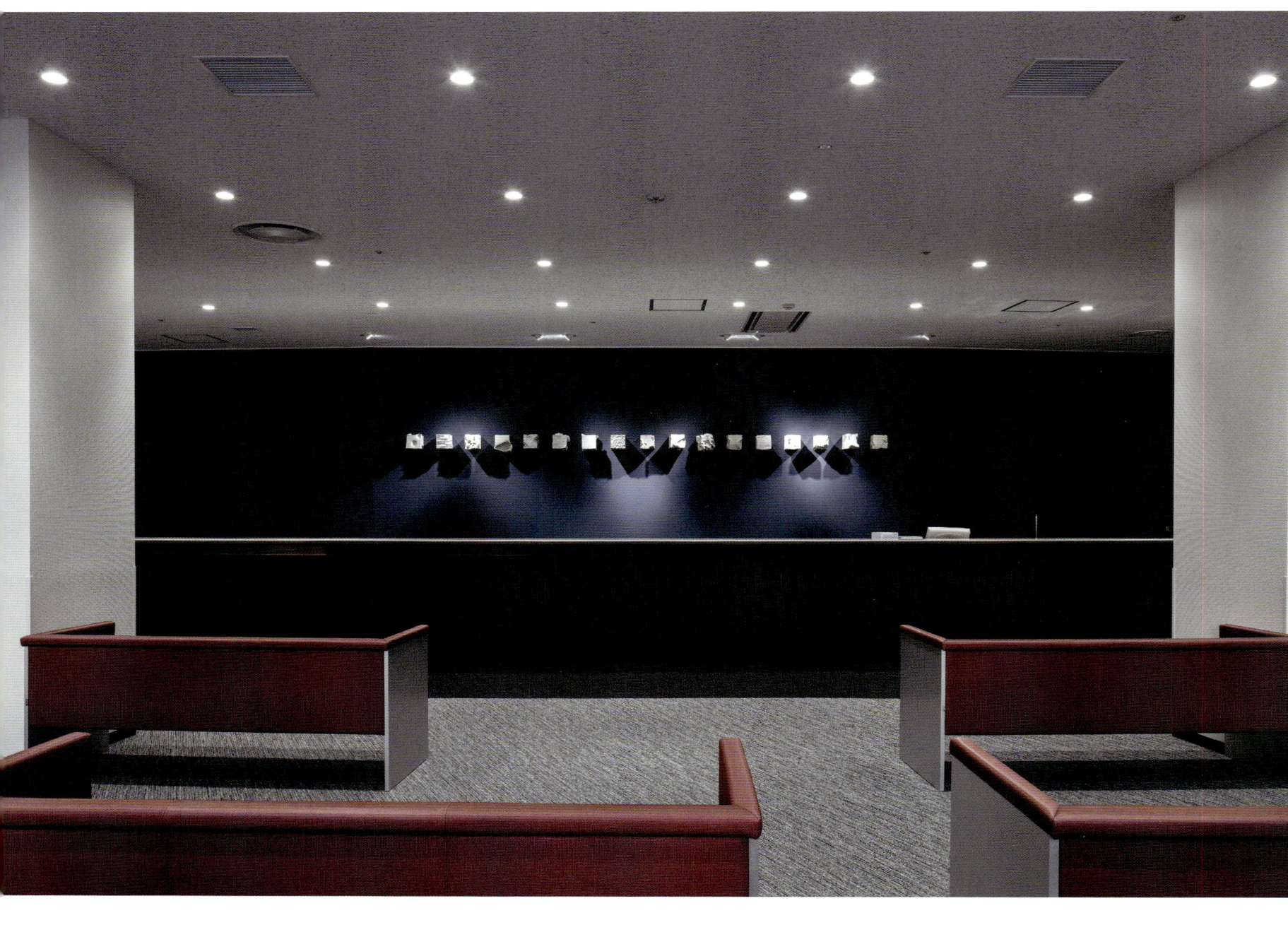

2-25 Light of Pinneshiri
Sapporo Teishinkai Hospital
Sapporo, Hokkaido, Japan, 2015

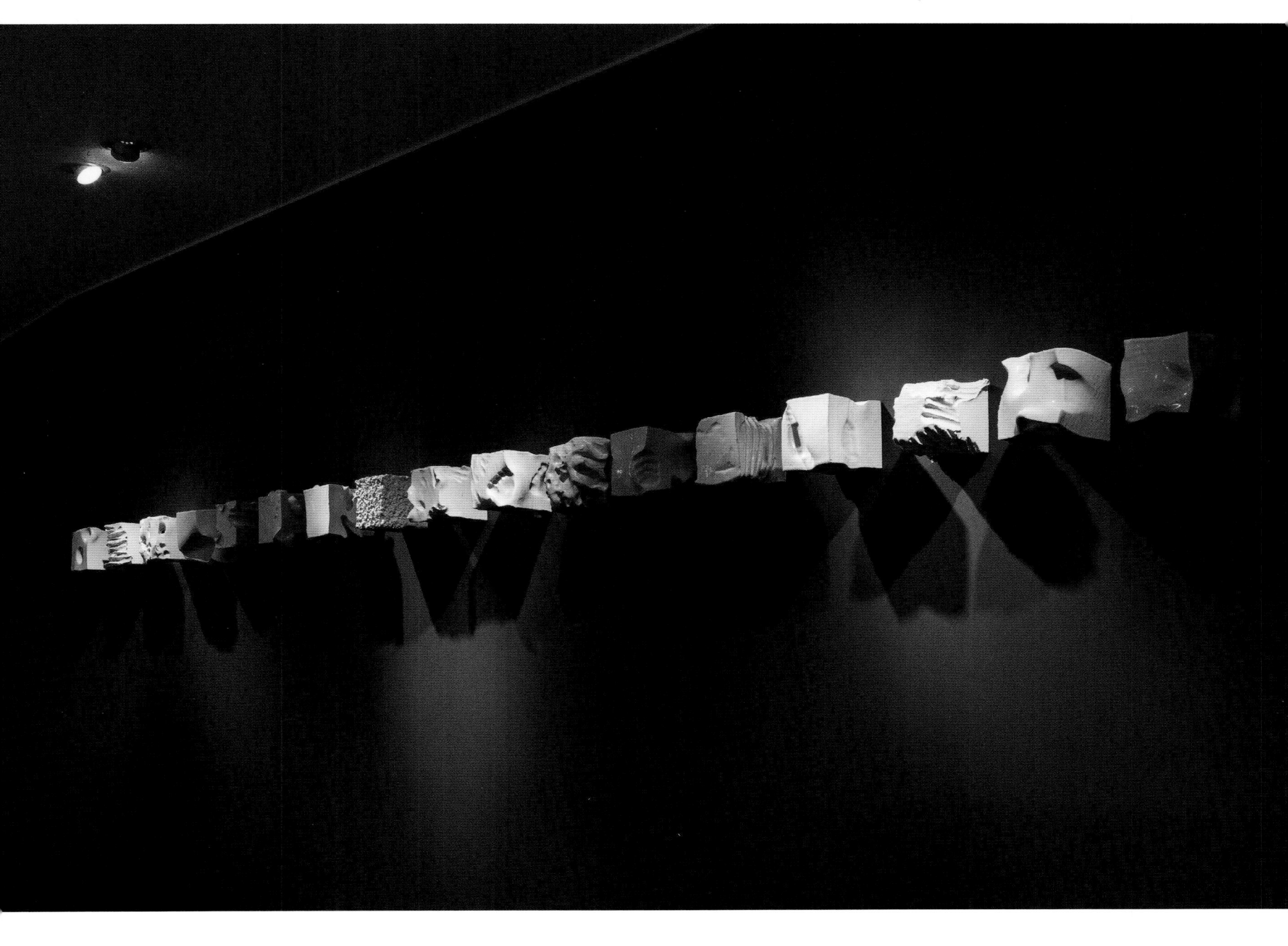

At the workshop in Yugawara, I used soft clay for pottery and made sculpture without any tools. I used only my hands and feet. (TI)

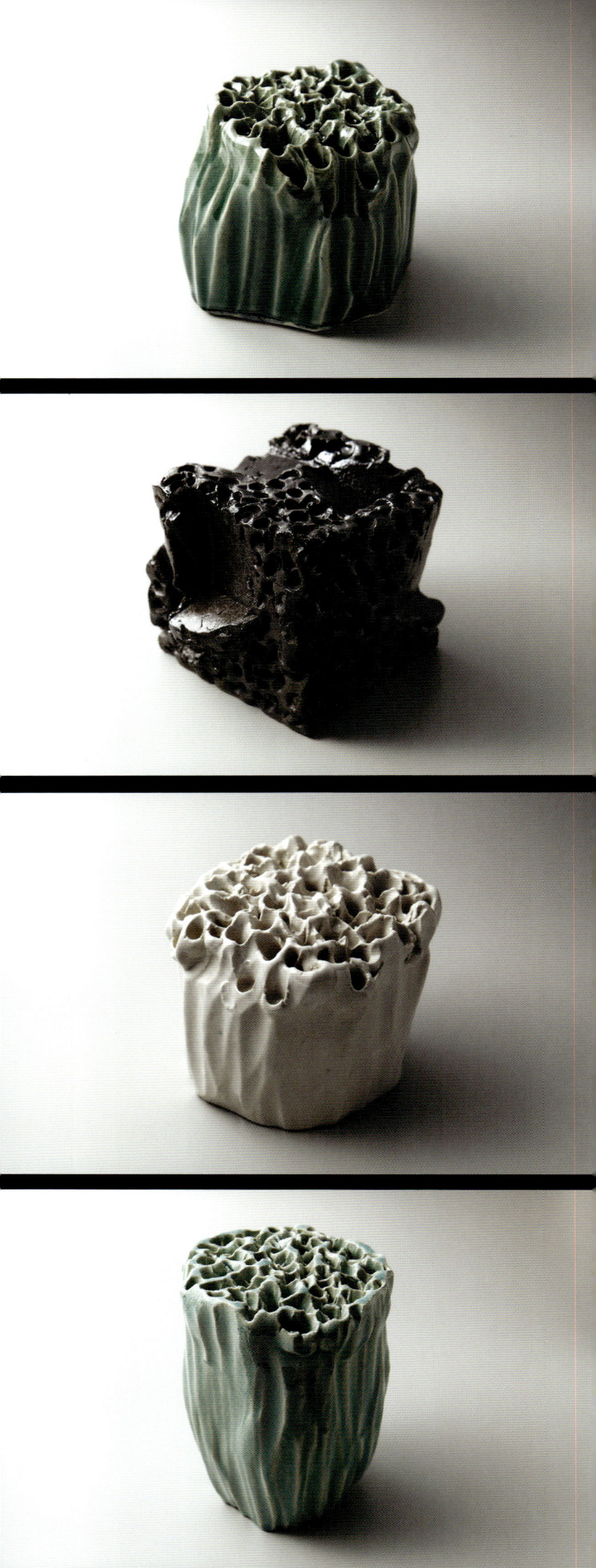

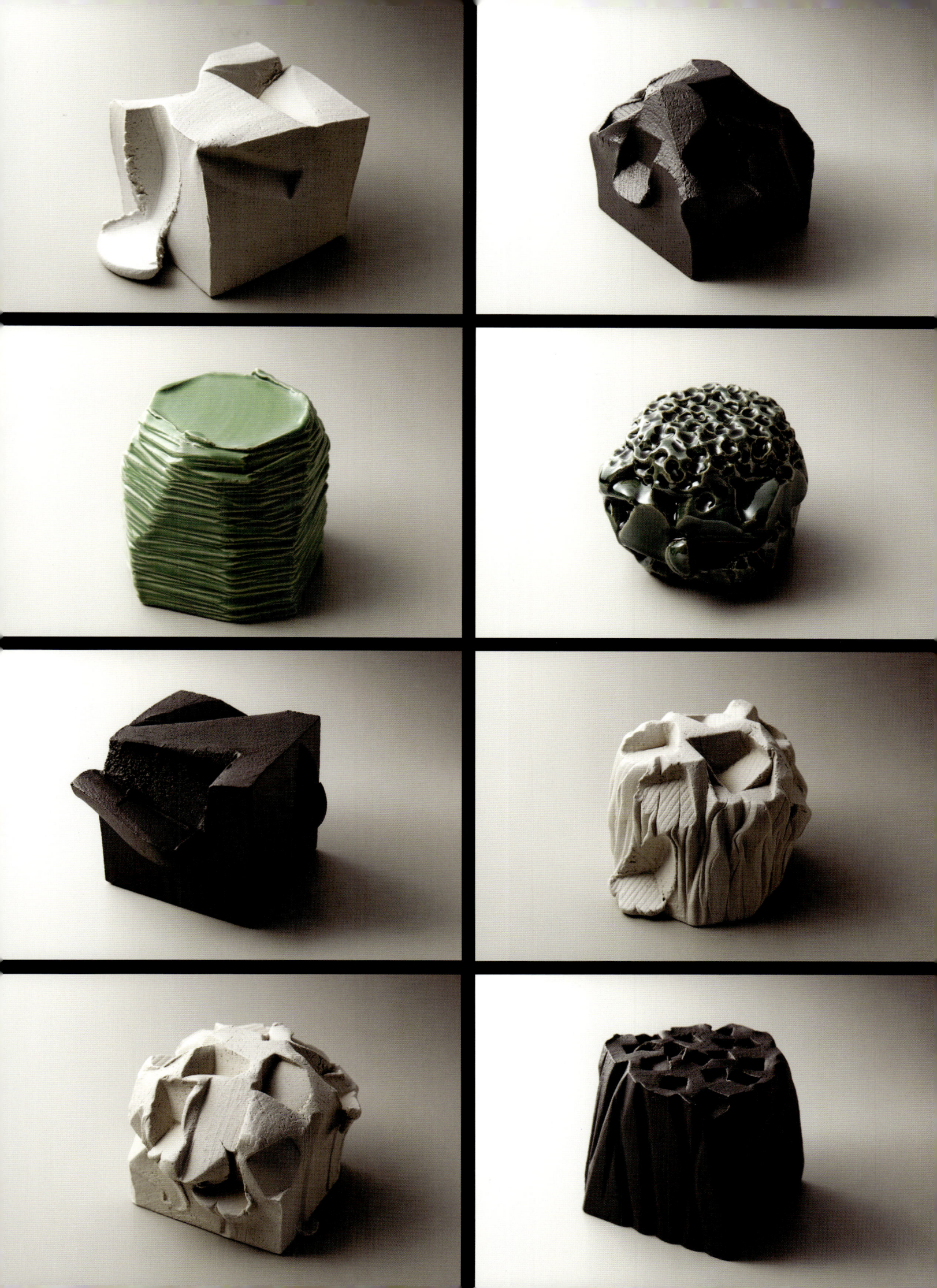

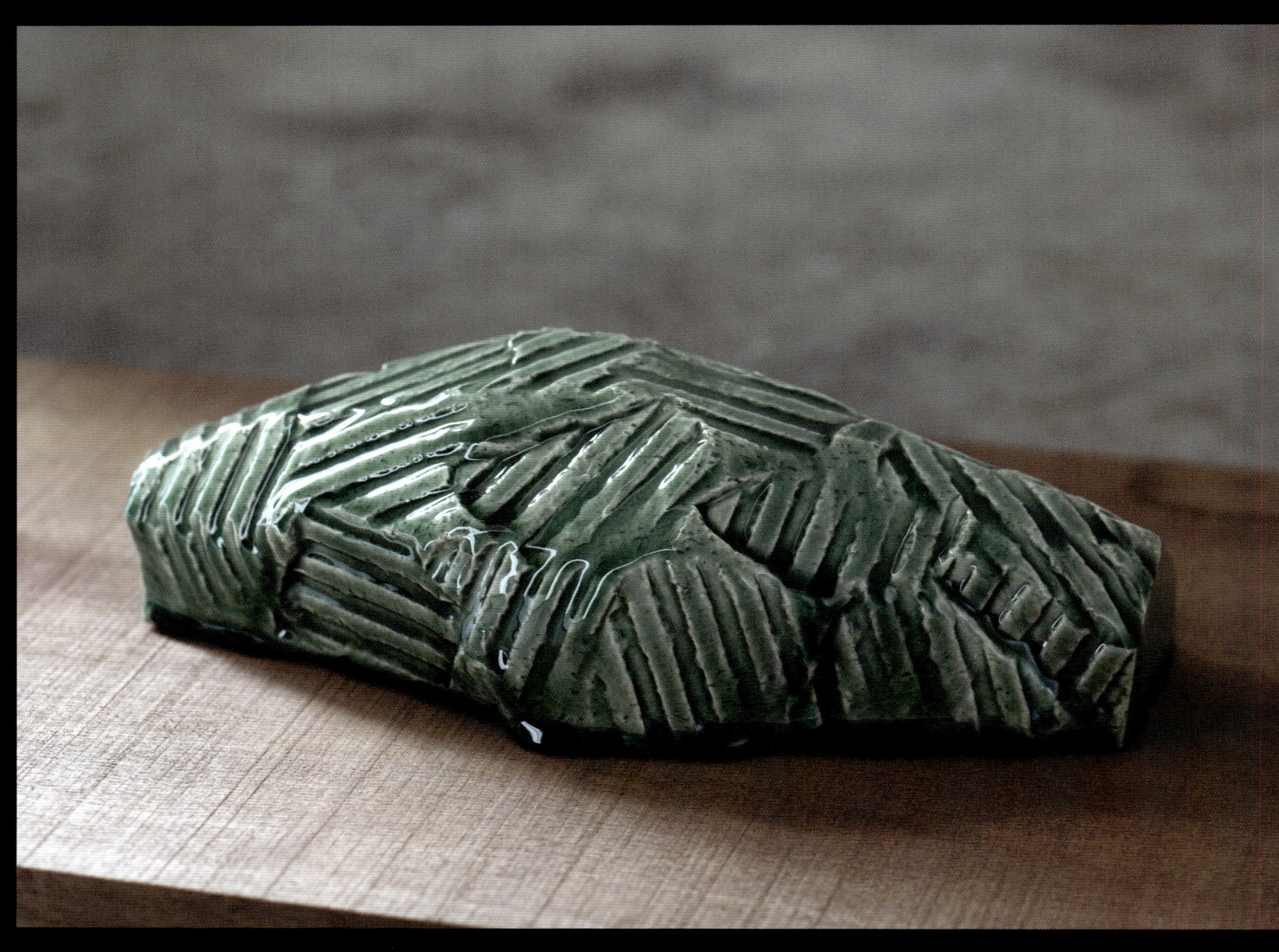

2-27 Bud, 2013

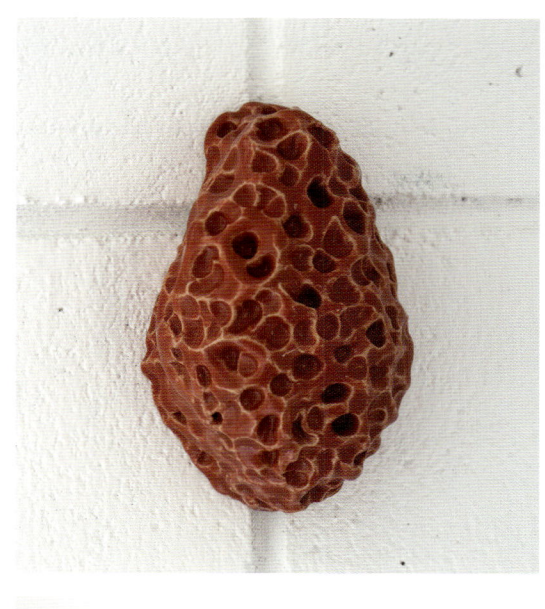
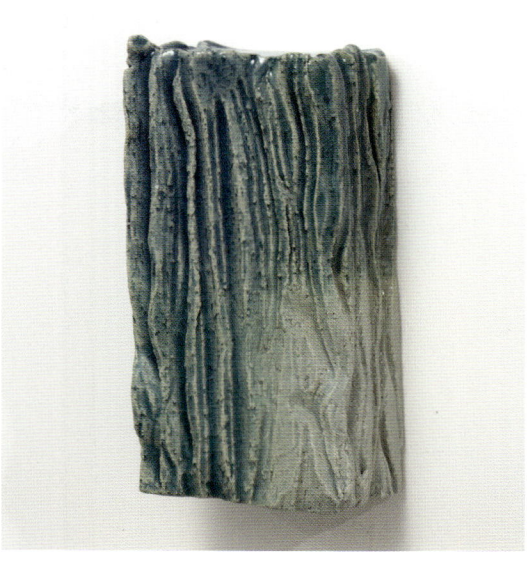
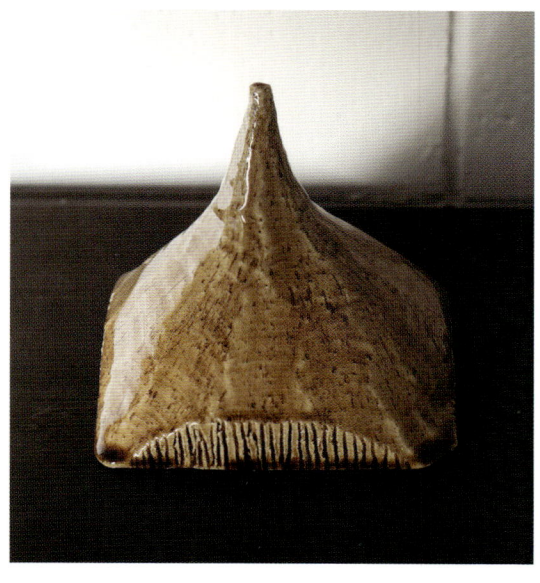
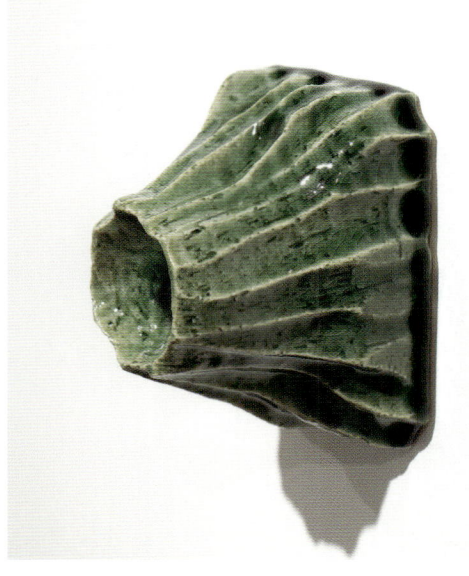
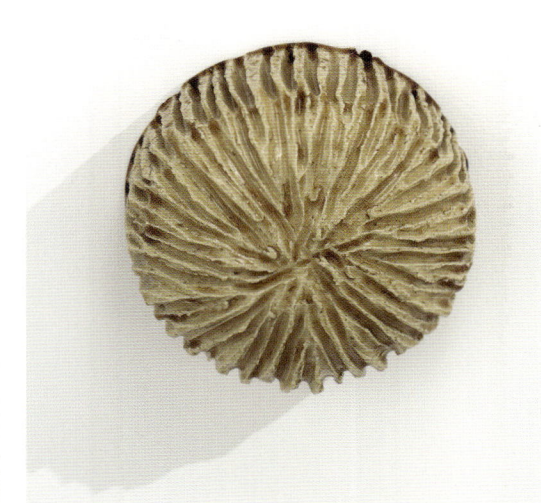
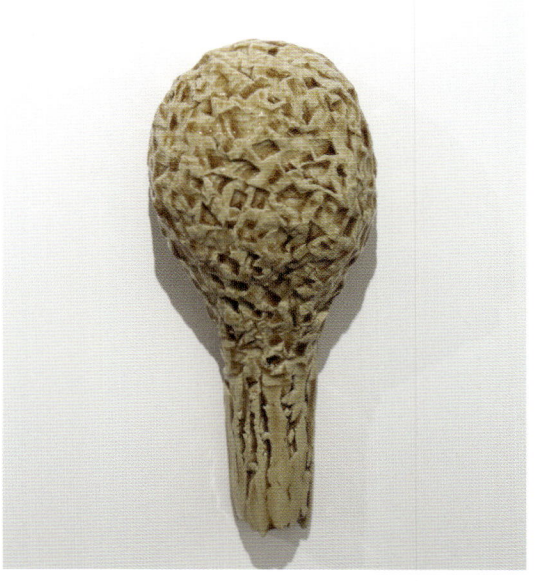
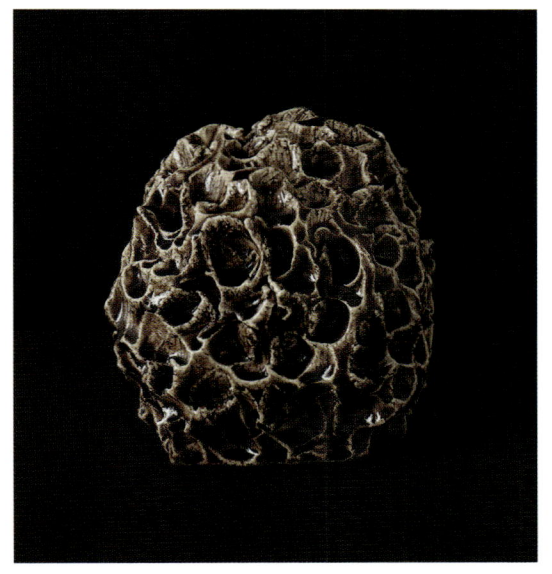
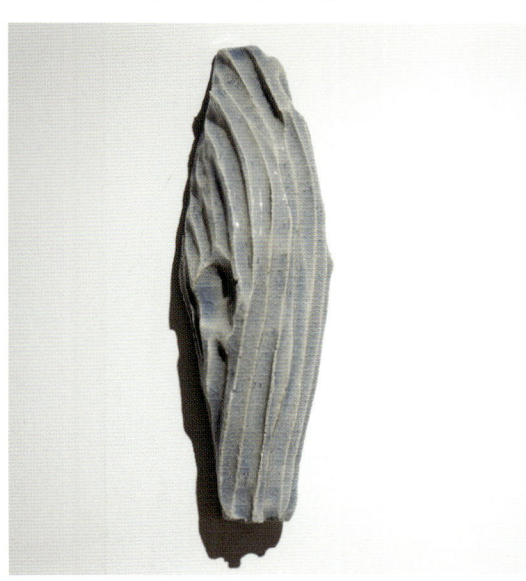
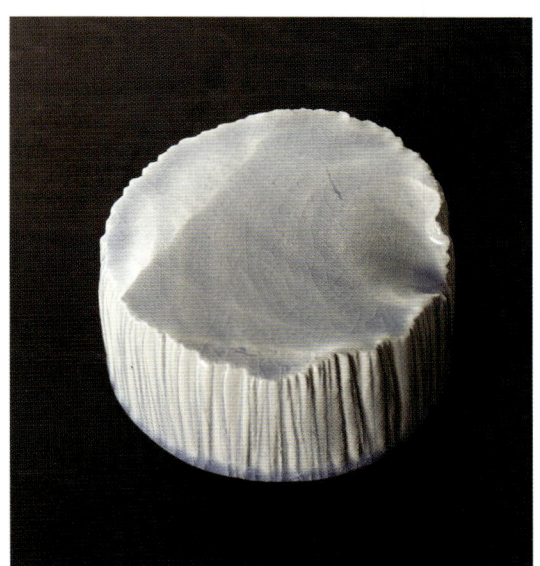

2-28 Seed 6, 2013

2-29 Spring Water, 2013

2-30 Mountain House, 2013

2-31 Snow Water, 2013

2-32 Field, 2013

2-33 Flowing Water, 2013

2-34 Mountain, 2013

2-35 Horsetail, 2013

2-36 Lake, 2013

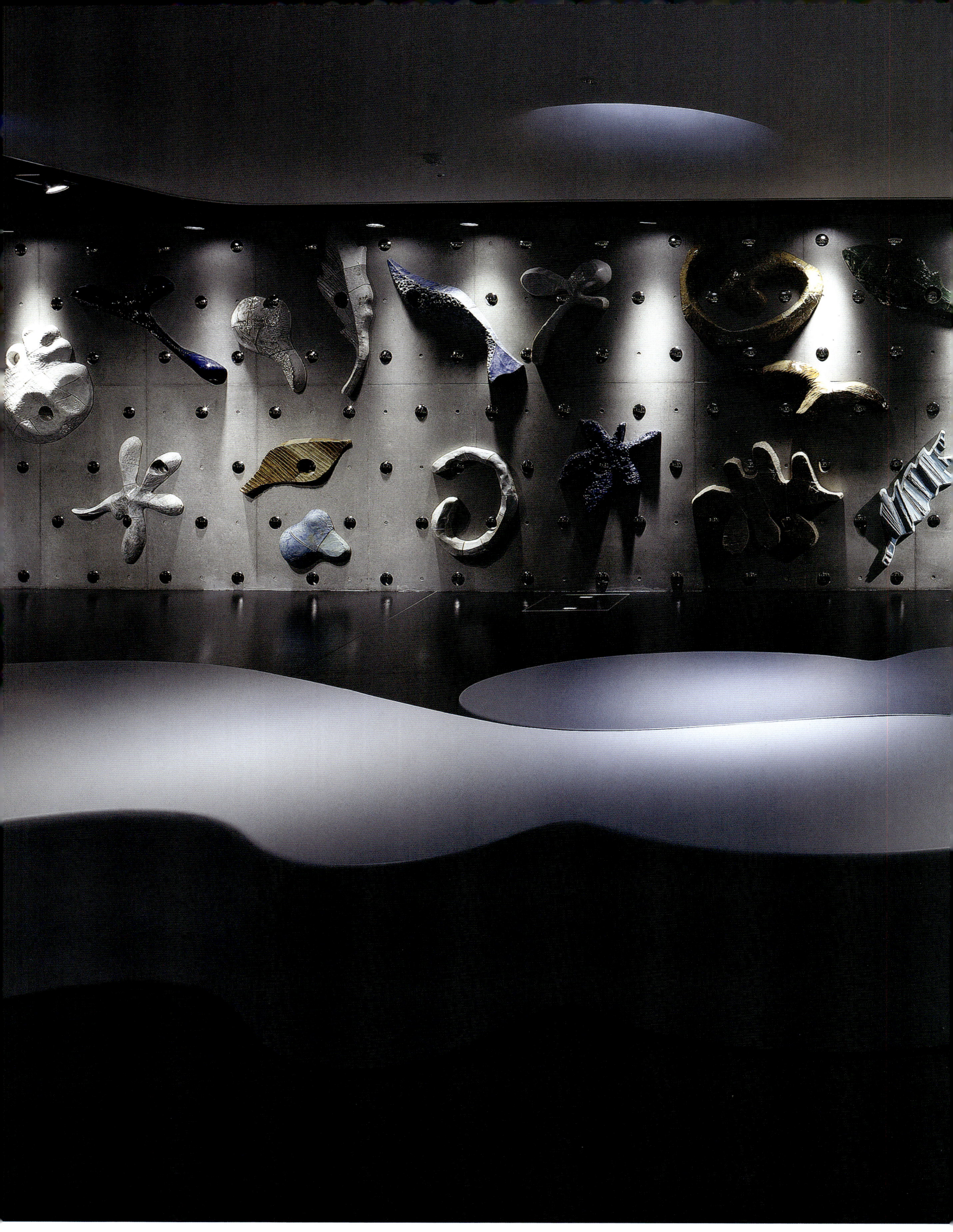

2-37 In Praise of Forest, Ocean and People
Ota-ku General Gymnasium
Tokyo, Japan, 2012

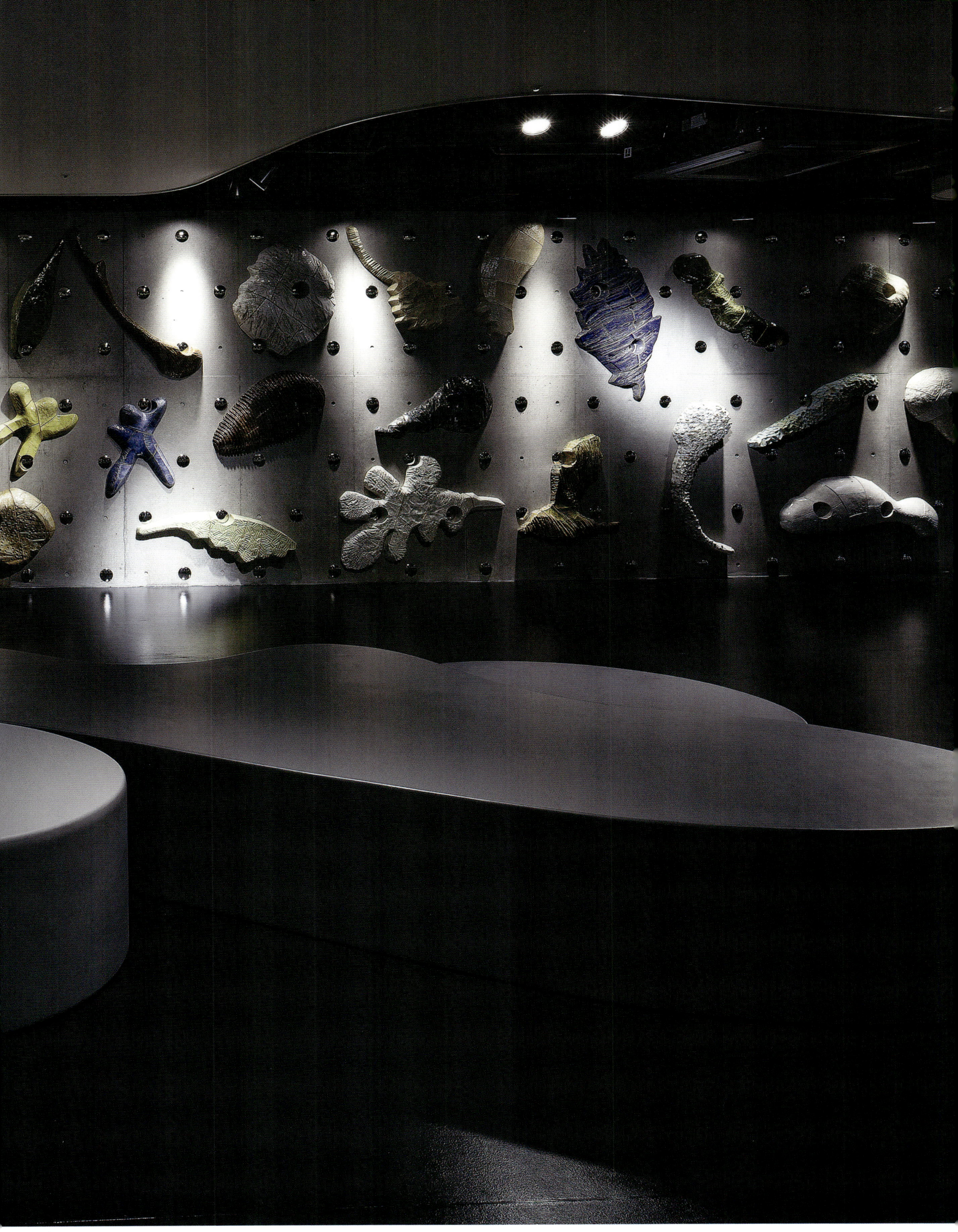

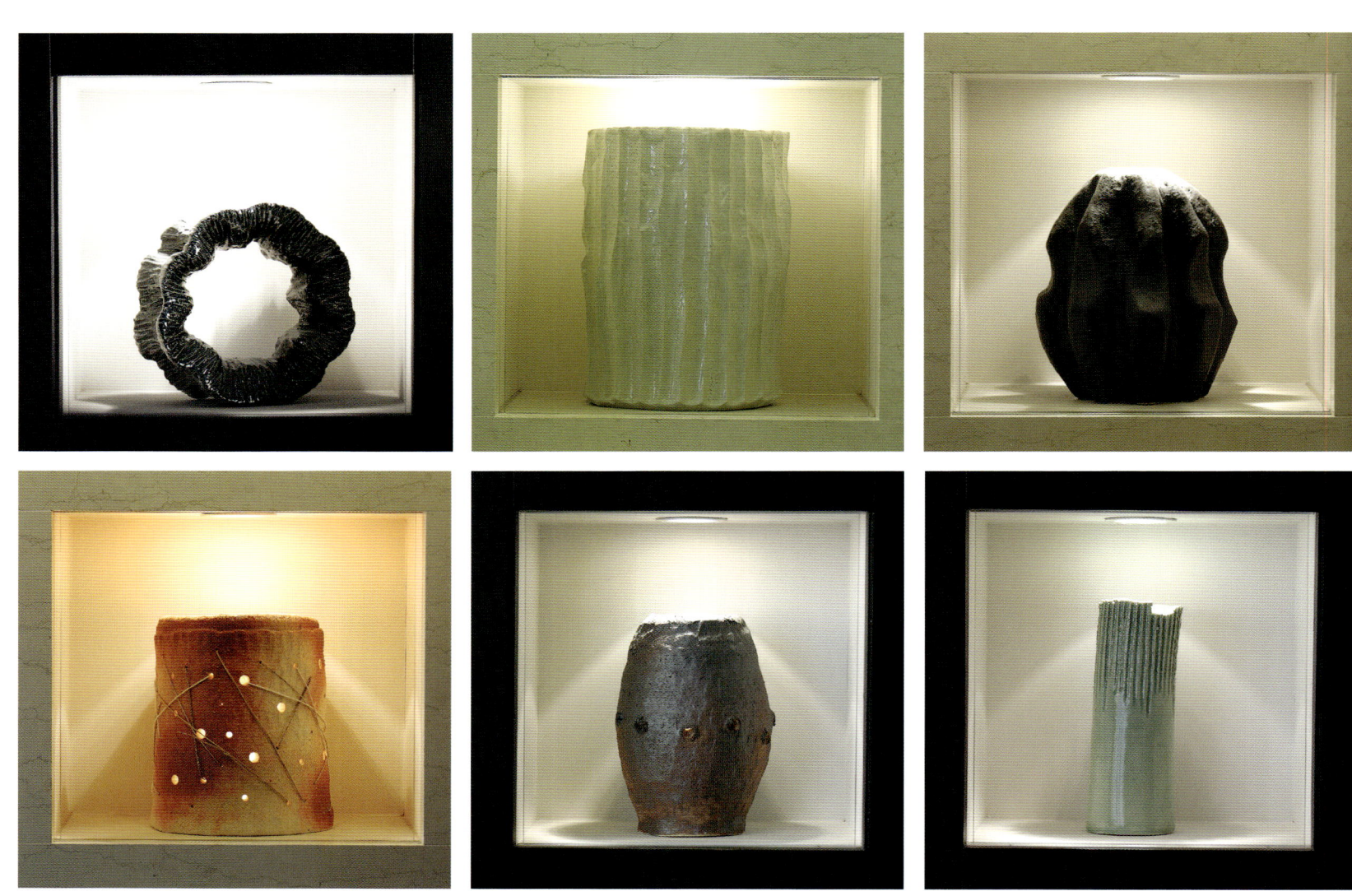

2-38 Small Ceramic Sculptures
La·Maree Shirokane
Tokyo, Japan, 2003

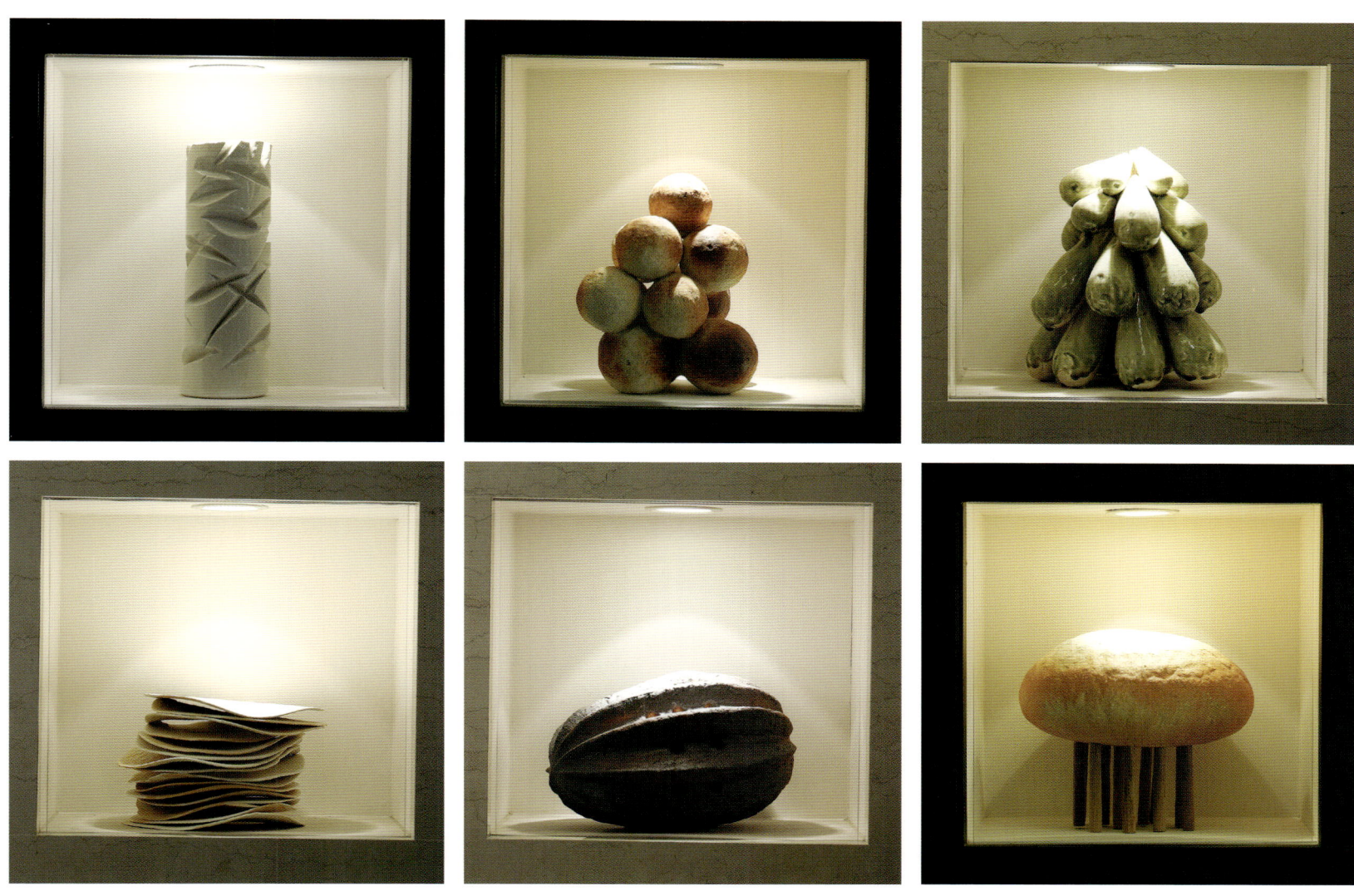

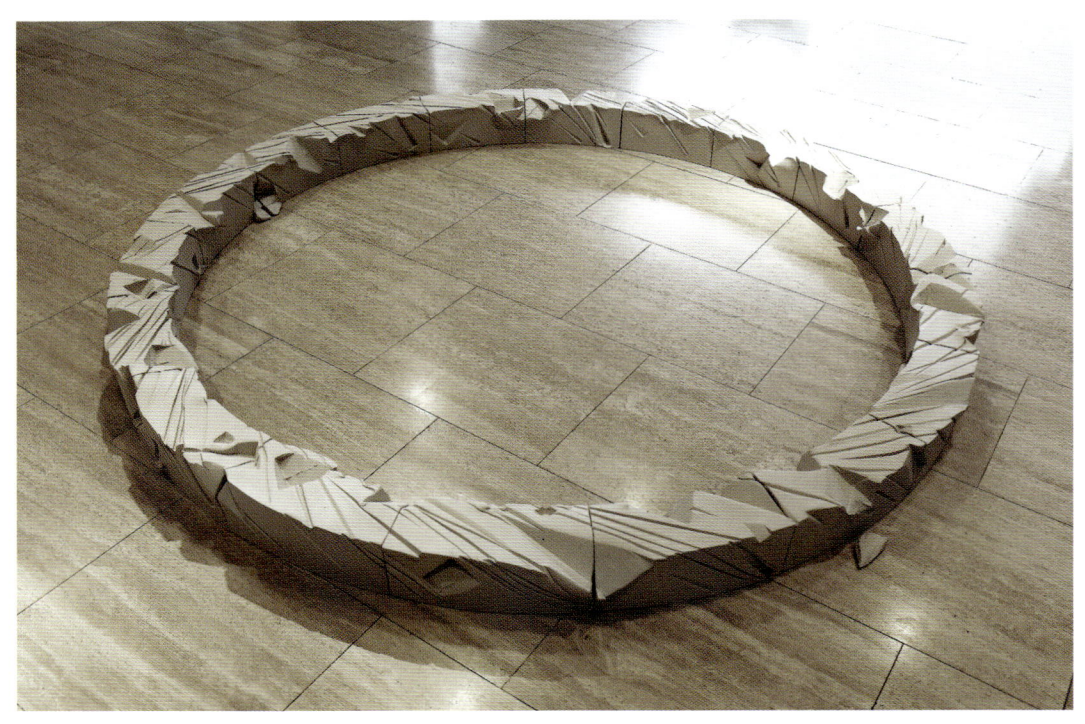

2-39 Never Ending Road, #1
AIJ Gallery
Tokyo, Japan, 2012

2-40 Motherland
Planis Hall
Sapporo, Japan, 2011

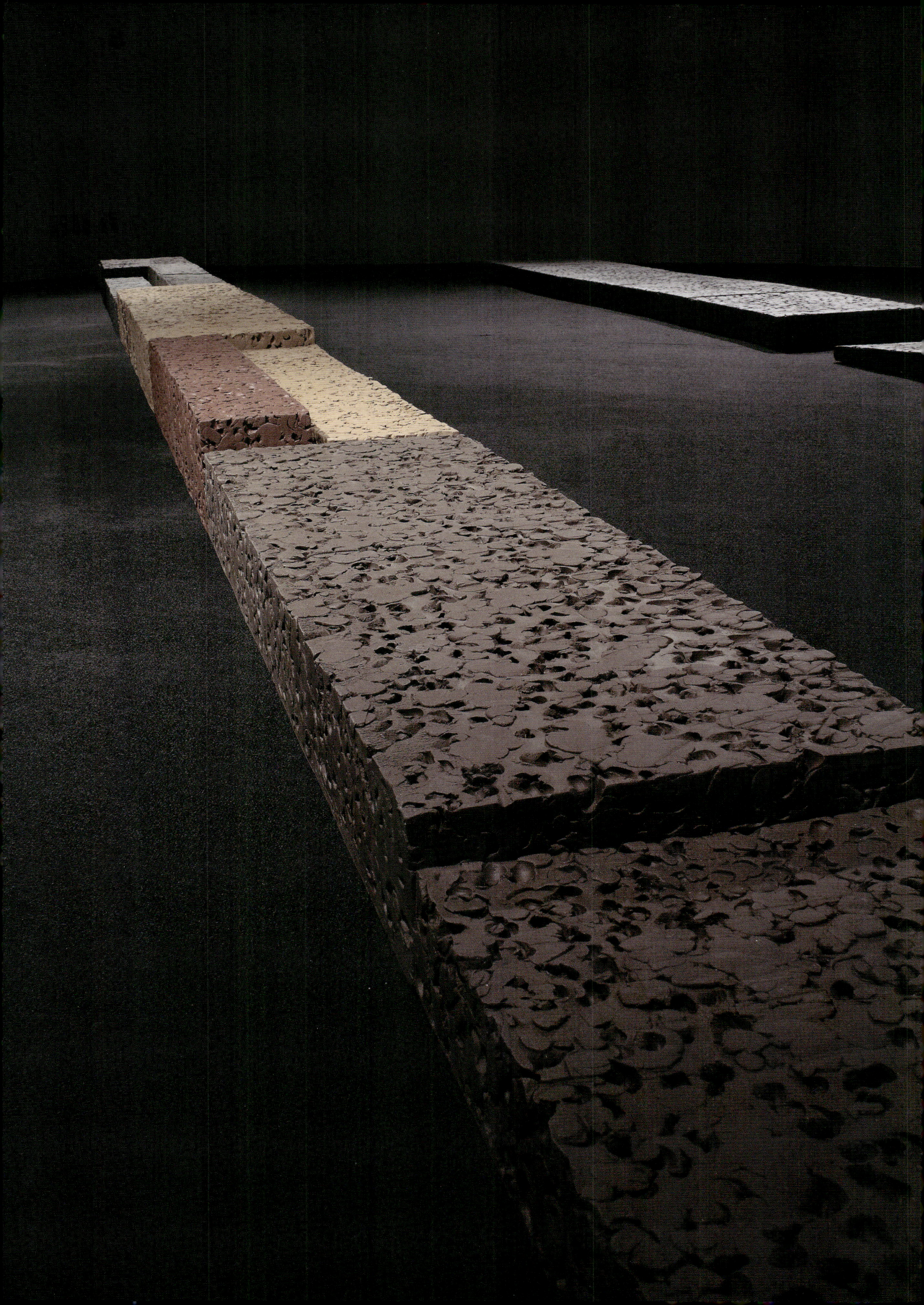

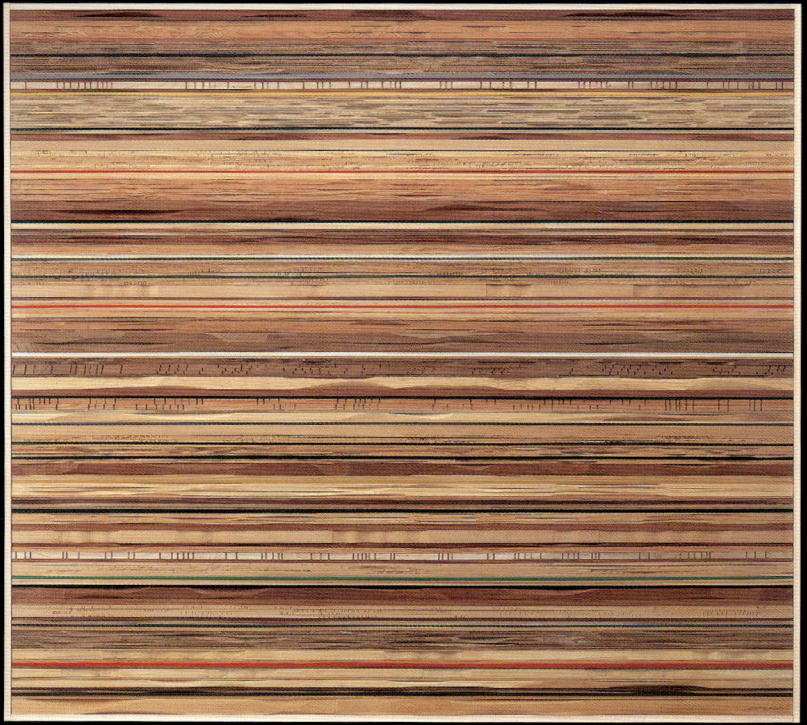 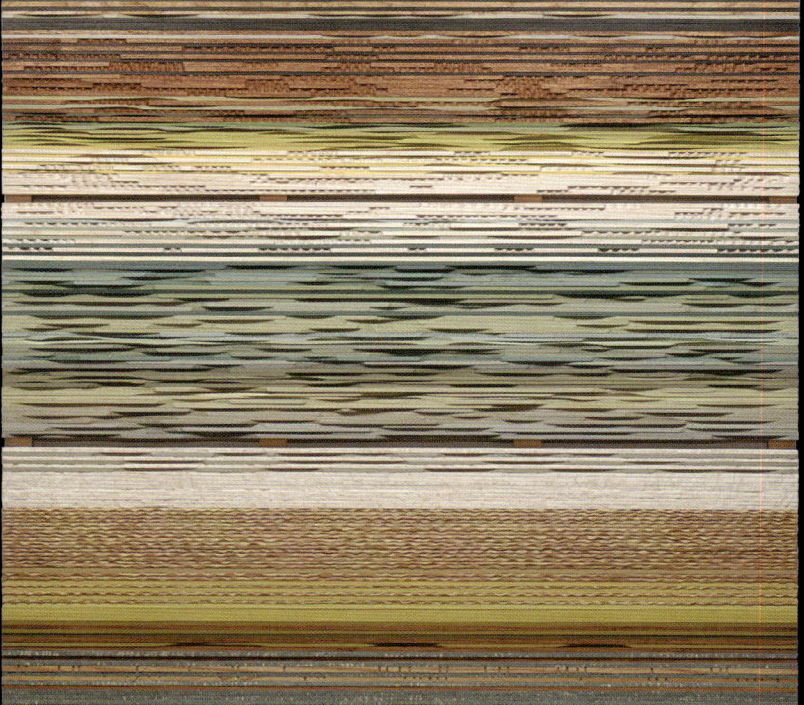

2-41 Horizontal Feeling/Loan Pine, 2000

2-42 Horizontal Feeling/Yakushima, 2002

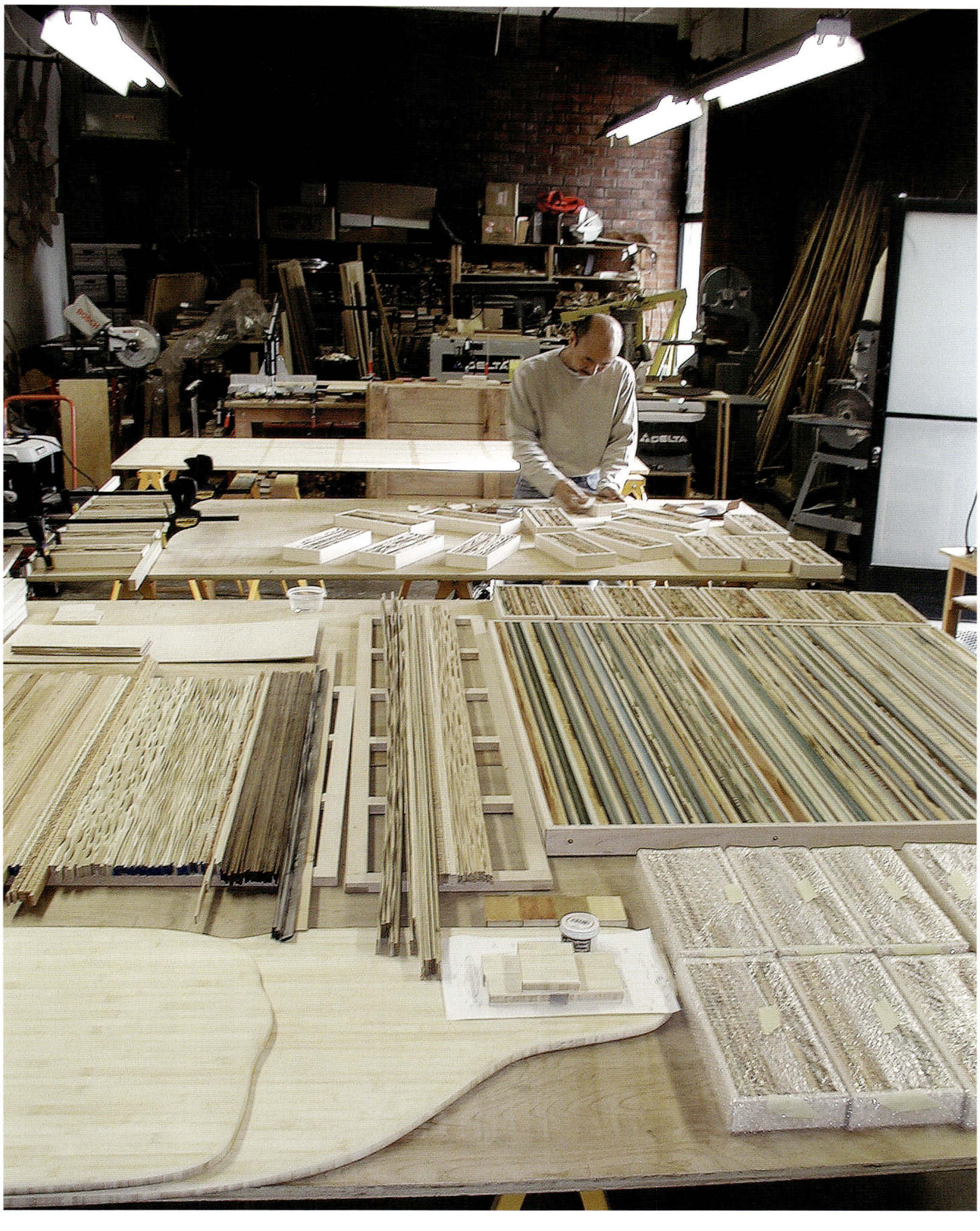

Igarashi at his Atelier in Los Angeles, CA, USA, 2003
I began to use wood pieces from used shipping crates for the Horizontal Feeling sculpture series. (TI)

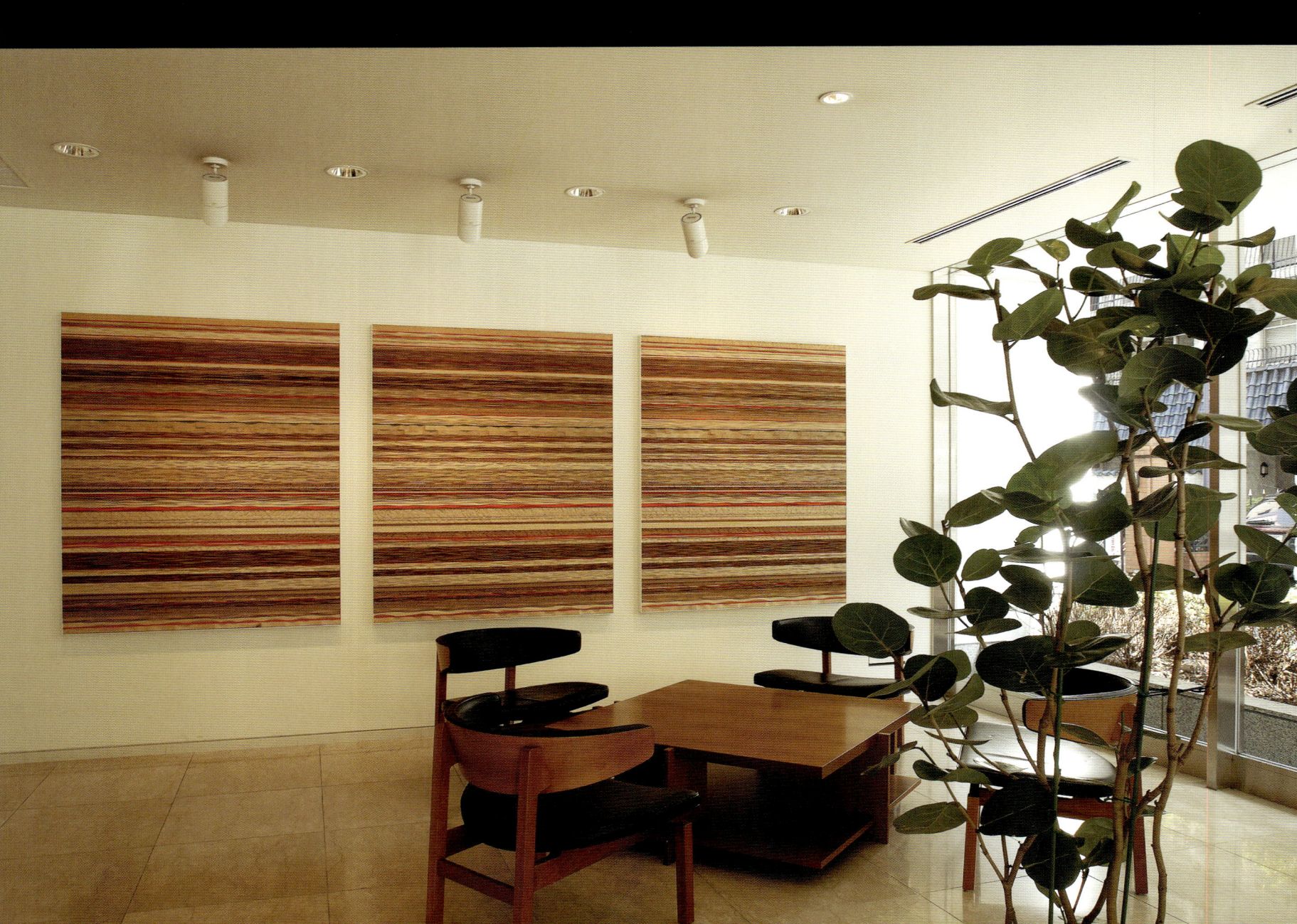

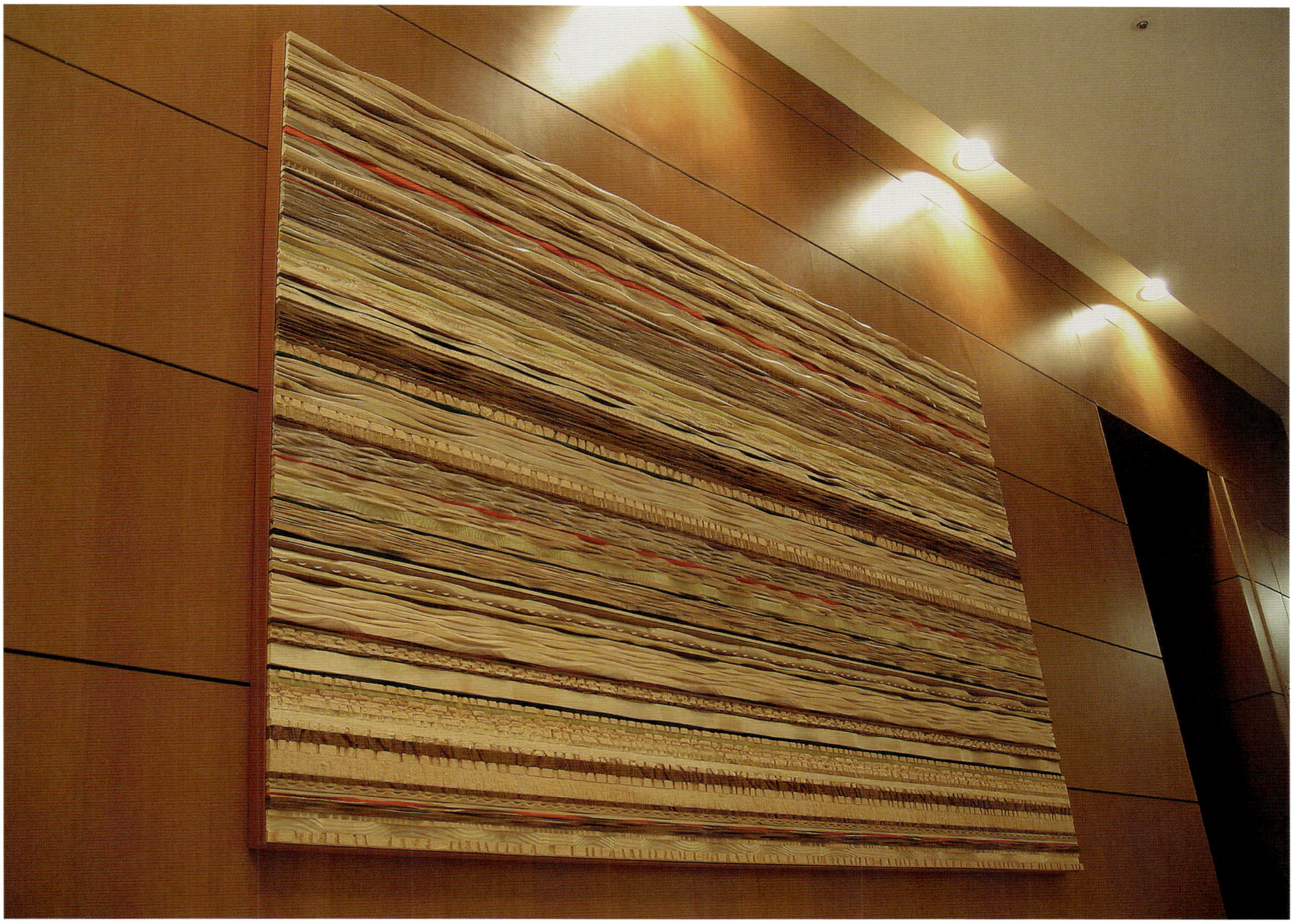

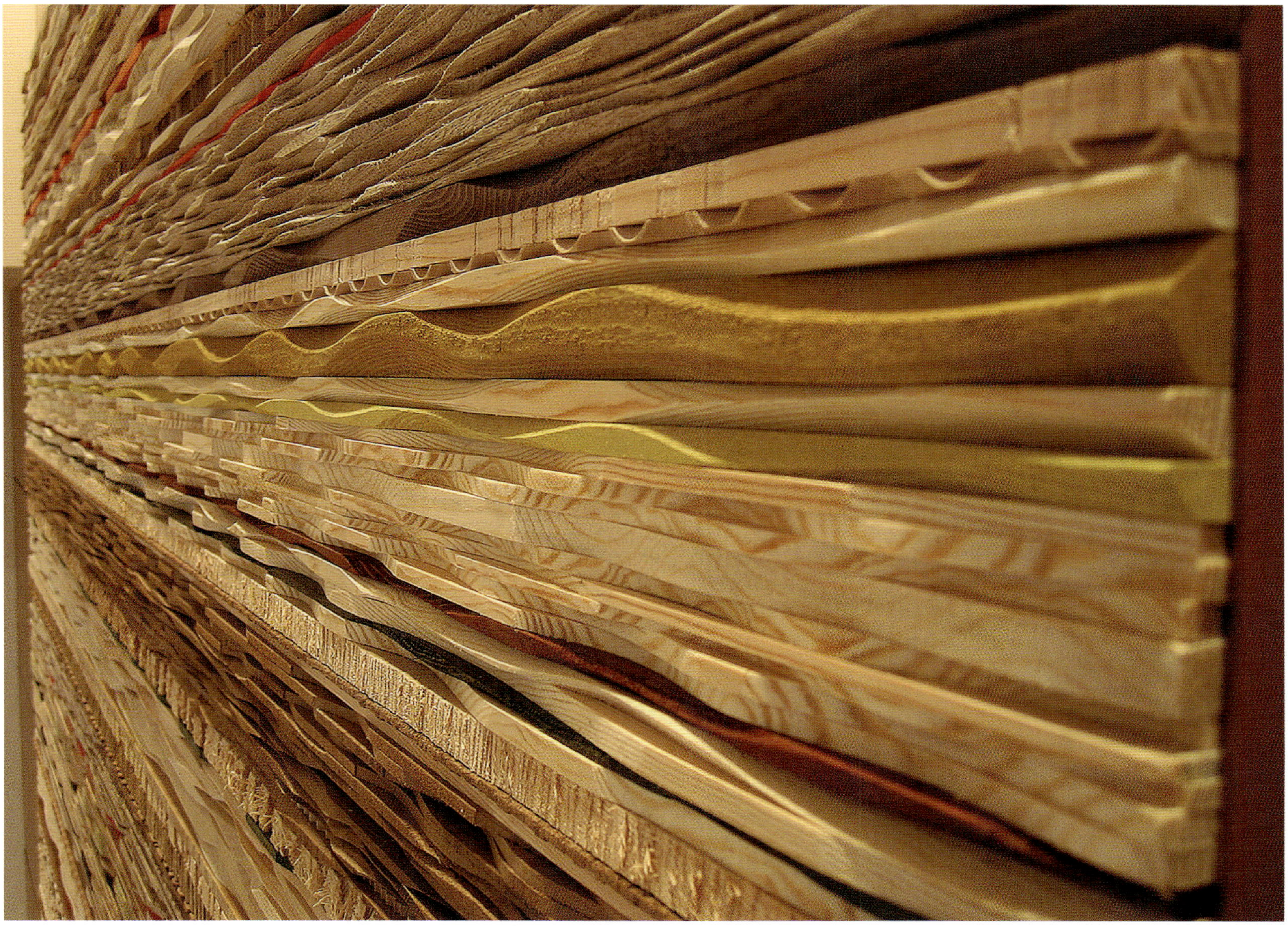

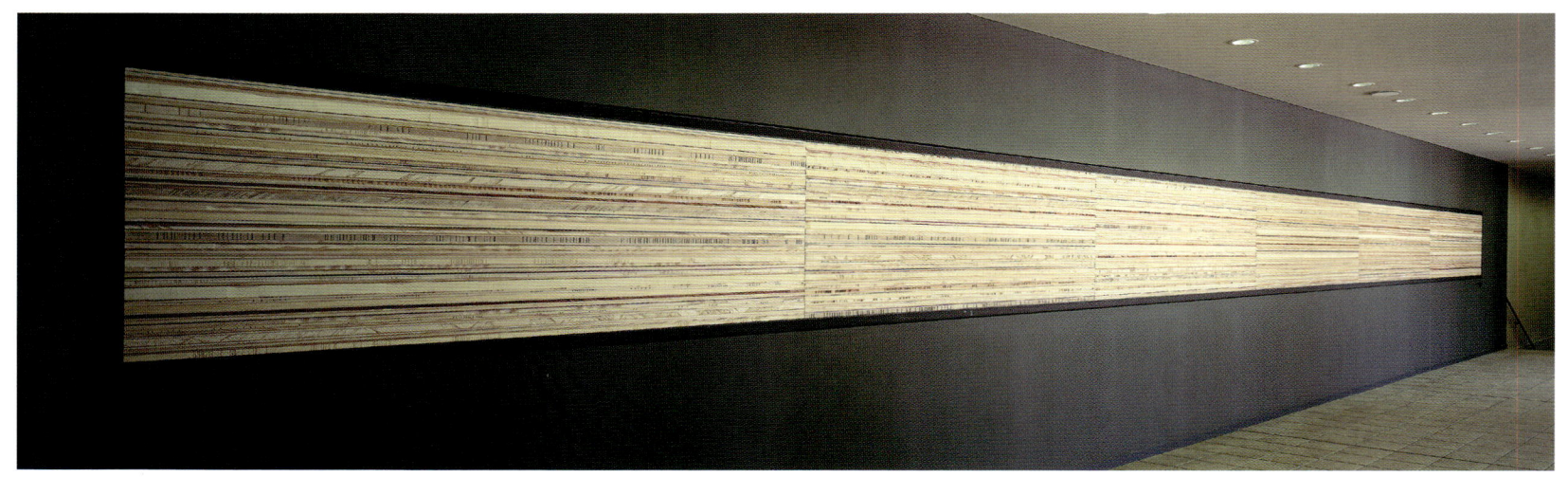

2-45 Sea of Words
Tokyo University of Foreign Studies
Tokyo, Japan, 2000

Details (pp.187–191)

Sea of Words

Horizontal Feeling

Horizontal Feeling/Palmdale

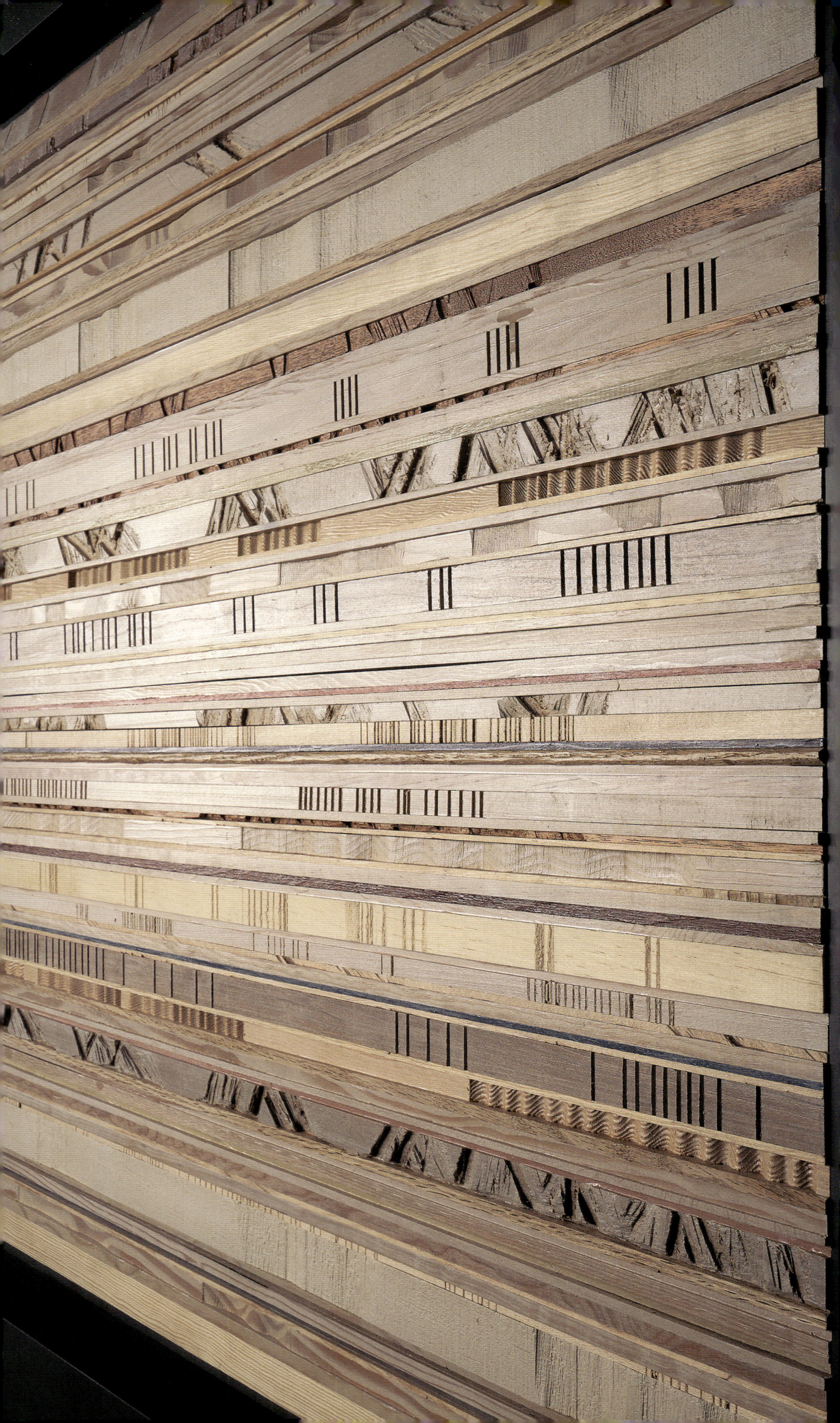

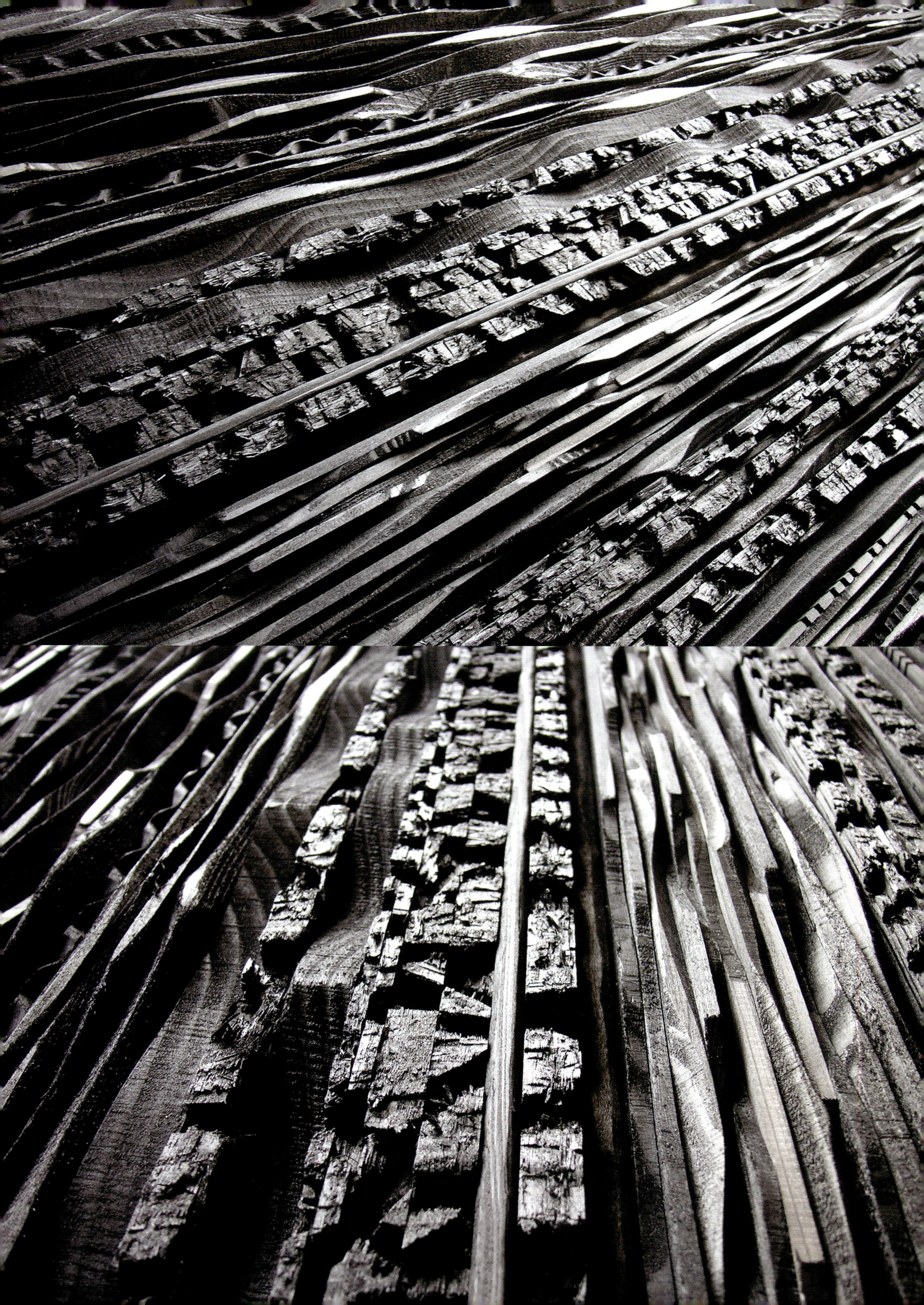

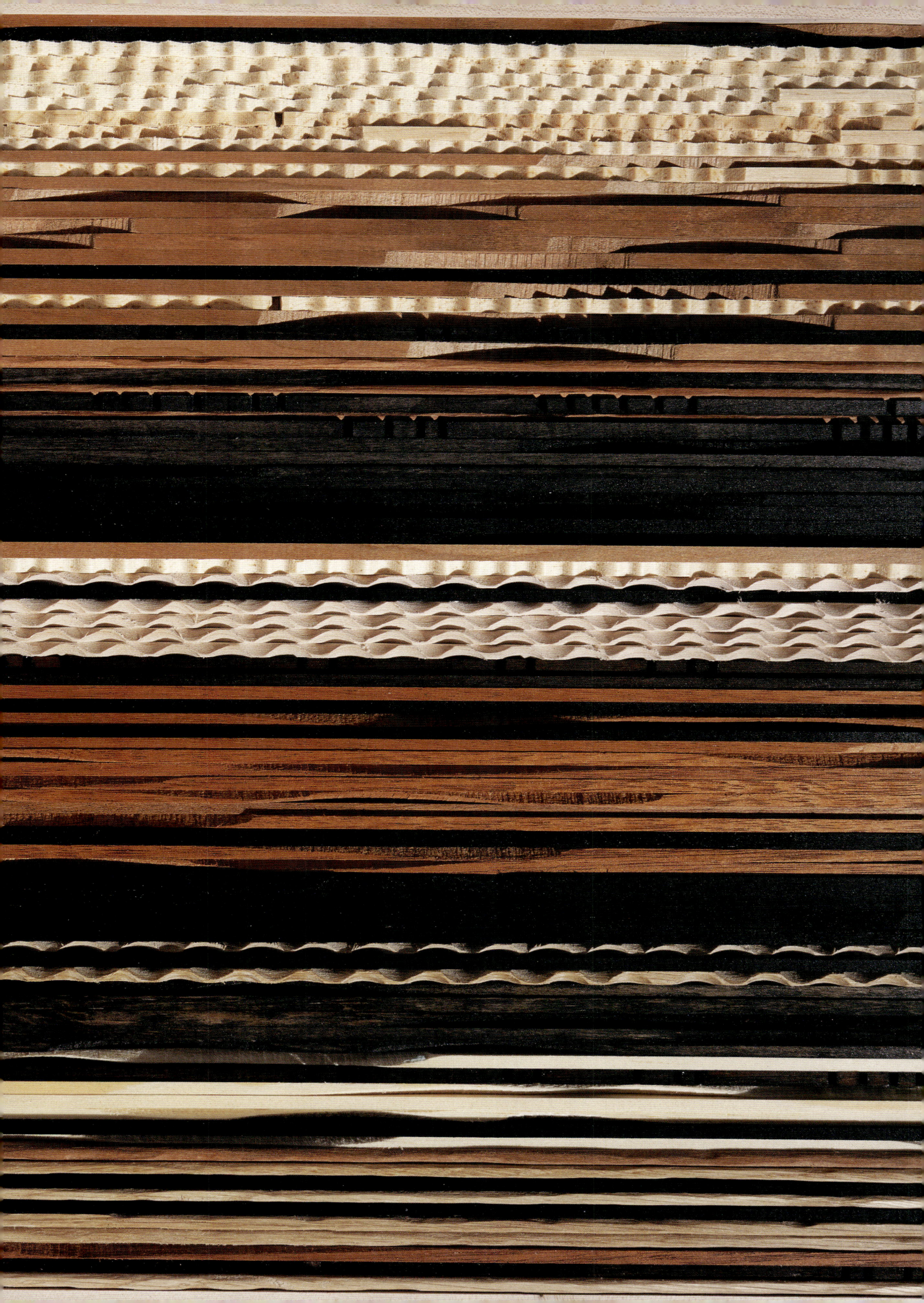

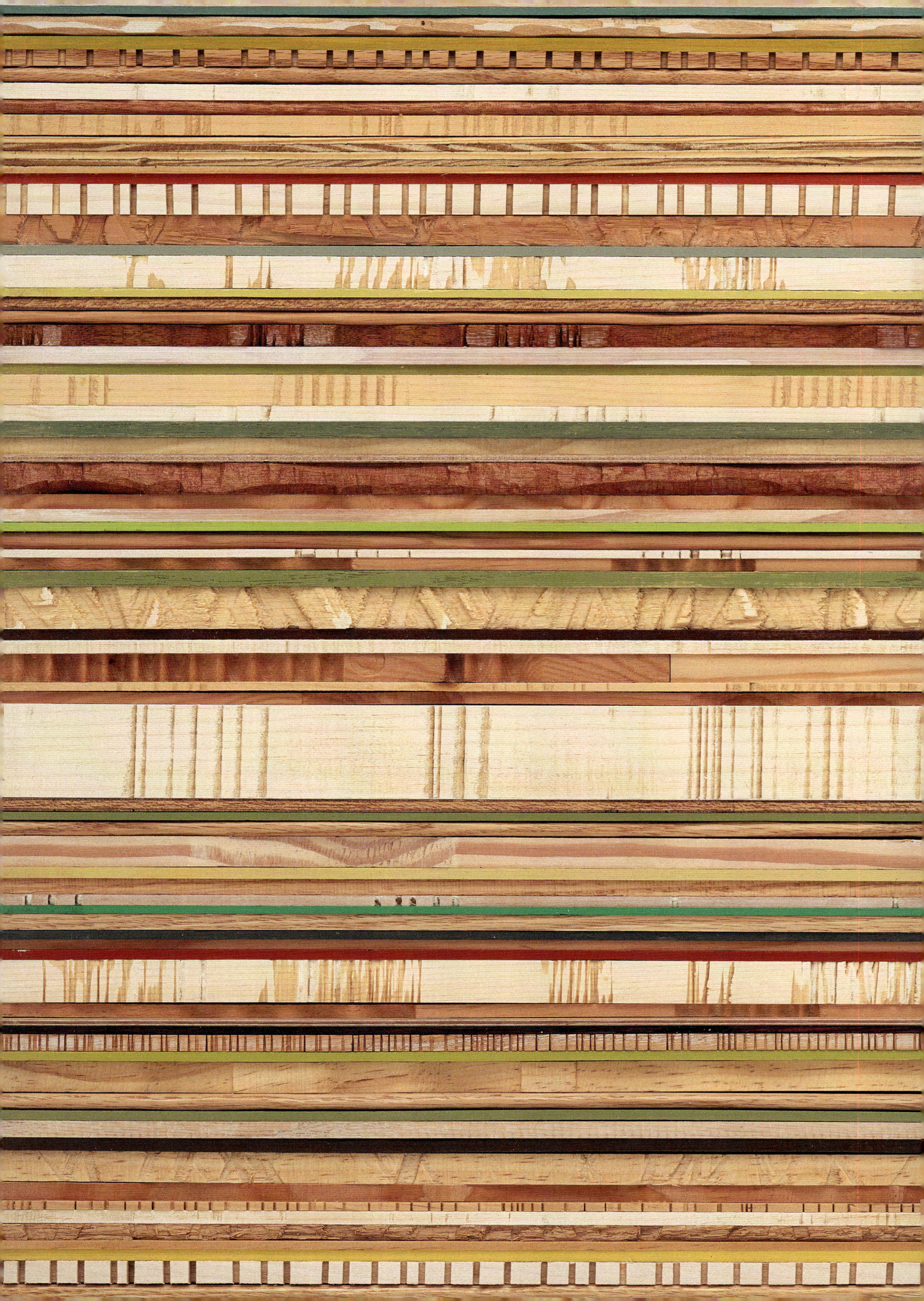

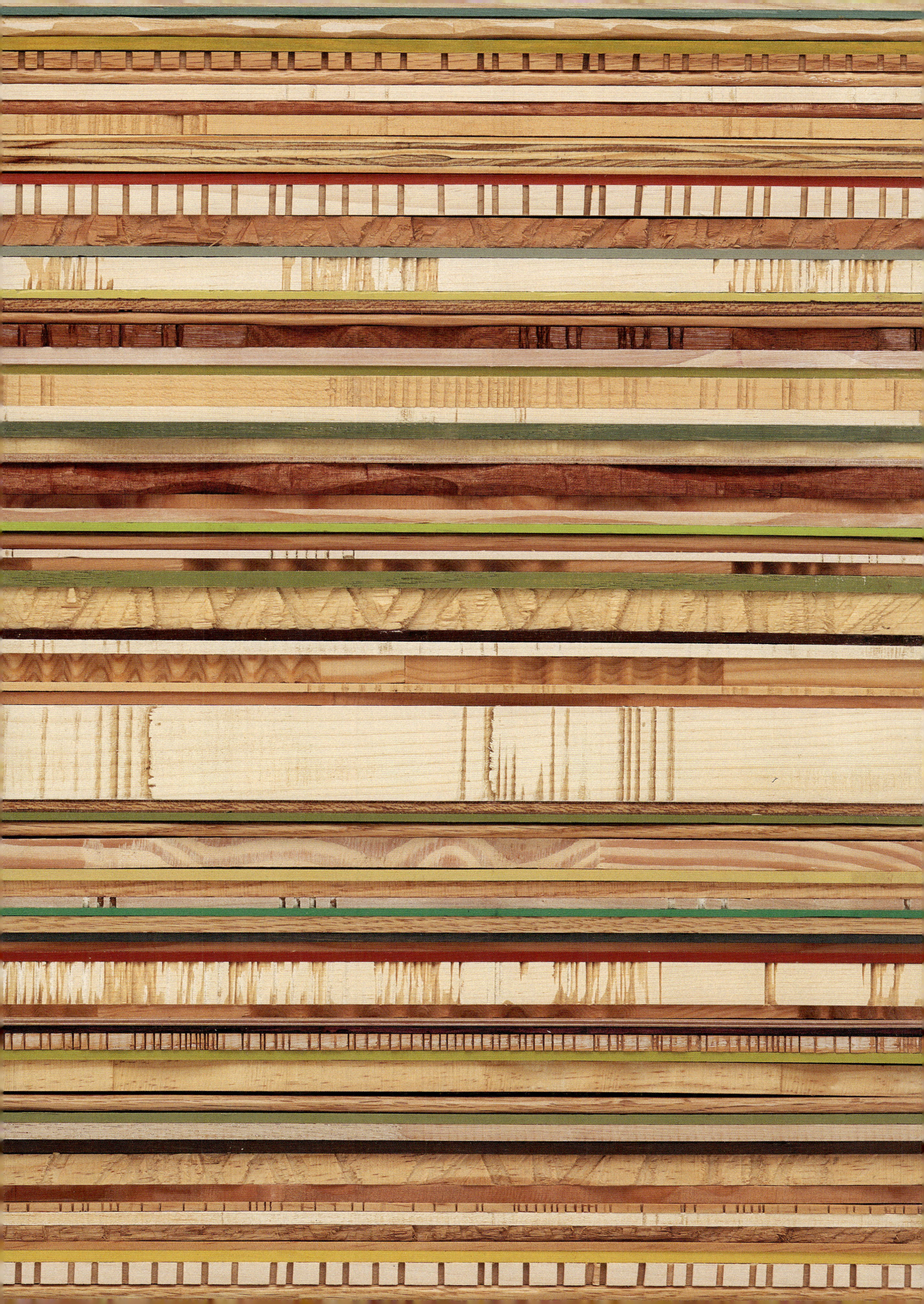

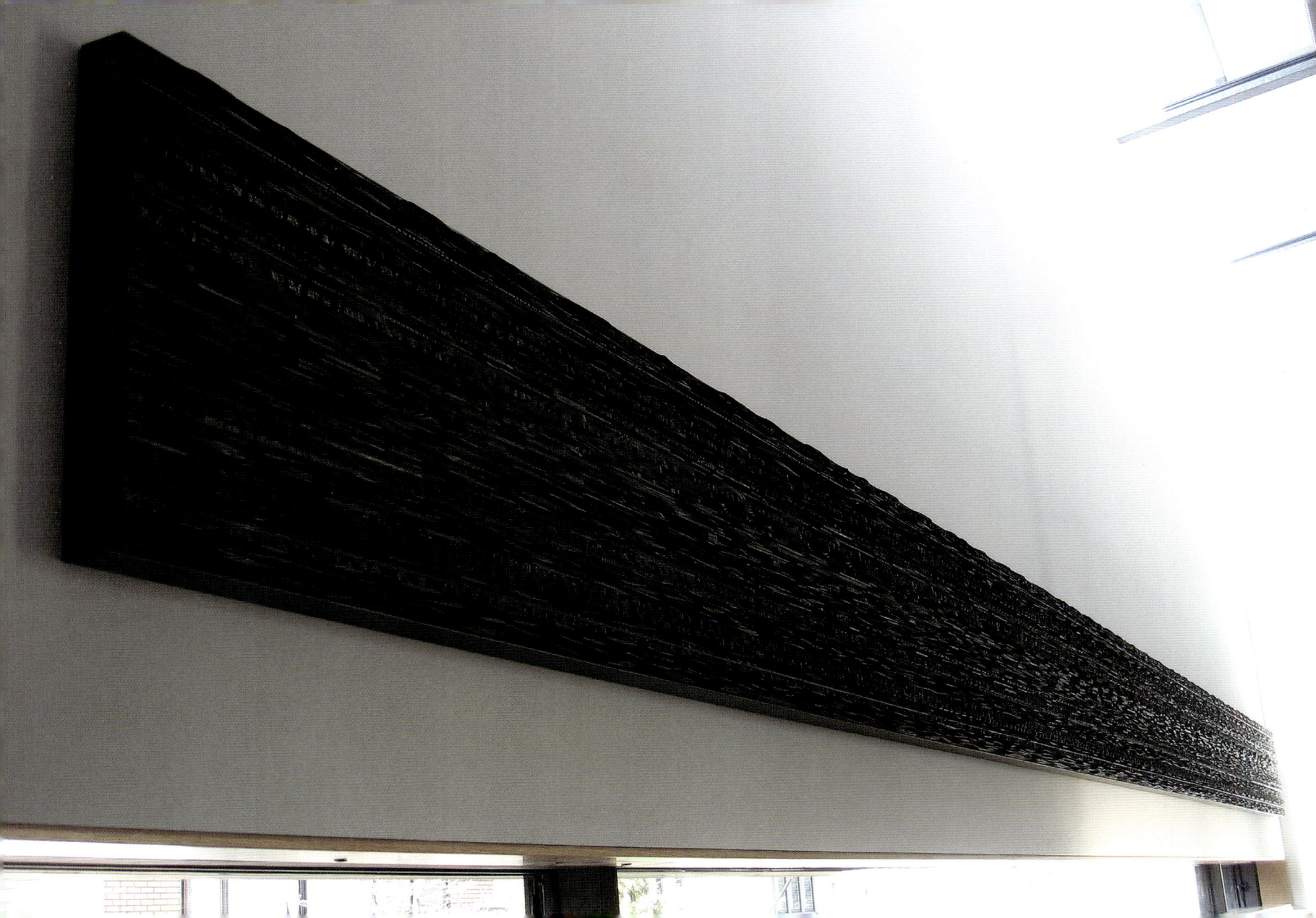

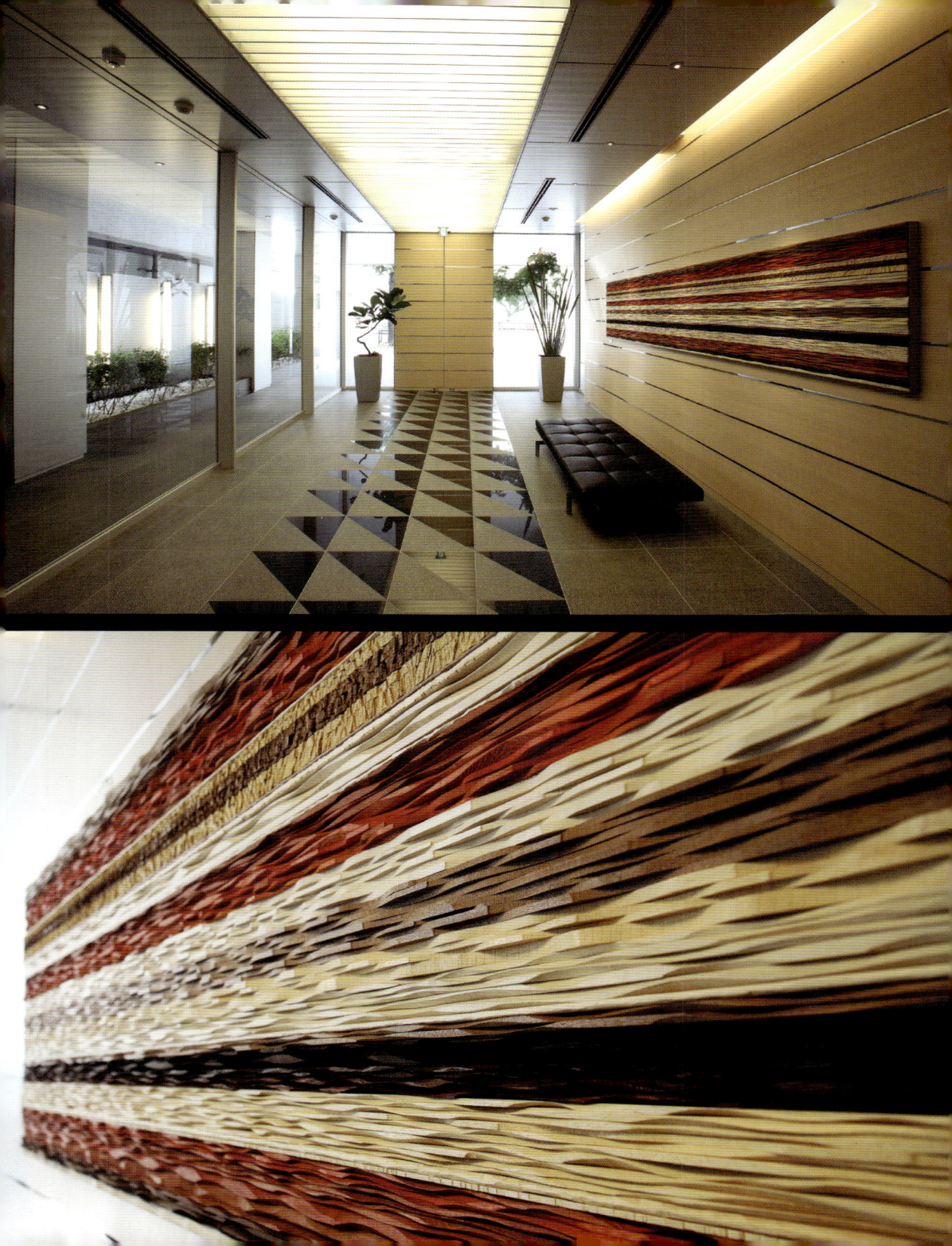

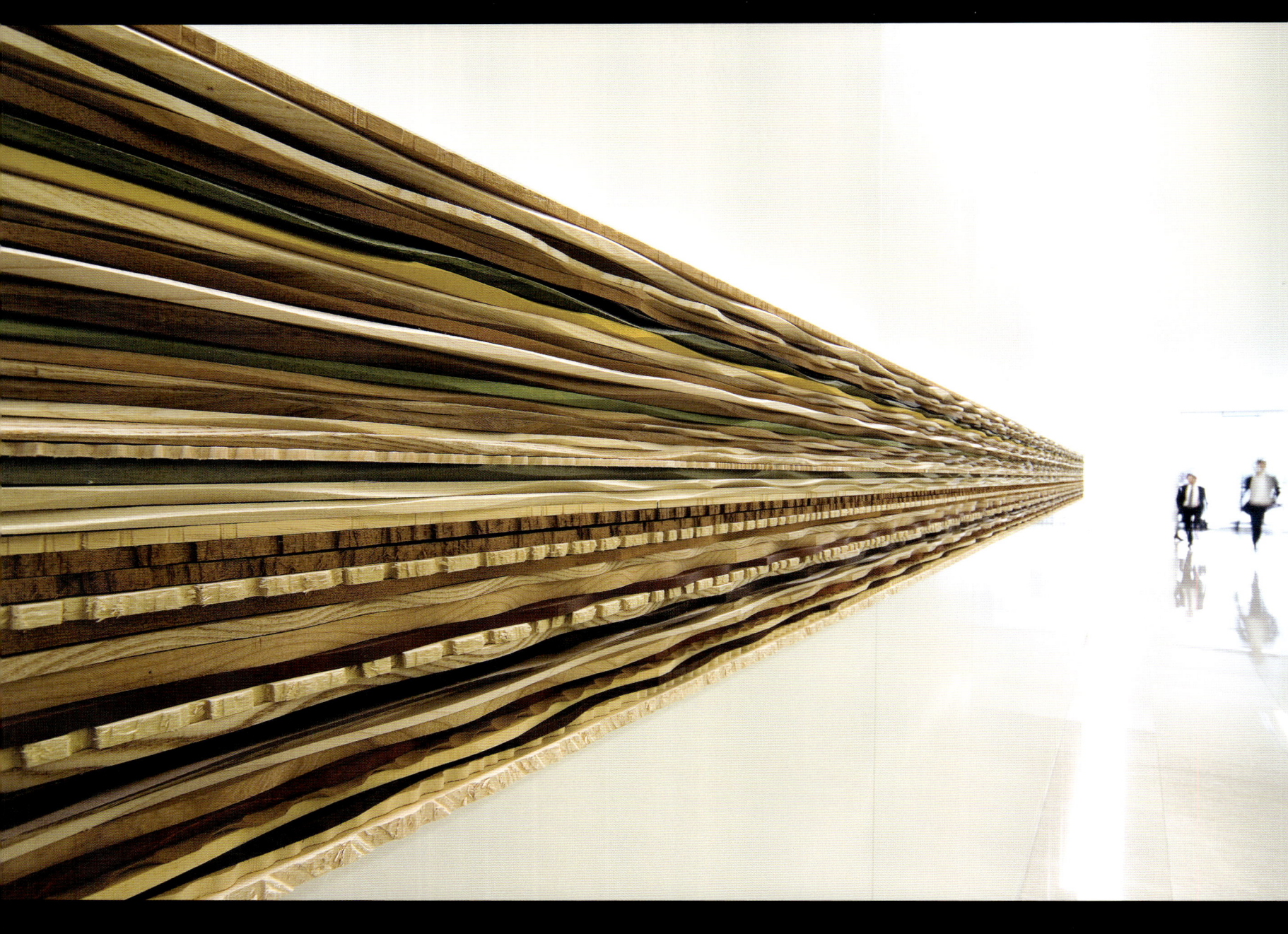

2-48 Horizontal Feeling
Kajima Akasaka Annex
Tokyo, Japan, 2007

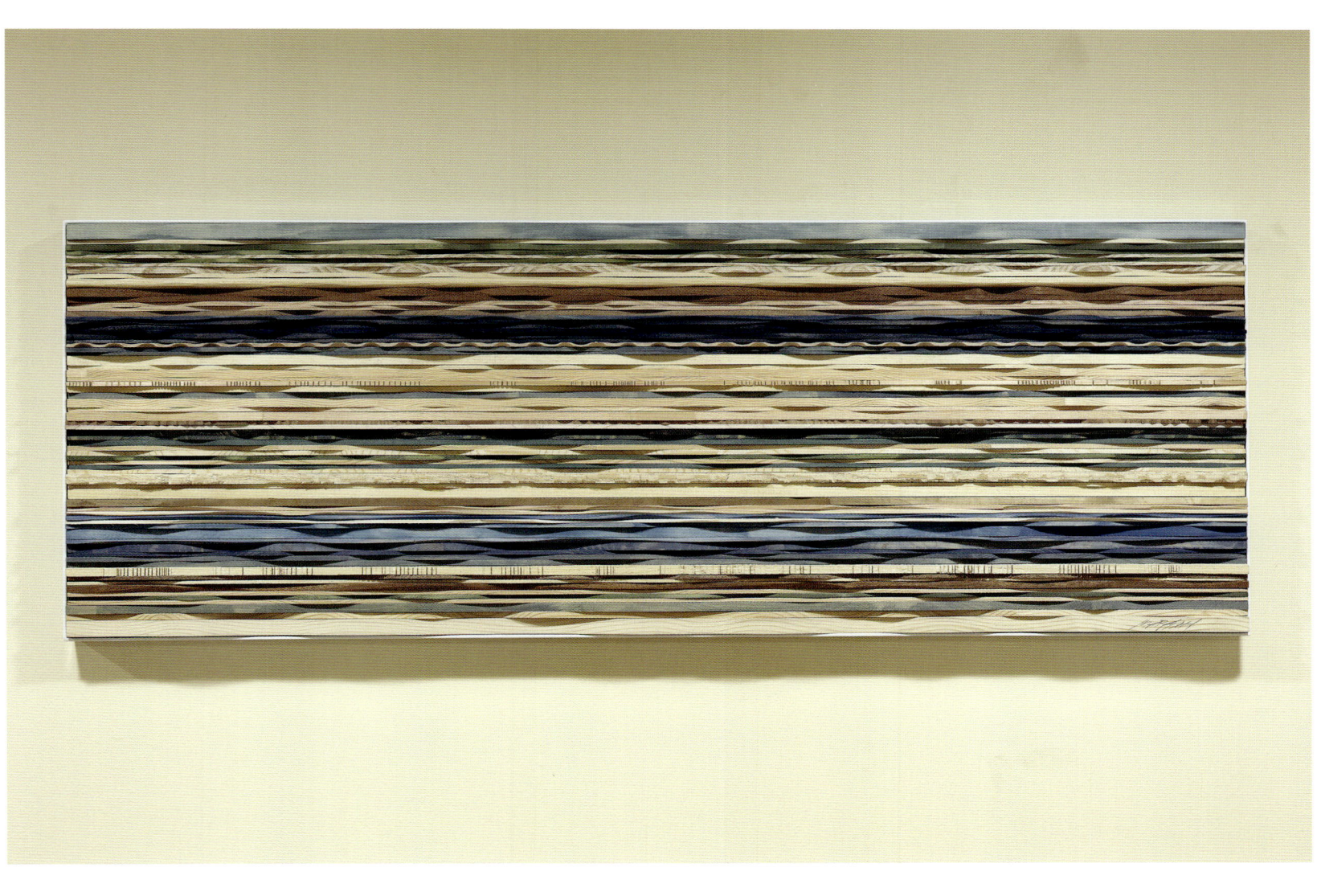

2-49 Horizontal Feeling LHH-3
Laguna Honda Hospital
San Francisco, CA, USA, 2008

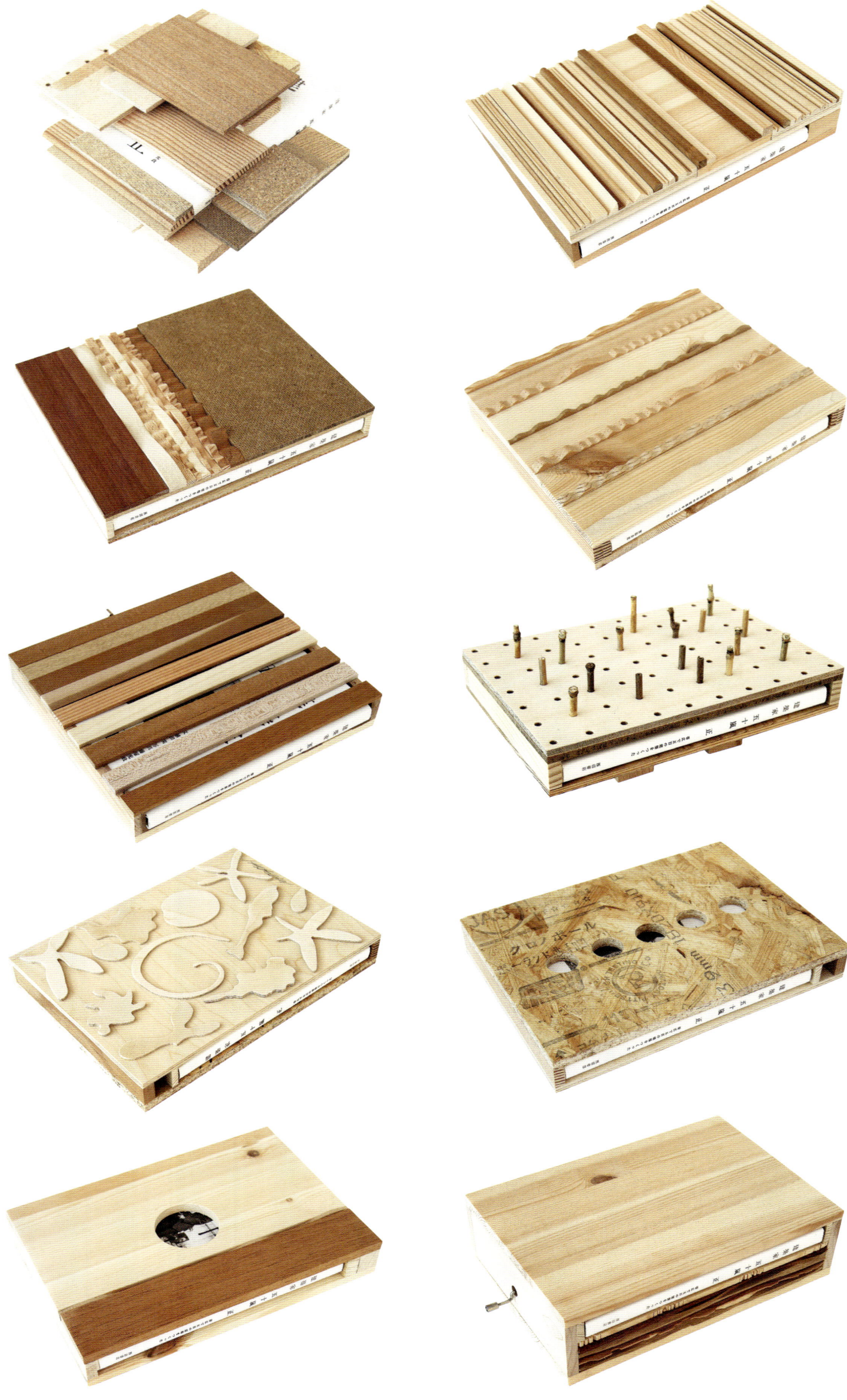

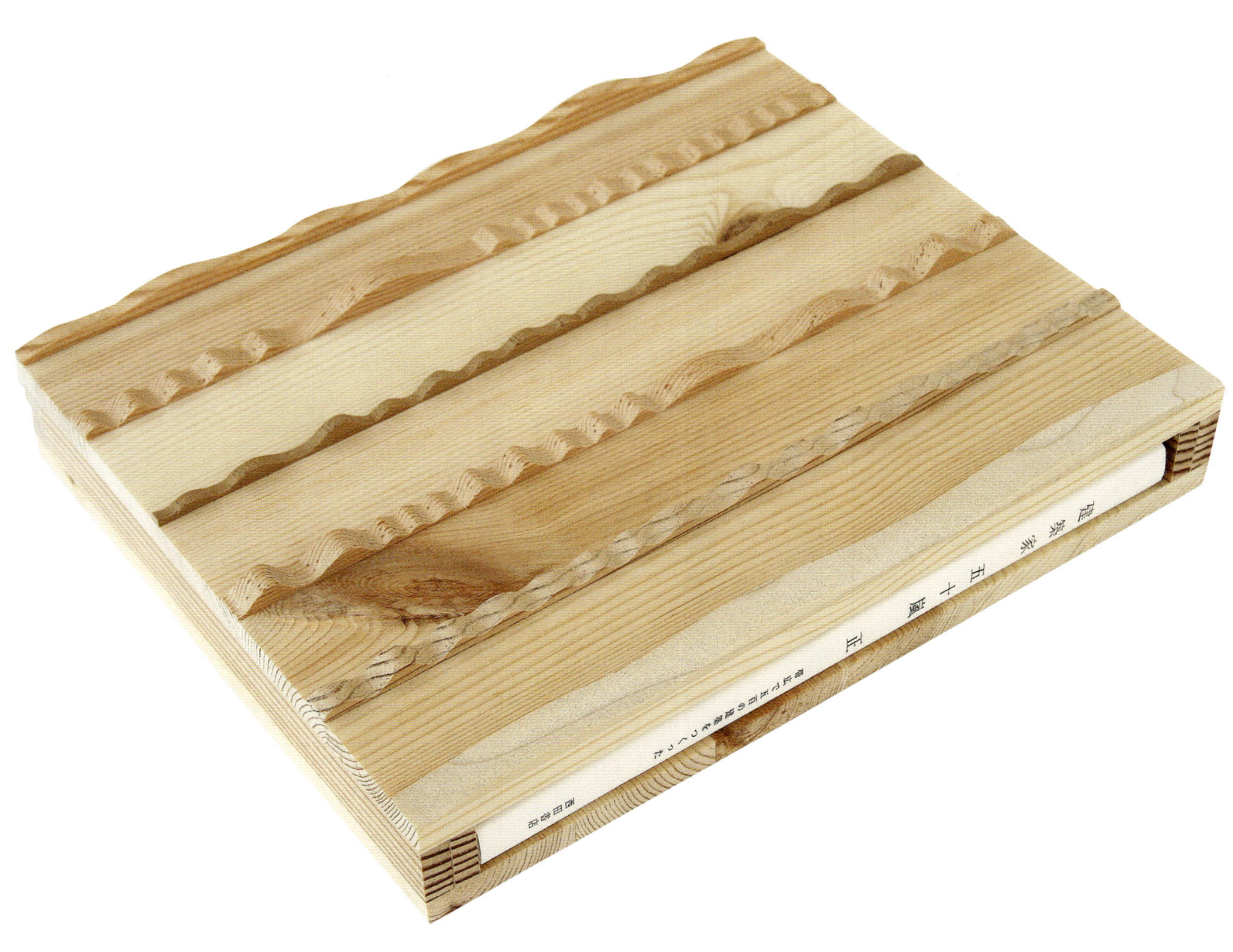

2-50 Art Box #01–20, 2007

Ad lib guarantees freedom. These are different variations of bookcases that I created ad lib for one book– one is accompanied with a music box, one has wheels, etc. (TI)

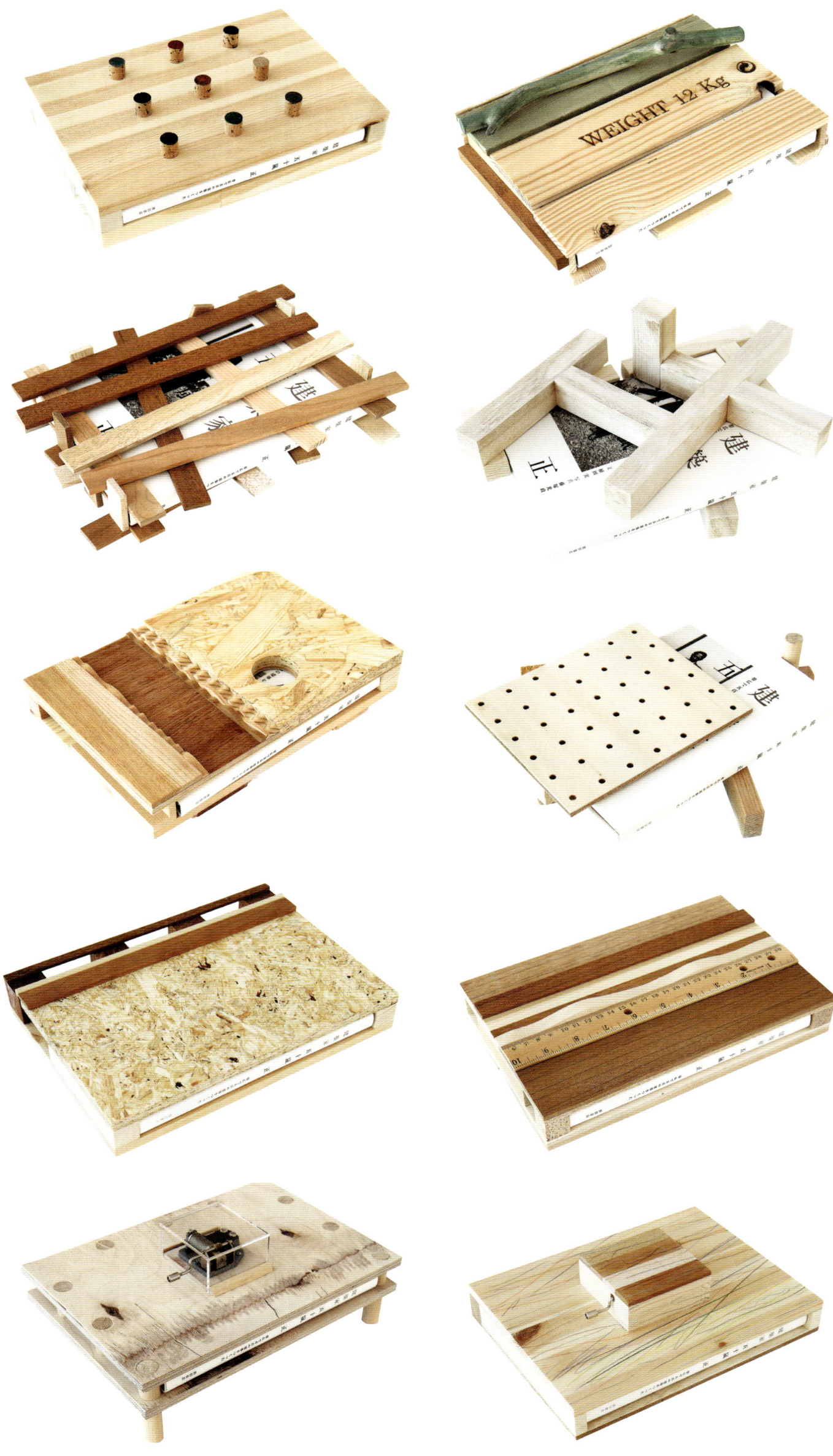

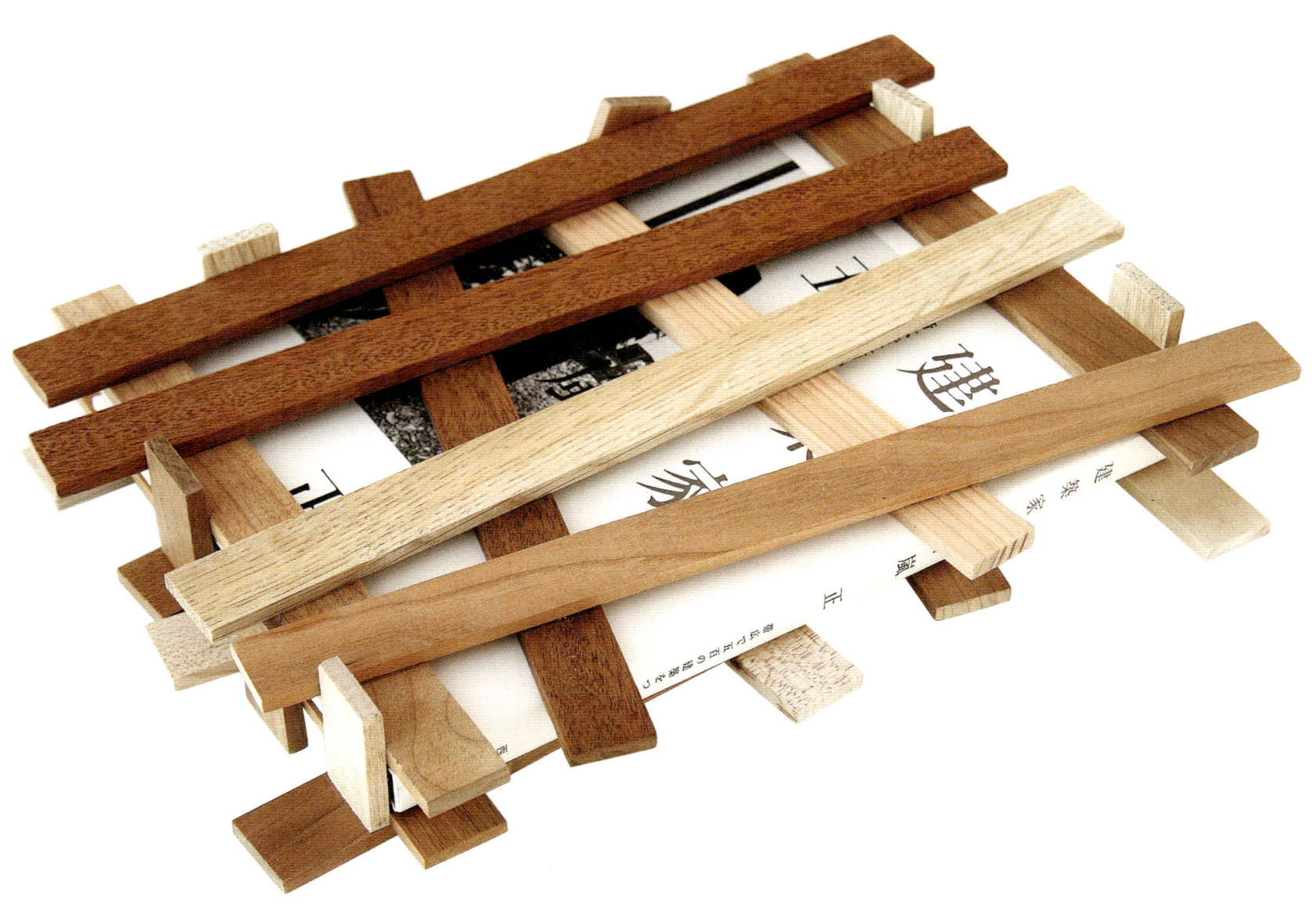

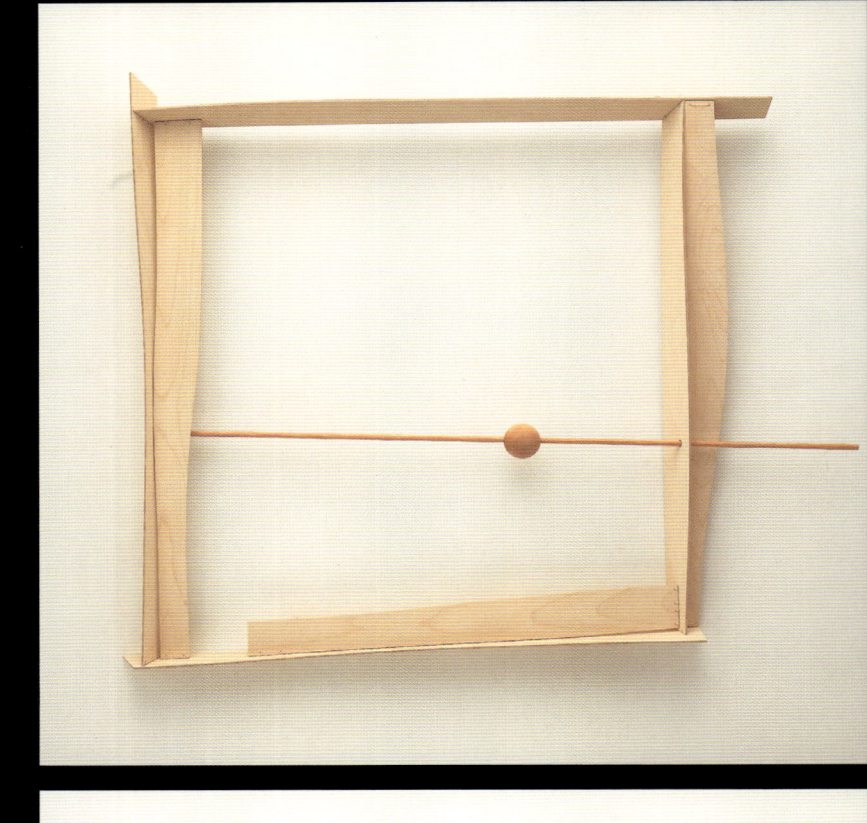

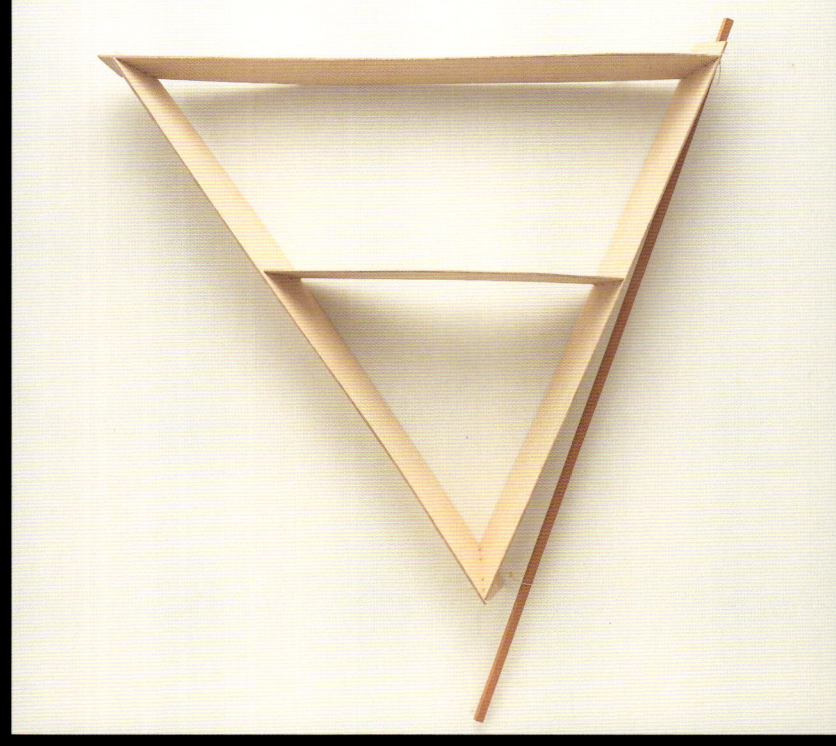

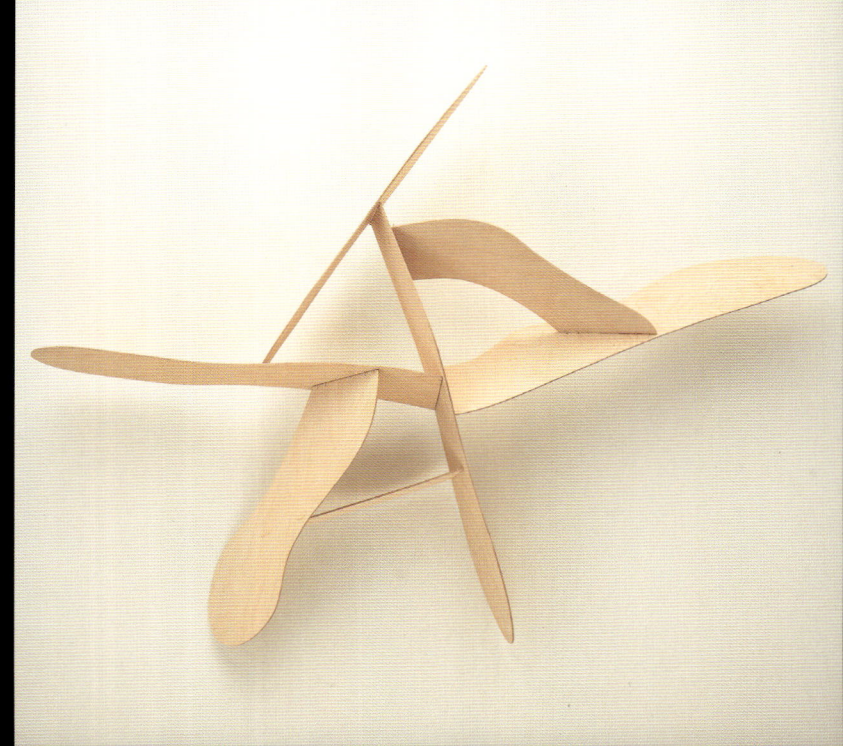

51 Flow, 2000

52 Illusion, 2000

53 Moment, 2000

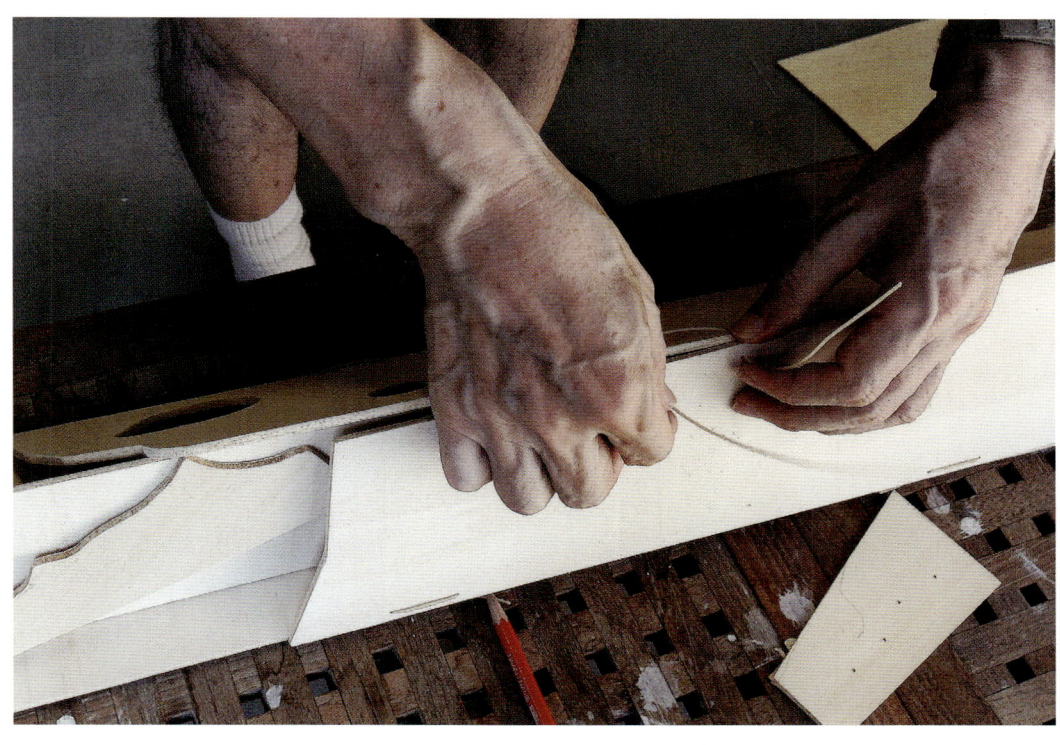

Making of Calligraphy series
*Making lightweight sculpture was an important goal.
I came up with the idea of using silk strings and putting
pieces of plywood together without glue and screws. (TI)*

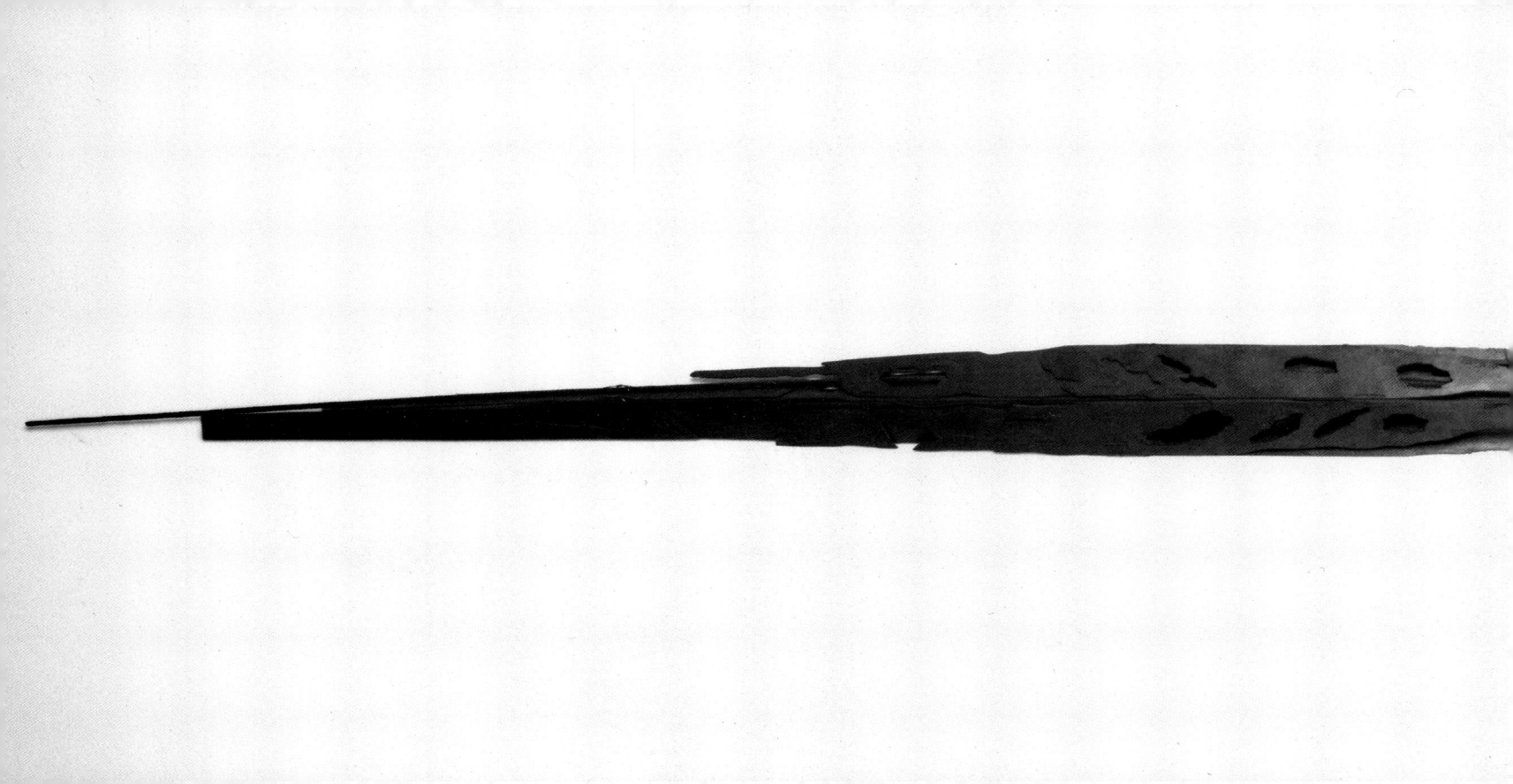

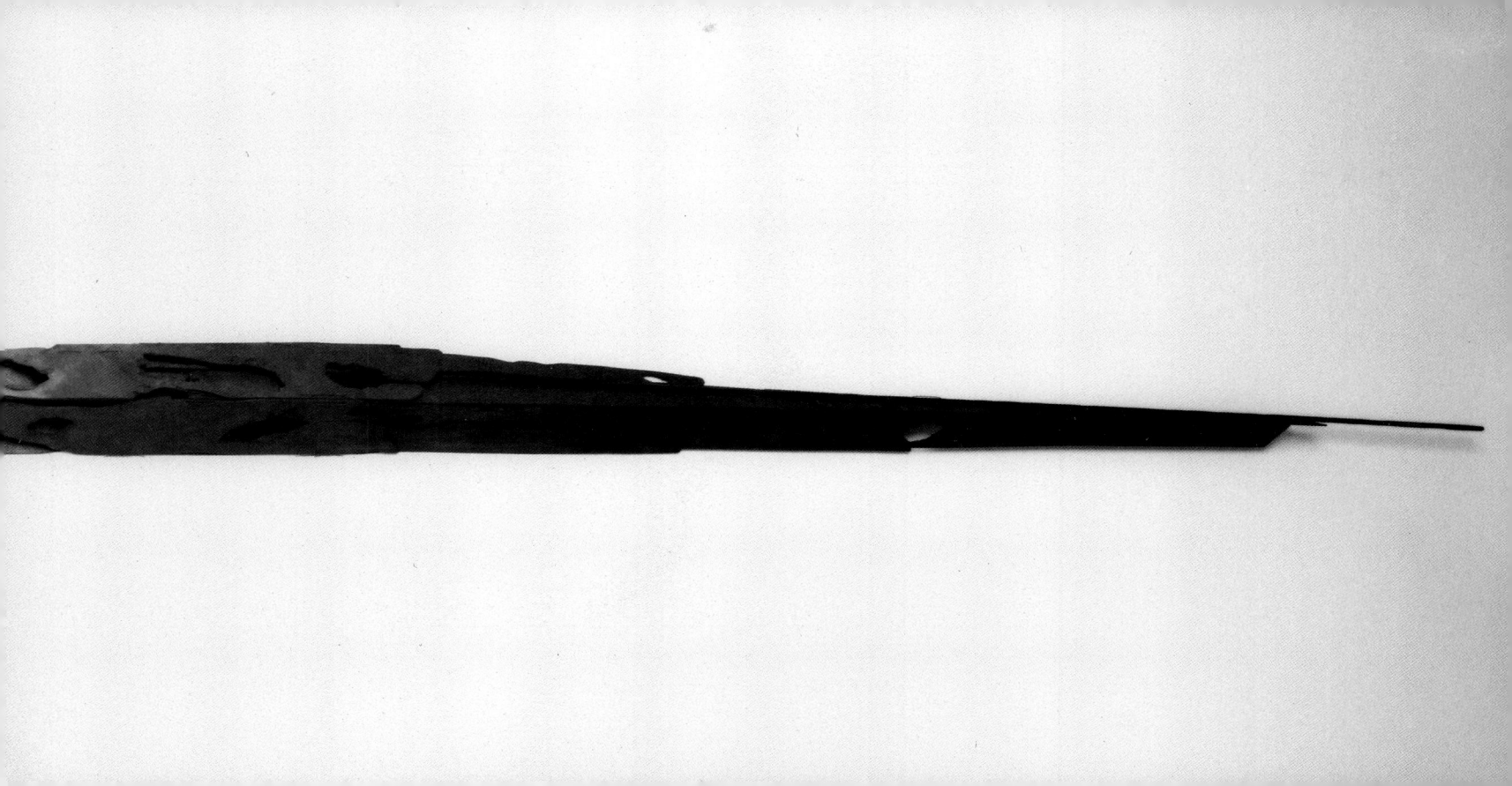

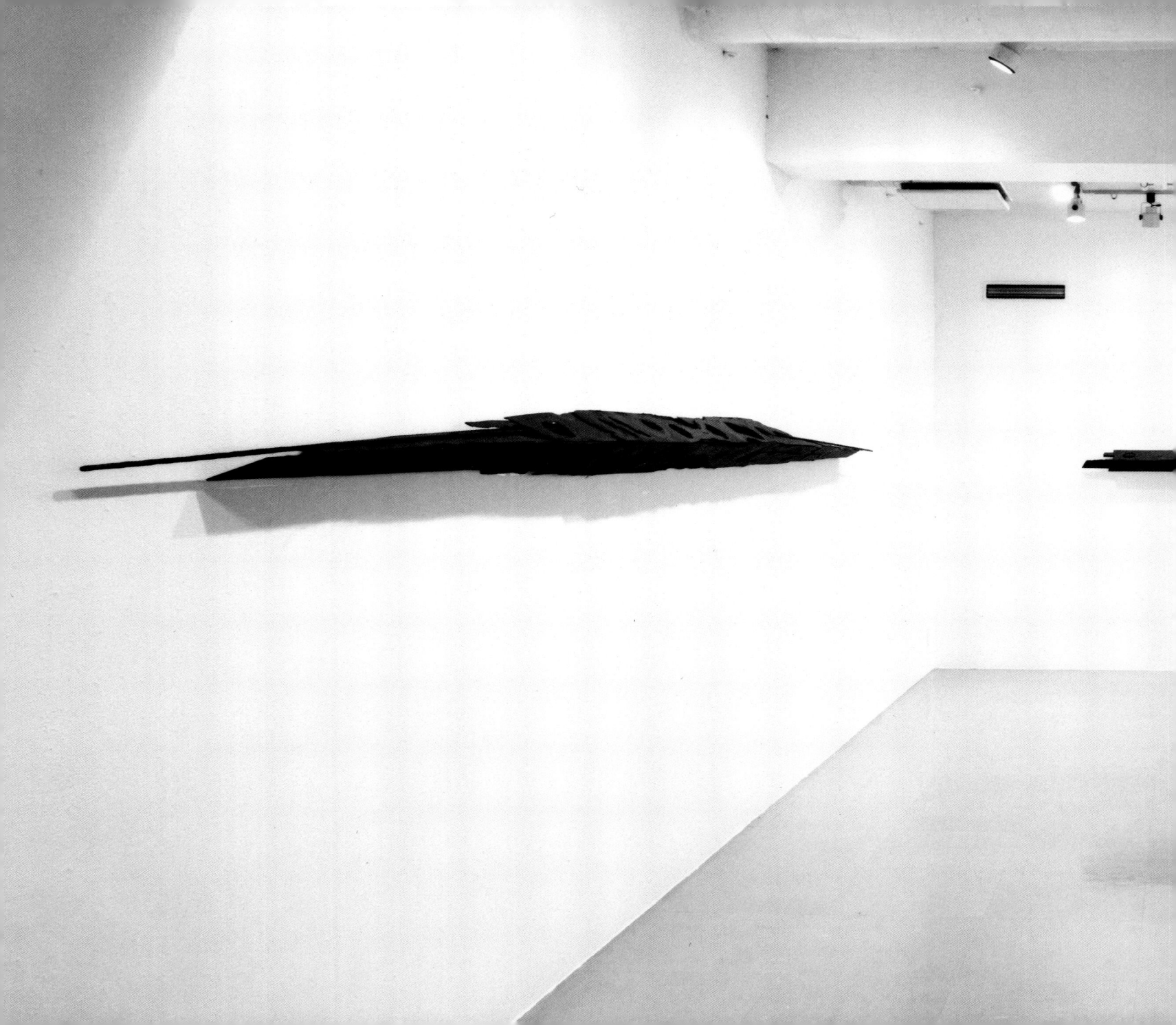

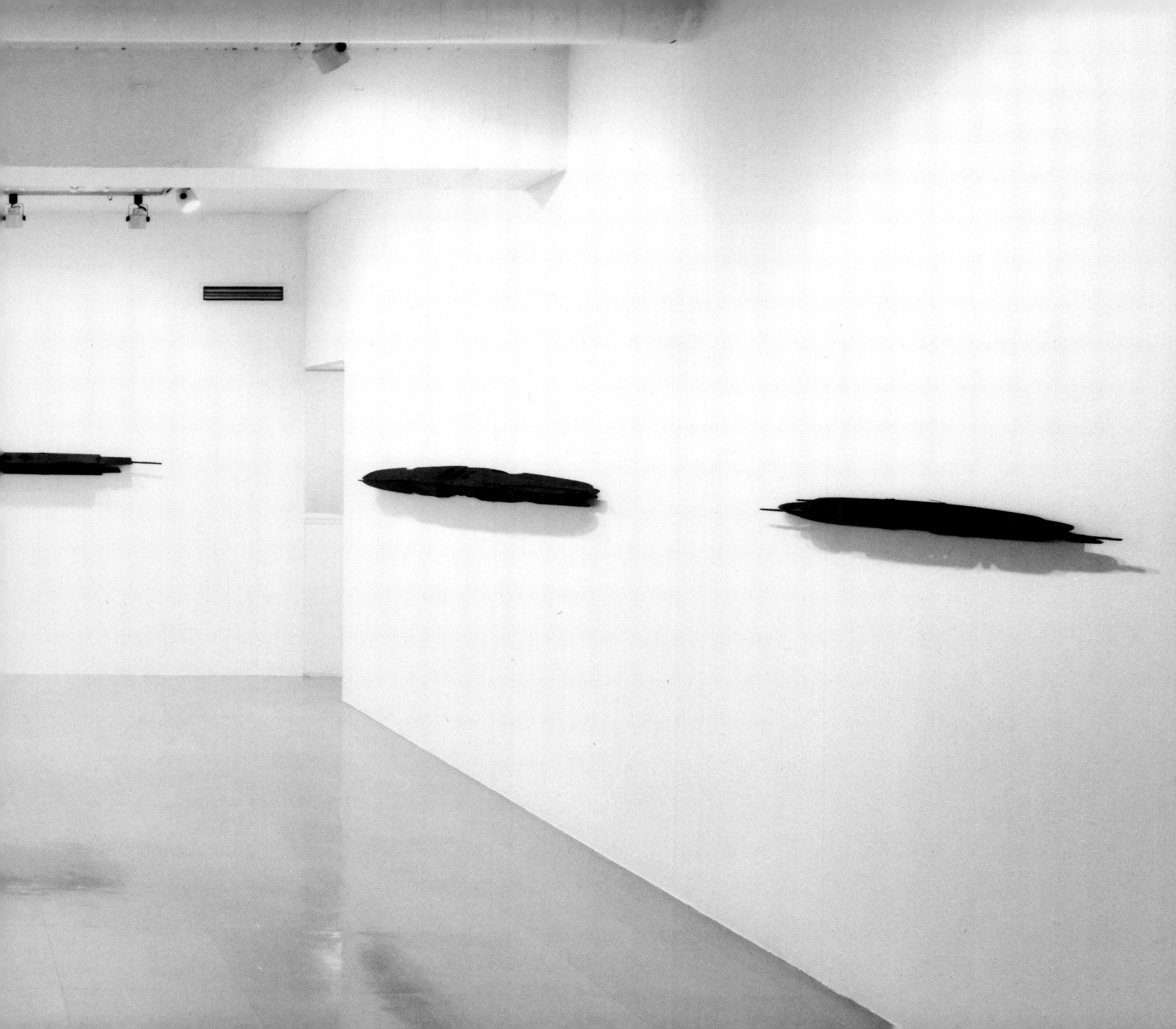

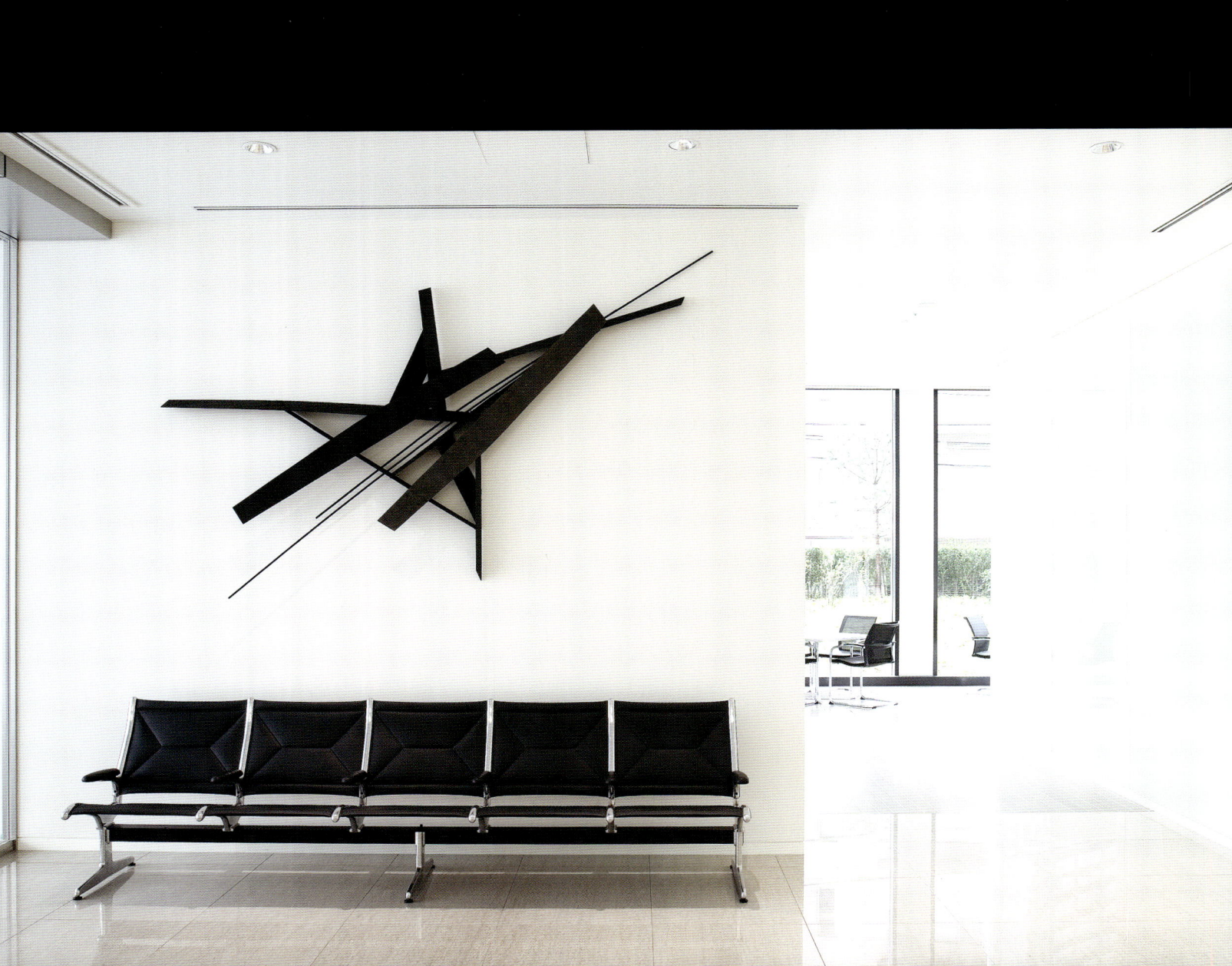

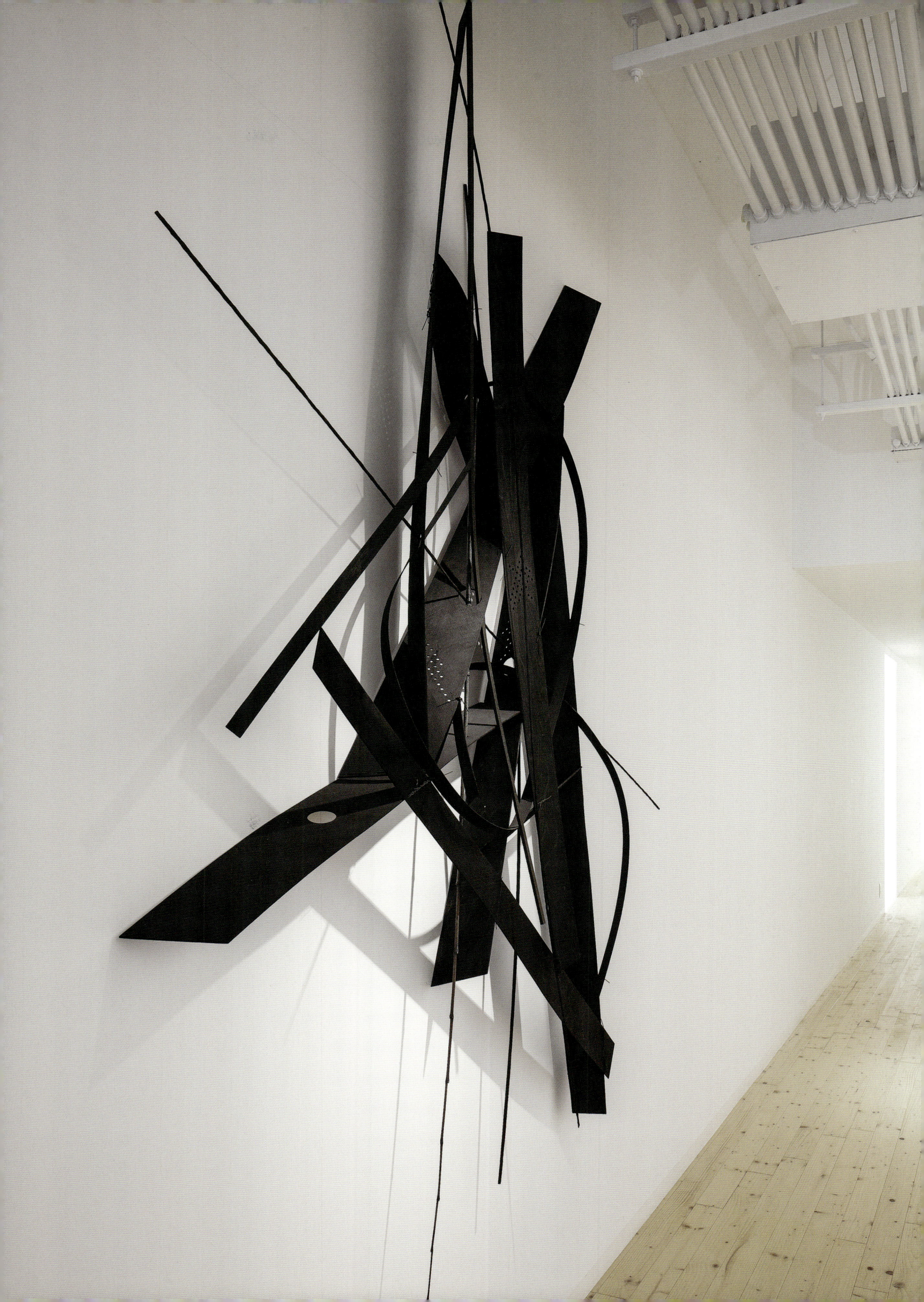

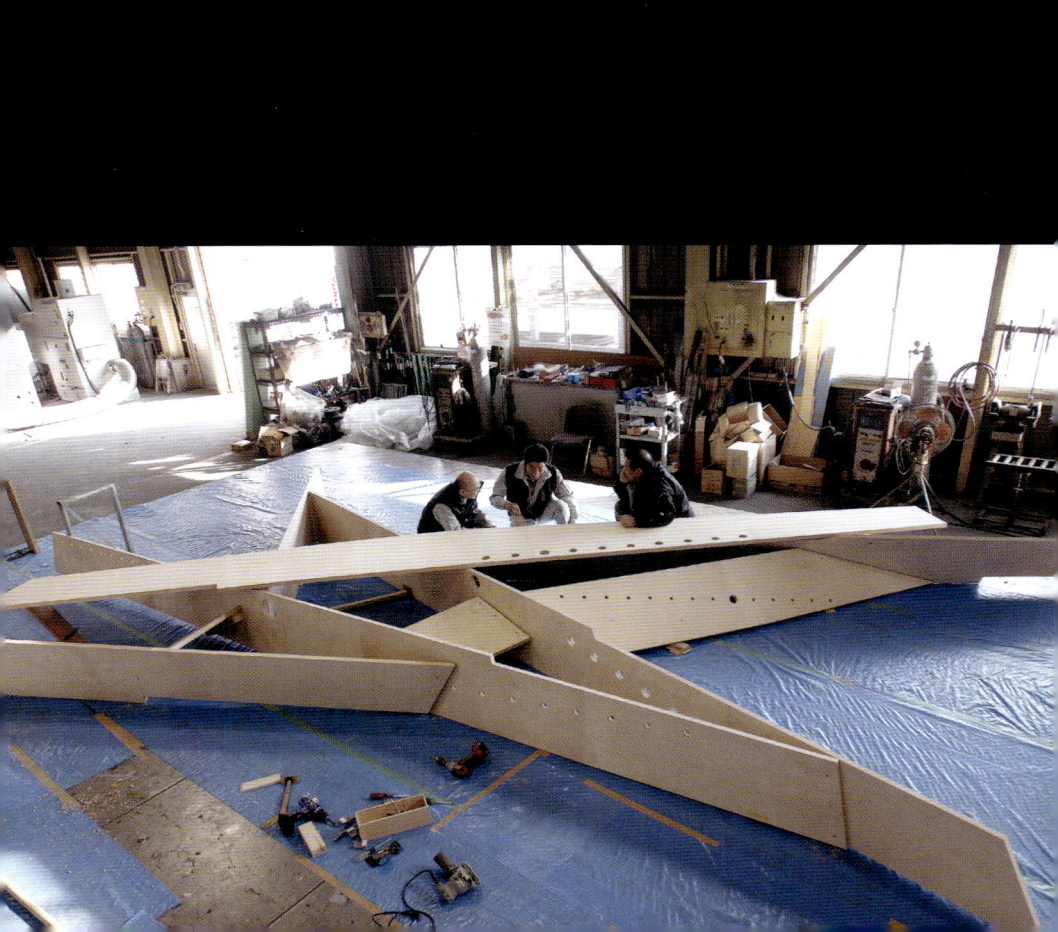

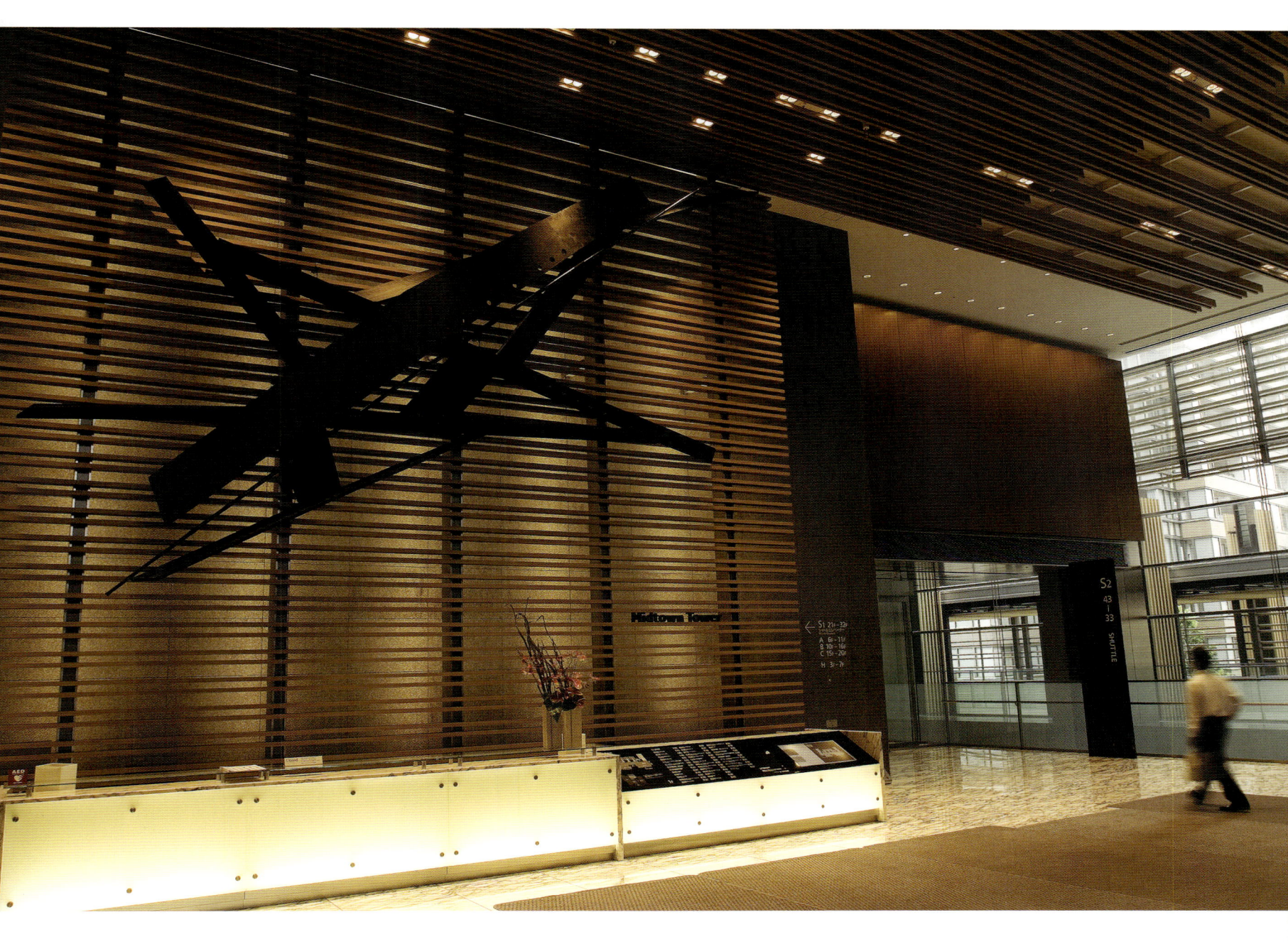

2-57 To the Sea of Premonition
Tokyo Midtown, Tokyo, Japan, 2006

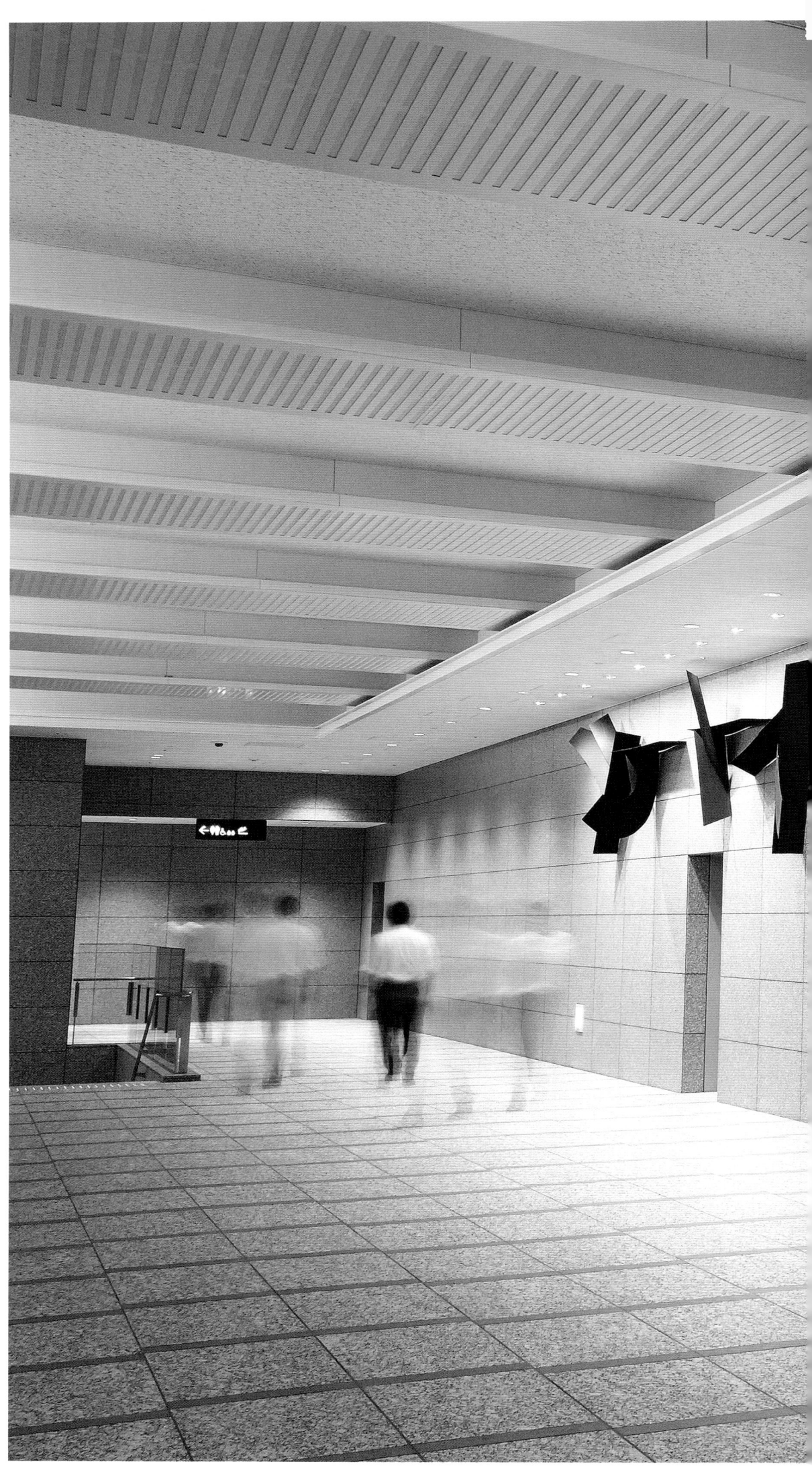

2-58 Zawa Zawa/ Hyun Hyun/ Giggi
Osaki Bright Core, Tokyo, Japan, 2015

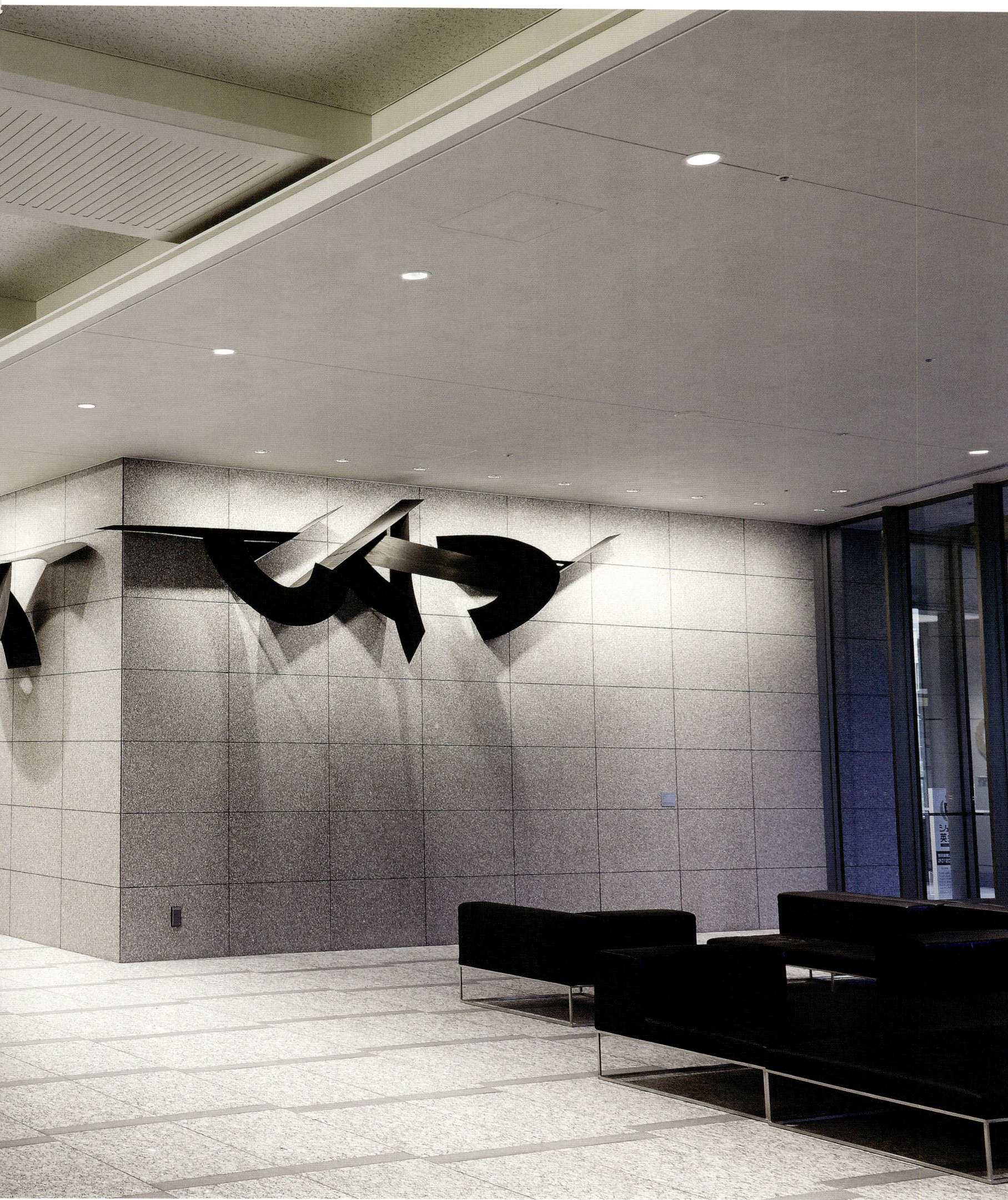

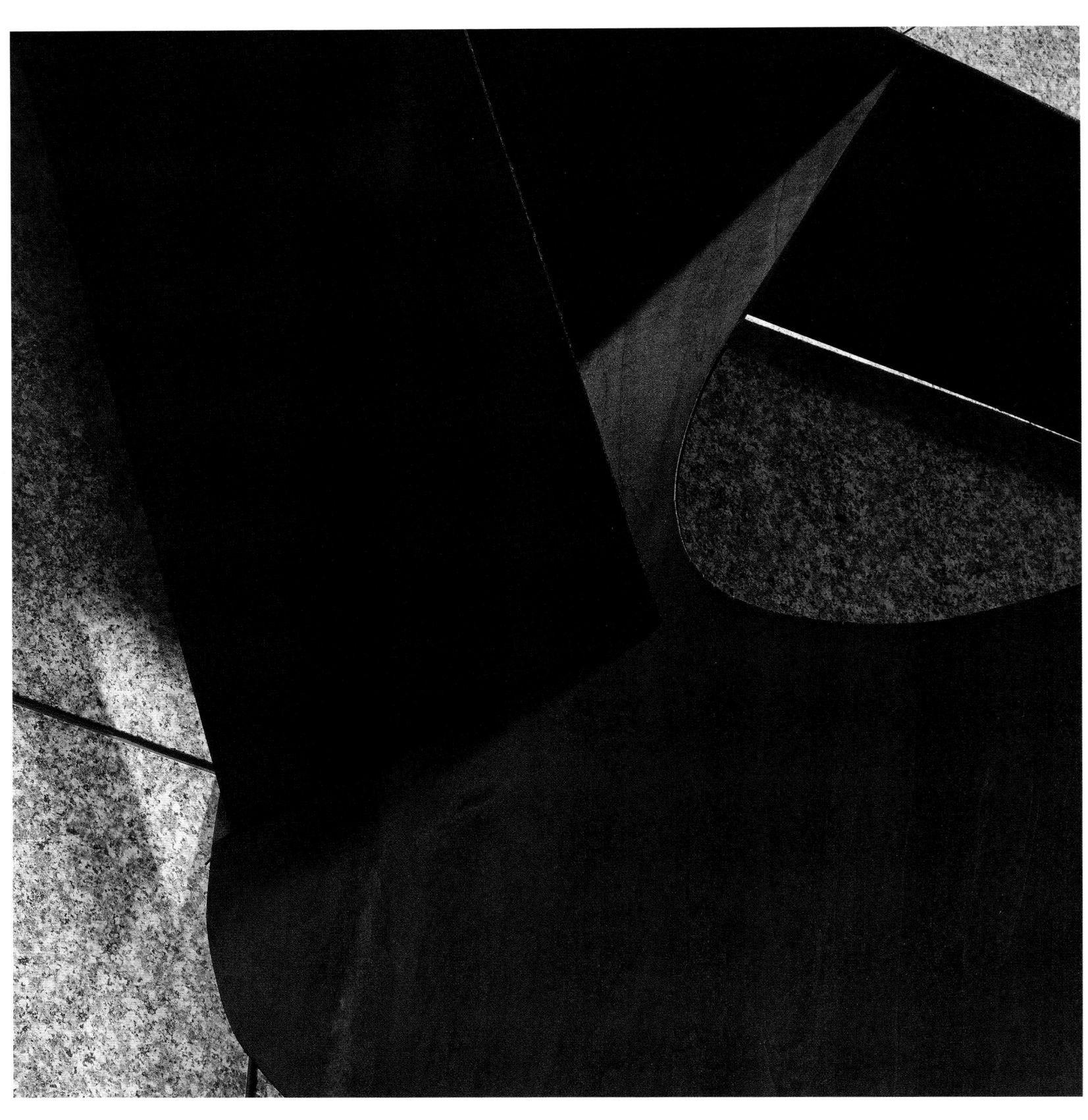

Zawa Zawa/ Hyun Hyun/ Giggi, detail

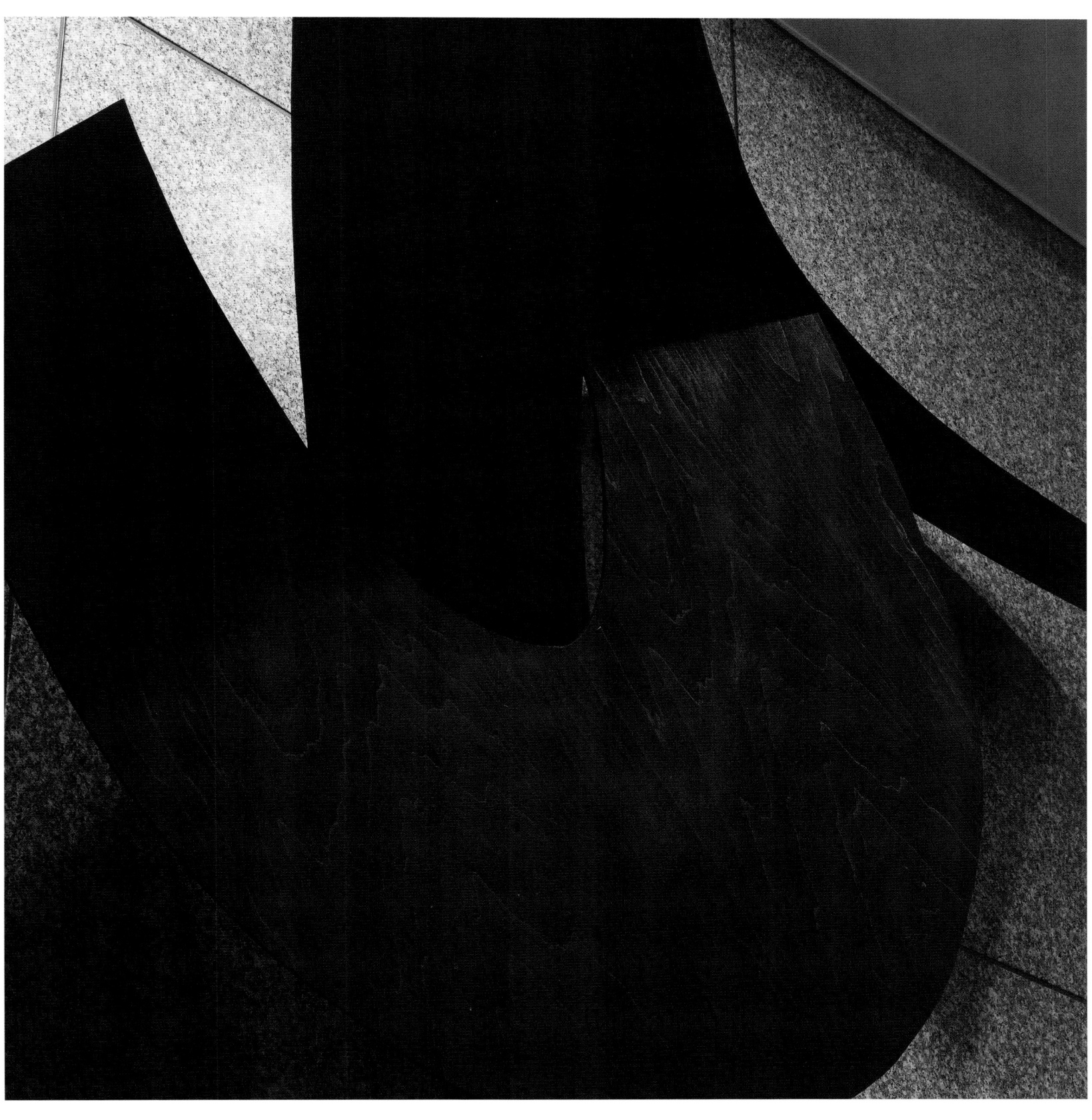

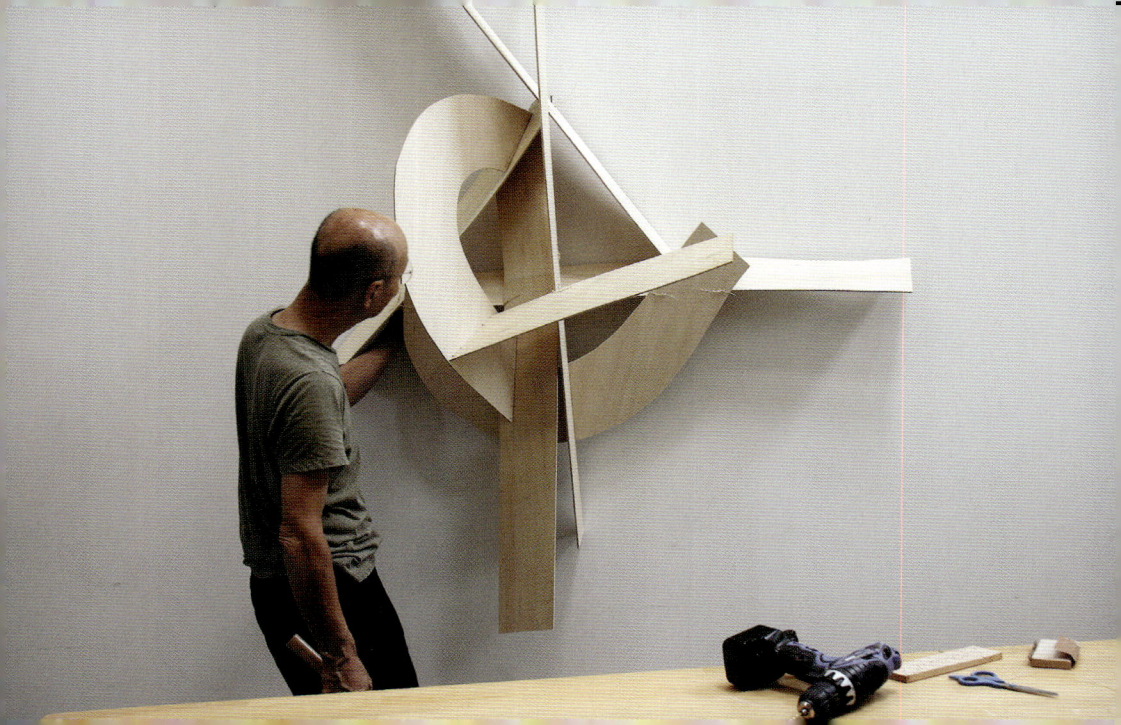

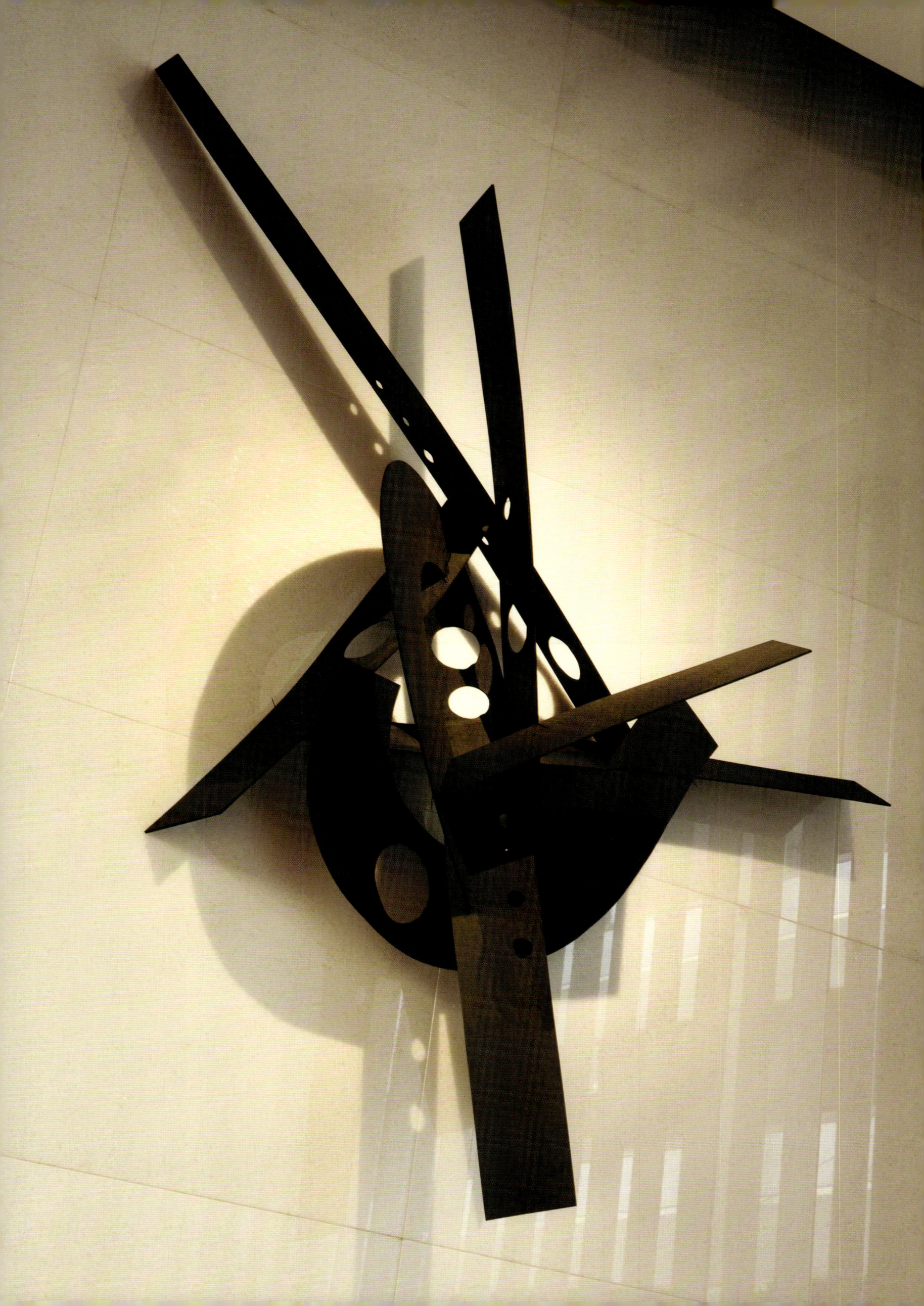

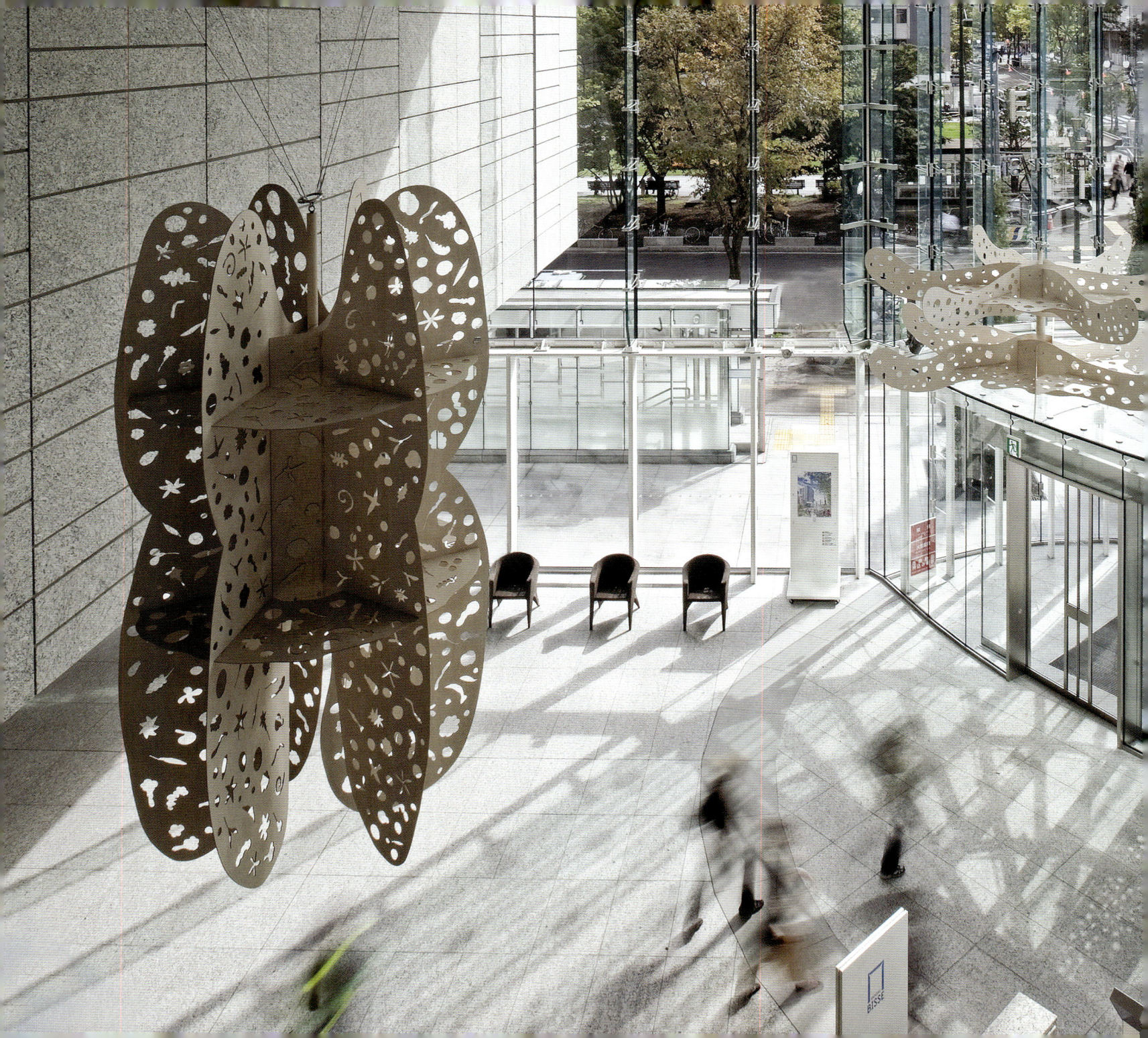

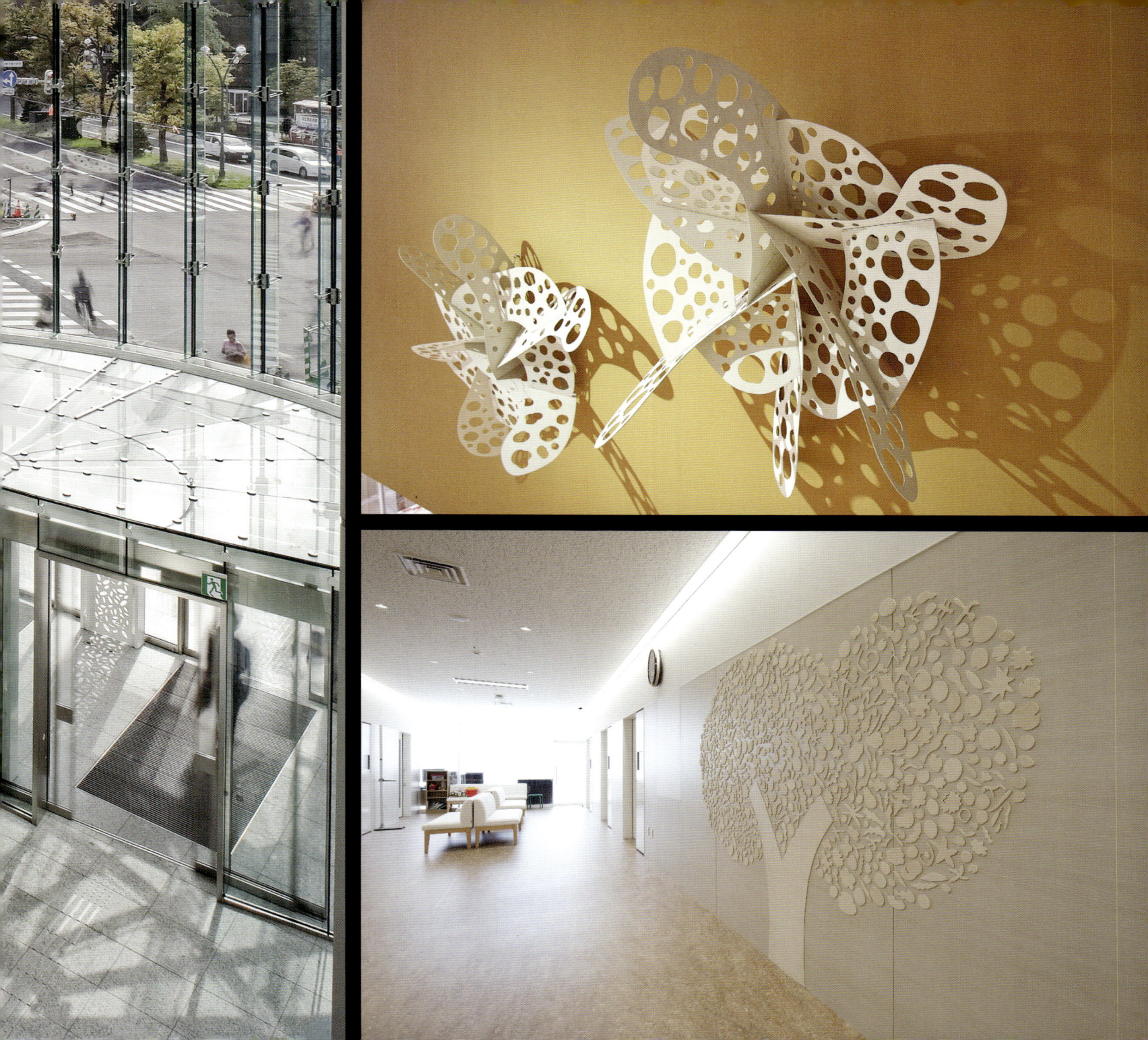

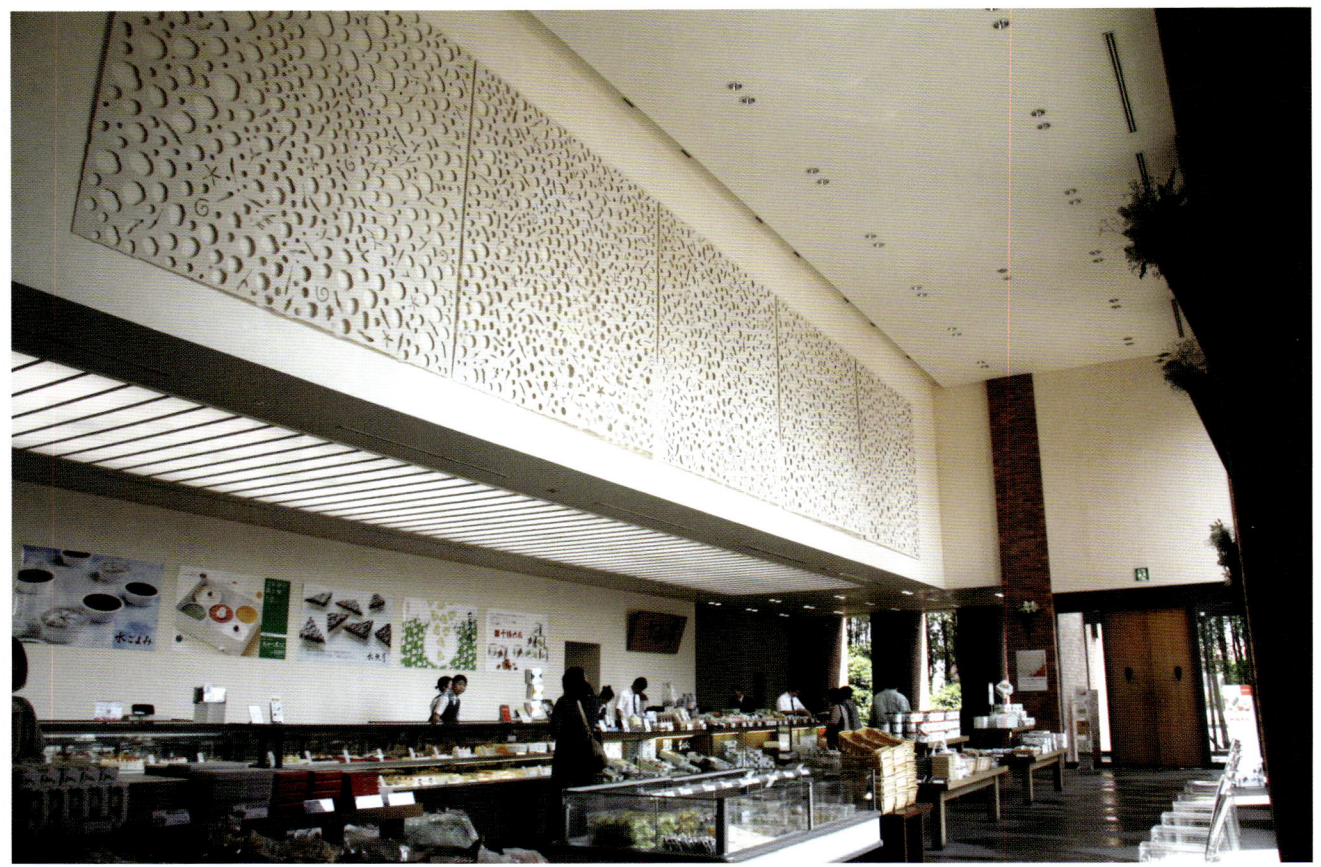
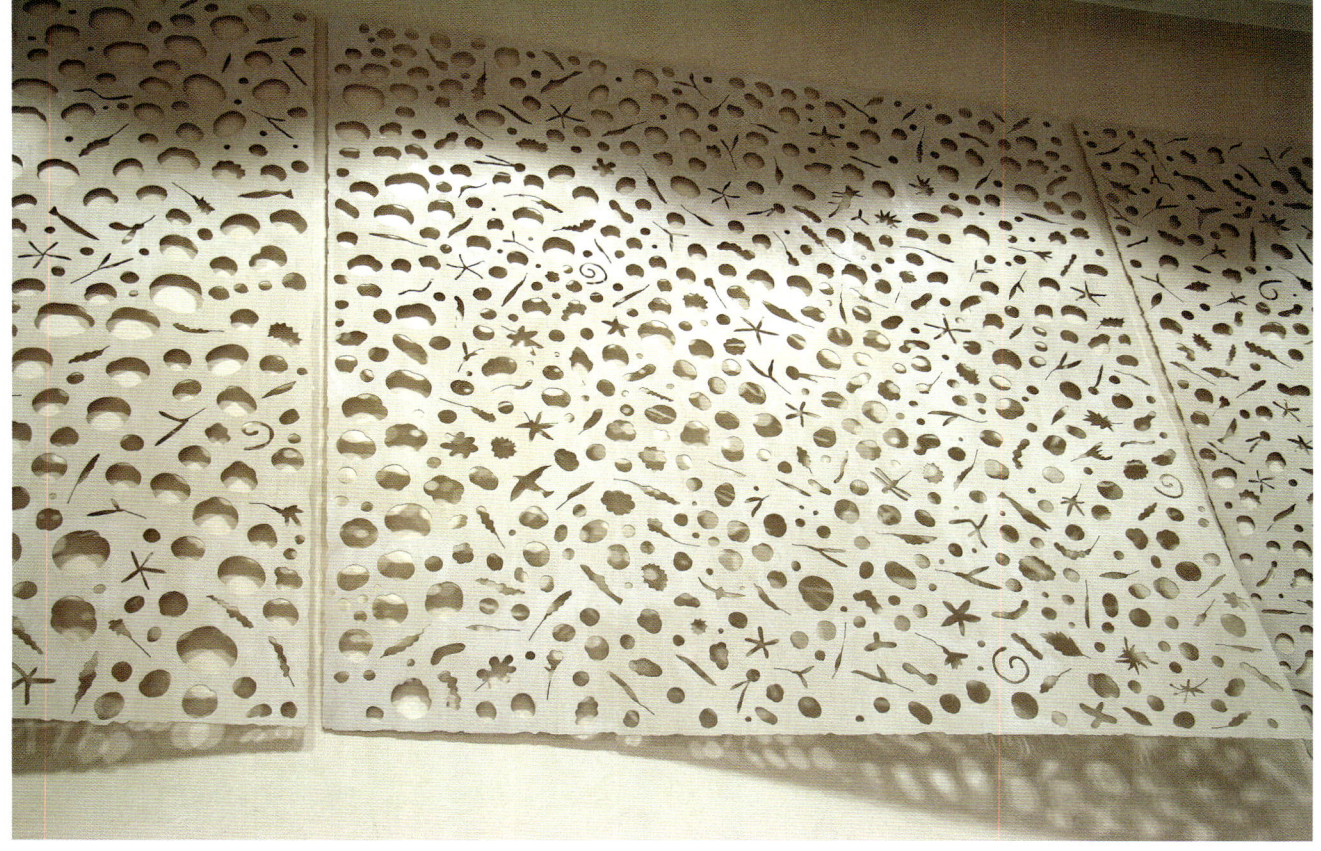

2-63 Komorebi
Rokkatei, Obihiro
Hokkaido, Japan, 2008

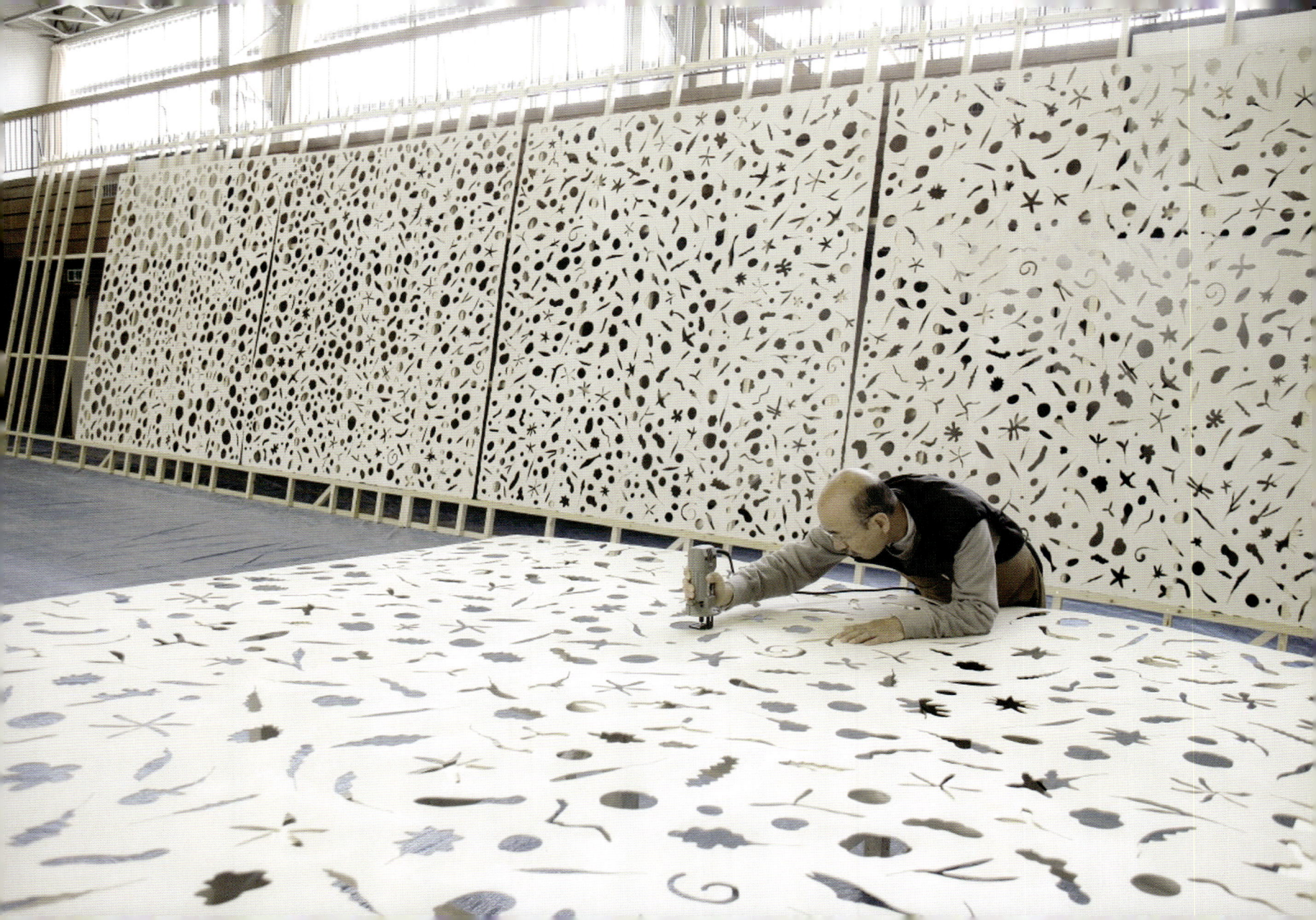

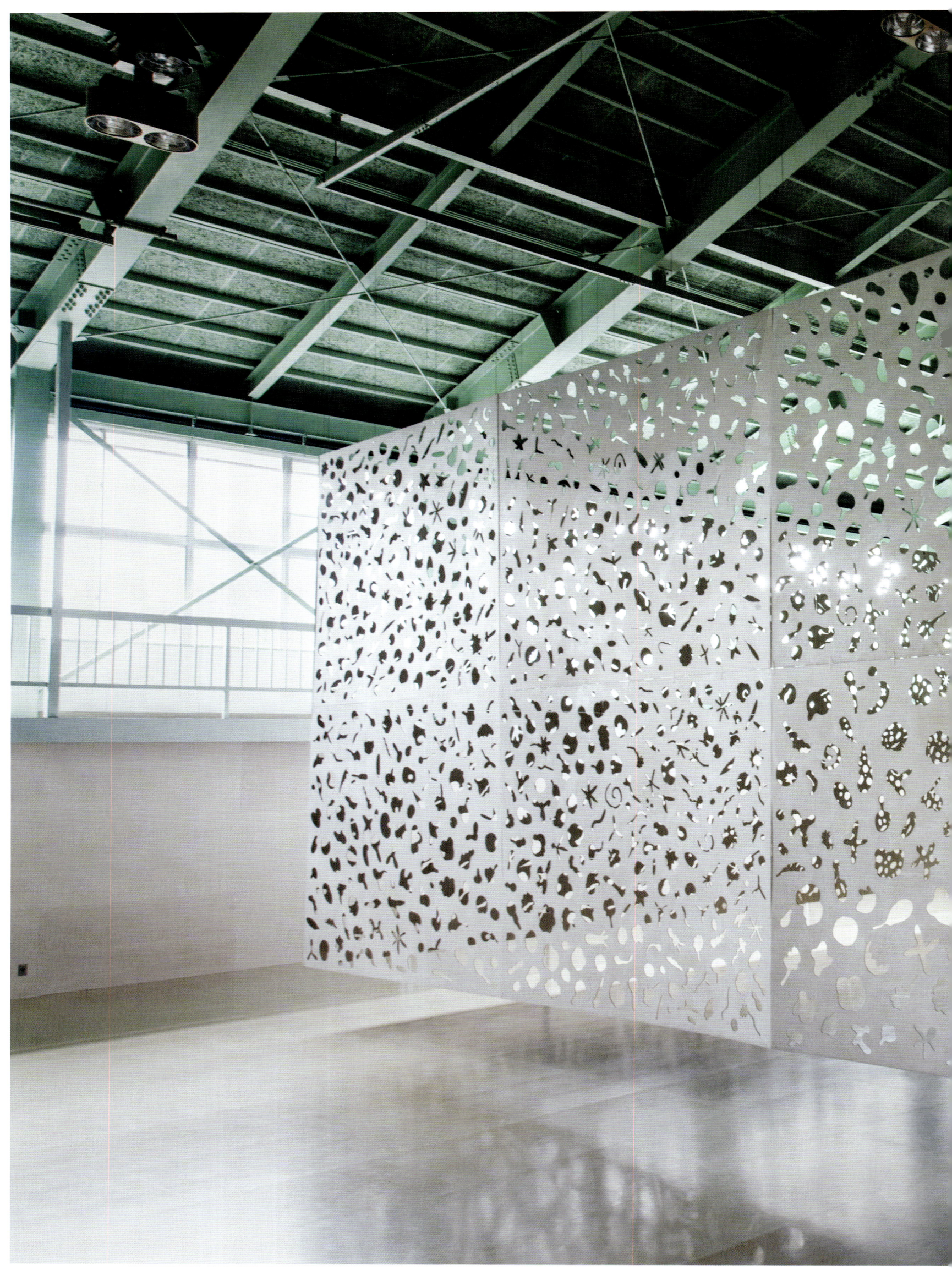

2-64 Sculpture Yu·Fu·Ru·Ji
Kazenobi, Shintotsukawa, Hokkaido, Japan, 2016

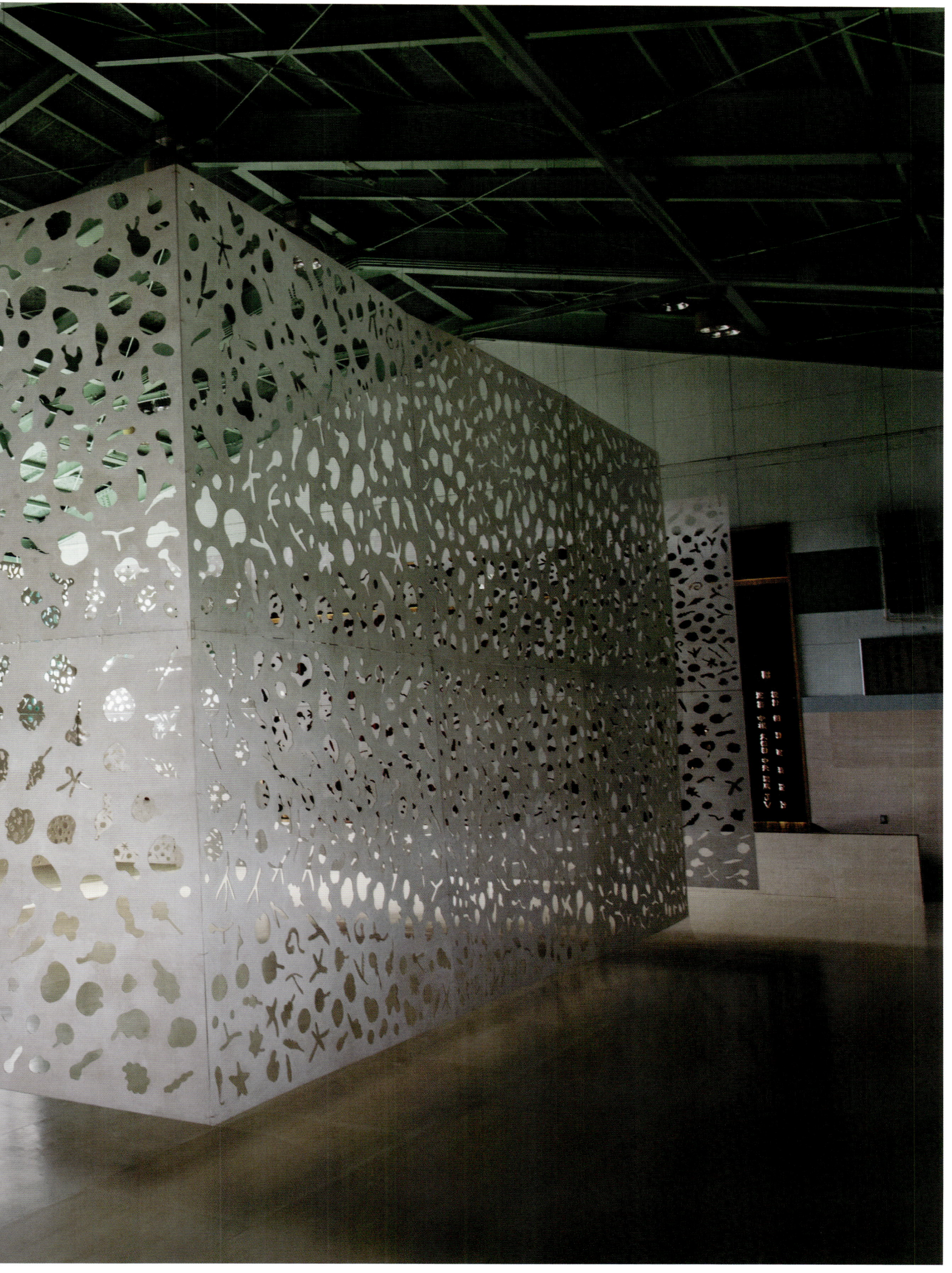

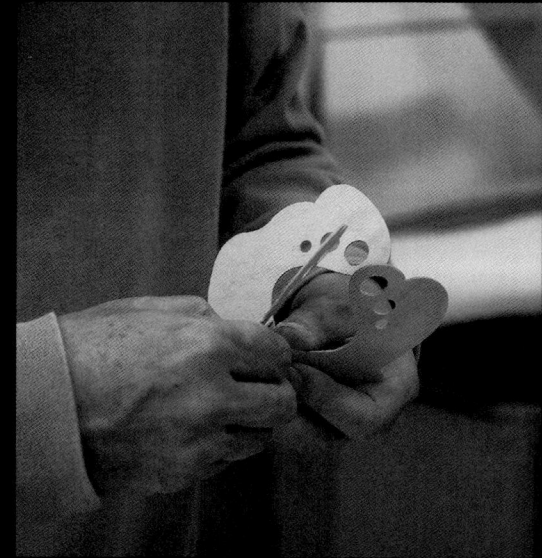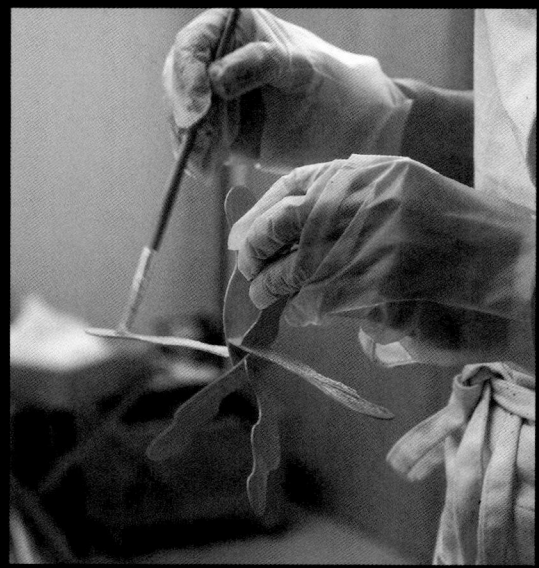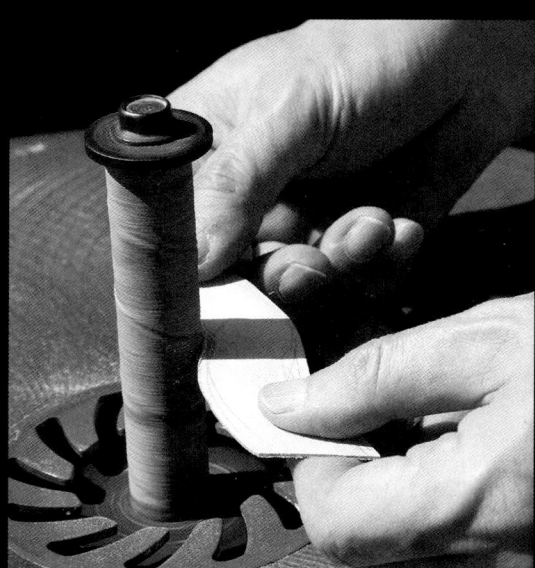

Various Maquettes
These Maquettes were produced mainly at my ateliers in Los Angeles and Akiya between 1995–2009. (TI)

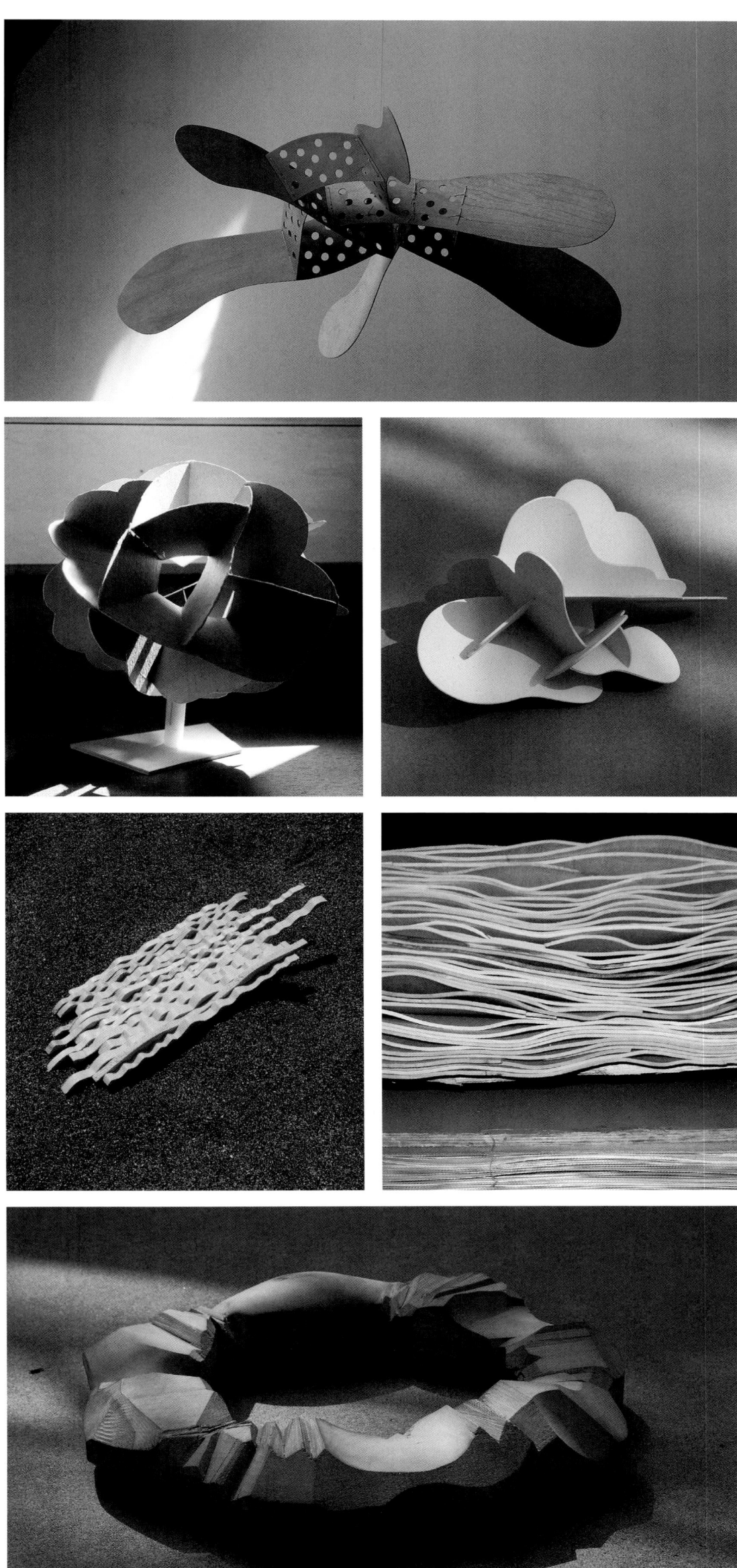

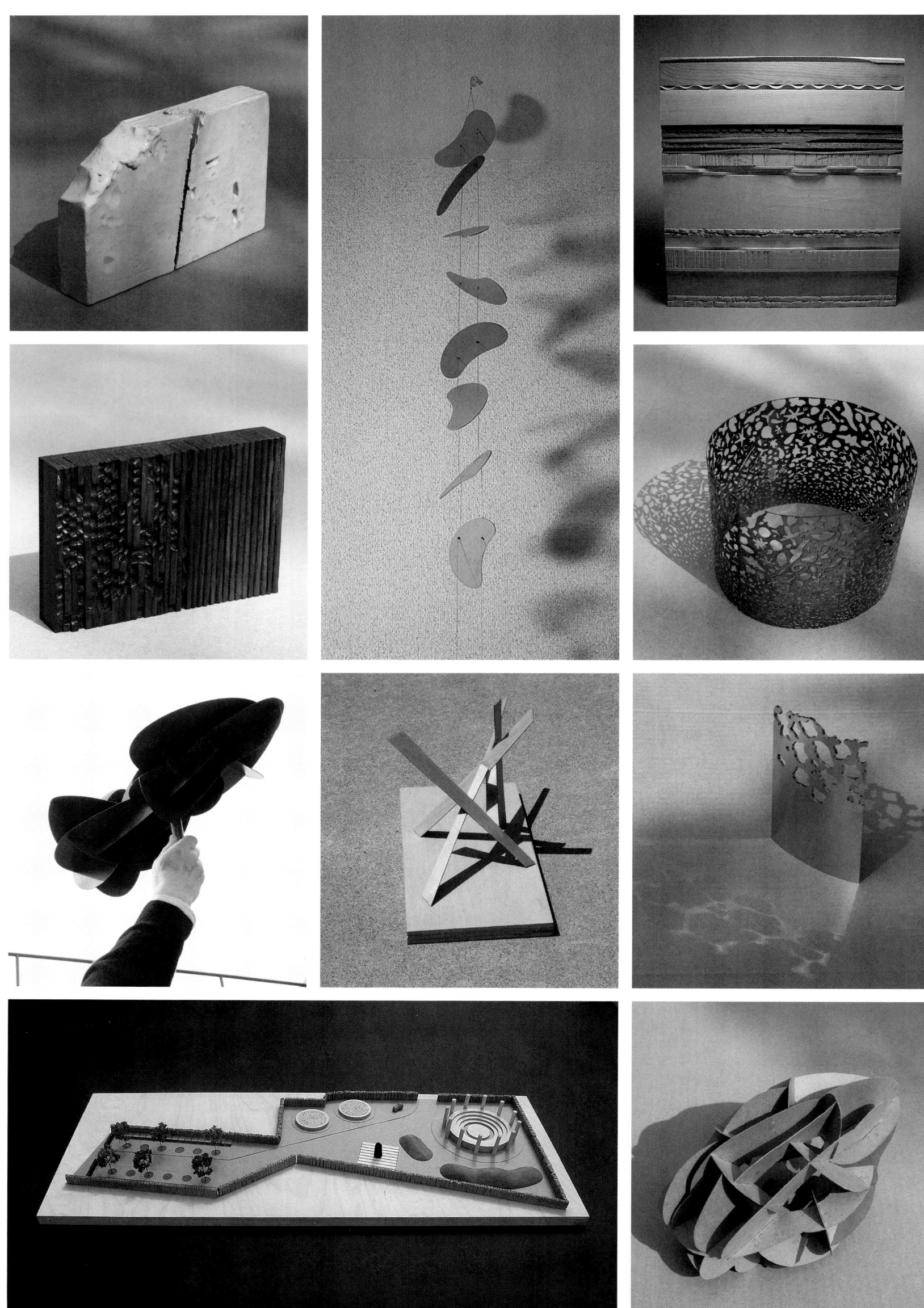

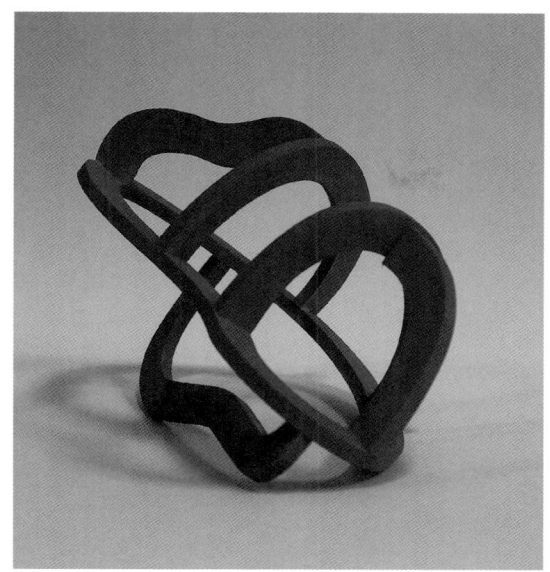
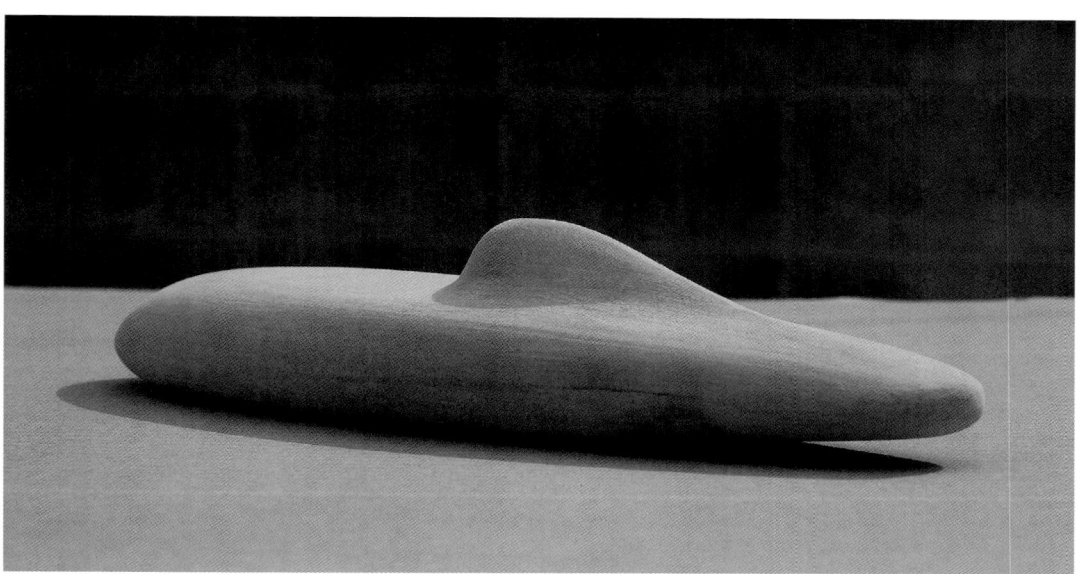
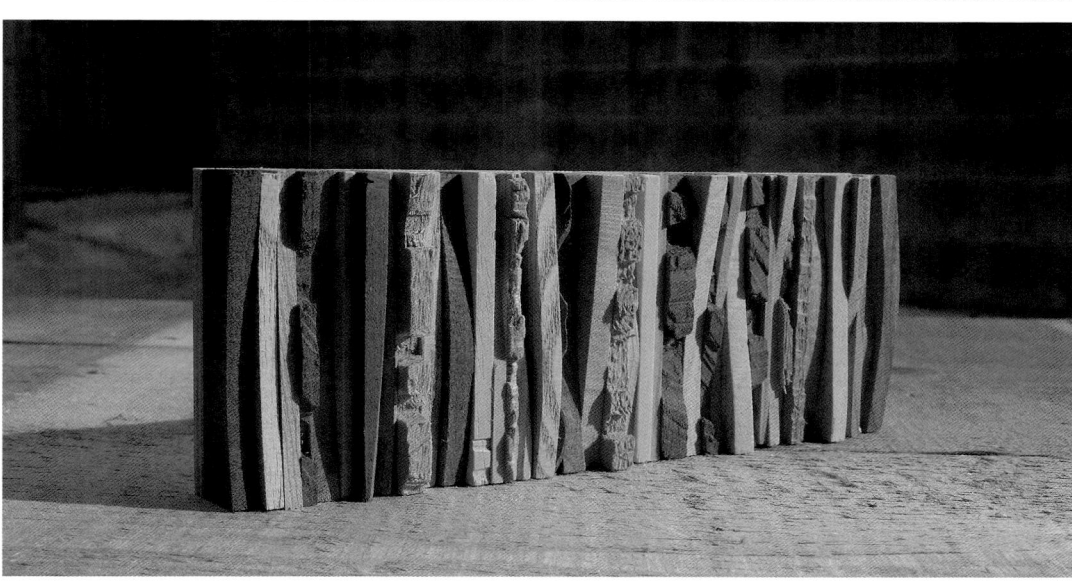
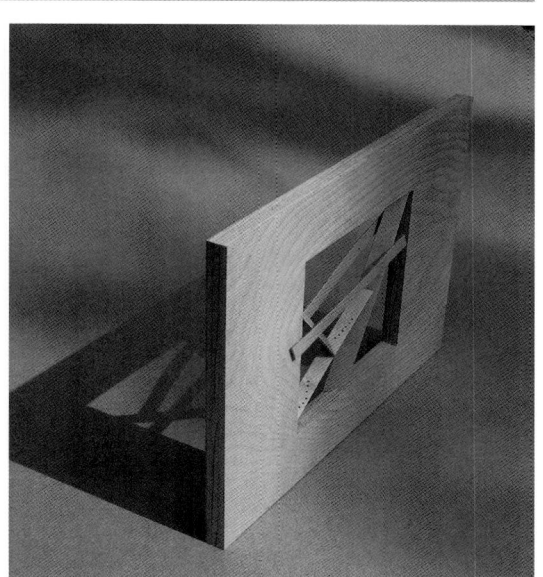
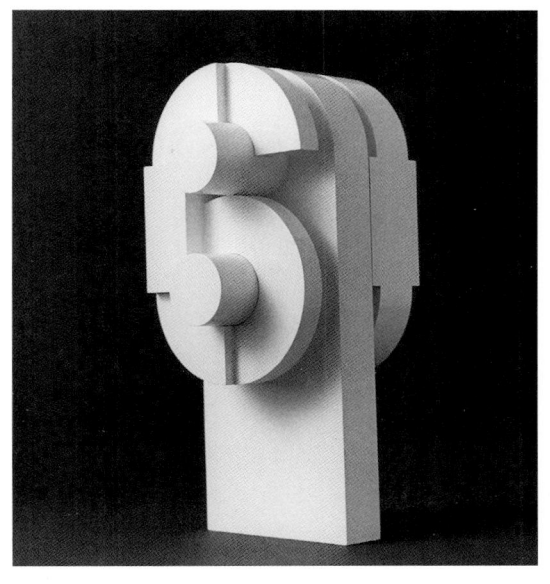
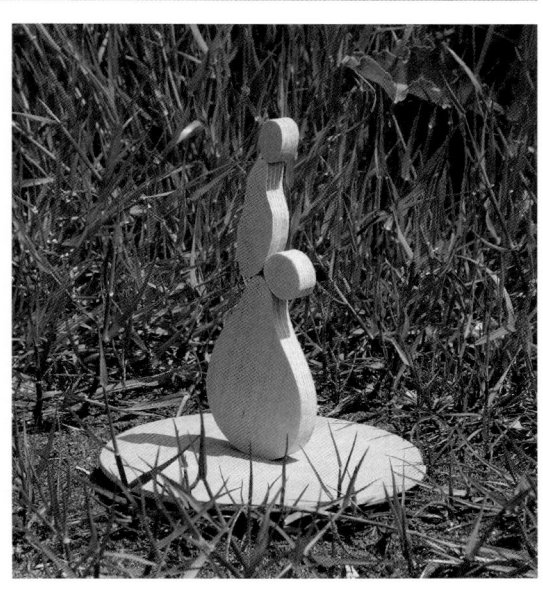
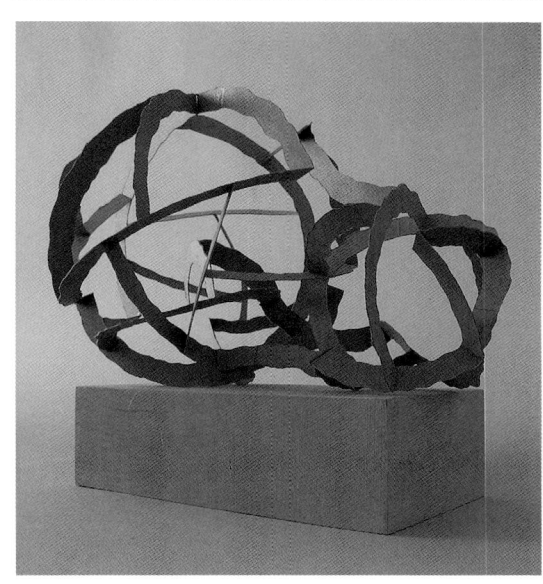
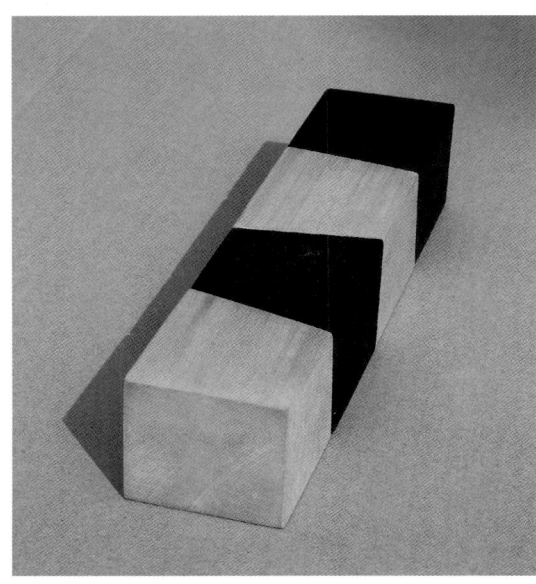
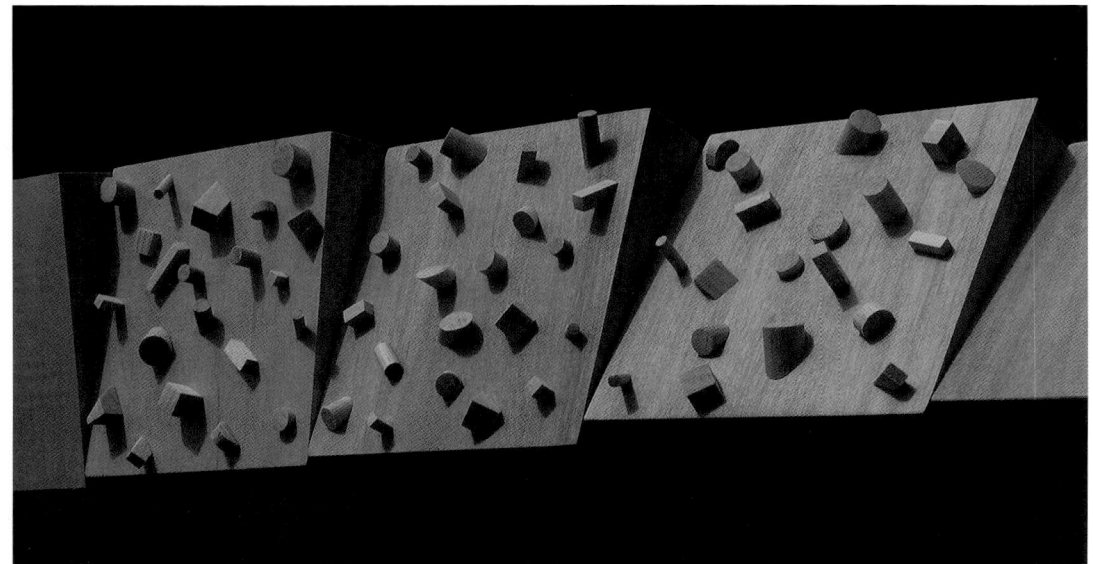

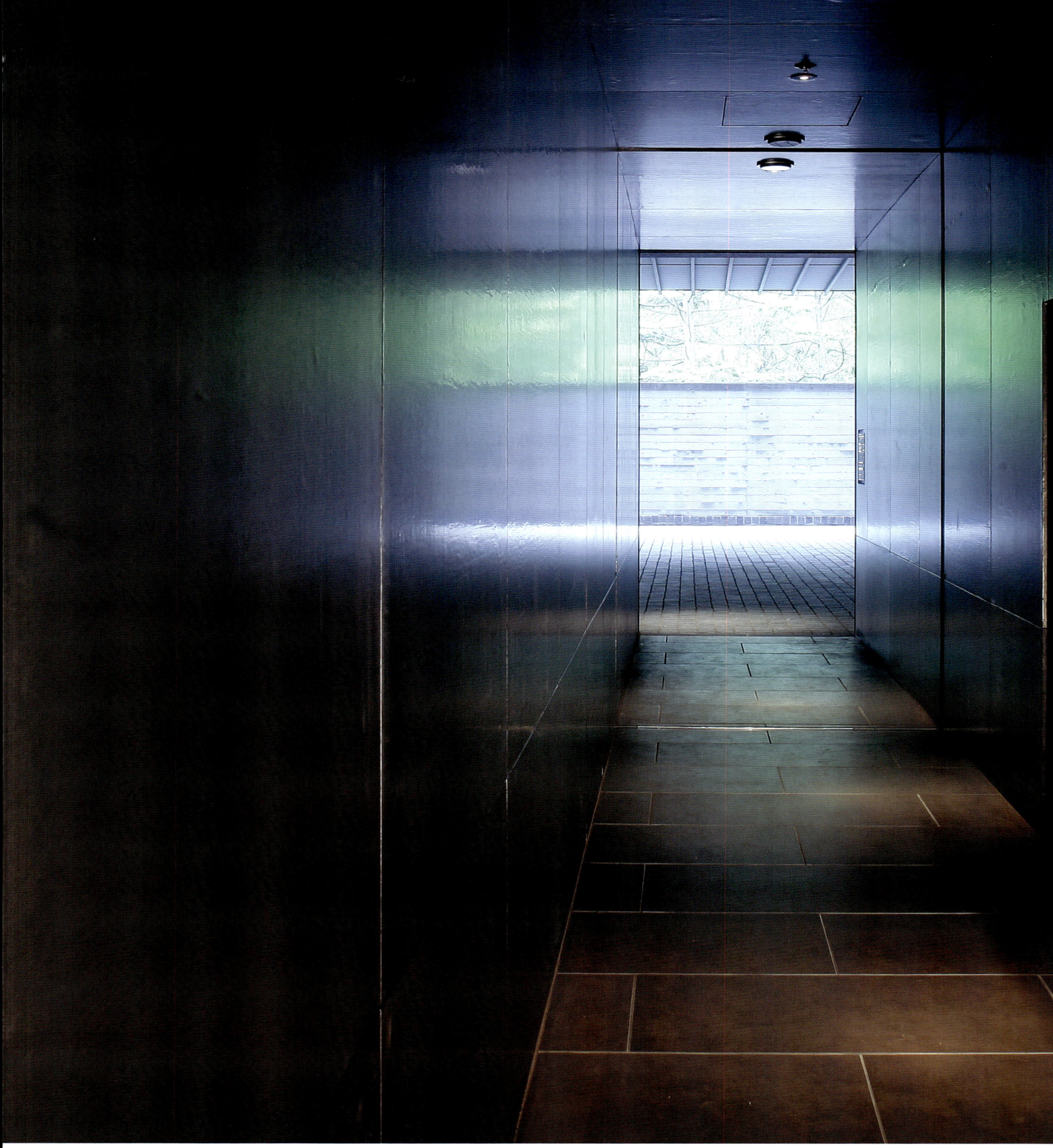

2-65 Komorebi
Borou Noguchi Noboribetsu
Hokkaido, Japan, 2006

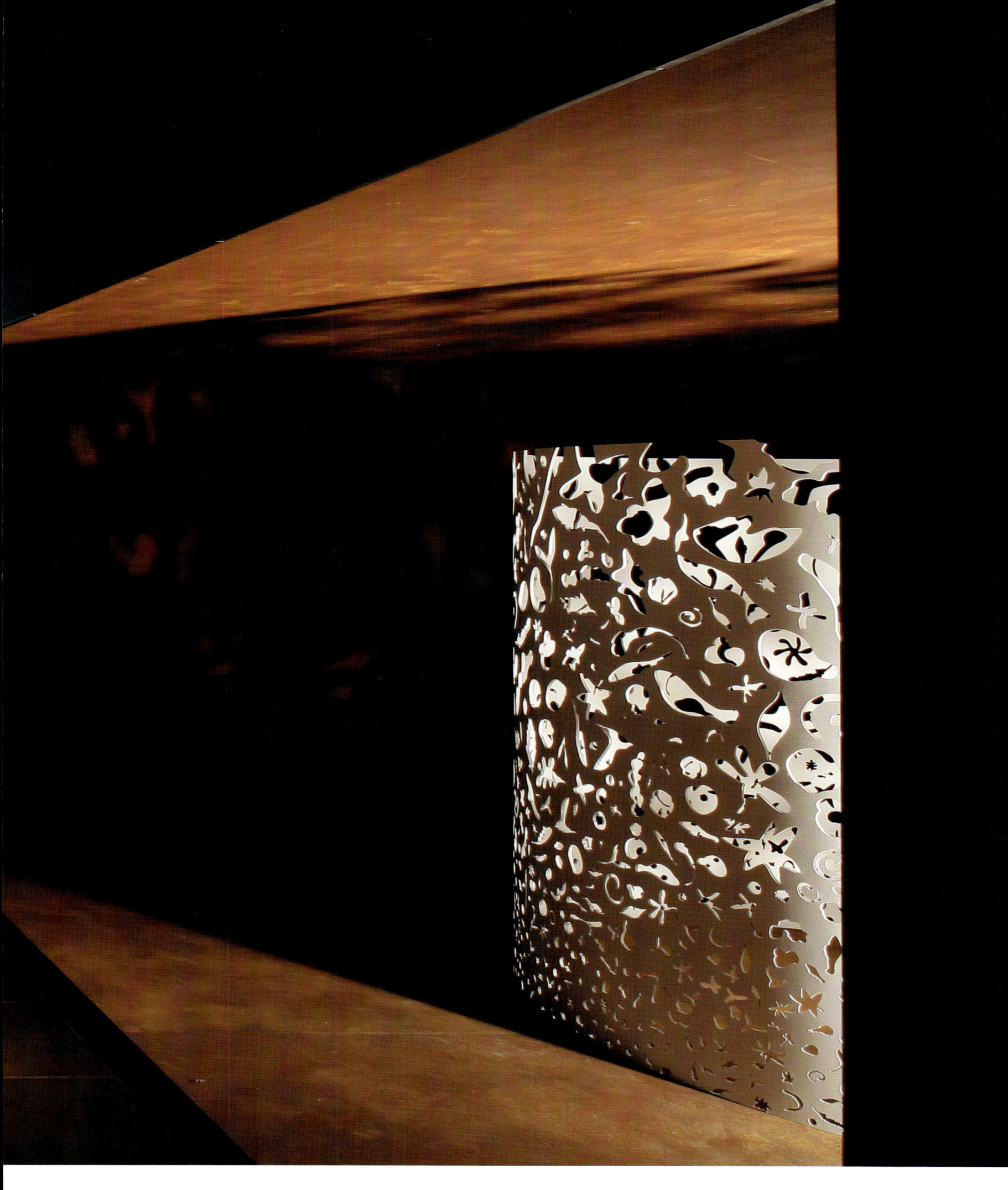

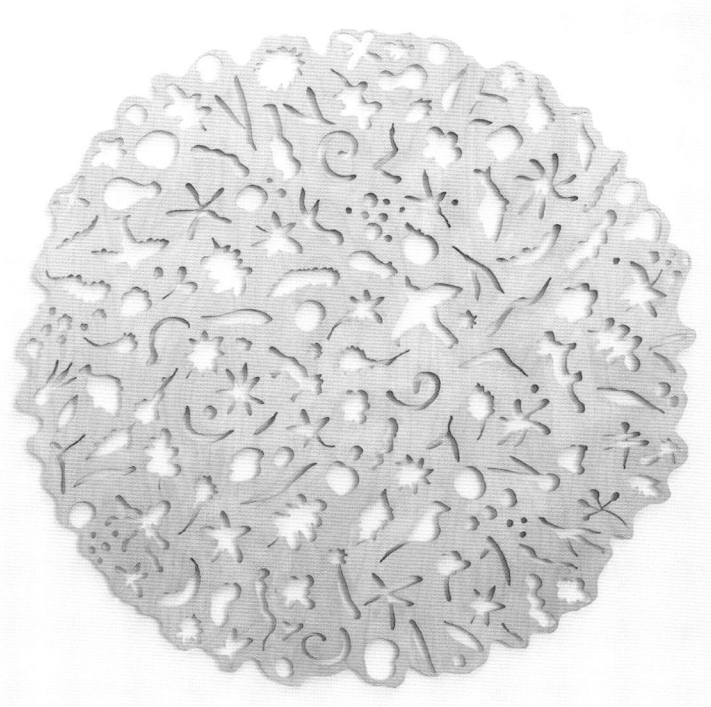

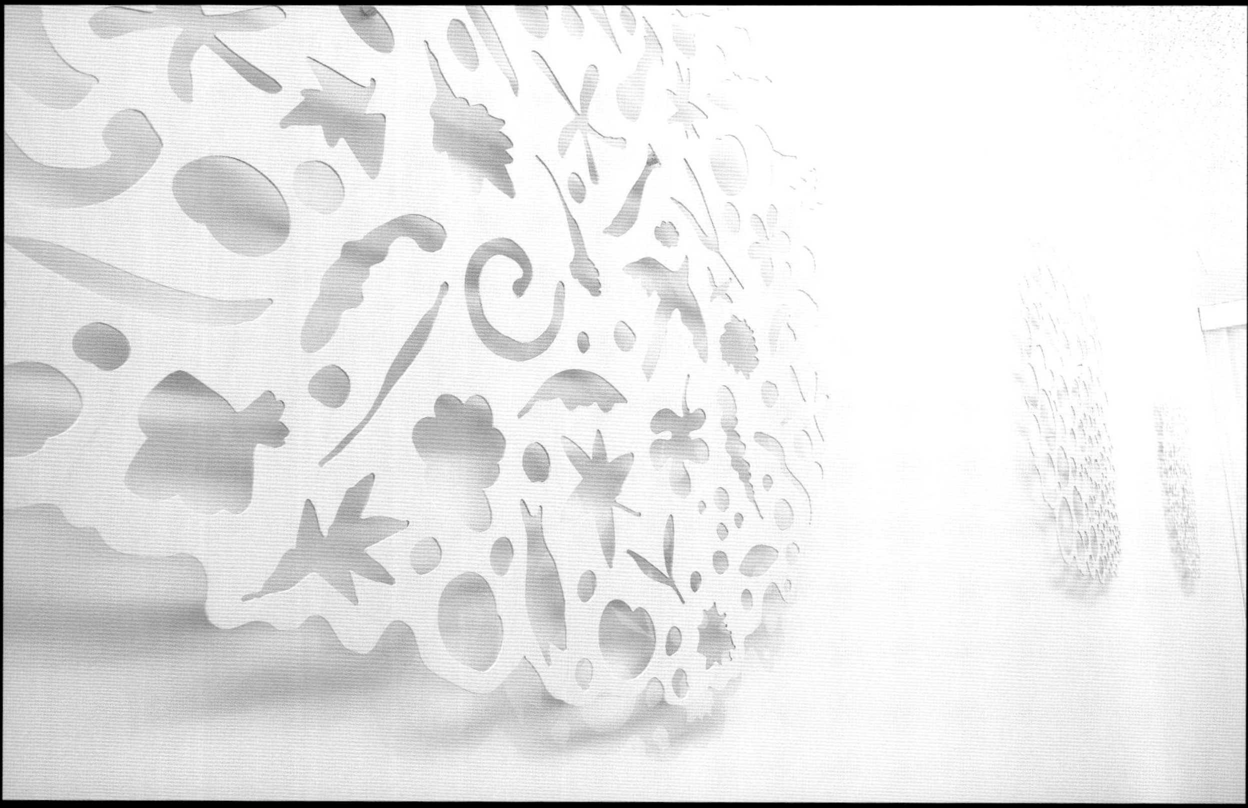

2-66 Komorebi
Kazenobi, Hokkaido, Japan, 2007

2-67 Komorebi
Kajima Corporation headquarters
Tokyo, Japan, 2007

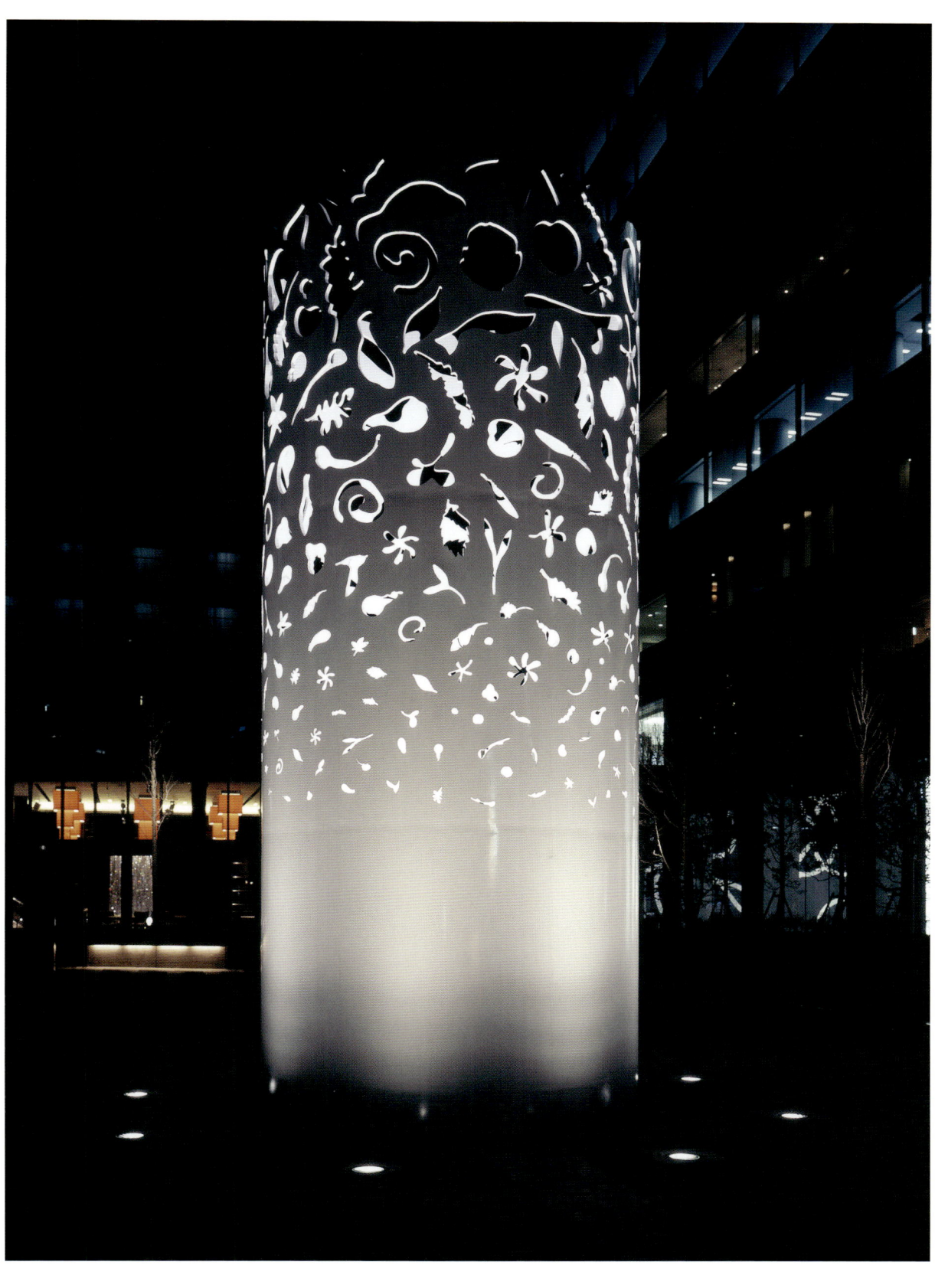

2-68 Komorebi
Nagoya Lucent Tower
Aichi, Japan, 2006

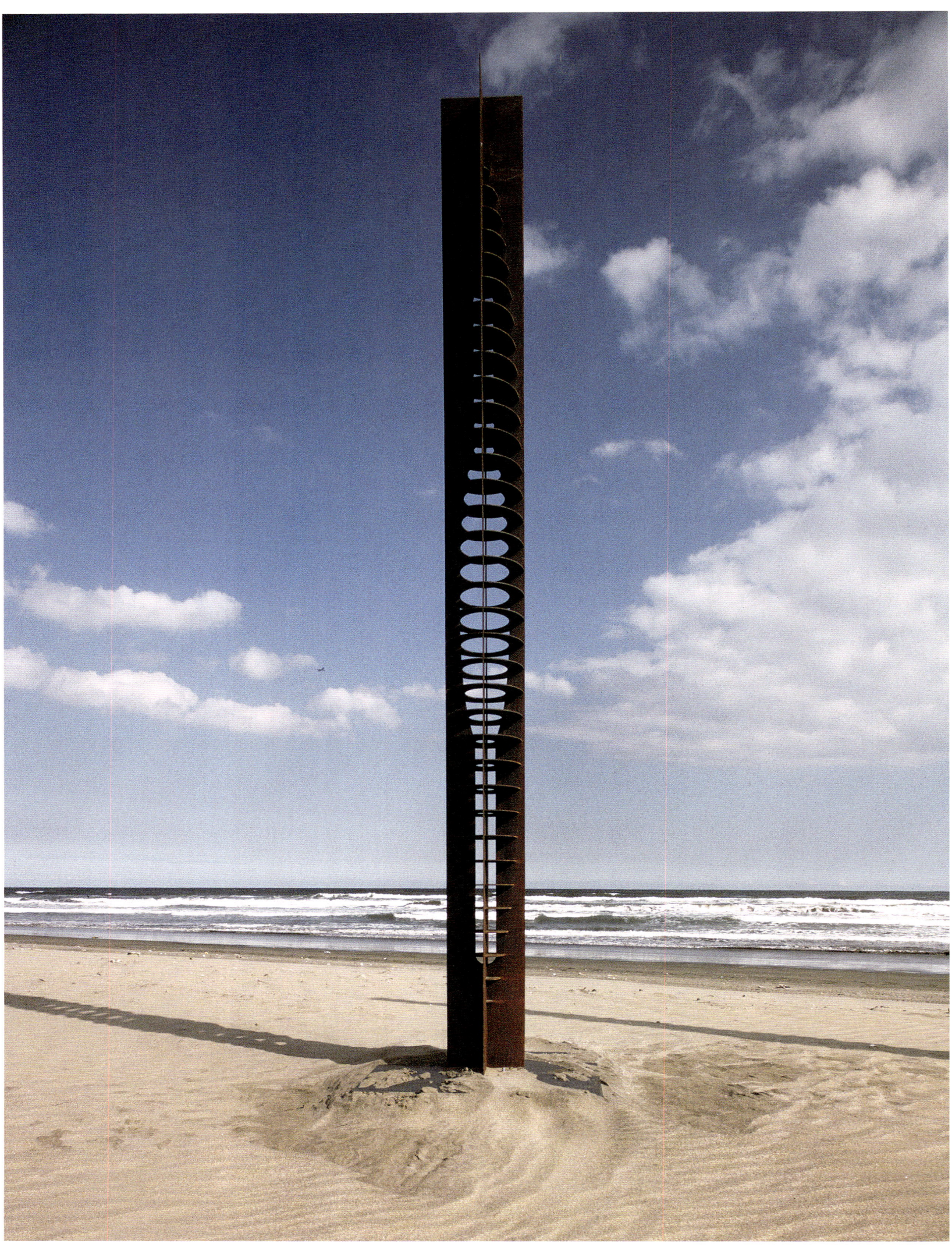

2-69 Wind in Space, 1995

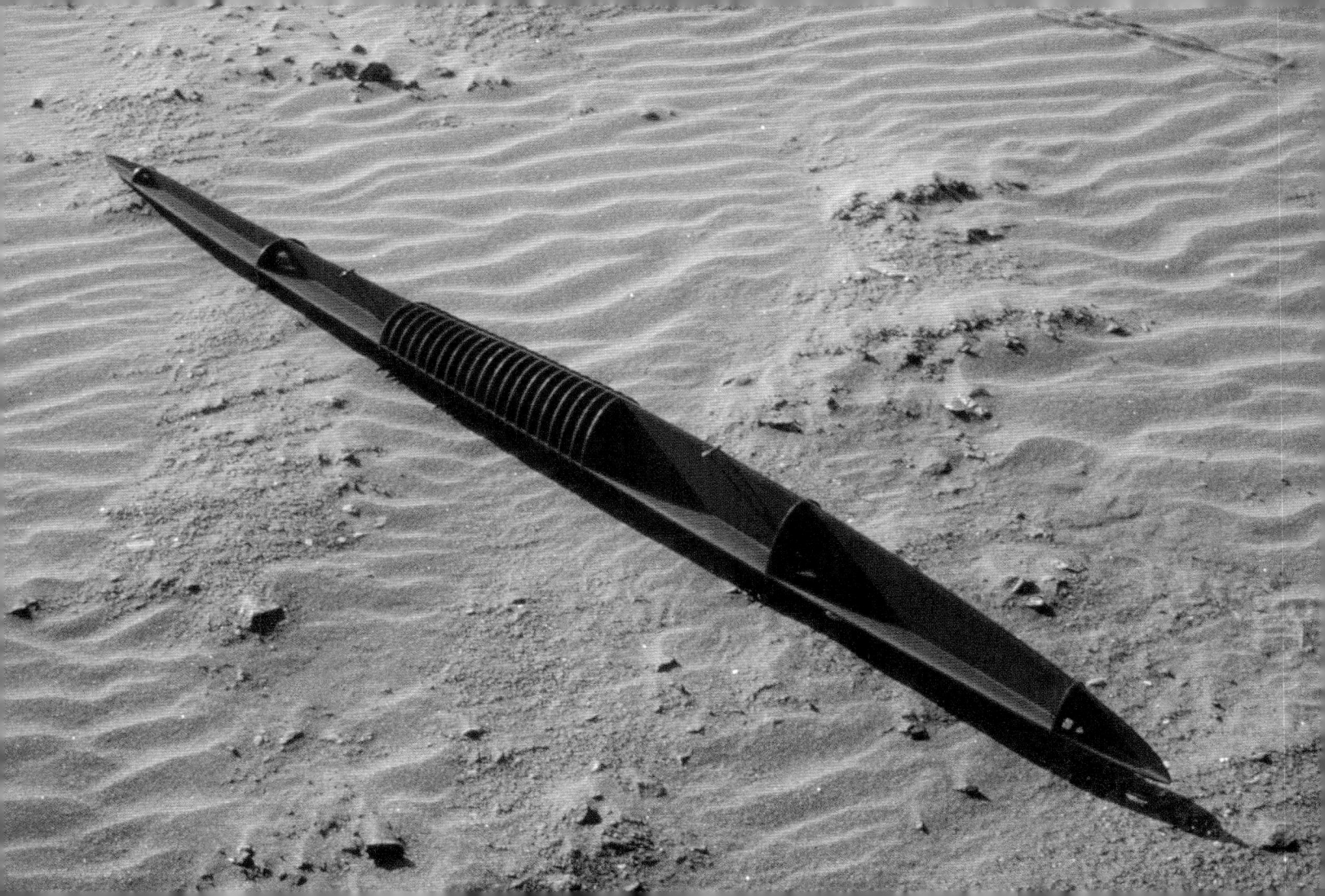

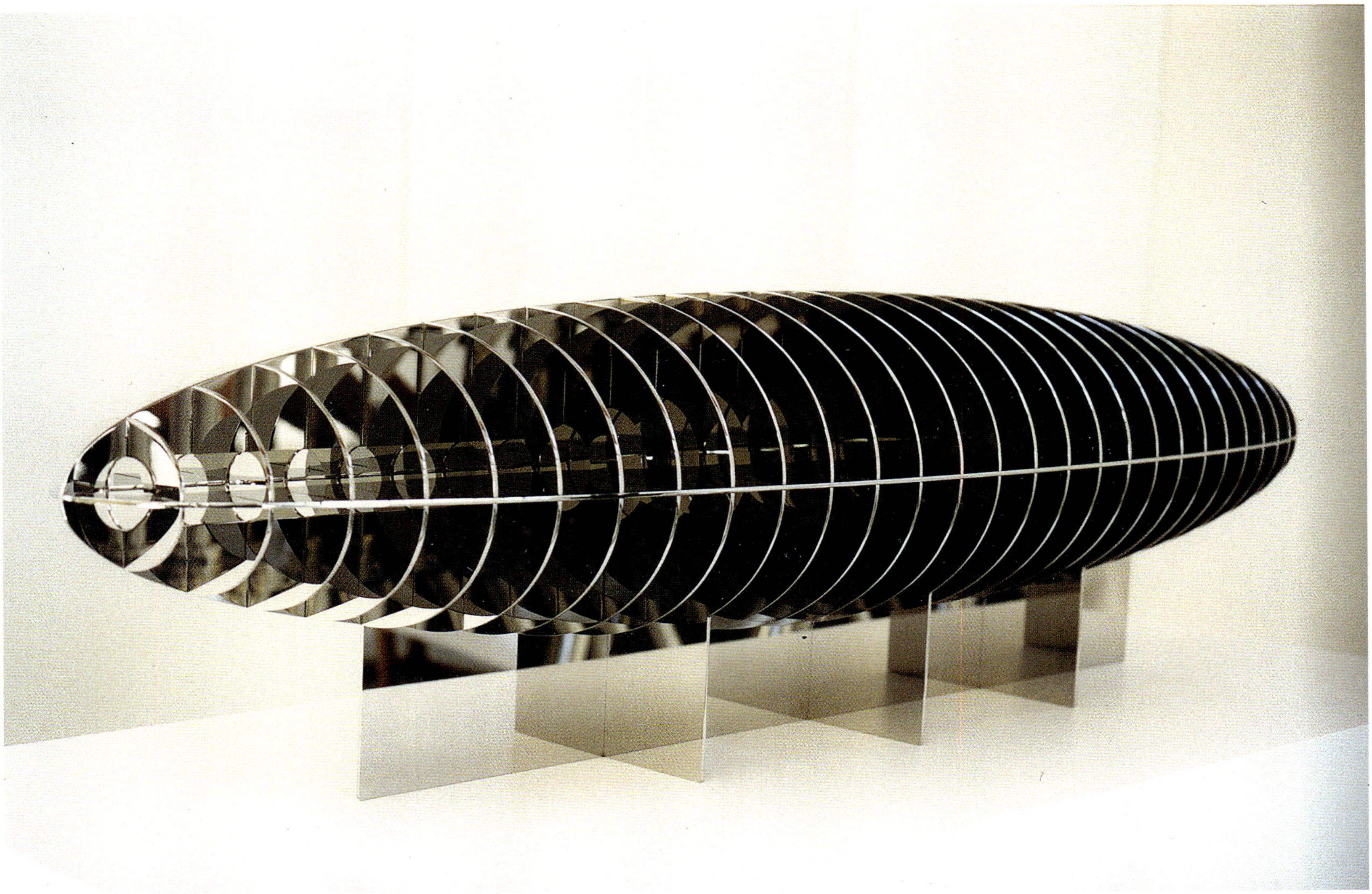

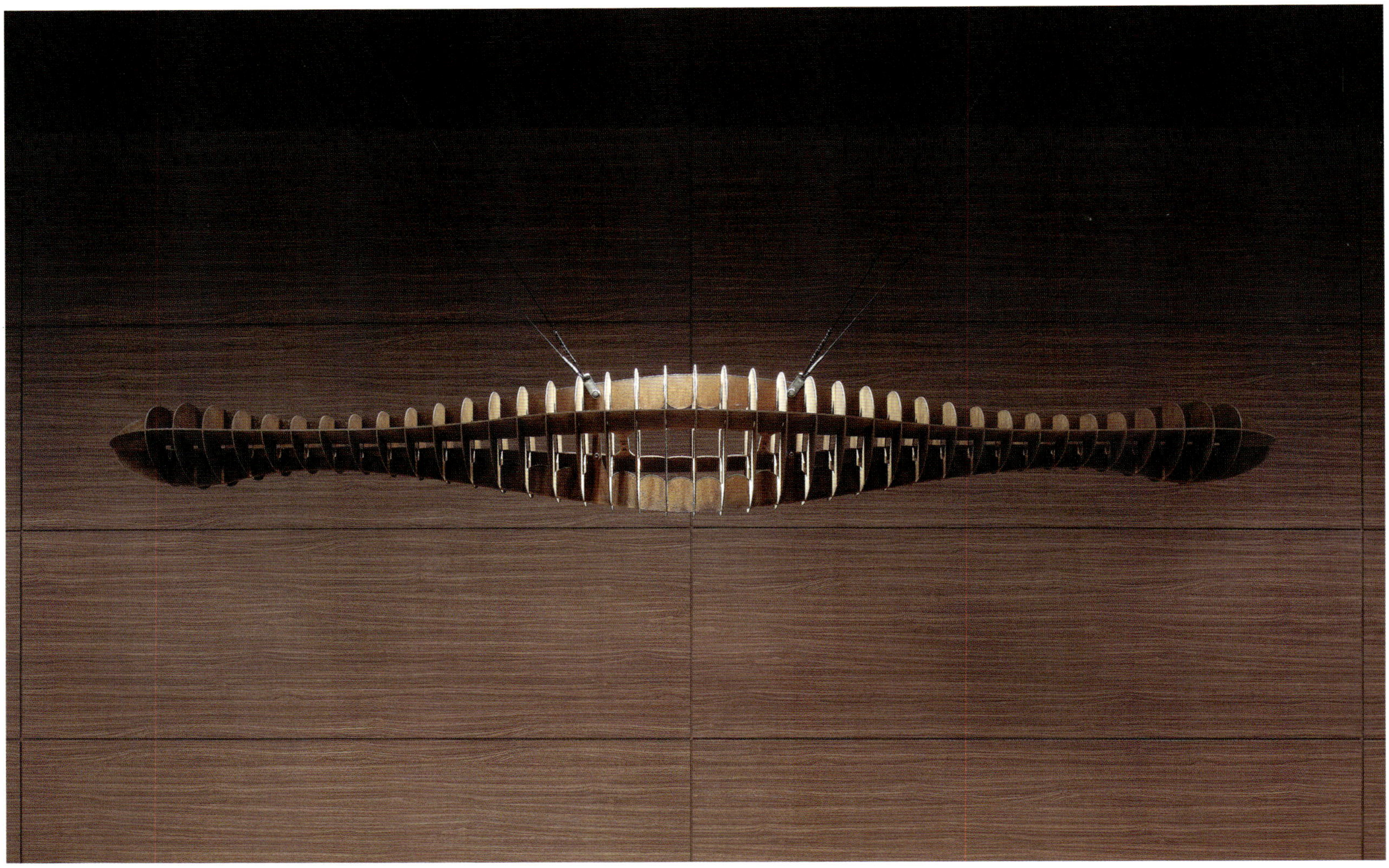

2-71 Untitled, 1994

2-72 Windstorm
Hokuyo Odori Center
Sapporo, Hokkaido, Japan, 1995

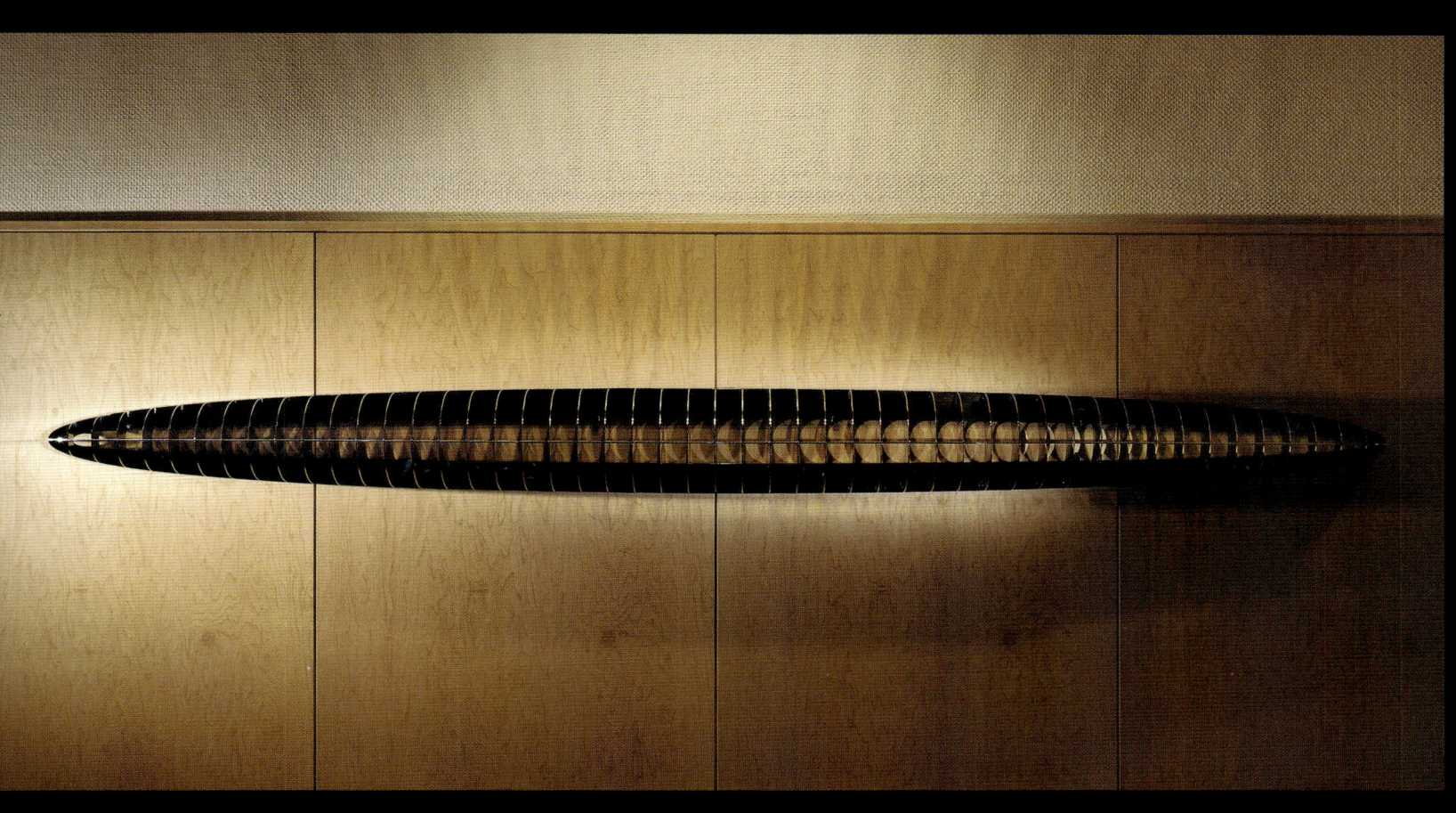

2-73 Boat
Niigata Community Hall Annex, Niigata, Japan, 2000

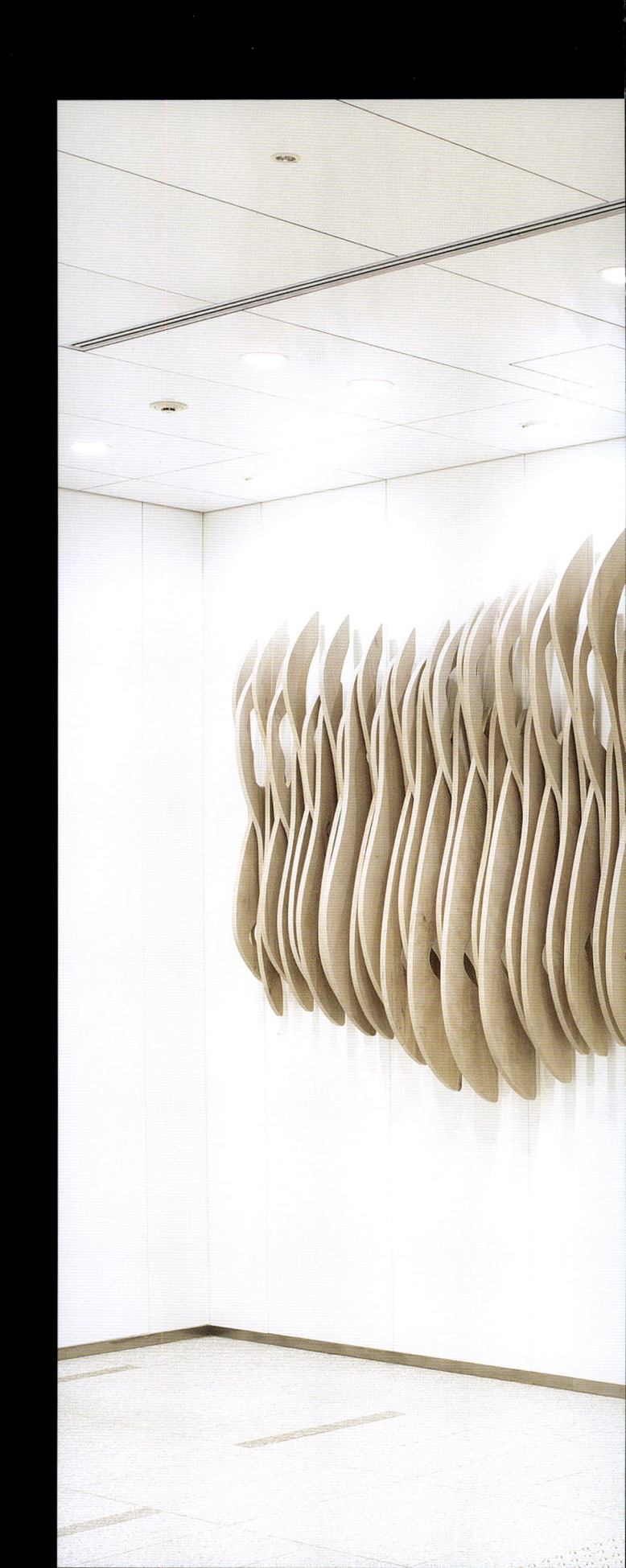

Rhythm of Mountain Range
City Hall, Kofu, Yamanashi, Japan, 2013

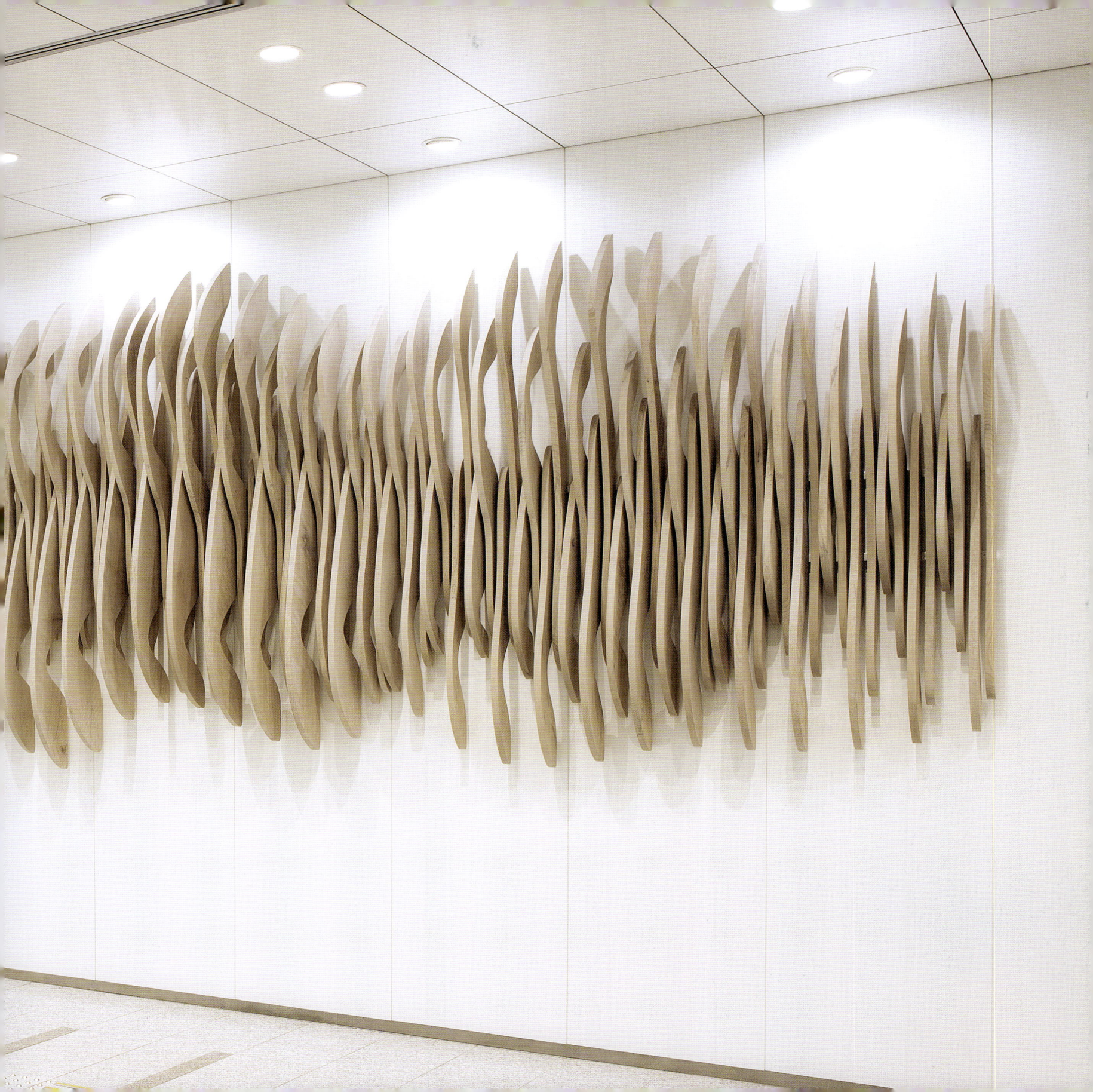

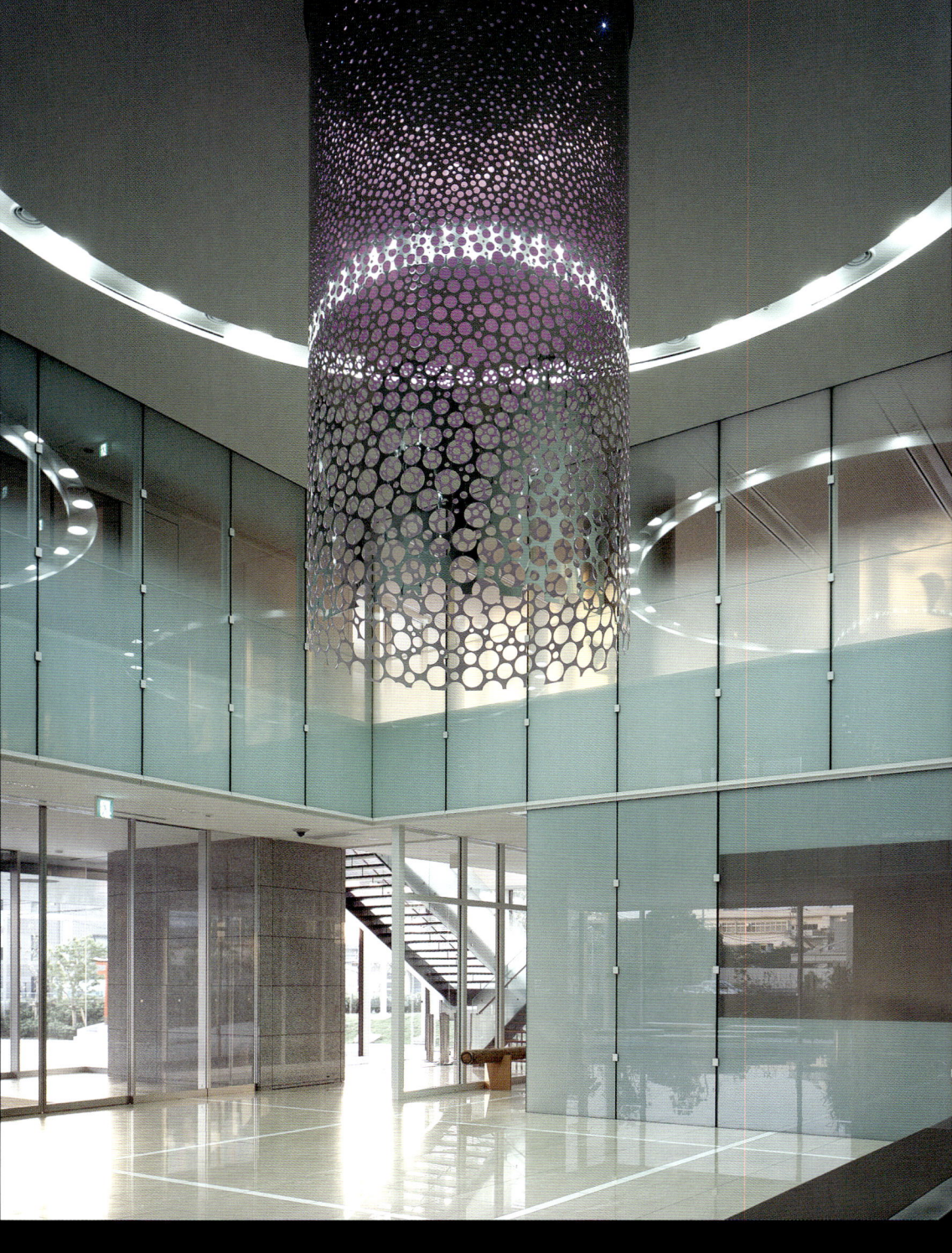

2-75 Fuu-ka-kou-sei (Wind, Flowers, Stars, Light)
Adeka headquarters, Tokyo, Japan, 2006

*The color of lights that illuminate my works slowly changes.
I am always aware of light and shadow in sculpture. (TI)*

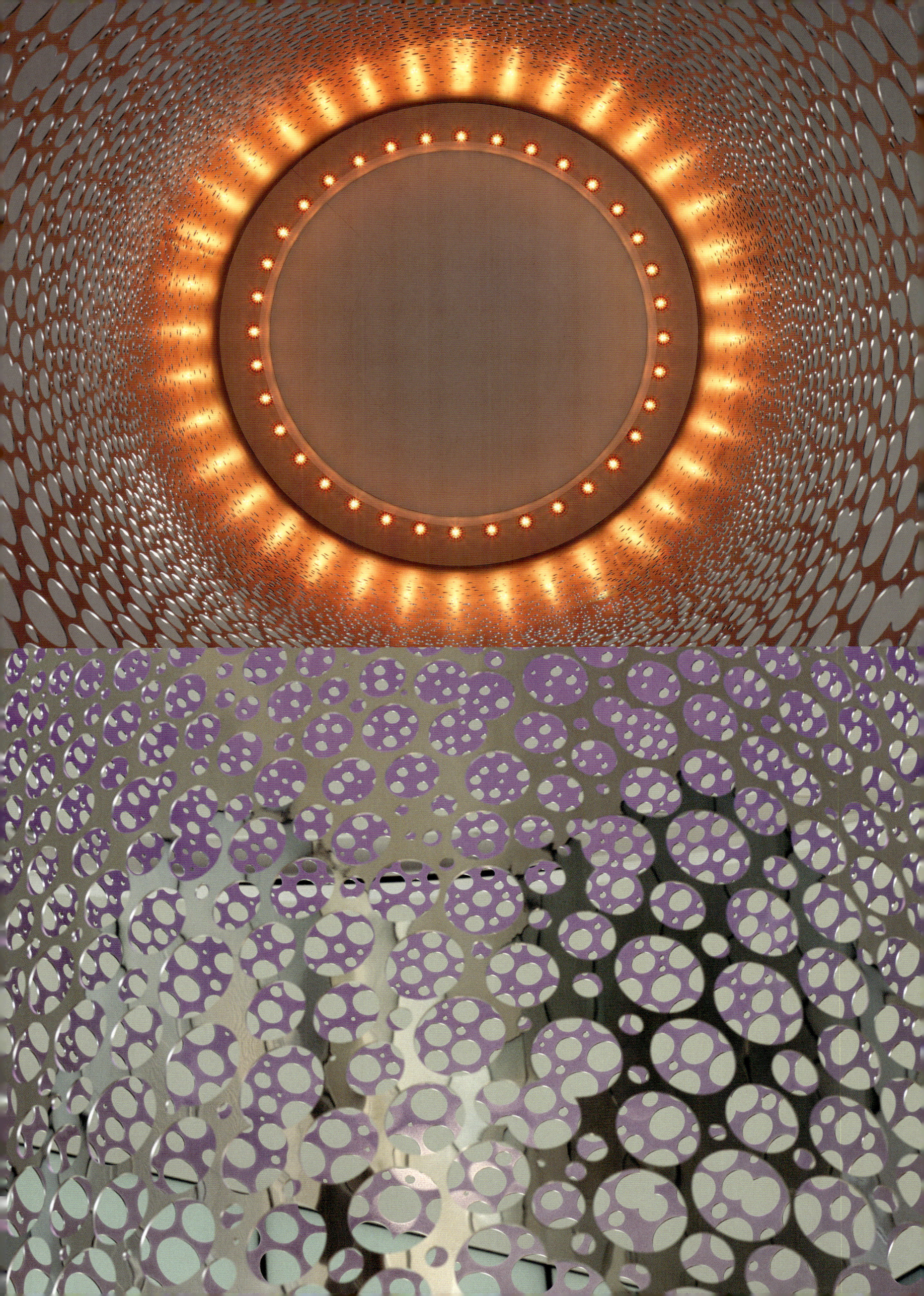

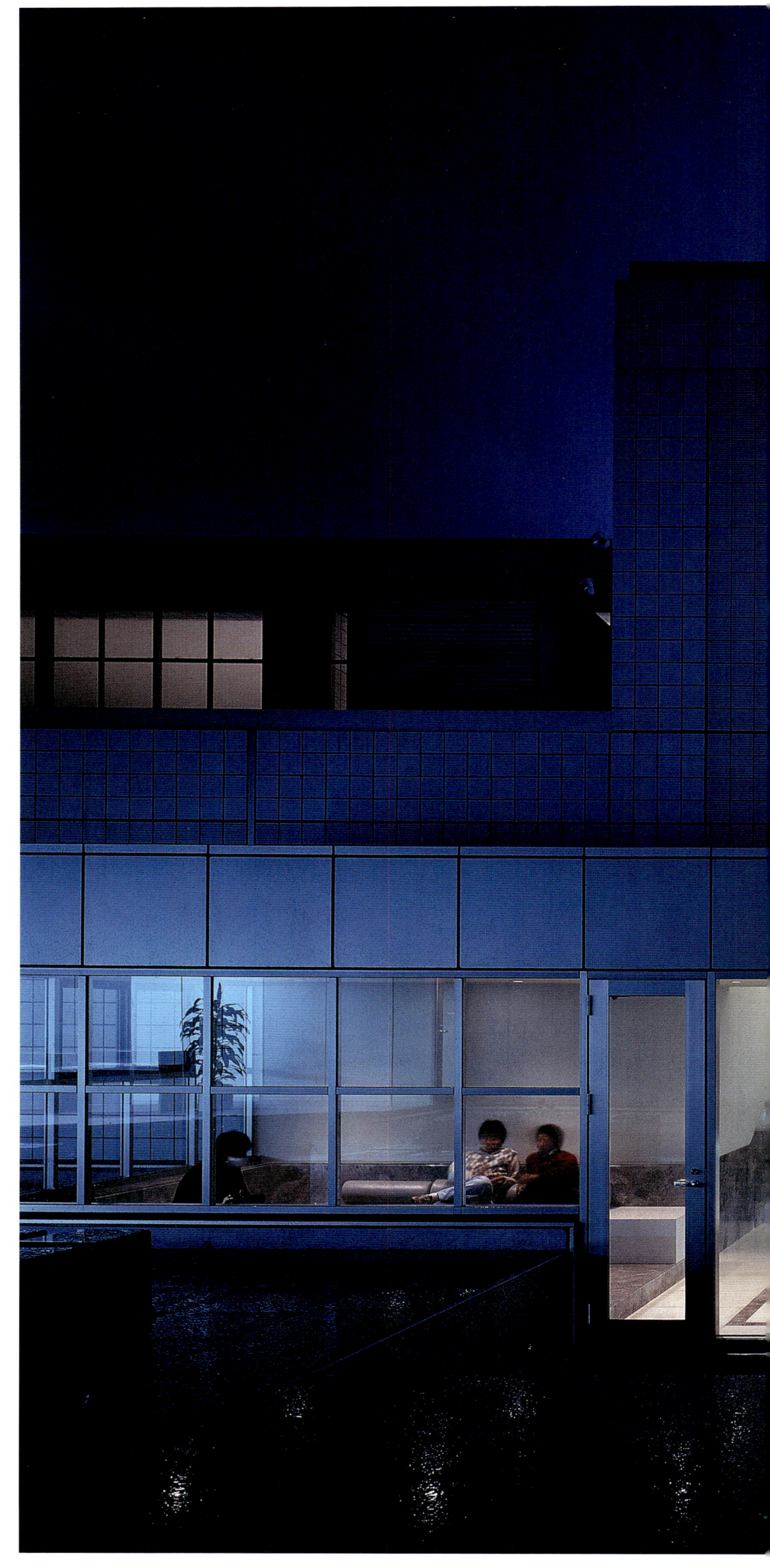

2-76 Stained Glass
Akita City Central Library
Akita, Japan, 1982

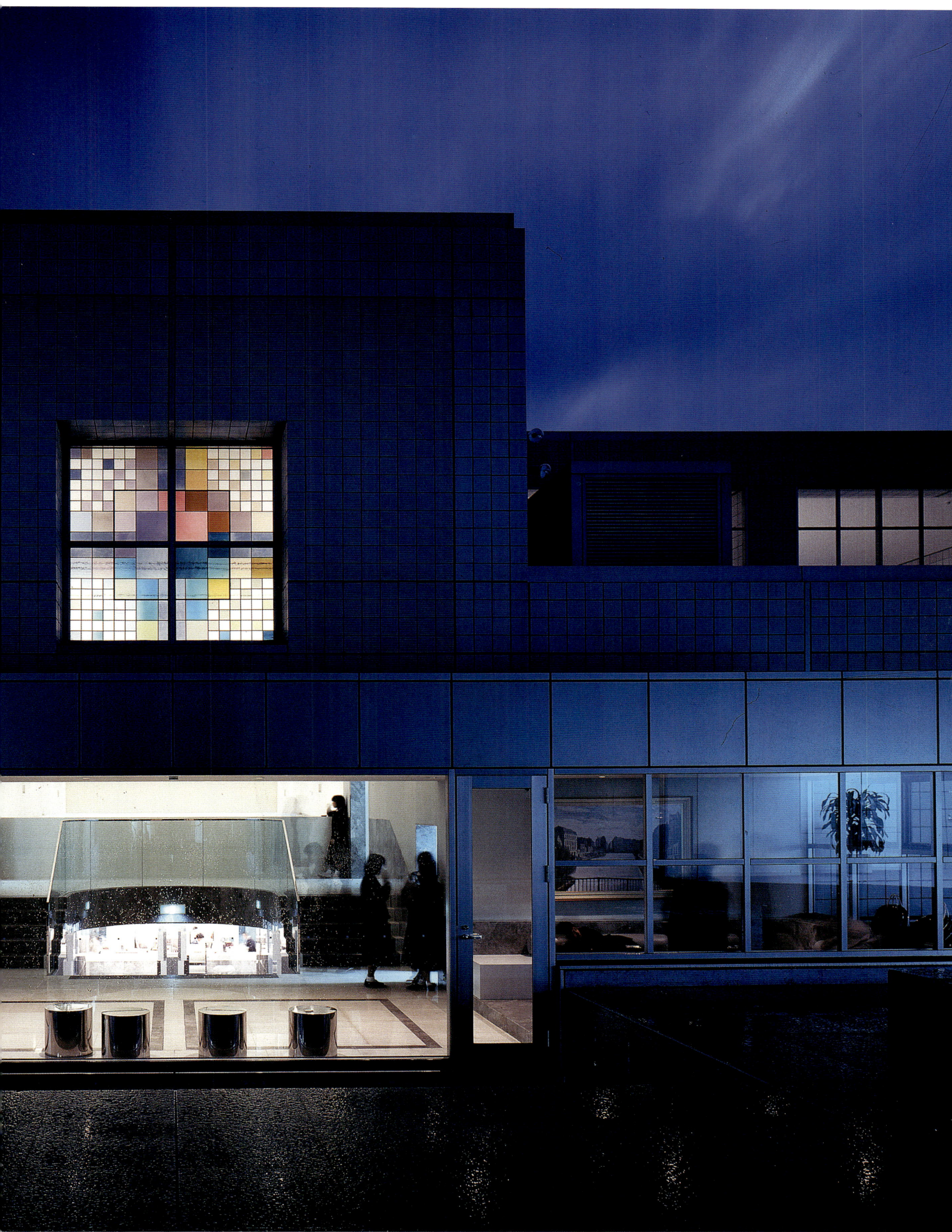

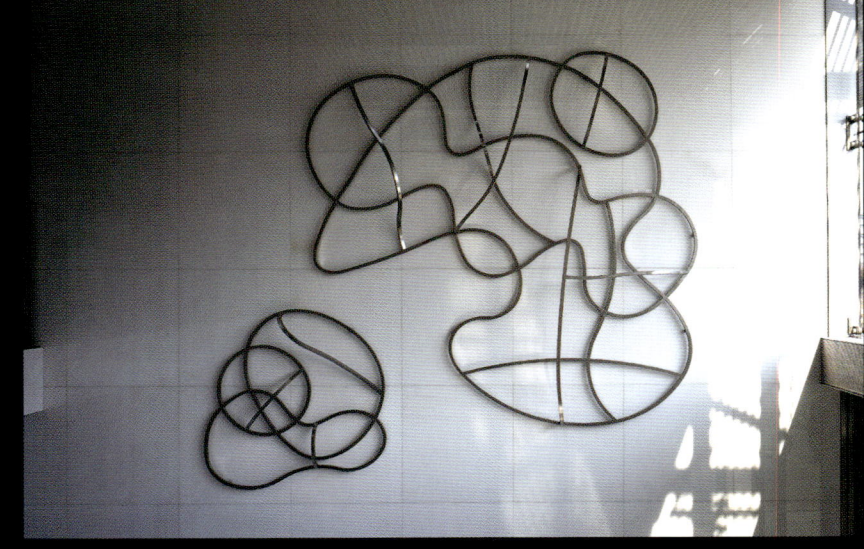

2-77 In the Sky
Emergency Medical Care
Training Center
Tokyo, Japan, 1998

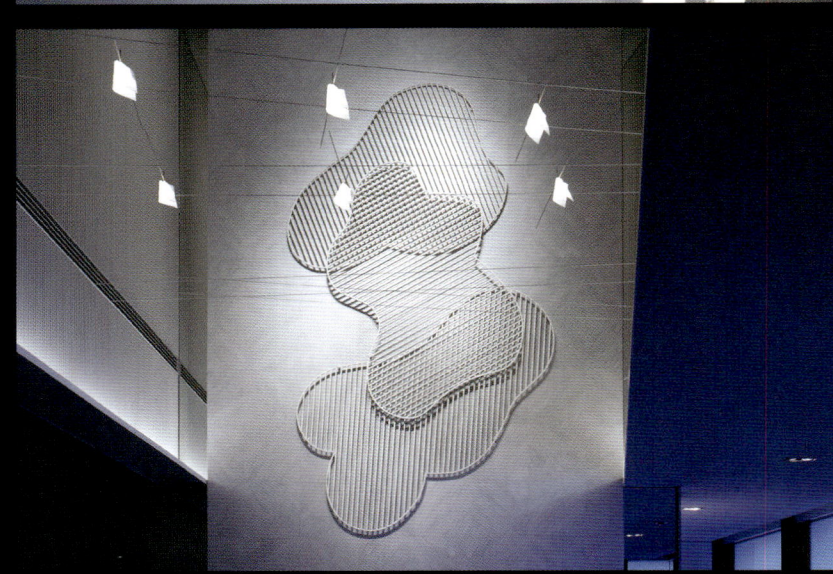

2-78 Cloud
Niigata Self-Governing Hall Annex
Niigata, Japan, 2000

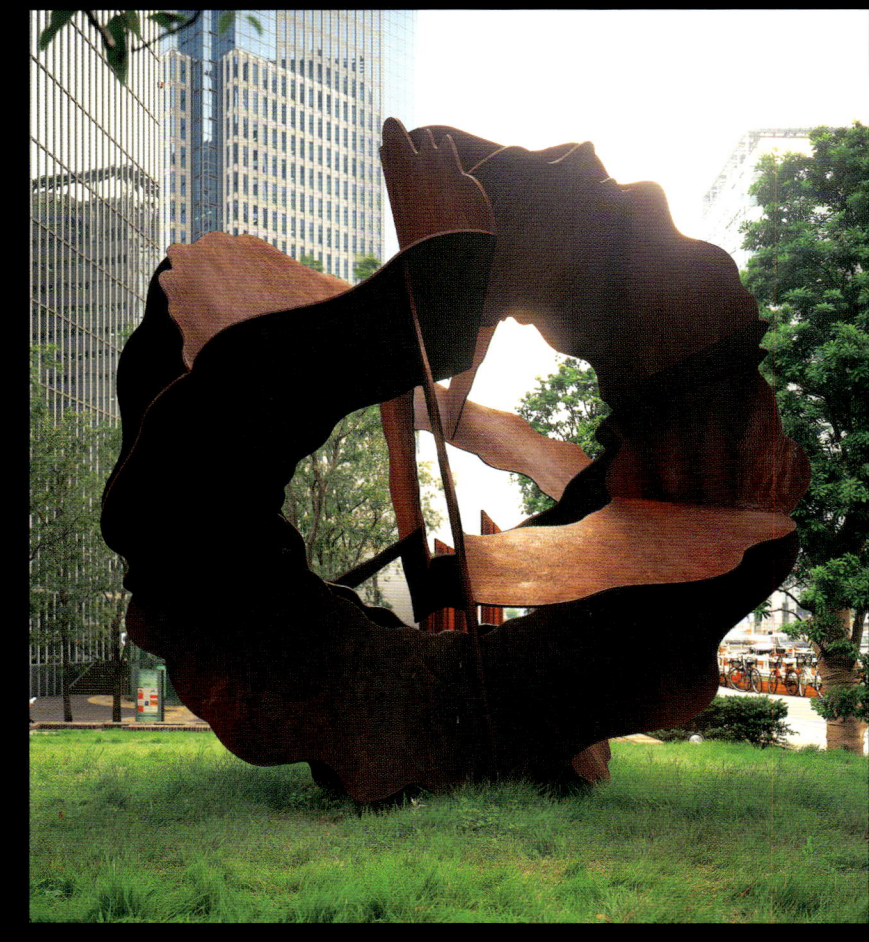

2-79 Wave Light
Across City Nakanosakaue
Tokyo, Japan, 1999

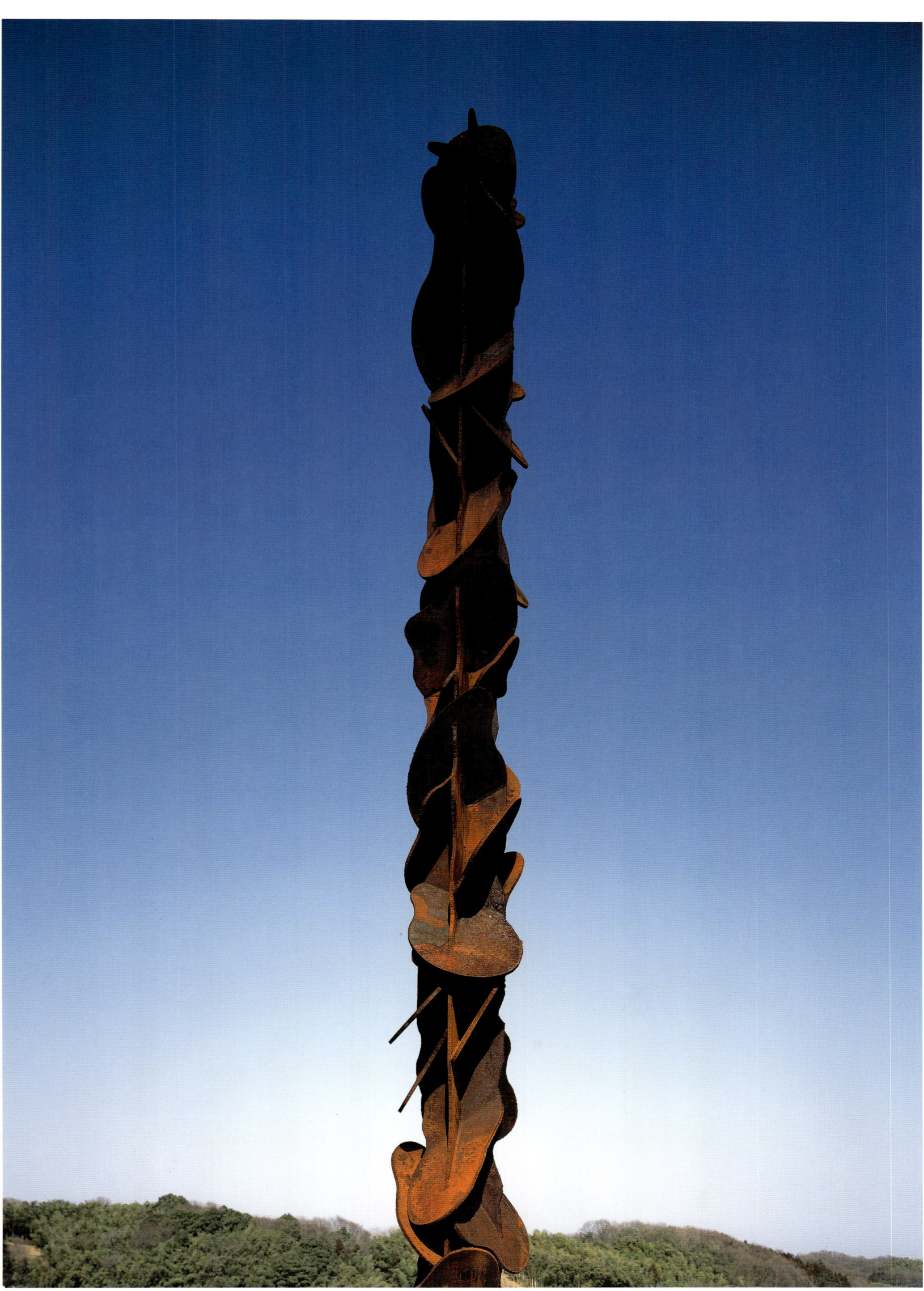

2-80 Dragon Spine
Tama Art University
Hachioji, Tokyo, Japan, 2000

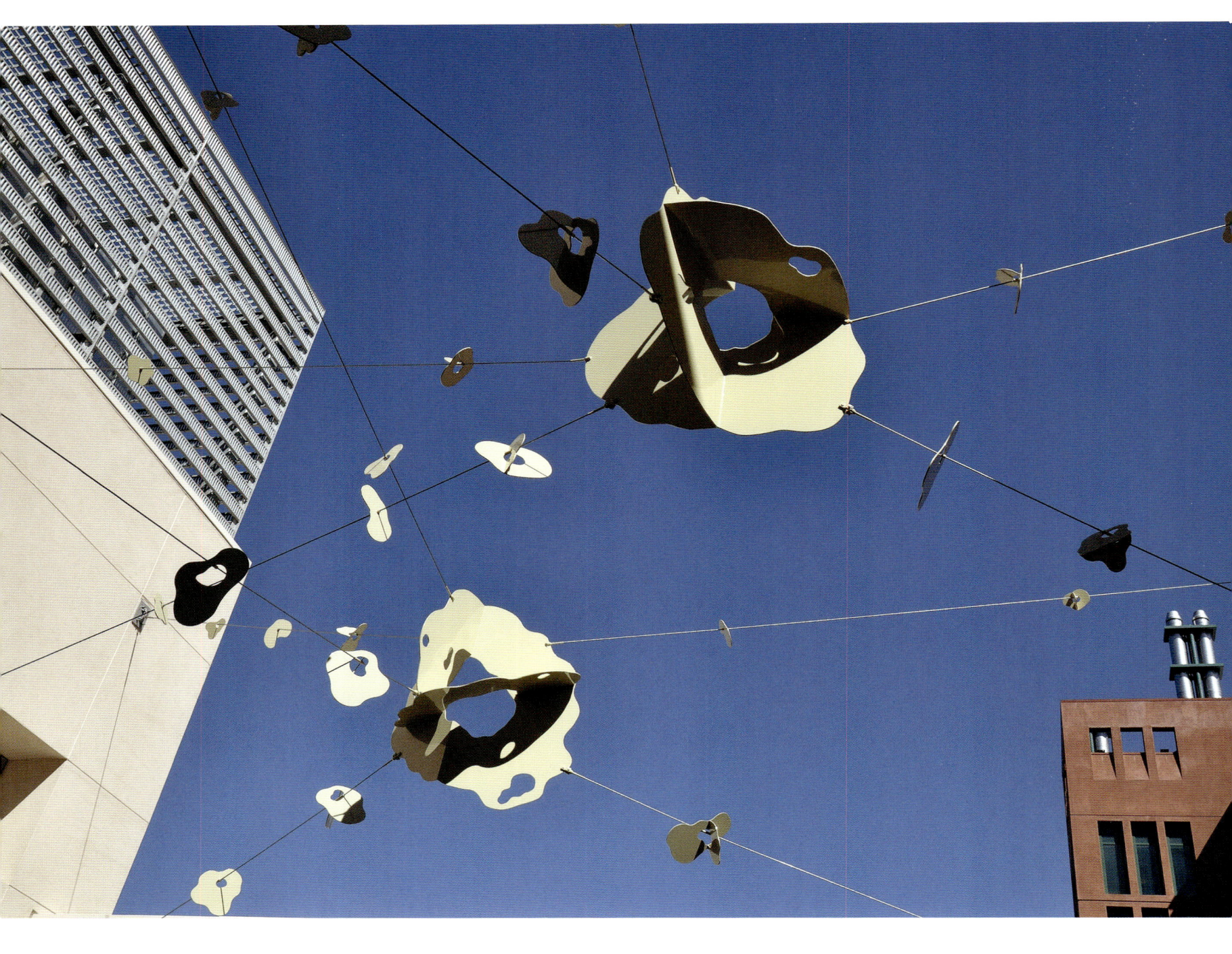

2-81 Sky Dancing
Laguna Honda Hospital
San Francisco, CA, USA, 2008

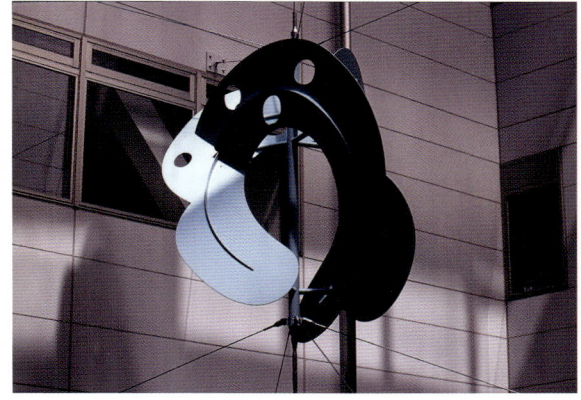
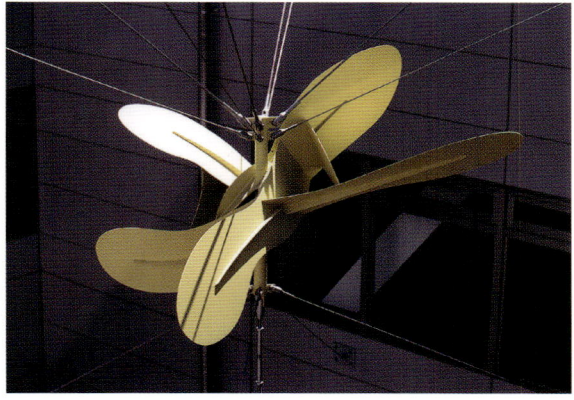

2-82 Bouquet
Kyushu University Hospital
Fukuoka, Japan, 2002

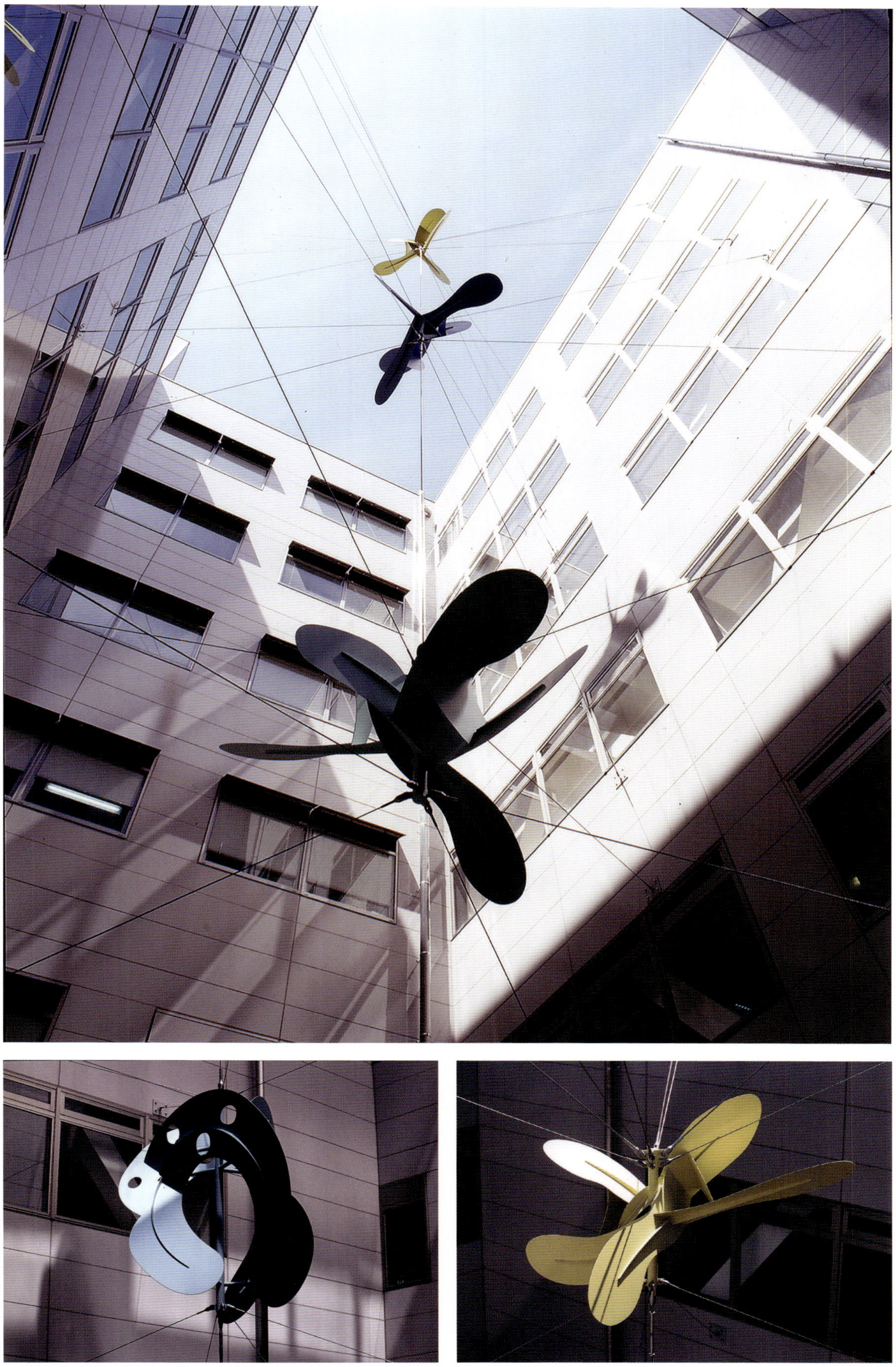

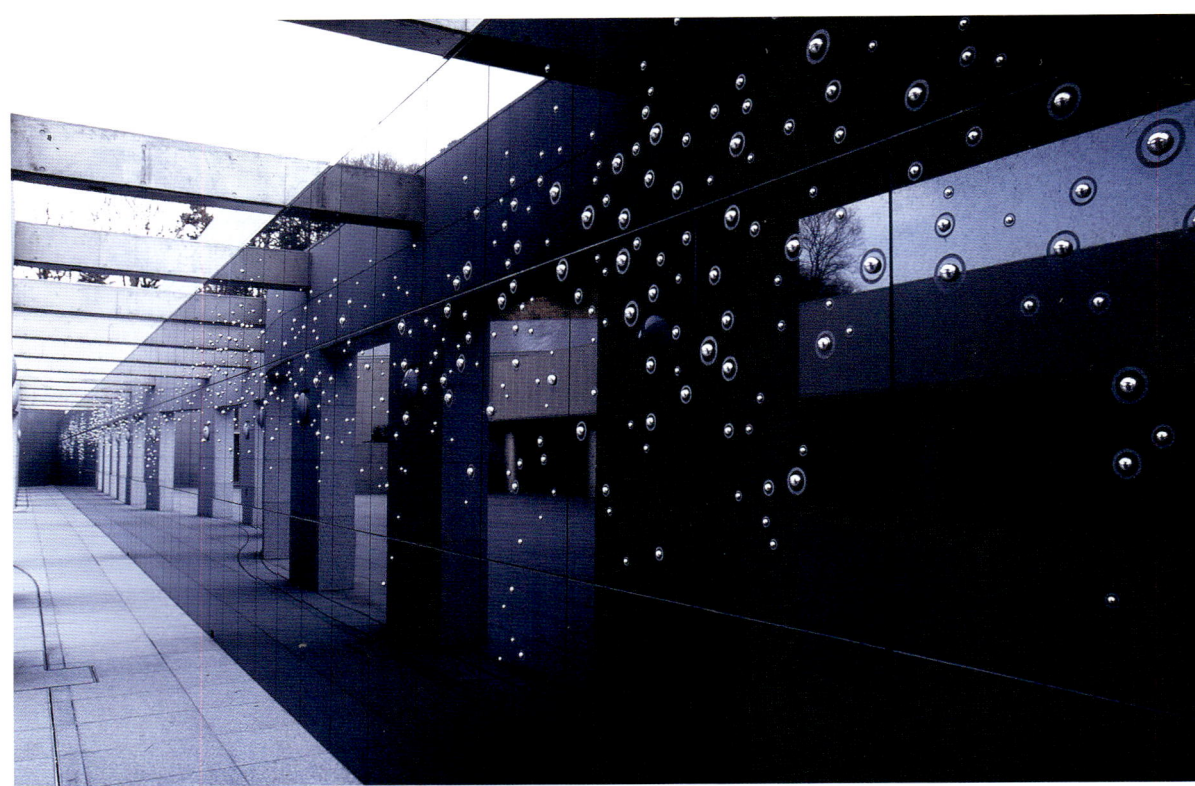
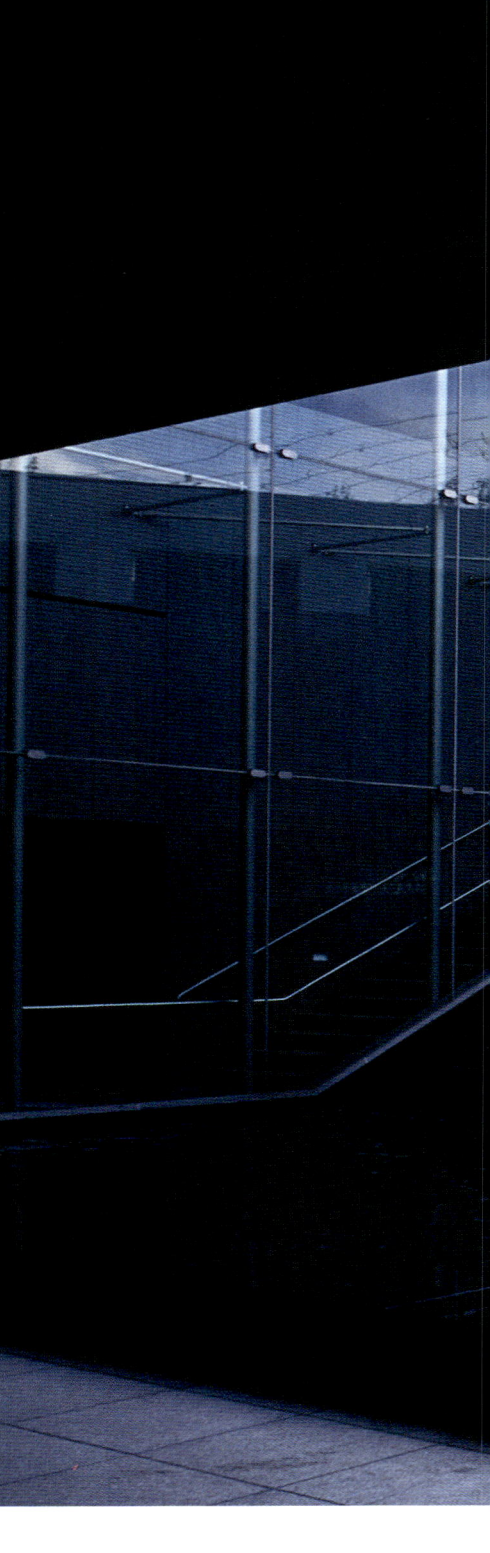
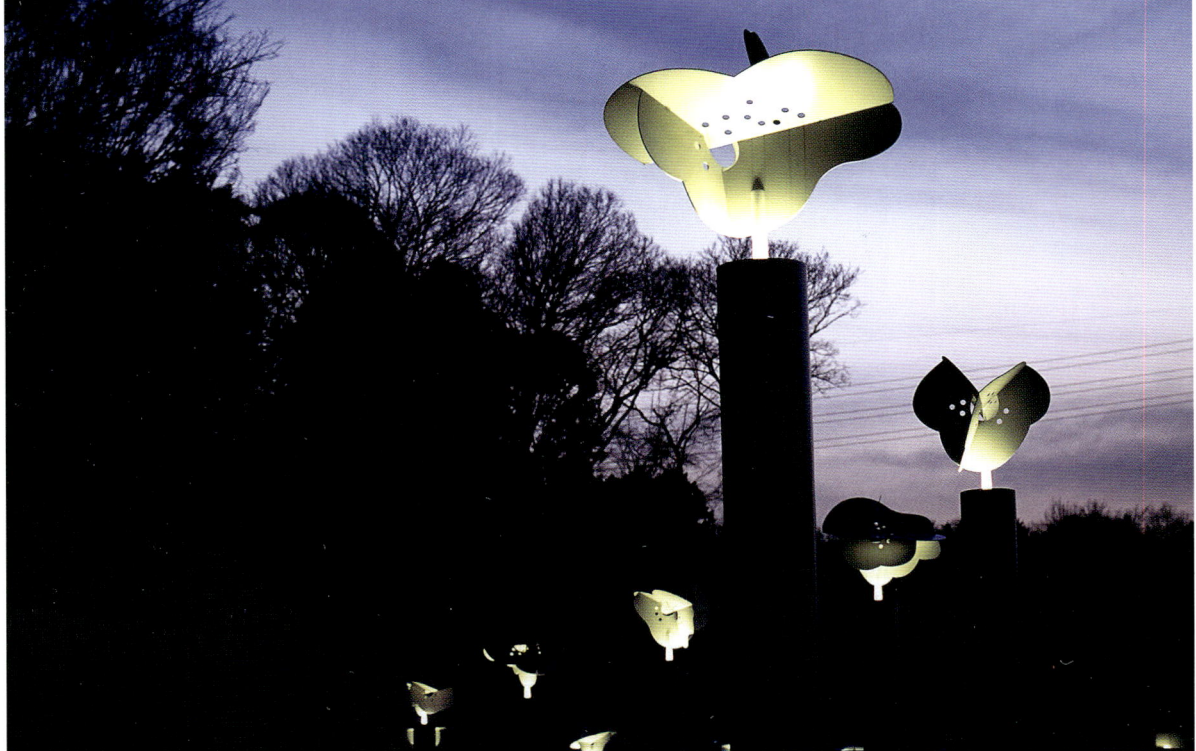

2-83 Milky Way
North Yokohama Funeral Hall
Kanagawa, Japan, 2001

2-84 Untitled, Lighting
North Yokohama Funeral Hall
Kanagawa, Japan, 2001

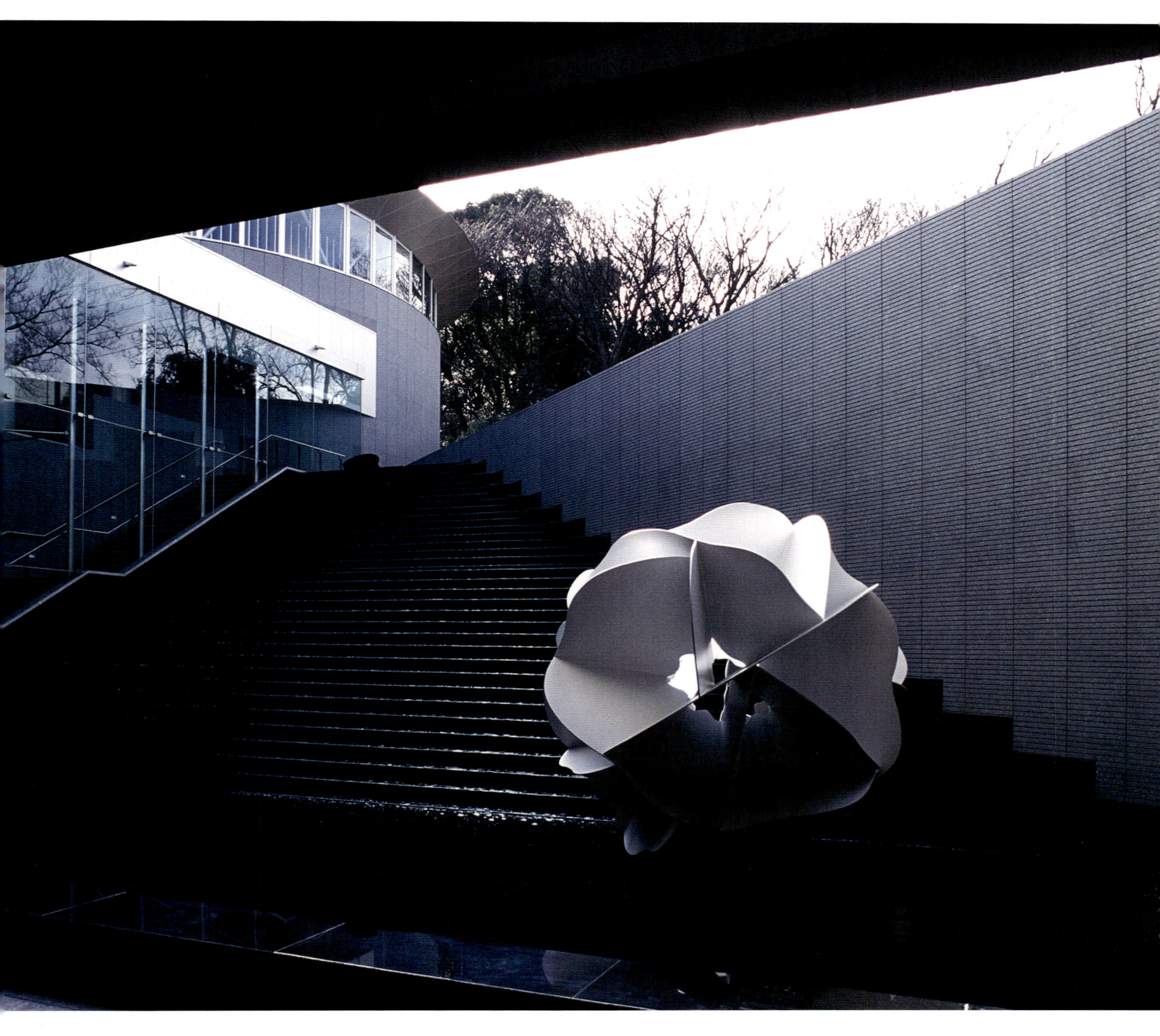

2-85 Untitled
North Yokohama Funeral Hall
Kanagawa, Japan, 2001

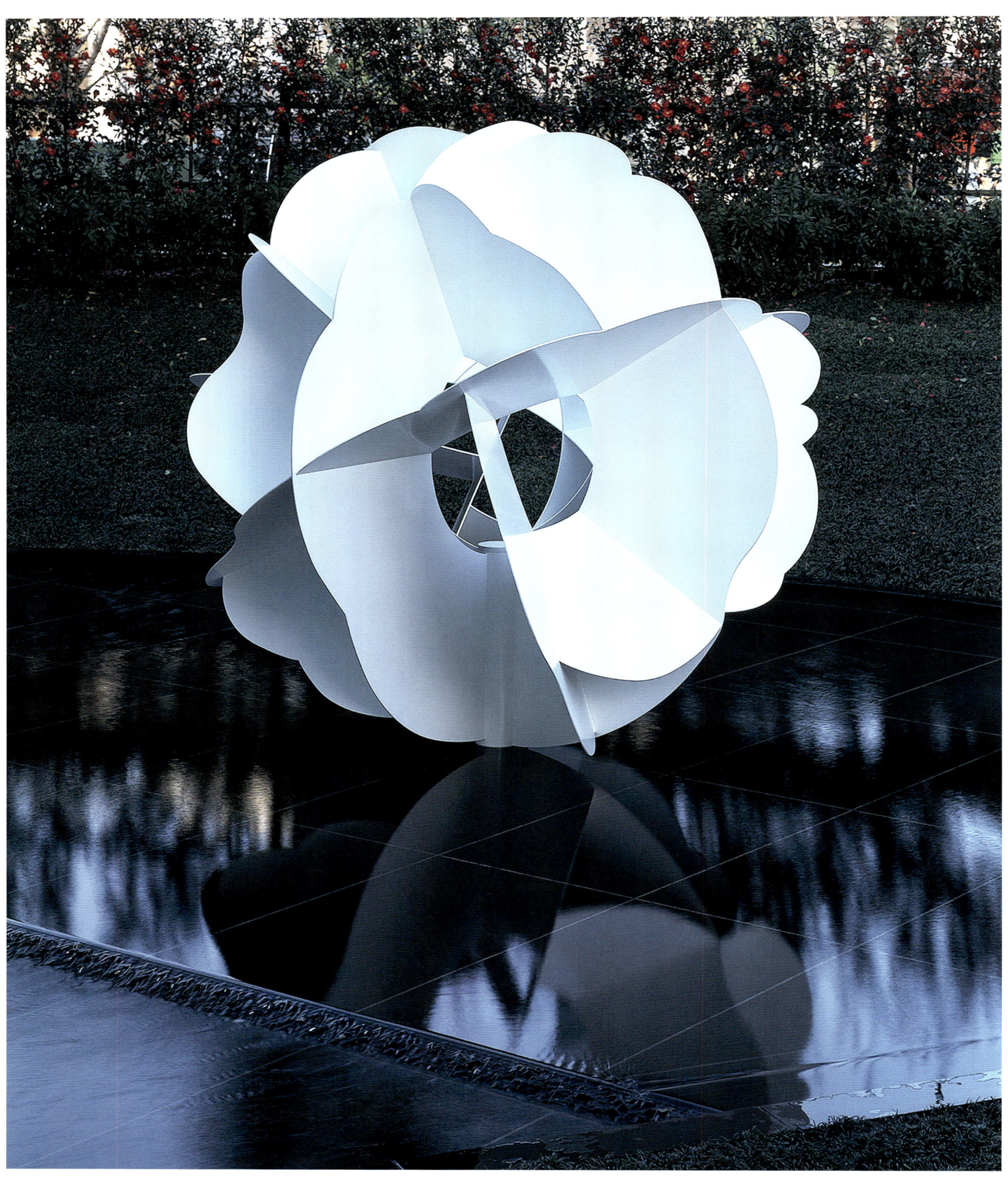

2-86 Lotus
Yamanouchi Lotus Garden
Tokyo, Japan, 1997

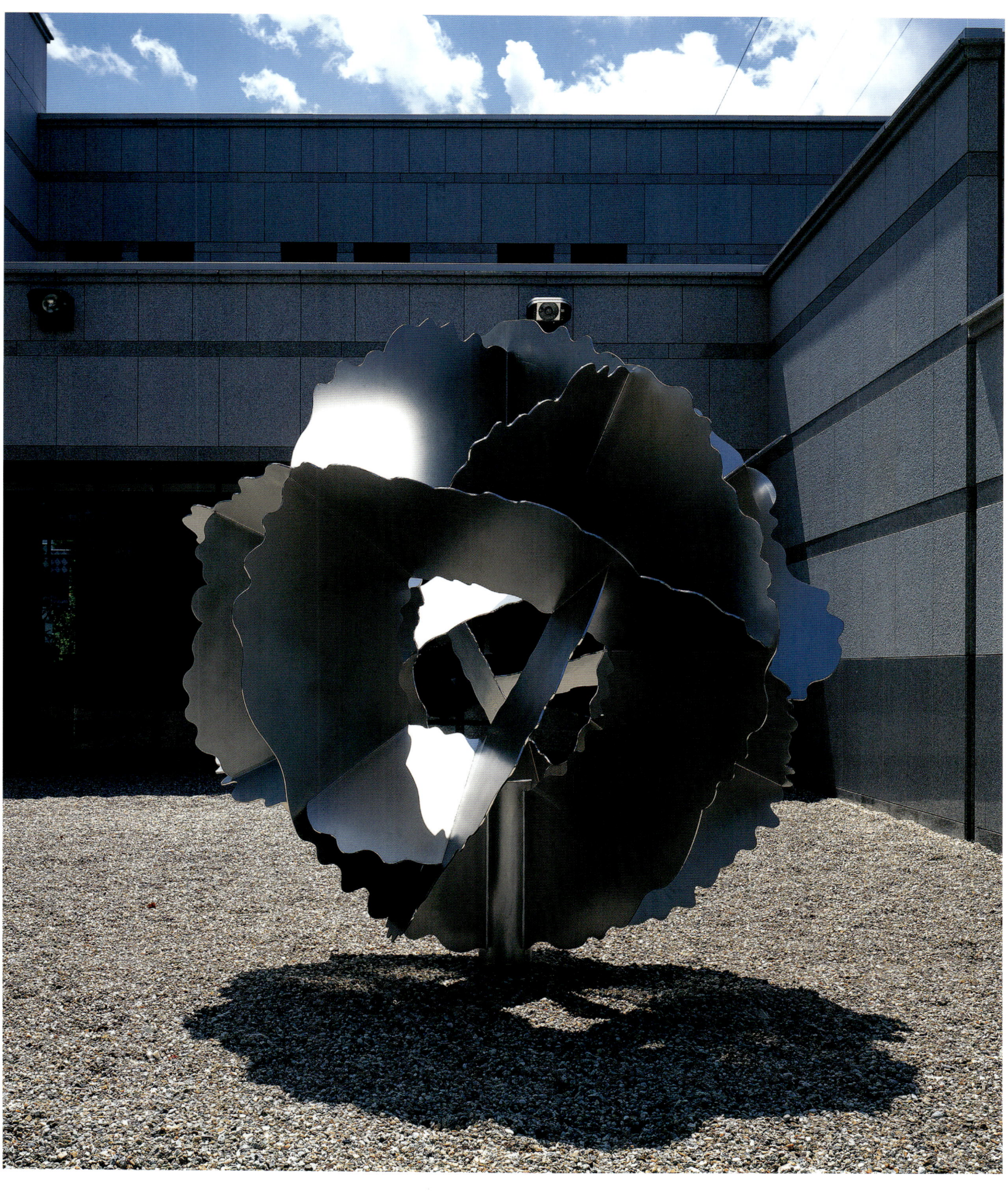

2-87 Crystal in Space
Hida Takayama Museum of Art
Gifu, Japan, 1997

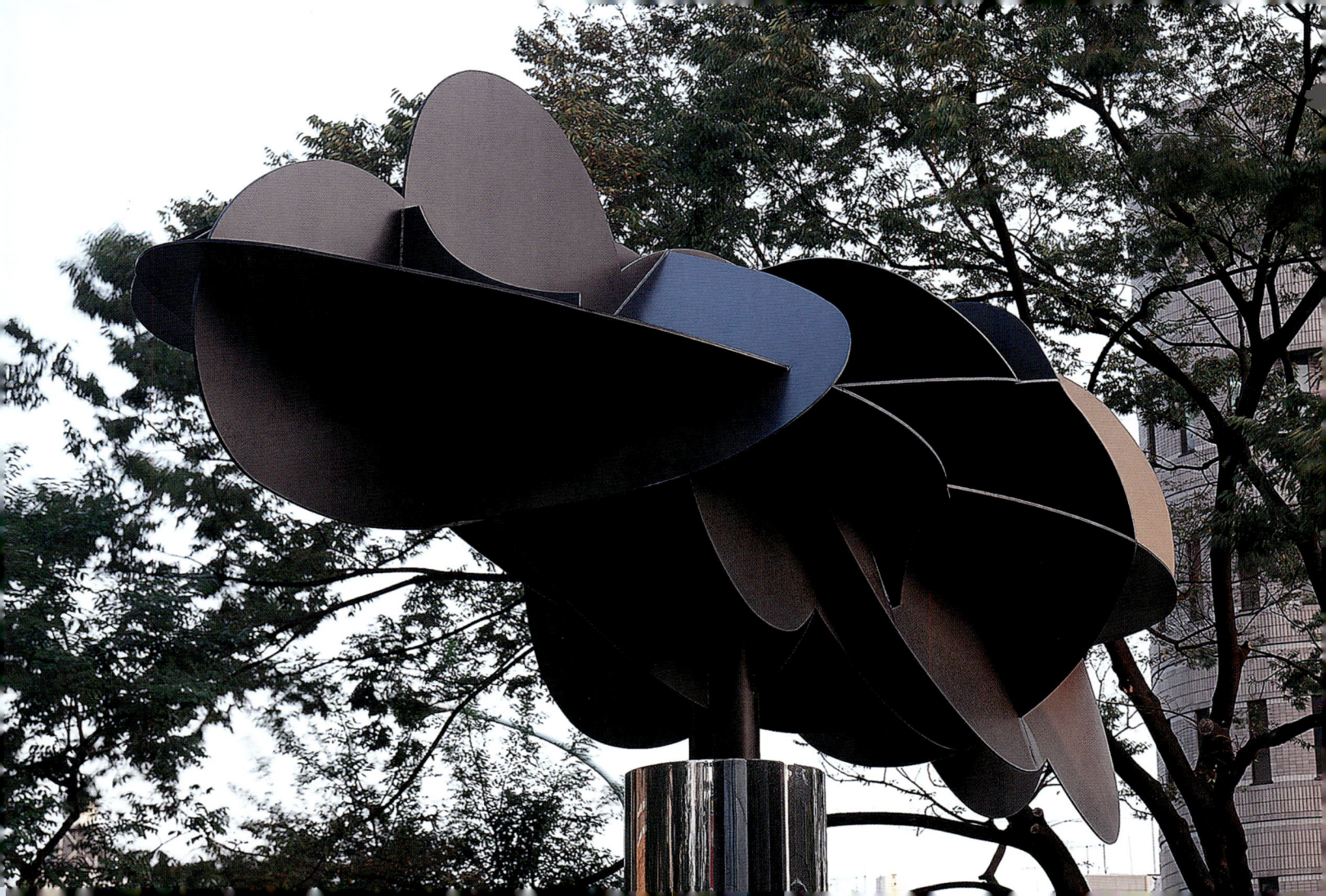

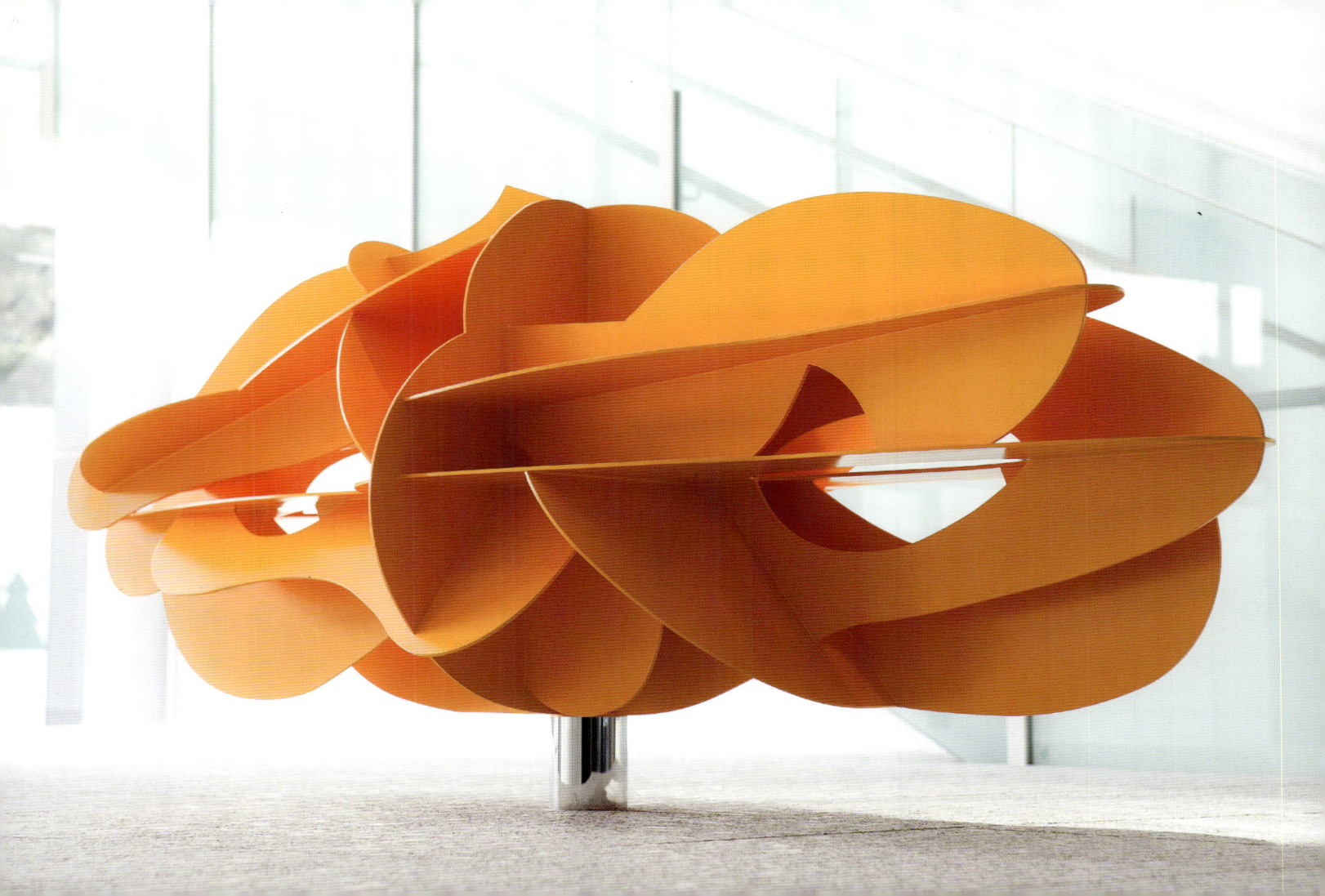

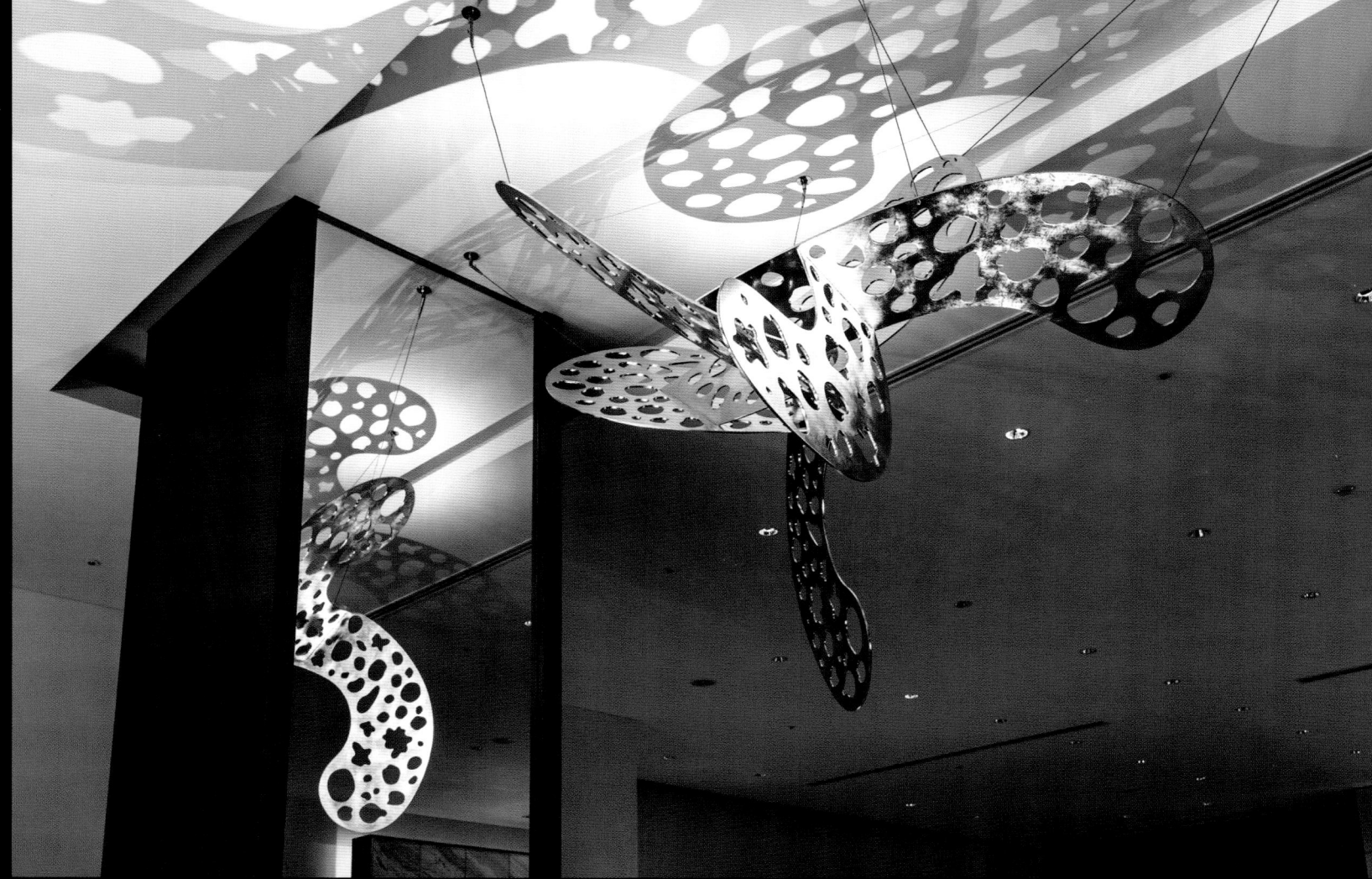

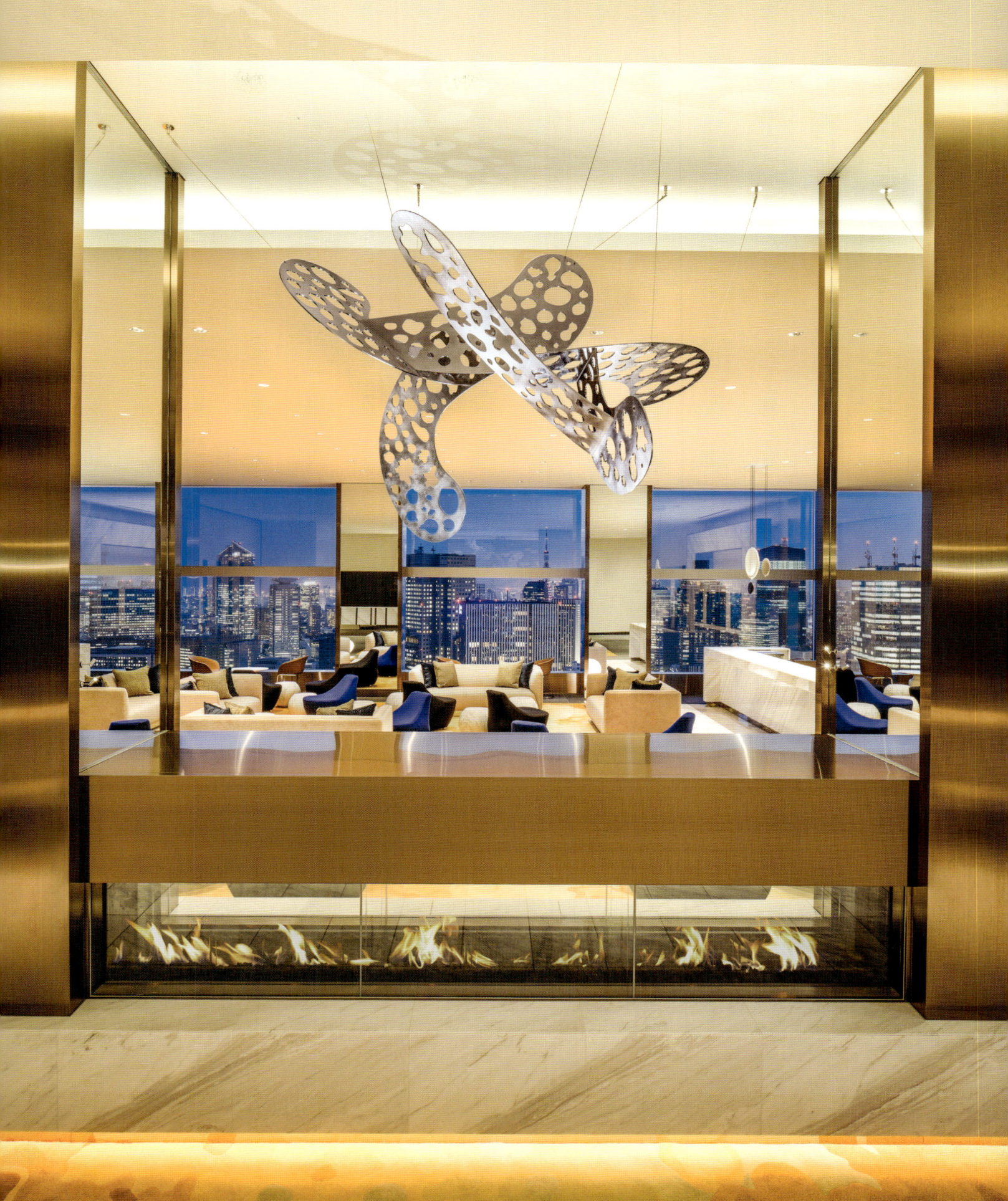

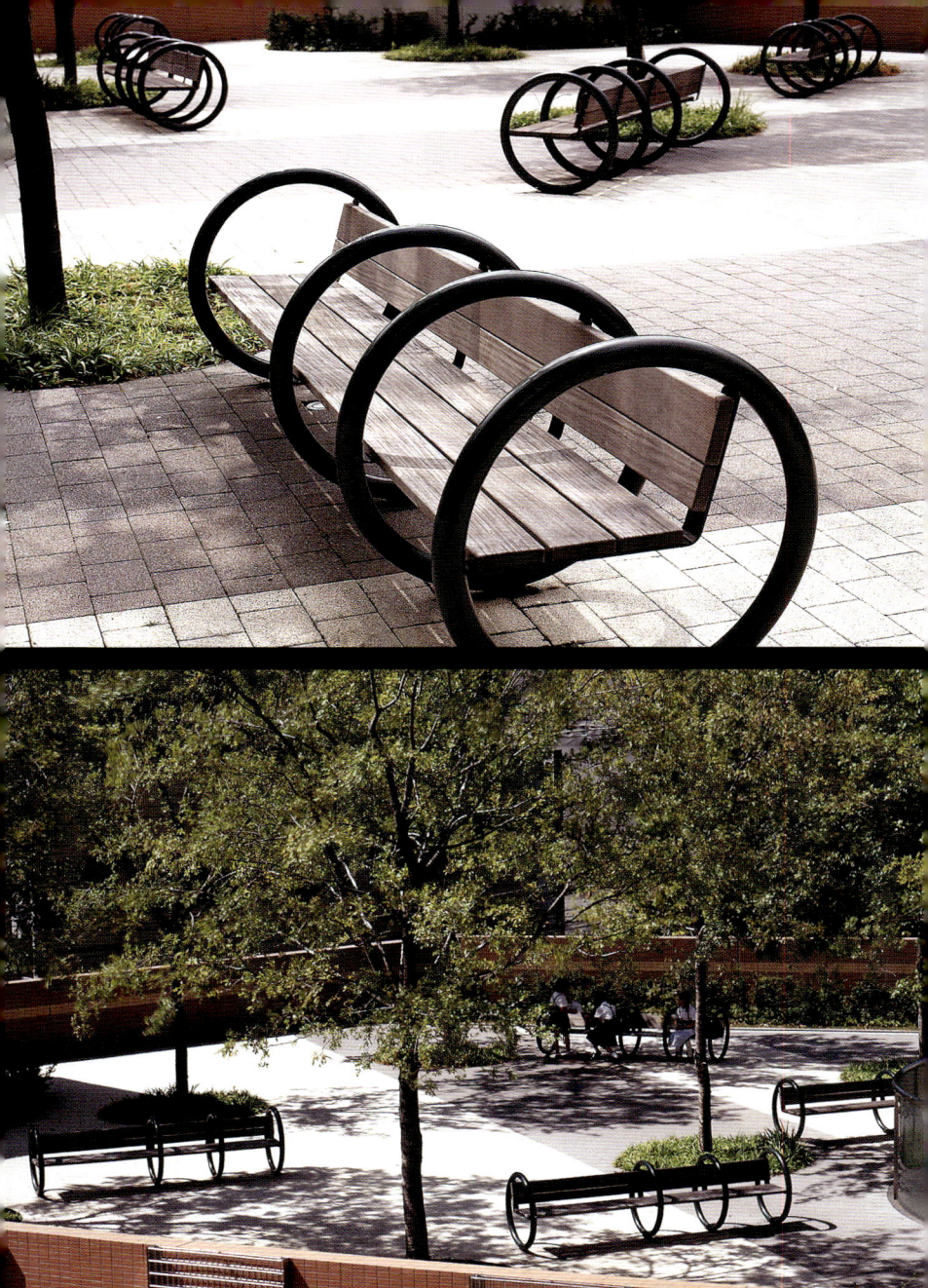

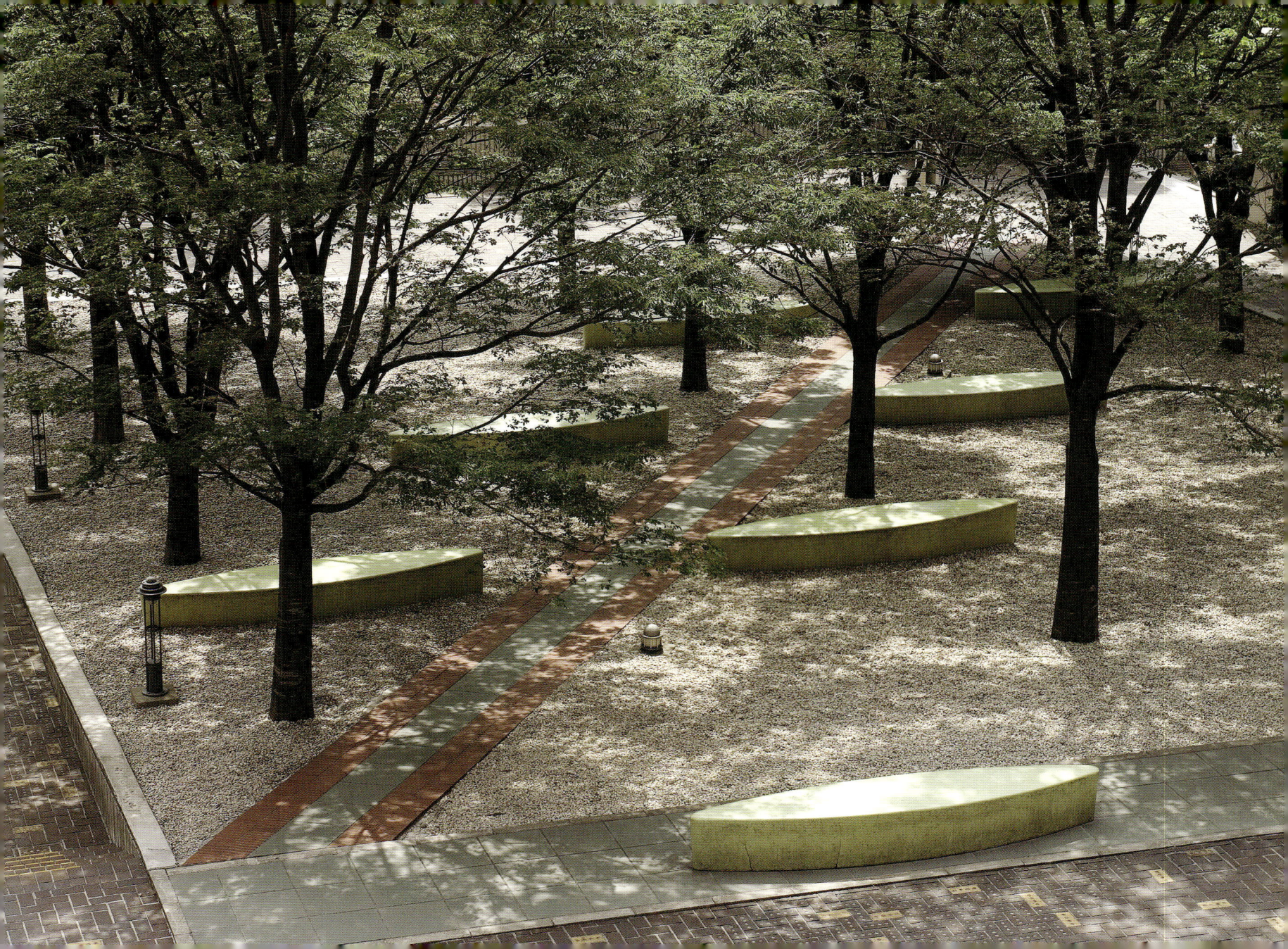

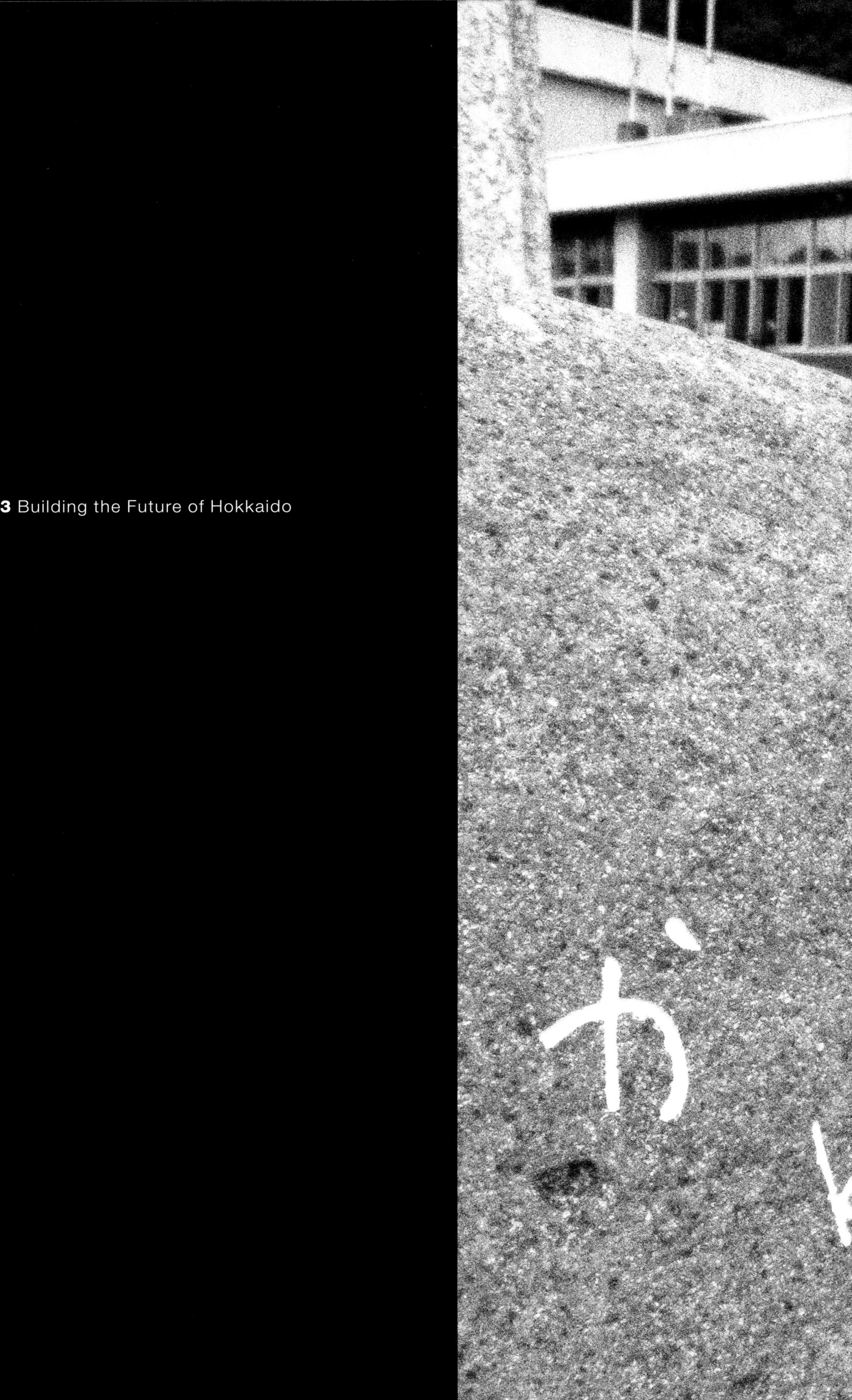

3 Building the Future of Hokkaido

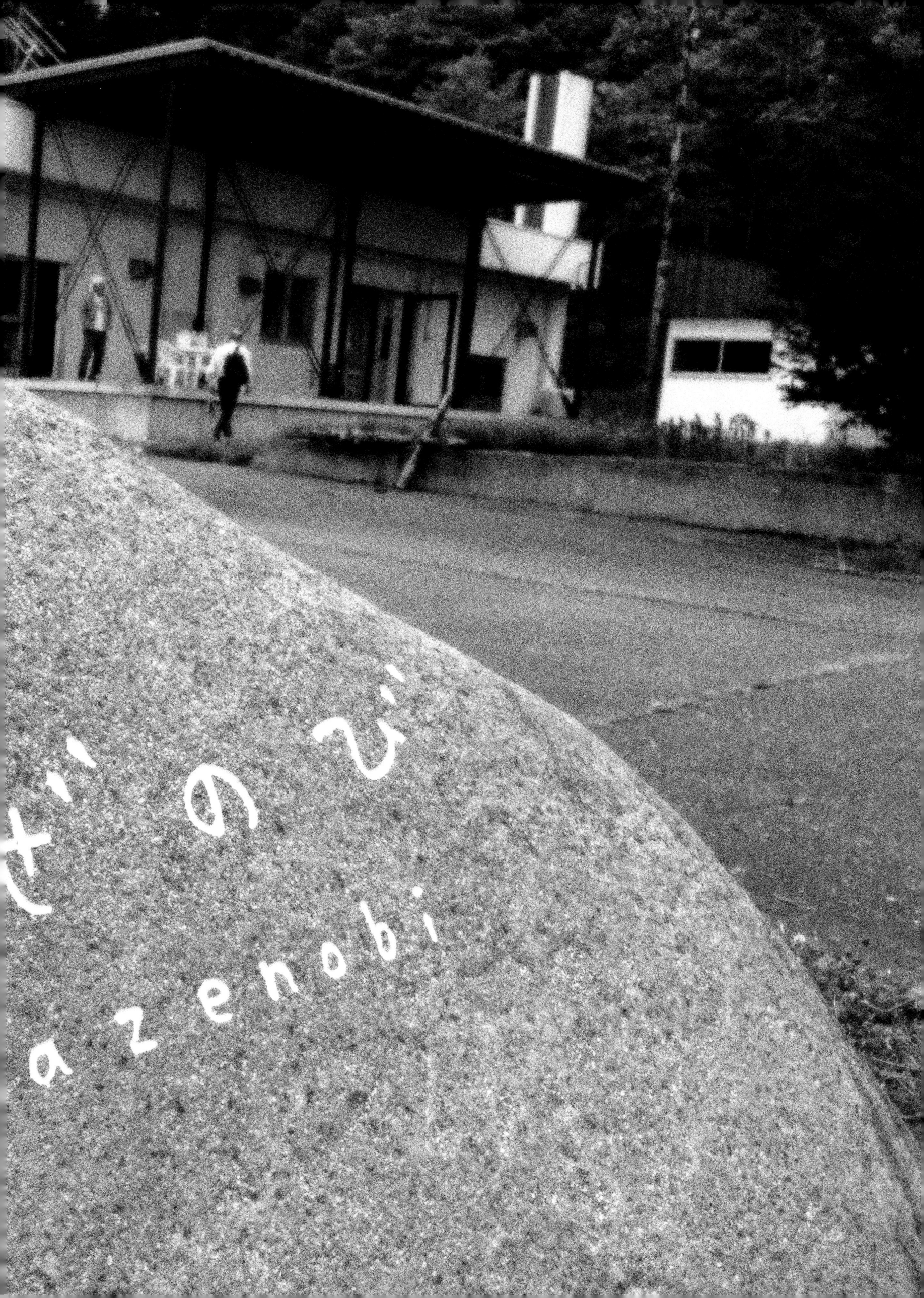
あぜのび
azenobi

"Having spent my childhood in the Sorachi area of Hokkaido, I learned a lot from the environment, rich in nature. Without knowing, I understood what it means to make, or create, through experiencing the joy of freedom in working with the material and connecting my body to nature. It is not an exaggeration to say that the foundation of my creative activity leading to what I am today was laid during that time."[4]

Home Calling Me Back

Since the 1970s, Takenobu Igarashi had positioned himself as a leading figure in the international design scene as a young Japanese graphic designer. When he turned 50 in 1994, he closed his design office in Tokyo and moved to Los Angeles to become a sculptor. After six years of being absorbed in his own creative world, suddenly in 2000, orders started coming in from Hokkaido—four within one month. "My home was calling me back, I thought, and flew back to Takikawa, my hometown in the Sorachi area in central Hokkaido, to the place that nurtured my sensitivity…My teacher and classmates from elementary school arranged to meet together for dinner. Everybody wanted to know what I had been doing. I was away from home for over forty years, so nobody knew anything about me. They asked me to do a lecture, which turned out to be on September 11, 2001—the day of the terror attack in New York! After the lecture we were out drinking and late at night I turned on the television and saw scenes like those in a movie. It was just unforgettable."

Since then Igarashi traveled between Los Angeles and Hokkaido, frequently crossing the Pacific Ocean. His first work was the sculpture *Dragon Spine* (2004), affectionately called *Nyoki Nyoki*, (an onomatopoeia meaning to grow or shoot up rapidly) made for Ichinosakanishi Park in Takikawa, and followed by involvement in the development project of JR Sapporo Station. For the observation deck of Sapporo's new landmark, the high-rise JR Tower, he made *Landscape* (2003), a relief in terracotta. He also designed the symbol mark for the JR Tower and a clock facing the station plaza. Later, for the adjoining underground plaza PASEO, Igarashi designed the entire space including another terracotta piece entitled *Forest of "Terminus"* (2011). *Dragon Spine* was commissioned by the city of Takikawa, a provincial city lacking in tourist attractions and notable characteristics.

"My aim was to make a sculpture that would be known as number one in Hokkaido. Since the budget was limited, I thought maybe I could stand out in height. However, it turned out that the estimated expense was four times as much as the budget…Luckily I had enough time, so I kept negotiating with the factory in Sapporo. At the same time, I thought of possibilities in cutting down costs. Meanwhile, the local government officials tried to raise the budget by persuading the municipal assembly. It was just around the time when 'wasting tax money' was being criticized in the news, but somehow they managed to double the budget. Finally, I was also able to persuade the factory to reduce the price, and the sculpture was realized. *Dragon Spine* was really only possible with everyone's help." *Dragon Spine* is a weathering steel sculpture measuring 21 meters in height. Like its title, countless organic forms climb up to the sky like the spine of a dragon. It is a powerful work, full of hope for the future.

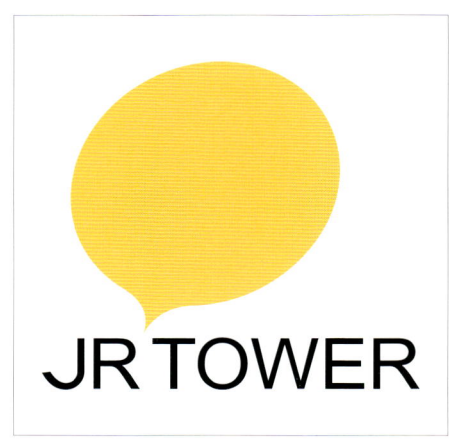

3-1 Logo Mark for JR Tower
Sapporo Station General Development Co., Ltd.
Sapporo, Hokkaido, Japan, 2003

This symbol mark with a yellow balloon nicely compliments the blue sky. There are a variety of ways to apply a symbol, such as drawing a picture and writing some text in the yellow balloon. (TI)

3-2 Dragon Spine (Nickname Nyoki Nyoki)
Ichinosaka West Park, Takikawa,
Hokkaido, Japan, 2004

I produced one, 9m high, for the campus of Tama Art University and another one, 21m high, for the park in my hometown. For the latter, I also designed a water square and placed a concrete sphere and hemisphere there. (TI)

[4] Takenobu Igarashi, From text to exhibition *Igarashi Takenobu: Kioku no katachi*, Granvista Gallery Sapporo, May 29–July 22, 2014.

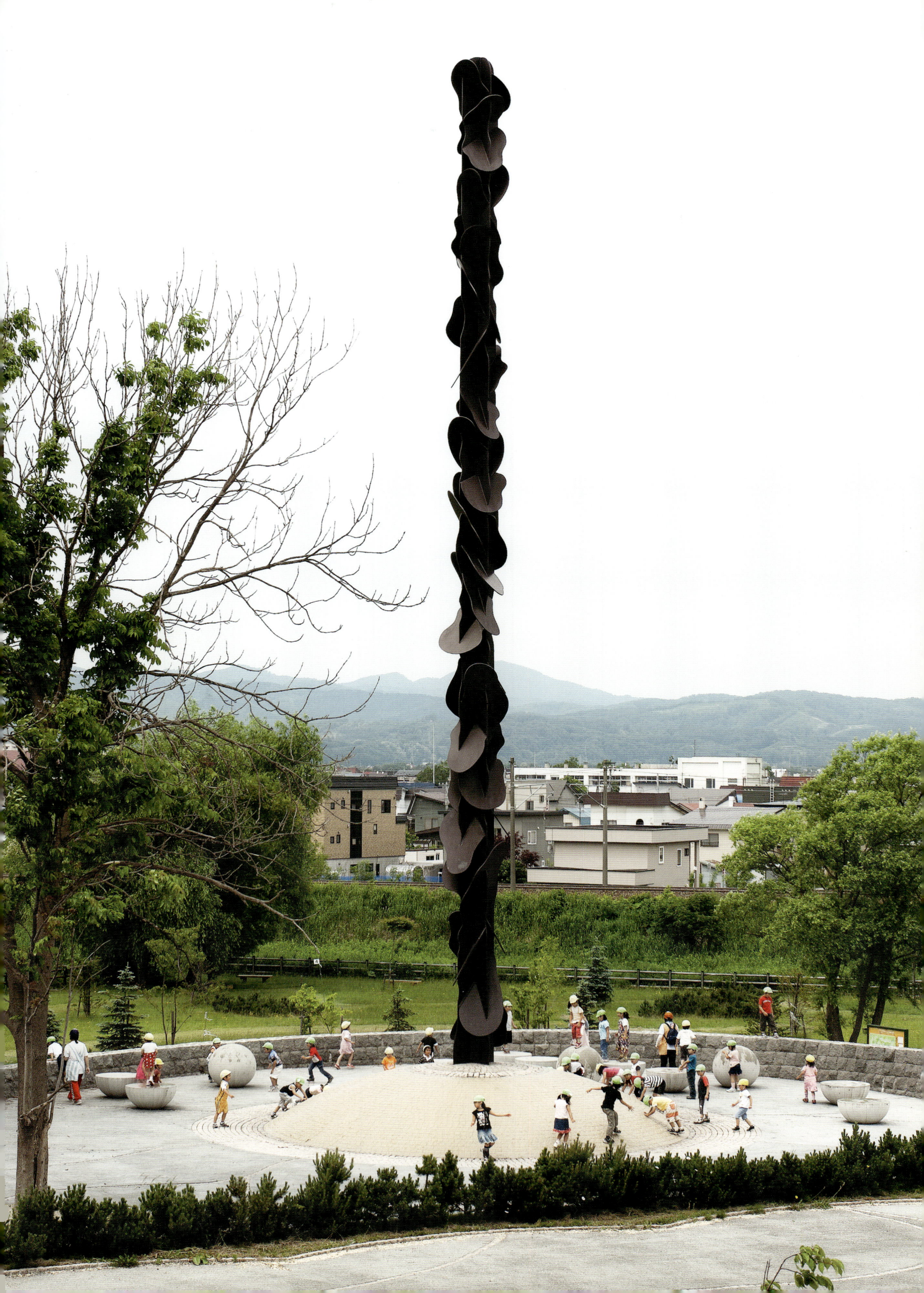

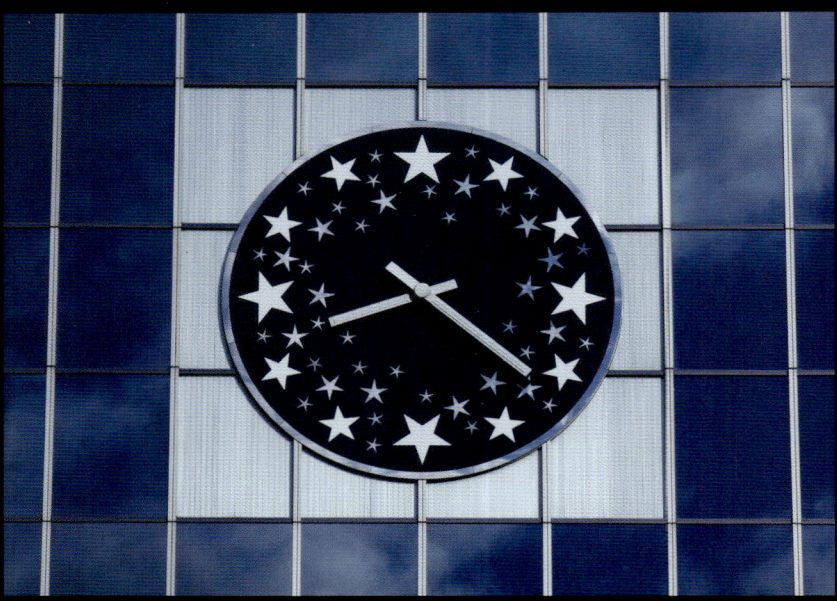

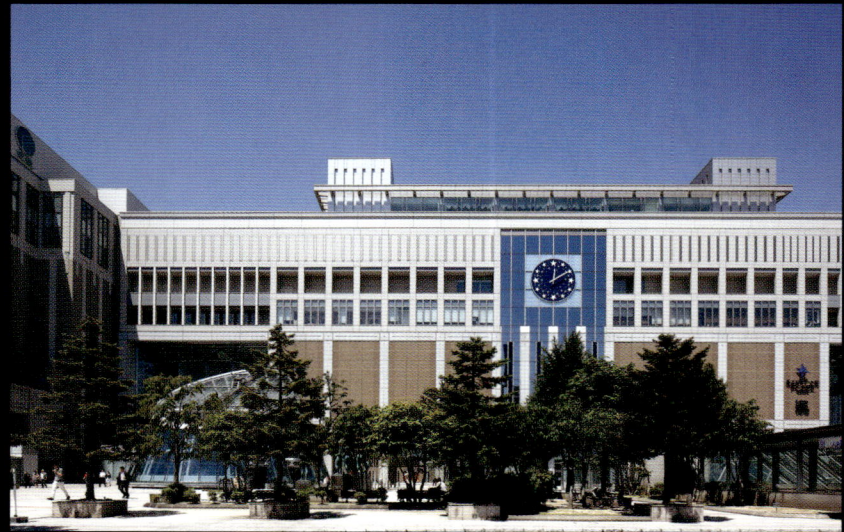

3-3 Sapporo Station, Big Star Clock
JR Tower, Sapporo Station, Sapporo, Hokkaido, Japan, 2003
This big clock, 7m across, required a flat surface to prevent icicles. That was the restriction when I designed it. The star is the symbol of Hokkaido and it was natural for me to use it as a motif for a big clock at Sapporo station. (TI)

Front view of South Gate, JR Tower

3-4 Landscape
JR Tower Observation deck T38
Sapporo Station
Sapporo, Hokkaido, Japan, 2003

3-5 Graphic Work for the Walkway to Forest of Terminus
JR Sapporo Station
Paseo, Sapporo, Hokkaido, Japan,

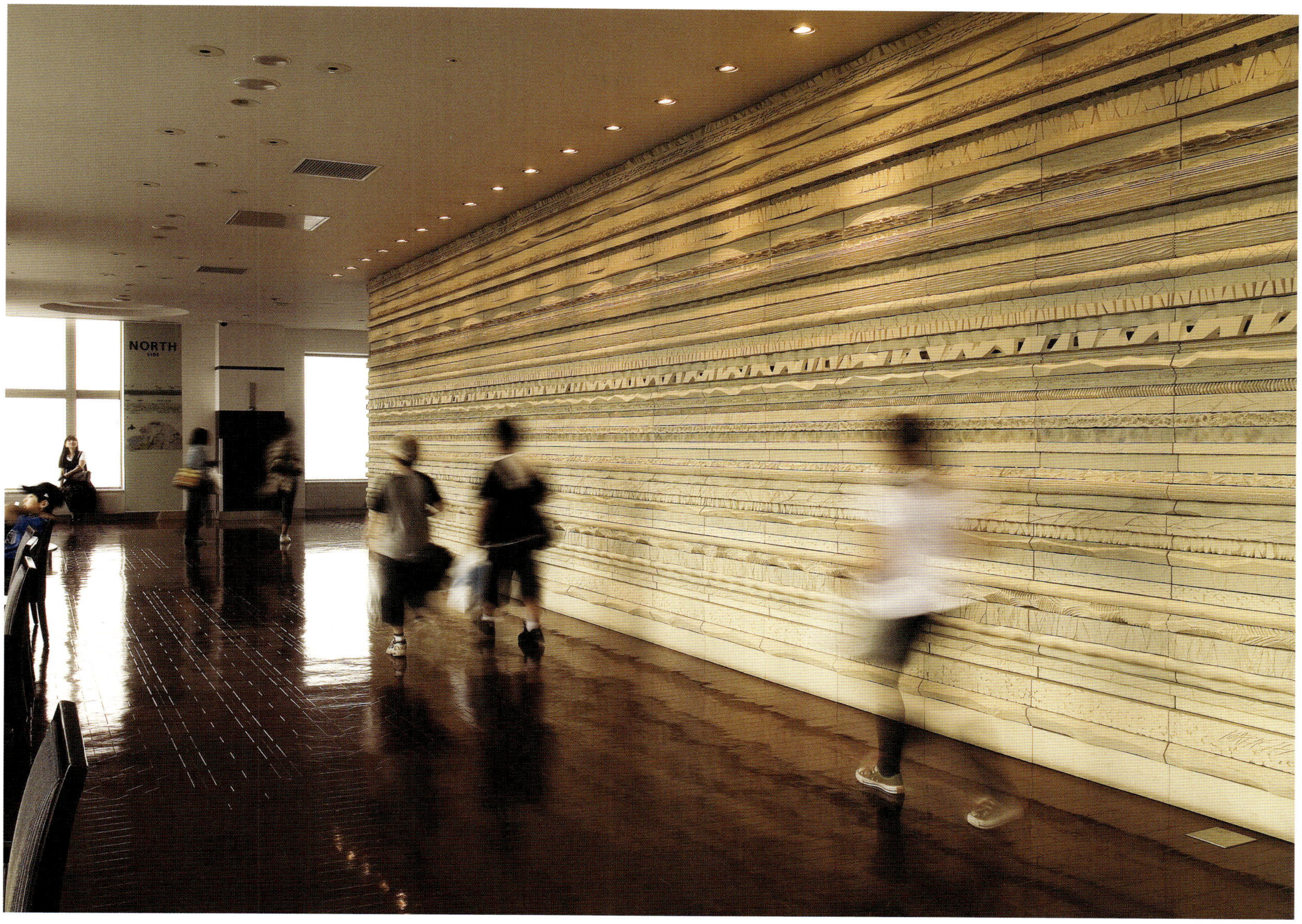

Chapter **3** Building the Future of Hokkaido

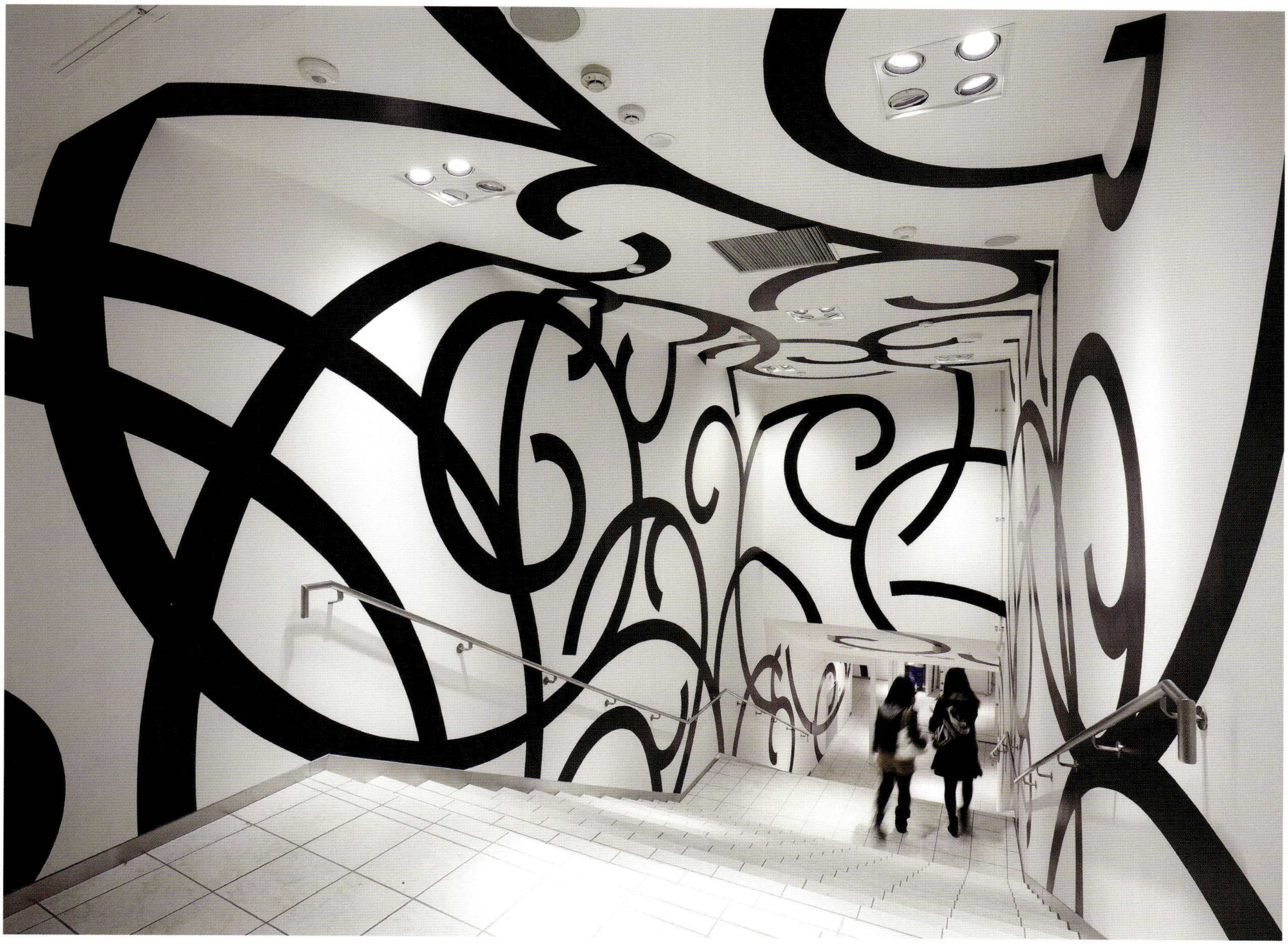

Revitalization of Tarokichigura—Grandfather's Legacy

Tarokichigura is a short walk from the railroad station toward the city center of Takikawa. Built by Igarashi's grandfather Tarokichi Igarashi, a sake brewer, it was a granary for storing rice used in making sake. During his childhood the granary was a perfect playground for Igarashi and his friends. Plans were made to use the historical stone building for concerts, but the building was in very poor condition. "There were holes in the roof and it was doubtful whether the stone granary would survive the winter. Yukihiko Usui, Deputy General Manager of JR Hokkaido Development Project and others wanted to save the granary if possible. Landscape designer Koji Saito, graphic designer Masami Yamagishi, design coordinator Mihoko Furuya, former classmate Ayako Kanbe, and other people of Sapporo as well as local citizens of Takikawa all endorsed the idea, and architect Yoshifumi Nakamura was asked to plan the renovation…Although I did not know him personally, I called and visited him. I told him about the granary and that I wanted him to do the complete renovation of it. He said, 'I have to go to Asahikawa next week, so I will stop by and look at it.' He then called me from his cell phone and said, 'I am here at the granary, but it looks much better than I had imagined.'"

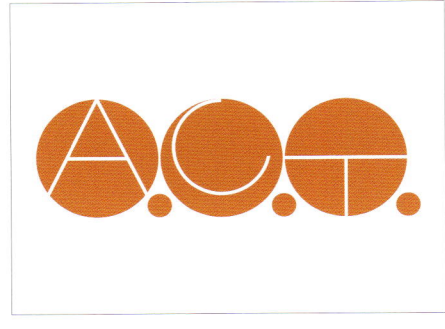

3-6 Logo Design
Incorporated non-profit organization Art Challenge Takikawa (A.C.T) that supports activities at Tarokichigura, 2003

Nakamura also planned the atelier in Akiya, Yokosuka, where Igarashi settled after moving back from Los Angeles. Igarashi also asked his photographer friend Mitsumasa Fujitsuka to take photos of the granary before the renovation work started, to record it in its original state. "He said he will do it when he goes to Hokkaido for work. I later heard from local people that before entering the granary he took off his hat, bowing his head and said, 'Tarokichi-san, may I come in?' They were so impressed about his respectful behavior, saying that 'only a real photographer acts that way.' Fujitsuka was moved by the old granary, that is a very 'rare' example of its kind still in existence. He did a feature in the *Modern Living Magazine*, calling it 'Tarokichigura.' So that's where it got its name…as Fujitsuka writes, it is dark inside the granary. Photos were made by sliding the door open to its fullest. However, he thought, 'it's nicer when it's darker inside.' There were little windows high up on each end, but they were unreachable. Just as he was thinking, 'it would be most beautiful if there would be light coming down from the window,' the wind blew and opened the iron shade shedding light from above. Such things happen (laughs)."

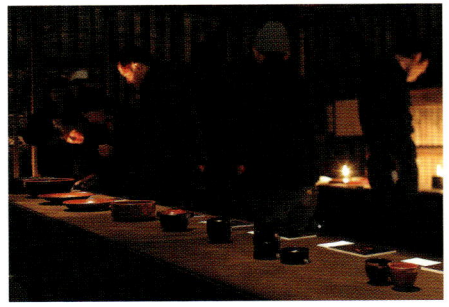

Exhibition at Tarokichigura

Art Challenge Takikawa (A.C.T.)

Igarashi and his siblings owned the granary but within half a year, NPO Art Challenge Takikawa (A.C.T.) was established and through government subsidy and support of all the people involved, it was restored and reborn as Tarokichigura. It was like a miracle. Donated to A.C.T. in 2004, Tarokichigura became the center of their activity, spreading out in all directions. As an example of a successful restoration, Tarokichigura was included in the book *Saisei Meikenchiku–Toki o Koeru Design*. One of the first exhibitions held at Tarokichigura was Ryoji Ikeda's one-man show. Igarashi came to know Ikeda, also a native of Hokkaido, in Los Angeles. Ikeda contacted Akira Tatehata, art critic and poet, who became interested in Tarokichigura and came to visit. Together with Igarashi, they worked on a book of poetry and prints, which was presented at the exhibition.

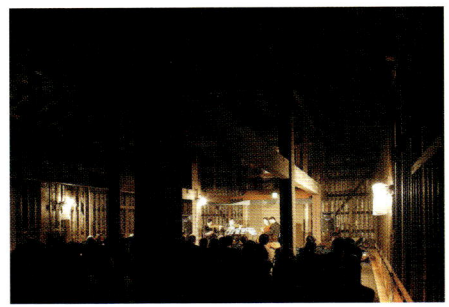

Tarokichigura is a stone-built warehouse with great acoustic properties.

As an NPO, A.C.T. needs to continuously plan and implement activities. As Igarashi states: "We wanted to make Takikawa more attractive through art, so we thought of using the granary as a place to hold concerts and exhibitions. However, it is a lot of work to continuously plan activities. So we came up with the idea of 'Igarashi Art Workshop'…We invited many people to come here, which would in turn help the development of Takikawa. We ourselves were learning a lot, and the project started moving. But the most important thing is the network of human relationships. It is important that great personalities come to use our space. For this reason, we collected members for the NPO all around Japan. There were times when we had about 250 members. So we had people doing design and architecture all over Japan involved in our project."

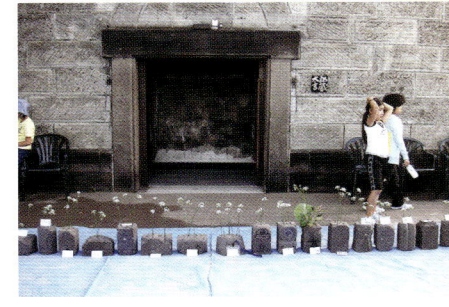

Flower vases with freestone, were made by children at a craft workshop.

*Art Challenge Takikawa changed its name to Art Challenge Tarokichigura in 2016.

Over the years, Igarashi and members of A.C.T. organized many different activities, such as summer festivals and a sculpture workshop for children. A beer garden was set up during the summer and weddings were held there. However, as the time passed by members started drifting away, leaving only the core members.

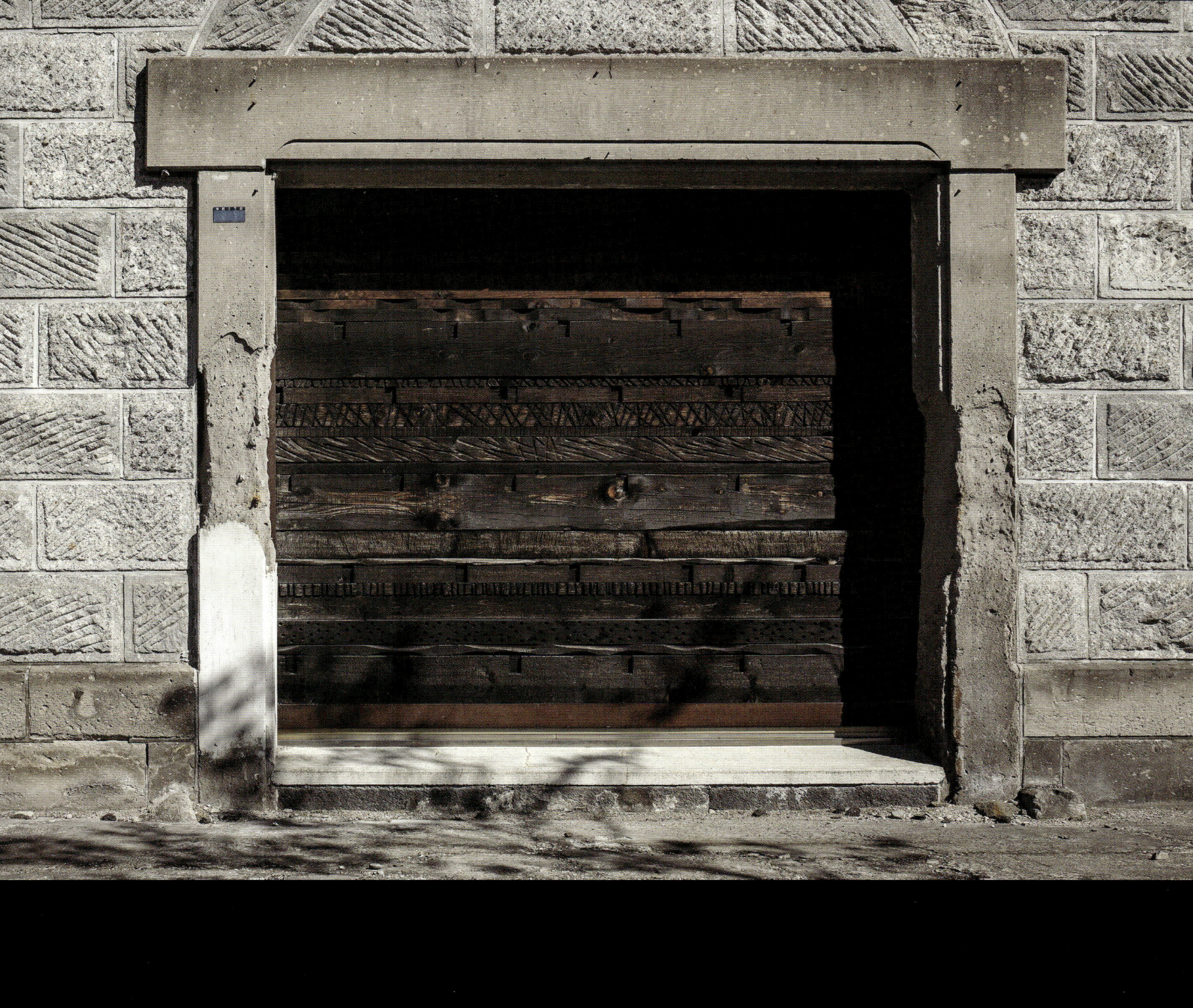

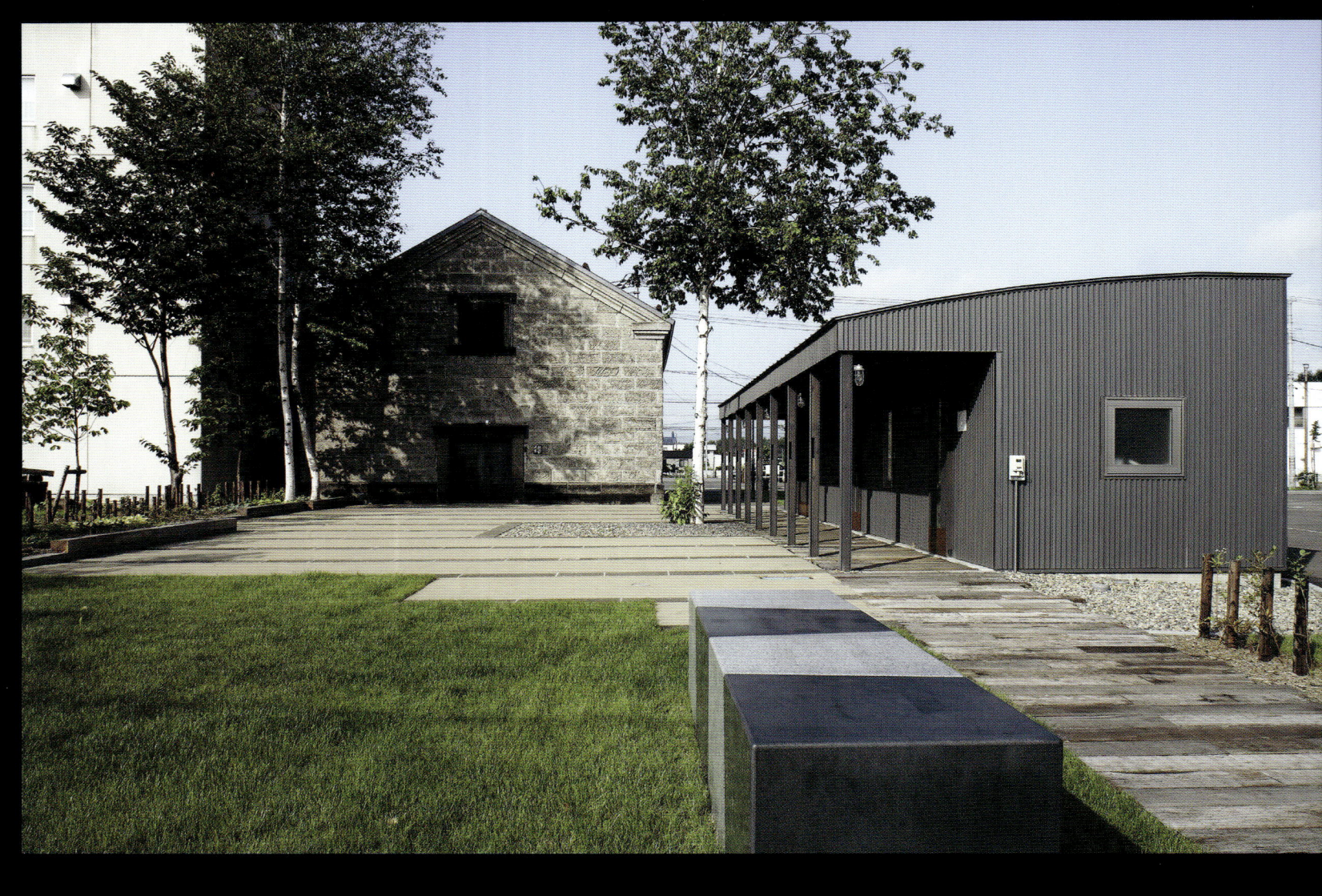
Various activities took place in the courtyard of Tarokichigura.

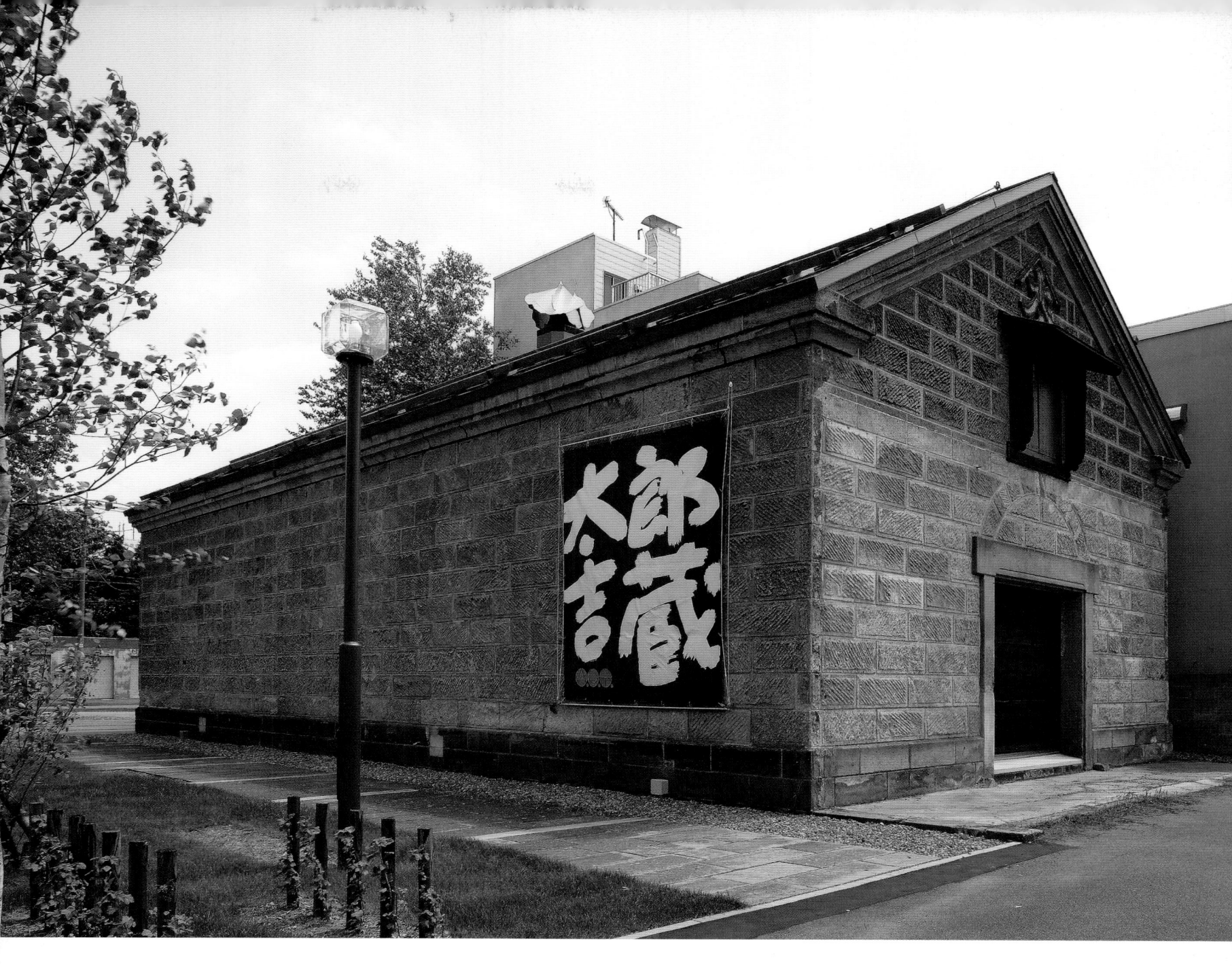

Full view of Tarokichigura opened in 2004

Renovation Planning Team
Architectural Planning:
Yoshifumi Nakamura/Lemminghouse
Lighting: Hiroyasu Shoji
Exterior Planning: Koji Saito
Report Design: Kenya Hara
Ventilation Tower, southwest facing door
Logo Design: Takenobu Igarashi
Sign Planning: Kenichi Hada

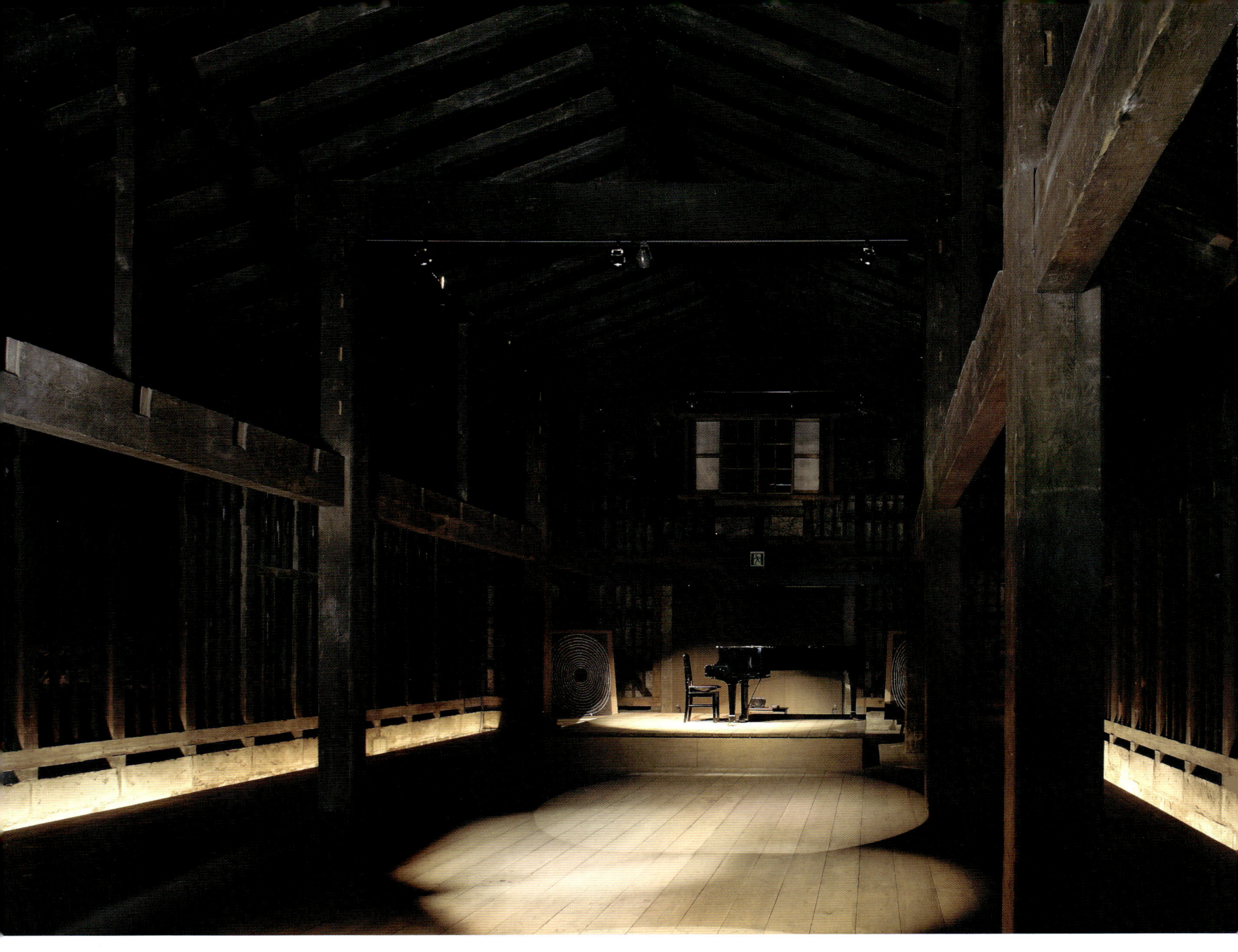

The lighting plan for Tarokichigura was carried out with the best use of the dimness of Kura, traditional Japanese storage structure.

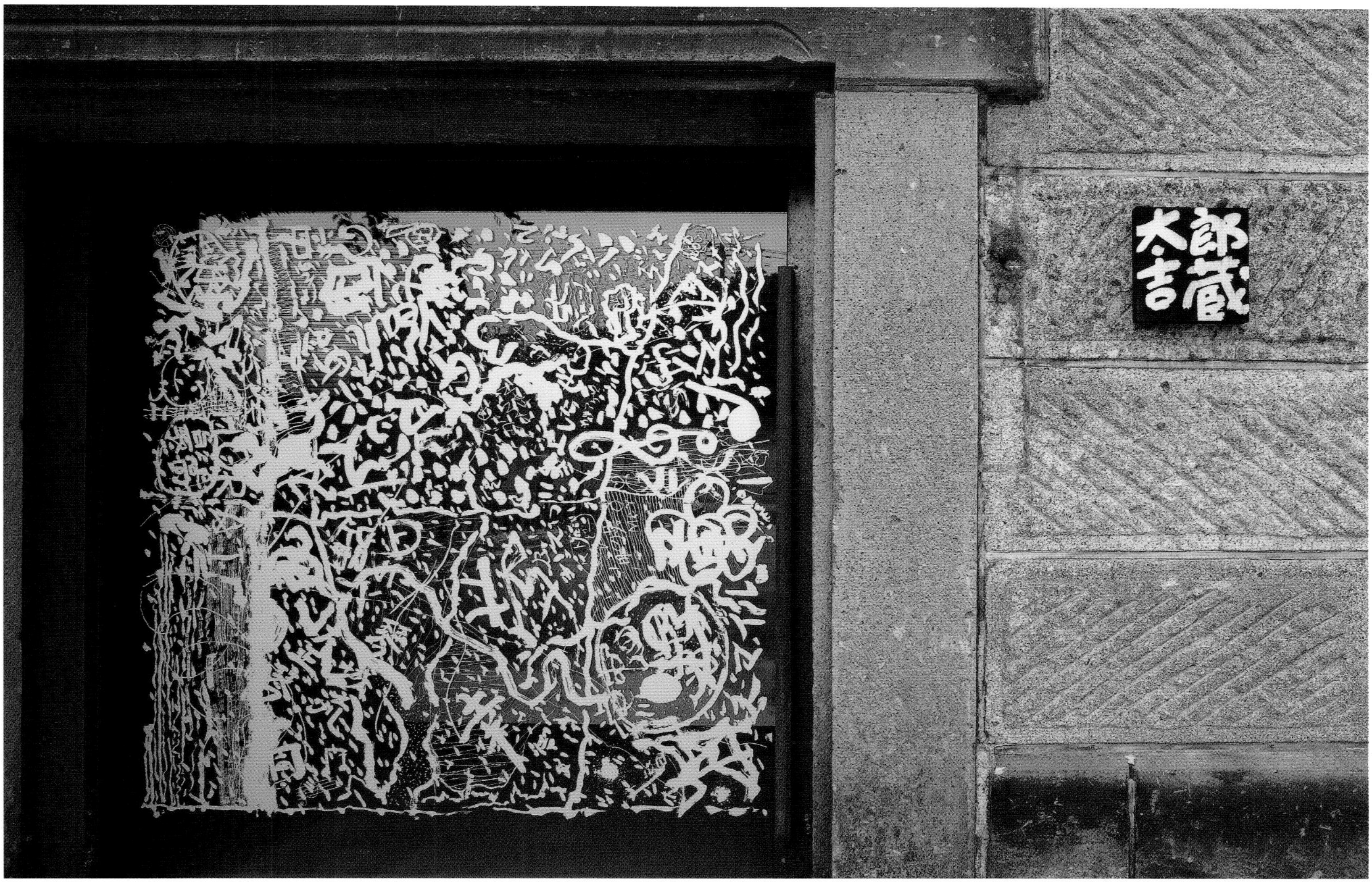

Automatic door at the entrance of Tarokichigura.
Igarashi silkscreened a design on the door
which was produced based on the hand drawings
of the local people.

"Operating costs are covered by membership fees and donations. We were able to get support from corporations, foundations, and government organizations at the beginning, but as time went on it became difficult to get support, partly due to competition with other NPOs. In spite of difficulties, we set up a design shop and an Italian restaurant within Hotel Miura kaen located just a few steps from Tarokichigura and Gallery COYA at the corner of the hotel's parking lot." The most successful activity of A.C.T. is the *Takikawa Kamibukuro Lantern Festival*. In 2014, over 14,000 lanterns made out of paper bags (kamibukuro) were displayed all over town for the 12th festival. The festival had become so popular that an executive committee was set up as an independent activity. With every citizen taking part in spite of freezing temperatures, the festival established itself as part of the winter landscape of Takikawa.

Igarashi Art Workshop has been held over thirty times, although its activities have been decreasing over the past seven or eight years. To solve this problem, Igarashi started the *Tarokichigura Design Conference*, a summer event in which seven to ten designers, architects, and artists talk openly and honestly about design. At the beginning, renowned designers were invited as panelists, but in recent years local designers and artists, including those working outside of Hokkaido, as well as other young promising talents, have also been invited, providing a generation change. All panelists and audiences participate at their own expenses, and the organization staff is made up of volunteers and A.C.T. members.

Kazenobi—Atelier and Gallery

While Igarashi was steadily active, he received an unexpected proposal from the Board of Education of Shin-Totsukawa-cho, the town neighboring Takikawa, asking him to renovate the old Yoshino Elementary School to use as an atelier and an exhibition space for his works. As if sent from heaven, the proposal came just when Igarashi was looking for a suitable space to store his sculptures. The old school is situated about a thirty-minute car ride from Takikawa, crossing the Ishikari River. The lush green hills are covered in snow during the harsh winter and on both sides of the road there are red arrows indicating the edge of the road as orientation for drivers in deep snow.

In 1889, approximately 2500 former residents of Totsukawa village in Nara prefecture moved to Hokkaido after a devastating flood destroyed their homes and fields. They established Shin-Totsukawa-cho, which means New Totsukawa-cho. The citizens of Shin-Totsukawa did not want to see the one-hundred-and-three-year-old elementary school with a rich history fall into decay, and were thinking of ways to preserve it after it closed. Igarashi's friend Yoshihiko Iida, architect and former professor at Yokohama National University, planned the restoration of the school building. Iida has also participated as a panelist at the Tarokichigura Design Conference. During the fourth *Tarokichigura Design Conference*, Kazenobi celebrated its grand opening on July 17, 2011. The name Kazenobi, deriving from the Japanese "kaze no bijutsukan," means "museum of the wind," which implies the nature of a new and refreshing art space like a wind blowing through the blessed land of the North. Among the works exhibited, *White Legend* is a gigantic piece in white ceramic, measuring 21 meters in length, and expressing the beauty of the winter landscape of Shin-Totsukawa. Every now and then Igarashi also holds workshops for children. In addition to the exhibition space, there is a café and a gift shop within the museum.

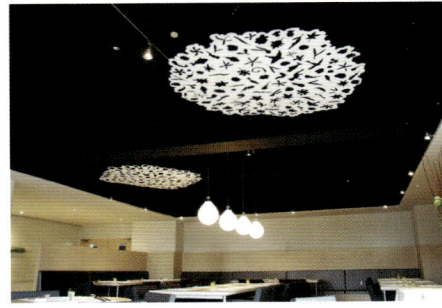

Interior design for the Italian restaurant il cielo. Team members from A.C.T. designed it for the hotel miura kaen, as an example of revitalization of the city.

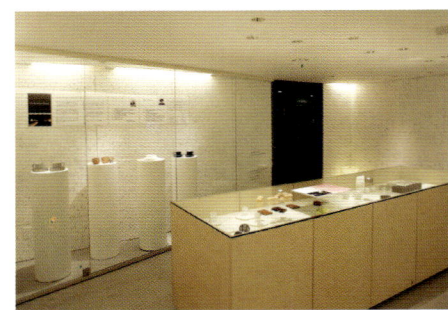

Located in hotel miura kaen, Takikawa design shop was created by Igarashi with the concept of "bringing nicely designed small products from all over the world to Takikawa."

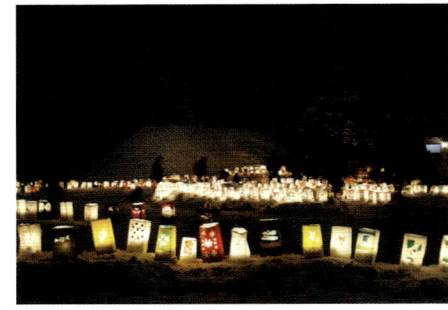

Takikawa Paper Lantern Festival, an event that A.C.T. has organized and managed with people from Takikawa since its establishment.

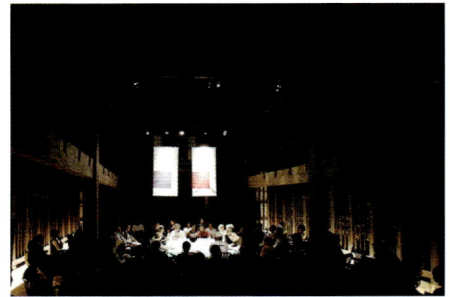

Tarokichigura Design Conference, started in 2007

Full view of Kazenobi in winter and autumn

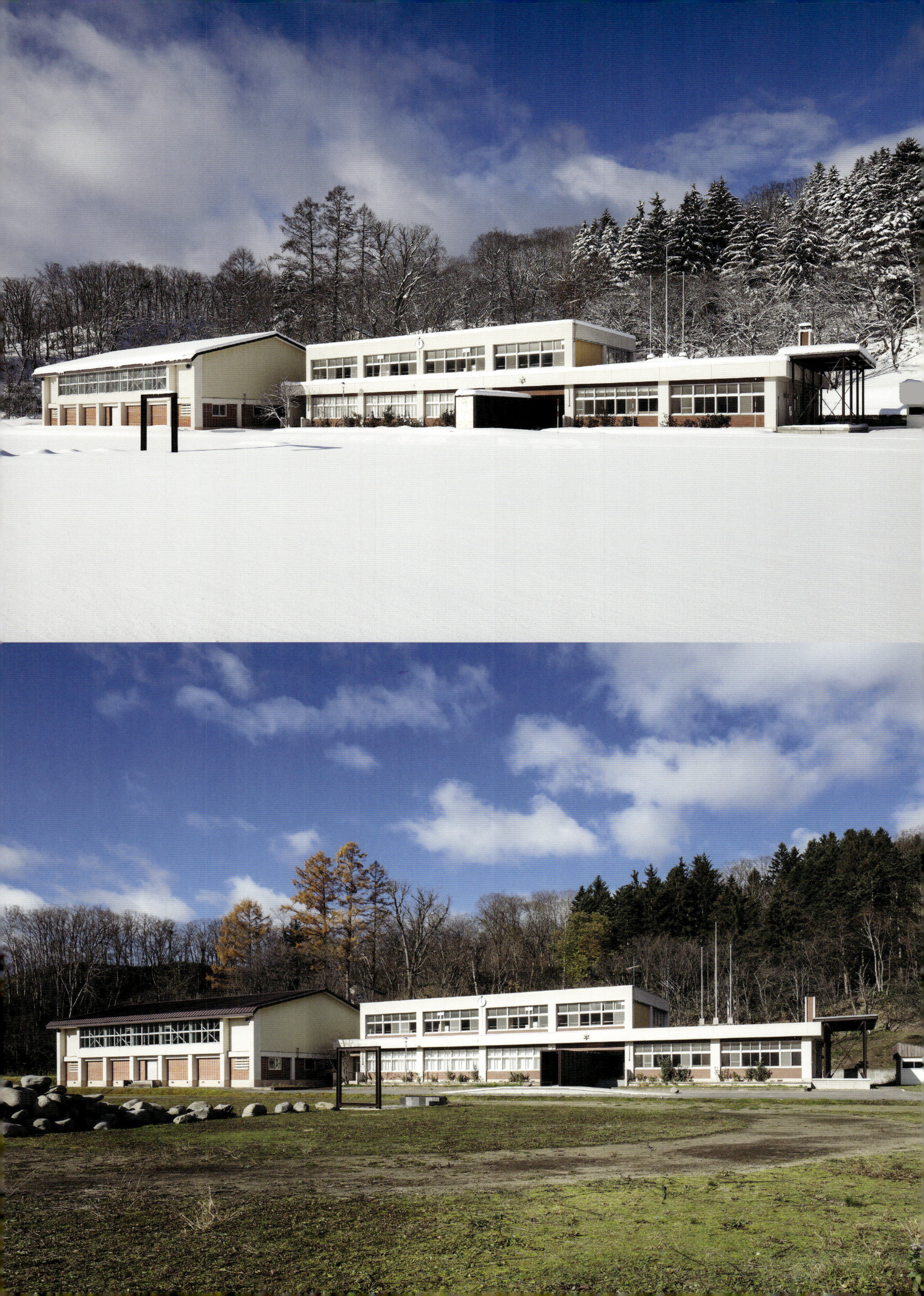

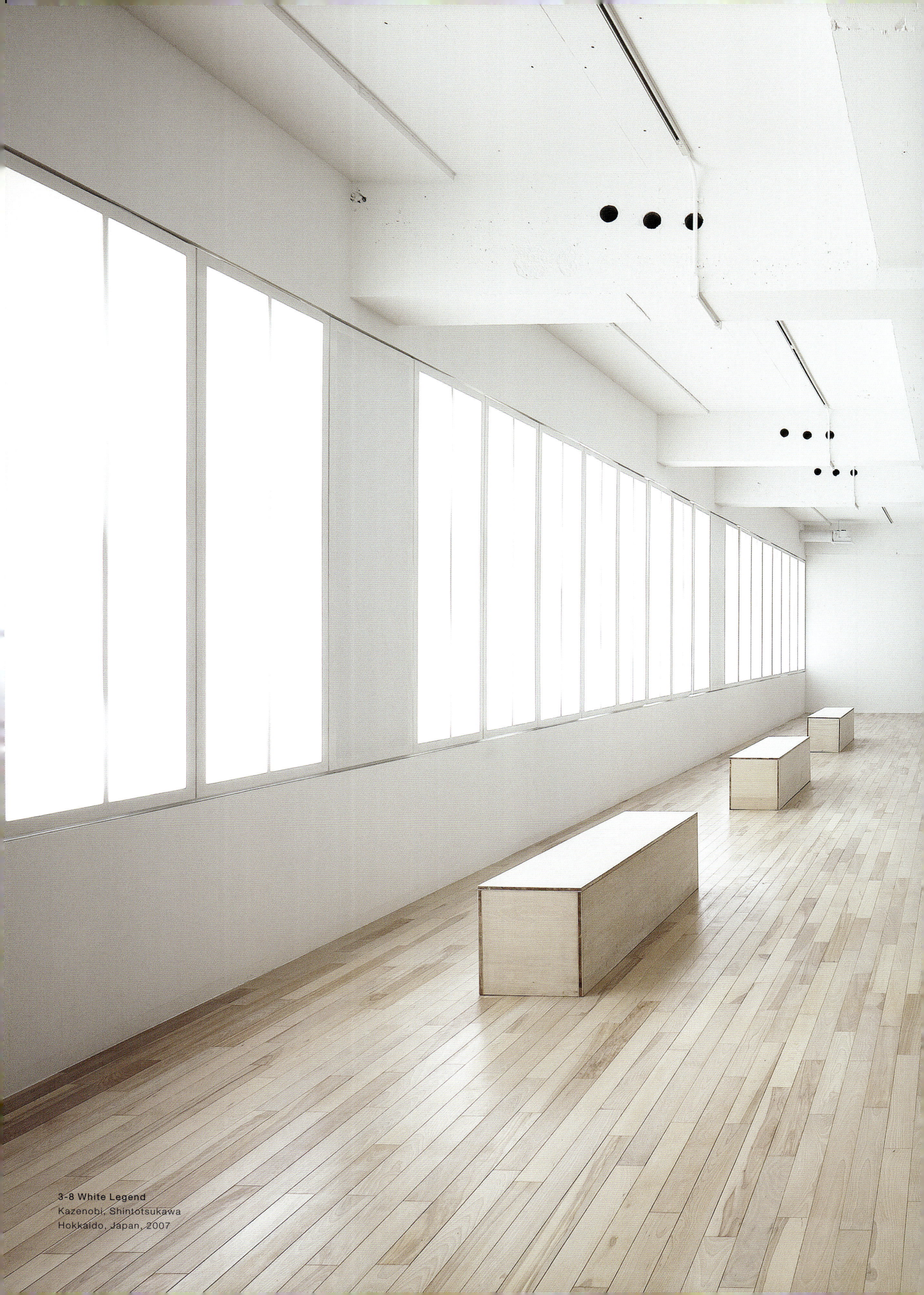

3-8 White Legend
Kazenobi, Shintotsukawa
Hokkaido, Japan, 2007

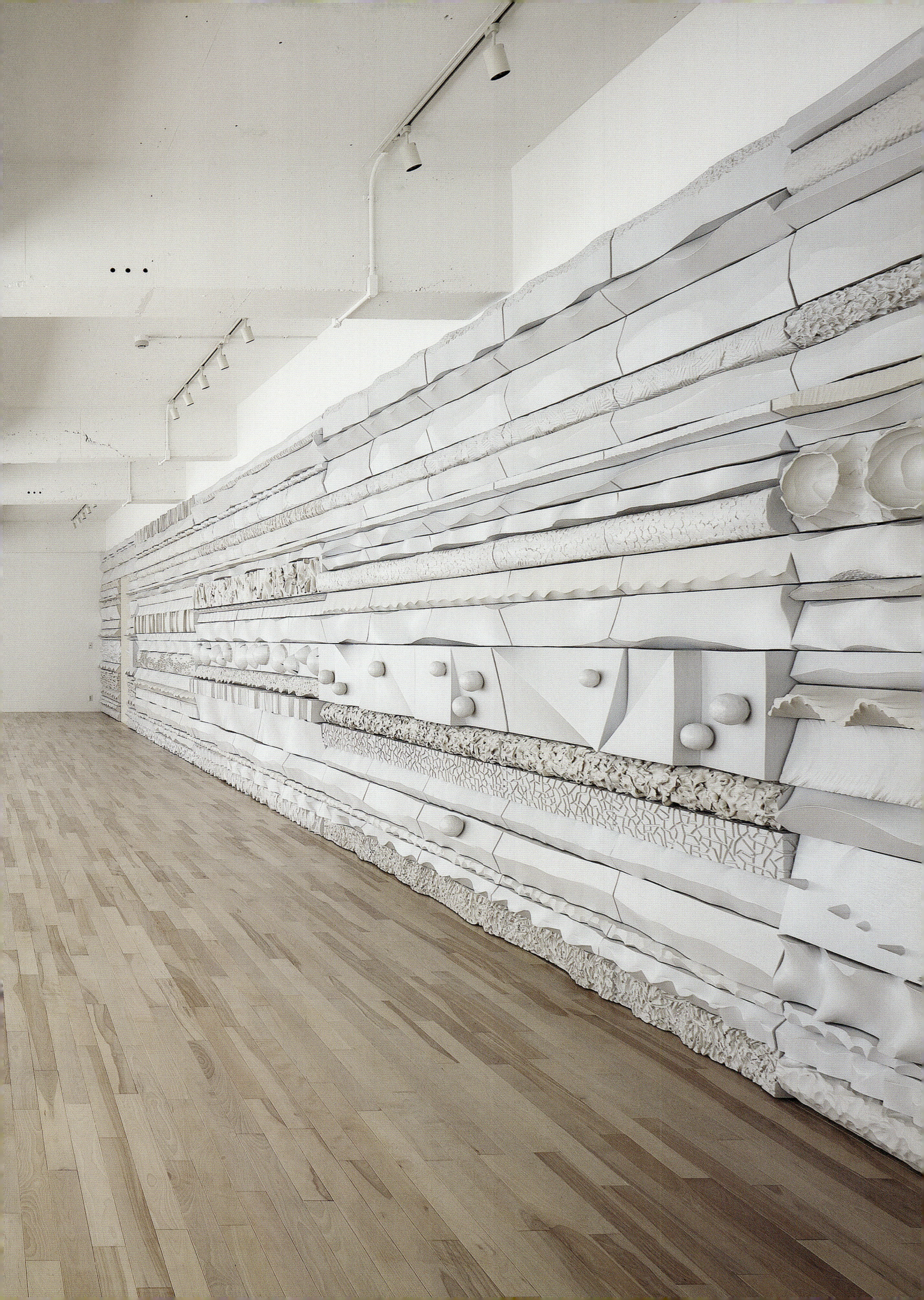

Activities Taking Root

Igarashi restored an old bakery at the corner of Hotel Miura Kaen's parking lot by his own initiative and expense, and created a new gallery named Gallery COYA, which was opened in 2013. Since Igarashi himself and his core collaborators were getting older, the gallery was made with the hopes of passing on the movement to the younger generation. This was thirteen years after he started his activities in Hokkaido, and nine years after the founding of A.C.T. The opening exhibition showed Igarashi's small ceramic pieces depicting the northern landscape. From the spring of 2014, young local artists have taken over to show their works. "Usually NPOs do not own real estate, but in our case we had Tarokichigura, our own space from the very beginning, which is very unique. And now we even have a gallery, and are expanding our sphere of activities."

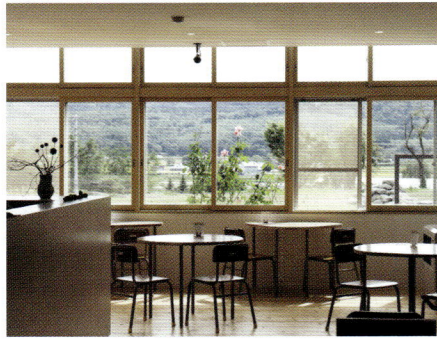

Cafe in Kazenobi

In keeping his personal activities separate from A.C.T.'s, Igarashi set up Kazenobi, that is an independent organization, as a general incorporated association with Yasushi Fujishima as Chairman. The rebuilding of Takikawa Dai-San (meaning 3rd) Elementary School where Igarashi attended as a child was planned to make it earthquake-proof. One of the requirements for the architecture competition was to incorporate art into the entire concept, which is very rare in Japan.

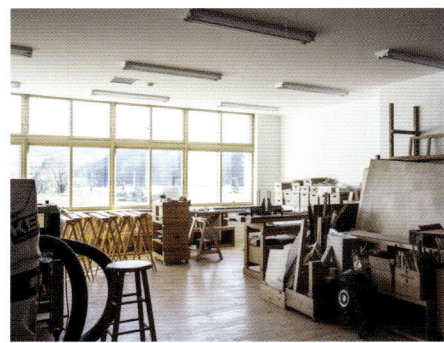

Atelier in Kazenobi

"The consciousness of the people had changed in the past years, that the members of the assembly, the administration, local people involved, and the citizens all took it for granted that art should also be incorporated into the new school building. There was no criticism like in the past against wasting tax money. It made me so happy to realize that all the activities we had been doing over the years were meaningful. They have totally changed the society and the way people think...for the new school building, three different art projects were planned. I worked together with all 400 children of the school on a relief piece using the wood floor of the old school gym. With the steel frame of the gym, I made an abstract sculpture in red placed outside, and then there is the number 3 sculpture placed on the outer wall of the building...Actually, I was thinking of using the 3 that I made for designer Michael Peters of London, whose design office had the address number 3. I wrote him a letter asking if he could donate the piece to the school, and he answered, 'When I sold the office, I took the sculpture to my vacation house, and my grandchild is always playing with it climbing up and down. So, if you could wait a few years...' (laughs).

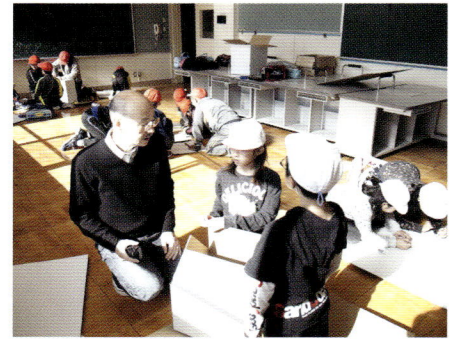

Workshop held in Kazenobi

So not being able to count on the old sculpture, it became difficult to realize the idea. But then those involved in the project managed to raise funds, and so I made a new 3, a variation of the 3 in London. Since the area has heavy snowfall, I had to shape it so that the snow does not slide down and injure the children."

As is apparent, the challenge Igarashi and his collaborators have taken on in shaping the future of the city through art is bearing fruit. As Igarashi states: "what is wonderful about art is that it crosses all boundaries like gender, age, nationality, and experience."[5]

[5] Chihiro Minato, "Art Challenge Takikawa: Creating an 'Ideal Homeland,'" *Art Bridge*, Vol. 1, March 23, 2015.

Entrance Hall on the first floor of Kazenobi

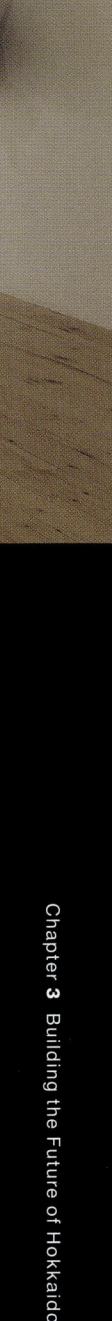

The Essence of Creativity

2015 marked another new phase in Igarashi's life. After being relieved of his heavy responsibilities as President of Tama Art University, he moved to Sapporo, choosing Hokkaido as his new center of activity and setting up his atelier within Kazenobi. Still seeking new challenges past the age of seventy is Igarashi's style and his way of life.

There is a famous Japanese proverb that states: "To return to one's hometown in glory," which is a triumphant return after achieving success and fame. In Igarashi's case, it is a bit different. In spite of his international fame, his activities in his hometown are not those of looking down from above, but those of grass taking root in the Mother Earth of the North, with his affection for the nature of Sorachi that nurtured him. Through setting up Gallery COYA and by actively appointing young panelists for the *Tarokichigura Design Conference*, Igarashi supports the next generation. He has not forgotten his debt of gratitude toward Ikko Tanaka and Shiro Kuramata, who had advised and supported him in his young days. The expression of his gratitude combined with his strong sense of responsibility form the basis of his unselfish efforts in building the future of his hometown.

One of his most recent works is a stained glass piece for the Shin-Hakodate-Hokuto Station of the new Hokkaido Shinkansen Line that opened in 2016. It is a massive piece measuring 16 meters in width. Unlike the usual method of placing the design within a straight metal frame or a circle, the piece, using German hand-blown glass and the newest technology, is made of free forms and LED lights replacing natural light. Another project is the ceramic relief for the Tancho Kushiro Airport. Both works are based on Igarashi's methodology of improvisation and chance. "Basically, it is made by cutting out different colored pieces of paper and dropping them on a piece of white paper. The accidentally resulting picture is then photographed and used as the original. Of course, I do choose the angle and adjust the perspective. I use Japanese curved scissors to cut the colored paper. The scissors are handy and can cut very fine curves. It is just amazing how a simple tool can help."

Igarashi's discovery of a new tool leads him to an unknown world. His playfulness and free will in creating his sculptures is similar to that found in Henri Matisse's cutouts. "The wonderful environment really eases my soul. The fields and paddies around change their appearance and color in time. Nature is full of life manifesting and asserting itself. You cannot see such colors in the city, such as you see here like the colors of trees and fields or clouds. And all the colors vanish and become white in winter. There is nothing comparable to the experience of working within this drama of nature."

At present time, several assistants help Igarashi at different stages of production, which is a relief that allows him more time. Visitors also bring fresh motivation and encouragement. All these changes are reflected in his new works. In summer 2016, Igarashi made a gigantic piece, *Komorebi*, which consisted of 28 plywood panels measuring 3x2.3 meters each for the former gym in Kazenobi, where he has set up his atelier. *Fragments of Memory*, mostly forms of nature as motifs, are cut out using a hand router. Compared to the earlier *Komorebi* series, the cutout pieces have become larger in size and more dynamic. Now Igarashi is more at ease while working, relieves the strain put on the tools and allows him to accomplish tasks faster—in the past the blade would burn and break, which seldom happens now.

The essence of Igarashi's creative journey is expressed in his own words: "I make. I just make without planning, whether it be logos, illustrations, modeling, or sculptures. I feel that it is not a pure act to plan the making...the pure act of making is just doing. In the process of doing, I am guided through inspiration, giving birth to new images. I think this is, after all, what fulfills my heart with satisfaction."

Written by: Shoji Usuda
Design journalist
Born 1943 in Nagano prefecture, Japan

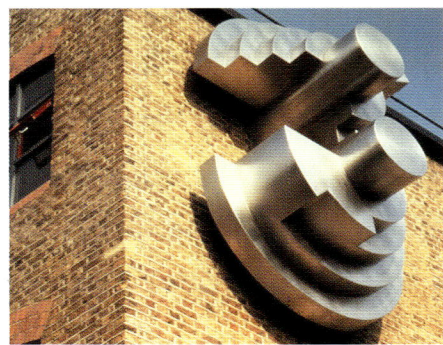

3-9 Sculpture 3
Michael Peters Group, London, England, 1985

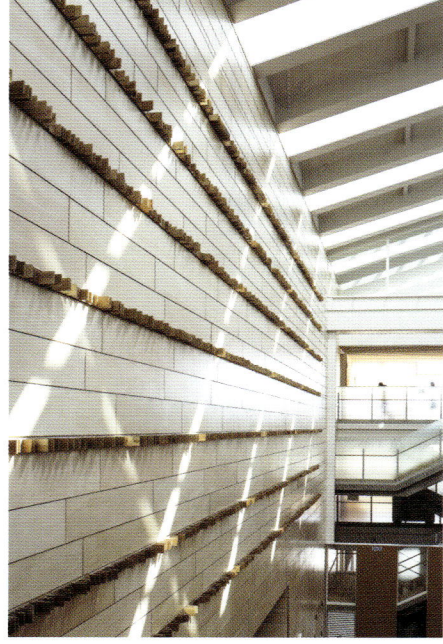

3-10 Wooden Relief
Takikawa Daisan Elementary School
Takikawa, Hokkaido, Japan, 2015
Produced with the corporation of the whole school, 400 elementary students in total.

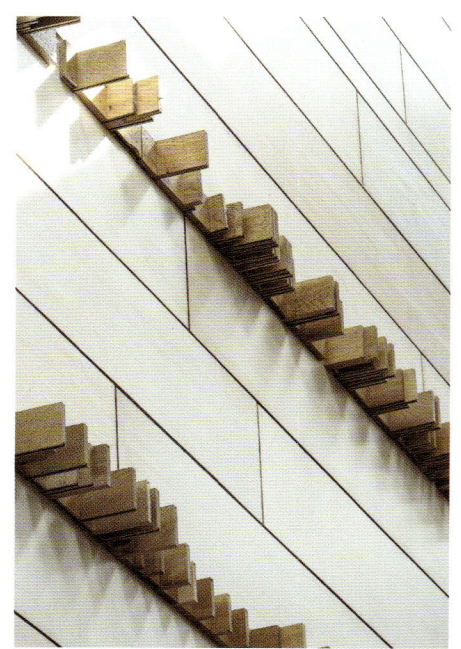

Wooden Relief, detail

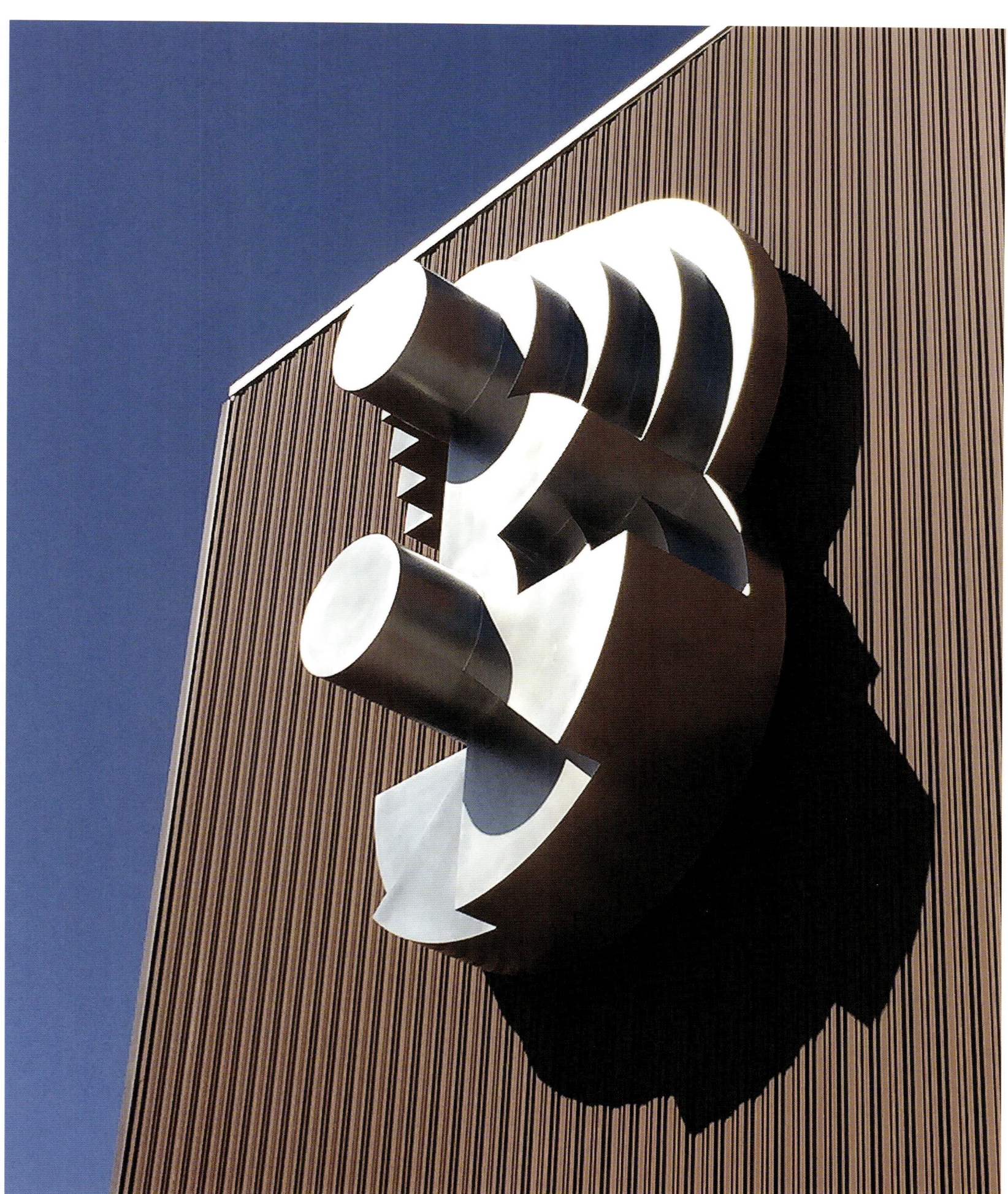

3-11 Sculpture 3
Stainless Steel, Takikawa Daisan Elementary School
Takikawa, Hokkaido, Japan, 2015

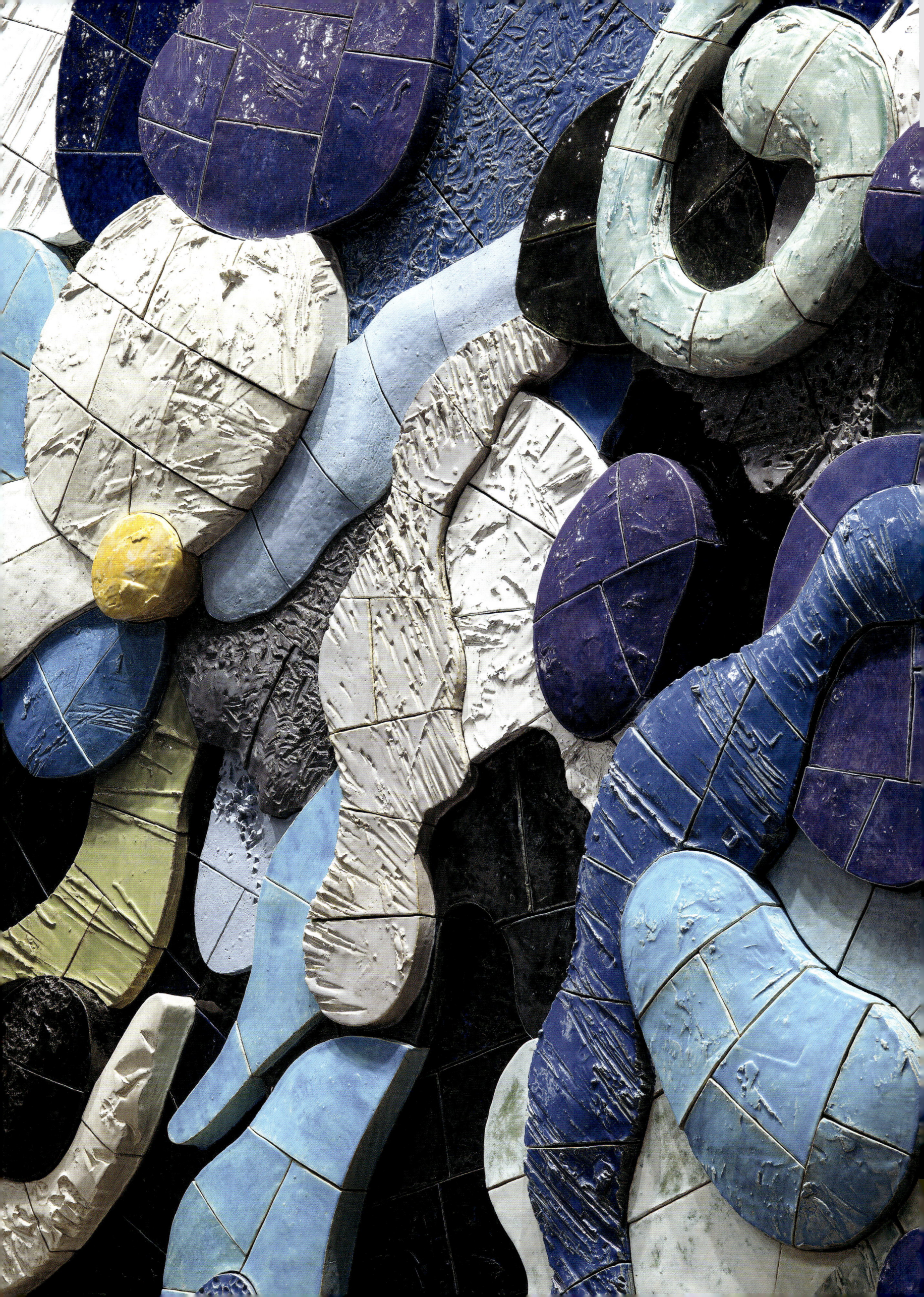

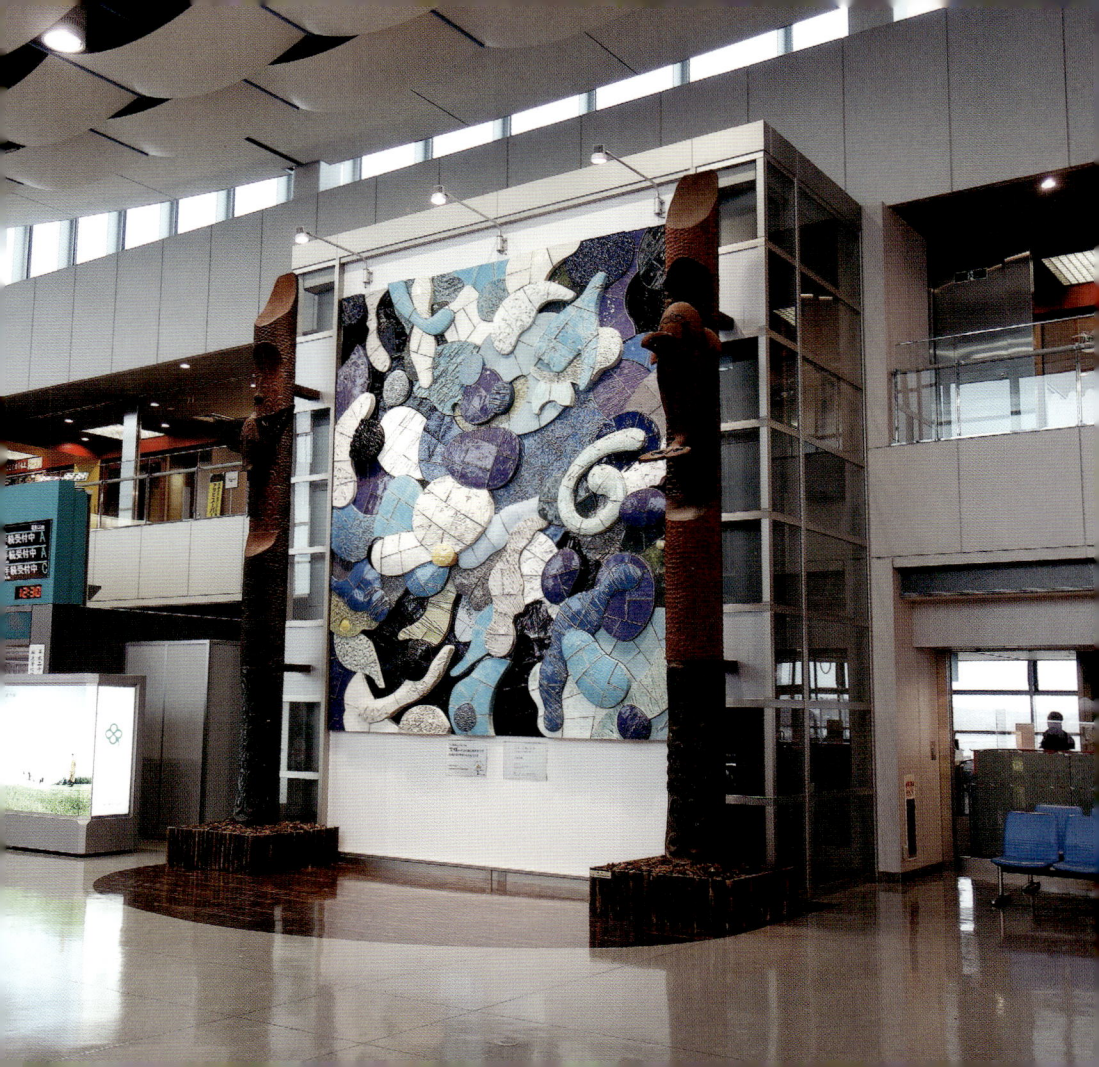

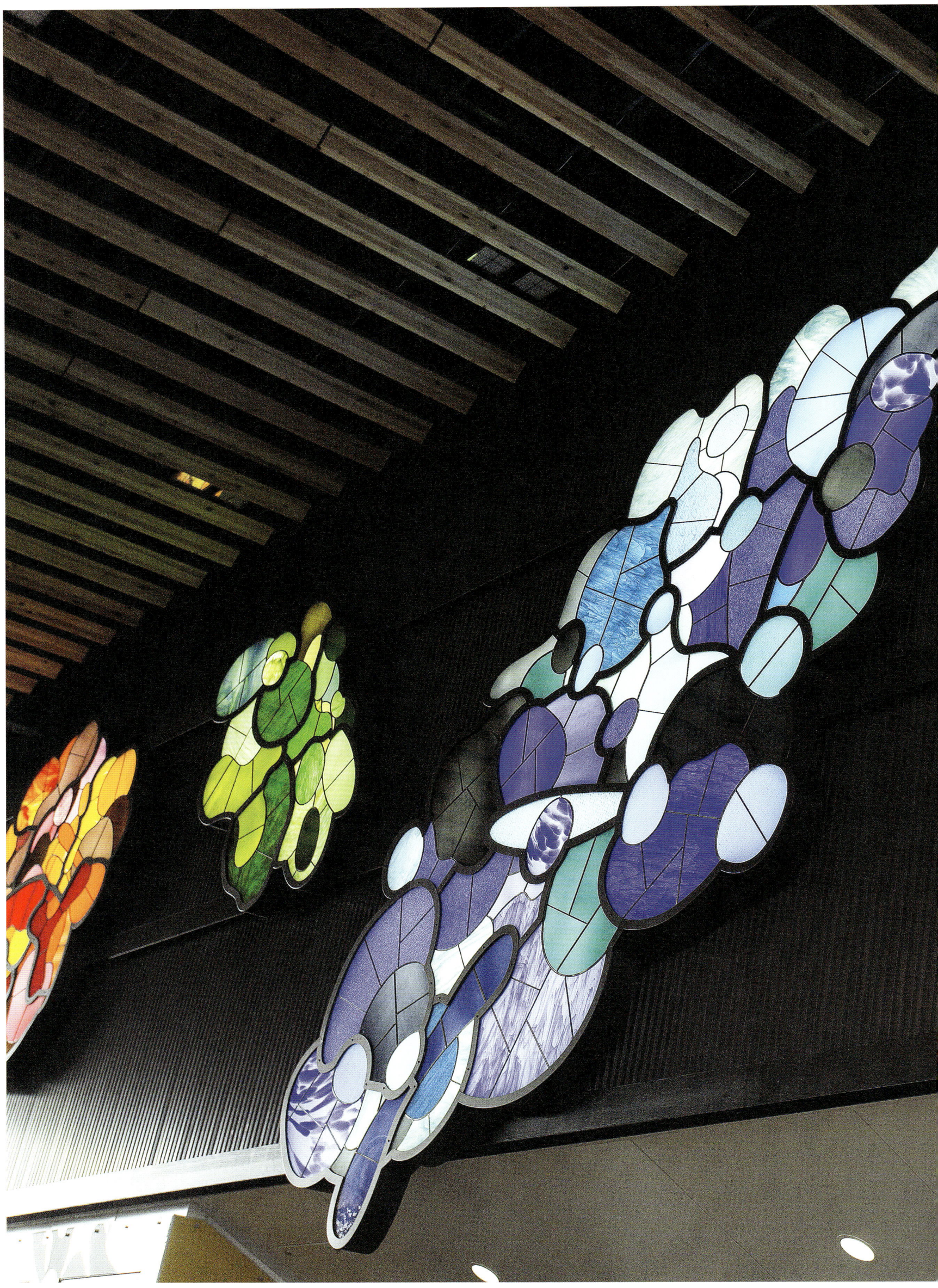

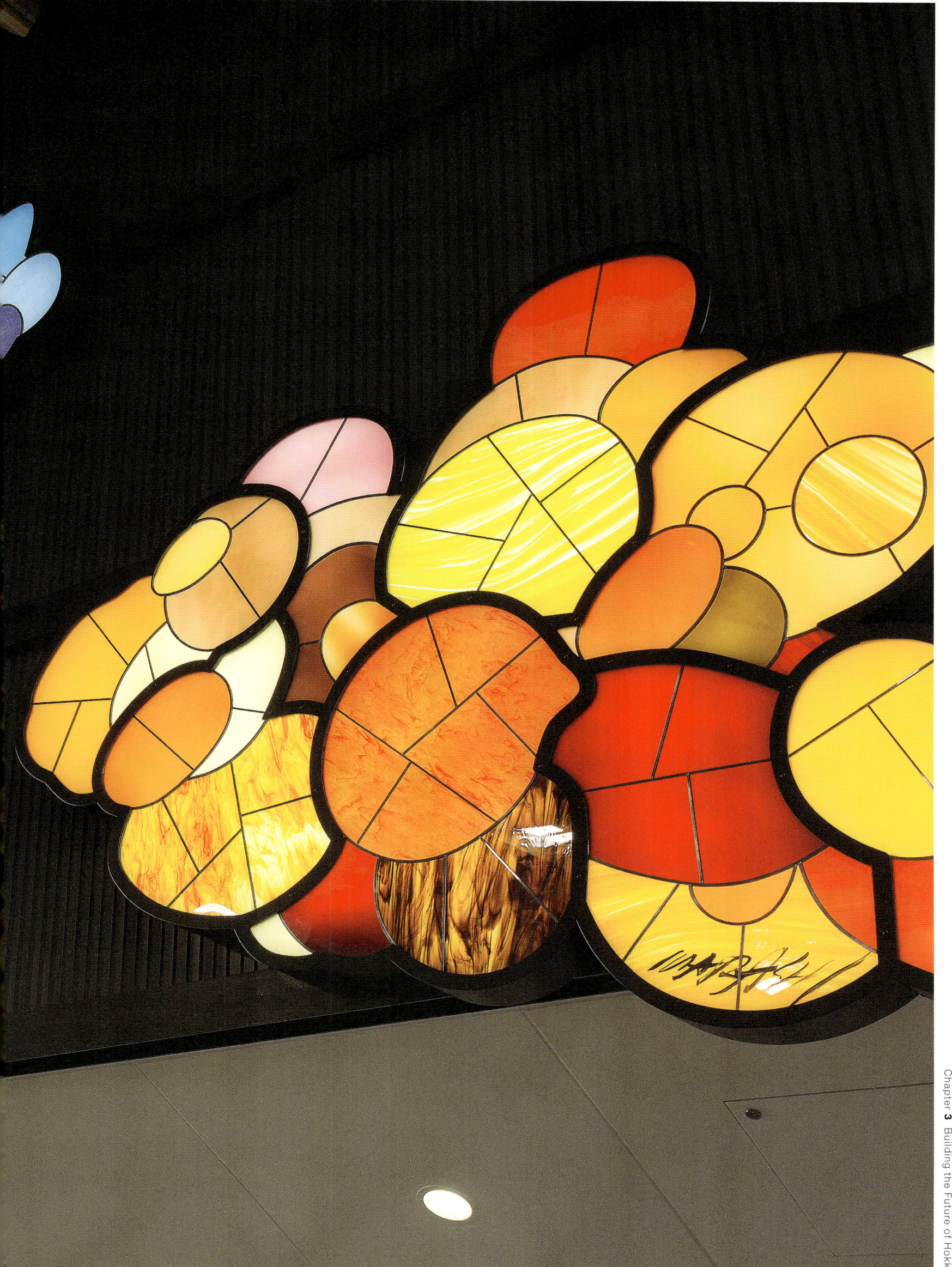

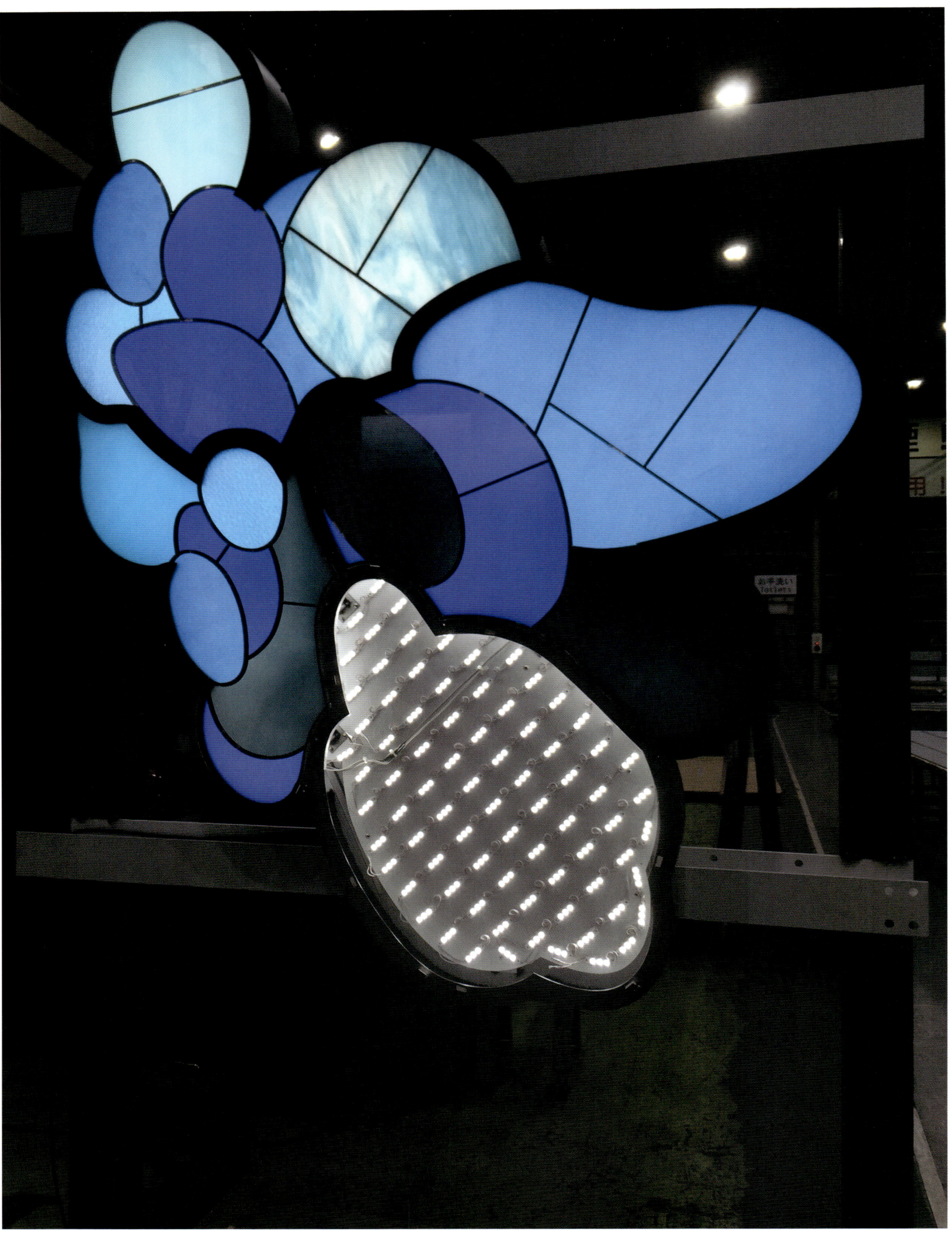

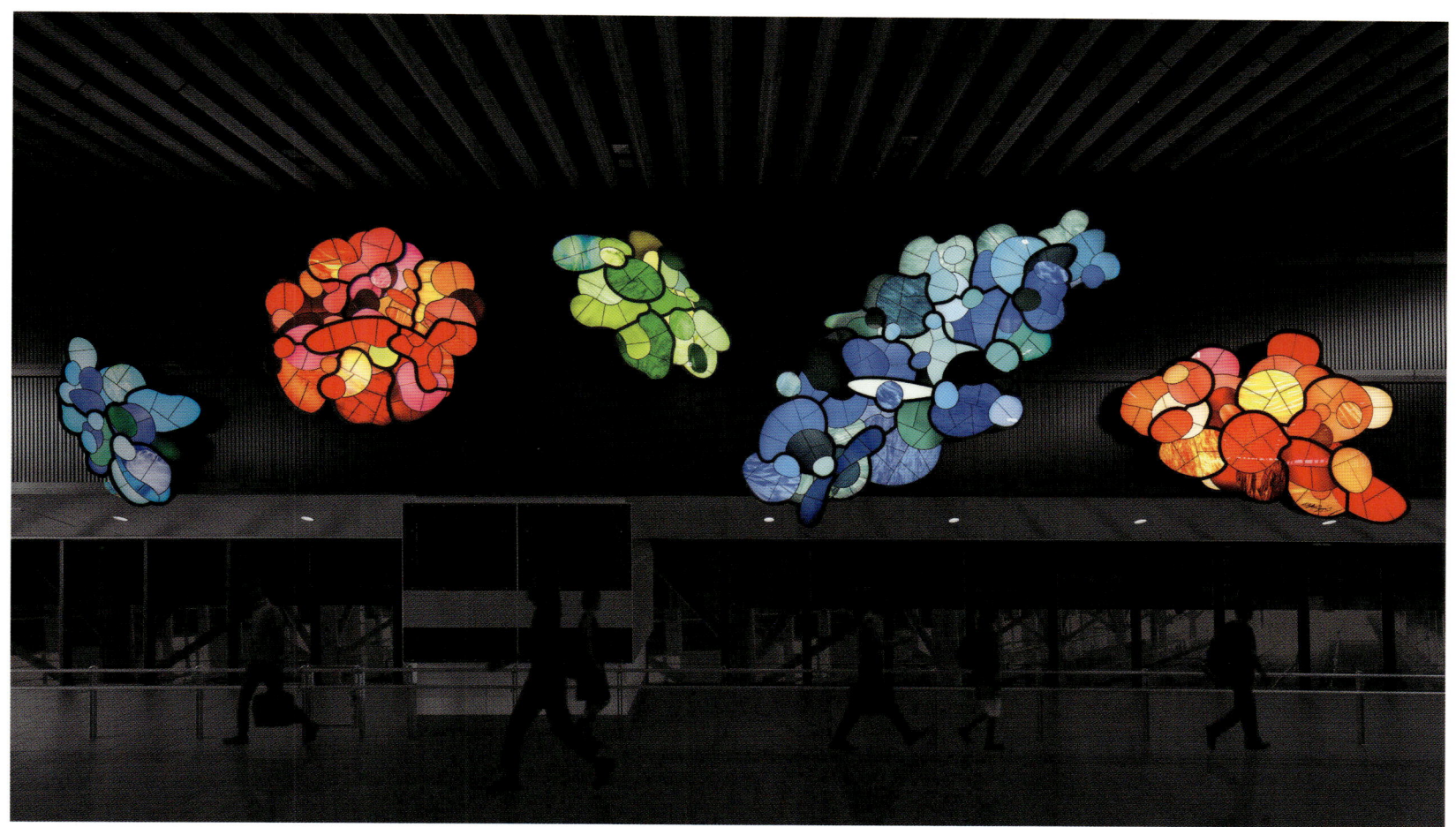

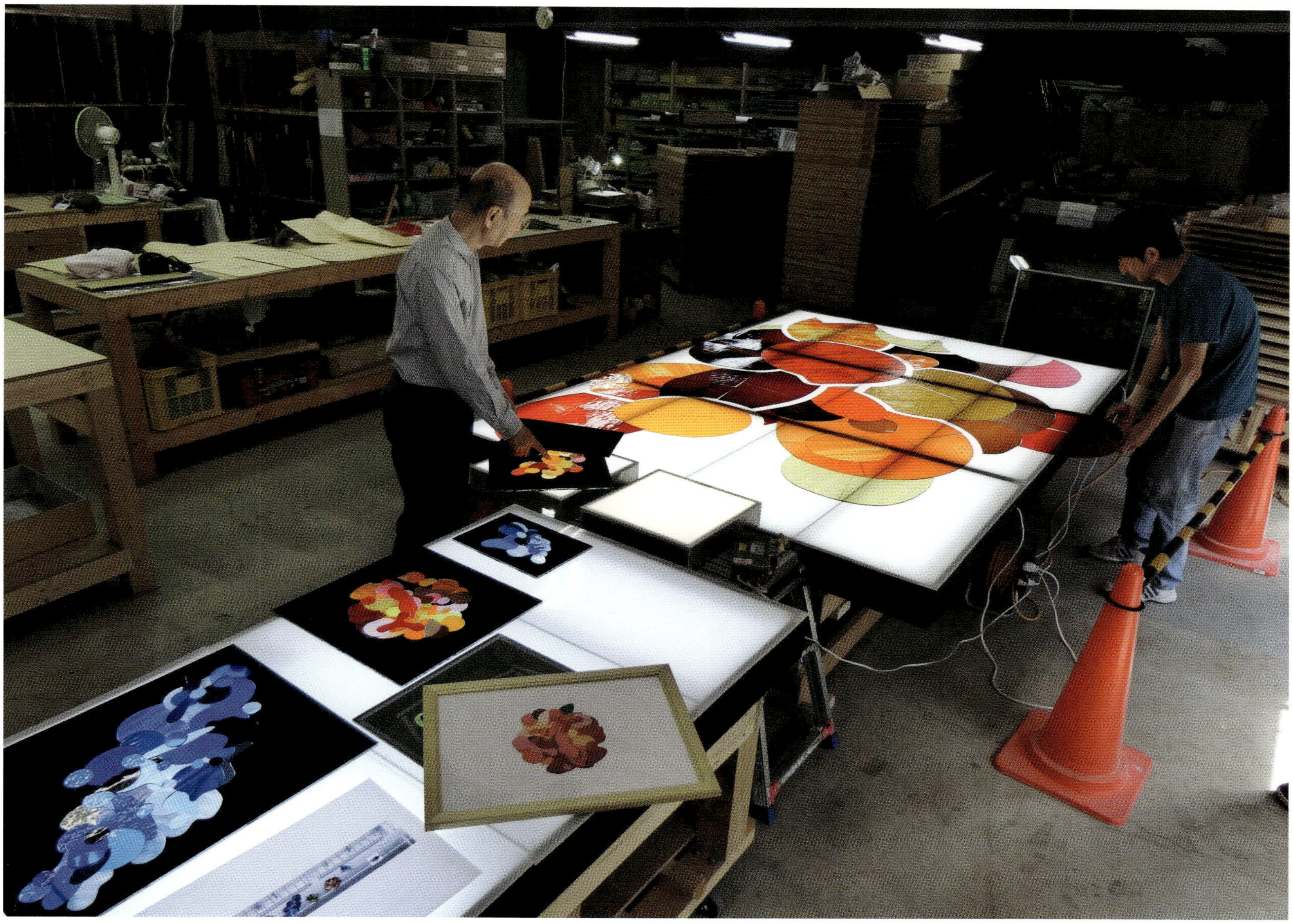

3-13 Muku Muku
Homage to Water, Sun and Land
Shin Hakodate Hokuto Station
Hokuto, Hokkaido, Japan, 2016

279

Igarashi producing Komorebi series at a workshop in Kazenobi

3-14 Memorial Monument for Shintotsukawa Municipal
Shintosukawa, Hokkaido, Japan, 2009

I used 103 stones to represent the 103-year-long history of the elementary school. (TI)

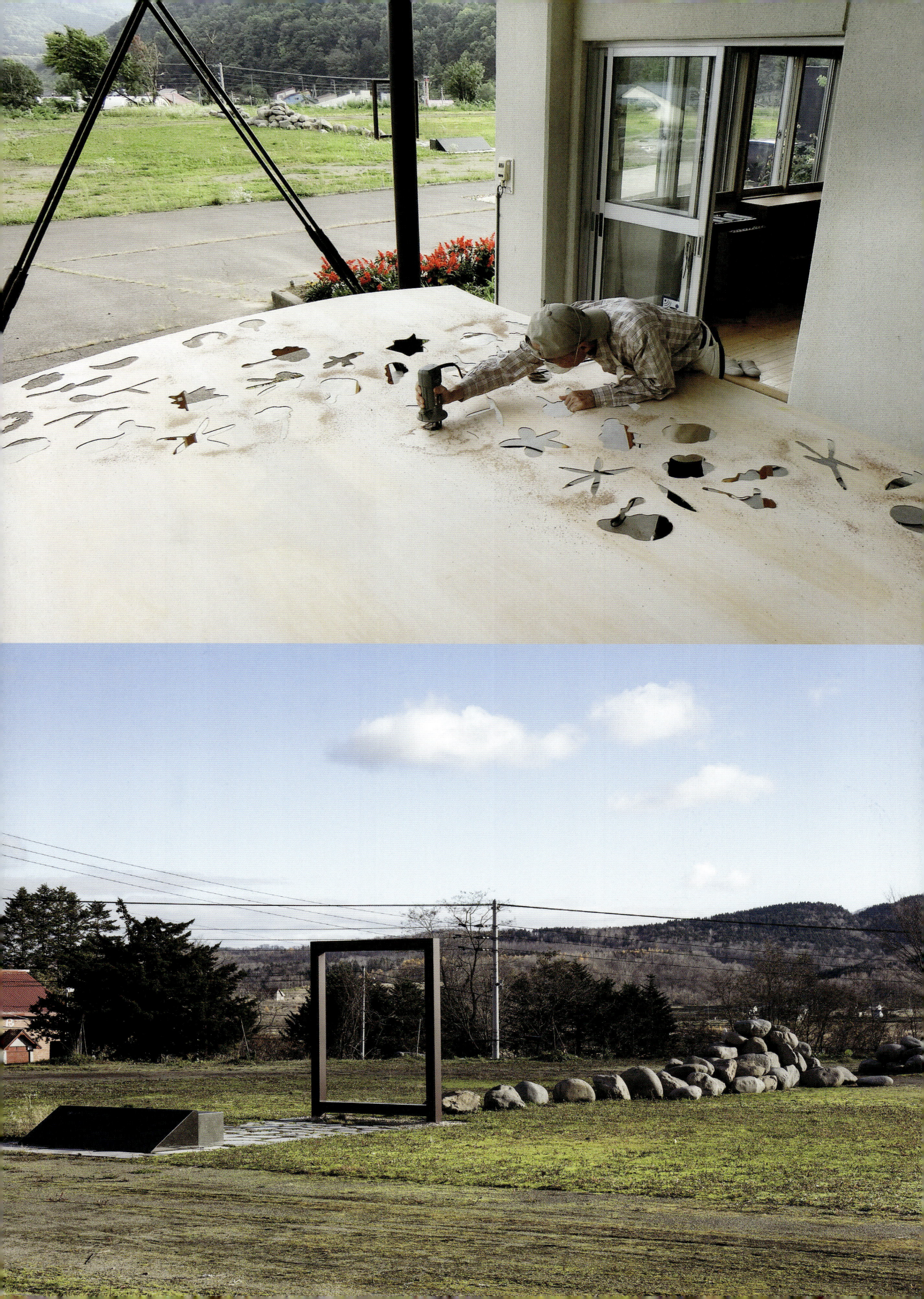

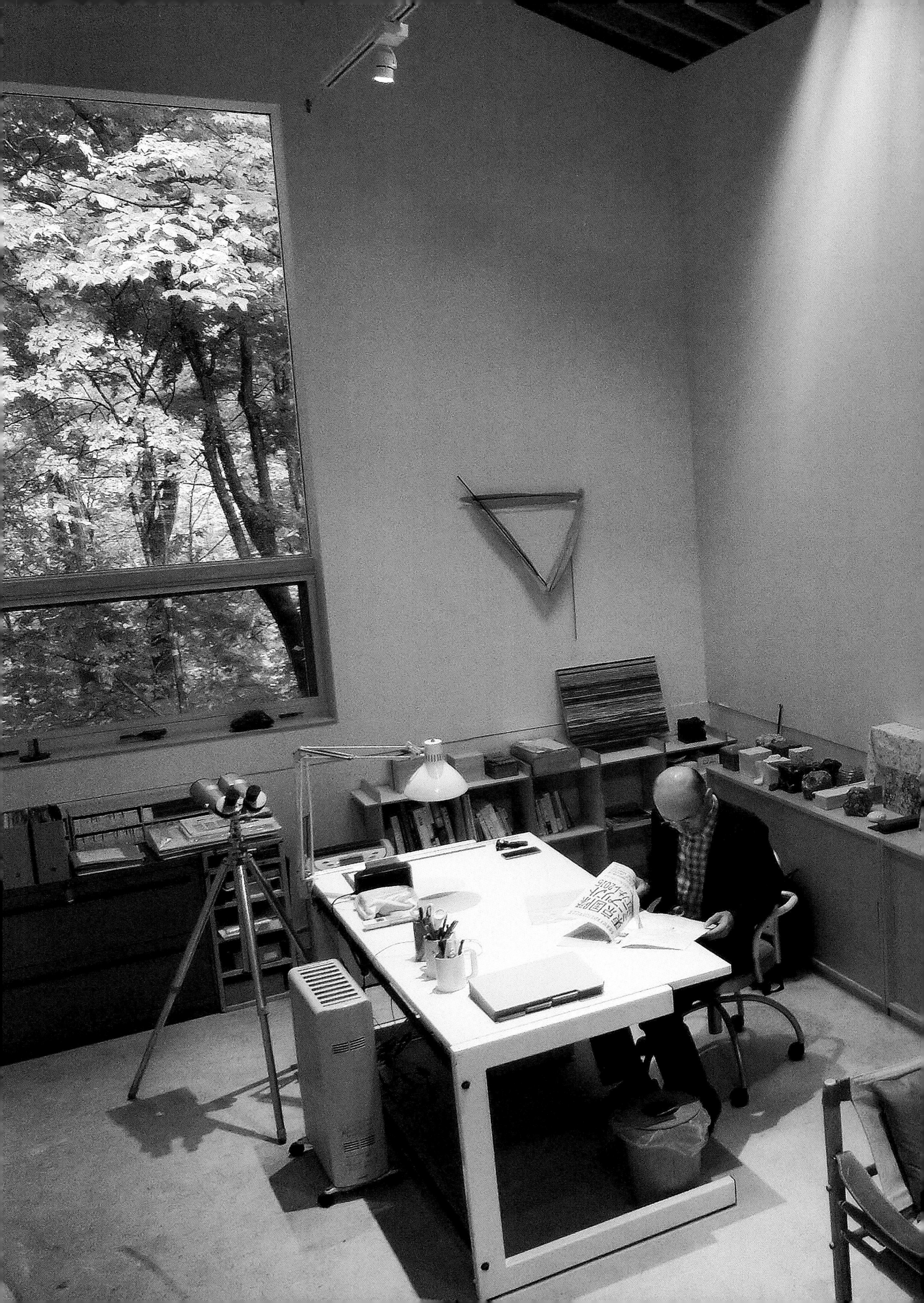

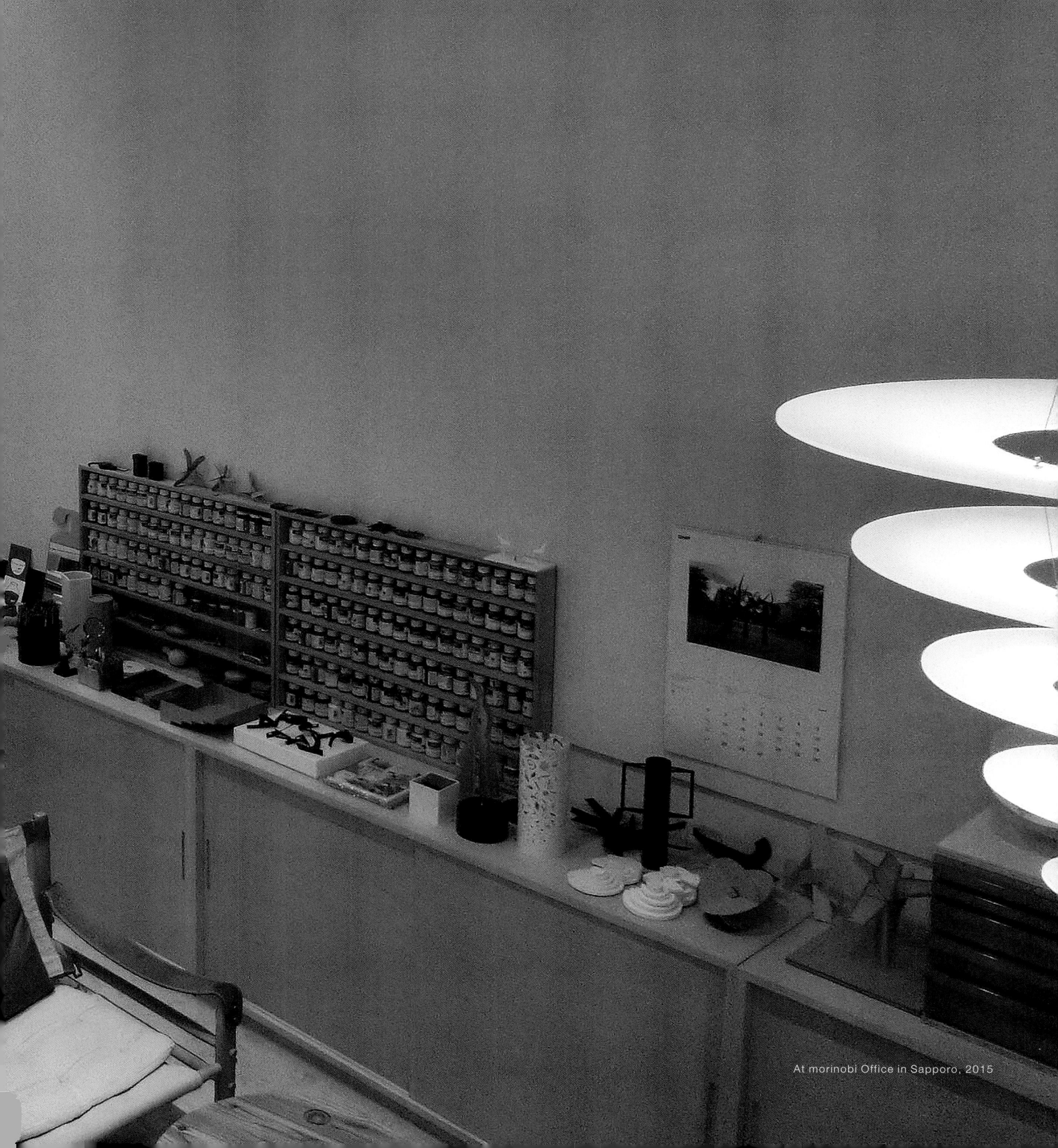

At morinobi Office in Sapporo, 2015

Bibliography

Adachi, Hiroshi. et al. (2009) *Saisei Meikenchiku – Toki o Koeru Design 1*. Tokyo: Kajima Institute Publishing Co., Ltd.

Igarashi, Takenobu. (2012) *Terra-cotta*. Igarashi Atelier.

Igarashi, Takenobu. (1987) *Igarashi Alphabets From Graphics to Sculptures*. Zurich: ABC Verlag.

Igarashi, Takenobu. (1983) *Igarashi Space Graphics*. Tokyo: Shoten Kenchiku-sha Co., Ltd.

Ingold, Tim. (2007) *Lines: A Brief History*. Abingdon: Routledge.

Meggs, Philip B. (1998) *A History of Graphic Design*. New York: John Wiley & Sons, Inc.

Minato, Chihiro. (2015) "Art Challenge Takikawa: Creating an 'Ideal Homeland.'" *Art Bridge*. Vol. 1, March 23.

Nachmanovitch, Stephen. (1990) *Free Play: Improvisation in Life and Art*. New York: Jeremy P. Tarcher/Penguin.

Appendix

Takenobu Igarashi | Biography

1944 — Takenobu Igarashi was born in Takikawa, Hokkaido as the youngest son of Ichiro and Katsuno Igarashi.

1951 Age 7 — Moved to Kugenuma Beach, Kanagawa-ken for a year of convalescence by a physician's recommendation.

1952 Age 8 — Returned to Takikawa and started to take lessons in watercolor and oil painting from Masumi Ichiki every Sunday.
Started making his own toys using a set of carpenter's tools given to him by his parents.

1955 Age 11 — His father died.

1956 Age 12 — Moved to Tokyo to live with older brother and sister. Got to know sculptor Michio Ihara.
Through the influence of his architect uncle Tadashi Igarashi, became interested in design.

1960 Age 16 — Entered Toyama Metropolitan High School, but not being able to adjust to the stiff atmosphere, transferred to Seijo Gakuen High School after a year.

1961 Age 17 — Was disappointed to find out that the World Design Conference was held in Tokyo a year before.

1962 Age 18 — Attended the Visual Design Institute led by Professor Masato Takahashi at the Tokyo University of Education and learned about Bauhaus-style basic design. Became interested in Max Bill's work. Impressed by poster design of Kohei Sugiura, Kiyoshi Awazu, Yusaku Kamekura, Ikko Tanaka, Kazumasa Nagai, and Makoto Wada.

1964 Age 20 — Entered the Design Department of Tama Art University. Was strongly influenced by Akio Kanda (graphic design), Yasutaka Kokubu (psychology), and Kenji Imai (architecture).
Parallel to his studies worked for Akio Kanda.

1968 Age 24 — Graduated from Tama Art University with "Pictograms as International Language" as his Bachelor's degree final project.
After graduation worked as assistant at the newly established design laboratory.
Entered graduate school at University of California, Los Angeles (UCLA).
Participated in a design seminar held by the Danish Institute. After staying three weeks in Copenhagen, Denmark, traveled to Paris and New York.

1969 Age 25 — Received master's degree from UCLA after a year and a half, studying under Professors Mitsuru Kataoka, Robert Heinecken, John Neuhart, and Morio Shinoda.
Was invited to prominent art-collector Frederick R. Weisman's house.
Traveled through the United States, driving 16,000 km with a car.
Visited Professor Gyorgy Kepes at MIT.
Impressed by Claes Oldenburg's soft sculpture exhibited at MoMA.

1970 Age 26 — Established his office in Tokyo.
Became acquainted with Shiro Kuramata, Shigeru Uchida, Takamichi Ito, Shintaro Tanaka, Tomio Miki, Mitsumasa Fujitsuka, and Hiroshi Awatsuji.

1973 Age 29 — Had a one-man show titled Animal Illustrations at Fujie Gallery through Shiro Kuramata's recommendation, marking his breakthrough as a designer.

1974 Age 30 — Logo and poster design for ZEN Environmental Design resulting in a long-lasting friendship with Zenichi Nakamura.

1975 Age 31 — Was a full-time lecturer at UCLA.
Became acquainted with John Whitney, Don Chadwick, and Charles and Ray Eames, with whom he maintained a long-lasting relationship.

1979 Age 35 — Was invited by Akira Sazen to be a part-time lecturer at Chiba University, Department of Design (1979–1983).

1980 Age 36 — On Board of Directors for JAGDA until 1996.
Became the youngest member of Alliance Graphique Internationale (AGI) through recommendations from Walter Herdeg of Graphis and British graphic designer F.H.K. Henrion.

1981 Age 37 — His mother died.

1982 Age 38 — Became acquainted with Katsumie Masaru.

1983 Age 39 — Served six years (two terms) as Executive Committee (IEC) member of AGI.
Became friends with Alan Fletcher, Ruedi Rüegg, Rolf Müller, Pierre Mendell, and Massimo Vignelli.
Architectural Alphabet exhibition at Reinhold Brown Gallery, New York.

1984 Age 40 — Designed a shopping bag for MoMA and started to design calendars with three-dimensional numbers. Designed different items for MoMA until 2004.
Lecture on alphabet works at the Smithsonian Institution in Washington D.C.
Around this time got to know Saul Bass, April Greiman, Deborah Sussman, John Follis, James Miho, Lou Dorfsman, Henry Wolf, and Ivan Chermayeff.

1986 Age 42 — Lecture at the Stanford Conference on Design at Stanford University.
Hibiki sculpture and logo, poster, and sign design for Suntory Hall.

1987 Age 43 — Takenobu Igarashi's Sculpture and Print exhibition at Yurakucho Asahi Gallery, Tokyo.
Igarashi Alphabets was published by ABC Verlag, Switzerland.
Served as executive consultant for Suntory's OUN project together with Alan Fletcher and Massimo Vignelli.

1988 Age 44 — Lecture at the International Design Conference, Aspen, Colorado.
Set up secretariat for the AGI Congress in Tokyo.
Due to the changes occurring in the organization, the relationship to AGI became distant after finishing his term as IEC the following year.

1989 Age 45	Was visiting professor at UCLA Design Department until 1991. Set up Faculty of Art and Communication Evening Division at Tama Art University. Served as Head of Design Department until 1993. Developed YMD products for Yamada Shomei Lighting Co., Ltd. in collaboration with local and traditional industries known for their outstanding craftsmanship. The products were sold in American and European museum stores. Selected as one of 100 members of AppleMasters. Won the Japan Design Committee's Second Katsumie Masaru Award. Awarded the Commendation of the Minister of Foreign Affairs for contributing to the success of the Poster Contest for the conservation of nature in Africa.		**2002** Age 58	Designed the giant Star Clock for JR Sapporo station. Started traveling frequently to Hokkaido. Started "Igarashi Art Workshop" in Takikawa. Terracotta sculpture Landscape for Sapporo JR Tower.
			2003 Age 59	Established NPO Art Challenge Takikawa (A.C.T.) together with friends. Invited by Japan Society in New York to give a lecture about recent activities.
			2004 Age 60	Sculpture Dragon Spine (Nyoki Nyoki) for Ichinosakanishi Park, Takikawa including the design of the surrounding environment Mizu no Hiroba with Koji Saito. 20 years after attaining his US permanent residency, he returned to Japan in June, setting up his atelier in Akiya, Kanagawa-ken. With the opening of Tarokichigura, activities in Hokkaido increased.
1990 Age 46	Lecture about his work at the TED2 Conference, Monterey, California. Designed the opening visual image of a 3D number for the conference. Got acquainted with Richard Saul Wurman.		**2005** Age 61	DVD "Mirai e no Tobira – Jonetsu, Hakken, Chosen" produced by Sapporo's UHB television station.
			2006 Age 62	Received Special Prize of Mainichi Design Award.
1993 Age 49	Had a one-man exhibition Takenobu Igarashi Grafik, Produkt, Skulptur at the Deutsches Plakat Museum in Essen as part of the events for "Year of Japan 1993" in Germany. Got acquainted with Dieter Rams of Braun GmbH.		**2007** Age 63	First Design Conference held at Tarokichigura.
			2009 Age 65	Maquette Exhibition at designshop+gallery, Tokyo. Was featured in NHK's program "Kagai Jugyo Youkoso Senpai / Omoi o Katachi ni Shitemiyou."
1994 Age 50	Had a one-man exhibition Takenobu Igarashi Graphics, Products, Sculptures at the Modern Art Museum, Ostend, Belgium. Moved to Los Angeles to work as a sculptor.		**2010** Age 66	Opening of Kazenobi, Takenobu Igarashi's atelier and museum at Shin-Totsukawa-cho, Hokkaido.
			2011 Age 67	Became the ninth president of Tama Art University. Forest of Terminus installed at Sapporo station's underground plaza PASEO.
1995 Age 51	Lectured at the Smithsonian Institution. Had a one-man sculpture exhibition at Hosomi Gallery, Tokyo. Logo design of Tama Art University.		**2012** Age 68	The Mother Earth, sculpture with fountain and bench installed at Akasaka K-Tower, Tokyo. In Praise of Forest, Ocean and People installed at Ota City General Gymnasium.
1996 Age 52	Kumo sculpture installed at Azabu Juban shopping district.		**2014** Age 70	Was invited to do a lecture "Shunkan ni Umareru Mono" by the Japanese Society for the Science of Design. North Wind installed at Higashikawa-cho International Center.
1997 Age 53	Started sharing studio with Minoru Ohira, with whom he spent countless intensive and valuable hours discussing everything from technical matters to sculpture, life, and society. Started working with marble. Crystal in Space sculpture for Hida Takayama Museum of Art.		**2015** Age 71	Retired as President of Tama Art University, and became professor emeritus. Moved to Sapporo. Sculpture 3 for Takikawa Dai-San Elementary School. Ceramic relief Shu, Sha, Shi installed at Tancho Kushiro Airport.
1998 Age 54	Takenobu Igarashi was published by Edition Axel Menges, Germany. Had a one-man exhibition at Museo José Luis Cuevas, Mexico City.		**2016** Age 72	Stained glass sculpture Muku Muku installed at Shin-Hakodate-Hokuto station of the new Hokkaido Shinkansen Line.
1999 Age 55	Moved his studio to a part of a factory in Culver City and start working with wood. Completion of a private residence in Brentwood, California.		**2018** Age 74	The solo exhibition The World of Takenobu Igarashi is held at Sapporo Art Park, Sapporo, Hokkaido, Japan.
2000 Age 56	First terracotta sculpture Rhythm of Wave installed at Daimon Station of Oedo Subway Line, Tokyo.			
2001 Age 57	Dragon Spine sculpture for Tama Art University's Hachioji campus.			

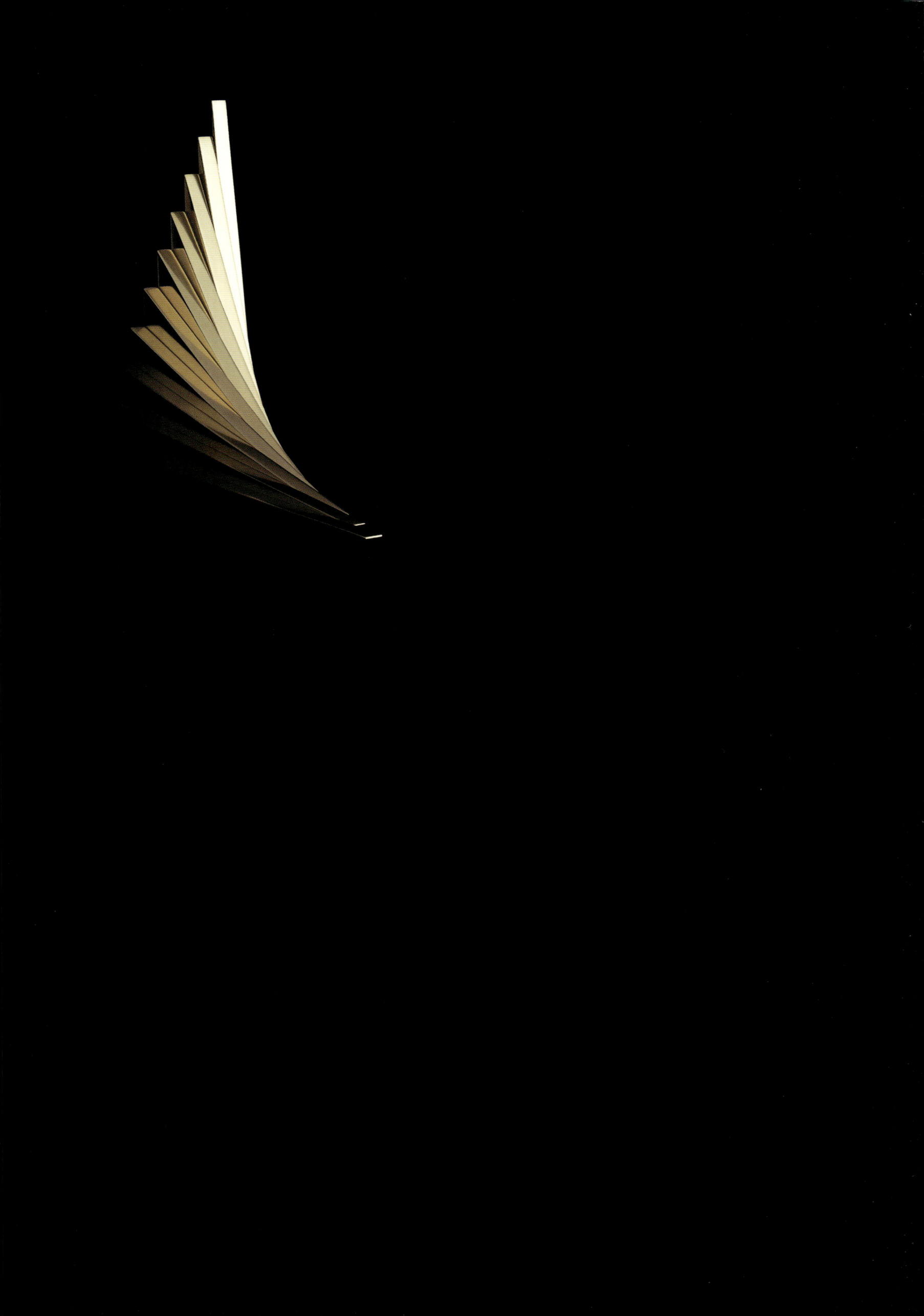

"In the process of doing, I am guided through inspiration."

APPENDIX

Chapter 1

1-1 Logo Sign
Mokuba, Jazz Cafe
Tokyo, Japan
1973

1-2 Wall Graphics with Logotype
Zen Environmental Design
Fukuoka, Japan
1974
Interior Design: Shoei Yoh

1-3 Poster
UCLA, USA
1976
Offset Printing
W1,030xH728mm

1-4 Cover
Graphis Magazine
1986, Issue #245
Graphis Press Corp.
Switzerland
1986
Offset Printing
W235xH300mm
Photo: Tatsuro Hirose

1-5 Poster "Summer Jazz"
Nippon Cultural Broadcasting Inc.
1976–84
Offset Printing
W515xH728mm

1-6 Stainless Steel Alphabet "B"
1984
Stainless Steel
W300xH300xD300mm

1-7 "Stainless Steel Alphabet "D"
1984
Stainless Steel
W300xH300xD300mm

1-8 Art Print
1985

1-9 Postcard
"Takenobu Igarashi Exhibition 2"
Gallery Fujie, Tokyo, Japan
1975
Offset Printing
W105xH150mm

1-10 Alphabet Greeting Card
Alphabet Gallery
Tokyo, Japan
1983
Silkscreen Printing
W105xH150mm (26 cards)

1-11 Poster
"Shigeru Uchida Exhibition"
Gallery Fujie
Tokyo, Japan
1975
Offset Printing
W728xH515mm

1-12 Wall Graphics
Misawa Homes Institute of Research
and Development Co., Ltd.
Tokyo, Japan
1977
Architect: Minoru Takeyama
Architect & U/A

1-13 Floor Graphics for Tokyo Port
Harumi Passenger Ship Terminal
Bureau of Port and Harbor, Tokyo
Metropolitan Government
Tokyo, Japan
1991
Ceramic Tile
Architect: Minoru Takeyama
Architect & U/A
Photo: Nacása & Partners Inc.

1-14 Logotype Sign for Apita
Shopping Mall
Uny Co., Ltd.
Aichi, Japan
1983

1-15 Cover
"Shitsunai" Interior Design Magazine
Kosakusha Publishing Co., ltd.
Tokyo, Japan
1980–97
Offset Printing
W182xH257mm
Cover Photo: Mitsumasa Fujitsuka

1-16 Cover
"Seko" Architecture Magazine
Shokokusha Publishing Co., ltd.
Tokyo, Japan
1976–82

1-17 Logotypes for "OUN"
OUN Corp., Tokyo, Japan
1987

1-18 Animal Illustration
1973
Silkscreen Printing
W900xH900mm

1-19 Logotype
Meiji Dairies Corporation
Tokyo, Japan
1986

1-20 Symbol Mark
Calpis Co., Ltd.
Tokyo, Japan
1983

1-21 VI Design
Mitsui Bank
Tokyo, Japan
1984

1-22 Symbol Mark
Tama Art University
Tokyo, Japan
1995

1-23 CI Design
Summit Store Inc.
Tokyo, Japan
1976–85

1-24 Logotype and Architectural
Graphic
Parco Part 3
Tokyo, Japan
1981

1-25 Symbol Mark and Model
Japan Typography Association
Tokyo, Japan
1978
Wood
Photo: Mitsumasa Fujitsuka

1-26 Logotype and Sign
AIM, Kita-Hiroshima
Hokkaido, Japan
1991
Stainless Steel
Photo: Mitsumasa Fujitsuka

1-27 VI Design
Suntory Holdings Limited
Tokyo, Japan
1990
Photo: Mitsumasa Fujitsuka

1-28 Metamorphosies of "Hibiki" logo
Suntory Holdings Limited
Tokyo, Japan
1990

1-29 "Hibiki" Model
1986

1-30 Architecture Sign
Suntory Hall
Tokyo, Japan
1986

1-31 VI Manual
Suntory Holdings Limited
Tokyo, Japan
1990

1-32 Sculpture
"Hibiki" Suntory Hall
Tokyo, Japan
1986
Bronze
W2,500xH1,800xD3,600mm
Photo: Masaru Mera

1-33 VI Design
Kanazawa Institute of Technology
Kanazawa, Ishikawa, Japan
1983

1-34 Symbol Mark
Noritz Corporation
Tokyo, Japan
1984

1-35 VI Design
UHAG, COSA, Libermann Group
Zurich, Switzerland
1985

1-36 VI Design
Kubota Computer
Osaka, Japan
1987

1-37 Logotype
OUN Vision
Sapporo, Hokkaido, Japan
2004

1-38 VI Design
Polygon Pictures
Tokyo, Japan
1987

1-39 VI Design
Field Stone Why Group
Tokyo, Japan
1987

1-40 VI Design
Talvas Golf & Resort
Nasu, Tochigi, Japan
1989

1-41 Symbol Mark
Oji Hall, Oji Paper Co., Ltd.
Tokyo, Japan
1992

1-42 VI Design
Hida Takayama Museum of Art
Hida-Takayama, Gifu, Japan
1997

1-43 VI Design
Oji Paper Co., Ltd.
Tokyo, Japan
1996

1-44 VI Design
Bourou Noguchi Noboribetsu
Noboribetsu, Hokkaido, Japan
2006

1-45 VI Design
Okazaki Women's University
Seiko Gakuen Educational Corporation
Okazaki, Aichi, Japan
2015

1-46 Poster
"All Night Jazz '84~'85" Revlon
Tokyo, Japan
1984
Offset Printing
W1, 030xH728mm

1-47 Poster
"The 9th Kanagawa Art Festival"
Kanagawa Prefecture
Kanagawa, Japan
1984
Offset Printing
W728xH1, 030mm

1-48 Poster
Zen Environmental Design
Fukuoka, Japan
1976
Offset Printing
W1, 030xH728mm

1-49 Illustration
"Dave Brubeck Quartet 25th Anniversary
Reunion," A&M Record, USA
1976
Offset Printing
W315xH315mm

1-50 Poster
Idea Special Issue
"Graphic Designer on the West Coast"
Seibundo Shinkosha
Tokyo, Japan
1975
Offset Printing
W728xH1, 030mm

1-51 Poster
"Noh," UCLA Asian Performing Arts
Institute, USA
1981
Offset Printing
W1, 030xH728mm

1-52 Poster
"Hawaiian Graphics" Japan Graphic
Designers Association Tokyo, Japan
1982
Offset Printing
W728xH1, 030mm

1-53 Pineapple Building (Model)
1982
Wood, Acrylic
W500xD300mm

1-54 Poster
"New Polaroid Impulse"
Polaroid Corp, USA
1988
Offset Printing
W594xH841mm

1-55 Poster
"Sevilla World Exposition 1992"
EXPO '92 Executive Committee
Spain

1988
Offset Printing
W700xH1,000mm

1-56 Poster
"EXPO '85"
International Science and Technology
Expo Association
Tokyo, Japan
1982
Offset Printing
W728xH1,030mm

1-57 "JAZZ15"
Tokyo Designers Space
Tokyo, Japan
1976
Print Gallery
Amsterdam, Netherlands
1978

1-58 Wrapping Paper
Seibu Department Store, Book Center
Tokyo, Japan
1975

1-59 Shopping Bag
The Museum of Modern Art
New York, USA
1984
Plastic
W330xH420xD175mm

1-60 Enigmatic Alphabet
HQ Magazine, Germany
1986

1-61 Poster
"New Music Media"
New Music Media Committee
Tokyo, Japan
1974
Offset Printing
W728xH1,030mm

1-62 Poster
"Sylph," Sylph, Tokyo, Japan
1981

1-63 Poster
"World Design Expo '89"
World Design Expo Association
Nagoya, Aichi, Japan
1987
Offset Printing
W728xH1,030mm

1-64 A to Z IBM Alphabet
IBM Japan, Tokyo, Japan
1984–90

1-65 Cover Illustration
Design News Magazine
Japan Institute of Design Promotion
Tokyo, Japan
1980–81

1-66 Graphic Chart for Igarashi
Poster Calendar
The Museum of Modern Art
New York, USA
1984–1991

1-67 Igarashi Poster Calendar
June
The Museum of Modern Art
New York, USA
1986
Offset Printing
W1,030xH728mm

1-68 Igarashi Poster Calendar
July
The Museum of Modern Art
New York, USA
1989
Offset Printing
W1,030xH728mm

1-69 Igarashi Poster Calendar
March
The Museum of Modern Art
New York, USA
1988
Offset Printing
W1,030xH728mm

1-70 Igarashi Poster Calendar
November
The Museum of Modern Art
New York, USA
1985
Offset Printing
W1,030xH728mm

1-71 Igarashi Poster Calendar
July
The Museum of Modern Art
New York, USA
1985
Offset Printing
W1,030xH728mm

1-72 Igarashi Poster Calendar
March
The Museum of Modern Art
New York, USA
1989
Offset Printing
W1,030xH728mm

1-73 Igarashi Poster Calendar
October
The Museum of Modern Art
New York, USA
1988
Offset Printing
W1,030xH728mm

1-74 Igarashi Poster Calendar
December
The Museum of Modern Art
New York, USA
1985
Offset Printing
W1,030xH728mm

1-75 Igarashi Poster Calendar
(Full Size) September
The Museum of Modern Art
New York, USA
1989
Offset Printing

1-76 Igarashi Poster Calendar
(Full Size) April
The Museum of Modern Art
New York, USA
1988
Offset Printing

1-77 Igarashi Poster Calendar
(Full Size) June
The Museum of Modern Art
New York, USA
1984
Offset Printing

1-78 Aluminum Alphabet "A"
1983
W140xH130xD120mm
Photo: Mitsumasa Fujitsuka

1-79 Aluminum Alphabet "B"
1983
W140xH130xD120mm
Photo: Mitsumasa Fujitsuka

1-80 Aluminum Alphabet
1983
"C": W140xH140xD110mm
"D": W140xH130xD110mm
"E": W140xH120xD94mm
"F": W140xH120xD140mm
"G": W140xH140xD94mm
"H": W140xH120xD104mm
"I": W140xH40xD120mm
"J": W140xH120xD110mm
"K": W140xH130xD110mm
"L": W140xH110xD110mm
"M": W140xH140xD120mm
"N": W140xH130xD110mm
Photos: Mitsumasa Fujitsuka

1-81 Aluminum Alphabet
1983
"O": W140xH140xD90mm
"P": W140xH125xD140mm
"Q": W140xH140xD140mm
"R": W140xH125xD120mm
"S": W140xH120xD120mm
"T": W140xH120xD126mm
"U": W140xH120xD140mm
"V": W140xH146xD120mm
"W": W140xH160xD120mm
"X": W140xH140xD94mm
"Y": W140xH140xD104mm
"Z": W140xH140xD110mm
Photos: Mitsumasa Fujitsuka

1-82 Mirror Alphabet "T/Y"
1987
Brass (Chrome Plating),
Aluminum
W350xH410xD220mm
Photo: Mitsumasa Fujitsuka

1-83 Mirror Alphabet "A"
1981
Brass (Chrome Plating),
ABS Plastic
W140xH300xD300mm
Photo: Mitsumasa Fujitsuka

1-84 Mirror Alphabet "H"
1981
Brass (Chrome Plating),
ABS Plastic
W140xH300xD300mm
Photo: Mitsumasa Fujitsuka

1-85 ABS Resin Alphabet "F"
1981
ABS Resin + Painted Lacquer
W300xH230xD230mm
Photo: Masaru Mera

1-86 ABS Resin Alphabet "V"
1981
ABS Resin + Painted Lacquer
W300xH300xD300mm
Photo: Masaru Mera

1-87 ABS Resin Alphabet "A"
1981
ABS Resin + Painted Lacquer
W300xH300xD300mm
Photo: Masaru Mera

1-88 ABS Resin Alphabet "D"
1981
ABS Resin + Painted Lacquer
W300xH300xD300mm
Photo: Masaru Mera

1-89 Concrete Alphabet "H"
1981
Formwork Concrete
W300xH300xD300cm
Photo: Masaru Mera

1-90 Concrete Alphabet "B"
1981
Formwork Concrete
W300xH300xD300mm
Photo: Masatu Mera

1-91 Wood Alphabet "D"
1981
Laminated Wood
W300xH300xD300cm
Photo: Masaru Mera

1-92 Wood Alphabet "H"
1981
Laminated Wood
W300xH285xD270cm
Photo: Masaru Mera

1-93 Expo Paper Asia
Tokyo, Japan Exhibition
Zanders Feinpapiere AG,
Germany
1989
Photo: Masaru Mera

1-94 DRUPA Exhibition Stand
Düsseldorf International Comprehensive
Printing Equipment Fair
Zanders Feinpapiere AG
Germany
1986
Photo: Wim Cox

1-95 Library Sign
Keio University Library Mita Media
Center, Tokyo, Japan
1985
Steel, Paint Finish
Architect: Maki and Associates

1-96 Directory Sign
Nippon Life Insurance Company
Toranomon NN Building
Tokyo, Japan
1981
Aluminum
W2,400xH2,400xD2,400mm
Architect: Maki and Associates

1-97 Sculpture "D"
For Magazine Cover Domus Magazine
Italy
1992
Aluminum and Gold Plated Brass
W140xH140xD125mm
Photo: Mitsumasa Fujitsuka

1-98 Sculpture "K"
For Catalog Cover
Kokuyo, Tokyo, Japan
1988
Aluminum+Gold Plated Brass
W180xH170xD150mm
Photo: Masaru Mera

1-99 Sculpture
For Nike 180 Air Shoes Campaign
Nike, USA
1990
Aluminum
W225xH155xD80mm
Photo: Mitsumasa Fujitsuka

1-100 Sculpture for the Cover of
"Kajima Corporation 150th
Anniversary Publication"

Kajima150, Kajima Corporation
Tokyo, Japan
1989
Aluminum and Brass
W190xH200xD390mm
Photo: Yukio Shimizu

1-101 Africa Prize Trophy
The Hunger Project
New York, USA
1987
Aluminum
W250xH250xD120mm
Photo: Mitsumasa Fujitsuka

1-102 CS Design Award Trophy
Nakagawa Chemical
Tokyo, Japan
1982
Brass (Gold & Chrome Plate)
W100xH75xD170mm–100x175mm
Photo: Masaru Mera

1-103 Clock
OUN Corp., Tokyo, Japan
1987
Plastic
W128.5xH66.5xD13.2mm
Photo: Mitsumasa Fujitsuka

1-104 Clock
OUN Corp., Tokyo, Japan
1987
Brass
W100xH100xD100mm
Photo: Mitsumasa Fujitsuka

1-105 Desktop Accessories
Raymay Fujii
Tokyo, Japan
1988
Aluminum, Stainless Steel,
Plastic, Rubber
Photo: Mitsumasa Fujitsuka

1-106 Lighting Equipment
Yamada Shomei Lighting Co. Ltd.
Y.M.D. Division
Tokyo, Japan
1994
Glass, Handmade Paper, String
Tube:170xH350mm
Shade: W550xH545mm
Photo: Masaru Mera

1-107 Flower Vase
Yamada Shomei Lighting Co. Ltd.
Y.M.D. Division
Tokyo, Japan
1990
Ceramic
Manufacture: Ceramic Japan
Photo: Masaru Mera

1-108 Sapporo Station Concourse
Clock, Sapporo Station General
Development Co., Ltd.
Sapporo, Hokkaido, Japan
2006
Manufacture: Seiko Holdings
Corporation
Photo: Mitsumasa Fujitsuka

1-109 Illustration for Watch
m+h unit Inc.
Tokyo, Japan
Manufacture: Costante Co.
2005

1-110 Stool
Yamada Shomei Lighting Co. Ltd.
Y.M.D. Division, Tokyo, Japan
1989
Cast Iron, Aluminum
W400xH460xD410mm
Manufacturer: Yamasho Chuzo,
Takenaka Seisakusho Co., Ltd.
Photo: Mitsumasa Fujitsuka

1-111 Platter/Triangle
Yamada Shomei Lighting Co., Ltd.
Y.M.D. Division
Tokyo, Japan
1989
Cast Iron
W450xH385xD80mm
Manufacture: Yamasho Chuzo
Photo: Masaru Mera

1-112 Platter/Dot
Yamada Shomei Lighting Co., Ltd.
Y.M.D. division
Tokyo, Japan
1989
Cast Iron
364x53mm
Manufacture: Yamasho Chuzo
Photo: Masaru Mera

1-113 Platter/Line
Yamada Shomei Lighting Co., Ltd.
Y.M.D. division
Tokyo, Japan
1989
Cast Iron
364x53mm
Manufacture: Yamasho Chuzo
Photo: Masaru Mera

1-114 Platter/One Crack
Yamada Shomei Lighting Co., Ltd.
Y.M.D. division
Tokyo, Japan
1989
Cast Iron
364x53mm
Manufacture: Yamasho Chuzo
Photo: Masaru Mera

1-115 Soy Sauce Dispenser
Kimura Glass Co., Ltd.
Tokyo, Japan
1995
Glass
80x95mm
Manufacture: Kimura Glass Co., Ltd.
Photo: Masaru Mera

1-116 Dinnerware
Yamada Shomei Lighting Co., Ltd.
Y.M.D. Division
Tokyo, Japan
1989–94
Stainless Steel
Manufacture: Tsubame shinko
Industrial Co., Ltd.
Photo: Masaru Mera

1-117 Photo Album
OUN Corp.
Tokyo, Japan
1988
Vinyl, Plastic
W375xH295xD40mm
Photo: Masaru Mera

1-118 Cordless Telephone
Entex Corp.
Tokyo, Japan
1989
Plastic
Station: W166xH222xD99.5mm
Cordless Phone: W55xH85.5xD224mm
Photo: Mitsumasa Fujitsuka

Chapter 2

2-1 "Infiniti"
Nissan Infiniti, USA
1989
Bronze
W350xH585xD145mm
Photo: Dale Berman

2-2 "Listen to Music"
Sumida Triphony Hall
Tokyo, Japan
1997
Cast Aluminum, Aluminum Sheet
W3,700xH2,400mm
Architect: Nikken Sekkei Ltd.
Interior design: Nikken Space
Design Ltd.
Photo: Masaru Mera

2-3 "Fuchujin"
Fuchu Intelligent Park
Tokyo, Japan
1991
Aluminum
W1,000xH5,000xD1,000mm (3 pieces)
Client: Mitsui Fudosan Co., Ltd.
Photo: Masaru Mera

2-4 "Snow Mountain"
2000
Marble
W483xH216xD330mm
Photo: Masaru Mera

2-5 "White Sun"
2000
Marble
W457xH406xD152mm
Photo: Masaru Mera

2-6 "Puppy"
2000
Marble
W216xH330xD216mm
Photo: Masaru Mera

2-7 "Sky Dancing"
Shibaura Institute of Technology
Toyosu Campus
Tokyo, Japan
2005
Plywood, Acrylic Paint, Silk String,
Bamboo, Stainless Wire
H600x3,500mm (10 pieces)
Architect: Nikken Sekkei Ltd., NTT
Facilities Inc.
Art consultant: AIM
Photo: Hiroyuki Oki

2-8 "Komorebi"
Hokkaido Medical Center for
Child Health and Rehabilitation
Sapporo, Hokkaido, Japan
2007
Plywood, Acrylic Paint
W3,000xH2,400mm (2 pieces)
Art consultant: Town Art Co., Ltd.
Photo: Shigeru Ohno

2-9 "Sky Tree"
Akasaka Garden City
Tokyo, Japan
2005
Granite
H4,000mm
Architect: Nihon Sekkei Inc.
Client: Sekisui House, Ltd.
Art consultant: AIM
Photo: Hiroyuki Oki

2-10 "Earth Mother"
Akasaka Garden City
Tokyo, Japan
2005
Granite
H2,000mm
Architect: Nihon Sekkei Inc.
Client: Sekisui House, Ltd.
Art consultant: AIM
Photo: Hiroyuki Oki

2-11 "Fire Ball"
Akasaka Garden City, Tokyo, Japan
*Including Background Window Drawing
2005
Granite
W1,200mm
Pedestal: Stainless Steel
W890xH400xD500mm
Architect: Nihon Sekkei Inc.
Client: Sekisui House, Ltd.
Art consultant: AIM
Photo: Hiroyuki Oki

2-12 "Water Glass"
Akasaka Garden City
Tokyo, Japan
*Including Background Window Drawing
2005
Granite
W890xH1,200mm
Pedestal: Stainless Steel
W890xH400xD500mm
Architect: Nihon Sekkei Inc.
Client: Sekisui House, Ltd.
Art consultant: AIM
Photo: Hiroyuki Oki

2-13 "Rhythm of Wave"
Daimon Station of Metropolitan Subway
Ooedo line, Tokyo, Japan
2000
Terra-Cotta
W10,000xH2,500mm
Architect: Ken Yokogawa Architect
& Associates Inc.
Photo: Mitsumasa Fujitsuka

2-14 "Landscape"
JR Tower Observation Deck T38,
Sapporo Station, Hokkaido, Japan
2003
Terra-Cotta
W11,890xH3,030mm
Architect: Nihon Sekkei Inc.
Client: Sapporo Station General
Development Co., Ltd.
Photo: Mitsumasa Fujitsuka

2-15 "The Mother Earth" (Sculpture),
"Fountainhead" (Fountain)
*Including Bench, Plaza Design
Akasaka K-Tower
Tokyo, Japan
2012
Photo: Mitsumasa Fujitsuka

2-16 "Forest of Terminus"
*Including Bench, Plaza Design
Basement Plaza of Paseo,
JR Sapporo Station
Sapporo, Hokkaido, Japan
2011
Photo: Mitsumasa Fujitsuka

2-17 From the "Land of Memory"
Tokyo Midtown
Tokyo, Japan
2006
Terra-Cotta
170xH3,000mm
Architect: SOM, Nikken Sekkei Ltd.
Client: Mitsui Fudosan Co., Ltd.

Art Consultant: Toshio Shimizu
Art Office
Photo: Eri Iwata

2-18 "Land of Intelligence"
Fukuoka, Japan University Library,
Fukuoka, Japan
2012
Terra-Cotta
W5,544xH792xD180mm (3 pieces)
Architect: Nikken Sekkei Ltd.
Art Consultant: Art Front Gallery
Photo: Hiroyuki Kawano

2-19 "Horizontal Feeling Landscape"
Laguna Honda Hospital
San Francisco, CA, USA
2008
Terra-Cotta
W4,810xH2,900xD50mm
Photo: Kai-Yee Woo

2-20 "Horizontal Feeling Landscape"
Laguna Honda Hospital
San Francisco, CA, USA
2008
Terra-Cotta
W6,300xH2,900xD50mm
Photo: Noreen Rei Fukumori

2-21 "Horizontal Feeling LHH"
Laguna Honda Hospital
San Francisco, CA, USA
2008
Ceramic
W2,121xH241xD50mm
Photo: Bruce Damonte

2-22 Untitled
Galleria Grande
Tokyo, Japan
2006
Terra-Cotta
W2,800xH2,800mm
Client: Properst
Photo: Hiroyuki Oki

2-23 "North Wind"
Higashikawa-cho International House
Higashikawa, Hokkaido, Japan
2014
Ceramic
W6,000xH1,400xD80–160mm
Client: Higashikawa
Photo: Shinya Fujiwara

2-24 "Diversity and Harmony"
Xinzhuang Joint Office Tower,
Executive Yuan
New Taipei City, Taiwan
2014
Ceramic
W14,220xH1,020xD150mm
Architect: M.H.Wu & Associates
Client: Executive Yuan
Art Consultant: Town Art Co., Ltd.
Photo: Hoho Lin

2-25 "Light of Pinneshiri"
Sapporo Teishinkai Hospital
Sapporo, Hokkaido, Japan
2015
Ceramic
W150xH150xD150mm (17 pieces)
Art Consultant: Kazenobijutsukan
Photo: Koji Sakai

2-26 Small Ceramic Sculptures
2014
Ceramic
W150xH150xD150mm etc.
Photo: Masaru Mera

2-27 "Bud"
2013
Ceramic
W280xH90xD125mm
Photo: Koji Sakai

2-28 "Seed 6"
2013
Ceramic
Private Collection

2-29 "Spring Water"
2013
Ceramic
W115xH120xD80mm
Private Collection

2-30 "Mountain House"
2013
Ceramic
W150xH160xD155mm

2-31 "Snow Water"
2013
Ceramic
W90xH180xD70mm

2-32 "Field"
2013
Ceramic
145xD95mm

2-33 "Flowing Water"
2013
Ceramic
W85xH275xD60mm

2-34 "Mountain"
2013
Ceramic
W160xH160xD160mm

2-35 "Horsetail"
2013
Ceramic
W125xH275xD90mm

2-36 "Lake"
2013
Ceramic
150xH90mm
Above 9 photos: Koji Sakai

2-37 "In Praise of Forest, Ocean
and People"
*Ceramic art and benches
Ota-City General Gymnasium
Tokyo, Japan
2012
Ceramic, Mirror
Various Sizes
Architect: Ishimoto Architectural and
Engineering Firm, Inc.
Client: Ohta
Art Consultant and Production:
Creare Atami-Yugawara Studio
Photo: Mitsumasa Fujitsuka

2-38 Ceramic Sculptures
La Maree Shirokane
Tokyo, Japan
2003
Ceramic, String
Client: Properst
Architect: Yasui Architects &
Engineers, Inc.
Art consultant: Otsuka Ohmi
Ceramics Co., Ltd.
Photo: Masaru Mera

2-39 "Never Ending Road #1"
2012
Terra-Cotta
2,400mm
Photo: Masaru Mera
Exhibition: AIJ Architectural
Institute of Japan Gallery
Tokyo, Japan

2-40 "Motherland"
2011
Terra-Cotta
W7,660xD360xH90mm
Photo: Koji Sakai
Exhibition: Planis Hall
Sapporo, Hokkaido, Japan

2-41 "Horizontal Feeling/Lone Pine"
2000
Various Woods, Acrylic Paint
W1,581xH1,474xD51mm
Photo: Masaru Mera

2-42 "Horizontal Feeling/Yakushima"
2002
Various Woods, Acrylic Paint
W900xH900mm

2-43 Untitled
Bureau Ginza
Tokyo, Japan
2004
Various Woods, Acrylic Paint
W1,241xH1,531xD50mm (3 pieces)
Architect: Jun Aoki & Associates,
Irie Miyake Architects & Engineers
Interior Design: Peter Hahn
Associates Limited
Client: Space Design, Inc.
Photo: Eri Iwata

2-44 "Redwood Forest"
Yotsuya Medical Cube
Tokyo, Japan
2005
Various Woods, Acrylic Paint
W2,500xH1,573xD55mm
Art consultant: Town Art Co., Ltd.

2-45 "Sea of Words"
Tokyo University of Foreign Studies,
Fuchu, Tokyo, Japan
2000
Various Woods, Acrylic Paint
W4,600xH800xD65mm
W13,800xH800xD65mm
Architect: Tokyo University of Foreign
Studies, Kume Sekkei Co., Ltd.
and others
Art Consultant: Town Art Co., Ltd.
Photo: Masaru Mera

2-46 Untitled
Private Residence
Tokyo, Japan
2005
Various Woods, Sumi Ink
W9,328xH508xD55mm
Architect: Kidosaki Architects Studio

2-47 "California Desert"
Valore Kudan Minami
Tokyo, Japan
2008
Various Woods, Acrylic Paint
W4,000xH760xD65mm
Architect: Minoru Takeyama
architect & U/A
Client: Komura Agency Co., Ltd.
Photo: Hiroyuki Oki

2-48 "Horizontal Feeling"
Kajima Akasaka Annex
Tokyo, Japan
2007
Various Woods, Acrylic Paint
W6,000xH300xD50mm
Architect: Kajima Corporation
Interior Design: Ilya Corporation
Photo: Eri Iwata

2-49 "Horizontal Feeling LHH-3"
Laguna Honda Hospital
San Francisco, CA, USA
2008
Various Woods, Acrylic Paint
W1,118xH406xD55mm
Photo: Bruce Damonte

2-50 "Art Box" #01–20
2007
Wood, Music Box, Wheels etc.

2-51 "Flow"
2000
Plywood, Silk String, Acrylic Paint
W965xH813xD76mm
Photo: Masaru Mera

2-52 "Illusion"
2000
Plywood, Silk String, Acrylic Paint
W739xH813xD165mm
Photo: Masaru Mera

2-53 "Moment"
2000
Plywood, Silk String, Acrylic Paint
W1,364xH1,029xD203mm
Photo: Masaru Mera

2-54 "Black Horizon"
2002
Plywood, Silk String, Sumi Ink
W4,570xH190xD150mm
Photo: Mitsumasa Fujitsuka
Exhibition: Gallery Natsuka

2-55 "Beyond the Horizon"
Kajima Akasaka Annex
Tokyo, Japan
2007
Plywood, Silk String, Sumi Ink
W2,800xH1,800xD300mm
Architect: Kajima Corporation
Interior Design: Ilya Corporation
Photo: Eri Iwata

2-56 "Depth of the Sea"
Kazenobi, Shintotsukawa
Hokkaido, Japan
2002
Various Wood, Silk String, Sumi Ink
W1,900xH2,560xD250mm
Architectural Renovation Design:
Yoshihiko Iida+IAS
Photo: Koji Sakai
Exhibited in Pacific Asia Museum
2003

2-57 "To the Sea of Premonition"
Tokyo Midtown, Tokyo, Japan
2006
Wood, Bamboo, String, Sumi Ink
W8,000xH6,000xD650mm
Architect: SOM, Nikken Sekkei Ltd.
Client: Mitsui Fudosan Co., Ltd.
Art Consultant: Toshio Shimizu Art Office
Photos of sculpture and
production scene: Eri Iwata

2-58 "Zawa Zawa/Hyun Hyun/Giggi"
Osaki Bright Core
Tokyo, Japan
2015
Plywood, Silk String, Sumi Ink

Client: Kitashinagawa 5-chome Daiichi District Urban Redevelopment Union
Art consultant: Toshio Shimizu Art Office
Artist Rep: Yukitoshi Maekawa
Photo: Daishi Saito

2-59 "Full of Spirit and Vigor"
Toranomon First Garden
Tokyo, Japan
2010
Plywood, Silk String, Sumi Ink
W1,450xH2,000xD580mm
Architect: Nikken Sekkei Ltd.
Client: Hulic Co., Ltd.
Art Consultant: Toshio Shimizu Art Office
Photo: Eri Iwata

2-60 "Sky Dancing"
Odori Bisse
Sapporo, Hokkaido, Japan
2010
Plywood, Silk String, Acrylic Paint, Stainless Steel Wire
Left: H2,800xΦ1,450mm
Right: H1,500xΦ3,250mm
Architect: Nikken Sekkei Ltd., Hokkaido Nikken Sekkei Ltd., Docon Co., Ltd.
Client: North Pacific Bank, LTD., Koyo Real Estate Co., Ltd.
Art Consultant: Toshio Shimizu Art Office
Photo: Masahide Sato

2-61 "Cosmos"
Takikawa Municipal Hospital
Takikawa, Hokkaido, Japan
2011
Plywood, Silk String, Acrylic Paint
W2,650xH2,700xD1,000mm
W2,000xH2,000xD800mm
Architect: Yamashita Sekkei Inc.
Client: Takikawa

2-62 Untitled
Chutoen General Medical Center,
Kakegawa, Shizuoka, Japan
* Collaborative work with hospital staff, architects, design related persons, and art consultants
2013
Plywood, Acrylic Paint
W3,160xH2,840mm
Architect: Kume Sekkei Co., Ltd.
Art Consultant: Art Now Co., Ltd.
Photo: Ken Kato

2-63 "Komorebi"
Rokkatei, Obihiro, Hokkaido, Japan
2008
Plywood, Acrylic Paint
W15,000xH3,000mm

2-64 "Yu·Fu·Ru·Ji"
Kazenobi, Shintotsukawa, Hokkaido, Japan
2016
Plywood, Acrylic paint
9,000x12,000x4,600mm
Client: Shintotsukawa
Photo: Kenzo Chose

2-65 "Komorebi"
Bourou Noguchi Noboribetsu, Noboribetsu, Hokkaido, Japan
2006
Steel
H1,100x1,400mm
Architect: Nakayama Architects Co., Ltd.
Client: Noguchi-Kanko Co., Ltd.
Photo: Koji Sakai

2-66 "Komorebi"
Kazenobi, Shintotsukawa, Hokkaido, Japan
2007
Plywood, Acrylic Paint
1,550mm
Photo: Koji Sakai

2-67 "Komorebi"
Kajima Corporation Head Office
Tokyo, Japan
2007
Plywood, Acrylic Paint
W800xH800mm (3 pieces)
Architect: Kajima Corporation
Interior Design: Ilya Corporation
Photo: Eri Iwata

2-68 "Komorebi"
Nagoya Lucent Tower
Nagoya, Aichi, Japan
2006
Steel
H6,000x2,500mm
Architect: Nikken Sekkei Ltd.
Lighting Design: Sawada Lighting Design & Analysis
Client: Ushijima Shigaichi Saikaihatsu Kumiai
Art Consultant: Toshio Shimizu Art Office
Photo: Hirofumi Tani

2-69 "Wind in Space"
1995
Steel
W305xH3,000xD250mm
Photo: Mitsumasa Fujitsuka

2-70 "Sky Wind"
1995
Steel
W1,800xH115xD70mm
Photo: Mitsumasa Fujitsuka

2-71 Untitled
1994
Stainless Steel
W1,200xH320xD320mm

2-72 "Windstorm"
Hokuyo Odori Center
Sapporo, Hokkaido, Japan
1995
Steel
W2,400xH300xD630mm
Architect: Nikken Sekkei Ltd., Hokkaido Nikken Sekkei Ltd., Docon Co., Ltd.
Client: North Pacific Bank, Ltd., Koyo Real Estate Co., Ltd.
Art Consultant: Toshio Shimizu Art Office
Photo: Koji Sakai

2-73 "Boat"
Niigata Self-Governing Hall Annex
Niigata, Japan
2000
Stainless Steel
W3,000xH240xD210mm
Architect: Nikken Sekkei Ltd.
Client: Niigata
Art Consultant: AIM
Photo: Nacása & Partners Inc.

2-74 "Rhythm of Mountain Range"
Kofu City Hall, Kofu
Yamanashi, Japan
2013
Wood (Beech)
W7,230xH2,490xD300mm
Architect: Nihon Sekkei Inc.
Photo: Eri Iwata

2-75 "Fuu-ka-kou-sei"
(Winds Flowers Stars Lights)
Adeka Corporation Head Office
Tokyo, Japan
2006
Stainless Steel, LED
H4,000xΦ2,000mm
Architect: Shimizu Corporation
Interior Design: Field Four Design Office
Art Consultant: AIM
Photo: Mitsumasa Fujitsuka

2-76 Stained Glass
Akita City Central Library
Akita, Japan
1982
Glass
W2,400xH2,400mm
Architect: Yoshio Taniguchi and Associates
Photo: Masaru Mera

2-77 "In the Sky"
Emergency Medical Care Training Center, Hachioji
Tokyo, Japan
1998
Stainless Steel
Architect: Ina Institute of New Architecture Inc.
Client: Foundation for Ambulance Service Development
Art Consultant: AIM
Photo: Masaru Mera

2-78 "Cloud"
Niigata Self-Governing Hall Annex]
Niigata, Japan
2000
Steel
W2,100xH3,700xD69mm
Architect: Nikken Sekkei Ltd.
Client: Niigata
Art Consultant: AIM
Photo: Nacása & Partners Inc.

2-79 "Wave Light"
Across City Nakanosakaue
Tokyo, Japan
1999
Corten Steel
H3,000x3,000mm
Architect: Ina Institute of New Architecture Inc.
Landscape design: Placemedia
Client: Nakano-Sakaue Re-Development District Association
Art Consultant: AIM
Photo: Masaru Mera

2-80 "Dragon Spine"
Tama Art University Hachioji Campus, Hachioji, Tokyo, Japan
2000
Corten Steel
W406xH8,990xD406mm
Architect: Mohri Architect & Associates Inc.
Photo: Mitsumasa Fujitsuka

2-81 "Sky Dancing"
Laguna Honda Hospital
San Francisco, CA, USA
2008
Aluminium, Stainless Steel Wire
Architect: Anshen+Allen, Architects
Photo: Noreen Rei Fukumori

2-82 "Bouquet"
Kyushu University Hospital
Fukuoka, Japan
2002
Stainless Steel
W2,250xH1,650mm (3 pieces)
W1,575xH1,575mm (4 pieces)
Art consultation and photograph provided by: Town Art Co., Ltd.

2-83 "Milky Way"
Yokohama North Funeral Hall
Yokohama, Kanagawa, Japan
2001
Black Granite, Stainless Steel
W40,000xH2,500mm
Architect: Minoru Takeyama Architect & U/A
Client: Yokohama
Photo: Mitsumasa Fujitsuka

2-84 Untitled
Yokohama North Funeral Hall
Yokohama, Kanagawa, Japan
2001
Stainless Steel
W750–1,000xH270–460mm
Architect: Minoru Takeyama Architect & U/A
Client: Yokohama
Photo: Mitsumasa Fujitsuka

2-85 Untitled
Yokohama North Funeral Hall
Yokohama, Kanagawa, Japan
2001
Stainless Steel
W2,350xH2,600xD2,350mm
Architect: Minoru Takeyama Architect & U/A
Client: Yokohama
Photo: Mitsumasa Fujitsuka

2-86 "Lotus"
Lotus Garden
Tokyo, Japan
1997
Sculpture: Stainless Steel
H2,460xΦ2,400mm
Fountain: Black Granite
W40,000x20,000mm
Architect: Nikken Sekkei Ltd.
Client: Yamanouchi Pharmaceutical Co., Ltd. (Now Astellas Pharma Inc.)
Photo: Masaru Mera

2-87 "Crystal in Space"
Hida Takayama Museum of Art
Hida-Takayama
Gifu, Japan
1997
Stainless steel
H2,050x2,000mm
Architect: Kajima Corporation
Landscape Design: Placemedia
Photo: Masaru Mera

2-88 "Kumo"
Azabu Juban Shopping District
Tokyo, Japan
1996
Corten Steel
W5,500xH5,200xD2,200mm
Client: Azabu Juban Shopping District Union
Art Consultant: Sanwa Technology Research Institute
Photo: Masaru Mera

2-89 "Departing Future"
Hamarikyu Mitsui Building
Tokyo, Japan

2011
Steel, Stainless Steel
W2,000xH855xD725mm
Client: Mitsui Fudosan Co., Ltd.,
Mitsui Engineering &
Shipbuilding Co., Ltd.
Art Consultant: Toshio Shimizu
Art Office
Photo: Eri Iwata

2-90 Wind Flower
The Prince Gallery Tokyo Kioicho
Tokyo, Japan
2016
Steel, Platinum foil
W2,000 x H1,400 x D1,650 mm
Architect: Nikken Sekkei Ltd.
Lighting Design: Lighting Planners
Associates
Client: Seibu Holdings Inc., Prince
Hotels and Resorts
Photo: Franco Tadeo Inada

2-91 Bench
Kawadacho Comfo Garden
Tokyo, Japan
2003
Steel Pipe, Wood
W2,640x750mm
Architect: Caesar Pelli and Associates
Japan, Nihon Sekkei Inc.
Landscape design: Placemedia
Client: Urban Development Corporation
Photo: Hiroyuki Oki

2-92 Bench
Wayo Women's University, Ichikawa,
Chiba, Japan
2000
Concrete (GRC)
W3,000xH460xD650mm
Architect: Ishimoto Architectural and
Engineering Firm, Inc.
Client: Tama Art University
Art Consultant: AIM
Photo: Eri Iwata

Chapter 3

3-1 Logo
JR Tower
Sapporo Station General Development
Co., Ltd.
2003

3-2 "Dragon Spine"
Ichinosakanishi Park
Takikawa, Hokkaido, Japan
2004
Corten Steel
W1,400xH21,000xD1,400mm
Park Design: Kitaba Landscape
Planning Co. Inc.
Client: Takikawa
Photo: Eri Iwata

3-3 "Big Star Clock"
JR Tower, Sapporo Station
Sapporo, Hokkaido, Japan
2003
Stainless Steel
7,200mm
Client: Sapporo Station General
Development Co., Ltd.
Manufacture: Seiko Time Systems Inc.
Photo: Koji Sakai

3-4 "Landscape"
JR Tower Observation deck T38
Sapporo Station
Sapporo, Hokkaido, Japan
2003
Terra-Cotta
W11, 890xH3,030mm
Architect: Nihon Sekkei Inc.
Client: Sapporo Station General
Development Co., Ltd.
Photo: Eri Iwata

3-5 Graphic Work for the Walkway to
"Forest of Terminus"
JR Sapporo Station Paseo
Sapporo, Hokkaido, Japan
2011
Paint, Various Sizes
Client: Sapporo Station General
Development Co., Ltd.
Photo: Mitsumasa Fujitsuka

3-6 Logo Design
NPO Art Challenge Takikawa (A.C.T.)
2003
Tarokichigura

3-7 Untitled
(Door Facing Southwest, Tarokichigura)
NPO Art Challenge Takikawa (A.C.T.)
Takikawa, Hokkaido, Japan
2004
Wood (Various Old Materials), Sumi Ink
W2,550xH2,300mm
Architectural Renovation Design:
Yoshifumi Nakamura
Photo: Koji Sakai

3-8 "White Legend"
Kazenobi, Shintotsukawa
Hokkaido, Japan
2011
Ceramic
W21,000xH3,000mm
Client: Shintotsukawa
Architectural Renovation Design:
Yoshihiko Iida+IAS
Photo: Mitsumasa Fujitsuka

3-9 Sculpture "3"
Michael Peters Group
London, England
1985
Stainless Steel
W2,400xH3,400xD2,200mm
Photo: Lu Jeffery

3-10 Wooden Relief
Produced with the corporation from
the whole school, 400 elementary
students in total.
Takikawa Daisan Elementary School
Takikawa, Hokkaido, Japan
2015
Wood
Architect: Kume Sekkei Co., Ltd.
Client: Takikawa
Photo: Koji Sakai

3-11 Sculpture "3"
Takikawa Daisan Elementary School
Takikawa, Hokkaido, Japan
2015
Stainless steel
W2,200xH3,600xD1,400mm
Architect: Kume Sekkei Co., Ltd.

3-12 "Shu, Sya, Shi,"
Homage to Sky, Water and Sun
Tancho Kushiro Airport
Kushiro, Hokkaido, Japan
2015
Ceramic
W4,500xH5,100mm
Client: Japan Traffic Culture Association
Art consultation and production:
Creare Atami-Yugawara Studio

3-13 "Muku Muku," Homage to Water,
Sun and Land
Shin Hakodate Hokuto Station, Hokuto,
Hokkaido, Japan
2016
Stained Glass
Client: Seibu Holdings Inc.,
Prince Hotels and Resorts
Art consultant and production:
Creare Atami-Yugawara Studio

3-14 Memorial Monument
Shintotsukawa Municipal Yoshino
Elementary School
Kazenobi, Shintotsukawa,
Hokkaido, Japan
2009
Stone, Steel
Client: Shintotsukawa
Photo: Shinkenchiku-sha

PHOTO CREDITS

*Photo Credits for Images that are
not numbered throughout the book.*

Takenobu Igarashi's Portrait
Page: 7
Photo: John Madere

Igarashi Studio
Page: 8-9
Photo: Paos

CI, Summit Store
Tokyo, Japan, 1976
Page: 12
Photo: Igarashi Studio

Igarashi Studio
Akasaka, Tokyo, Japan, c.1976
Page: 12
Photo: Igarashi Studio

Takenobu Igarashi Alphabet Art
Exhibition, Matsuya Design Gallery
Tokyo, Japan, 1981
Page: 15
Photo: Igarashi Studio

Alphabet Sculptures Exhibition
Ginza Mikimoto Hall, Tokyo, 1983
Page: 15
Photo: Mitsumasa Fujitsuka

Exhibition at the Reinhold Brown
Gallery
New York, NY, USA, 1983
Page: 15
Photo: Igarashi Studio

Igarashi Studio
Aoyama, Tokyo, c. 1992
Macintosh computers were introduced
to staff members.
Page: 19
Photo: Paos

Igarashi International
Santa Monica, CA, USA
Interior design by Ken Tanaka, c. 1989
Page: 29
Photo: Kenji Shirato

Page: 37
Photo: Unknown

Summit Store Supermarket
Tokyo, Japan, 1976–1985
Page: 40
Photo: Igarashi Studio

AIM, Sapporo
Hokkaido, Japan, 1991
Page: 45
Photo: Mitsumasa Fujitsuka

Igarashi is making a plan with a drafter
at the studio in Aoyama, Tokyo, 1980.
Page: 62
Photo: Igarashi Studio

Page: 130
Photo: Igarashi Atelier

Igarashi's Atelier
Los Angeles, CA, USA
Page: 132
Photo: Igarashi Atelier

Work model for a hospital in
San Francisco, CA, USA
Page: 132
Photo: Igarashi Atelier

Making Sculptures
Pasadena, CA, USA, 1998
Page: 136
Photo: Yoshi Hashimoto

Working with clay at Creare Workshop
Page: 138
Photo: Igarashi Atelier

Igarashi's atelier in Akiya
Yokosuka, Kanagawa, Japan
Page: 138
Photo: Igarashi Atelier

Making Komorebi series
at the Atelier in Akiya
Page: 139
Photo: Igarashi Atelier

Exhibition Catalog for
Takenobu Igarashi Maquettes
Page: 140
Photo: Koji Sakai

Making Maquettes
Page: 141
Photo: Igarashi Atelier

Akasaka K Tower The Mother Earth,
Fountain Head and Bench, Land Detail
*I came up with the idea of a place with a
fountain, bench, sculpture, and floor. (TI)*
Page: 150–151
Photo: Mitsumasa Fujitsuka

Page 154–155
Photo: Mitsumasa Fujitsuka

Igarashi used self-made tools to shave,
carve and hit the clay at the factory of
Shigaraki.
Page: 160
Photo: Eri Iwata

Making of Land of Intelligence
*Photographer Shigeo Anzai came to
capture this moment. (TI)*
Page: 161
Photo: Igarashi Atelier

Making of Diversity and Harmony
Page: 168–169
Photo: Igarashi Atelier

*At the workshop in Yugawara, I used
soft clay for pottery and made sculpture
without any tools.
I used only my hands and feet. (TI)*

Page: 171
Photo: Koji Sakai

Igarashi at his Atelier in Los Angeles
CA, USA, 2003
I began to use wood pieces from used shipping crates for the Horizontal Feeling sculpture series. (TI)
Page: 183
Photo: Igarashi Atelier

Horizontal Feeling, Horizontal Feeling/Palmdale
Page: 190–191
Photo: Masaru Mera

Making of Calligraphy series
Making lightweight sculpture was an important goal. I came up with the idea of using silk strings and putting pieces of plywood together without glue and screws. (TI)
Page: 201
Photo: Igarashi Atelier

Page: 204-205
Photo: Mitsumasa Fujitsuka

Making of the Sea of Premonition, 2006
Page: 208
Photo: Eri Iwata

Zawa Zawa/ Hyun Hyun/ Giggi, detail
Page: 212-213
Photo: Daishi Saito

Making of Full of Spirit and Vigor
Page: 214
Photo: Igarashi Atelier

Making of Komorebi at a former elementary school building in Nakasatsunai village, Hokkaido, Japan.
After returning to Japan, I started making the Komorebi series. There were no sketches and there was no draft drawing. I just cut out the shapes and relied on my intuition. (TI)
Page: 219
Photo: Yoshihiko Tobari

Various Maquettes
These Maquettes were produced mainly at my ateliers in Los Angeles and Akiya between 1995–2009. (TI)
Page: 222–225
Photo: Igarashi Atelier

Page: 254–255
Photo: Igarashi Atelier

Exhibition at Tarokichigura
Page: 260
Photo: Koji Sakai

Tarokichigura is a stone-built warehouse with great acoustic properties.
Page: 260
Photo: Koji Sakai

Flower vases with freestone were made by children at a craft workshop.
Page: 260
Photo: Kazuhiro Ito

Various activities took place in the courtyard of Tarokichigura.
Page: 262
Photo: Koji Sakai

Full view of Tarokichigura opened in 2004
Page: 263
Photo: Koji Sakai

The lighting plan for Tarokichigura was carried out with the best use of the dimness of Kura, traditional Japanese storage structure.
Page: 264
Photo: Koji Sakai

Automatic door at the entrance of Tarokichigura. Igarashi silkscreened a design on the door which was produced based on the hand drawings of the local people.
Page: 265
Photo: Koji Sakai

Interior design for the Italian restaurant il cielo. Team members from A.C.T. designed it for the hotel miura kaen, as an example of revitalization of the city.
Page: 266
Photo: Igarashi Atelier

Located in hotel miura kaen, Takikawa design shop was created by Igarashi with the concept of "bringing nicely designed small products from all over the world to Takikawa."
Page: 266
Photo: Koji Sakai

Takikawa Paper Lantern Festival, an event that A.C.T. has organized and managed with people from Takikawa since its establishment.
Page: 266
Photo: Machiko Kosuge

Tarokichigura Design Conference, started in 2007
Page: 266
Photo: Koji Sakai

Full view of Kazenobi in winter and autumn
Page: 267
Photo: Shinkenchiku-sha

Cafe in Kazenobi
Page: 270
Photo: Mitsumasa Fujitsuka

Atelier in Kazenobi
Page: 270
Photo: Koji Sakai

Workshop held in Kazenobi
Page: 270
Photo: Machiko Kosuge

Entrance Hall on the first floor of Kazenobi
Page: 271
Photo: Shinkenchiku-sha

Wooden Relief, detail
Page: 272
Photo: Koji Sakai

Page: 276–277
Photo: Create Atami – Yugawara Studio

Page: 278
Photo: Igarashi Atelier

Page: 279 (top)
Photo: Create Atami – Yugawara Studio

Page: 279 (bottom)
Photo: Igarashi Atelier

Page: 281 (top)
Photo: Igarashi Atelier

Page: 281 (bottom)
Photo: Shinkenchiku-sha

Page: 282–283
Photo: Igarashi Atelier

PUBLIC COLLECTIONS

ICOGRADA Audio Visual Archive
England
Logo, Poster, Announcement, Signage, Magazine Cover, Illustration,
1974–79

Kunstgewerbemuseum der Stadt
Zurich, Switzerland
Posters
1979

Fachhochschule Düsseldorf, Germany
Posters:
"UCLA"
"Zen"
"Graphic Designers on the West Coast"
1979

Heidenheimer Modell, Werkgymnasium
Heidenheim, Germany
Posters:
"UCLA"
"Zen"
"Graphic Designers on the West Coast"
1979

Museum des 20. Jahrhunderts
Vienna, Austria
Posters
1980

Santa Rosa Junior College Art Gallery
Santa Rosa, CA, USA
Posters
1981

The Library of Congress
Washington DC, USA
Poster: "NOH"
1981

Seattle Art Museum
Seattle, WA, USA
Poster: "NOH"
1981

Portland Art Museum
Portland, OR, USA
Poster: "NOH"
1981

Honolulu Academy of Arts
Honolulu, HI, USA
Poster: "NOH"
1981

Cooper-Hewitt Museum
The Smithsonian Institution's National Museum of Design, New York, NY, USA
Posters:
"Graphic Designers on the West Coast"
"NOH"
1981

Flat Wear:
8 pieces
Product: "Imono Stool" (Triangle)
Shopping Bag:
The Museum of Modern Art
Silkscreen:
Letter "P"

Letter "Q"
1981

Art Center College of Design
Pasadena, CA, USA
14 Posters/7 Silkscreen Prints
1981

The Museum of Modern Art
New York, NY, USA
Posters:
"NOH"
"ZEN"
1981

The Museum of Modern Art
New York, NY, USA
Posters:
"Expo'85"
"Creative Pillars"
1982

Toyama Prefectural Museum of Art & Design
Posters:
"Modern Japan Poster Exhibition"
"MoMA"
"Kanagawa Art Exhibition"
"Kanagawa Art Festival"
1983

General Electric Art Collection
Aluminum Sculptures:
"G"
"E"
"C"
"O"
1984

Die Neue Sammlung Staatliches Museum fur angewandte Kunst
Munich, Germany
Poster: "Expo'85"
1985

Lords Gallery Ltd. London
Philip Granville Collection, England
Posters:
"Expo'85"
"Igarashi Atlanta"
1985

The Israel Museum, Jerusalem
Posters:
"IGARASHI Atlanta"
"EXPO'85"
"1st Winter Asian Games"
"12th/14th/15th/17th Summer Jazz Festival"
1986

The Library of Congress
Washington DC, USA
Book:
"Alphabet Book, A to Z"
"Brochure of Aluminum Sculptures"
1986

The Chicago Athenaeum
Chicago, IL, USA
Posters:
"UCLA "
"Identity"
"NOH"
"Expo'85"
"Kanagawa Art Festival"
"4 Mitsumura, Seven"
1990

Cooper-Hewitt Museum
New York, NY, USA
Products:

"Imono Platter" (1crack)
"Imono Stool" (triangle)
"Stainless Flatware" (5)
1990

Design Zentrum
Nordrhein Westfalen, Germany
Product: "Imono Stools"
1990

The Israel Museum, Jerusalem
Products:
"Imono Platter" (Holes)
"Imono Stool" (Triangle)
"Hyvalysti" Garden Kit
Stainless Flatware (5)
1991

Die Neue Sammlung. Staatliches
Museum fur Angewandte Kunst,
Germany
Book: "Living Objects"
1991

The Denver Art Museum,
Colorado, USA
Products:
"Imono" Platter (dots)
"Imono Stool"
1992

Musee des Arts Decoratifs de Montreal
Canada
Sculpture: "Architectural View 91"
Products:
Particle Board
"Imono" Platter (Triangle, Circle, Square)
1993

Colorado State University
College of Applied Human Sciences
Department of Design, Merchandising
and Consumer Sciences
Fort Collins, CO of Applied Human
Sciences, CO, USA
Products:
"Fisso Postage Scale"
"Kai Razor"
1993

National Museum in Poznan
Poznan, Poland
Posters:
"World of Shigeru Uchida"
"Identity"
"Creative Pillars"
"Expo'85"
"Rights for All: Equality, Security,
Liberty, Property"
"Morisawa"
"East Looks West"
1993

Dansk Plakatmuseum Abyhoj, Denmark
Posters:
"Expo'85"
"Hawaiian Graphics"
"MoMA"
"Kanagawa Art Festival"
"World Design Expo"
"Morisawa"
1994

The Chicago Anthenaeum
The Museum of Architecture
and Design, IL, USA
Posters:
"4 of Mitsumura, Seven
"Identity"
"NOH"
"Expo'85"
"Hawaiian Graphics"

"MoMA"
"Kanagawa Art Festival"
"Atlanta"
"World Design Expo"
"New Polaroid Impulse"
"Living Objects"
"Morisawa"
1994

Philadelphia Museum of Art, PA, USA
Product: "Fisso Desktop"
1995

Glasgow Museums, Scotland, UK
Products: 3 "Imono" Platters
(Nami & Dots & One more)
1996

Centre Georges Pompidou
Paris, France
Product: Lighting fixture "Andon-Zukin"
1996

San Francisco Museum of Modern Art
San Francisco, CA, USA
Product: Garden Tool Kit
2000

Hida Takayama Museum of Art
Sculpture: "Crystal in Space"
1997

Takeo Co., Ltd. Poster Collection
(Reinhold-Brown Collection)
1997

Takeo Archives, Takeo Co., Ltd.
All existing design works and
Alphabet Sculpture
2014

Takikawa City Art Natural History
Museum, Hokkaido, Japan
Poster Calendar and 267 products
2014

Los Angeles County Museum of Art
CA, USA
26 Posters
2015

San Francisco Museum of Modern Art
CA, USA
51 Posters and Printed Works
22 Products
2016

PUBLIC ART AND COMMISSION WORKS

The numbers indicate posted work number or posting page.

1982
Stained Glass/Akita City Central Library, Akita, Japan [2-76]

1983
Sculpture "3"/Michael Peters Group, London, England [3-9]
Sculpture "G," "E," "C," "O"/General Electric Art Collection, USA
Sculpture "O"/The Square Shopping Center, Tama, Tokyo, Japan

1986
Sculpture "Hibiki"/Suntory Hall, Tokyo, Japan [1-32]

1989
Sculpture "Infiniti"/Infinity Showroom, Many places in the United States [2-1]

1990
Sculpture "Nike180"/Nike, Inc., USA [1-99]

1991
Sculpture "Fuchujin"/Fuchu Intelligent Park, Tokyo, Japan [2-3]

1992
Floor Graphics/Harumi Passenger Ship Terminal, Tokyo, Japan [1-13]
Sculpture "D"/ "Domus" Magazine Cover, Italy [1-97]

1996
Sculpture "Kumo" [2-88]
"Numo"/Azabu Juban Shopping District Tokyo, Japan
Sculpture "Wind Flower"/Hachinohe Country Club, Aomori, Japan

1997
Sculpture "Listen to Music"/Sumida Triphony Hall, Tokyo, Japan [2-2]
Sculpture "Crystal in Space"/Hida Takayama Museum of Art, Hida-Takayama, Gifu, Japan [2-87]

1998
Sculpture "Lotus"/Yamanouchi Pharmaceutical Co., Ltd.
(Now Astellas Pharma Inc.)
Tokyo, Japan [2-86]
Sculpture "In the Sky"/Ambulance Service Development Tokyo Institute of Training, Tokyo, Japan [2-77]
Sculpture "Hydrangea"/Special nursing home for the elderly Ajisai-so Tokyo, Japan
Sculpture "Skywards"/Grand Arc Hanzomon, Tokyo, Japan

1999
Sculpture "Wave Light"/Across City Nakanosakaue, Tokyo, Japan [2-79]

2000
Sculpture "Rhythm of Wave"/Daimon Station of Metropolitan Subway Ooedo Line, Tokyo, Japan [2-13]
Sculpture "Sea of Words"/Tokyo University of Foreign Studies, Tokyo, Japan [2-45]
Sculpture "Shinano River," "Cloud" [2-78], "Rain," "Icicle," "Boat"] [2-73] / Niigata Self-Governing Hall Annex, Niigata, Japan
Sculpture "Shall I Go Soon?"
"Shall I Have a Break?"/
Rafre Saitama, Saitama, Japan
Entrance Gate /Maita Park, Yokohama, Kanagawa, Japan
Bench/Wayo Women's University, Ichikawa, Chiba, Japan [2-92]
Sculpture "Dragon Spine"/Tama Art University, Hachioji, Tokyo, Japan [2-80]
Sculpture "Cantabile," Relief "Prelude"/ Moiwa Shalom Church, Sapporo, Hokkaido, Japan

2001
Sculpture "Caligraphy 112901"
The Diplomat Hotel, Miami, USA
Sculpture "Untitled," "Milky Way," Lighting pole Sculpture/Yokohama North Funeral Hall, Yokohama, Kanagawa, Japan [2-85, 2-83, 2-84]
Outer Wall Sculpture "Untitled"/Kitakyusu Museum of Natural History & Human History, Kitakyushu, Fukuoka, Japan

2002
Sculpture "Woven Nest"/CHA Medical Clinic, Los Angeles, USA
Sculpture "Bouquet"/Kyushu University Hospital, Fukuoka, Japan [2-82]
Sculpture "Horizontal Feeling-Connecticut"/Nissei Eblo Inc., Tokyo, Japan
Sculpture "Friends"/Musashimurayama City General Center, Tokyo, Japan
Sculpture "Untitled"/Pentagram, San Francisco, CA, USA

2003
Sculpture "Landscape"/JR Tower, Sapporo, Hokkaido, Japan [2-14]
Sculpture "Goka-kyoso"/Ina Central Hospital, Ina, Nagano, Japan
Fountain/Suntory Kyushu Kumamoto Plant, Kumamoto, Japan
Sculpture, Ceramic 10 pieces [2-38] / La Maree Shirokane, Tokyo, Japan
Sculpture "To the Sky"/Tokyo University of Science Noda Campus, Noda, Chiba, Japan
Pillar Art/Bureau Shinagawa, Tokyo, Japan
Sculpture "Untitled"/TAIKO, Santa Barbara, CA, USA
Sculpture "Horizontal Feeling"/Kidosaki residense, Tokyo, Japan
Carillon/Sino Omiya, Saitama, Japan
Bench/Kawadacho Comfo Garde, Tokyo, Japan [2-91]

2004
Sculpture "Untitled"/Bureau Ginza, Tokyo, Japan [2-43]
Sculpture "Dragon Spine" and the Water Square/Ichinosaka Nishi Park, Takikawa, Hokkaido, Japan [3-2]
Bridge, Los Angeles, USA
Door (Southwest side and entrance)/ Tarokichigura, Takikawa, Hokkaido, Japan [3-7]
Ventilation Tower /Tarokichigura, Takikawa, Hokkaido, Japan [p.261]

2005
Sculpture "Untitled," Private Residence in Nakameguro, Tokyo, Japan [2-46]
Sculpture "Redwood Forest," [2-44]
"Ballade"/Yotsuya Medical Cube, Tokyo, Japan
Sculpture "To the Sky"/Takikawa City Hall, Takikawa, Hokkaido, Japan
Sculpture "Moment"/I Residence, Kanagawa, Japan
Sculpture "Earth Mother," [2-10]
"Sky Tree," [2-9] "Fire Ball," [2-11] "Water Glass," [2-12] /Akasaka Garden City, Tokyo, Japan
Sculpture "Horizontal Feeling #102601"/ Cosmo Kawaguchi Station Front, Saitama, Japan
Sculpture "Untitled" Alphabet ORI Sculpture, Chiba, Japan
Walkway/Aomori Museum of Art Side (Aomori Prefecture General Art Park Project), Aomori, Japan
Sculpture "Horizontal Feeling"/Toyooka Public Hospital, Hyogo, Japan
Sculpture "Land"/Wako Municipal General Welfare Center, Saitama, Japan

2006
Sculpture "Sky Dancing"/Shibaura Institute of Technology Toyosu Campus, Tokyo, Japan [2-7]
Sculpture "Untitled"/Galleria Grande, Tokyo, Japan [2-22]
Sculpture "Fuu-ka-kou-sei

(Winds Flowers Stars Lights)"/ADEKA Corporation Head Office, Tokyo, Japan [2-75]
Sculpture "Komorebi"/Me Mo Ru Kagetsu nursery school, Takikawa, Hokkaido, Japan
Sculpture "Kaze Hana Tori"/Kagetsu Children's Center, Takikawa, Hokkaido, Japan
Sculpture "Komorebi" / Bourou Noguchi Noboribetsu, Noboribetsu, Hokkaido, Japan [2-65]
Sculpture "Windy Fish"/The Yomiuri Shimbun, Sapporo, Hokkaido, Japan
Bench "Friends"/Tarokichigura, Takikawa, Hokkaido, Japan
Sculpture "Komorebi"/Hyatt Regency Kyoto, Kyoto, Japan
Sculpture "Komorebi"/Nagoya Lucent Tower, Nagoya, Aichi, Japan [2-68]
Sculpture "To the Sea of Premonition," [2-57] "From the Land of Memory" [2-17] /Tokyo Midtown, Tokyo, Japan

2007
Sculpture "Santa Monica Breeze"/ Sapporo City Regional Family Court Takikawa Branch Office Building, Takikawa, Hokkaido, Japan
Sculpture "To the Sky," "Horizontal Feeling#103101"/Midland Square, Nagoya, Aichi, Japan
Sculpture "Komorebi"/Hokkaido Medical Center for Child Health and Rehabilitation, Sapporo, Hokkaido, Japan [2-8]
Sculpture "Untitled"/Takekawa Hospital, Tokyo, Japan
Sculpture "Komorebi"/il cielo, Hotel miura kaen, Takikawa, Hokkaido, Japan [p.264]
Sculpture "Asparagas"/il cielo, Hotel miura kaen, Takikawa, Hokkaido, Japan
Sculpture "Untitled (Ceramic Sculpture)" /il cielo, hotel miura kaen, Takikawa, Hokkaido, Japan
Sculpture "Komorebi"/Kajima Corporation Head Office, Tokyo, Japan [2-67]
Sculpture "Beyond the Horizon"/Kajima Corporation Head Office, Tokyo, Japan
Sculpture "Beyond the Horizon"/Kajima Akasaka Annex, Tokyo, Japan [2-55]
Sculpture "Horizontal Feeling"/Kajima Akasaka Annex, Tokyo, Japan [2-48]

2008
Sculpture "California Desert"/Valore Kudan Minami Building, Tokyo, Japan [2-47]
Sculpture "Komorebi"/Kidosaki residense, Tokyo, Japan
Sculpture "Komorebi"/Rokkatei, Obihiro, Hokkaido, Japan [2-63]
Sculpture "Komorebi"/Almeida Memorial Hospital, Oita, Japan
Sculpture "Horizontal Feeling Landscape" 2 Pieces [2-19,2-20], "Sky Dancing" [2-81], "Horizontal Feeling LHH-1," "Horizontal Feeling LHH-2," "Horizontal Feeling LHH-3," [2-49]
"Horizontal Feeling LHH-4," "Horizontal Feeling LHH-5" /Laguna Honda Hospital, San Francisco, USA
Sculpture "From Deep Under Ground" /Tarokichigura, Takikawa, Hokkaido, Japan
Sculpture "To the Sky"/Hitachi Omori Building, Tokyo, Japan
Sculpture "Untitled"/Lions Residence Nakano Prase, Tokyo, Japan

2009
Sculpture "Sunrise Mountain"/A Certain Guest House, Nagano, Japan
Sculpture "Horizontal Feeling"/Chita Kosei Hospital, Chita, Aichi, Japan
Sculpture "Away from the Ground"/ Nipponkoa Nihombashi Bldg., Tokyo, Japan
Sculpture "Komorebi"/Makuhari Baytown Patios 19th Avenue, Chiba, Japan
Sculpture "Present of Wind"/Yawaragi Fushimi Bettei, Sapporo, Hokkaido, Japan
Sculpture "BIRD"/Soka Gakkai Cultural Hall, Takikawa, Hokkaido, Japan
Memorial Monument for a Colosed Elementary School/Kazenobi, Shintotsukawa, Hokkaido, Japan [3-14]

2010
Sculpture "Windstorm"/Hokuyo Odori Center, Sapporo, Hokkaido, Japan [2-72]
Sculpture "Sky Dancing"/Odori Bisse, Sapporo, Hokkaido, Japan [2-60]
Sculpture "Full of Spirit and Vigor"/ Toranomon First Garden, Tokyo, Japan [2-59]
Sculpture "Forest of Terminus" including bench, plaza design and graphic work for the walkway/ JR Sapporo station Paseo, Sapporo, Hokkaido, Japan [2-16, 3-5]
Sculpture "Tie/Proud Hongo Yumimachi, Tokyo, Japan

2011
Sculpture "White Legend"/Kazenobi, Shintotsukawa, Hokkaido, Japan [3-8]
Sculpture "Komorebi"/Kazenobi, Shintotsukawa, Hokkaido, Japan [2-66]
Sculpture "Depth of the Sea"/Kazenobi, Shintotsukawa, Hokkaido, Japan [2-56]
Sculpture "Sailing Future"/Hamarikyu Mitsui Building, Tokyo, Japan [2-89]
Sculpture "Cosmos"/Takikawa Municipal Hospital, Takikawa, Hokkaido, Japan [2-61]

2012
Sculpture "The Mother Earth," Fountain "Fountainhead" [2-15] / Akasaka K-Tower, Tokyo, Japan
Sculpture "Land of Intelligence"/ Fukuoka, Japan University Library, Fukuoka, Japan [2-18]
Sculpture "Full of Spirit and Vigor"/ Proud Ooi James-zaka, Tokyo, Japan
Sculpture "In Praise of Forest, Ocean and People"/Ota-City General Gymnasium, Tokyo, Japan [2-37]

2013
Sculpture "Komorebi/Spring Sunlight," "Komorebi/Autumn Sunlight"/Proud Tower Shinonome Canal Court, Tokyo, Japan
Sculpture "Rhythm of Mountain Range"/ Kofu City Hall, Kofu, Yamanashi, Japan [2-74]
Sculpture "Komorebi" etc./Chutoen General Medical Center, Kakegawa, Shizuoka, Japan [2-62]
Sculpture "The Pleiades"/Kichijyoji Gotenyama House, Tokyo, Japan
Sculpture "Wing"/Certain office, Tokyo, Japan

2014
Sculpture "Diversity and Harmony"/ Xinzhuang Joint Office Tower, Executive Yuan, Taiwan [2-24]
Sculpture "Life· Time · Land", Hot Spring Apartment, Taiwan
Sculpture "North Wind" [2-23], "Mi Zu No Ne," "Spirit of Mountain"/ Higashikawa-cho International House, Higashikawa, Hokkaido, Japan

2015
Sculpture "Komorebi - Yo"/Proud Tower Ooizumi-gakuen, Tokyo, Japan
Sculpture "Zawa Zawa/Hyun Hyun/ Giggi"/Osaki Bright Core, Tokyo, Japan [2-58]
Sculpture "3"/Takikawa Daisan Elementary School, Takikawa, Hokkaido, Japan [3-11]
Relief (Collaboration with Elementary School Students) Takikawa Daisan Elementary School, Takikawa, Hokkaido, Japan [3-10]
Sculpture "Komorebi"/Park Homes Maruyama Ura-Sando Terrace, Sapporo, Hokkaido, Japan
Sculpture "North latitude 35 degrees, 36 minutes and 15 seconds East longitude 139 degrees, 42 minutes and 32 seconds"/Bunkyo University Affiliated Junior High School · Senior High School, Tokyo, Japan
Sculpture "Shu, Sya, Shi Homage to Sky, Water and Sun"/Tancho Kushiro Airport, Kushiro, Hokkaido, Japan [3-12]
Sculpture "Present of Wind"/Yawaragi Funeral hall Takikawa, Takikawa, Hokkaido, Japan
Sculpture "Light of Pinneshiri," [2-25] "Homage to The Forest" / Sapporo Teishinkai Hospital, Sapporo, Hokkaido, Japan

2016
Sculpture "Muku Muku Homage to Water, Sun and Land"/Shin Hakodate Hokuto Station, Hokuto, Hokkaido, Japan [3-13]
Sculpture "Nami no Oto"/The Parkhouse Harumi Towers Tiaro Residence, Tokyo, Japan
Sculpture "Wind Flower"/The Prince Gallery Tokyo Kioicho, Tokyo, Japan
Sculpture "Yu·Fu·Ru·Ji"/Kazenobi, Shintotsukawa, Hokkaido, Japan [2-90]
Sculpture "Horizontal Feeling"/KT Building, Tokyo, Japan

2017
Sculpture "Suhtto"/Proud Tower Nagoya Sakae, Nagoya, Aichi, Japan

EXHIBITIONS

Solo Exhibitions:

Takenobu Igarashi Exhibition Animal Illustration
1972
Gallery Fujie, Tokyo, Japan
Cooperation: Kumazawa Screen Printing, Inc., Shigeru Uchida (Display Design)

Takenobu Igarashi Poster Exhibition 2
February 21–March 4, 1975
Gallery Fujie, Tokyo, Japan
Cooperation: Light - Printing Co.,Ltd.
The 274th Design Gallery 1953
Takenobu Igarashi's Alphabet Sculpture
1981
Matsuya Ginza 7th Floor Design Gallery 1953, Tokyo, Japan
Organizer: Japan Design Committee.

Takenobu Igarashi Alphabet Sculpture Exhibition
July 9–19, 1983
Mikimoto Hall, Tokyo, Japan

Takenobu Igarashi, Architectural Alphabets, Sculpture, Drawing, Design
October 4–December 3, 1983
Reinhold Brown Gallery, New York, USA
An Exhibition of Works by Takenobu Igarashi
November 17–December 15, 1984
Portfolio Center and the Art Directors Club of Atlanta, USA

The 335th Design Gallery 1953
Designer and Company Series 40
"Shitsunai Magazine" Cover 50 months
1985
Matsuya Ginza 7th Floor Design Gallery1953, Tokyo, Japan
Organizer: Japan Design Committee

Posters by Takenobu Igarashi
January 15–February 28, 1987
Woodbury University Gallery
Los Angeles, CA, USA

Takenobu Igarashi
January 26–February 5, 1987
University of Washington,
The School of Art Gallery, USA

Artist from Nation of Words
Takenobu Igarashi Sculpture Exhibition
November 6–25, 1987
Yurakucho Asahi Gallery, Tokyo, Japan
Organizer: The Asahi Shimbun

Takenobu Igarashi Poster Exhibition
1987
Mac Quaries Gallery, Sydney, Australia

Artist from Nation of Words
Takenobu Igarashi Sculpture
Art Print Exhibition
May 13–24, 1988
Keihan Gallery of Arts and Science (Keihan Department Store 7th Floor)
Osaka, Japan
Organizer: The Asahi Shimbun
Graphic Design Takenobu Igarashi
1988
Galerie Von Oertzen, Frankfurt, Germany

Takenobu Igarashi's Casting Exhibition
Japan Creative Gallery
April 14–May 10, 1989
Seibu Department Store Ikebukuro Branch, Tokyo, Japan
Organizer: Seibu Department Stores, Limited

Takenobu Igarashi · Living Objects
October 6–November 15, 1989
Yurakucho Seibu Creators' Gallery, Tokyo, Japan

Designer's Saturday · IDCNY
October 11–18, 1989
International Design Center, New York (IDCNY),
New York, NY, USA

Living Objects
October 25–November 18, 1989
Gallery 91, New York, NY, USA

Living Objects
November 2–December 29, 1989

Gallery of Modern Art,
Los Angeles, CA, USA

Igarashi Poster Design + Lecture
September 12, 1990
Landhaus, Bregenz, Austria

Products of <Urushi> on Desktop
Exhibition, Product development
collaboration between Aizu lacquerware
Union and Takenobu Igarashi Part 1
October 18–20, 1990
Axis Gallery Annex, Tokyo, Japan
Co-host: Aizu Lacquerware Union,
Igarashi Studio
Design '90, Takenobu Igarashi Exhibition
1990
Hong Kong Shanghai Bank, Hong Kong
Tai Tak Takeo Fine Paper Co., Ltd. &
Hong Kong Designers Association

Dream to be Formed in Shape ·
From 50 projects
Takenobu Igarashi Exhibition
June 26–July 8, 1995
Tokyo Design Center
Planning: Design

East Looks West Exhibition
Takenobu Igarashi in Germany
April 16–June 6, 1993
Deutsches Plakat Museum
Essen, Germany

Multiplex −17 Takenobu Igarashi
May 18–June 18, 1993
Green Collection Multiplex,
Tokyo, Japan

The 471st Design Gallery Exhibition
The Futon by Takenobu Igarashi
October 27–November 15, 1993
Matsuya Ginza 7th Floor Design Gallery,
Tokyo, Japan
Organizer: Japan Design Committee

Takenobu Igarashi's Sculpture
March 22–April 12, 1995
Hosomi Gallery, Tokyo, Japan

Takenobu Igarashi Design
June 24–July 29, 1998
Museo Jose Luis Cuevas Arte
Contemporaneo, Mexico City, Mexico

Takenobu Igarashi
Wood and String Works
September 4–22, 2000
Gallery Natsuka, Tokyo, Japan

Takenobu Igarashi
Wood and Stone Works
October 4–24, 2000
Space T·R·Y, Tokyo, Japan

83rd Art Exhibition
Featuring work by Takenobu Igarashi
June 13, 2001
Gensler, Santa Monica, CA, USA

Takenobu Igarashi Exhibition
December 10–22, 2001
Gallery Natsuka, Tokyo, Japan

Takenobu Igarashi Exhibition
"Mirage in the Pitch Dark"
March 3–13, 2002
Hokusen Gallery Ivory
Sapporo, Hokkaido, Japan

Invisible Moment,
Works of Artist Takenobu Igarashi

May 24–July 12, 2002
AZ Los Angeles, Inc.,
Los Angeles, CA, USA

Invisible Moment, Takenobu Igarashi
Plywood & String Works
June 27–August 23, 2002
Gensler San Francisco
San Francisco, CA, USA
Takenobu Igarashi Evolving
September 2–21, 2002
Gallery Natsuka, Tokyo, Japan

UCLA Extension Catalog Covers
1990–2004
March 25–May 14, 2004
AIGA National Design Center
American Institute of Graphic Arts
Featuring the Graphic Design
and Illustration Work of the Fifty
World's Leading Creative Talent
New York, NY, USA
Takenobu Igarashi Exhibition
Flat Works with Cutouts
December 5–22, 2005
Gallery Natsuka, Tokyo, Japan

Takenobu Igarashi Series Exhibition
Design and Art Trajectory
Takenobu Igarashi, Sky's Wood Carving
Relief Exhibition
October 15–30, 2005
JR Tower 36F Observation Deck,
Sapporo, Hokkaido, Japan
Organizer: Sapporo Station General
Development Co., Ltd.

Takenobu Igarashi Series Exhibition
Design and Art Trajectory
Time Tunnel Series Vol. 21
(Takikawa/First venue)

Takenobu Igarashi Exhibition
"The World of Plane and
Three Dimensional"
October 18–25, 2005

Takikawa City Art Natural History
Museum, Takikawa, Hokkaido, Japan
Takenobu Igarashi Series Exhibition
Design and Art Trajectory
Time Tunnel Series Vol. 21
(Takikawa/Second Venue)
Takenobu Igarashi Poster
Calendar Exhibition
October 22–23, 2005

Takikawa Dai3 Elementary School
Playroom, Takikawa, Hokkaido, Japan
Takenobu Igarashi Series Exhibition
Design and Art Trajectory
Time Tunnel Series Vol. 21
(Tokyo / First and Second Venues)

Takenobu Igarashi Exhibition
"The world of Plane and
Three Dimensional"
October 31–November 25, 2005
[First Venue] Creation Gallery G8,
Tokyo, Japan
[Second Venue] Guardian Garden,
Tokyo, Japan

Takenobu Igarashi
Whereabouts of the Book
20 Art Box Exhibition
June 5– 23, 2007
Space T·R·Y, Tokyo, Japan

Takenobu Igarashi: Maquette
"Precious Models of a Sculpture"
June 12–28, 2009

designshop+gallery, Tokyo, Japan

Takenobu Igarashi Terra-Cotta Exhibition
September 18–24, 2012
AIJ Architectural Gallery, Tokyo, Japan

Why Don't You Come and Meet
the Pieces of Sorachi ·
Takenobu Igarashi Ceramic Sculpture
Exhibition
July 21–August 31, 2013
Gallery COYA
Takikawa, Hokkaido, Japan
Organizer: Kazenobijutsukan

JAZZ1976+2013 · Takenobu Igarashi
"The Reappearance of the Visionary
JAZZ 15 Amsterdam Exhibition and Time
Space of Creativity by New Terra-Cotta"
August 14–September 22, 2013
Gallery Retara
Sapporo, Hokkaido, Japan
Why Don't You Come and Meet the
Pieces of Sorachi
Takenobu Igarashi Ceramic Sculpture
Exhibition
December 9–21, 2013
Gallery Natsuka, Tokyo, Japan

Surrounded by Sorachi Shape
Takenobu Igarashi
April 14–May 3, 2014
Gallery Iriya, Tokyo, Japan

Group Exhibitions:

Tama Art University · Design Group ·
Epui Exhibition
March 23–28, 1964
HBC Sanjo Building Gallery, Sapporo,
Hokkaido, Japan
Sponsor: The Hokkaido Shimbun
Press, Hokkaido Broadcasting Co., Ltd.
Perspective of Contemporary Japanese
Posters "Identity"
1976
Seibu Museum of Modern Art
Tokyo, Japan

Japanese Posters
1979
Kingstgewerbemuseum der Stadt
Zurich, Switzerland

Design '79, Hongkong/Japan Design
Exhibition
November 16–20, 1979
Hong Kong City Hall, Hong Kong

Co-hosted by Hong Kong Designers
Association and Japan Typography
Association
Contemporary Japanese Posters
1980
Museum des 20, Jahrhunderts
Vienna, Austria

Exhibition of Creative Labyrinth
1980
Seibu Museum of Modern Art, Tokyo
Designer's Space, Tokyo, Japan

Contemporary Japanese Poster Exhibition
1981
Santa Rosa Junior College Art Museum,
Santa Rosa, CA, USA
Takenobu Igarashi + Hirokatsu Hijikata
Exhibition
1981
Art Center College of Design
Pasadena, CA, USA

Writing and Reading
1981
Cooper–Hewitt Museum
New York, NY, USA

Takenobu Igarashi+Koichi Sato
Poster exhibition
1985
G7 Gallery, Tokyo, Japan

Seven Graphic Designers
Poster Exhibition
1985
Itoya Gallery, Tokyo, Japan

"L'Image de Mots"
1985
Georges Pompidou Center
Paris, France
"Napoli Exhibit"
1986
The Naples Ninety-Nine Foundation
Italy

The Modern Poster
June 6–September 6, 1988
The Museum of Modern Art
New York, NY, USA
Organized by Stuart Wrede, Director,
Department of Architecture and Design

The Image of Thinking in Visual Poetry
"Computer Riddles"
by Takenobu Igarashi
May 19–September 10, 1989
Guggenheim Museum
New York, NY, USA

INFLUENCE4
Exhibit of Work of Featured Speakers
Posters for Design Expo89
by 20 leading Japanese Designers
March 3–April 10, 1989
Marshall University, Birke Art Gallery,
Huntington, WV, USA

EAST MEETS WEST IN DESIGN
March 26–May 10, 1989
Huntington Museum of Art
Huntington, WV, USA

91 Objects by 91 Designers
September 19–November 16, 1991
Gallery 91, New York, NY, USA

The World of Graphic Design
at the Galerie von Oertzen
September 6–October 5, 1997,
Staditische Galerie im Kameliterkloster,
Frankfurt, Germany
March 26–May 3, 1998, The Deutsches
Plakatmuseum, Essen, Germany

Seven Japanese Artists Show
Tetsuji Aono, Sush Hachida Gaikotsu,
Naotake Hiro, Takenobu Igarashi,
Kyoko Kawahata, Masayuki Oda,
Mai Shimohana
May 3–July 3, 2002
LIMN Gallery, San Francisco, CA, USA

Asia Print Adventure 2003
Spirit of 81 Artists from 33 Countries
International Contemporary Art Exhibition
- Representation of Expanding Prints
September 18–28, 2003
Hokkaido Museum of Modern Art,
Sapporo, Hokkaido, Japan

Drawing the Line: Contemporary Artists
Reassess Traditional East Asian
Calligraphy

Featuring: Therese Hak Kyung Cha,
Wenda Gu, Takenobu Igarashi,
So Moon Kim, Linda Nishio, Qin Feng,
Kazuaki Tanahashi, Wang Nanming,
Jane Park Wells, Fio Oy Wang,
and Xu Bing
May 31, 2003
Pacific Asia Museum
Pasadena, CA, USA

Typo & Konstrukcja
2006
The Poster & Design Gallery of the
National Museum in Poznan, Poland

Light, Memory, Form
Takenobu · Tomoko · Shoko Igarashi
Exhibition
June 5–23, 2007
Space T·R·Y, Tokyo, Japan

KATACHI-FORM Zeitgenossische
Angewandte Kunst aus Japan
zwischen Handwerk und Industrie
May 3–August 26, 2007
Ausstellung im Museum fur Angewandte Kunst Frankfurt, Germany

Poster of the 20th Century [Typography]
- Power of Design · Power of Letters
January 29–March 27, 2011
Tokyo Metropolitan Teien Art Museum,
Tokyo, Japan
Organizer: Tokyo Metropolitan
Foundation for History and Culture,
Tokyo Metropolitan Teien Art Museum,
Nihon Keizai Shimbun

Masayuki Nagare, Noriko Tamura,
Haruhisa Hattori, Takenobu Igarashi
Exhibition
"Terminus Story" and Artists of Beauty
September 3–25, 2011
Planis Hall, Sapporo, Hokkaido, Japan

Watery Landscapes by FEAA Project
Sayuli, Takenobu Igarashi, Han Jiyoun
September 29–October 5, 2014
Nest Gallery, Geneva, Switzerland

LECTURES

Recent Work
February 1981
Graphic Designer's Association
University of Hawaii
Honolulu, HI, USA

Contemporary Japanese Posters
February 11, 1981
Santa Rosa Junior College Newman
Auditorium, Santa Rosa, CA, USA

Architectural Alphabet
November 1984
The Smithsonian Institution,
Washington D.C., USA

My Work
November 15, 1984
Portfolio Center and Art Directors Club
of Atlanta
Atlanta, GA, USA

Recent Work
January 1985
American Institute of Graphic Arts/
Genslar Associates
San Francisco, CA, USA

My Recent Work
February 11–12, 1985
11th ICOGRADA Student Seminar
Odeon Cinema Leicester Square
London, England
Chairman: FHK Henrion
Speaker: Keith Godard, F. Gottschalk,
Takenobu Igarashi, Malcolm Lewis

A to Z alphabet
May 1985
AGI California
Santa Barbara, CA, USA

Igarashi Alphabets
July 24–26, 1986
Stanford Conference on Design
Stanford University, Stanford, CA, USA

The Design and Sculpture of Igarashi
A Free Public Lecture
February 4, 1987
University of Washington/AIGA
Seattle, WA, USA

My Recent Work
June 1987
Art Direction & Design in Orange County
Orange County, CA, USA

The Design-Made Object:
International Expressions
June 1987
NEOCON 19 Seminars:
Merchandise Mart
Chicago, IL, USA
Takenobu Igarashi, Dakota Jackson,
Jack Lenor Larsen and Tobia Scarpa

3D Alphabet
August 1987
Annual Convention of Environmental
Graphic Designers Association
Cranbrook Academy of Art
Bloomfield, MI, USA

My Work
August 1987
AIGA Boston
Boston University,
Boston, MA, USA

My Work & Poster Show
October 1987
Australia Type Directors Club
Sydney Opera House, Australia

Looking for the Ultimate CI
CI in Imaging Society
1980s
CI Graphics Symposium
Co-Host: The Yomiuri Shimbun,
CI Graphics Executive Committee
Imperial Hotel Fuji Room, Tokyo, Japan

Aspen Design Conference
June, 1988
Colorado, USA

Takenobu Igarashi ·
My Experience in Design
June 30, 1988
Toyota Motor Corporation Endowed
Lecture Program at Art Center
Art Center Auditorium,
Pasadena, CA, USA

Influence 4
Sharpening the Creative Edge:
Japan and the United States
April 5–8, 1989
Marshall University
Huntington, WV, USA
Saul Bass, Gerald Hirshberg,
Takenobu, Igarashi, Katherine McCoy,
Hiroshi, Morishima, Koich Sato,
Tadao Shimizu, Massimo Vignelli,
Charles Helmken, Karen Nulf,
Richard Thornton

My Recent Works
May 25, 1989
Norske Grafiske Designere
Oslo, Norway

Designer's Saturday · IDCNY
October 14, 1989
International Design Center,
New York, NY, USA

The Connecticut Art Directors Club
October 19, 1989
Bruce Museum, Greenwich, CT, USA

Parson's School of Design
October 1989
Parson's School of Design,
New York, NY, USA

Pratt Institute
October 1989
New York, NY, USA

Focus: Igarashi
October 14, 1989
Designer's Saturday IDCNY
New York, NY, USA

Pan-Pacific Design Conference
November 1989
Tokyo, Japan

An Evening with Takenobu Igarashi
January 17, 1990
American Center for Design
Chicago Historical Society
Chicago, IL, USA

About Recent Work
February 22–25, 1990
TED2, Technology Entertainment Design
The Second Conference
Monterey CA, USA

Takenobu Igarashi
September 19, 1990
Art Center College of Design (Europe)
Montreux, Switzerland

International Design Plaza Nagoya '90
Aiming at Creation of a New Era of
21st Century Design
"International Design Business
Front Line"
October 12–13, 1990
Nagoya International Convention
Center
Speaker: Sam Lopata (USA), Friedrich
Frenkler (Germany), Takenobu Igarashi
(Japan), Kenji Oki (Japan)
Coordinator: Takuo Ikegame
Nagoya, Aichi, Japan

The New York Chapter of the American
Institute of Graphic Arts and Champion
International Presents an Evening with
Takenobu Igarashi
February 27, 1991
Fashion Institute of Technology,
New York, NY, USA

"Design as an Economic Success
Strategy-Japan and Germany
Compared"
May 7–8, 1993
The Design Zentrum Hordrhein
Westfalen
Essen, Germany

Fachhochschule fur Gestaltung
Schwabisch Gumund
May 5, 1993
Germany
Takenobu Igarashi Modern Design
und Handwerk in Japan
Kultur Bregenzerwald Forum and
Handwerk & Forum Bregenzerwald
May 7, 1996
Gymnasium Egg
Bregenzerwald, Austria

Industrial Design Lecture Series
Fall 89 Pratt Takenobu Igarashi
Igarashi Studio, L.A.
Tuesday October 3, 1989
Pratt Institute
New York, NY, USA

Domus Academy
1991
Domus Academy, Milan, Italy

The public lecture for the 20th
anniversary year festival of Hokkaido
Tokai University
Possibility of Design
October 12, 1991
Asahikawa, Hokkaido, Japan

MACWORLD Expo/Tokyo
February 20–22, 1992
Creative Design and Macintosh
Kazuo Kawasaki, Yukimasa Okumura,
Takenobu Igarashi
Japan Convention Center Makuhari
Messe
Chiba, Japan

The Society of Typographic Designers
STD Lecture Series
September 20, 1994
St Bride Institute, London, England

The Inter-Relationship Between Graphic
and Product Design
April 1995
The Smithsonian Institution
Washington D.C., USA

International Influences & Inspiration
Takenobu Igarashi Alain le Quernec
Ben Bos
Katie Murphy Amphitheatre, FIT
AIGA New York Chapter
March 18, 1998
New York, NY, USA

Inside the Studio Takenobu Igarashi
January 16, 2002
Japan Society
New York, NY, USA

Tama Art University Public Lecture 2011
10th Anniversary Commemorative Public
Lecture Program
Beginning and Design, Influence,
Background, Thought and Image
Takenobu Igarashi
October 8, 2011
Tama Art University Kaminoge Campus,
Tokyo, Japan

The Japan Institute of Architecture
Kanto Branch Series,
Viewpoint of Architecture
4th Takenobu Igarashi,
The New World of Terra-Cotta
Talk: Takenobu Igarashi · Shigeo Anzai
· Yoshihiko Iida

Photo: Yoshihiko Iida
September 24, 2012
Architectural Hall Tokyo, Tokyo, Japan

MAIN LITERATURE LIST

Work Collection:

1975
『五十嵐威暢デザイン事務所1970–1975』
Private Edition

1980
『五十嵐威暢デザイン事務所1970–1980』
Private Edition

1982
『五十嵐威暢デザイン事務所1970–1982』
Private Edition

1983
『五十嵐威暢デザイン事務所スペースグラフィック』
Shotenkenchiku-sha Publishing Co., Ltd., Tokyo, Japan

1985
ABCDEFGHIJKLMNOPQRSTUVWXYZ /
Sculpture by Takenobu Igarashi
Photography: Yasuhiro Ishimoto
Book Design: Debi Shimamoto
Published by Alphabet Gallery
Tokyo, Japan

1987
Igarashi Alphabets
ABC Verlag, Zurich, Switzerland

1991
Takenobu Igarashi
Rock Scissors Paper
『デザインのぐう・ちょき・ぱぁー』
Graphic-sha Publishing Co., Ltd.
Tokyo, Japan

1992
Takenobu Igarashi
Igarashi Sculptures
Robundo Publishing Inc.
Tokyo, Japan

1996
Takenobu Igarashi
『デザインすること、考えること』
Asahi Press, Tokyo, Japan
The World Master: Takenobu Igarashi
Hei-Long-Jiang Province Fine Arts
Publishing House of China

1998
Takenobu Igarashi
Edition Axel Menges, Fellbach, Germany

2000
"Dezain suru koto, kangaeru koto"
by Takenobu Igarashi
Cho hyung sha, Seoul, Korea

2002
五十岚威畅—国际设计大师丛书
主编: 余 秉楠, 余 璐
河北美术出版社 中国

2005
『タイムトンネルシリーズVol.21
五十嵐威暢展 平面と立体の世界』
Recruit Holdings Co., Ltd.
Tokyo, Japan

2008
Takenobu Igarashi
『あそぶ、つくる、くらす
デザイナーを辞めて彫刻家になった』
Rutles Inc.
Tokyo, Japan

2012
『Takenobu Igarashi Terra-Cotta』
Private edition

DVD:

2005
Takenobu Igarashi
『―彫刻家 五十嵐威暢の世界―』
Hokkaido Cultural Broadcasting Co., Ltd., Hokkaido, Japan

Single Line Books:

1977
『世界のレターヘッド 五十嵐威暢編』
Seibundo Shinkosha, Tokyo, Japan

1980
『環境のグラフィックデザイン 五十嵐威暢編』
Shotenkenchiku-sha Publishing Co., Ltd., Tokyo, Japan

1982
『日本のタイポグラフィ』
Seibundo Shinkosha, Tokyo, Japan

1985
『SEVEN 7人のグラフィックデザイナーが、ここで出会った。』
Graphic-sha Publishing Co., Ltd.,
Tokyo, Japan

1988
Stuart Wrede
The Modern Poster
The Museum of Modern Art,
New York, NY, USA

1989
Ruedi Ruegg
Basic Typography: Design with Letters
ABC Verlag, Zurich, Switzerland
B. Martin Pedersen
Graphis Corporate Identity 1
Graphis Press Corp.
Zurich, Switzerland

1993
Brody Neuenschwander
Letterwork
Creative Letterforms in Graphic Design
Phaidon Press Ltd., England
Maggie Kinser Saiki
『Y・M・D モノ・ヒト・デザイン 飛躍する地場産業への提言』
Photo: Masaru Mera
Robundo Publishing Inc., Tokyo, Japan
Nancy Williams
Paperwork
The Potential of Paper in
Graphic Design
Phaidon Press Ltd., England
Designed by Williams and Phoa

1994
B. Martin Pedersen
Graphis Products by Design 1
Graphis Press Corp.
Zurich, Switzerland

1997
Essays on Design 1
AGI's Designers of Influence
Booth-Clibborn Editions, England
Edited by Robyn Marsak
Designed by David Hillman and
JaneChipchase and Pentagram

Design Limited
Novum Press: Plakate · Posters
A Selection of more than 400 works
by first-rate Designers
Edited by Dieter Urban
F. Bruckmann KG, Germany

1999
『日本のタイポグラフィックデザイン
1925–95』
Supervision: Seigo Matsuoka, Ikko
Tanaka, Katsumi Asaba
Trans art, Tokyo, Japan

2001
Masters of the 20th Century
The Icograda Design Hall of Fame
Conceived, Designed and Edited by
Mervyn Kurlansky
Graphis Inc., New York, NY, USA

2002
Maggie Kinser Saiki
12 Japanese Masters
Graphis Inc., New York, NY, USA

Richard Saul Wurman
1000 Who's Really Who
The Most Creative Individuals
in the USA
First Company Inc., USA

2005
U&lc Influencing Design & Typography
Edited by John D. Berry
Mark Batty Publisher, USA

2007
『東京ミッドタウンのアートとデザイン』
Supervision: Toshio Shimizu
Tokyo Shoseki Co., Ltd, Tokyo, Japan

Alliance Graphique Internationale
AGI Graphic Design Since 1950
Edited by Ben & Elly Bos
Thames & Hudson, England

2008
『グラフィックデザインの世紀
明治世代、山名文夫、杉浦非水から昭和世代まで』
Edit: Century of Graphic Design
Editorial Committee
Bijutsu Shuppan-sha Co., Ltd., Tokyo, Japan

2009
『グラフィックデザイナーの肖像』
Planning: Keiko Hirano
Produce and Edit: Takeo Co., Ltd.
Shinchosha, Tokyo, Japan

Jason Godfrey
Bibliographic 100 Classic Graphic
Design Books
Laurence King Publishing Ltd., London,
England

『駅とアートは求め合う 札幌・JRタワーの秘密』
Edited: Sapporo Station General
Development Co., Ltd.
Gentosha Media Consulting Inc.,
Tokyo, Japan

Masaharu Taniguchi
『札幌アートウォーク』
Photo: Keiji Tsuyuguchi
The Hokkaido Shimbun Press
Hokkaido, Japan

『再生名建築 時を超えるデザイン1』
「凍結保存した「神聖なガランドウ」太郎吉蔵」
Writer: Yukihiro Kado
Kajima Institute Publishing Co., Ltd.,
Tokyo, Japan

2011
Richard Poulin
The Language of Graphic Design
An Illustrated Handbook for
Understanding
Fundamental Design Principles
Rockport Publishers, Inc., USA

2012
Richard Poulin
Graphic Design + Architecture
A 20th-Century History
Takenobu Igarashi and
The Architectural Alphabet 1983
Rockport Publishers, USA

2013
Takenobu Igarashi
『Yell（エール）』
Takeo Co., Ltd., Tokyo, Japan

Exhibition Catalogs:

1986
Ventiquattro Manifesti per Napoli
Twenty-Four Posters for Naples
Napoli, Museo Villa Pignatelli Cortes,
Italy
Explorations
Catalog of the International Design
Congress and Exhibition in Stuttgart
Germany

1987
『文字の国のアーティスト五十嵐威暢彫刻・版画展1987年11月6日〜25日』
Supervision+Text: Nobuo Abe
Text: Koichi Inakoshi
Yurakucho Asahi Gallery, Tokyo, Japan

1989
Takenobu Igarashi LIVING OBJECTS
Private edition

1998
Takenobu Igarashi Design
June 24–July 29
Text by Takenobu Igarashi at The Jose
Luis Cuevas Museum by Bertha Cuevas
Type Design by Ereira Melendez Torres
Museo Jose Luis Quevas Arte
Contemporaneo, Mexico City

2000
『五十嵐威暢 木と紐の仕事』
Text: Akira Tatehata
Gallery Natsuka, Tokyo, Japan

『五十嵐威暢 木の仕事と石の仕事』
Text: Akira Tatehata
Space T·R·Y, Tokyo, Japan

2004
『時代のアイコン 1950–2004』
Text: Takenobu Igarashi
Japan Design Committee, Tokyo,
Japan

『水色のガラス―消失と出現のイメージ』
Micro Technology Co., Ltd., Tokyo, Japan

2005
『五十嵐威暢展―カットアウトによる平面作品』
Text: Toshio Shimizu
Gallery Natsuka, Tokyo, Japan
『五十嵐威暢シリーズ展
―デザインとアートの軌跡―＋イベント

ガイドブック[札幌+滝川+東京]2005.
OCT-DEC』
Takenobu Igarashi Series Exhibition
Executive Committee, Tokyo, Japan

『五十嵐威暢 そらの木彫レリーフ展』
Sapporo station General Development
Co., Ltd., Hokkaido, Japan

2006
Type & Construction 3
Text by Anna Grabowska-Konwent
The National Museum in Poznan, Poland

2007
248th Exhibition
Exhibitions Graphic Messages from
Ginza Graphic Gallery & ddd Gallery
1986-2006
29th Anniversary
Ginza Graphic Gallery, Tokyo, Japan
[Part 1] January 11-31, 2007
[Part 2] February 6-28, 2007
Katachi-Form Zeitgenossische
Angewandte Kunst aus Japan zwischen
Handwerk und Industrie Ausstellung im
Museum fur Angewandte Kunst
Frankfurt 3. May 26-August 2007
Text by Unrich Schneider
and Miki Shimokawa
Museum fur Angewandte Kunst
Frankfurt, Germany

2009
Takenobu Igarashi: Maquette
designshop+gallery Tokyo

2013
Jazz 1976+2013 Takenobu Igarashi
Text: Chihiro Minato
Gallery Retara, Hokkaido, Japan

『アトリエの赤ん坊たち・五十嵐威暢展』
JR Tower Hotel Nikko Sapporo,
Hokkaido, Japan

『空知のかけらに会いに来ませんか・五
十嵐威暢』
Text: Takenobu Igarashi
Gallery COYA, Hokkaido, Japan

Sequential Publications:

1973
『アイデア』1973/07
五十嵐威暢とその作品
Writer: Mitsuru Kataoka
Seibundo Shinkosha, Tokyo, Japan

1975
『アイデア』1975/05
五十嵐威暢とさわやかな象徴の世界
Writer: Ikko Tanaka
Seibundo Shinkosha, Tokyo, Japan

『季刊デザイン』1975/9 -Spring
五十嵐威暢のかたち
アルファベットに知的な操作
Writer: Akio Okuda
Bijutsu Shuppan-sha Co., Ltd.,
Tokyo, Japan

1977
『グラフィック デザイン』68 /1977
世界の新人展望 '70 日本その1 五十嵐
威暢
Kodansha Ltd., Tokyo, Japan

『家庭画報』1977
Serialization Town Design 1-12
Composition・Sentence:
Takenobu Igarashi
Sekaibunka Publishing Inc., Tokyo, Japan

1979
Graphis 205 Volume 35 1979 / 80
Takenobu Igarashi by John Follis
Switzerland

1981
The Japan Times Weekly 1981
キャリアを切り開くデザイナー
(Japanese translation articles)
by Ruth Stevens
Tokyo, Japan

『グラフィック デザイン』83 / 1981
五十嵐威暢のアルファベット・アート
Writer: Hiroshi Awatsuji
Kodansha Ltd, Tokyo, Japan

1982
『アイデア』1982 / 03
[特集2]―五十嵐威暢の最近作
Writer: Shigeru Uchida
Seibundo Shinkosha, Tokyo, Japan

1983
『ミセス』1983 / March Issue-
December Issue
Serialization DESIGN NOW
Composition・Sentence:
Takenobu Igarashi
Photo: Mitsumasa Fujitsuka
Bunkagakuen Bunka Publishing
Bureau, Tokyo, Japan

『美術手帖』1983 / October Issue
All That Art 29
五十嵐威暢 立体アルファベット
Bijutsu Shuppan-sha Co., Ltd.,
Tokyo, Japan

JAPAN INTERIOR DESIGN
No.296 November 1983 Issue
書評 五十嵐威暢と環境のグラフィック
Writer: Mitsumasa Fujitsuka
Interior publishing, Tokyo, Japan

1984
『アイデア』1984 / 01
五十嵐威暢／アーキテクチャル・アルファ
ベット デザインのしなやかな骨
Writer: Koichi Sato
Seibundo Shinkosha, Tokyo, Japan

Express Winter 1984.1
"IGARASHI"
USA

Japan Interior Design 1984 No.302
特集―プロフェッショナル・オフィス・スペー
ス／日本編 グラフィックデザイナーの
アトリエ
Takenobu Igarashi Design Studio
Interior Publishing Tokyo

Novum 1984/9
Works by Takenobu Igarashi
by Kurt Weidemann
Germany

Atlanta Journal, December 1, 1984
A Guide to the Arts・Currents
Igarashi Sculpts in 3 Dimensions
USA
Graphis 229 Volume 40 1984
Takenobu Igarashi Architectural
Alphabets
by Stanley Mason
Switzerland

1985
『グラフィックデザイン』99 / 1985
鮮やかな光芒―2つのオーソドックス展
Writer: Yoshio Hayakawa
Kodansha Ltd, Tokyo, Japan

『アイデア』1985 / 1 158
五十嵐威暢とニューヨーク近代美術館
の仕事
Writer: Ruth P. Stevens
Seibundo Shinkosha, Tokyo, Japan

『新美術新聞』1985.4.1 +7.11
時代精神1985― 美術と状況
デザインは何を伝えるか 五十嵐威暢氏
に聞く
Bijutsu-Nenkansha Co.,Ltd.,
Tokyo, Japan

1986
HQ High quality #5 1986
Enigmatic Alphabet
Germany

『室内』1986 / 381 September issue
人物登場 サントリーと電通が始めたデザ
イン会社
由里正雄、稲生一平、五十嵐威暢、アラン・
フレッチャー、マッシモ・ビニエリ
Kosakusha Publishing Co., Ltd.,
Tokyo, Japan

1987
Portfolio1987 / 013
Igarashi Studioの華麗な海外での最新作
Writer: Yoshihisa Ishikawa
Seibundo Shinkosha, Tokyo, Japan
『日本経済新聞』February 9, 1987
(Morning Education Culture Column)
せめて便箋に薄化粧
ワープロ時代、「レターヘッド」で人間味を
Writer: Takenobu Igarashi

『読売新聞』November 20, 1987
CIグラフィックス・シンポジウム
第三部 飽情報時代の企業イメージ創造
活力を生む優れたデザイン
類似への配慮持て・五十嵐

『朝日新聞』November 14, 1987
(Evening Publication Art)
「遊び」を新発想で

Badener Tagblatt, Baden 1987.1.31
"Takenobu Igarashi Alphabet Neuheit in
der ABC-Verlagsreihe «Grafik+Design»"
by Hans Hunziker
Baden, Germany

TM Typograpfische Monatsblatter,
No.2 / 1987
Igarashis Alphabete Von der Graphick
zur Plastik
Zurich, Switzerland

Zur ichsee-Zeitung, Stafa 1987.3.14.
"Igarashi Alphabets
Buchstaben-grafisch, statisch"
by Irene Stoll-Kern

『朝日新聞』June 30, 1987
(Evening Publication)
点描：アルファベットに触覚的な存在感
五十嵐氏が英・独・仏語の本

『タテ組ヨコ組』1987 Summer No. 17
From the Front Line Personal Magazine
・17 Takenobu Igarashi
Morisawa Tokyo, Japan

1988
『デザインの現場』1988 / 12
Igarashiグラフィックとプロダクトの二刀流
Bijutsu Shuppan-sha Co., Ltd.,
Tokyo, Japan

Graphis 254 Volume 44 1988
"Takenobu Igarashi Capital Letters"
by Stuart I. Frolick
USA

『アイデア』1988 / 5
五十嵐威暢の記号シリーズ
Writer: Susumu Kitahara
Seibundo Shinkosha, Tokyo, Japan

The New York Times
February 4, 1988
An International Set of
Desk Accessories
USA
『アイデア』1988 / 5
サントリーアートポスター
Writer: Junji Ito
Seibundo Shinkosha, Tokyo, Japan

1989
『毎日新聞』December 13, 1989
「汎太平洋デザイン会議'89」を終えて
21世紀の生活の美とは
いまデザインが問われている！

The New York Nichibei
November 2. 1989
五十嵐威暢・リビングオブジェクト展
Writer: Toshiya Masuda
New York, USA

The New York Times
November 16. 1989
Traveling Eastward
USA

Monthly Design March 1989
Foreign Designer Japanese Designer
Takenobu Igarashi
Korea 1990

Axis1990 Summer/36
TED2 創造性を支えるテクノロジー
五十嵐威暢のアートワーク
Axcis, Inc., Tokyo, Japan

Design News1990/210
リビング・オブジェクトの視点
五十嵐威暢のプロダクト・デザイン活動
Japan Institute of Design Promotion,
Tokyo, Japan

Axis 1990 Autumn/37
Topics: Y・M・D地場産業の技術力を基礎
に、国際的なプロダクトへの試み
Axcis, Inc., Tokyo, Japan

Metropolitan Home March 1990
Takenobu Igarashi Design Diplomats
Past and Future Merge Ehen a Graphics
Guru Marries High Tech to Tradition
by Fred A. Bernstein
USA

『アイデア』1990 / 219
第2回勝見勝賞を受賞した五十嵐威暢
Seibundo Shinkosha, Tokyo, Japan
Omuni May 1990
Building Character
by Phil Scott
New York, USA

CREATION 1990 / 07
Takenobu Igarashi
Writer: Toshifumi Kawahara
Recruit Holdings Co., Ltd.,
Tokyo, Japan

Blueprint 65 March 1990
Cologne Fair Report:
Germany Moves into the Big Time

Progressive Media International
London, UK

1991
Esquire April 1991 Vol.115 No.4
Man at His Best Iron with Irony
by Phil Patton
Hearst Corporation, New York, NY, USA

1992
Graphis 277 Volume 48 1992
Takenobu Igarashi
by Maggie Kinser Saiki
USA

1993
LINEA GRAFICA 1993 / 286
Pieces of Writing
by Giovanni Baule
Azzurra Editrice, Milan, Italy

1995
Design New 1995 / 12
「五十嵐威暢の近作
デザインの再生という手法について」
Japan Institute of Design Promotion,
Tokyo, Japan

1996
TIME 1996/October–December
Golden Anniversary Issue ASIA
Time Inc., New York, NY, USA

1998
Graphis 317, 1998
Takenobu Igarashi: Carving New Dreams
by Michael Kaplan
USA

2001
『北海道新聞』September 7, 2001
「海外での芸術活動知って」
滝川出身 米国在住の彫刻家 五十嵐さん
11日、故郷で講演 小学校同期生が後押し
Hokkaido, Japan

2002
『プレス空知』27th April 2002
ロサンゼルスからの手紙
(下)コペンハーゲンで考えたこと
滝川を芸術公園都市に
Writer: Takenobu Igarashi
Hokkaido, Japan

設計交流
"5 design exchange 三位日本著名設計家
Three Japanese Graphic Designers"
by Henry Steiner
Hong Kong

2003
Sculpture April 2003 Vol.22 No.3
"Los Angeles Takenobu Igarashi by
Collete Chattopadhyay"
International Sculpture Center, USA

『展評』2003 / 014
五十嵐威暢 手作業でダイレクトに伝える
Writer: Yumi Takaishi
Art Village, Tokyo, Japan

『芸術新潮』2003 / 05
Art News 札幌上空160メートルに出現!
五十嵐威暢の圧巻重層レリーフ
Shinchosha, Tokyo, Japan

2004
『北海道新聞』October 22, 2004
そらネット27 芸術でまちに活気と夢
「アートチャレンジ滝川」設立から間もな
く1年
Writer: Susumu Yamamura
Hokkaido, Japan

『北海道新聞』June 2, 2004
NPO法人・アートチャレンジ滝川の挑戦
歴史、文化残るまちづくり
Writer: Kazuhiro Ito ("Art Challenge
Takikawa" Director)
Hokkaido, Japan

『プレス空知』September 1, 2004
彫刻家・五十嵐氏が自ら裏口ドアの制作
手がける
10月9日プレオープン
Writer: Manabu Sato
Hokkaido, Japan

2005
U&lc Influencing Design & Typography
Edited by John D. Berry
Mark Batty Publisher, USA

『IP NEWS インテリアプランナーニュ
ース』
2005 vol.20
即興的につくるということ
デザインを誰が評価するのか
The Special Event Dialogue Takenobu
Igarashi x Suguru Mori
Hokkaido Interior Planner Association,
Information Committee
Hokkaido, Japan

2006
『毎日新聞』March 2, 2006
毎日デザイン賞特別賞五十嵐威暢シリーズ
展の活動 特別賞 多様な展開、意義深く
Tokyo, Japan

『デザインの現場』2006 / 2月
彫刻家 五十嵐威暢の挑戦
Writer: Keiichiro Fujisaki
Bijutsu Shuppan-sha Co., Ltd.,
Tokyo, Japan

『エル・デコ』February 2006 issue
ArtとDesignで町が変わる 北海道・滝川市
彫刻家・五十嵐威暢が蒔いた奇跡の種
Hearst Fujingaho, Tokyo, Japan

『北海道新聞』March 14, 2006
(Evening Education Culture Column)
滝川出身の彫刻家五十嵐さん
毎日デザイン賞特別賞受賞
札幌などでの作品展に評価
Hokkaido, Japan

『北海道新聞』March 5, 2006
日曜インタビュー 彫刻家 五十嵐威暢さん
50歳からの再出発 アトリエで彫刻をつくる
ことと街づくりへの参加の間に溝はない
Hokkaido, Japan

2007
『東京新聞』June 16, 2007
芸術・現代美術にみる父と子
創造生む伝承と拒絶
Writer: Toshio Shimizu
Tokyo, Japan

『北海道新聞』June 28, 2007
(Evening Publication)
彫刻家・五十嵐さん企画 故郷の滝川で「デ
ザイン宣言」志求め「賢人会議」
Writer: Takao Sato (Editorial committee)
『第一回 太郎吉蔵デザイン会議テーマ：「
デザインの近未来」』
Text: Takenobu Igarashi etc.
Tarokichigura Design Conference
Secretariat, Hokkaido, Japan

2008
『北海道新聞』September 18, 2008
滝川第2回太郎吉蔵会議を終えて
寄稿 デザイナーは高い志抱け
Writer: Takenobu Igarashi

『第二回 太郎吉蔵デザイン会議
テーマ：「ローカルとデザイン」』
Text: Takenobu Igarashi etc.
Tarokichigura Design Conference
Secretariat, Hokkaido, Japan

2009
『第三回 太郎吉蔵デザイン会議
テーマ：「デザイナーの新しい役割」』
Text: Takenobu Igarashi etc.
Tarokichigura Design Conference
Secretariat, Hokkaido, Japan

2010
『芸術新潮』Serialization1st (April
2010)–24th Final Round (March 2012)
デザインと彫刻とぼくのクロニクル
Writer: Takenobu Igarashi
Shinchosha, Tokyo, Japan

2011
『くれあーれにゅーす』2011 / No.9
座談会 豊かさを育てる芸術の力
—パブリックアートの更なる可能性を目
指して
Japan Traffic Culture Association,
Creare News Editorial Office
Tokyo, Japan

『第四回 太郎吉蔵デザイン会議
テーマ：「本当の問題」』
Text: Takenobu Igarashi etc.
Tarokichigura Design Conference
Secretariat, Hokkaido, Japan

『JRタワーアートシーン』2011 / No.09
アートから触れる新パセオ
Sapporo station General Development
Co., Ltd., Hokkaido, Japan

2012
『芸術新潮』2012 / 09
Art News Takenobu Igarashi
つち、いろ、かたちうごめく体育館
Shinchosha, Tokyo, Japan

『第五回 太郎吉蔵デザイン会議
テーマ：「アジアの時代」』
Text: Takenobu Igarashi etc.
Tarokichigura Design Conference
Secretariat, Hokkaido, Japan

2014
『日本デザイン学会誌』
2014 Vol.21-3 / Vol. 83
デザイン学研究特集号
特集／実践するデザイナーたちのデザ
イン知
瞬間に生まれるもの
Writer: Takenobu Igarashi
Tokyo, Japan

『第六回 太郎吉蔵デザイン会議
テーマ：「デザインのいまとこれから」』
Text: Takenobu Igarashi etc.
Tarokichigura Design Conference
Secretariat, Hokkaido, Japan

2015
『くれあーれにゅーす』2015 / No.11
Special interview
『1%フォー・アーツ』を日本に
Japan Traffic Culture Association,
Creare News Editorial Office
Tokyo, Japan

PAPER'S
Takeo newsletter No.51, Winter 2015
対談 紙について話そう。五十嵐威暢・田
中義久
Takeo Co., Ltd., Tokyo, Japan

Takeo Desk Diary 2016
タイピングスケープス
—モダニズム以降のレターヘッド
Text: Takenobu Igarashi
Takeo Co., Ltd., Tokyo, Japan

Web Reports:

2014
Otsuka Ohmi Repor + Artist Series
彫刻家・五十嵐威暢〜つくることは、生き
ること〜
『第1回 であい』October 27, 2014
www.ohmi.co.jp/report/index.php?c:
topics2_view&pk: 1466485219
『第2回 しごと』November 25, 2014
www.ohmi.co.jp/report/index.php?c:
topics2_view&pk: 1466487909
『第3回 むかし いま みらい』December
17, 2014
www.ohmi.co.jp/report/index.php?c:
topics2_view&pk: 1466490061

Published by:
Graphis Inc.
389 Fifth Avenue, New York, NY 10016
Phone: 212-532-9387
www.graphis.com
help@graphis.com

Distributed by:
National Book Networks, Inc.
15200 NBN Way, Blue Ridge Summit, PA 17214
Toll Free (U.S.): 800-462-6420
Toll Free Fax (U.S.): 800-338-4550
Email orders or Inquires: customercare@nbnbooks.com

Legal Counsel:
John M. Roth
3140 Bryant Avenue South, #3
Minneapolis, MN 55408
Phone: 612-360-4054
johnrothattorney@gmail.com

ISBN 13: 978-1-931241-63-2
ISBN 10: 1-931241-63-5

Copyright © 2018 Graphis, Inc. All rights reserved.
Jacket and book design copyright © 2018 by Graphis, Inc.
No part of this book may be reproduced, utilized or
transmitted in any form without written permission of
the publisher. Printed in China.

Credits:
Writer: **Shōji Usuda**
Creative Director: **B. Martin Pedersen**
Designers: **B. Martin Pedersen, Hee Ra Kim**
English translation: **Naoko Metzler-Nakayama**
English text editor: **Roshanak Keyghobadi**
Associate editor: **Angela Sabarese**
Coordinator: **Sakura Nomiyama**

Portrait photograph of Takenobu Igarashi by: **John Madere**
All the other photographs in this book are by various
photographers, who are credited in the Appendix.

This publication is based on the Japanese version of *Takenobu Igarashi's*
Book published by Takeo Co., Ltd., Takeo Archives in 2016.

Production team for the original Japanese version were:
Editor: **Naoko Hasegawa**
Art Director: **Yasuhiro Nagahara**
Designer: **Iuko Matsukawa**
Designer: **Miho Hirabayashi**
Special thanks to: **Asako Hada**